EXAMKRACKERS MCAT®

101 PASSAGES:
CHEMISTRY
GENERAL & ORGANIC CHEMISTRY

Major Contributors:
Jacob Chevlen
Austin Mattox
Kaitlyn Barkley, M.D.
Jennifer Birk Goldschmidt, M.S.
Andrew Elson

Contributors:
Jay Li
Laura Burkbauer
Joshua Novack

Art Director:
Erin Daniel

Designer:
Dana Kelley

Illustrator:
Poy Yee

Copyright © 2017 by Examkrackers, Inc.,

All rights reserved under International and Pan-American Copyright Conventions.

Published in the United States of America by Osote Publishing, New Jersey.

ISBN 13: 978-1-893858-94-7

To purchase additional copies of this book or other books of the 101 Passage series, call 1-888-572-2536.

Examkrackers.com
Osote.com

FAIR USE NOTICE. This book is an independent educational guide for students who are preparing to take the Medical College Admission Test® exam, also known as the MCAT® exam. This book has been prepared and published by Examkrackers, Inc. and is not endorsed or sponsored by, or otherwise affiliated with, the Association of American Medical Colleges (AAMC), which publishes the MCAT® exam and owns the foregoing trademarks. The trademarks owned by AAMC are used for information and identification only, and are not intended to claim or suggest any affiliation with AAMC.

Printed and bound in the United States of America.

PHOTOCOPYING & DISTRIBUTION POLICY

The illustrations and all other content in this book are copyrighted material owned by Osote Publishing. Please do not reproduce any of the content, illustrations, charts, graphs, photos, etc., on email lists or websites.

Photocopying the pages so that the book can then be resold is a violation of copyright.

Schools and co-ops MAY NOT PHOTOCOPY any portion of this book.
For more information, please contact Osote Publishing:
email: support@osote.com or contact Examkrackers:
email: support@examkrackers.com or phone 1.888.KRACKEM.

No part of this work may be reproduced or transmitted in any form or by any means, electronic or mechanical, including photocopying, and recording, or by any information storage or retrieval system without prior written permission of the copyright owner unless such copying is expressly permitted by federal copyright law, or unless it complies with the Photocopying & Distribution Policy listed above.

© 2017 Osote Publishing
All rights reserved.

Read this First

Practice is essential to success on the MCAT®. MCAT® practice is the best way to develop the key skills you will need to get a high score.

The 101 passages and associated questions in this book were carefully designed to simulate exactly the content, length, style, tone, difficulty and format of real AAMC MCAT® passages, questions, and answer choices. Each chapter in this book has two tests. The first one is of exact MCAT® section length and the second is a mini-MCAT® section for additional practice. Both passage-based questions and stand-alone questions are just like the questions you'll see on MCAT® day, and are included in a 3:1 ratio, just like the real MCAT®.

The Examkrackers 101 series covers every single topic and subtopic tested by the MCAT®. Topics that require more drilling and topics that are especially difficult are covered by multiple questions. Each chapter in *101 Passages: Chemistry* tests the content covered by the corresponding chapter in Examkrackers *Chemistry* manual. To maximize your MCAT® preparation, take the tests in each chapter following your review of that chapter in the manual. To stay in touch with how the science you review is tested on the MCAT®, coordinate your content review with simulated MCAT® practice, chapter by chapter.

The MCAT® is all about how flexible and adaptable you are with the basics. Real MCAT® passages and questions will always present you with new and unfamiliar situations. It is only through simulated MCAT® practice that you will learn to see what simple science is relevant and then recall and apply the basics with confidence. Through practice and focus on the questions you get wrong, you will develop essential skills that bring a high score on MCAT® day.

In this section you will find information on:

- Using the warm-up passage to assess your skills
- MCAT® Timing
- MCAT® Simulation
- How to use this book to increase your MCAT® score
- Scoring your practice tests
- Complete MCAT® preparation with Examkrackers

How to Begin: Assessing Your Skills

This book begins with one "warm-up" passage. Use it to familiarize yourself with the look, feel, and format of MCAT® chemistry passages and questions. Give yourself about eight minutes to take the warm-up test. While working through the passage and the associated questions, observe yourself and notice your own approach. Immediately after taking the warm-up test, look at the following checklist of strategies and skills. Based on the passage and questions in the warm-up, evaluate which skills come naturally to you and which skills you will work to build as you continue through this book.

- Energy
- Focus
- Confidence
- Timing
- Narrating the passage
- Identifying and answering research questions
- Applying simple science in new situations
- Clear, simple, and connected organization of the content in your mind
- Simplifying the questions and answers
- Eliminating weak answer choices

Choose two or three skills to focus on throughout Test 1 and continue to build new skills as you proceed through the book. Return to this page and check off strategies and skills as you master them.

MCAT® Timing

Examkrackers 101 books are great tools with which to master MCAT® timing before MCAT® day. The tests can be taken untimed or timed. As you initially practice brand-new skills, go slowly in order to master them. Take timed tests to prepare for timing on MCAT® day. The practice tests in this book are exactly like the real MCAT®: 10 passages and 59 questions in 95 minutes. The mini-tests are precisely scaled to AAMC MCAT® timing: 29 questions in 45 minutes. Timing on MCAT® day is a skill that you will build through timed practice.

Take a 5 second break before reading each passage. Look at the clock only once, at the halfway point (the 29th question). If you are before the 47-minute mark, slow down. If you are after the 47-minute mark, speed up. Developing an intuitive sense for good MCAT® timing and pace is an essential skill. Eventually, you will come to know whether you are on pace as you go without looking at a clock. You will know when you are getting sandbagged in order to speed up and when you are rushing so that you can slow down.

After you take a test, assess your timing skills. If you did not finish the test before the allotted time, determine where you are spending time that you could save. If you finished with time to spare, determine how you could spend more time toward a higher score on your next practice test.

Plan a schedule in advance. Choose a distribution for these tests throughout your study period. For example, if you are studying over a ten-week period, take one test from this book every week on the same day. Do not save all the tests for the weeks immediately prior to the MCAT®, as MCAT® skills require time and practice to develop. It is important to stay in touch with the MCAT® and MCAT® practice throughout your study period. Between tests, give yourself adequate time to review the test you take each week. Consciously plan what you will do differently on the next test in order to increase your MCAT® score.

MCAT® SIMULATION

When you are ready to take your first simulated, full-length test, choose an environment that is not familiar or comfortable, e.g. a public library, not your couch at home. Ensure that you will maximize focus and minimize distraction for one sitting of at least 95 minutes. If needed, you may use disposable earplugs, just as on MCAT® day. During the test, do not look at or answer the telephone, do not sit and stare out the window, and do not get up for any reason, such as to get a drink or to go to the bathroom. Treat each practice test like the real thing.

It is always a good idea to mark up the multiple choice questions *on the test itself* as you go through them. If 'A' can't be correct, then mark it off and go to 'B'. If 'B' is *possible*, circle it, and go to 'C', and so on. That way you are eliminating and narrowing choices that are *not possible* or are *less likely*. Using the process of elimination is a very helpful technique on the MCAT®. The computer-based test allows the use of strikethrough and highlight functions right on the screen to help with narrowing down choices. It is not very practical or helpful to write your answers or considerations on a piece of notebook paper as this does not simulate MCAT® day.

How to Use This Book to Increase Your MCAT® Score:

REVIEW

Test and question review is the single most important thing you will do to change your MCAT® score.

Always leave time for review of each test. Your score will change through careful review of each practice test you take, not through repetitive practice.

Every question you get wrong is a gift, an opportunity to increase your score. Always think about how questions you get wrong are valuable – they are the pearls that will lead you directly to a high MCAT® score.

You will need ninety-five minutes to take the test and at least ninety minutes to review it.

Immediately after completing each test, take notes on what happened during the test.

Then, take a short break for an hour or less. Next sit down and check your answers. At the end of each test, you will be directed to the page in the back of the book where you can find the answers, and answer explanations, for that test. Every page of the tests has a tab and footer telling you what test you're working on. Every page of the answers and explanations has a tab and footer telling you which test is being covered. Always be sure these match when checking your answers. No need to flip through pages and pages of explanations looking for the right test.

Make a list of question numbers you marked and/or got wrong. Do not yet read the answer explanations.

Compare your score to the last practice test you took. Your raw score is the number you answered correctly out of 59. Did your raw score increase since the last test? If yes, what did you do differently? Make a note to keep doing what worked. If no, what was different today? Make a commitment to change strategies that did not work.

Make time to retake the questions you answered incorrectly before looking at the answer explanations. This allows you to build the most important MCAT® muscles of all: problem solving and independent thinking. Once you see the answer explanation, you lose the opportunity to learn how to solve the MCAT® question yourself. This may sometimes require multiple attempts or reinforcement of science, but the purpose of practice is for you to learn how to *solve* the questions. Reading the explanation of how to get to the right answer should come only after you have tried your hardest to find your own way there.

Once you have made a second attempt, read the answer explanation for each question you got wrong in order to learn to think in ways that will get you a high score. Examkrackers answer explanations are uniquely process-oriented, meaning that they reveal the way to think like the MCAT®. The answer explanations show you the reasoning process that leads to the elimination of each weak answer and the selection of the best answer. Our answer explanations will help you identify new strategies that work and will help you learn to think in ways that bring a high score.

It can also help to review those questions you got right in order to reinforce the skills, confidence and concepts that allowed you to solve those problems.

SMART PRACTICE

There are two kinds of practice: practice that is repetitive and practice that is smart. Practice that is repetitive, in which you do the same thing over and over again, will reinforce skills that you already have and will also reinforce any habits you may have that are not working.

1. Before each test, plan on what skills you want to add, build, reinforce or replace with this practice test. Use the list provided above as well as any skills you have added. Make specific "When… Then…" commitments (see below).
2. Be conscious or self-aware during each test, in order to evaluate what you are doing while you are doing it. Take notes during the test on what you are thinking or feeling, what skills you are struggling with, what is happening that you notice, etc.
3. Smart practice finally means evaluating immediately *after* each test how the commitments helped. If your score increased, what did you do differently that accounts for the increase—commit to continuing with this new skill. If your score decreased, what in your approach or environment was different—commit to replacing what is not working.
4. Repeat this process throughout the study period.

MAKING COMMITMENTS

Immediately after each test, make specific commitments for what you plan next – what will you keep doing more of and what still needs to change?

Commitments work best if new, good habits are linked to old, bad habits. I can make a commitment not to speed on the highway tomorrow, but inevitably I will find myself speeding yet again. Change comes when I decide that

When I speed, **then** I will immediately slow down to 54 mph.
Similarly:
When I fall into negative thinking while taking the test,
Then I will take a five-second break and refocus on the question in front of me.
Or
When I have trouble understanding what I am reading,
Then I will take a five-second break and resume reading, narrating with the basics that I know

When you commit to avoiding the mistakes that led you to incorrect answers in one test, you will see improvement in your raw score on the next test.

Look toward the next date you will take a practice test. Document your commitments and keep them ready at hand to review before you begin your next practice test.

Scoring Your Practice Tests

The goal is to see your scores on Examkrackers practice materials improve over time.

The best way to utilize your raw score is to be sure it increases with each practice test you take, whether as skill-building or simulation. The best way to do this is to make specific commitments to replace what isn't working with effective MCAT® skills.

Note: Even if Examkrackers derived a scaled score from thousands of our students, it would not accurately predict your AAMC MCAT® score. Unlike the AAMC MCAT® which includes easy questions, Examkrackers practice questions simulating the MCAT® are largely of the medium and difficult level, in order to improve your MCAT® skills and to help you learn how to think like the MCAT®. Our students are at different stages of preparation for the MCAT® and do not represent the MCAT® day student population. Any scaled score other than that directly from the AAMC does not correlate to AAMC MCAT® scores. Only a scaled score from the AAMC can accurately predict your AAMC MCAT® score.

Your goal should be to get more items right and fewer wrong with each Examkrackers practice test you take. A higher score with each practice test reflects that you are using the questions you get wrong and those you get right to learn and practice new skills that will increase your score.

Complete Your MCAT® Preparation

Note: *101 Passages: Chemistry* contains only chemistry passages and questions to maximize your chemistry practice. The AAMC MCAT® integrates biological systems with biochemistry. For integrated MCAT® simulation, use our full-length, online *EK-Tests*®. Visit www.examkrackers.com for details.

To complete your preparation for the Chemical and Physical Foundations MCAT® section, use this book along with the Examkrackers *Chemistry, Biology 1: Molecules*, *Biology 2: Systems*, and *Reasoning Skills* manuals, and *MCAT® 101 Passages Biology 1: Molecules*. Together these tools provide in-depth instruction in the skills needed to get a high score on the "*Chemistry*" MCAT® section.

To prepare fully for the four sections of the MCAT®, Examkrackers *Complete Study Package* includes six manuals packed with content review, MCAT® strategy, and guided practice. The corresponding *MCAT® 101 Passages* series allows you to practice the methods and build the skills taught in Examkrackers study manuals. Take an online or in person Examkrackers Comprehensive MCAT® Course (information available at our website, below).

Examkrackers Live MCAT® Hotline is a service available ten hours per week so your questions can be addressed directly and interactively by expert, high scoring MCAT® instructors.

EK-Tests® are the best full length simulated MCAT® product available on the market. Each electronic test matches the MCAT® in sources, style, format, question types, length, skills and content tested. Tools to maximize review and score improvement are built-in.

Regularly visit the Examkrackers Forums where students' questions are answered and any errata are posted.

Go to www.examkrackers.com or call 1.888.KRACKEM to learn more about Examkrackers materials, support and live MCAT® preparation, both online and in-person.

Toward your success!

TABLE OF CONTENTS

PHYSICAL SCIENCES

DIRECTIONS. Most questions in the Physical Sciences test are organized into groups, each preceded by a descriptive passage. After studying the passage, select the one best answer to each question in the group. Some questions are not based on a descriptive passage and are also independent of each other. You must also select the one best answer to these questions. If you are not certain of an answer, eliminate the alternatives that you know to be incorrect and then select an answer from the remaining alternatives. A periodic table is provided for your use. You may consult it whenever you wish.

PERIODIC TABLE OF THE ELEMENTS

1 **H** 1.0																	2 **He** 4.0
3 **Li** 6.9	4 **Be** 9.0											5 **B** 10.8	6 **C** 12.0	7 **N** 14.0	8 **O** 16.0	9 **F** 19.0	10 **Ne** 20.2
11 **Na** 23.0	12 **Mg** 24.3											13 **Al** 27.0	14 **Si** 28.1	15 **P** 31.0	16 **S** 32.1	17 **Cl** 35.5	18 **Ar** 39.9
19 **K** 39.1	20 **Ca** 40.1	21 **Sc** 45.0	22 **Ti** 47.9	23 **V** 50.9	24 **Cr** 52.0	25 **Mn** 54.9	26 **Fe** 55.8	27 **Co** 58.9	28 **Ni** 58.7	29 **Cu** 63.5	30 **Zn** 65.4	31 **Ga** 69.7	32 **Ge** 72.6	33 **As** 74.9	34 **Se** 79.0	35 **Br** 79.9	36 **Kr** 83.8
37 **Rb** 85.5	38 **Sr** 87.6	39 **Y** 88.9	40 **Zr** 91.2	41 **Nb** 92.9	42 **Mo** 95.9	43 **Tc** (98)	44 **Ru** 101.1	45 **Rh** 102.9	46 **Pd** 106.4	47 **Ag** 107.9	48 **Cd** 112.4	49 **In** 114.8	50 **Sn** 118.7	51 **Sb** 121.8	52 **Te** 127.6	53 **I** 126.9	54 **Xe** 131.3
55 **Cs** 132.9	56 **Ba** 137.3	57 **La*** 138.9	72 **Hf** 178.5	73 **Ta** 180.9	74 **W** 183.9	75 **Re** 186.2	76 **Os** 190.2	77 **Ir** 192.2	78 **Pt** 195.1	79 **Au** 197.0	80 **Hg** 200.6	81 **Tl** 204.4	82 **Pb** 207.2	83 **Bi** 209.0	84 **Po** (209)	85 **At** (210)	86 **Rn** (222)
87 **Fr** (223)	88 **Ra** 226.0	89 **Ac**= 227.0	104 **Unq** (261)	105 **Unp** (262)	106 **Unh** (263)	107 **Uns** (262)	108 **Uno** (265)	109 **Une** (267)									

*	58 **Ce** 140.1	59 **Pr** 140.9	60 **Nd** 144.2	61 **Pm** (145)	62 **Sm** 150.4	63 **Eu** 152.0	64 **Gd** 157.3	65 **Tb** 158.9	66 **Dy** 162.5	67 **Ho** 164.9	68 **Er** 167.3	69 **Tm** 168.9	70 **Yb** 173.0	71 **Lu** 175.0
=	90 **Th** 232.0	91 **Pa** (231)	92 **U** 238.0	93 **Np** (237)	94 **Pu** (244)	95 **Am** (243)	96 **Cm** (247)	97 **Bk** (247)	98 **Cf** (251)	99 **Es** (252)	100 **Fm** (257)	101 **Md** (258)	102 **No** (259)	103 **Lr** (260)

Passage: 1

Time: 8 minutes

DIRECTIONS: Use this warm-up passage and questions to become familiar with MCAT® chemical science questions and to assess your skills before beginning Practice Test 1A.

Read the passage, then select the best answer to each associated question. If you are unsure of an answer, rule out incorrect choices and select from the remaining options. Indicate your selection beside the option you choose. A periodic table can be found on the last page of this book for you to use at any point during this test section.

Passage 1 (Questions 1-5)

Influenza has caused outbreaks every 1-3 years repeatedly throughout the past 400 years. Influenza RNA-dependent RNA polymerase (RdRP) is a heterotrimeric complex of one acidic subunit (PA) and two basic subunits (PB1 and PB2). The PA subunit, truncated to its approximately 209 N-terminal domain (PA-Nter), has full endonuclease activity, involving the binding of bivalent metal ions Mn^{2+} or Mg^{2+}. This mechanism implies that the first ion, located at site M1, supports formation an atom that is susceptible to an attacking nucleophile by withdrawing electrons, while the second ion at site M2 facilitates the exit of leaving group through neutralization of its negative charge. Both ions likely stabilize the transition state.

Structural reports are not consistent concerning the type and number of ions. The Mg^{2+} ion may occupy site M2 and would be directly coordinated by Glu80, Asp108 and three water molecules. The M1 site may be occupied by a water molecule coordinated by His41. Due to the ambiguity of the location of the metal ions, scientists used Equation 1 to predict PA-Nter ion occupancy, where K_{M1} and K_{M2} are the equilibrium binding constants for both M1 and M2 sites for Mg^{2+} and Mn^{2+}. Assuming non-cooperative binding, the average number of ions bound to PA-Nter, v, is given by Equation 1, where x denotes the molar concentration of ions.

$$v(x, K_{M1}, K_{M2}) = \frac{x}{K_{M1}+x} + \frac{x}{K_{M2}+x}$$

Equation 1

Next, the scientists quantified the kinetics of catalysis in the presence of Mg^{2+} and Mn^{2+} ions and in the excess of enzyme. The results are shown in Figure 1.

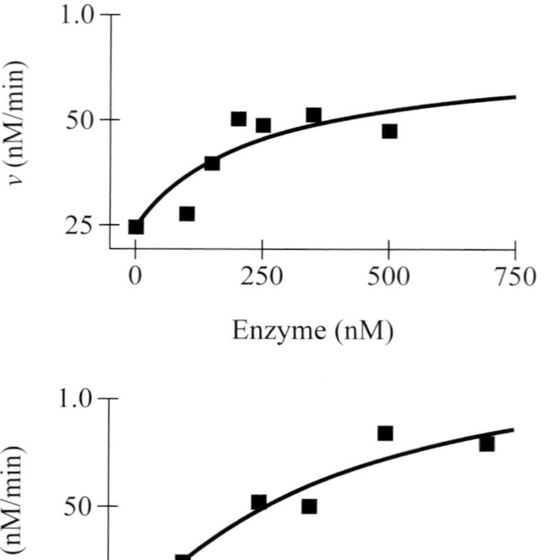

Figure 1 Cleavage kinetics of various PA-Nter concentrations in the presence of Mg^{2+} and Mn^{2+}

This passage is adapted from "New Insights into Metal Ion-Driven Catalysis of Nucleic Acids by Influenza PA-Nter." Kotlarek D and Worch R. *PLoS ONE.* 2016. doi:10.1371/journal.pone.0156972 for use under the terms of the Creative Commons CC BY 4.0 license (http://creativecommons.org/licenses/by/4.0/legalcode).

Question 1

Magnesium is most likely to form which of the following bonds?

- O **A.** Ionic
- O **B.** Covalent
- O **C.** Hydrogen
- O **D.** Van der Waals

Question 2

What is the electron configuration of manganese?

- O **A.** $[Ar]3d^5 4s^2$
- O **B.** $[Kr]5s^1$
- O **C.** $[Ar]2d^6 3s^3$
- O **D.** $[He]2s^2$

Question 3

Which of the following statements best describes the results of the experiment conducted with Mg^{2+} in Figure 1?

- O **A.** DNA cleavage proceeds the most rapidly in the presence of excess paramagnetic ions and an excess of enzyme.
- O **B.** DNA cleavage proceeds the most rapidly in the presence of excess diamagnetic ions and an excess of enzyme.
- O **C.** DNA cleavage proceeds the most rapidly in the presence of excess paramagnetic ions and minimal enzyme.
- O **D.** DNA cleavage proceeds the most rapidly in the presence of excess diamagnetic ions and minimal enzyme.

Question 4

Asp in an enzyme active site is likely to stabilize Mg^{2+} and water by:

- O **A.** sharing electrons between metals.
- O **B.** donating electrons from magnesium to non-metals.
- O **C.** transient associations of oppositely charged electron clouds.
- O **D.** complete sharing of electrons between atoms.

Question 5

Which of the following properties of RNA most likely allows it to associate with RdRP?

- O **A.** The oxygen of the phosphodiester backbone binds various Lysine and Arginine residues in RdRP.
- O **B.** The pyrimidine and purine bases covalently bond to magnesium in the RNA polymerase active site.
- O **C.** The nitrogen of the purine ring is unable to participate in hydrogen bonding with opposing bases.
- O **D.** Nucleic acids bond only through disulfide bonds to RdRP.

STOP. If you finish before time is called, check your work. You may go back to any question in this test.

ANSWERS & EXPLANATIONS for the Warm-Up Passages can be found on p. 213.

Introduction to General Chemistry

TEST 1A

Time: 95 minutes
Questions 1–59

DIRECTIONS: Most of the questions in this test section are grouped with a passage. Read the passage, then select the best answer to each question. Some questions are independent of any passage and of one another. Select the best answer to each of these questions. If you are unsure of an answer, rule out incorrect choices and select from the remaining options. Indicate your selection beside the option you choose. A periodic table can be found on the last page of this book for you to use at any point during this test section.

Passage 1 (Questions 1-4)

Exposure of the skin to ultra violet radiation (UVR) is associated with an increased risk of cancer. The UVR spectrum is divided into three regions: UVA, UVB, and UVC, as shown in Figure 1.

[UVC] [UVB] [UVA]

200 300 400

Nanometers

Figure 1 Division of UVR spectrum

The higher energy photons of UVR are mutagenic, leading to the photochemically induced dimerization of pyrimidines at their Carbon-Carbon double bond site, shown in Figure 2.

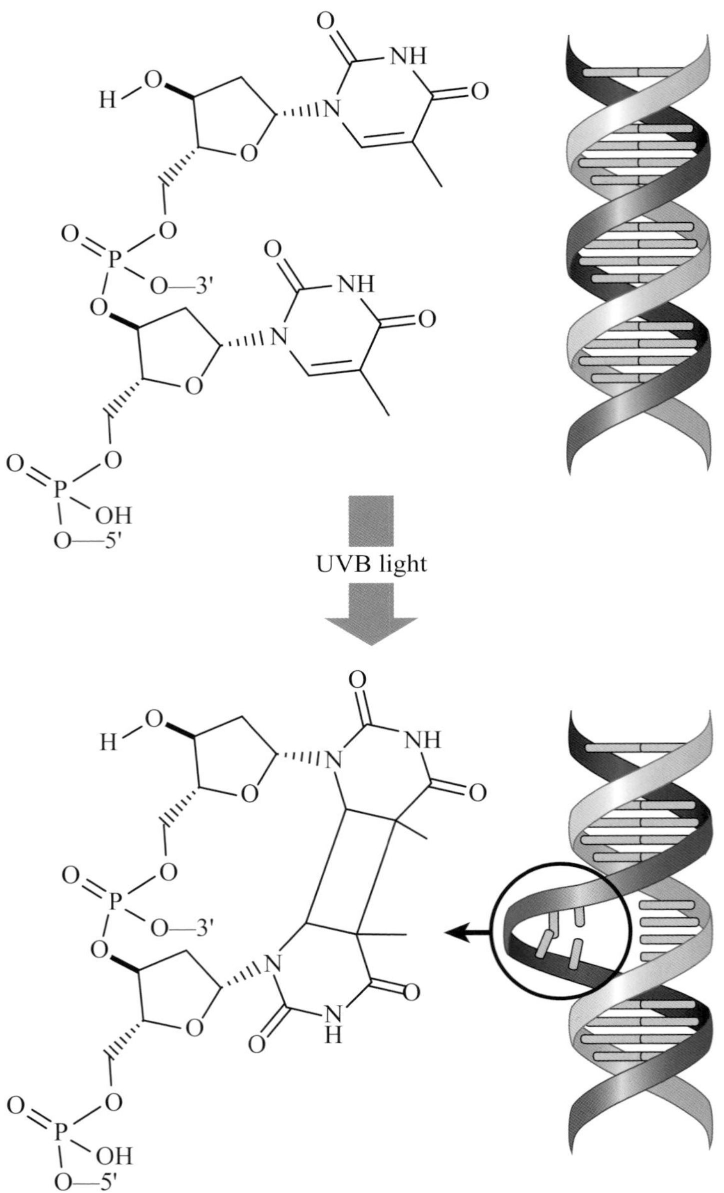

Figure 2 Photochemically induced dimerization reaction

The incorrect repair of these lesions leads to permanent mutations, which, overtime, may promote cutaneous oncogenesis.

Tanning beds are particularly dangerous, as they provide a much greater exposure to UVR than sunlight. The bulbs in tanning beds rely on the UVR emission spectrum of excited gaseous mercury. The technology used in these lamps can be understood with the principles of Bohr's model of the hydrogen atom.

In the Bohr model, electrons orbit the nucleus of an atom in orbitals of fixed energy. Electrons can gain or lose energy by absorbing or releasing photons, respectively, and moving from one discrete orbital to the next.

The energy provided to the mercury in the arc lamp promotes electrons to higher energy levels. When they relax, they release energy in the form of UVR. Advances in quantum mechanics have since antiquated Bohr's model, but it is still valid for hydrogenic species, or atomic systems comprised of one point charge orbiting another. In particular, the Bohr model predicts that the wavelength of light λ released during an electronic transition is dependent on the atomic number Z, principal quantum numbers n, and a constant R.

$$\frac{1}{\lambda} = RZ^2\left(\frac{1}{n_f^2} - \frac{1}{n_i^2}\right)$$

Equation 1

Question 1

All of the following atomic species can be modeled by the Bohr model EXCEPT:

- **A.** H.
- **B.** Be^{3+}.
- **C.** Li^{+}.
- **D.** He^{+}.

Question 2

The cytotoxicity of UVR increases with increasing photon energy. What region of the light spectrum is best for sterilizing water?

- **A.** UVA
- **B.** UVB
- **C.** UVC
- **D.** Infrared region

Question 3

Which of the following phrases accurately describes photon emission from a hydrogen arc lamp?

- A. Photon emission is endothermic; $\Delta E > 0$ kJ/mol.
- B. Photon emission is exothermic; $\Delta E < 0$ kJ/mol.
- C. The wavelength of the photon released during the $n = 3$ to $n = 2$ transition is shorter than the $n = 4$ to $n = 2$ transition.
- D. The energy of the photon released during the $n = 3$ to $n = 2$ transition is greater than the $n = 4$ to $n = 2$ transition.

Question 4

Approximately what minimum wavelength can be achieved during an electronic transition that ends at the 3rd energy level for a He^+ atom?

- A. 0.44R
- B. 1.5/R
- C. 4.5/R
- D. 2.25/R

Passage 2 (Questions 5-9)

Glioblastoma (GBM) is the most common and malignant tumor of the central nervous system with a poor overall survival rate. Genetic alterations such as epidermal growth factor receptor (EGFR) gene amplification and mutation are main drivers promoting GBM progression and malignancy. The most common mutant of EGFR, EGFRvIII, occurs at an overall frequency of 25–64%.

The need for molecular imaging probes with easier syntheses, better thermal stability, smaller size, lower immunogenicity, and more versatile chemistry has led to the development of radiolabeled aptamers as promising candidates. Aptamers are single-stranded oligonucleotides with excellent affinity and specificity for their target.

^{188}Re is a useful option for radiolabeling aptamers and pharmaceuticals by virtue of its favorable physical and nuclear properties. ^{188}Re decays via β^- particle emission, suitable for radiotherapy, and its β^- decay is also accompanied by a high energy γ-ray emission.

A recent study evaluated the performance of a group of aptamers (U2, U8, U19, and U31) to be radiolabeled with ^{118}Re, designed to target EGFRvIII cells. EGFRvIII cells were dissociated with protease K at 37°C for 3 min and 10 min respectively. Further digestive action was halted by addition of a protease inhibitor. After washing, samples were incubated with fluorescein isocyanate (FITC)-labeled aptamers (Figure 1), and then subjected to flow cytometry analysis.

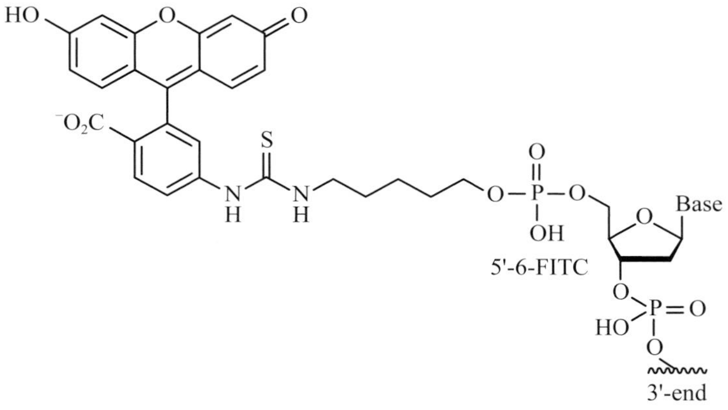

Figure 1 FITC labeled oligonucleotide

FITC fluoresces, allowing labeled cells to be counted based on fluoresced light following laser excitation Their results of this study for all aptamers is shown below, in Figure 2.

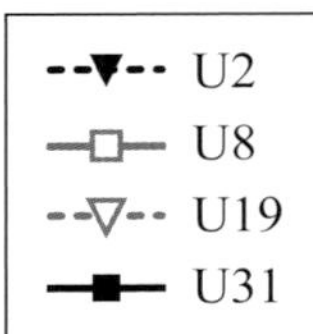

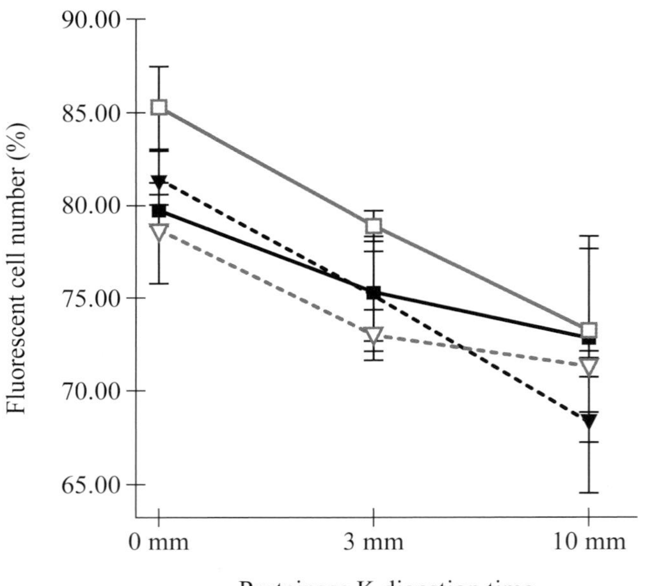

Figure 2 Digestion time influence on cell number fluorescence

This passage was adapted from ""Cell-SELEX Aptamer or Highly Specific Radionuclide Molecular Imaging of Glioblastoma In Vivo." Wu X, Liang H, Tan Y, Yuan C, Li S, Li X, et al. *PLoS ONE*. 2014. 9(3) doi: 10.1371/journal.pone.0090752 for use under the terms of the Creative Commons CC BY 4.0 Attribution license (http://creativecommons.org/licenses/by/4.0/legalcode).

Question 5

What is the molecular weight of the product of the decay of ^{188}Re?

- **A.** 189 g/mol
- **B.** 190 g/mol
- **C.** 188 g/mol
- **D.** 187 g/mol

Question 6

FITC contains a carboxylate moiety, and the ribose sugar contains an ether group in its heterocycle. What are the effective nuclear charges (Z_{eff}) of each of these oxygen atoms, respectively?

- **A.** −1, 0
- **B.** −½, 0
- **C.** 7, 6
- **D.** 6, 6

Question 7

The work function, ϕ, is the minimum work required to eject an electron from the surface of a solid. If the surface of a lead apron is struck with a γ-ray with an energy of 50 keV following ^{188}Re decay, which of the following will most likely occur? (Note: $\phi_{Pb} = 4.1$ eV)

- **A.** One electron will be ejected with a kinetic energy of 8×10^{-15} J.
- **B.** A multitude of electrons will be ejected; the sum of their kinetic energy will be equal to 50 keV − ϕ_{PB}.
- **C.** No electrons will be ejected from the lead apron.
- **D.** One electron will be ejected with a kinetic energy of 7.3×10^{-18} J.

Question 8

Solid ^{188}Re is best described under which of the following categories?

- **A.** Representative element
- **B.** Alkaline earth metal
- **C.** Chalcogen
- **D.** Transition metal

Question 9

Which conclusion is best supported by the results of this experiment?

- **A.** U8 shows the greatest affinities for the defective EGFRvIII gene.
- **B.** U2 shows the greatest affinity for enzymes coded by the EGFRvIII gene.
- **C.** U8 shows the greatest affinity for transmembrane receptors coded by the EGFRvIII gene.
- **D.** U2 shows the greatest affinities for the defective EGFRvIII gene.

Passage 3 (Questions 10-13)

Zinc is an important essential trace element for growth, metabolism, and wound healing in both human and animals. Zinc oxide (ZnO) is generally considered as a cheap inorganic material with low toxicity, which is commonly used as a nutritional or medical additive for the zinc-deficient children. Additionally, zinc oxide nanoparticles (nano-ZnOs) are widely used in personal care products, including cosmetics and sunscreens.

It is an emerging need to investigate the toxicity of nano-ZnOs, which can easily enter cells due to their smaller size and introduce oxidative stress. Previous studies have shown that nano-ZnOs could interfere with zinc ion hemostasis via enhanced absorption and transported to the target organs.

Body and organ weights are sensitive indicators for identification of the potentially harmful effects of drugs on animals. In order to evaluate the long term effects of doses of nano-ZnOs on development, zinc metabolism, and mineral bio-distribution of Zn, Fe, Cu, and Mn in different tissues, scientists randomly divided 48 mice into four groups. The mice were fed diets as follows for 32 weeks and their weights recorded weekly: (1) the control group: basal diet; (2) 50 mg/kg nano-ZnO group: basal diet + 50 mg/kg nano-ZnOs; (3) 500 mg/kg nano-ZnO group: basal diet + 500 mg/kg nano-ZnOs; (4) 5000 mg/kg nano-ZnO group: basal diet + 5000 mg/kg nano-ZnOs. The recorded weights are shown in Figure 1.

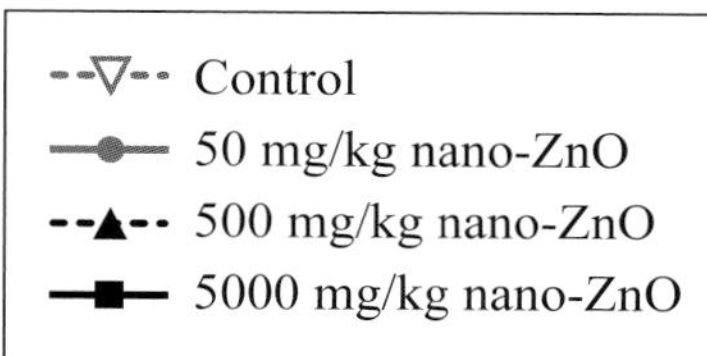

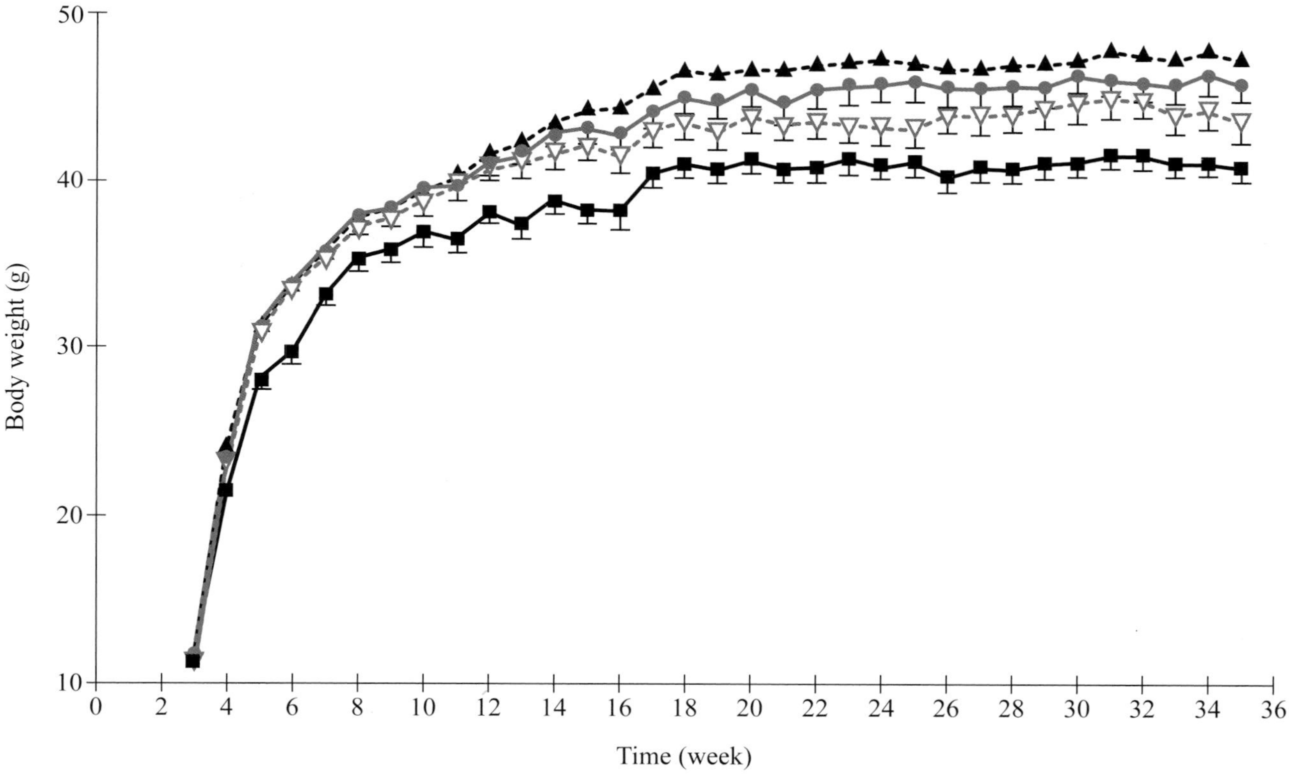

Figure 1 Mean body weights of male mice in control and 50, 500, and 5000 mg/kg groups

This passage is adapted from "Effects of Long-Term Exposure to Zinc Oxide Nanoparticles on Development, Zinc Metabolism and Biodistribution of Minerals (Zn, Fe, Cu, Mn) in Mice." Wang C, Lu J, Zhou L, Li J, Li W, et al. *PLoS ONE.* 2016. 11(10) doi:10.1371/journal.pone.0164434 for use under the terms of the Creative Commons CC BY 4.0 license (http://creativecommons.org/licenses/by/4.0/legalcode).

Question 10

The bond between the atoms in ZnO is most likely to be characterized by:

- A. even sharing of electrons between Zn and O.
- B. polarization of electrons shared between Zn and O towards Zn.
- C. polarization of electrons shared between Zn and O towards O.
- D. transfer of electrons from Zn to O.

Question 11

Dietary Cu is most likely to be classified as a(n):

- A. metalloid.
- B. transition metal.
- C. non-metal.
- D. lanthanide.

Question 12

In a follow up study, scientists also discovered variations in body weight after treatment with another compound. The greatest reduction in body weight was also likely seen with which of the following compounds?

- A. 500 mg/kg NiF
- B. 500 mg/kg PdO
- C. 5000 mg/kg RbB
- D. 5000 mg/kg FeN

Question 13

Researchers discovered that certain transporters showed variations in mRNA expression, depending on the concentration of nano-ZnO that cells were treated with. The supplemental data suggest that MT1 and MT2 likely:

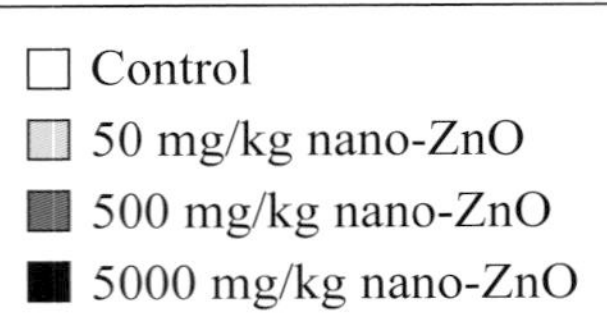

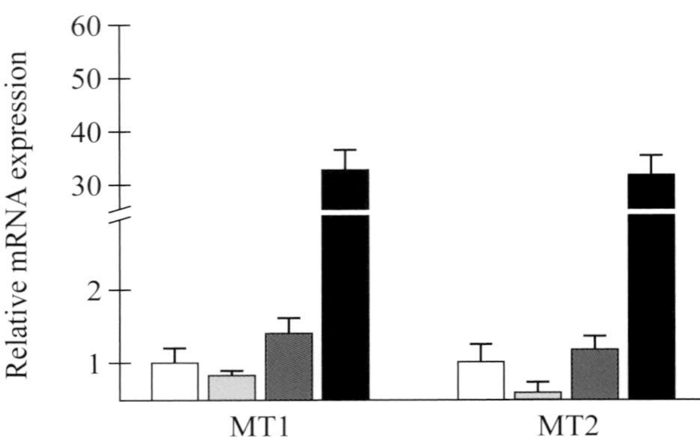

- A. transport paramagnetic transition metals.
- B. transport diamagnetic transition metals.
- C. transport anionic metalloids.
- D. transport cationic non-metals.

Questions 14 - 17 do not refer to a passage and are independent of each other.

Question 14

By the Pauli Exclusion Principle, which of the following is impossible?

- O **A.** Two electrons sharing the same quantum state
- O **B.** Two electrons having the same spin
- O **C.** Two electrons sharing an orbital
- O **D.** Two electrons sharing the same ionization energy

Question 15

Under the Heisenberg uncertainty principle, which of the following cannot be known when defining the position of an electron in an electronic structure?

- O **A.** Velocity
- O **B.** Acceleration
- O **C.** Momentum
- O **D.** Time

Question 16

Compared to the ground state, the excited state of the electrons in Ta_2PdSe_5 would:

I. have a higher energy.
II. release a proton.
III. exist at higher temperatures.

- O **A.** I only
- O **B.** I and II only
- O **C.** I and III only
- O **D.** I, II, and III

Question 17

Electrons in which orbital experience the greatest Z_{eff}?

- O **A.** 3*d*
- O **B.** 3*p*
- O **C.** 1*s*
- O **D.** 4*d*

Passage 4 (Questions 18-21)

Magnetic Resonance Imagine (MRI) is an imaging technique that is a relatively new addition to medical technology. MRI is capable of providing exquisite contrast between tissues that otherwise appear the same on CT scan. Additionally, the images are less pixilated, and various sequences on the MRI scanner can be used to highlight certain structures. MRI scanners rely on super conductive metals to function. Development of superior superconductors is therefore a highly valuable field of research.

Superconductivity with very large upper critical fields has been reported in several layered compounds $M_2Pd_xCh_5$ where M = Nb or Ta and Ch = S or Se. An important chemical feature of these compounds is that one of the Pd sites in the unit cell is chemically less favorable than the other, leading to a tendency for Pd deficiency.

Researchers studied the electronic structure and related properties of the superconductor Ta_2PdSe_5. The crystal structure is shown in Figure 1. The Fermi surface has two disconnected sheets, both derived from bands of primarily chalcogenide p states. These are a corrugated hole cylinder and a heavier complex shaped electron sheet. The sheets contain 0.048 holes and a compensating number of electrons per formula unit, making the material a semimetallic superconductor. The results support the presence of two band superconductivity, although a discrepancy in the specific heat is noted.

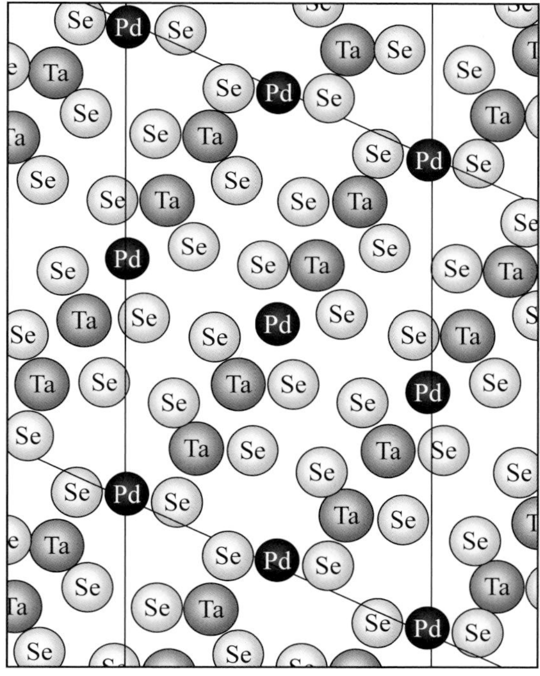

Figure 1 Crystal structure of Ta_2PdSe_5

This passage was adapted from "Multiband Semimetallic Electronic Structure of Superconducting Ta_2PdSe_5." Singh DJ. *PLoS ONE*. 2015. 10(4). doi:10.1371/journal.pone.0123667 for use under the terms of Creative Commons CC BY 4.0 license. (http://creativecommons.org/licenses/by/4.0/legalcode).

Question 18

Of the possible atoms denoted Ch in the molecular formula, which of the following has the greatest partial negative charge (δ^-)?

- O **A.** S
- O **B.** Se
- O **C.** Pd
- O **D.** F

Question 19

What is the expected electronic structure of the monoatomic uncharged atom in Ta_2PdSe_5?

- O **A.** $[Kr]4d^8\ 5s^1$
- O **B.** $[Xe]4f^{14}\ 5d^5$
- O **C.** $[Xe]4f^{14}\ 5d^3\ 6s^2$
- O **D.** $[Kr]4d^{10}$

Question 20

Which of the following correctly describes Ta_2PdSe_5?

- O **A.** All of the atoms are metals.
- O **B.** Two of the atoms are metals, and one is a nonmetal.
- O **C.** One of the atoms is a metal, and two are nonmetals.
- O **D.** All of the atoms are nonmetals.

Question 21

The following figure depicts the experimental results of the electronic structure of Ta_2PdSe_5. Which of the following statements is accurate?

Pd *d* orbital
Td *d* orbital

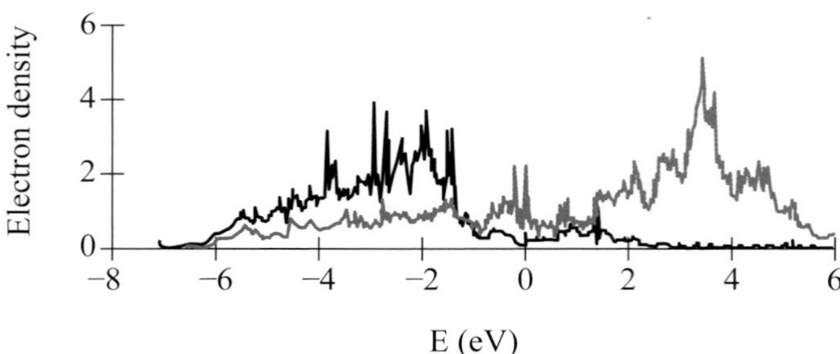

- O **A.** At high energy, many electrons occupy the *d* orbital of Pd.
- O **B.** At very low energy, few electrons occupy the *d* orbitals of Ta or Pd.
- O **C.** Moving from low to high energy, the electrons move from Ta to PD.
- O **D.** The *s* orbitals of both Ta and Pd are full at low energy.

Passage 5 (Questions 22-25)

Halogens are the only group in the periodic table whose elements, under ambient conditions, can represent all three states of matter. Fluorine and chlorine are gasses and bromine is a liquid. Iodine is a solid, with a reflective metallic luster.

In the gas phase, all four of these elements have characteristic colors as shown in Table 1.

Table 1 Gaseous Halogen Colors

Halogen	Color
Fluorine	Very pale yellow
Chlorine	Yellow to green
Bromine	Red
Iodine	Violet

Elemental halogens are toxic to most organisms, and have even been intentionally exploited for lethal purposes in chemical warfare. Nonetheless, metal halide salts are essential for the health of most living things. In the human body, fluoride is present in bone and dental structures. Chloride is the primary anion in all bodily fluids, making up ≈ 70% of the total negative ion content in the body. Bromide is a cofactor for the biosynthesis of collagen. Iodide is a vital constituent in thyroid hormones such as thyroxine (T_4), shown in Figure 1.

Figure 1 Structure of thyroxine

Iodine is unique in other respects as well. Under atmospheric conditions, solid iodine lacks a melting point, and after absorbing sufficient thermal energy, sublimation occurs. It is this effect that is utilized in the "purple smoke" reaction, where powdered iodine is reduced with powdered aluminum into a covalently bonded dimeric solid through Reaction 1. The exothermicity of the reaction causes excess iodine to sublime into a rich violet colored gas. Reaction 1 is initiated by adding a drop of hot water to a mixture of the two powders.

$$2Al(s) + 3I_2(s) \rightarrow Al_2I_6(s)$$

Reaction 1

Question 22

Which of following hypotheses is best supported by the data in Table 1?

I. Of the elements in Table 1, fluorine absorbs the highest energy visible light, and after undergoing an electron transition, reemits it. Unabsorbed light is transmitted through the gas.

II. Of the elements in Table 1, fluorine absorbs the highest energy visible light, which is converted to heat, and does not undergo an electron transition. Unabsorbed light is reflected from the gas.

III. Of the elements in Table 1, iodine absorbs the highest energy visible light, which is converted to heat, and does not undergo an electron transition. Unabsorbed light is reflected from the gas.

IV. Of the elements in Table 1, iodine absorbs the highest energy visible light, and after undergoing an electron transition, reemits it. Unabsorbed light is transmitted through the gas.

- O **A.** I and III only
- O **B.** I and IV only
- O **C.** II and III only
- O **D.** II and IV only

Question 23

Under ambient conditions, which factor explains the decreasing entropy of the halogens from fluorine to iodine?

- O **A.** Decreasing polarity
- O **B.** Decreasing electronegativity
- O **C.** Increasing quantity of valence electrons
- O **D.** Increasing mass

Question 24

What type of reaction is Reaction 1?

- O **A.** Single displacement
- O **B.** Lewis acid/Lewis base
- O **C.** Combination
- O **D.** Decomposition

Question 25

Which protocol would produce the most "purple smoke"?

- O **A.** 7.62 g I_2 and 0.54 g Al
- O **B.** 0.54 g I_2 and 7.62 g Al
- O **C.** 12.20 g I_2 and 0.54 g Al
- O **D.** 0.54 g I_2 and 12.20 g Al

Questions 26 - 29 do not refer to a passage and are independent of each other.

TEST 1A

Question 26

The emission spectra of many atomic species were tested for conformity with the Bohr model. Which of the tested atomic species below have the largest ionic or atomic radius?

- O **A.** Li^{2+}
- O **B.** He^{+}
- O **C.** B^{4+}
- O **D.** H

Question 27

The alpha decay of ^{187}Re, another radioisotope of Re, leads to:

I. a product with a larger atomic radius.

II. a product with a smaller atomic radius.

III. a product with a smaller mass number.

IV. a product with a smaller atomic number.

- O **A.** I, III, and IV only
- O **B.** II, III, and IV only
- O **C.** I and IV only
- O **D.** II and III only

Question 28

Tritium, $^{3}_{1}H$, is often formed in the water that cools fuel rods. Under standard conditions, what phase does tritium occupy?

- O **A.** Solid
- O **B.** Liquid
- O **C.** Gas
- O **D.** Plasma

Question 29

Which of the four important dietary elements has the greatest electron affinity?

- O **A.** Ca
- O **B.** S
- O **C.** Se
- O **D.** P

Passage 6 (Questions 30-33)

An emerging environmental health concern for urban populations is the presence of photochemical smog. Photochemical smog is a mixture of particulate matter and ground level ozone, which can lead to difficulty breathing, and in some individuals, may induce asthma attacks. Current research suggests that chronic exposure may permanently compromise pulmonary function.

In large cities, a major contributor to the formation of photochemical smog is exhaust gas from vehicles. The high temperatures achieved in an internal combustion engine cause nitrogen and oxygen to react, generating the nitrogen oxide species (NO_x), NO and NO_2. In addition, incomplete combustion products, such as CO, and other volatile organic compounds (VOCs) are released.

The first step in ozone formation is when a naturally occurring tropospheric hydroxyl radical attacks a VOC, creating a peroxy radical.

$$^{\bullet}OH(g) + CO(g) \rightarrow {}^{\bullet}HOCO(g)$$

Reaction 1

$$^{\bullet}HOCO(g) + O_2(g) \rightarrow HO_2{}^{\bullet}(g) + CO_2(g)$$

Reaction 2

The peroxy radical then attacks nitrogen oxide, forming nitrogen dioxide, which is subsequently photolyzed by light with a minimum $\lambda < 410$ nm. The highly reactive atomic oxygen product reacts with atmospheric oxygen to form surface level ozone.

$$HO_2{}^{\bullet}(g) + NO(g) \rightarrow {}^{\bullet}OH(g) + NO_2(g)$$

Reaction 3

$$NO_2(g) + h\upsilon \rightarrow NO(g) + O(g)$$

Reaction 4

$$O(g) + O_2(g) \rightarrow O_3(g)$$

Reaction 5

Under atmospheric conditions with an excess of oxygen, NO will form NO_2 in a concentration dependent manner as shown in Table 1.

Table 1 Concentration Dependent Rate of Formation of NO_2

NO concentration in air (ppm)	Time required for half NO to be oxidized to NO_2 (min)
20,000	0.125
10,000	0.25
1,000	2.5
100	25
10	250
1	2500

Question 30

Which of the following graphs best illustrates the relationship between the concentration of NO and the time required to form NO_2?

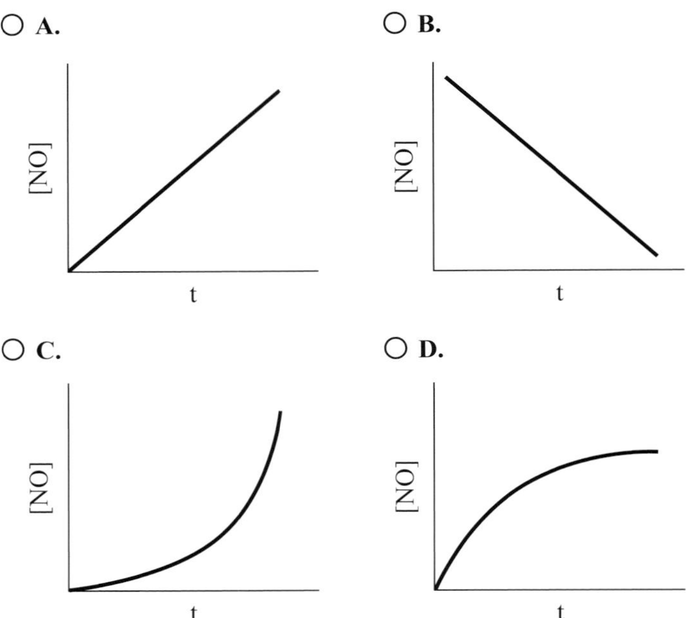

Question 31

What net reaction describes the formation of surface level ozone?

- A. $O(g) + O_2(g) \rightarrow O_3(g)$
- B. $NO_2(g) + h\upsilon + O_2(g) \rightarrow NO(g) + O_3(g)$
- C. $CO(g) + 2O_2(g) + h\upsilon \rightarrow CO_2(g) + O_3(g)$
- D. $CO(g) + O_2(g) + h\upsilon \rightarrow CO_2(g) + O_3(g)$

Question 32

What is the Lewis dot structure of ozone?

- A. ·Ö–Ö–Ö·
- B. :Ö–Ö=Ö: (with − formal charge on the left O and + on the central O)
- C. $[\ddot{O}{=}O{=}\ddot{O}]^{2+}$
- D. :Ö–Ö≡O:$^{+}$

Question 33

Atomic oxygen will:

- A. be attracted to a magnetic field, since it has completely paired electrons in its *p* orbital.
- B. be attracted to a magnetic field, since it has unpaired electrons in it *p* orbital.
- C. not be attracted to a magnetic field, since it has unpaired electrons in it *p* orbital.
- D. not be attracted in a magnetic field, since it has completely paired electrons in it *p* orbital.

Passage 7 (Questions 34-37)

Gamma radiation is responsible for many hazardous impacts on living tissue such as DNA damage, genomic instability, apoptosis, and inflammation, by the generation of reactive oxygen species (ROS). Although several synthetic radioprotectors like lipoic acid, deoxyspergualin, cysteine, and cysteamine are effective at preventing these hazards, systemic toxicity at their optimum protective doses limits their practical application. As a result, the investigation of non-toxic radioprotective compounds of biological origin is crucial.

Ferulic acid (FA), shown in Figure 1, is commonly found in wheat, rice bran, and broccoli, and has strong *in vitro* antioxidant properties. It is used in a variety of contexts, including in its monoanionic sodium salt form, sodium ferulate, as a flavor enhancer in artificial sweeteners. In a recent study, its capacity to reduce the lethality of acute radiation sickness, a direct manifestation of radiation induced tissue damage, was explored.

Ferulic acid

Figure 1 Structure of ferulic acid

During the study, inbred mice were subjected to 10 Gy of gamma irradiation (IR) from a ^{60}Co source. They were given various doses of FA for five days prior to the exposure. Their survival probability as a function of FA dosage/day during the course of the experiment is plotted in Figure 2.

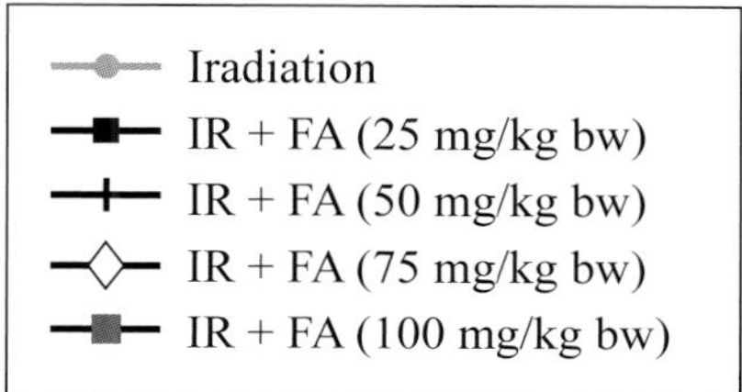

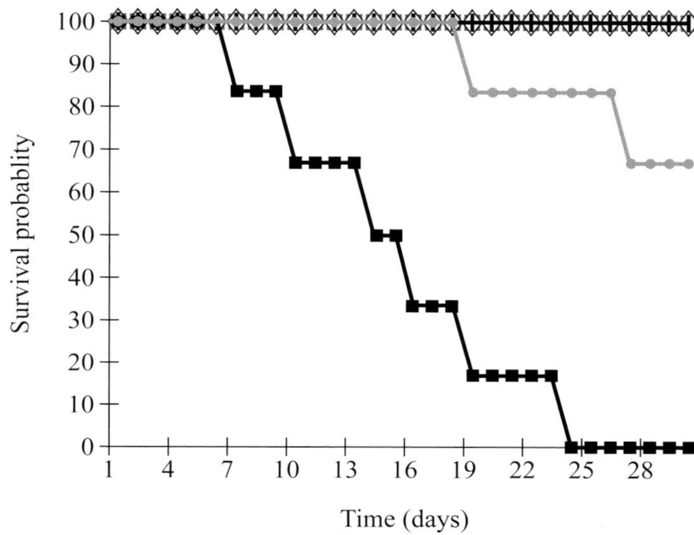

Figure 2 Survival probability for 30 days

This passage is adapted from "Role of Ferulic Acid in the Amelioration of Ionizing Radiation Induced Inflammation: A Murine Model". Das U, Manna K, Sinha M, Datta S, Das DK, et al. *PLoS ONE*. 2014. 9(5) doi:10.1371/journal.pone.0097599. For use under the terms of the Creative Commons CC BY 4.0 license.

Question 34

Which of the following solutions would form the most sodium ferulate from 97.1 g of FA? (Note: MW_{FA} = 194.18 g/mol)

- **A.** 500 mL of a 0.1 M solution of NaOH
- **B.** 500 mL of a 1 M solution of NaOH
- **C.** 250 mL of 0.25 M solution of NaOH
- **D.** 500 mL of a 2 M solution of NaOH

Question 35

What is the minimum daily dose of FA required to protect a 750 g rat from the lethal effects of acute radiation sickness for thirty days?

- **A.** 37.5 mg
- **B.** 50 mg
- **C.** 187.5 mg
- **D.** 45 mg

Question 36

Which ionization energy chart below best illustrates the ionization energies of the radiation source?

○ **A.**

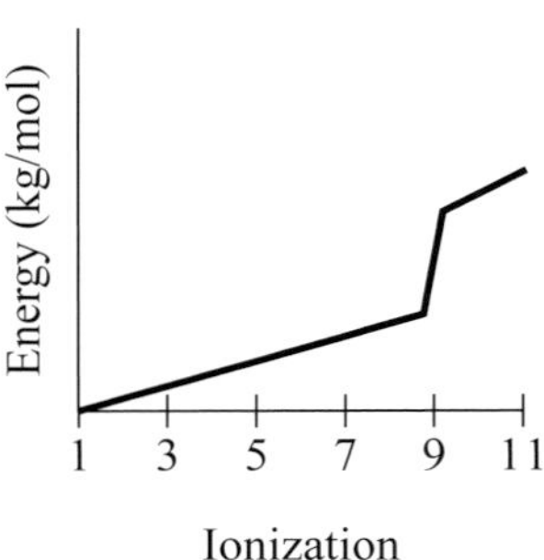

○ **B.**

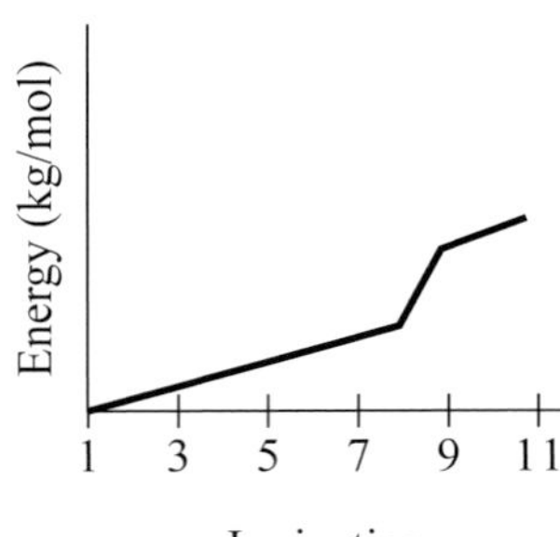

○ **C.**

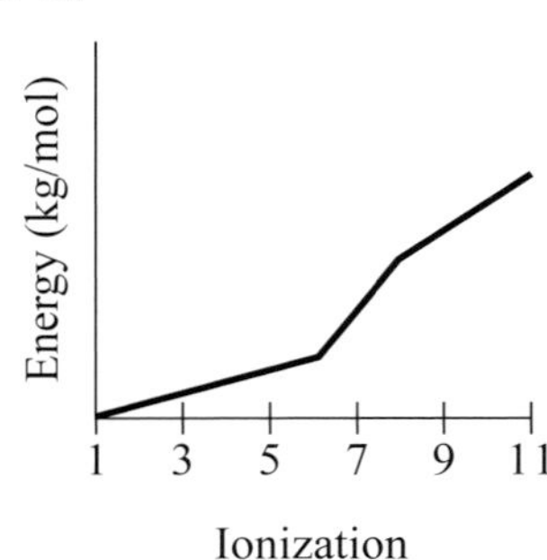

○ **D.**

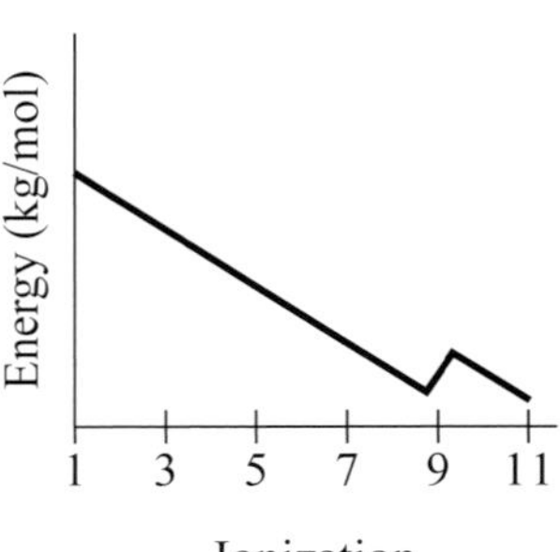

Question 37

The α plot of FA is shown below. What is its pK_{a2}?

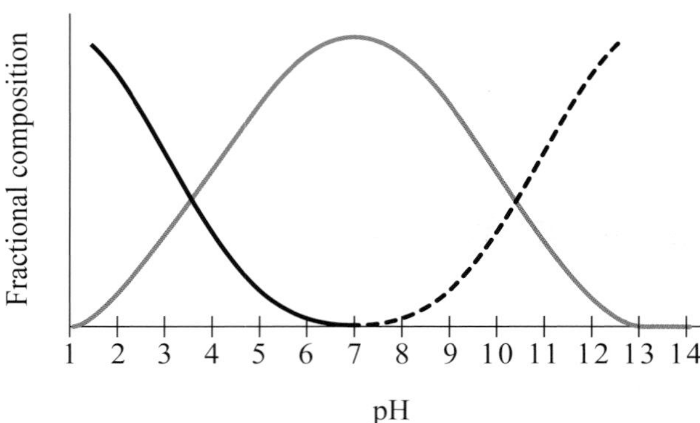

○ **A.** 3.5

○ **B.** 10.2

○ **C.** 12

○ **D.** 8

Passage 8 (Questions 38-42)

Strontium (Sr) can promote the process of bone formation. To improve bioactivity, porous allograft bone scaffolds (ABS) were doped with Sr and the mechanical strength and bioactivity of the scaffolds were evaluated. Sr-doped ABS were prepared using the ion exchange method.

The density and distribution of Sr in bone scaffolds were investigated by inductively coupled plasma optical emission spectrometry (ICP-OES), X-ray photoelectron spectroscopy (XPS), and energy-dispersive X-ray spectroscopy (EDS). Results are shown in Figure 1. The X-axis represents the distance from the starting point and the Y-axis represents the relative quantity of each element recorded during the examination.

A.

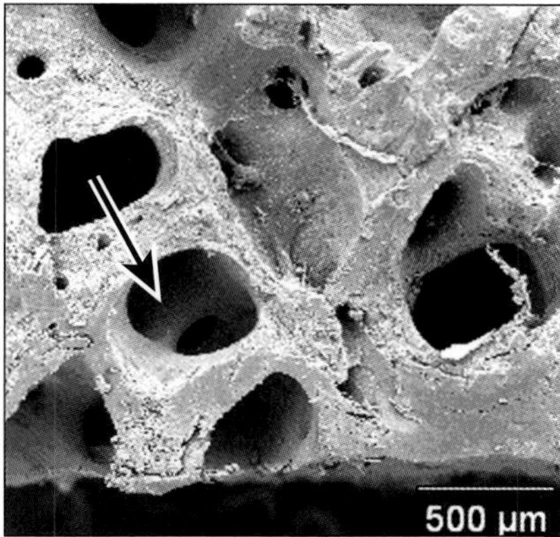

B.

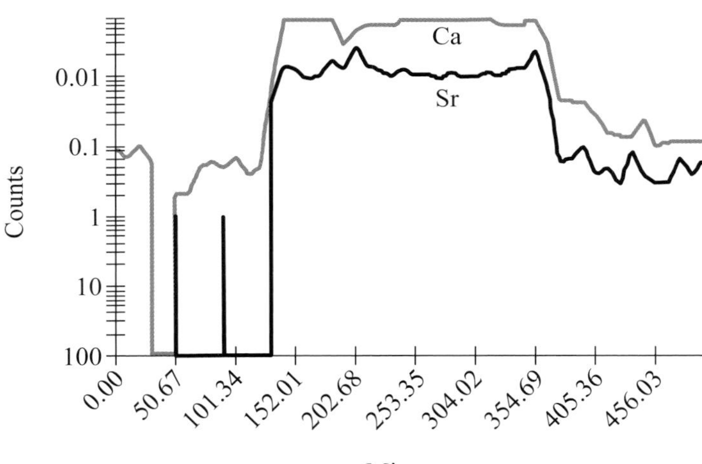

Figure 1 The relative quantity of Ca and Sr elements across the scanning route (arrow).

Controlled release of strontium ions was measured and mechanical strength was evaluated by a compressive strength test. The bioactivity of Sr-doped ABS was investigated by a simulated body fluid (SBF) assay, cytotoxicity testing, and an *in vivo* implantation experiment. The Sr molar concentration [Sr/(Sr + Ca)] in ABS surpassed 5% and Sr was distributed nearly evenly. XPS analyses suggest that Sr combined with oxygen and carbonate radicals. The compressive strength of the Sr-doped ABS did not change significantly. The bioactivity of Sr-doped material, as measured by the *in vitro* SBF immersion method, was superior to that of the Sr-free freeze-dried bone and the Sr-doped material did not show cytotoxicity compared with Sr-free culture medium. The rate of bone mineral deposition for Sr-doped ABS was faster than that of the control at 4 weeks (3.28 ± 0.23 µm/day vs. 2.60 ± 0.20 µm/day; $p < 0.05$).

This passage was adapted from "Porous Allograft Bone Scaffolds: Doping with Strontium." Zhao Y, Guo D, Hou S, Zhong H, Yan J, et al.. *PLoS ONE*. 2013. 8(7). doi:10.1371/journal.pone.0069339 for use under the terms of Creative Commons CC BY 3.0 license. (http://creativecommons.org/licenses/by/3.0/legalcode).

Question 38

Which of the follow properties do calcium and strontium share?

I. The preferred oxidation state is 2^+ outer *s* orbital is full of electrons in the resting state.
II. They are shiny silver solids at room temperature.
III. They are red on the flame test.

- A. I only
- B. II only
- C. II and III only
- D. I, II, and III

Question 39

The combination of Sr with a chalcogen as stated in the passage would produce a molecule with how many atoms?

- A. One
- B. Two
- C. Three
- D. Four

Question 40

Based on Figure 1, which of the following is true?

- A. There is a greater concentration of calcium, which has greater ionization energy, incorporated into the bone.
- B. There is a greater concentration of strontium, which has greater ionization energy, incorporated into the bone.
- C. There is a greater concentration of calcium, which has a lesser ionization energy, incorporated into the bone.
- D. There is a greater concentration of strontium, which has a lesser ionization energy, incorporated into the bone.

Question 41

Strontium is the primary metal found in strontianite ($SrCO_3$), which is popular in costume jewelry because it resembles a cloudy diamond and is fluorescent under UV light. Which of the following is true of the atoms in strontianite?

- O **A.** The strontium has the greatest electron affinity.
- O **B.** The carbon has the greatest electron affinity.
- O **C.** The oxygen has the greatest electron affinity.
- O **D.** The electron affinity of each atom is equal.

Question 42

Which of the following could be used instead of 176 g of Sr for doping bone?

- O **A.** 24 g Mg
- O **B.** 170 g Rb
- O **C.** 274 g Ba
- O **D.** 454 g Ra

Questions 43 - 46 do not refer to a passage and are independent of each other.

Question 43

The human body has about 5.5 L of blood which contains 3.5 g of dissolved chloride ion. What is concentration of chloride ion in the blood?

- O **A.** 17.9 mmol/L
- O **B.** 0.0179 mmol/L
- O **C.** 179 mmol/L
- O **D.** 8.9 mmol/L

Question 44

Which of the following compounds would most likely share similar reactivity to ZnO?

- O **A.** CoO
- O **B.** MnO
- O **C.** CaO_2
- O **D.** CdO

Question 45

The electrons that participate in amide bonding are most likely to be found closest to which of the following atoms?

- O **A.** Nitrogen
- O **B.** Hydrogen
- O **C.** Oxygen
- O **D.** Carbon

Question 46

The group of elements with the lowest first ionization energies are:

- O **A.** alkaline earth metals.
- O **B.** alkali metals.
- O **C.** noble gasses.
- O **D.** the oxygen group.

Passage 9 (Questions 47-51)

The interactions between the twenty natural amino acids (aa) are the dominant factors in determining protein structures and interactions. Due to structural diversity, the aa side chain interactions exhibit varying energetic contributions and physical properties, which cannot be explained simply by the familiar interaction types, such as hydrogen bonds, van der Waals interactions, and electrostatic interactions. In protein chemistry, strong aa interactions include salt bridges, cation-π bond interactions, and amide bridge interactions. Salt bridge interactions play an important role in the amyloid-beta plaque growth of Alzheimer's and related diseases. Amide bridge interactions may contribute to the pathogenesis of other neurologic diseases.

The energies of the three strong aa side chain interaction types were studied by quantum modeling in an effort to understand their role in protein stability. The energy of the interactions was defined as the energy difference $\Delta E(\mathrm{a}-\mathrm{b})$ between the energy $E(\mathrm{a}-\mathrm{b})$ of the aa pair-complex a – b and the energy summation $E(\mathrm{a}) + E(\mathrm{b})$ of the two amino acid monomers a and b, as shown in Equation 1. Positive values of $\Delta E(\mathrm{a}-\mathrm{b})$ represent repulsive interactions, while negative values describe attractive interactions.

$$\Delta E(\mathrm{a}-\mathrm{b}) = E(\mathrm{a}-\mathrm{b}) - [E(\mathrm{a}) + E(\mathrm{b})]$$

Equation 1

The two amide-containing amino acids, Asn and Gln, possess both a partially positively charged NH_2 group and a partially negatively charged C=O group (Figure 1). This allows two amide-containing amino acids to form an amide bridge.

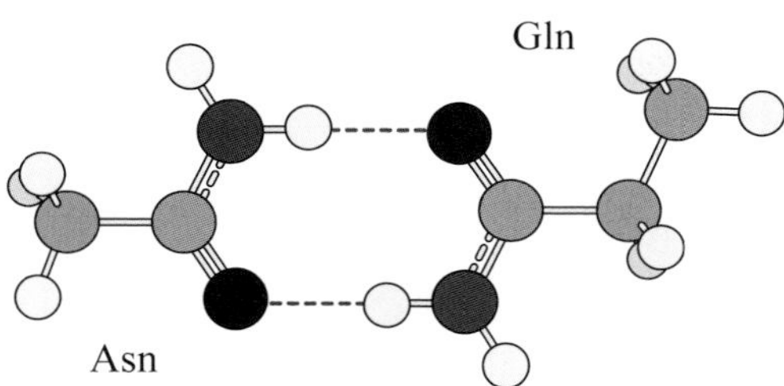

Figure 1 Amide bridge interactions between amino acids Asn and Gln

This passage is adapted from "Exploring Strong Interactions in Proteins with Quantum Chemistry and Examples of Their Applications in Drug Design." Xie N-Z, Du Q-S, Li J-X, and Huang R-B. *PLoS ONE.* 2015. 10(9) doi:10.1371/journal.pone.0137113 for use under the terms of the Creative Commons CC BY 4.0 license (http://creativecommons.org/licenses/by/4.0/legalcode).

Question 47

The electron configuration of nitrogen, one atom that participates in an amide bond, is shown below. Which of the following best explains the *p* orbital arrangement?

↿⇂	↿⇂	↿	↿	↿
1*s*	2*s*		2*p*	

- A. Orthogonal arrangement of electrons minimizes repulsion and lowers the energy of each suborbital.
- B. The *d* suborbitals of nitrogen had been filled, leaving the remaining valence electrons for the *p* suborbital.
- C. The valence shell of N contains three electrons.
- D. The electron configuration of N is the same as O^-.

Question 48

The electronic structure for the most electronegative atom in the Gln side chain is:

- A. [He]$2s^2 2p^3$
- B. [Ne]$1s^2 1p^5$
- C. [He]$2s^2 2p^4$
- D. [Ne]$2s^2 2p^5$

Question 49

Synthetic amino acids are often made by the Gabriel synthesis reactions in an atmosphere composed of Ar and Ne. Which of the following statements best explains why?

- A. Ar is used to protect the reducing end of the synthesized amine.
- B. Ne prevents atmospheric elements from reacting with potassium phthalimide.
- C. Ar reacts with an alkyl halide to activate it for addition to the phthalimide ring.
- D. Ne stabilizes the leaving group from the phthalimide ring to generate the amino acid.

TEST 1A

Question 50

Quantum modeling is unable to accurately describe the electron density of a cation-π bond interaction between amino acids because:

- A. a cation-π bond resembles a hydrogen bond, which does not have electron sharing.
- B. the speed and location of an electron cannot be simultaneously known.
- C. amino acids does not form cation-π bonds with one another.
- D. no amino contains an aromatic functional group that can contribute the π bond.

Question 51

In a separate experiment, scientists measured the $\Delta E(\mathrm{a}-\mathrm{b})$ of two atoms or ions that were expected to simulate strong amino acid interactions and found that the $\Delta E(\mathrm{a}-\mathrm{b}) = -100$ kJ. The two atoms or ions included in the experiment were most likely:

- A. Na^+ and Ca^{2+}.
- B. Li^+ and H.
- C. Mg^{2+} and O^{2-}.
- D. Kr and He^-.

Passage 10 (Questions 52-56)

Nuclear meltdown occurs when the cooling medium which surrounds the fuel rods in a reactor core is lost, and the fuel-rods' decay processes cause them to overheat and melt. Meltdown events pose a unique health threat, as they can release a profusion of carcinogenic radioactive materials.

The uranium fuel within the rods is encased in a zirconium alloy. During meltdown in water-containing reactors, high temperatures accelerate Reaction 1:

$$Zr(s) + 2H_2O(l) \rightarrow ZrO_2(s) + 2H_2(g)$$

Reaction 1

The hydrogen gas in this reaction poses a serious hazard. If exposed to air, it can explode violently when it combines with oxygen to form water.

Among the released waste of a meltdown are ^{134}Cs and ^{137}Cs. These radionuclides are of interest due to their long half-lives of 2 and 30 years, respectively. The release of ^{134}Cs and ^{137}Cs engenders the serious problem of radiocesium attachment to and/or uptake by agricultural plants such as bamboo.

A recent study used gamma-spectrometry to asses the degree of radionuclide uptake in bamboo in a city neighboring the meltdown site (N) and in a more distant city (D). The results are shown below in Figure 1.

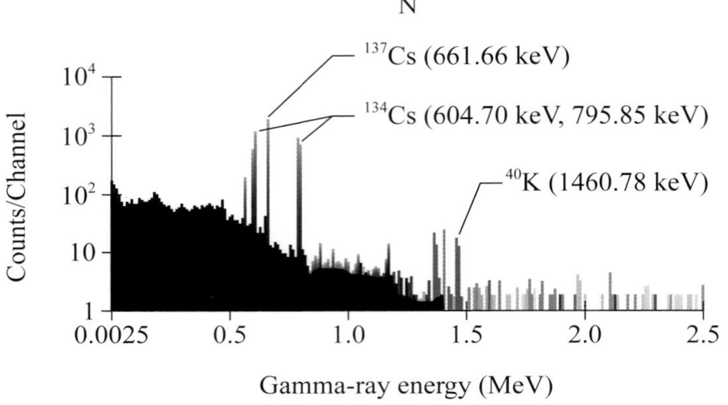

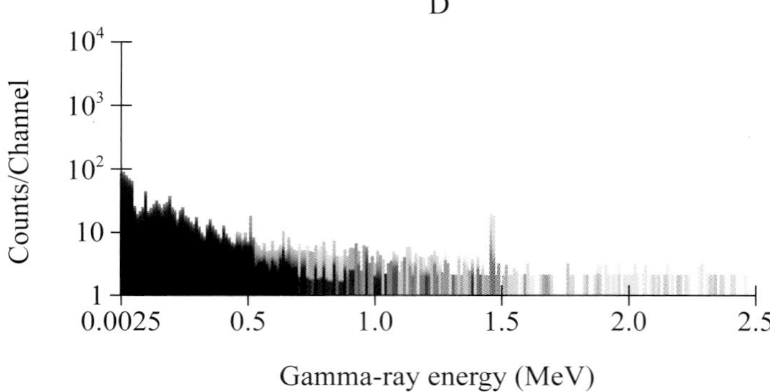

Figure 1 γ-ray spectrum of bamboo samples

Gamma-spectrometry takes advantage of detecting the characteristic γ-ray signature of specific elements. The specific signature is a consequence of three types of γ-ray interactions: photoelectron absorption (PA), Compton scattering (CS), and pair production (PP), as shown in Figure 2:

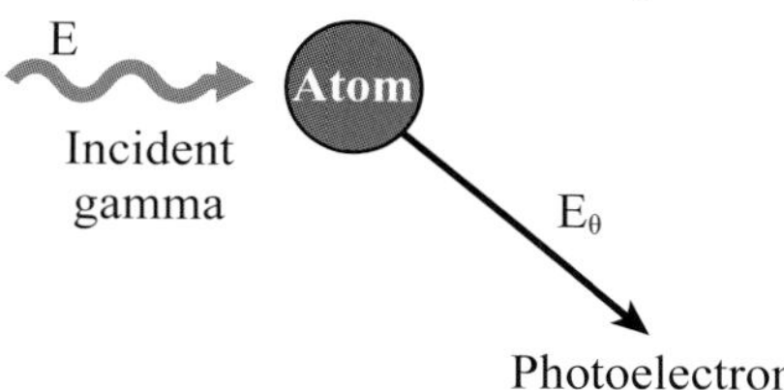

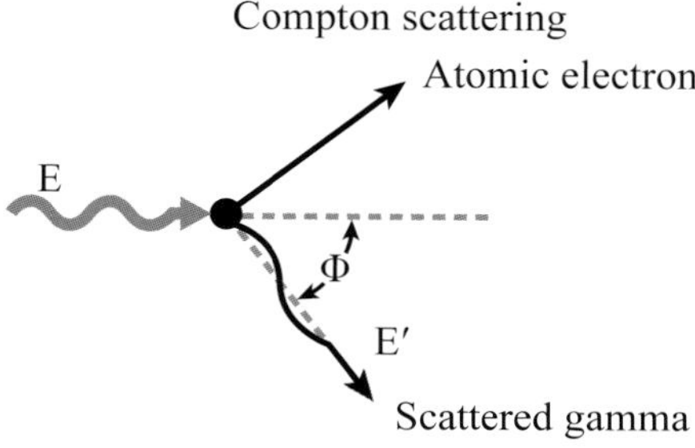

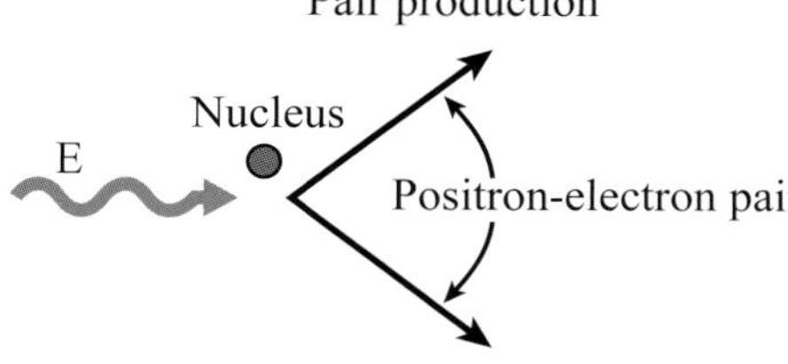

Figure 2 Schematic of γ-ray interactions

During PA, a photoelectron is ejected from the struck particle, and its energy is equal to the energy of γ-ray minus the electron binding energy of the material. CS results in the elastic scattering of the incident γ-ray after striking an electron. The remaining energy of the γ-ray *E′* is described with Equation 1.

$$E' = \frac{E}{1 + \frac{E}{m_0 c^2}(1 - \cos\theta)}$$

Equation 1

PP results in the generation of a positron and electron which carry the gamma ray energy minus $2m_0c^2$, where m_0 is their rest mass.

This passage was adapted from "Radionuclide analysis on bamboos following the Fukishima nuclear accident". Higaki T, Higaki S, Hirota M, Akita K, Hasezawa S. *PLoS ONE*. 2012. 7(4) doi:10.1371journal.pone.0034766 for use under the terms of the Creative Commons CC BY 3.0 Attribution license (http://creativecommons.org/licenses/by/3.0/legalcode).

Question 52

The energy of a γ-ray following Compton scattering:

- O **A.** is greatest when it has a small scattering angle.
- O **B.** is greatest when it has a large scattering angle.
- O **C.** is the same regardless of the scattering angle.
- O **D.** is greater than the energy of the incident gamma ray.

Question 53

During a reactor meltdown, how much steam could 20 L of hydrogen produce if it reacts with 20 L of oxygen, at SATP?

- O **A.** 40 L
- O **B.** 30 L
- O **C.** 20 L
- O **D.** 10 L

Question 54

The active volume of the detector used in this experiment had a binding energy of 360 keV. If a full energy ^{137}Cs γ-ray struck it, what maximum velocity could the ejected photoelectron have? (Note: $m_e = 9.1 \times 10^{-31}$ kg)

- O **A.** 3×10^5 m/sec
- O **B.** 2×10^7 m/sec
- O **C.** 2×10^8 m/sec
- O **D.** 5×10^{16} m/sec

Question 55

Reaction 1 is best described as which of the following types of reaction?

- O **A.** Combination reaction
- O **B.** Decomposition reaction
- O **C.** Oxidation-reduction reaction
- O **D.** Arrhenius acid/base reaction

Question 56

After 6.5 years, what will be the activity of the leaf sample's higher energy ^{134}Cs peak?

- O **A.** 62.5 counts/channel
- O **B.** 307 counts/channel
- O **C.** 130 counts/channel
- O **D.** 105 counts/channel

Questions 57 - 59 do not refer to a passage and are independent of each other.

Question 57

All of the following are true regarding the isotopic distribution of uranium on earth EXCEPT:

I. ^{235}U is not the isotope of greatest natural abundance.

II. if a mole of uranium dioxide is reduced to metallic uranium, the metallic uranium will have a mass of approximately 92 g.

III. an isotope of uranium with a mass number greater than 238 does not naturally exist.

IV. the alpha emission product of ^{238}U is ^{234}Th.

- A. I, II, and III only
- B. II, III, and IV only
- C. II and III only
- D. III and IV only

Question 58

The reaction between a metal and water was used to produce hydrogen gas that was used to hydrogenate an intermediate in a synthetic fatty acid synthesis pathway. The metal used was most likely:

- A. Ni.
- B. Ca.
- C. Li.
- D. Fe.

Question 59

Calcium gluconate, shown below, is often used to treat burns caused by industrial exposure to hydrofluoric acid. Which of the following statements best explains why calcium gluconate is effective at treating HF burns?

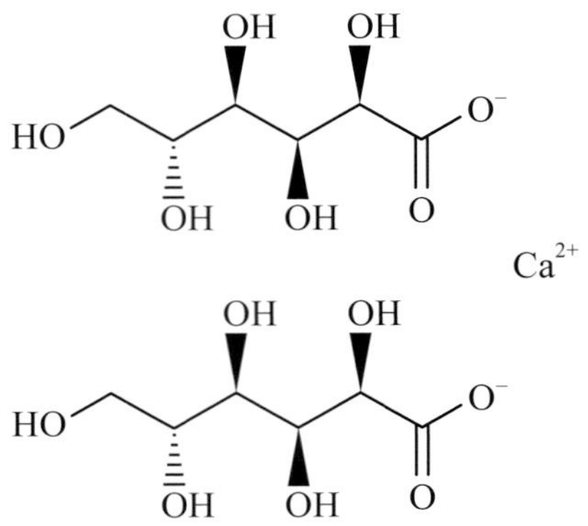

- A. Fluorine is highly reactive with six electrons in its outer valence shell and reacts to form insoluble CaF_2.
- B. Hydrogen combines with gluconate to form a protective layer over the skin that resists additional acid exposure.
- C. Calcium is an unstable element that rapidly combined with hydrogen to create insoluble CaH_2.
- D. Calcium neutralizes an atom with seven electrons in its valence shell, preventing additional reactive damage.

STOP. If you finish before time is called, check your work. You may go back to any question in this test.

ANSWERS & EXPLANATIONS for Test 1A can be found on p. 216.

Introduction to General Chemistry

MINI-TEST 1B

Time: 45 minutes
Questions 1–29

DIRECTIONS: Most of the questions in this test section are grouped with a passage. Read the passage, then select the best answer to each question. Some questions are independent of any passage and of one another. Select the best answer to each of these questions. If you are unsure of an answer, rule out incorrect choices and select from the remaining options. Indicate your selection beside the option you choose. A periodic table can be found on the last page of this book for you to use at any point during this test section.

TEST 1B

Passage 1 (Questions 1-6)

The modality of radiation therapy selected for use during cancer treatment is based on maximizing tumor death and sparing healthy tissues. A useful physical parameter for comparing the radioactive properties of different agents is their linear energy transfer (LET). LET describes the quantity of energy released by a travelling radioactive particle per unit distance that it travels. Larger LETs lead to a much more concentrated energy deposition and are associated with shorter effective ranges (Table 1).

Table 1 Properties of Radioactive Particles

Decay mode	Range	LET
α	Cellular 30-80 μm	≈ 100 keV/μm
β	Multi-cellular 0.5-15 mm	≈ 0.2 keV/μm

Actinium 225 (^{225}Ac) is a robust alpha emitter whose early clinical applications were limited by its toxicity and tendency to accumulate in the bones and liver after intravenous administration. To combat these limitations, scientists chelated ^{225}Ac to prevent its accumulation in the bones. This technique was further improved by binding chelated ^{225}Ac to monoclonal antibodies specific for proteins expressed on the surface of cancer cells.

The synthesis of radiolabeled monoclonal antibodies proceeds via two reactions (Reactions 1–2) shown below.

Reaction 1

Reaction 2

Question 1

What other SI derived unit can describe the LET?

- A. Coulomb
- B. Joule
- C. Newton
- D. Tesla

Question 2

^{225}Ac has a 10.0 day half-life. If a sample of freshly prepared ^{225}Ac had an initial count of 10 cpm, what is its count after 15 days?

- A. 6.0
- B. 4.2
- C. 3.5
- D. 1.3

Question 3

What is the electron configuration of the transition metal used in Reaction 2 prior to chelation in the product?

- A. $[Rn]7s^16d^2$
- B. $[Rn]6d^3$
- C. $[Rn]7s^1$
- D. $[Rn]7s^26d^1$

Question 4

What is the hybridization of the sulfur atom in the chelate?

- A. sp^3
- B. sp^2
- C. sp
- D. dsp^3

Question 5

Actinium 225 reaches a stable product by the subsequent release of four α-particles, two β^--particles, and one more α-particle. What is the identity of its stable daughter product?

- A. ^{205}Tl
- B. ^{227}Ac
- C. ^{205}Pb
- D. ^{213}Bi

Question 6

An unknown isotope decayed with the emission of a single particle that had an LET of 0.5 keV/μm. If the final product were ^{209}Bi, which of the following scenarios is most plausible, if the ejected particle entered the magnetic field below, as shown?

X X X

X X X

•⟶

X X X

- A. The parent atom was ^{209}Tl and the particle would move upwards.
- B. The parent atom was ^{209}Pb and the particle would move downwards.
- C. The parent atom was ^{209}Po and the particle would move downwards.
- D. The parent atom was ^{209}Pb and the particle would move upwards.

Passage 2 (Questions 7-11)

Fission chain reactions convert parent nuclides into smaller daughter nuclides, along with the release of energy. They are called chain reactions because the daughter products and energy released stimulate further reactions of other parent nuclides in the system. In this way, a single reaction can drive infinitely more reactions, until the fissile material is consumed, with an exponential amplification of released energy over time, if left uncontrolled. The controlled fission chain reaction of ^{235}U is exploited in nuclear power plants. Since each uranium atom releases three neutrons, the fission of one atom can drive that of three others.

$$ {}^{1}_{0}n + {}^{235}_{92}U \rightarrow {}^{141}_{56}Ba + {}^{92}_{36}Kr + 3\,{}^{1}_{0}n + \Delta mc^2 $$

Reaction 1

The rest mass of the fission products is less than the rest mass of the original uranium atom and the incident neutron. This loss of mass Δm, called the mass defect, is released as energy according to the mass-energy equivalence equation $E = \Delta mc^2$, where c is the speed of light *in vacuo*. The energy released by the fission of uranium within the fuel rods of a nuclear reactor is used to heat a pool of water. Steam produced from this pool powers the rotation of a turbine that generates electricity.

To prevent the reaction from producing too much heat, control rods can be lowered in between the fuel rods. These control rods absorb neutrons which would otherwise initiate further fission in the fuel rods, and reduces the rate of reaction.

The major limitation of nuclear energy is the safe disposal of spent fuel rods, which contain radioactive waste products such as ^{137}Cs or ^{90}Sr. Unshielded exposure to a recently spent nuclear fuel rod would provide a lethal dose of radiation to a human in a matter of seconds.

Question 7

^{141}Ba decays via β^- decay. What is the identity of its daughter isotope?

- A. ^{141}Cs
- B. ^{140}La
- C. ^{141}La
- D. ^{142}Ba

Question 8

The Arrhenius equation describes the dependence of the rate constant *k* on other parameters of a chemical reaction.

$$ k = Ae^{-\frac{E_a}{RT}} $$

Arrhenius equation

Lowering the control rods:

- A. increases the activation energy of this fission reaction.
- B. increases the value of pre-exponential factor, *A*.
- C. decreases the activation energy of this fission reaction.
- D. decreases the value of the pre-exponential factor, *A*.

Question 9

^{137}Cs has a half-life of 30 years. How long will it take for the activity of ^{137}Cs to be reduced to 1/1000 of its initial value?

- A. 255.3 years
- B. 597.1 years
- C. 299.7 years
- D. 330.0 years

Question 10

How much mass must be lost from an atom of ^{235}U if it is to be completely converted into light with a wavelength of 490 nm? (Note $h = 6.6 \times 10^{-34}$ m$^2 \cdot$ kg/s and $c = 3 \times 10^8$ m/s)

- A. $\dfrac{6.6 \times 10^{-34} \times 3 \times 10^8}{4.9 \times 10^{-7}}$ kg
- B. $\dfrac{6.6 \times 10^{-34}}{4.9 \times 10^{-7} \times 3 \times 10^8}$ kg
- C. $\dfrac{6.6 \times 10^{-34}}{490 \times 3 \times 10^8}$ kg
- D. $\dfrac{6.6 \times 10^{-34} \times 3 \times 10^8}{490}$ kg

Question 11

Which of the following graphs best illustrate ^{141}Ba ionization energies?

A.

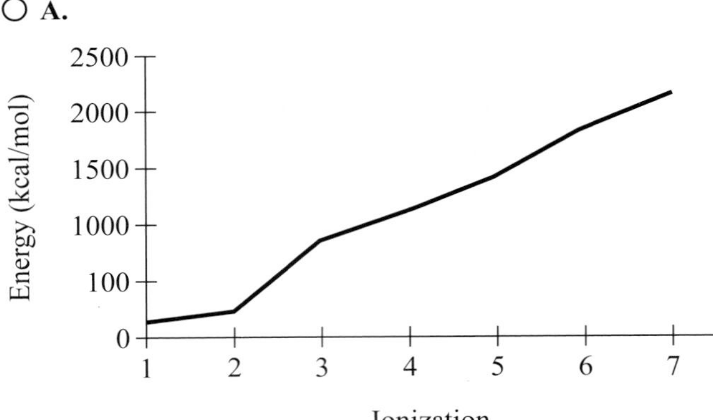

B.

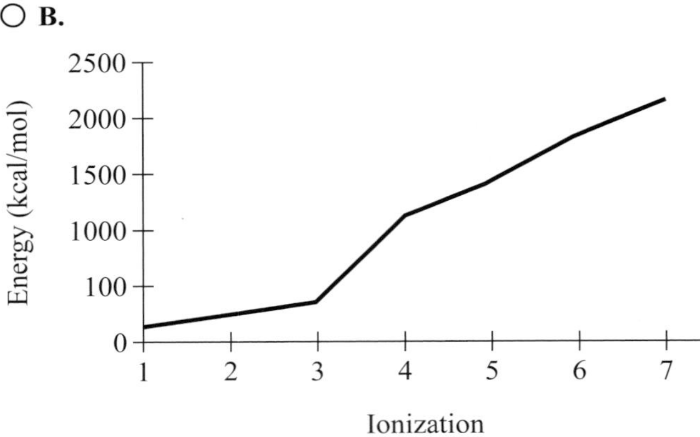

C.

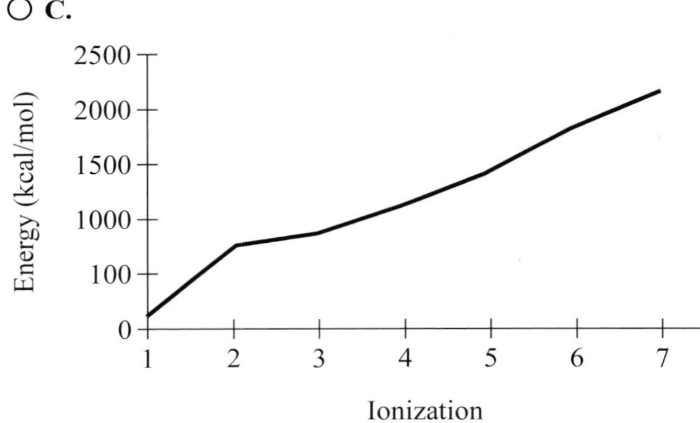

D.

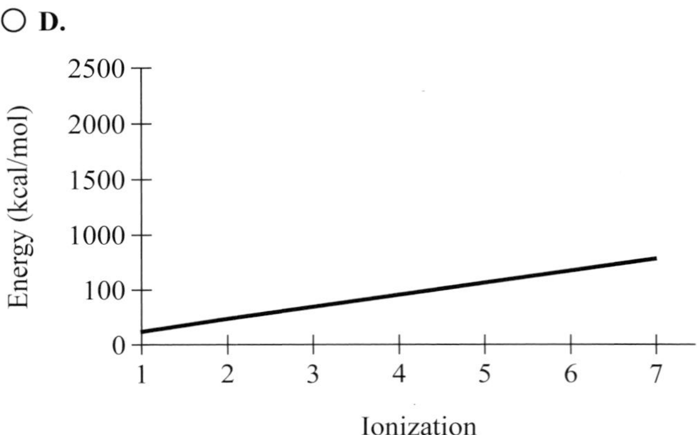

Questions 12 - 15 do not refer to a passage and are independent of each other.

Question 12

^{59}Co is the only stable isotope of cobalt. What property or properties could distinguish ^{59}Co from ^{60}Co?

I. Effective nuclear charge
II. Mass
III. Atomic number
IV. Radioactivity

- A. II only
- B. II and IV only
- C. I, II, and IV only
- D. I, II, III, and IV

Question 13

Redox reactions are common in biologic systems and chemistry laboratories. Which of the following would be least useful in a redox reaction?

- A. $LiAlH_4$
- B. CrO_3
- C. Mg^{2+}
- D. H_2O_2

Question 14

Fluoride-based compounds are often added to toothpaste to reduce the formation of cavities. The electron configuration of Ca in CaF_2 is most likely to be:

- A. [Ar].
- B. $[Ar]4s^1$.
- C. $[Ar]4s^2$.
- D. $[Ar]4s^2 3d^2$.

Question 15

Gases with low reactivity are often used to prevent unwanted atmospheric reactivity during cancer drug synthesis. Which of the following gases are likely to be used?

- A. Br_2
- B. Ar
- C. F_2
- D. S

Passage 3 (Questions 16-21)

Radionuclides are isotopes with unstable nuclei that emit energy during decay processes. Physicians rely on radionuclides as chemical labels in biomedical research, contrast agents in certain diagnostic tools, and as therapeutic agents in the treatment of certain types of cancer.

α-emitters are a specific class of radionuclides which decay with the emission of a helium nucleus, or alpha particles. Interestingly, the energy released during alpha particle emission only slightly varies across elements with different half-lives. This relationship is formally described by the Geiger-Nuttall law, where λ is the decay constant, Z is the atomic number, E is the energy of the emitted alpha particle, and a_1 and a_2 are constants.

$$\ln \lambda = \left[-a_1\left(\frac{Z}{\sqrt{E}}\right)\right] + a_2$$

Equation 1

Alpha particles are particularly useful in targeted chemotherapy because their high mass and low velocity leads to a short emission range, and prevents them from causing wider tissue damage. One such α-emitter is ^{223}Ra, a calcium-mimetic used in the treatment of cancer that has spreads to the bone. It forms complexes with hydroxapatite and is incorporated into the bony matrix, destroying cancer cells in areas of new-bone growth. ^{223}Ra exerts its cytotoxicity by breaking double stranded DNA.

^{223}Ra has a half-life of 11.4 days, and decays according follows the decay chain described in Figure 1.

$$^{223}Ra \xrightarrow{\alpha} {}^{219}Rn \xrightarrow{\alpha} {}^{215}Po \xrightarrow{\alpha} {}^{211}Pb \xrightarrow{\beta^-} {}^{211}Bi \xrightarrow{\alpha} {}^{207}Ti \xrightarrow{\beta^-} {}^{207}Pb$$

Figure 1 Decay chain of ^{223}Ra

The concentration of ^{223}Ra present in the patient's body after treatment is effectively modeled with a first order rate law.

$$[^{223}Ra]_t = [^{223}Ra]_o e^{(-\lambda t)}$$

Equation 2

Question 16

Aqueous solutions of radium-223-chloride are used to treat cancer in the bone. What is the charge on radium-223 in these solutions?

- A. −2
- B. +1
- C. −1
- D. +2

TEST 1B

Question 17

A sealed container of ^{223}Ra has a mass of 50 g. After 22.8 days, what is its mass?

- A. 12.5 g
- B. 25 g
- C. 37.5 g
- D. 50 g

Question 18

If element X emits more energetic α-particles than element Y, its half-life is:

- A. longer.
- B. shorter.
- C. equal.
- D. not enough information provided.

Question 19

The highest energy electron in ^{223}Ra is in the:

- A. 4*f* orbital
- B. 5*d* orbital
- C. 7*s* orbital
- D. 6*p* orbital

Question 20

Which graph correctly describes the decay of ^{223}Ra?

A.

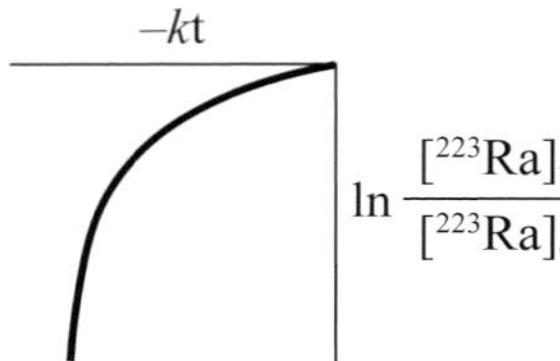

B.

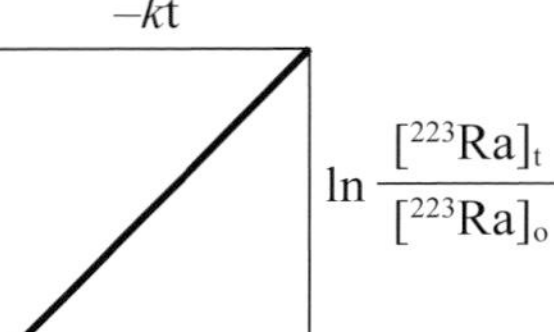

C.

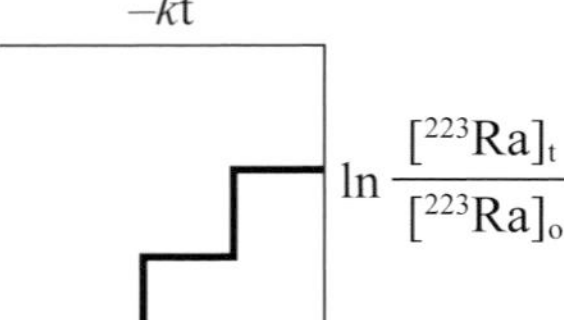

D.

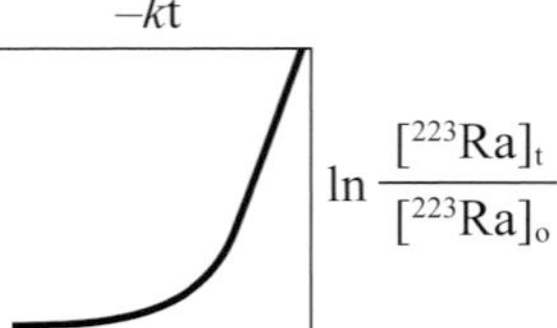

Question 21

How many protons have been lost by ^{223}Ra once it has decayed into ^{215}Po?

- A. 2
- B. 8
- C. 6
- D. 4

Passage 4 (Questions 22-26)

As a multifunctional material, tantalum oxide has attracted increasing attention in recent years and has been widely used in the fabrication of memory devices and orthopedic instruments. Tantalum oxide deserves such special recognition in many areas mainly because it has many excellent properties such as a wide band gap, high photocatalytic activity under UV irradiation, chemical resistance, a high melting point, and good mechanical strength and biocompatibility. Considering the promising application potential of tantalum oxide in industries, great efforts have been motivated to further refine and develop the synthesis techniques of tantalum oxide.

The tantalum foils used by researchers for the following synthesis were 0.5 mm × 2.5 cm × 5.0 cm, purity 99.95%. The platinum foil used was 0.1 mm × 2.5 cm × 5.0 cm, purity 99.95%. The method for preparing the coral-like tantalum oxide (named CLTO) was that a tantalum foil was polished firstly with abrasive papers and ultrasonically degreased in anhydrous ethanol and distilled water for 15 minutes in turn, and dried in nitrogen flow. This pretreated tantalum foil was then anodized for 1 hour at 20 V in a two–electrode configuration equipped with a platinum cathode at room temperature. The electrolyte was a mixture of ethylene glycol, phosphoric acid and NH_4F. The obtained CLTO was annealed in air for 3 hours to crystallize Ta_2O_5.

This passage was adapted from "Synthesis of Coral-Like Tantalum Oxide Films via Anodization in Mixed Organic-Inorganic Electrolytes." Yu H, Zhu S, Yang X, Wang X, Sun H, et al *PLoS ONE*. 2013. 8(6). doi:10.1371/journal.pone.0066447 for use under the terms of the Creative Commons CC BY 3.0 license (http://creativecommons.org/licenses/by/3.0/legalcode).

Question 22

The mass of the tantalum foil is which of the following? (ρ = 16.99 g/cm^3)

- A. 1 g
- B. 10.6 g
- C. 106 g
- D. 606 g

Question 23

How many moles of tantalum were used in the experiment?

- A. 0.06 moles
- B. 1900 moles
- C. 0.59 moles
- D. 19,000 moles

Question 24

What is the oxidation number of the tantalum in the final product?

- A. 0
- B. 2/5
- C. 2
- D. 5

Question 25

If a 1 M solution of the solvent used in the experiment was prepared, how many atoms of phosphorus were present in 1 L of solution?

- A. 3.01×10^{23}
- B. 6.02×10^{23}
- C. 12.04×10^{23}
- D. 18.06×10^{23}

Question 26

The researchers calculated a 90% yield for the overall reaction. How many grams of product were obtained?

- A. 9 g
- B. 11 g
- C. 23 g
- D. 30 g

Questions 27 - 29 do not refer to a passage and are independent of each other.

Question 27

The oxygen in the amide carbonyl of the chemotherapeutic compound shown below can be substituted for a sulfur, which lengthens the half-life of the drug. Which of the following statements best explains why?

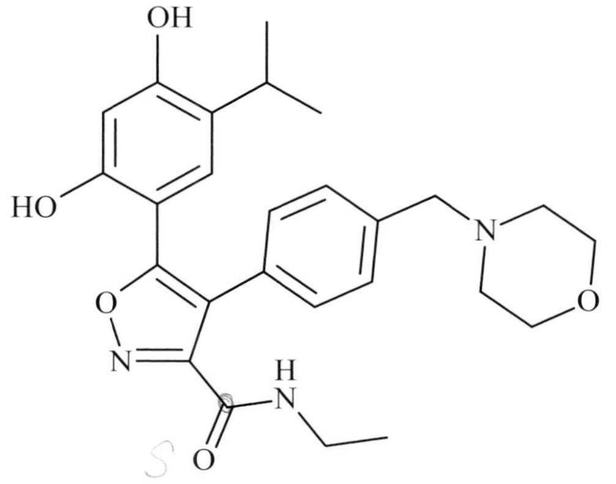

OH HO O N H N O

This figure is adapted from "Thermodynamics of Aryl-Dihydroxyphenyl-Thiadiazole Binding to Human Hsp90." Kazlauskas E, Petrikaite V, Michailoviene V, Revuckiene J, Matuliene J, et al. *PLoS ONE*. 2013. 7(5) doi:10.1271.0036899 for use under the terms of the Creative Commons CC BY 3.0 license (http://creativecommons.org/licenses/by/3.0/legalcode).

- A. Sulfur substitution reduces hydrolysis of the amide functional group of the chemotherapeutic.
- B. Sulfur substitution increases hydrolysis of the amide functional group of the chemotherapeutic.
- C. Sulfur substitution increases breakdown of the chemotherapeutic in the liver.
- D. Sulfur substitution decreases breakdown of the chemotherapeutic in the liver.

TEST 1B

Question 28

Potassium in potassium cyanide contributes 60% of the mass of the compound and is used to synthesize proteins *in vitro* to create antibodies to detect the influenza virus. The molecular formula of potassium cyanide is most likely:

- **A.** K_2CN.
- **B.** KC_2N.
- **C.** KCN_2.
- **D.** KCN.

Question 29

A soluble potassium solution is often used to normalize cardiac activity in patients with metabolite deficiency. In a laboratory test, KCl is dissolved in water and a gaseous product is detected. The molecular formula of this gaseous product is most likely:

- **A.** Cl_2.
- **B.** KCl.
- **C.** KO_2.
- **D.** Cl_2O.

STOP. If you finish before time is called, check your work. You may go back to any question in this test.

ANSWERS & EXPLANATIONS for Test 1B can be found on p. 216.

Introduction to Organic Chemistry

TEST 2A

Time: 95 minutes
Questions 1–59

DIRECTIONS: Most of the questions in this test section are grouped with a passage. Read the passage, then select the best answer to each question. Some questions are independent of any passage and of one another. Select the best answer to each of these questions. If you are unsure of an answer, rule out incorrect choices and select from the remaining options. Indicate your selection beside the option you choose. A periodic table can be found on the last page of this book for you to use at any point during this test section.

Passage 1 (Questions 1-5)

Short chain fatty acids (SCFAs), such as butyric acid (C4), are promising intermediates of many chemical and biofuel molecules. For example, butyric acid is a precursor for short chain fatty alcohols like butanol, which is superior to ethanol in terms of energy density, vapor pressure and hygroscopicity, and is a direct replacement of gasoline. Short chain alkanes like propane, with highly favorable physicochemical properties as a fuel and a major component of liquefied petroleum gas, has been produced in *E. coli* via butyric acid as an intermediate.

Butyric acid, which has therapeutic applications as its derivatives, is used for the treatment of diseases like cancer, sickle cell anemia and alopecia. Since *E. coli* does not natively produce butyric acid, scientists could either transfer the complete fermentative pathway from anaerobes into *E. coli*, thus restricting its growth to anaerobic condition, or exploit aerobically active fatty acid synthesis cycle (Figure 1). Engineering the *E. coli* fatty acid biosynthesis (FASII) pathway is a promising avenue to produce fatty acid-derived fuels and chemicals. Scientists selected three thioesterases, TesAT, TesBT, and TesBF from *Bryantella formatexigens*, for their ability to produce short chain fatty acids, overexpressed them in *E. coli* and analyzed the role of the host fatty acid synthesis pathway and its regulatory network in production of butyric acid.

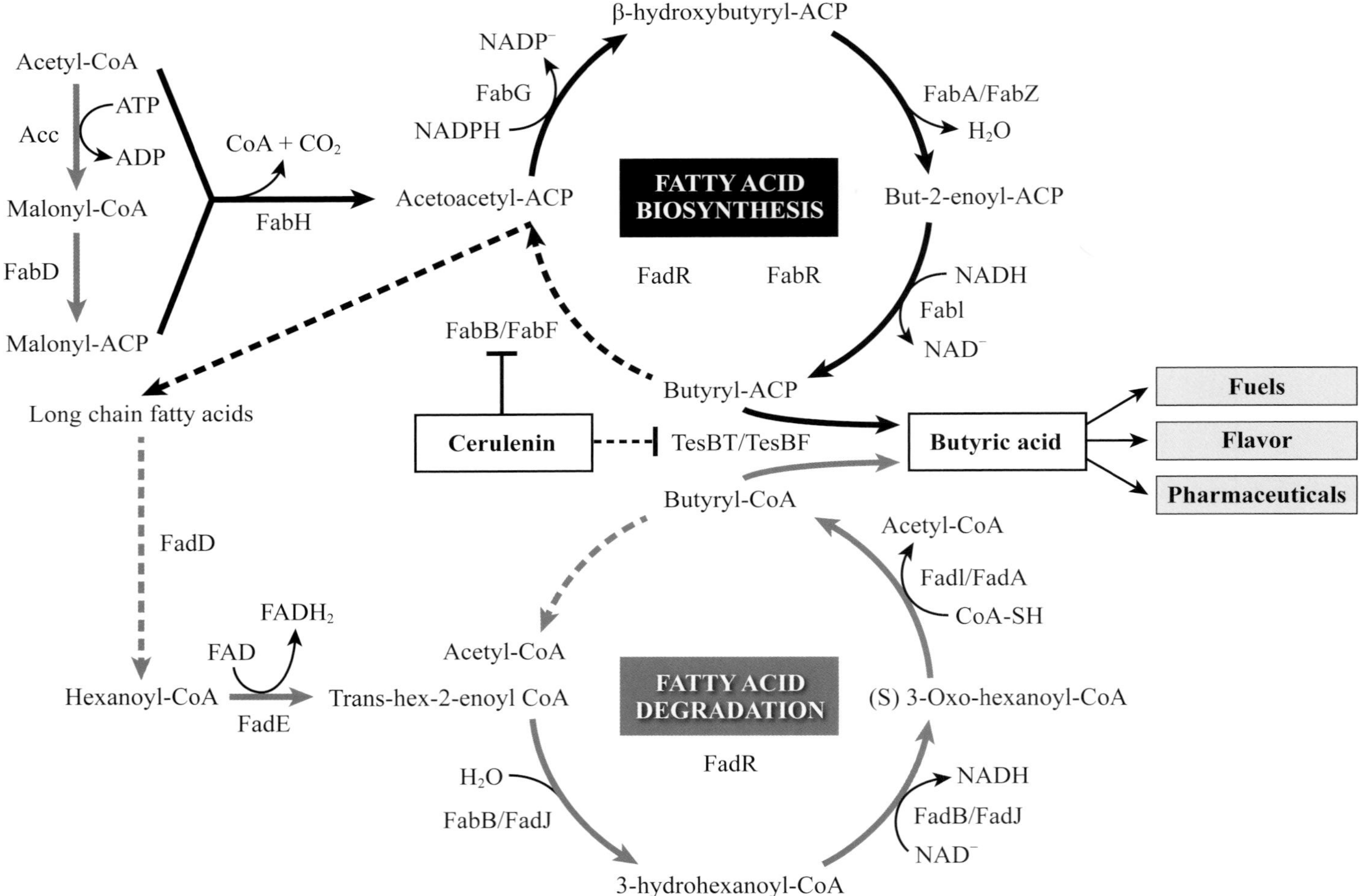

Figure 1 Schematic representation of various strategies adopted to engineer *E. coli* for production of butyric acid

Scientists knocked out specific genes in *E. coli* that were engineered to overexpress TesBF and TesBT and measured the production of various unsaturated and saturated fatty acids. The results are shown in Figure 2.

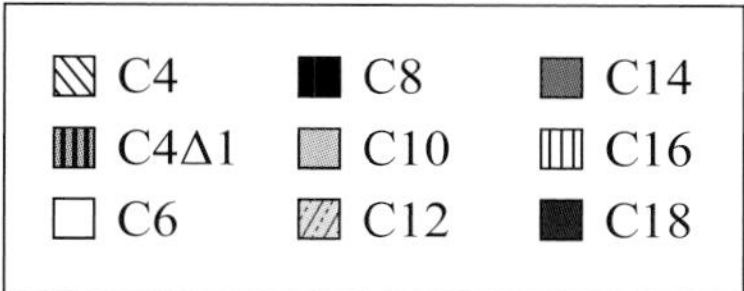

Δ means knock out for genes

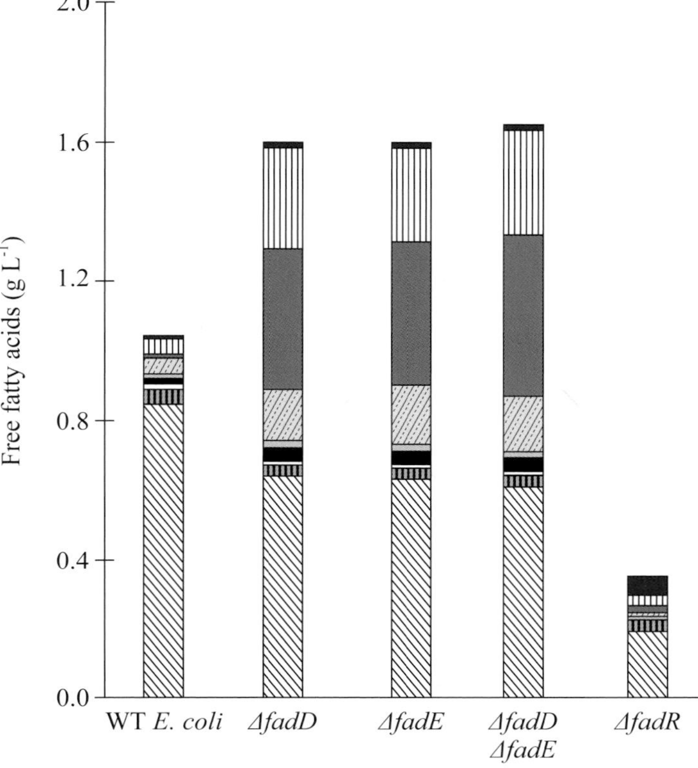

Figure 2 Production of various fatty acids in genetically modified *E. coli.*

This passage is adapted from "Engineered Production of Short Chain Fatty Acid in Escherichia coli Using Fatty Acid Synthesis Pathway." Jawed K, Mattam A, Fatma Z, Wajid S, Abdin M, et al. *PLoS ONE.* 2016. 11(7) doi:10.1371/journal.pone.0160035 for use under the terms of the Creative Commons CC BY 4.0 license (http://creativecommons.org/licenses/by/4.0/legalcode).

Question 1

Carbons one and four of butyric acid are most likely to have which of the following hybridizations, respectively?

○ **A.** sp and sp^2

○ **B.** sp^2 and sp^3

○ **C.** sp^3 and sp^3

○ **D.** sp^3d and sp

Question 2

A condensation reaction during synthesis of an unsaturated hydrocarbon is most likely to create:

○ **A.** a bond that is stronger, shorter, and contains atoms in a trigonal planar geometric arrangement.

○ **B.** a bond that is stronger, longer, and contains atoms in a tetrahedral geometric arrangement.

○ **C.** a bond that is weaker, shorter, and contains atoms in a tetrahedral geometric arrangement.

○ **D.** a bond that is weaker, longer, and contains atoms in a trigonal planar geometric arrangement.

Question 3

The formal charge on the carboxyl carbon of butyric acid is most likely to be:

○ **A.** 0.

○ **B.** +1.

○ **C.** −1.

○ **D.** +2.

Question 4

Following the results that generated Figure 2, scientists found that the concentration of but-2-enoyl-ACP was increased. Which of the following molecular bonds failed to form in a particular enzyme?

○ **A.** A double bond between carbons two and three of a hydrophobic chain in FabR

○ **B.** A triple bond between carbon and oxygen of a carbonyl in FabA

○ **C.** A single bond between carbon and sulfur in FabG

○ **D.** A single bond between carbons five and seven of a hydrophilic chain in FabB

Question 5

Free butyric acid produced by engineered *E. coli* is also likely to be useful for the molecular absorption of:

○ **A.** fructose.

○ **B.** glutamine.

○ **C.** vitamin.

○ **D.** cytosine.

Passage 2 (Questions 6-9)

Clinical improvement in inflammatory bowel disease (IBD) treated with methotrexate and 6-mercaptopurine (6-MP) is associated with a decrease in pro-inflammatory cytokines. Figure 1 shows the structure of methotrexate.

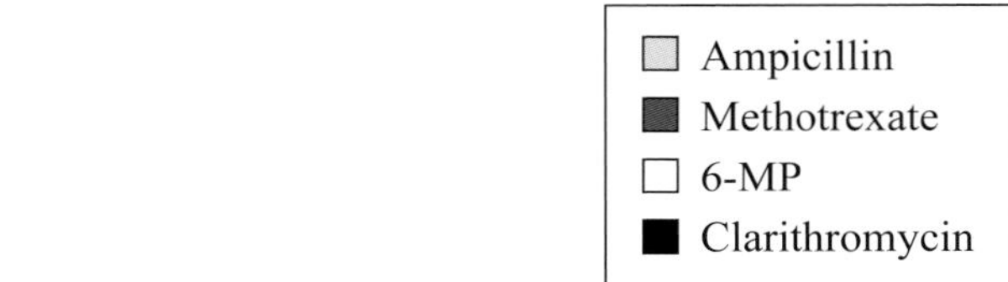

Figure 1 Methotrexate

Although controversial, there are increasingly compelling data that *Mycobacterium avium* subspecies paratuberculosis (MAP) may be an etiological agent in some or all of IBD. Researchers hypothesized that the clinical efficacy of methotrexate and 6-MP in IBD may be to simply inhibit the growth of MAP. The effect on MAP growth kinetics by methotrexate and 6-MP were evaluated in cell culture of two strains each of MAP and *M. avium* using a radiometric detection system that quantifies mycobacterial growth as arbitrary "growth index units" (GI). Efficacy data are presented as "percent decrease in cumulative GI" (% 2DcGI). The results are shown in Figure 2.

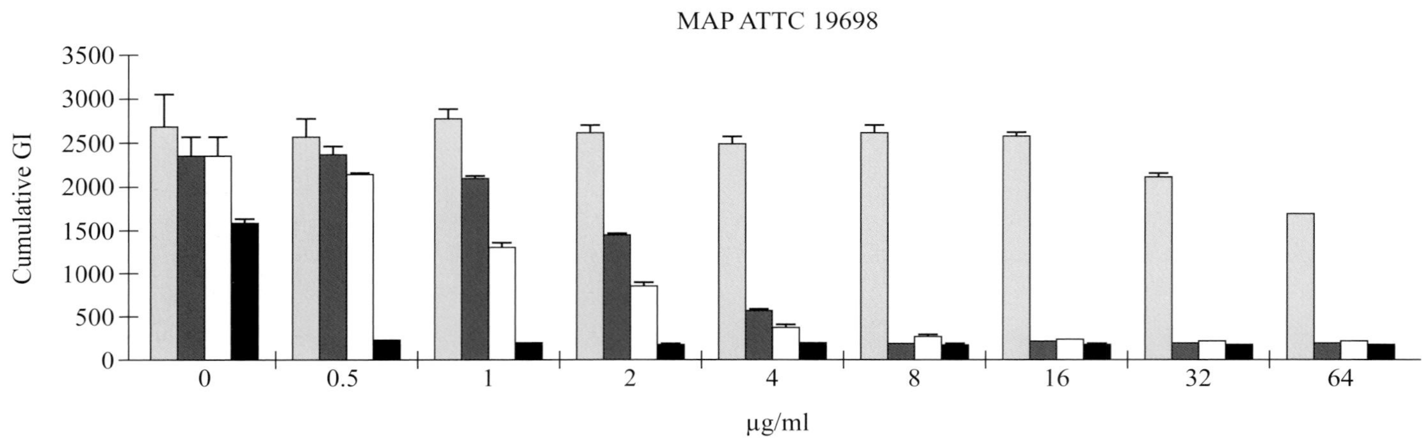

Figure 2 Growth studies

This passage was adapted from "On the Action of Methotrexate and 6-Mercaptopurine on M. avium Subspecies paratuberculosis." Greenstein RJ, Su L, Haroutunian V, Shahidi A, Brown ST. *PLoS ONE*. 2007. 2(1) doi:10.1371/journal.pone.0000161 for use under the terms of the Creative Commons CC BY 2.0 license (http://creativecommons.org/licenses/by/2.0/legalcode).

Question 6

The bonds in methotrexate are all covalent. Which of the following bonds is the most ionic in nature?

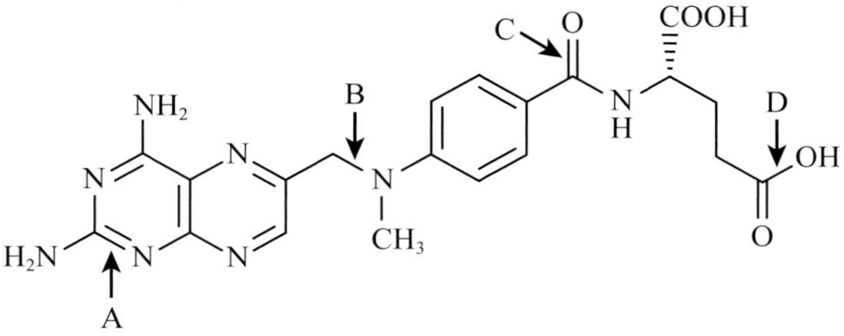

- A. Bond A
- B. Bond B
- C. Bond C
- D. Bond D

Question 7

Which of the following hybrid orbitals is/are present in methotrexate?

I. *sp*
II. sp^2
III. sp^3

- A. II only
- B. I and II only
- C. II and III only
- D. I, II, and III

Question 8

Which of the following statements is supported by the data in Figure 2?

- A. Increasing concentration of drug always results in more bacterial growth.
- B. Increasing concentration of drug always results in more bacterial death.
- C. Ampicillin is ineffective as a treatment for MAP.
- D. Ampicillin is the best treatment for MAP.

Question 9

What is the overall charge distribution of methotrexate?

- A.

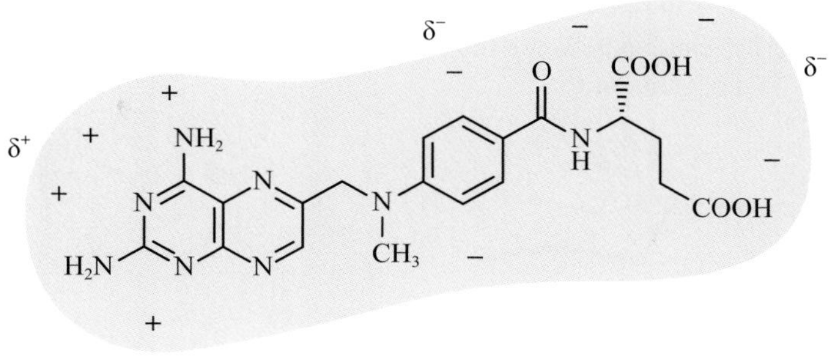

- B.

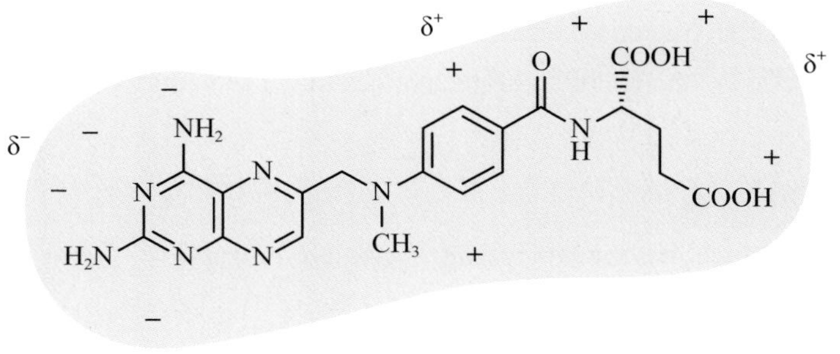

- C.

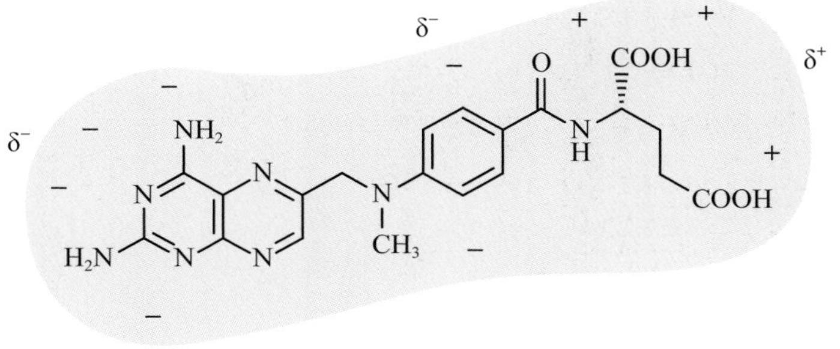

- D.

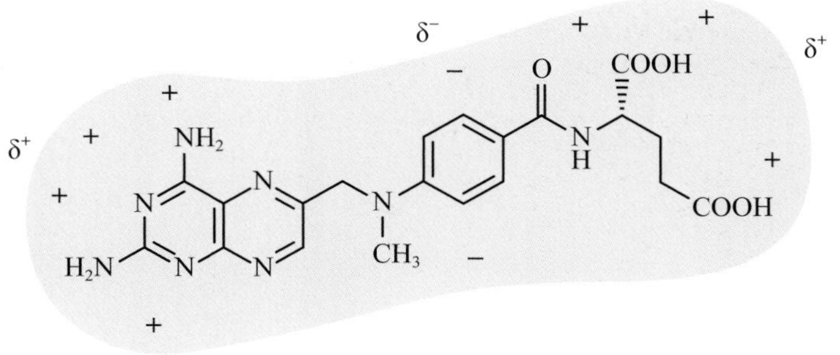

Questions 10 - 13 do not refer to a passage and are independent of each other.

Question 10

The reaction between the compound shown below and water is most similar to:

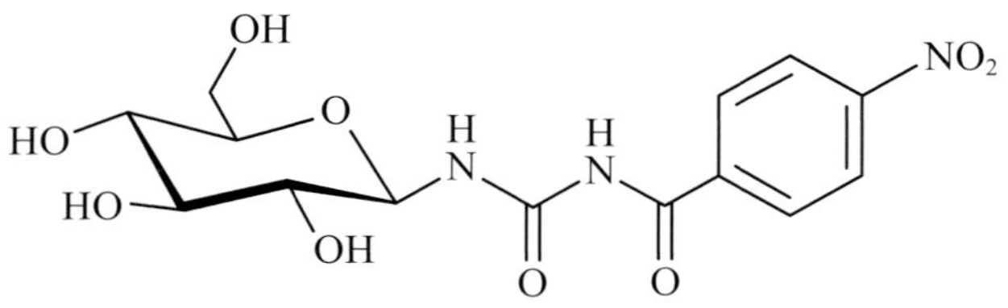

O A. the breakdown of glucose into pyruvate.

O B. the breakdown of proteins in the proteasome.

O C. the emulsification of fats in the small intestine.

O D. the coupling of nucleotides into a growing DNA strand.

Question 11

Which lists the bonds from shortest to longest?

O A. N–H, O–H, O=C, N=C

O B. O=C, N=C, N–H, O–H

O C. O–H, N–H, O=C, N=C

O D. N=C, O=C, N–H, O–H

Question 12

Creatine exists as which zwitterion in the body?

O A.

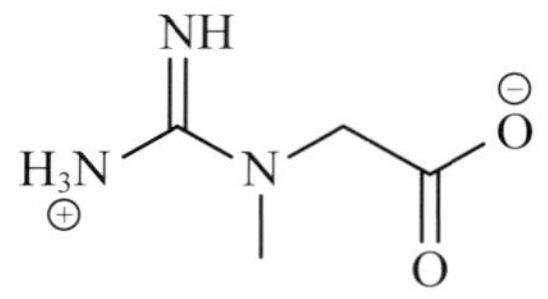

O B.

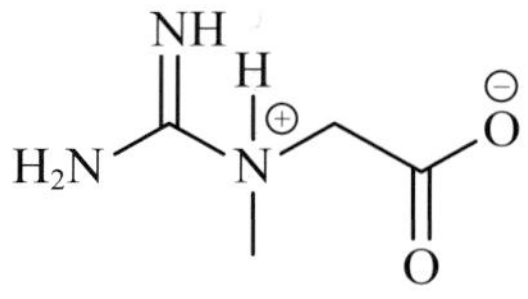

O C.

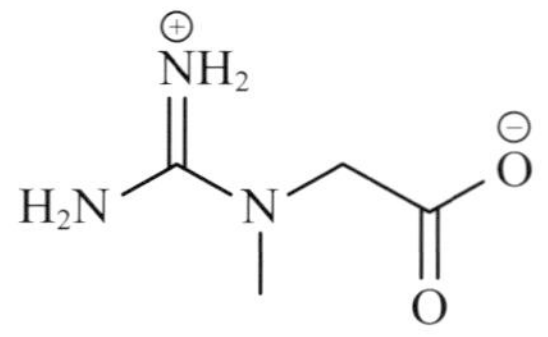

O D.

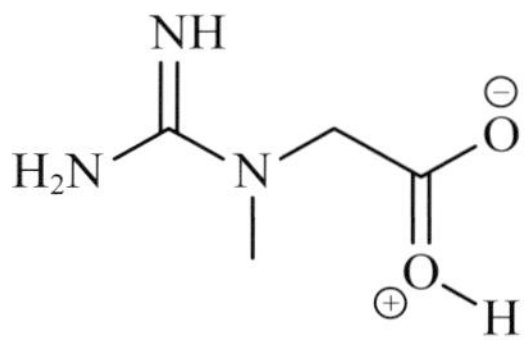

Question 13

The concentration of certain fatty acids may be determined by their absorption of visible light. Scientists would be most likely to detect an eight carbon fatty acid containing which of the following bonds?

O A. Seven sigma bonds

O B. Seven sigma bonds and two pi bonds

O C. One pi bond and seven sigma bond

O D. Three pi bonds and seven sigma bonds

TEST 2A

Passage 3 (Questions 14-17)

The tumor suppressor Programmed cell death 4 (Pdcd4) is lost in a number of different tumors such as lung, colon, breast, ovarian, and pancreatic cancer. Pdcd4 activity seems to be regulated at the post-translational level, and stabilization of Pdcd4 has emerged as an interesting concept for novel tumor therapeutics. Structure-activity relationship modeling indicated that six compounds had the potential to stabilize the DNA-binding domain of Pdcd4 in an allosteric fashion (Figure 1). Scientists decided to modify the linker between the aryl moieties, in addition to modifying the substituent groups on the rings themselves.

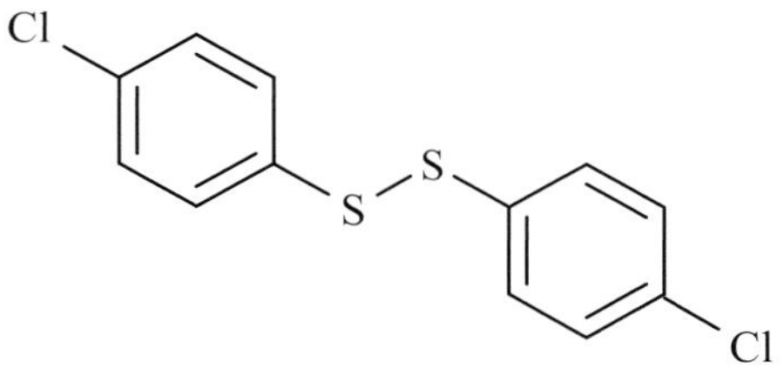

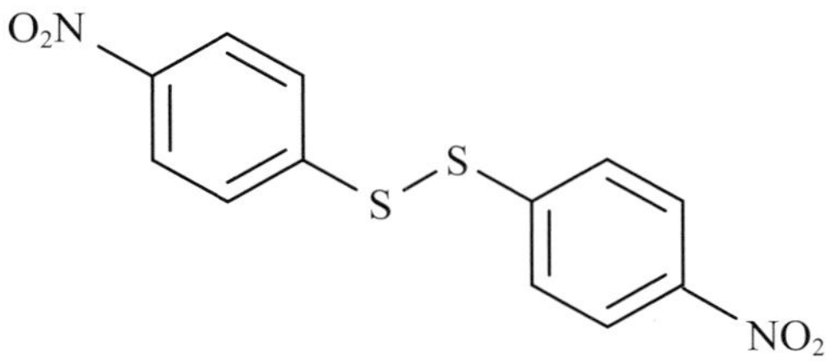

Figure 1 Chemical structure of putative Pdcd4-stabilizing compounds

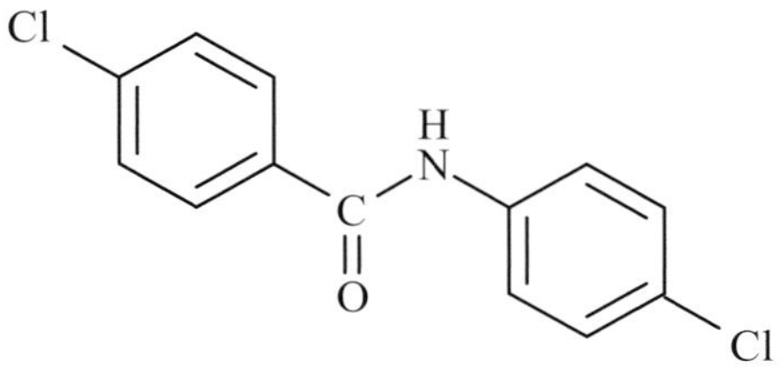

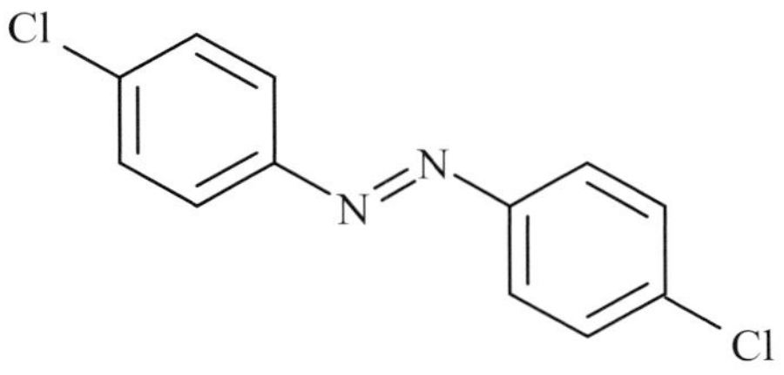

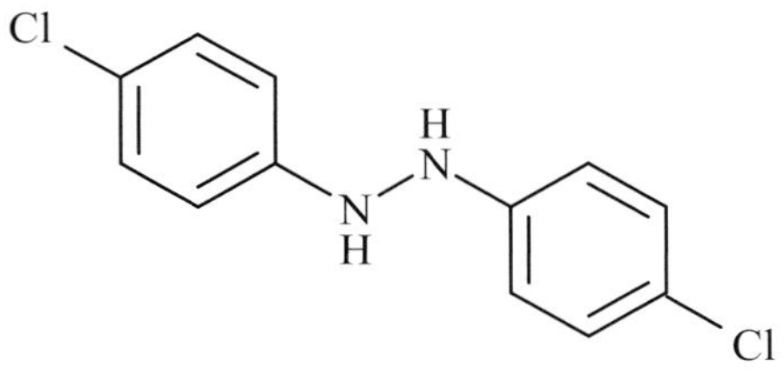

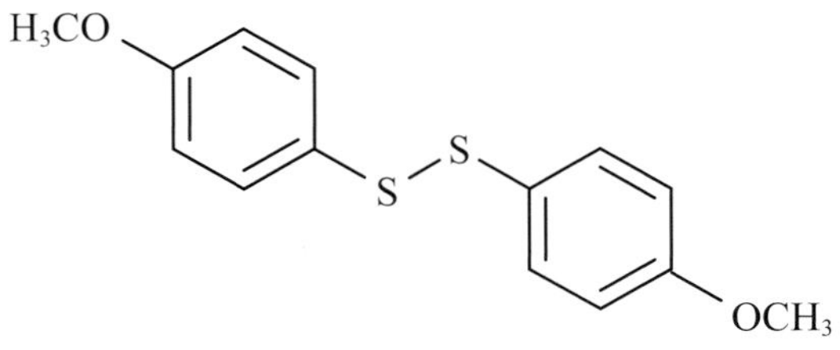

In an initial attempt to assess the influence of the conformational features of the linker region on the biological activity, scientists carried out a computational study on compounds 1, 2, and 4 by exploring the conformational space around the three rotatable bonds (σ1, σ2, σ3), as shown in Figure 2. They concluded that there were small but meaningful energy differences between the compounds, which would likely predict their efficacy *in vitro*.

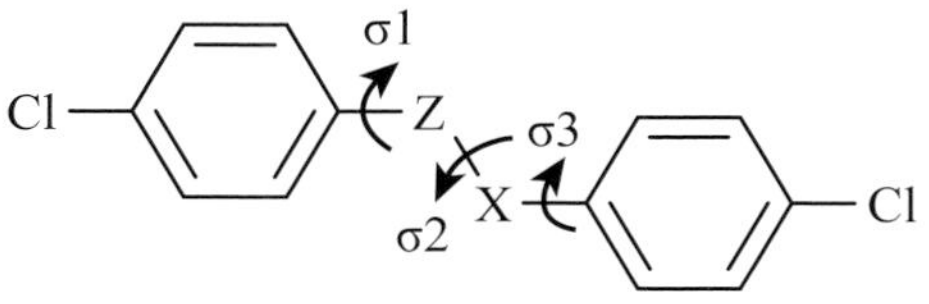

1: X = Z = –S–
2: X = –CO–; Z = –NH–
4: X = Z = –NH–

Figure 2 Conformational analysis of compounds 1, 2 and 4, modeled using rotation around σ1, σ2, and σ3

This passage is adapted from "Diaryl Disulfides as Novel Stabilizers of Tumor Suppressor Pdcd4." Schmid T, Blees J, Majer M, Wild J, Pescatori L, et al. *PLoS ONE*. 2016. 11(3) doi:10.1371/journal.pone.0151643 for use under the terms of the Creative Commons CC BY 4.0 license (http://creativecommons.org/licenses/by/4.0/legalcode).

Question 14

The potential energy plot around the σ2 bond of compound 2 is shown below. Which point on the plot is most likely to reflect the eclipsed conformation?

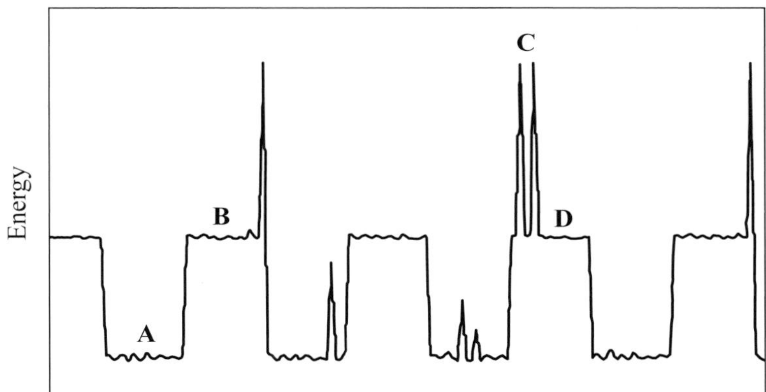

- A. Point A
- B. Point B
- C. Point C
- D. Point D

Question 15

Which of the following relationships best describes the relative dipole moment between the atoms connecting the aryl groups in the compounds depicted in Figure 1?

- A. 1 > 2
- B. 2 > 3
- C. 6 > 4
- D. 5 > 6

Question 16

How many free electrons are found on the nitrogen at the center of compound three?

- A. One
- B. Two
- C. Three
- D. Four

Question 17

Compound six is thought to stabilize Pdcd4 by binding to an allosteric regulatory site. Compared to the other compounds, which of the following bonds likely plays an increased role in the activity of compound six?

- A. Van der Waals
- B. Ionic
- C. Electrostatic
- D. Hydrogen

Passage 4 (Questions 18-21)

Flavonoids are among the most widespread secondary plant metabolites and play a significant role in the prevention of several chronic diseases, including cancer. Due to their numerous anticancer functions, including antiproliferative, cell cycle arresting and pro-apoptotic effects, certain members of this chemical group are believed to have potential not only in chemoprevention but also as future chemotherapy agents for treating cancer.

Protoapigenone (compound 1) was first isolated by our group from the Formosan fern *Thelypteris torresiana*. This compound has a close structural and likely biosynthetic relationship with apigenin (compound 2), a common 49-hydroxy-flavone (Figure 1) that is abundantly present in fruits and vegetables.

1

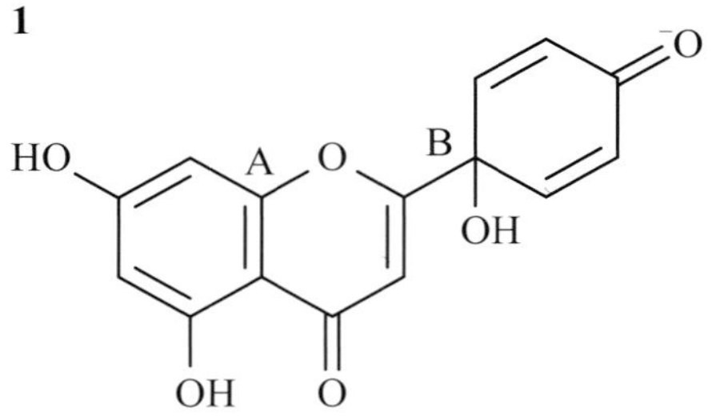

HO, A, O, B, O, OH, OH, O

2

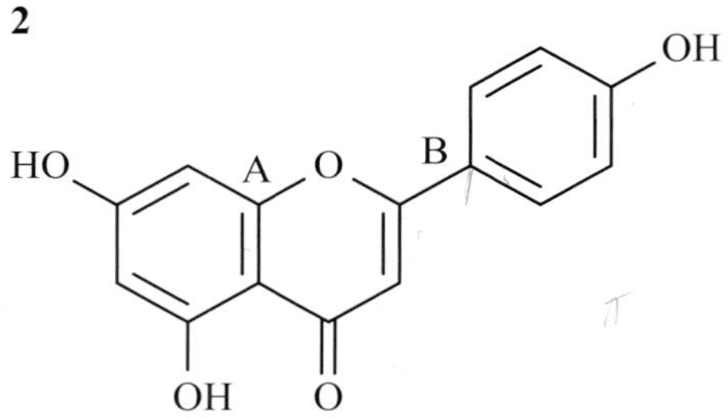

HO, A, O, B, OH, OH, O

Figure 1 Structures of protoapigenone (1) and apigenin (2)

The compound was also found to induce apoptosis in human prostate cancer cells and to selectively inhibit ovarian cancer cell growth both *in vitro* and *in vivo* in mice while causing no major side effects in the latter case. Potential clinical promise has created a need for an economical way to drastically increase the production of protoapigenone, potentially through conversion starting with apigenin.

This passage was adapted from "Direct Semi-Synthesis of the Anticancer Lead-Drug Protoapigenone from Apigenin, and synthesis of Further New Cytotoxic Protoflavone derivatives." Hunyadi A, Chuang D, Danko B, Chiang MY, Liee C et al. *PLoS ONE*. 2011. 6(8) doi:10.1371/journal.pone.0023922 for use under the terms of the Creative Commons CC BY 3.0 license (http://creativecommons.org/licenses/by/3.0/legalcode).

Question 18

Which of the following correctly describes a comparison between protoapigenone and apigenin?

- A. The two molecules have the same number of sigma bonds.
- B. Apigenin has one less pi bond.
- C. Protoapigenone is nonplanar while apigenin is planar.
- D. Apigenin has a higher molecular weight than protoapigenone.

Question 19

Which of the following correctly describes the hybridizations of the carbons in apigenin?

I. All carbons are sp^2 hybridized
II. All carbons are in the same plane
III. The bond angles are all 109.5°

- A. I only
- B. II only
- C. I and II only
- D. I and III only

Question 20

Which of the following types of intermolecular bonding is protoapigenone capable of?

I. London dispersion forces
II. Hydrogen bonding
III. Dipole-dipole interactions

- A. II only
- B. I and II only
- C. II and III only
- D. I, II, and III

Question 21

Stereochemistry is a key consideration in the formation of pharmacologic compounds. How many stereocenters and possible diastereomers does protoapigenone have?

- A. 0 stereocenters and 1 diastereomer
- B. 1 stereocenter and 2 diastereomers
- C. 2 stereocenters and 2 diastereomers
- D. 3 stereocenters and 8 diastereomers

Passage 5 (Questions 22-25)

Creatine is a guanidine compound synthesized by the kidneys, pancreas, and liver, as well as ingested from food (Figure 1). There is strong evidence showing that creatine exerts a vital role in cerebral energetic provision, corroborated by the presence of creatine kinase isoforms in both the brain and spinal cord. In addition, there exists an association between brain creatine depletion and mental retardation, autism, speech delay, and brain atrophy, and the reversal of these symptoms following oral creatine administration.

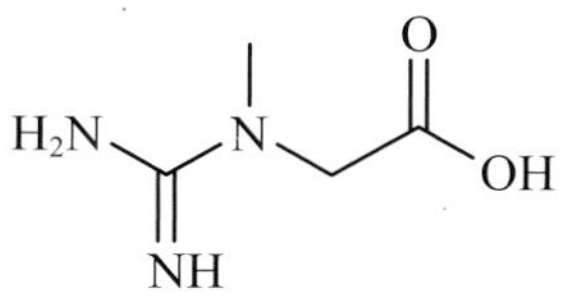

Figure 1 Structure of creatine

Recently, the combination of creatine supplementation and strength training has emerged as an efficient nonpharmacological tool for counteracting some aspects of age-related muscle weakness, including physical dysfunction, disability in activities of daily living, and low lean mass. The psychological benefits of exercise and creatine supplementation have not yet been explored.

A recent study sought to explore the additive effect of these behaviors on mood. The study grouped elderly women into four equally sized groups. Two of the groups engaged in regular exercise, and two did not. Creatine or placebo was administered to each group in a double blind fashion.

The mood of the participants was evaluated at the beginning, middle, and end of the study using a standard scale for the evaluation of depression (Figure 2). Positive scores on this scale indicate depressive symptoms, while negative numbers indicate healthy psychological processing.

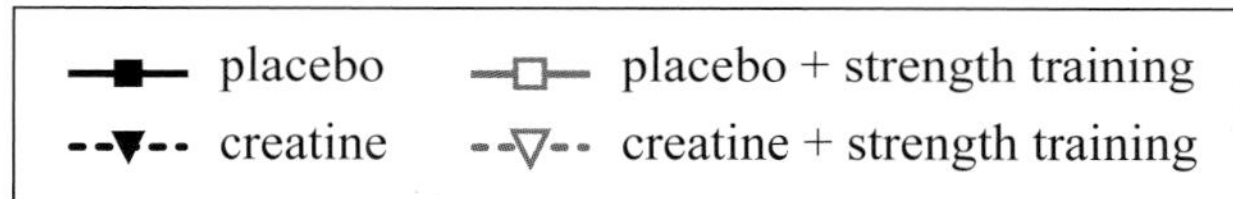

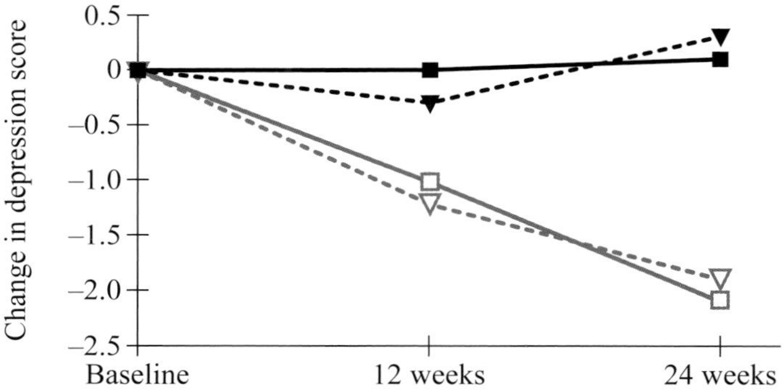

Figure 2 Change in depression score over the course of the study

This passage was adapted from "Creatine Supplementation Associated or Not with Strength Training upon Emotional and Cognitive Measures in Older Women: A Randomized Double-Blind Study." Alves C , Filho C, Benatti F, Brucki S, Pereira R, et al. *PLoS ONE*. 2013. 8(10) doi:10.1371/journal.pone.0076301 for use under the terms of the Creative Commons CC BY 3.0 Attribution license (http://creativecommons.org/licenses/by/3.0/legalcode).

Question 22

What can be concluded about the psychological and chemical functionality of creatine?

- ○ **A.** Creatine cannot cross the blood-brain barrier, as it is a polar zwitterion in the body.
- ○ **B.** Creatine is sufficient to reduce depression, as it is a non-catecholamine.
- ○ **C.** Creatine is necessary but insufficient to reduce depression, as only half of its racemic mixture is biologically active.
- ○ **D.** Creatine is neither necessary nor sufficient to reduce depression, as it is positively charged in the stomach.

Question 23

What is the empirical formula of creatine?

- ○ **A.** $C_3H_9N_3O_2$
- ○ **B.** $C_4H_6N_3O_2$
- ○ **C.** $C_4H_9N_3O_2$
- ○ **D.** $C_4H_8N_3O_2$

Question 24

Creatine contains:

- ○ **A.** 2 σ bonds; they have a lower net bond energy than 2 π bonds.
- ○ **B.** 2 π bonds; they have a lower net bond energy than 2 σ bonds.
- ○ **C.** 4 σ bonds; they have a lower net bond energy than 4 π bonds.
- ○ **D.** 4 π bonds; they have a lower net bond energy than 4 σ bonds.

Question 25

During muscle contraction, creatine is spontaneously converted to creatinine. What is the structure of creatinine?

○ **A.**

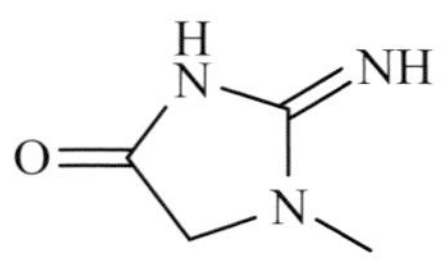

○ **B.**

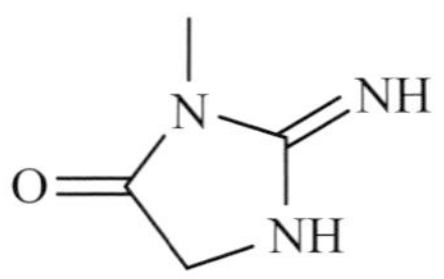

○ **C.**

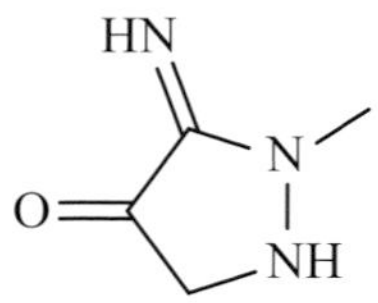

○ **D.**

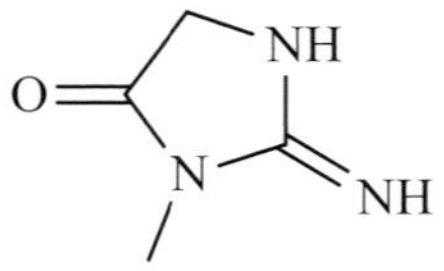

Questions 26 - 29 do not refer to a passage and are independent of each other.

Question 26

Which carbon is most acidic?

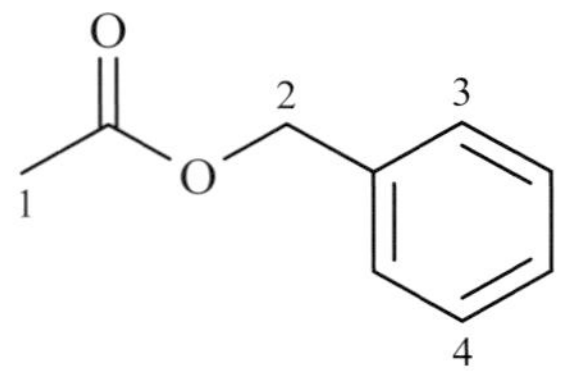

Benzyl acetate

- ○ **A.** 1
- ○ **B.** 2
- ○ **C.** 3
- ○ **D.** 4

Question 27

The general structure and carbon nitrogen bond lengths of some molecules are in the table below:

General structure	Average carbon-nitrogen bond length (Å)
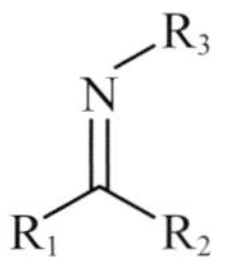	1.25
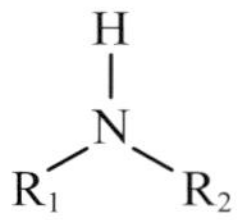	1.47
$R-C\equiv N$	1.16

Based on this table, what is the C–N bond length in pyridine (shown)?

Pyridine

- ○ **A.** 1.22
- ○ **B.** 1.37
- ○ **C.** 1.45
- ○ **D.** 1.20

Question 28

Levetiracetem is a medication used to prevent seizures in those with epilepsy. The structure is shown below. Which of the following are the empiric and molecular formulas, respectively?

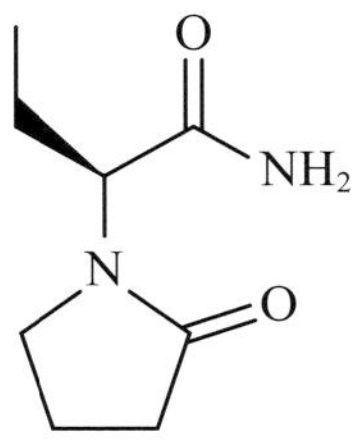

O
NH$_2$
N
O

- **A.** C_4H_7NO; $C_8H_{14}NO$
- **B.** $C_8H_{14}NO$; C_4H_7NO
- **C.** C_4H_7NO; $C_8H_{14}N_2O_2$
- **D.** $C_8H_{14}N_2O_2$; C_4H_7NO

Question 29

A researcher hopes to develop a new drug to treat chronic dry eye. The current drugs on the market utilize D-amino acids in polypeptide formation to suppress the immune system to decrease damage to the lacrimal gland. Which reaction could be used to convert D-amino acids to L-amino acids?

- **A.** S_N2 reaction
- **B.** E2 reaction
- **C.** Grignard reaction
- **D.** Strecker reaction

Passage 6 (Questions 30-33)

Cisplatin (CP) is a platinum based antineoplastic agent used against cervical, head and neck, and prostate cancers. The anticancer activity of this drug is attributed to its capability to form covalent bonds at N-7 position of purine residues of DNA leading to formation of 1, 2 or 1, 3-intrastrand crosslinks. These adducts of CP-DNA derail the cellular replication and transcription machinery if these lesions anyhow evade DNA repair system in the effected cells. Riboflavin (RF) is an essential vitamin that is required for normal cellular functions. It can undergo photo-addition, leading to generation of various free radicals. The combination of CP and RF seems to provide a synergistic effect on cell killing.

The proposed synergistic mechanism involves their excitable groups. Upon exposure of light, RF is excited and undergoes enolization. CP is also predicted to undergo an aquation reaction in water that ultimately forms diammoniumplatinum oxide. Light exposure can cleave the pi-bond between platinum (Pt) and oxygen of diammoniumplatinum oxide in heterolytic fashion, making Pt an unstable electron deficient species (Pt^+). This highly unstable species can be attacked by a lone pair of electrons on the nitrogen atoms of the alloxazine ring. Thus, Pt^+ can form four possible complexes through coordination bonding thereby engaging most of CP and RF in combination. The proposed mechanism is shown in Figure 1.

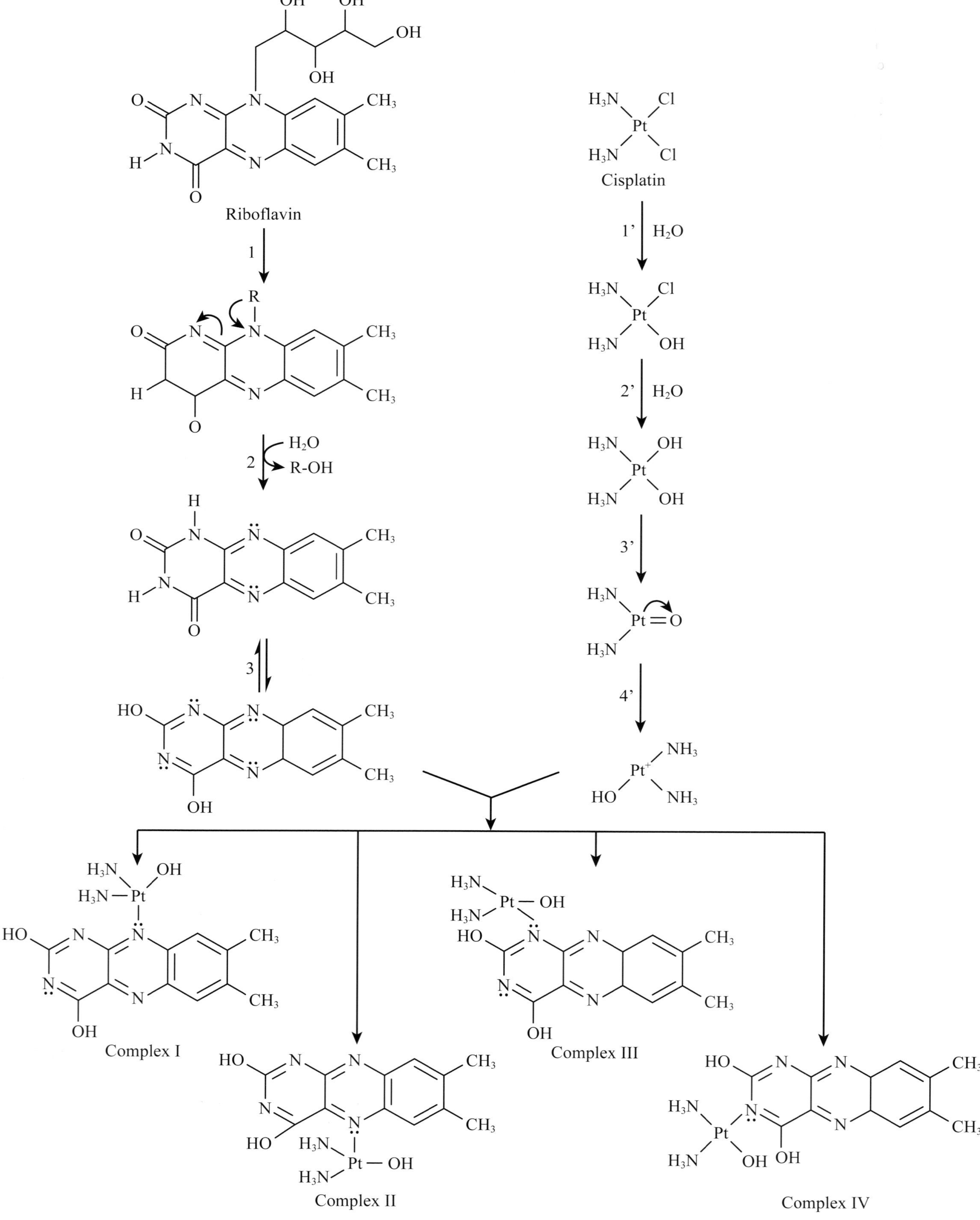

Figure 1 Putative mechanism of complex formation between riboflavin and cisplatin after photo-illumination

This passage is adapted from "Riboflavin Ameliorates Cisplatin Induced Toxicities Under Photoillumination." Hassan I, Chibber S, Khan A, and Naseem I. *PLoS ONE*. 2012. 7(5) doi:10.1371/journal.pone.0036273 for use under the terms of the Creative Commons CC BY 3.0 license (http://creativecommons.org/licenses/by/3.0/legalcode).

Question 30

Which of the following mechanisms best describes Reaction 1′ in Figure 1?

- **A.** E1
- **B.** E2
- **C.** S_N1
- **D.** S_N2

Question 31

Reaction 3 of the riboflavin pathway most likely involves:

- **A.** transfer of an oxygen to form a more stable conformational isomer.
- **B.** transfer of a nitrogen to form a less stable conformational isomer.
- **C.** transfer of a hydrogen to form a more stable constitutional isoform.
- **D.** transfer of a proton to form a less stable constitutional isoform.

Question 32

According to the information contained in Figure 1, the structure of the cisplatin derivative shown after reaction 3′ is:

A.
```
  H.  .H
H· ·N:
    :
   :Pt: :Ö
    :
H· ·N:
  H˙  ˙H
```

B.
```
  H.  .H
H· ·N
    :
   :Pt: :Ö
    :
H· ·N
  H˙  ˙H
```

C.
```
  H.  .H
H· ·N
    :
   :Pt: :Ö
    :
H· ·N
  H˙  ˙H
```

D.
```
  H.  .H
H· ·N
    :
   :Pt: ·Ö:
    :
H· ·N
  H˙  ˙H
```

Question 33

IR spectroscopy was performed on the four complexes and the results are presented below. The moderate intensity bands between 1400 – 1600 cm^{-1} are representative of functional groups that:

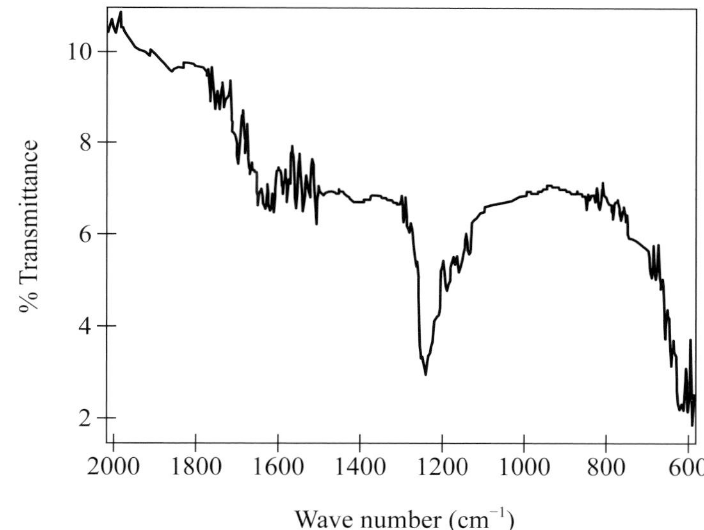

- **A.** have two pi bonds between atoms of unequal electronegativity.
- **B.** have two pi bonds and two sigma bonds between atoms of equal atomic sizes.
- **C.** have one sigma bond and one pi bond between atoms of equal electron affinities.
- **D.** have three sigma bonds between atoms of unequal atomic radii.

Passage 7 (Questions 34-37)

Microtubules (MTs) are cytoskeletal polymers formed by the polymerization of α- and β-tubulin heterodimers, which is followed by GTP hydrolysis. MTs are found within all dividing eukaryotic cells, as well as in most differentiated cell types, and play crucial roles in cell division, cell motility, cellular transport, the maintenance of cell polarity, and cell signaling.

Because microtubule dynamics play an important role in various cellular functions, such as mitosis, they are a potential target for development of anticancer drugs. One group of potential compounds is the microtubule-stabilizing agents. These compounds stimulate microtubule polymerization by binding to the inner surface of the microtubules in a deep hydrophobic pocket on β-tubulin, though they may also interact via a hydrophilic pocket on α-tubulin. Combretastatin A4 (CA-4, Figure 1) is thought to have anti-proliferative properties but has low water solubility, poor oral bioavailability, and a short half-life.

Figure 1 Chemical structure of combretastatin A-4 (CA-4)

Scientists were interested in increasing the bioavailability and cytotoxic activity of CA-4 by modifying the boxed ring structure shown in Figure 1. The indicated ringed structure was exchanged for the functional groups shown in Figure 2 to synthesize derivatives of CA-4. Subsequent *in vitro* testing of the CA-4 derivatives indicated that CA-4 substituted with rings d, e, f, or k had the greatest affinity for the tubulin heterodimer.

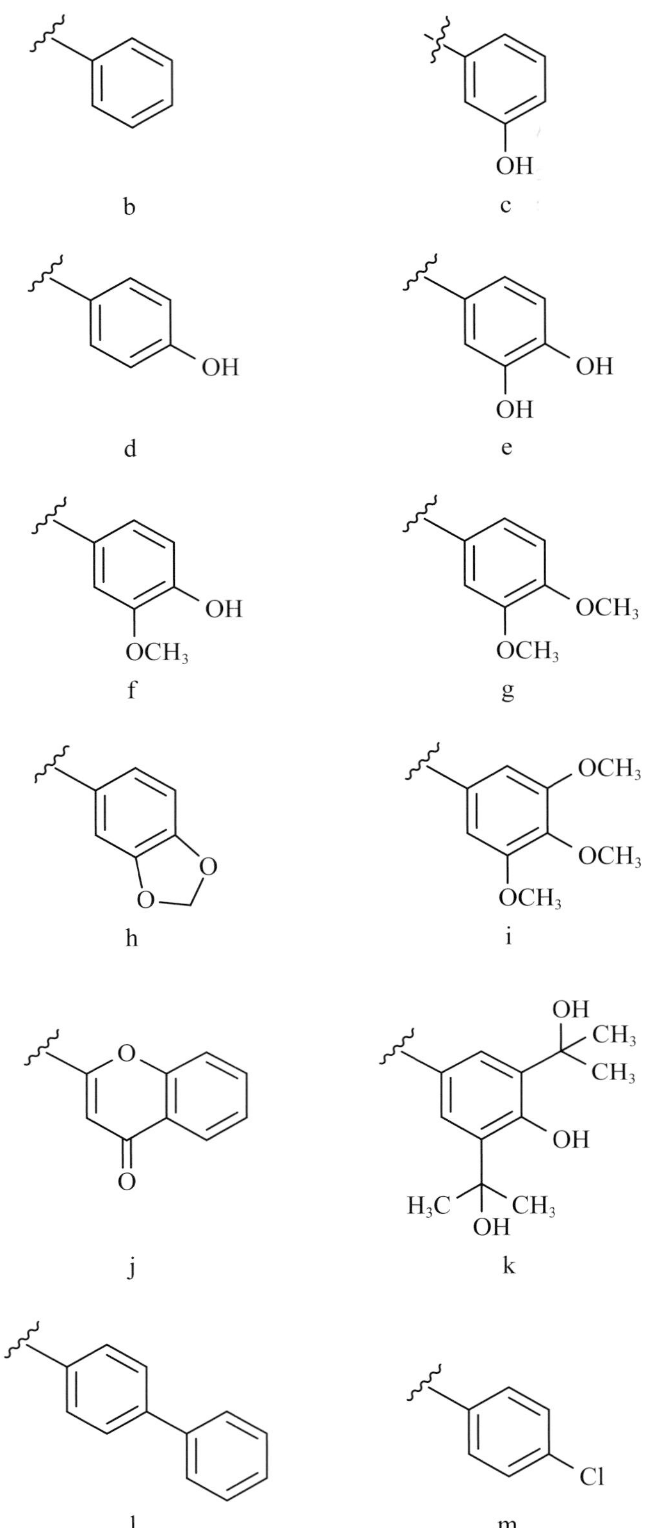

Figure 2 Ring substitutions used to synthesize derivatives of combretastatin A-4 (CA-4)

This passage is adapted from "Docking, Synthesis and Antiproliferative Activity of N-Acylhydrazone Derivatives Designed as Combretastatin A4 Analogues." Nascimento do Amaral D, Cavalcanti B, Bezerra D, Ferreira P, Castro R, et al. *PLoS ONE*. 2014. 9(3) doi:10.1371/journal.pone.0085380 for use under the terms of the Creative Commons CC BY 4.0 license (http://creativecommons.org/licenses/by/4.0/legalcode).

Question 34

In order to synthesize the substituent k shown in Figure 2, an iodine atom was replaced with a hydroxyl group. Which of the following best describes this reaction?

- A. Occurs by S_N1 chemistry with retention of stereochemistry
- B. Occurs by S_N1 chemistry with loss of stereochemistry
- C. Occurs by S_N2 chemistry with retention of stereochemistry
- D. Occurs by S_N2 chemistry with loss of stereochemistry

Question 35

Isomerization of CA-4 is thought to play a key role in limiting its affinity for β-tubulin, resulting in loss of cytotoxic activity. Isomerization is most likely to occur from:

I. *E* to *Z*.
II. *cis* to *trans*.
III. *R* to *S*.

- A. I only
- B. II only
- C. I and II only
- D. II and III only

Question 36

Modification of CA-4 with which of the following substituents would likely increase the binding of the CA-4 analogue to β-tubulin?

- A. c
- B. e
- C. j
- D. l

Question 37

A derivative of substituent d was modified in the reaction shown below. A scientist would most likely agree with which of the following statements?

C_{H_2}—Cl → C_{H_2}—F

- A. The reaction occurred in one step and used dimethyl sulfoxide (DMSO) as a solvent.
- B. The reaction occurred in one step and used ethanol as a solvent.
- C. The reaction occurred in two steps and used acetonitrile as a solvent.
- D. The reaction occurred in two steps and used acetic acid as a solvent.

Passage 8 (Questions 38-43)

Evidence for abiogenesis, the theory that all living things developed and evolved from simple inorganic chemicals, was explored in a recent experiment. The experimental protocol replicated a model of primitive earth, assuming an ocean beneath an atmosphere of ammonia, carbon dioxide, methane, and hydrogen. An electrode in the top compartment continuously produced electric sparks, simulating lightning strikes in the early atmosphere. A heater in the lower compartment vaporized water into the top compartment, where it could mix and react with the atmospheric gases, energized by the electric sparks. A condenser beneath the top compartment recovered the water and new products, allowing them to enter another reaction cycle. The apparatus used in this experiment is shown below in Figure 1.

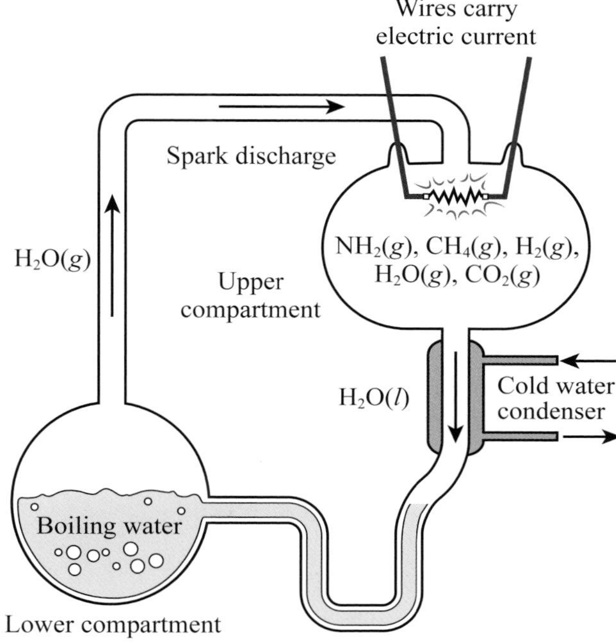

Figure 1 Simulation of primitive earth's capacity for abiogenesis

A variety of amino acids were collected after a week of continuous operation. The first step of their formation was the generation of radical monoatomic oxygen, through Reaction 1.

$$CO_2(g) \rightarrow CO(g) + O\cdot(g)$$

Reaction 1

Formaldehyde and hydrogen cyanide could evolve from Reactions 2 and 3, respectively.

$$CH_4(g) + 2O\cdot(g) \rightarrow CH_2O(g) + H_2O(l)$$

Reaction 2

$$CH_4(g) + NH_3(g) \rightarrow HCN(g) + 3H_2(g)$$

Reaction 3

Formaldehyde, hydrogen cyanide, and ammonia combined via a Strecker synthesis to generate glycine. Other amino acids formed when other carbonyl compounds reacted with the hydrogen cyanide and ammonia. At the end of the study, thin layer chromatography was used to determine the magnitude of the product variety. A developed chromatography plate from the experiment is shown in Figure 2.

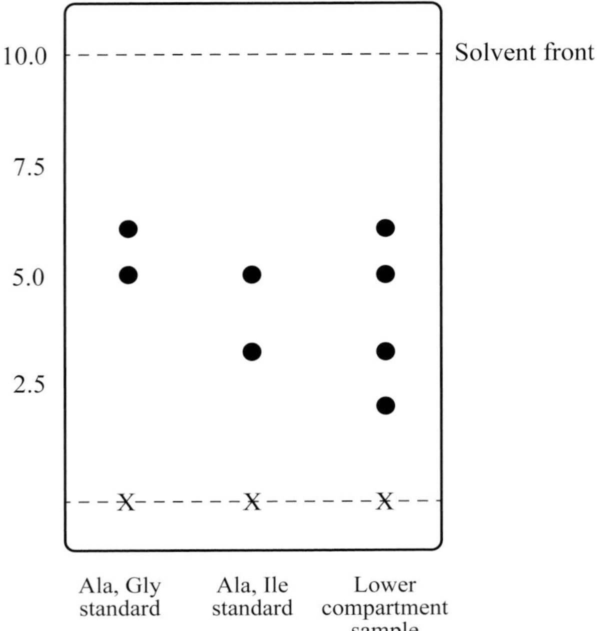

Figure 2 Developed chromatography plate

Question 38

During the formation of glycine, what functional groups are in the product that were not present in any of the reactants?

- A. cyano, amide
- B. imide, carboxylic acid
- C. amine, carboxylic acid
- D. amide, carboxylic acid

Question 39

A solution of alanine extracted from the lower compartment was tested in a polarimeter and had an $[\alpha]_D^{20} = 0$. Which of the following best explains this observation?

- A. Molecules of alanine lack the capacity to rotate polarized light.
- B. Nucleophilic attack on the imine intermediate by HCN is equally favored on each face of the intermediate.
- C. The alanine solution polymerized, resulting in a polypeptide.
- D. The pH of the solution exceeded the isoelectric point of alanine.

Question 40

What is the molecular geometry of ammonia?

- A. Tetrahedral
- B. Trigonal planar
- C. Trigonal pyramidal
- D. Square planar

Question 41

If the isoleucine in the lower compartment formed as described in the passage, which of the following electrochemically generated intermediates was formed in the upper compartment?

- A.

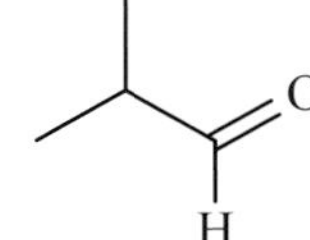

- B.

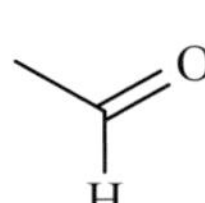

- C.

O
H

- D.

O
H

Question 42

What is the R_f of isoleucine from this experiment?

- A. 0.6
- B. 3.33
- C. 0.3
- D. 1.6

Question 43

What is true of the carbon-containing product of Reaction 1?

I. It has a longer carbon-oxygen bond than does $H_2C{=}O$.
II. The oxygen atom has a formal charge of +1.
III. The carbon atom does not have an octet of valence electrons.
IV. The carbon atom has a formal charge of −1.

- A. I, II, III, and IV
- B. II, III, and IV only
- C. II and IV only
- D. I only

Questions 44 - 47 do not refer to a passage and are independent of each other.

Question 44

Calcium gluconate (shown) is used to treat hydrofluoric acid burns. Solutions of calcium gluconate:

calcium gluconate

- A. will rotate polarized light because it is a chiral molecule.
- B. will not rotate polarized light because each anion in the compound is an enantiomer of the other.
- C. will not rotate polarized light because each anion in the compound is a meso structure.
- D. will rotate polarized light because they are more optically dense than water.

Question 45

Thalidomide's stereodependent plasma protein binding behavior is summarized in the table below:

	protein binding (%)	% absorbed into blood from stomach
R-(+)-thalidomide	55	90
S-(−)-thalidomide	66	90

If 100 mg of the thalidomide isomer shown below was administered to a patient, immediately after digestion, what mass of it can be found unbound in the blood?

Thalidomide

- A. 49.5 mg
- B. 40.5 mg
- C. 55 mg
- D. 30.6 mg

Question 46

The thiazolium ring of vitamin B_1 exchanges a hydrogen atom for a furfural residue during furoin production. During this exchange, this ring exists as the transiently lived intermediate shown below:

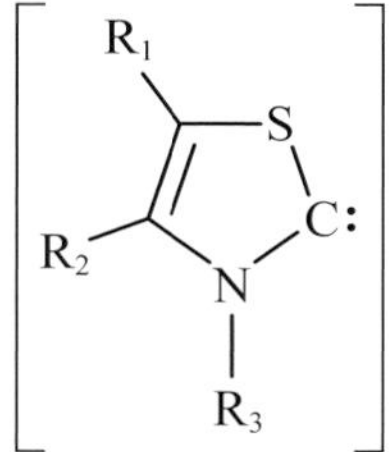

Intermediate

What is the hybridization and formal charge of the carbon radical in this intermediate?

- A. sp^3 and −1
- B. sp^2 and +1
- C. sp and 0
- D. sp^2 and 0

Question 47

What describes the relationship between structures I and II?

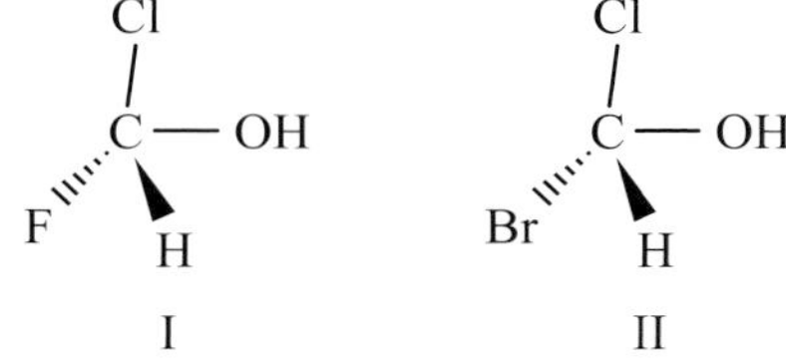

- A. I and II share the same absolute and relative configurations.
- B. I and II share the same absolute configuration.
- C. I and II share the same relative configuration.
- D. I and II do not share either absolute or relative configurations.

Passage 9 (Questions 48-51)

The glycogen content of tissues and cells depends on the concerted regulation of glycogen synthesis by glycogen synthase (GS) and glycogen breakdown by glycogen phosphorylase (GP). GP is a homodimeric enzyme existing in a phosphorylated (GPa) and an unphosphorylated form (GPb). Phosphorylase kinase phosphorylates GPb turning it to GPa, the active form. Effectors influence GP activity by switching between the tense (T, less active) and relaxed (R, more active) states of both GPa and GPb.

Glycogen phosphorylase inhibitors (GPi-s) may serve a synergistic role in combating aberrant handling of glucose in diabetes. Based on previous chemical designs, scientists synthesized a novel GPi, N-(3,5-dimethyl-benzoyl)-N′-(β-D-glucopyranosyl) urea by the process shown in Figure 1.

Scientists began by adding 3,5-dimethyl-benzamide (compound 2) to anhydrous 1,2-dichloroethane and oxalylchloride, and the mixture was heated at reflux temperature for 1 day. The volatiles were distilled off under diminished pressure and toluene was evaporated from the residue to remove the rest of oxalylchloride. The resulting acyl-isocyanate (compound 3) was mixed with a solution of β-D-glucopyranosylammonium carbamate (compound 1) in anhydrous pyridine, and the mixture was stirred at room temperature for 4 days. Pyridine was distilled off under diminished pressure and evaporation of toluene removed traces of pyridine. The crude product was purified by silica gel column chromatography with a $CHCl_3$-MeOH mobile phase to give the target compound 4.

Figure 1 Synthesis of the novel GPi N-(3,5-dimethyl-benzoyl)-N′-(β-D-glucopyranosyl) urea

This passage is adapted from "Glycogen Phosphorylase Inhibitor N-(3,5-Dimethyl-Benzoyl)-N'-(β-D-Glucopyranosyl) Urea Improved Glucose Tolerance under Normoglycemic and Diabetic Conditions and Rearranges Hepatic Metabolism." Nagy L, Docsa T, Szanto M, Brunyanszki A, Hegedus C, et al. *PLoS ONE*. 2013. 8(7) doi:10.1371/journal.pone.0069420 for use under the terms of the Creative Commons CC BY 4.0 license (http://creativecommons.org/licenses/by/4.0/legalcode).

Question 48

Which of the following shows the structural formula of oxalylchloride?

- A. $Cl-C(=O)-C(=O)-Cl$
- B. $Cl=C(-O)-C(=O)-Cl$
- C. $Cl-C(-O)=C(-O)-Cl$
- D. $Cl-C(=O)-H$

Question 49

Compound 1 and the compound shown below are most likely to be:

I. meso compounds.
II. epimers.
III. diastereomers.

- A. I only
- B. I and II only
- C. II and III only
- D. I, II, and III

Question 50

How many valence electrons are found on the carbons of the methyl substituents on compound 3?

- A. 0
- B. 1
- C. 3
- D. 4

Question 51

Compound 1 is most likely to have been formed from which of the following sugars?

- A. Fructose
- B. Sucrose
- C. Galactose
- D. Glucose

Passage 10 (Questions 52-56)

Counter-irritation describes a modality of pain relief mediated through the application of a substance that stimulates one location of the body, with the goal of relieving pain elsewhere in the body. Often, counter-irritants are chemicals that trigger sensations of heat or cold. In contrast to more common analgesics, their effects stem from stimulating pain receptors, as opposed to depressing them.

Methyl salicylate and menthol (Figure 1) are often coadministered as a topically applied liniment. Methyl salicylate induces the sensation of heat, analogous to the way hot peppers cause one's mouth to "burn." Menthol activates cutaneous TRPM8 receptors, resulting in sensations of cold, analogous to the cooling sensation experienced when cold air blows over the skin. Depending on the formulation of the liniment, these sensations can be made to follow one another, leading to analgesic action in the site of their administration.

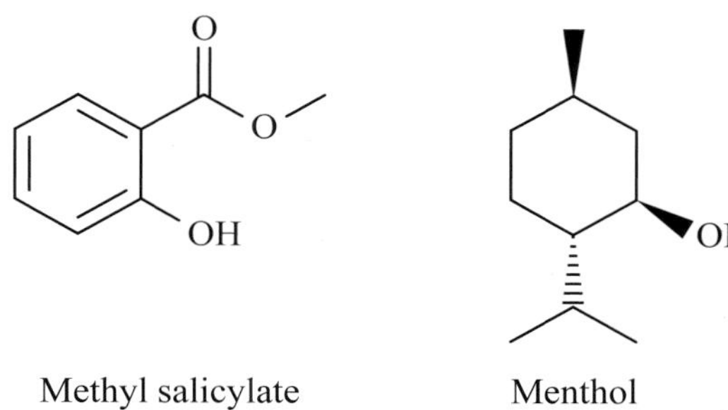

Figure 1 Structures of counter-irritants

Question 52

How many possible stereoisomers are there for menthol?

- A. 3
- B. 9
- C. 8
- D. 4

Question 53

What is the empirical formula of methyl salicylate?

- A. $C_8H_8O_3$
- B. $C_7H_8O_3$
- C. $C_6H_{10}O_3$
- D. C_4H_4O

TEST 2A

Question 54

Salicylic acid (shown) was historically extracted from the leaves and bark of the willow, *Salix alba*, and used in pain management.

Salicylic acid

Which of the following synthetic schemes could produce methyl salicylate from salicylic acid?

I. Combine excess methanol, salicylic acid, and catalytic H_2SO_4, followed by work-up and isolation.

II. Combine excess methanol, salicylic acid, and catalytic NaOH, followed by work-up and isolation.

III. Combine excess acetic anhydride and salicylic acid, followed by work-up and isolation.

IV. Combine methanoic anhydride and salicylic acid, followed by work-up and isolation.

- **A.** I, II, and III only
- **B.** I, II, and IV only
- **C.** I and II only
- **D.** I only

Question 55

If menthol were reacted with HCl, which of the following compounds is NOT a direct product (without rearrangement)?

A.

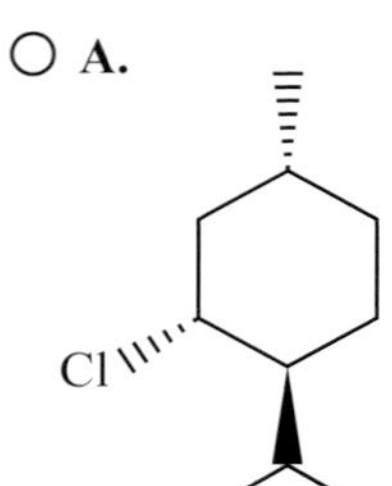

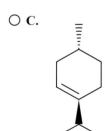

B.

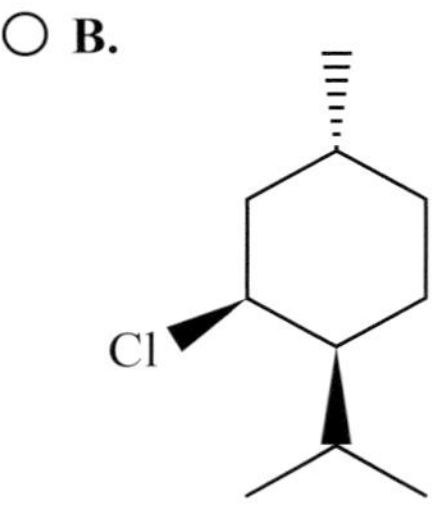

C.

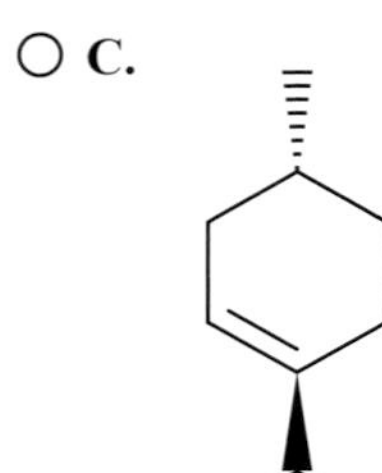

D.

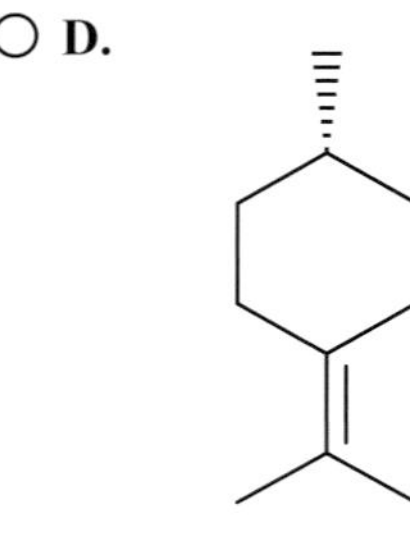

Question 56

The hydroxyl group of menthol is dramatically less acidic then that of methyl salicylate. Which of the following best explains the observation?

- **A.** The O–H bond in menthol is weaker than the O–H bond in methyl salicylate.
- **B.** The sp^2 hybridization of C3 in methyl salicylate reduces the basicity of methyl salicylate anion following deprotonation.
- **C.** Resonance allows for the positive charge following deprotonation of methyl salicylate to be delocalized throughout it aromatic ring; menthol is incapable of delocalizing the charge which follows deprotonation.
- **D.** The aromatic system of methyl salicylate delocalizes the negative charge which follows deprotonation; the hydroxyl oxygen of menthol does not have access to a π-bond, prohibiting resonance.

Questions 57 - 59 do not refer to a passage and are independent of each other.

Question 57

The specific rotation of light $[\alpha]_\lambda^T$ is measured with a polarimeter and calculated from the equation below, where l is the path length, *c* is the concentration of the analyte, and α is the observed rotation of light from its initial orientation. All of the following are true EXCEPT:

$$[\alpha]_\lambda^T = \frac{\alpha}{1 \times c}$$

- O **A.** doubling the path length will reduce the specific rotation of light by a factor of 2.
- O **B.** doubling the concentration of an enantiopure chiral solute will double the observed rotation of the light.
- O **C.** doubling the concentration of a racemic mixture will have no effect on the observed rotation of light.
- O **D.** a solution does not need to contain an enantiomerically pure solution to rotate polarized light.

Question 58

Tapentadol (shown) is an opioid analgesic of the bezenoid class. How many stereoisomers does it have?

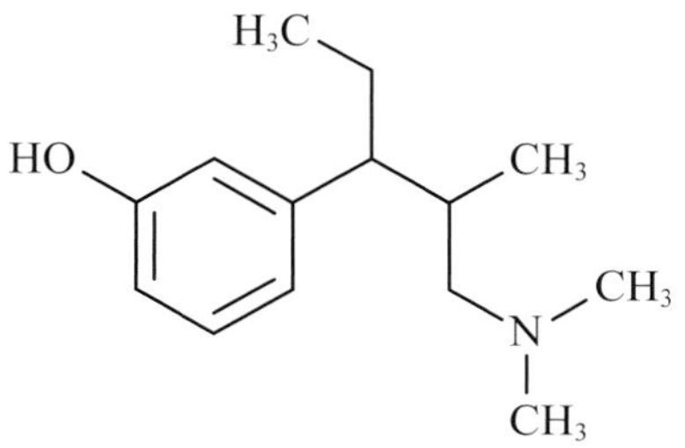

H_3C HO CH_3 CH_3 N CH_3

Tapentadol

- O **A.** 2
- O **B.** 4
- O **C.** 8
- O **D.** 16

Question 59

The compound shown below is used in the Strecker synthesis of tyrosine. How many σ and π bonds are in this compound?

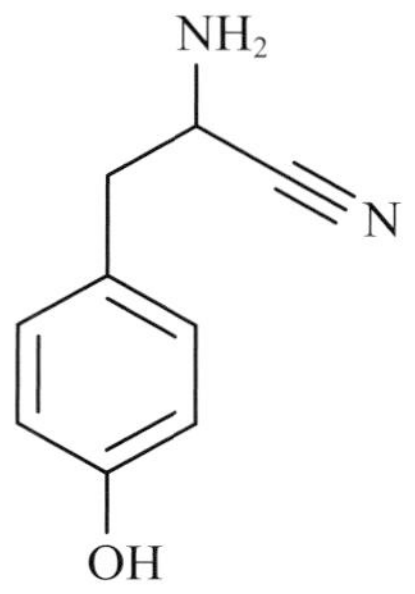

NH_2 N OH

- O **A.** 12 σ and 5 π bonds
- O **B.** 15 σ and 5 π bonds
- O **C.** 11 σ and 4 π bonds
- O **D.** 15 σ and 4 π bonds

STOP. If you finish before time is called, check your work. You may go back to any question in this test.

ANSWERS & EXPLANATIONS for Test 2A can be found on p. 240.

Introduction to Organic Chemistry

TEST 2B

Time: 45 minutes
Questions 1–29

DIRECTIONS: Most of the questions in this test section are grouped with a passage. Read the passage, then select the best answer to each question. Some questions are independent of any passage and of one another. Select the best answer to each of these questions. If you are unsure of an answer, rule out incorrect choices and select from the remaining options. Indicate your selection beside the option you choose. A periodic table can be found on the last page of this book for you to use at any point during this test section.

Passage 1 (Questions 1-4)

Without exogenous intervention, cessation of cardiac function leads to hypoxia, and rapid death of the brain and respiratory control centers. Bodily tissues consume what oxygen remains in the blood, releasing carbon-dioxide and creating an anoxic and slightly acidic environment. This environment allows endogenous anaerobic bacteria of the gut to flourish and consume bodily tissues.

The stench of decomposing flesh is a result of the gaseous products of these decomposition reactions. In particular, especially foul polyamines, such as putrescine or cadaverine (Figure 1), are generated from the decarboxylation of amino acids.

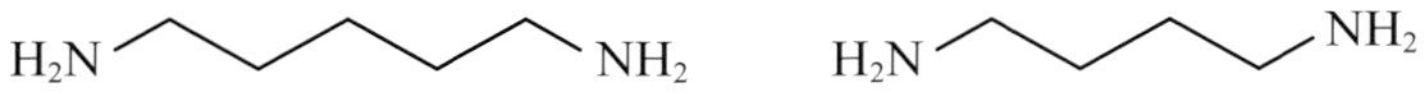

H_2N–(CH$_2$)$_5$–NH_2 Cadaverine H_2N–(CH$_2$)$_4$–NH_2 Putrescine

Figure 1 Structures of noxious polyamines

In a forensic test, a chemist was given a liquid sample from a decomposing human body. Gas chromatography revealed the presence of two volatile compounds, one of which was cadaverine. The sample was dissolved in dichloromethane, and cadaverine was removed by extraction, leaving the other volatile chemical, Compound A.

Solutions of compound A proved neutral to litmus paper. Refluxation in aqueous sulfuric acid yielded a solid, Compound B (melting point [MP] = 132–133°C), and a liquid, Compound C. Possible structures for Compound B are shown in Table 1, below.

Table 1 Potential structures for Compound B

Compound	Structure	MP (°C)
2,3-dimethyl-butanedioic acid	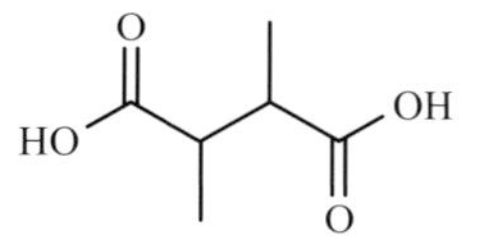	132
3,4-dimethyl-hexanedioic acid	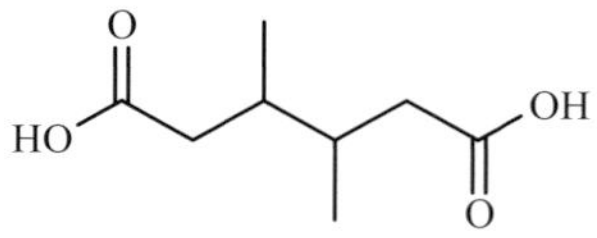	133
2-hydroxy-2-phenylacetic acid	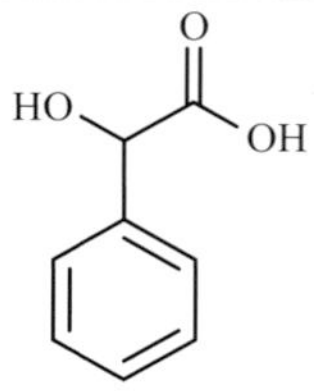	133
Cinnamic acid	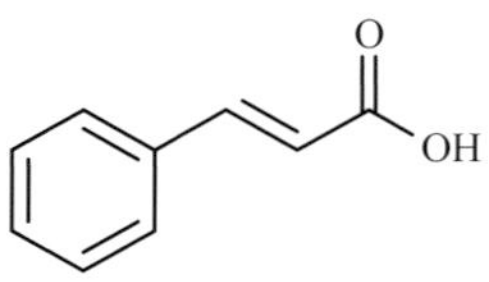	133
Furoic acid	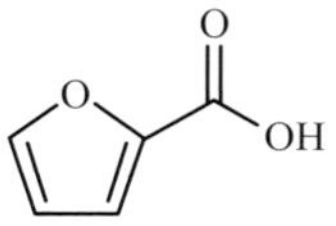	133

The IR spectrum of compound C indicated that it was an alcohol. Its structure was fully elucidated with ^{1}H NMR spectroscopy. With the potential identities for Compound B and the spectroscopic data for Compound C, it was possible to identify compound A by comparing its physical properties to those of reference samples.

Question 1

Which of the following solutions could most effectively extract cadaverine from the dichloromethane solution?

- **A.** Toluene
- **B.** Isopropyl alcohol
- **C.** 10% aqueous $NaHCO_3$
- **D.** 10% aqueous HCl

Question 2

Under proper conditions, all of the compounds in Table 1 could react with putrescine to form a corresponding:

- **A.** polymer.
- **B.** nitrile.
- **C.** amide.
- **D.** imine.

Question 3

Which of the following compound types could provide potential structures for Compound A?

- **A.** RC(O)H and R–NH_2
- **B.** RC(O)OR and R–O–R
- **C.** RC(O)OH and RC(O)OR
- **D.** R–O–R and RC(O)OH

Question 4

Which of the following is the correct IUPAC name for cinnamic acid?

- **A.** (*Z*)-3-phenylprop-2-enoic-acid
- **B.** (*E*)-3-phenylprop-2-enoic-acid
- **C.** (*Z*)-2-phenylprop-3-enoic-acid
- **D.** (*E*)-2-phenylprop-3-enoic-acid

Passage 2 (Questions 5-9)

AIDS, one of the leading threats for human health worldwide, is a disease of the human immune system caused by the human immunodeficiency virus (HIV). Although highly active antiretroviral therapy (HAART) is an available option for HIV treatment, many patients suffer from incomplete efficacy, severe toxicity, and the eventual emergence of resistance. Therefore, the development of potent antiretroviral agents with novel mechanism of action is of great interests in the field of medicinal chemistry and drug discovery.

C-C Chemokine Receptor 5 (CCR5), a G protein-coupled receptor (GPCR) for the chemokines MIP-1a, MIP-1b, and RANTES and a primary co-receptor with CD4 for macrophage-tropic HIV-1 viruses has been identified as a new target for HIV-1 epidemic prevention and treatment. Efforts devoted to the development of CCR5 antagonists have resulted in the discovery of a few small-molecule inhibitors against CCR5. The presence of one basic nitrogen center that tends to form a strong salt-bridge interaction with the Glu283 residue of the CCR5 receptor is one of the most important features for CCR5 antagonists. A hydrophobic interaction involving the Ile198 may also be important. Scientists were interested in synthesizing a novel CCR5 antagonist by the process shown in Figure 1. After synthesis and purification, compound 9 was shown to bind CCR5 with a K_M of 1.5×10^{-9} M.

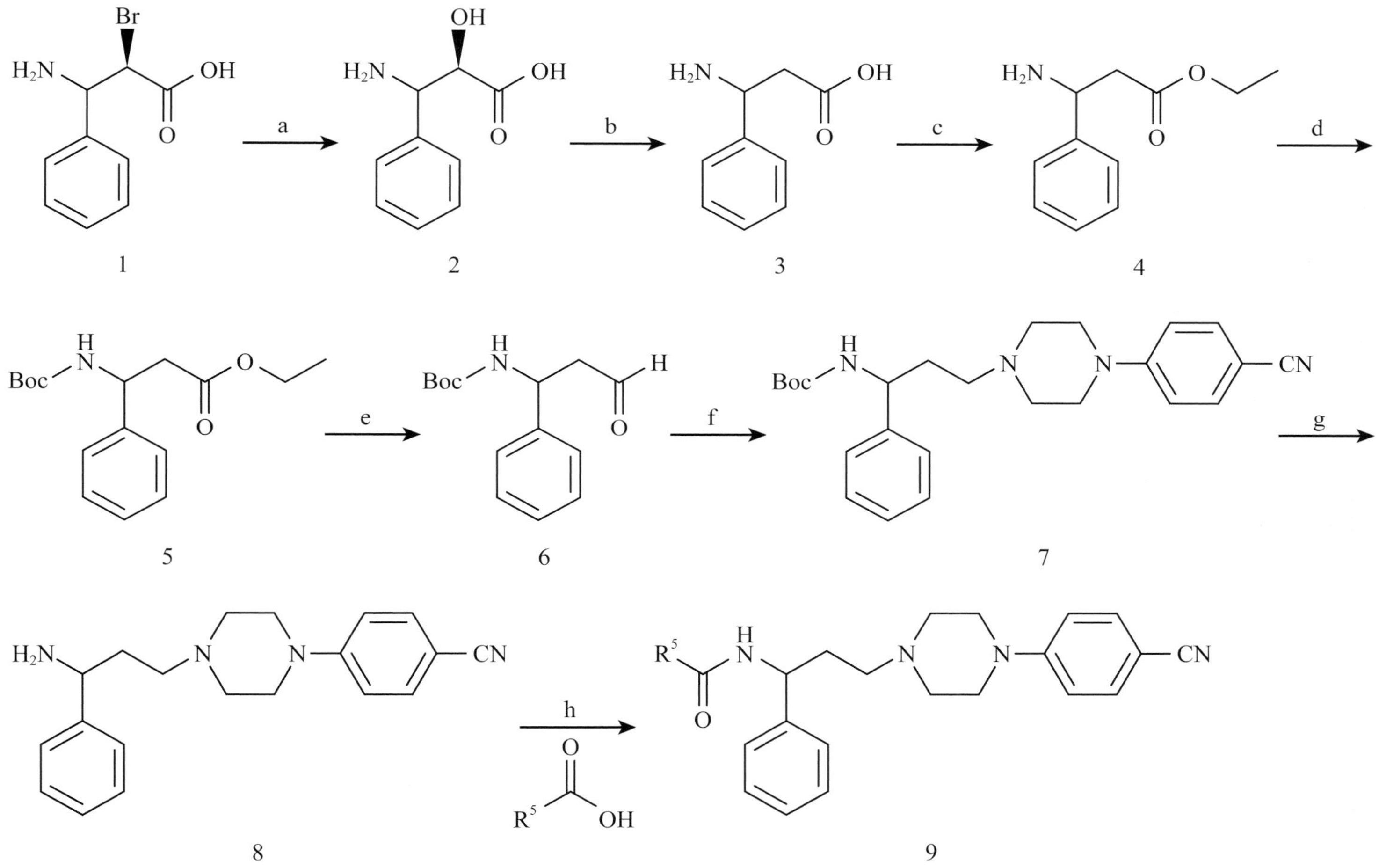

TEST 2B

Figure 1 Chemical synthesis of a novel CCR5 antagonist

This passage is adapted from "Design, Synthesis and Biological Evaluation of Novel Piperazine Derivatives as CCR5 Antagonists." Liu T, Weng Z, Dong X, Chen L, Ma L, et al. *PLoS ONE*. 2013. 8(1) doi:10.1371/journal.pone.0053636 for use under the terms of the Creative Commons CC BY 4.0 license (http://creativecommons.org/licenses/by/4.0/legalcode).

Question 5

The most likely mechanism of reaction a, shown in Figure 1, is:

- A. E1.
- B. E2.
- C. S_N1.
- D. S_N2.

Question 6

The *R* enantiomer of compound 2 is known to rotate light +80°. If a scientist assessed the rotation of plane-polarized light after reaction a, the observed rotation angle would be:

- A. 0°.
- B. −80°.
- C. +40°.
- D. +80°.

Question 7

The synthesis of compound 2 most likely occurred in which of the following solvents?

- A. Pentane
- B. Diethyl ether
- C. Acetone
- D. *t*-Butanol

Question 8

According to information contained in the passage, which of the following functional groups likely contributes to the interactions between compound 9 and Ile198 of CCR5?

- A. Nitrile
- B. Carbonyl
- C. Benzyl
- D. Amide

Question 9

What is the hybridization and geometry of the carbon in the nitrile group of compound 7?

- A. *sp* and linear
- B. sp^2 and trigonal planar
- C. sp^2 and tetrahedral
- D. sp^3 and tetrahedral

Passage 3 (Questions 10-13)

Alzheimer's disease (AD), a progressive neurodegenerative condition resulting in memory loss and neuropsychiatric disturbances, is the most common form of dementia. The experimental AD drugs (−)- and (+)-phenserine appear to ameliorate several cardinal features of AD. The structures of (−)- and (+)-phenserine are shown in Figure 1.

(−)-Enantiomeric series

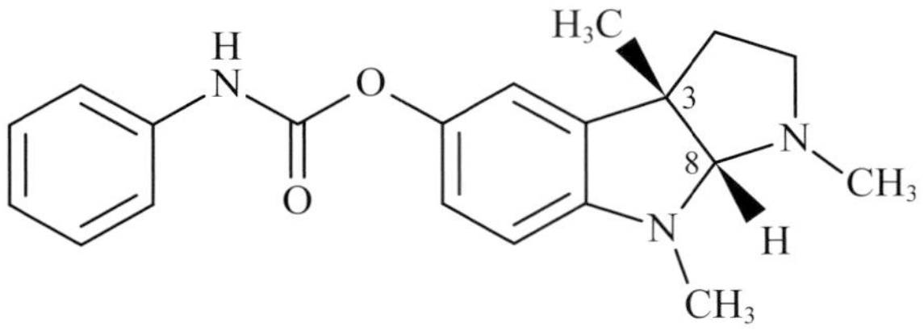

(−)-Phenserine

(+)-Enantiomeric series

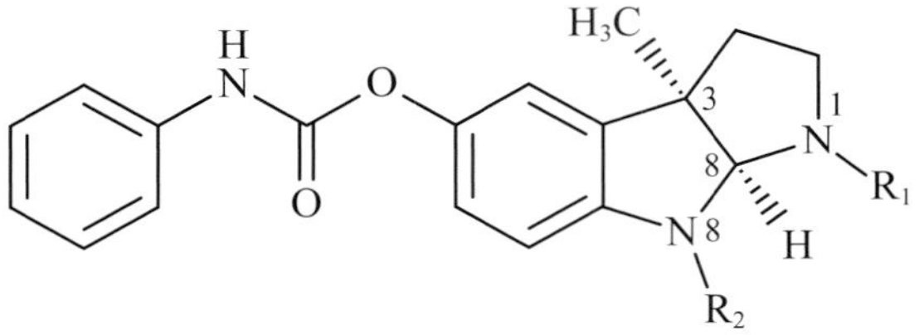

(+)-Phenserine: $R_1{=}CH_3$, $R_2{=}CH_3$
(+)-N1-Norphenserine: $R_1{=}H$, $R_2{=}CH_3$
(+)-N8-Norphenserine: $R_1{=}CH_3$, $R_2{=}H$
(+)-N1, N8-Binorphenserine: $R_1{=}H$, $R_2{=}H$

Figure 1 Structures of (−)-phenserine, (+)-phenserine and the derivatives of (+)-phenserine

(−)-phenserine ameliorates the cholinergic deficiency prominent in AD via its acetylcholinesterase inhibitory actions, augmenting cognition. (+)-phenserine augments neurogenesis and lowers both total and phosphorylated tau levels, the protein that forms the plaques and tangles in AD. In light of the decline in neurotrophins in AD brain, scientists characterized the cellular proliferation of neurons exposed to (−)- and (+)-phenserine, as well as derivatives of the drugs (+)-N1-norphenserine, (+)-N8-norpenserine, and (+)-N1,N8-bisnorpenserine. The results are shown in Figure 2.

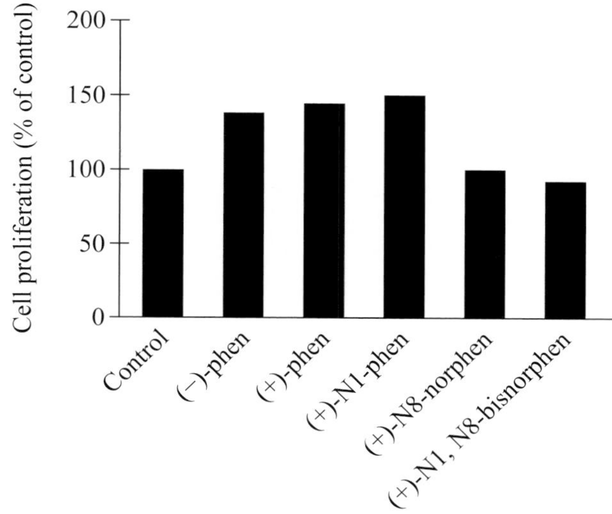

Figure 2 The effect of (−)- and (+)-phenserine and its derivatives on cell proliferation of adult neurons

This passage is adapted from "Neurotrophic and Neuroprotective Actions of (−)- and (+)-Phenserine, Candidate Drugs for Alzheimer's Disease." Lilja A, Luo Y, Yu Q-s, Röjdner J, Li Y, et al. *PLoS ONE*. 2013. 11(10) doi:10.1371/journal.pone.0164434 for use under the terms of the Creative Commons CC BY 4.0 license (http://creativecommons.org/licenses/by/4.0/legalcode).

Question 10

The stereochemistry of (−)-phenserine is best described as:

- **A.** 3*S*.
- **B.** 3*S*, 8*R*.
- **C.** 2*S*, 3*R*.
- **D.** 2*R*, 3*R*, 8*S*.

Question 11

According to the structure of (+)-phenserine in Figure 1, the bond length and strength of a carbon-carbon bond found in the phenyl substituent are likely to be:

- **A.** weaker and longer than the carbon-carbon bond in the heterocyclic nitrogen-containing pyrrolidine ring.
- **B.** weaker and shorter than the carbon-carbon bond in the heterocyclic nitrogen-containing pyrrolidine ring.
- **C.** stronger and longer than the carbon-carbon bond in the heterocyclic nitrogen-containing pyrrolidine ring.
- **D.** stronger and shorter than the carbon-carbon bond in the heterocyclic nitrogen-containing pyrrolidine ring.

Question 12

During preparation of (+)-phenserine, a scientist dissolves the compound in water with a pH of 12. Which of the following best describes the resulting reaction?

- **A.** Addition of a hydroxyl group to form a germinal diol
- **B.** Substitution of a methyl group on the heterocyclic nitrogen-containing pyrrolidine ring
- **C.** Hydrolysis of the electrophilic carbonyl of the amide bond
- **D.** Oxidation of the bridging carbon to a double bond

Question 13

Which of the following statements best describes the results shown in Figure 2?

- **A.** Decreasing the polarity of the compound decreases drug efficacy.
- **B.** Decreasing the number of groups with tetrahedral geometry decreases drug efficacy.
- **C.** Increasing the number of single bonds within the compound decreases drug efficacy.
- **D.** Decreasing the number of bonds with sp^2 hybridized carbons decreases drug efficacy.

Questions 14 - 17 do not refer to a passage and are independent of each other.

Question 14

Slowly decreasing the temperature of a solution containing aspirin is most likely to change the relative concentrations of aspirin:

- O **A.** structural isomers.
- O **B.** conformational isomers.
- O **C.** stereoisomers.
- O **D.** enantiomers.

Question 15

Which of the following choices best describes the relative hybridization of the 6 atoms of the cyclic ring in the molecule below?

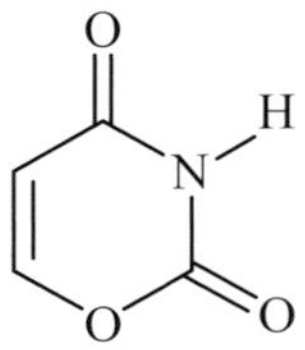

- O **A.** 1 *sp*, 2 sp^2, and 3 sp^3
- O **B.** 0 *sp*, 4 sp^2, and 2 sp^3
- O **C.** 2 *sp*, 1 sp^2, and 0 sp^3
- O **D.** 0 *sp*, 2 sp^2, and 4 sp^3

Question 16

Which of the following functional groups allows the concentration of aspirin, as shown below, to be determined by UV spectroscopy?

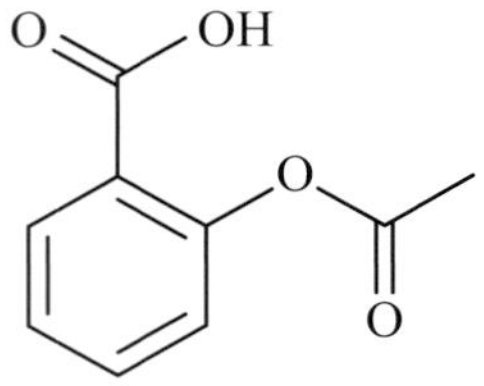

- O **A.** Benzyl
- O **B.** Carboxyl
- O **C.** Methyl
- O **D.** Ester

Question 17

Chemical synthesis a cancer drug is known to produce the byproduct shown below. Which of the following carbons is expected to have the least electron density?

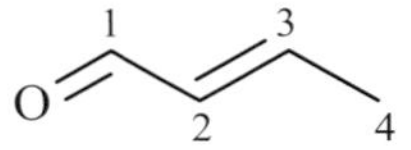

- O **A.** Carbon four
- O **B.** Carbon three
- O **C.** Carbon two
- O **D.** Carbon one

Passage 4 (Questions 18-21)

Intestinal gas or flatus has been associated, often humorously, with its malodorous properties. Curiously, the body contributes very little to the gaseous components of flatus. Rather, bacterial residents of the colon release organic sulfides during their metabolism of materials available during digestion, such as sugars and amino acids.

The vast majority of a flatus is composed of the odorless gasses nitrogen, oxygen, hydrogen, methane, and carbon dioxide. A recent study sought to elucidate the concentrations of the minority odiferous components. During the study, subjects had a tube inserted into the rectum and a gas impermeable bag attached to the tube. Prior to inserting the tube, participants were fed an identical breakfast and dinner associated with enhanced intestinal gas production. These meals consisted of 172 g of pinto beans, 450 mL of beer, and 1 Hebrew National standard size beef frankfurter. Water was provided to participants *ad libitum*.

The identities of three chief malodorous compounds were determined by subjecting several samples to gas-chromatographic–mass-spectroscopic (GC-MS) analysis. Afterwards, retention times were compared to reference samples to ensure proper identification.

The structures of these contributing odor molecules are shown below, in Figure 1.

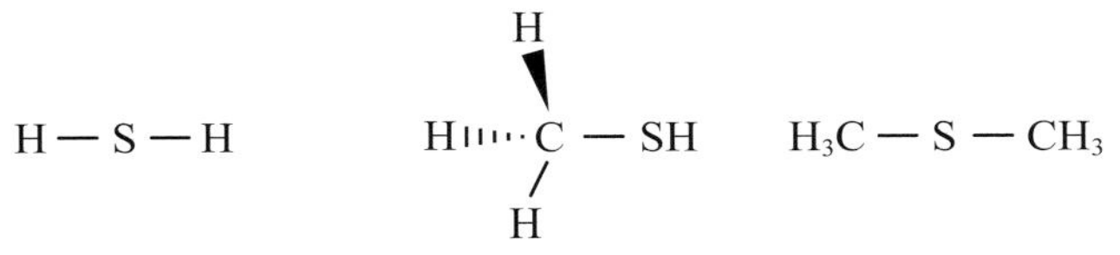

Hydrogen sulfide Methanethiol Dimethyl sulfide

Figure 1 Malodorous components in human flatus

A close up of a GC trace of the malodorous components is shown as well in Figure 2.

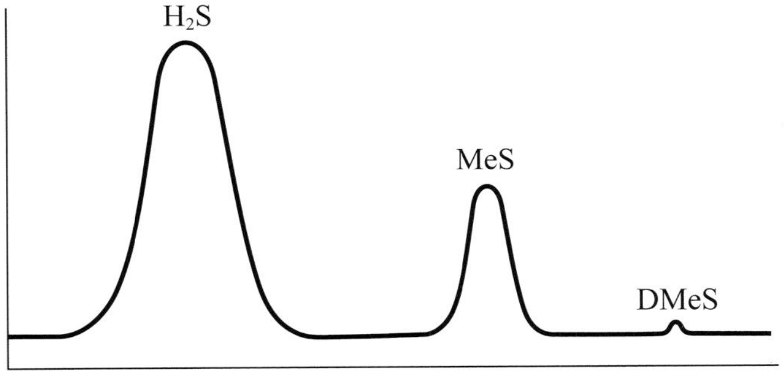

Figure 2 Labeled GC trace of malodorous components

Question 18

Which of the malodorous components has a net dipole moment?

I. Hydrogen sulfide
II. Methanethiol
III. Dimethyl sulfide

- A. I, II and III
- B. I and III only
- C. II only
- D. I only

Question 19

Methionine is dietary source of sulfur metabolized by colonic bacteria. Rotation is impossible along which bond axis in this methionine containing dipeptide?

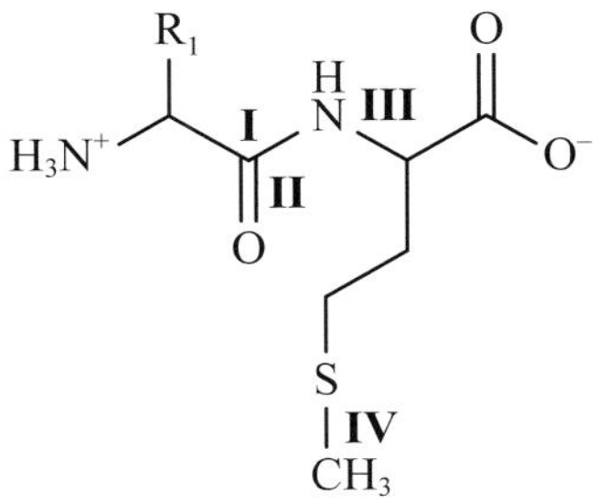

- A. I, II, and III only
- B. II and III only
- C. II only
- D. I and IV only

TEST 2B

Question 20

An organosulfide, II, along with compounds I and III are believed to contribute the smell associated with axillary odor. Which of the following lists organizes them in order of increasing acidity?

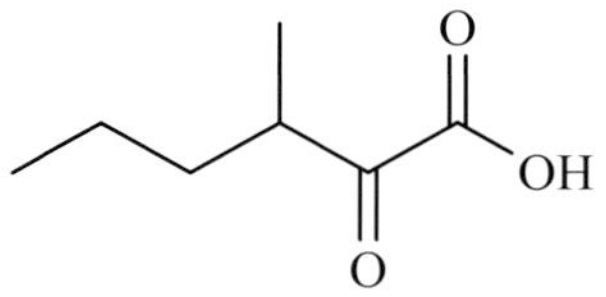

O

OH

O

I

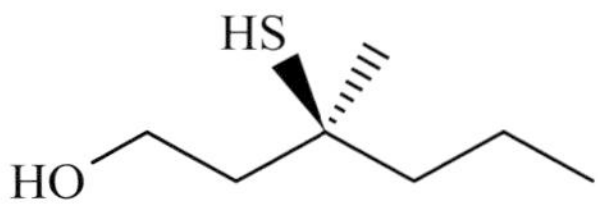

HS

HO

II

HO

O

OH

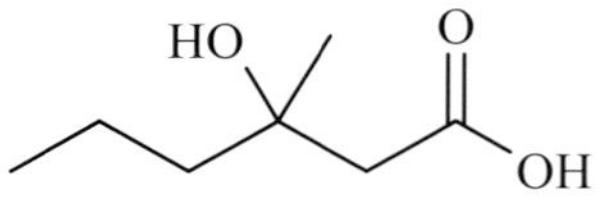

III

- A. II < III < I
- B. I < III < II
- C. II < I < III
- D. III < I < II

Question 21

Suppose methanethiol were labeled using hydrogen isotopes as shown below.

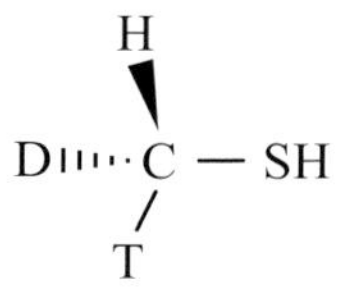

H

D····C — SH

T

How many possible stereoisomers of this labeled methanethiol exist?

- A. 1
- B. 2
- C. 3
- D. 4

Passage 5 (Questions 22-26)

STI-571 is a tyrosine kinase inhibitor (TKI) used in the treatment of Philadelphia chromosome positive chronic myelogenous leukemia (Ph+ CML). Ph+ CML is caused by a reciprocal translocation between chromosomes 9 and 22. The oncogenic fusion gene product encodes a dysfunctional tyrosine kinase (TK) protein which is constitutively active, leading to unregulated proliferation of granulocytes. In the pre-modern era, when TKIs were unavailable, a diagnosis of CML had a poor prognosis. Death via anemia, stroke, heart attack, or renal failure was expected as the blood "sludged" as a result of the dramatically increased white cell count.

STI-571 can be synthesized via a 2-step synthesis from commercially available precursors (reactions 1-2) executed in a THF/pyridine solvent system.

STI-571 is a remarkably selective, targeting the defective TK of Ph+ CML and acting on no other known TK in the body. It acts by blocking the ATP binding site. Since TKs rely on the transfer of a terminal phosphate from ATP to the tyrosine residue of their substrates, once this site is blocked, phosphorylation, which induces proliferative signaling, is disabled. 18 hours following administration of STI-571, it is found that 50% of the initial dose has been excreted from the body.

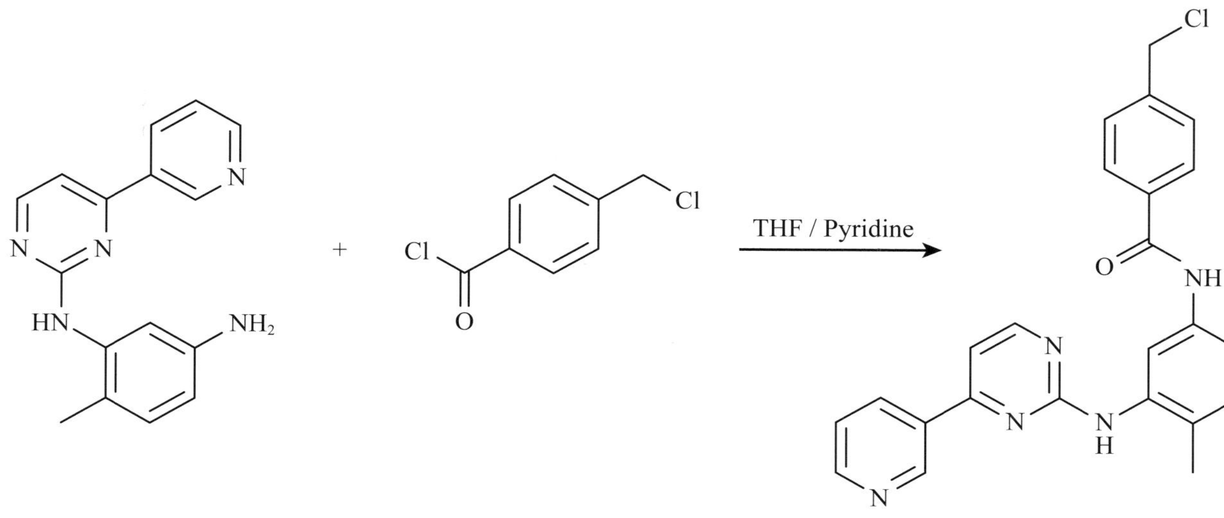

THF / Pyridine

NH2 HN N N N Cl O Cl Cl O NH N N N H N

Reaction 1

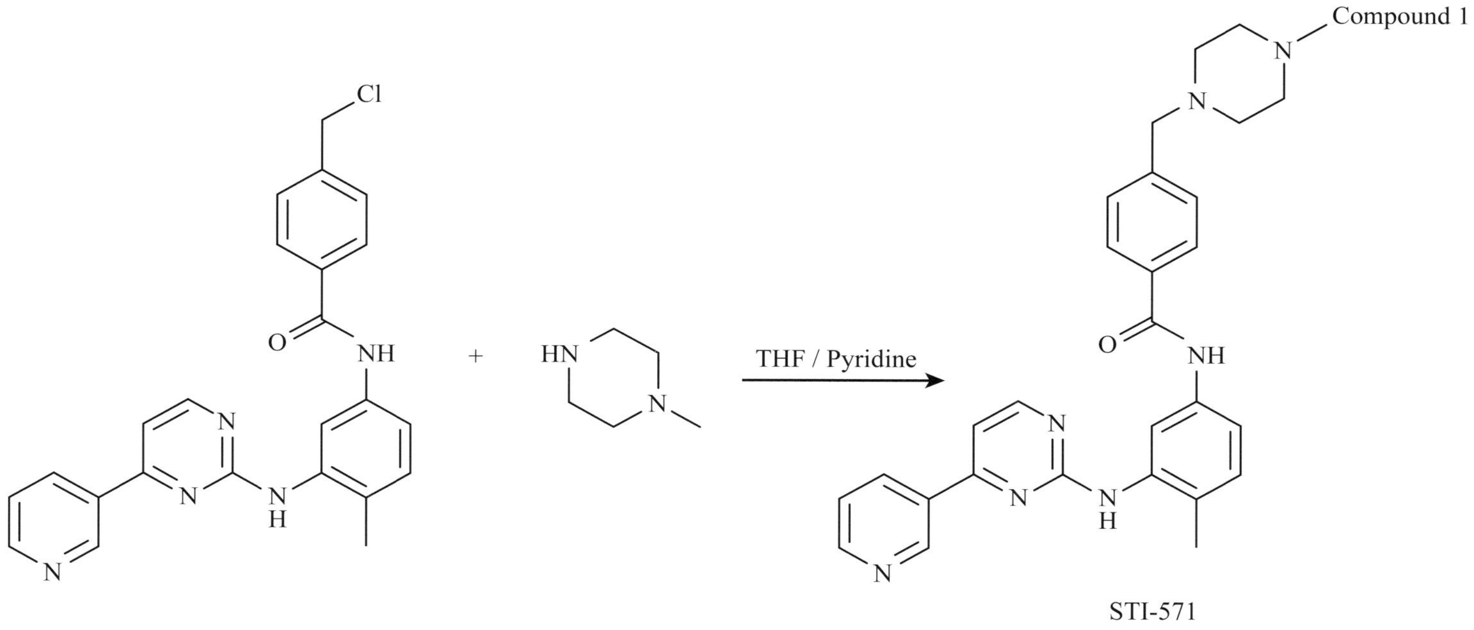

Compound 1

Cl O NH N N N H N HN N THF / Pyridine N N O NH N N N H N

STI-571

Reaction 2

TEST 2B

Question 22

A patient was administered 600 mg of STI-571 at the same time each day for two days. Immediately after receiving the second dose, how much STI-571 is in the patient's body?

- A. 1200 mg
- B. 839 mg
- C. 923 mg
- D. 695 mg

Question 23

No inversion of configuration is observed during Reaction 2 since:

- A. amines do not participate in bimolecular nucleophilic substitution reactions.
- B. the absolute configuration of a molecule is maintained during bimolecular nuclear substitution reactions.
- C. 1° alkyl halides do not always experience an observable inversion of configuration during bimolecular nucleophilic substitution reactions.
- D. steric interactions from the addition of a 2° amine prevent polyalkylation and its associated inversion of configuration.

Question 24

Why is it necessary to use pyridine in the solvent during Reaction 2?

- A. Pyridine reacts with the protons released during the reaction to form insoluble pyridinium chloride salts, which are easily removed during purification.
- B. Pyridine protects the amide product from hydrolysis.
- C. Pyridine prevents the protonation of the attacking amine, thereby preserving its nucleophilicity.
- D. Compound 1 is not soluble in THF without pyridine.

Question 25

Compounds I and II (shown) were considered for use in the second part of the synthesis described in the passage. What relationship do they have with one other?

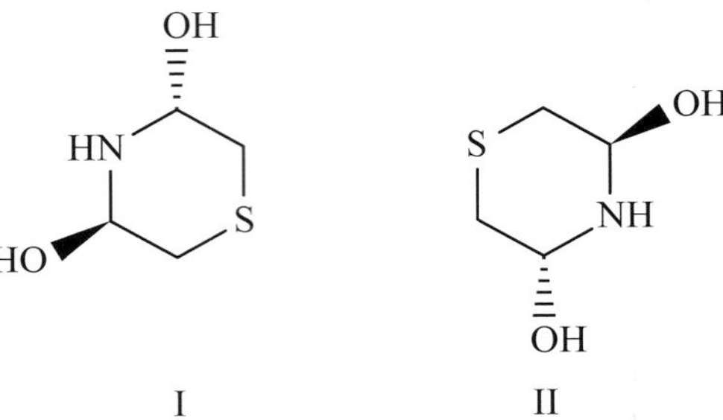

- A. They are enantiomers.
- B. They are diastereomers.
- C. They are stereoisomers.
- D. They are non-isomeric.

Question 26

Other heterocycles can be introduced into solvent systems. Which of the heterocycles below releases the most heat during combustion?

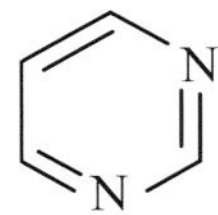

Pyrimidine

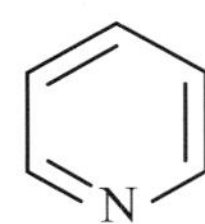

Pyridine

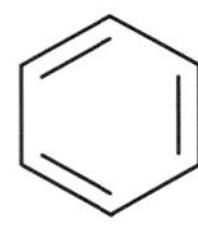

Benzene

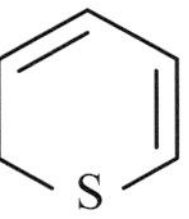

2H-thiopyran

- A. Pyrimidine
- B. Pyridine
- C. Benzene
- D. 2H-thiopyran

Questions 27 - 29 do not refer to a passage and are independent of each other.

Question 27

A certain chemotherapeutic is known to stabilize a tumor suppressor gene by covalently bonding to amino acids in an allosteric regulatory site in an additive manner. Which of the following plots most likely depicts the activity of this compound?

O **A.**

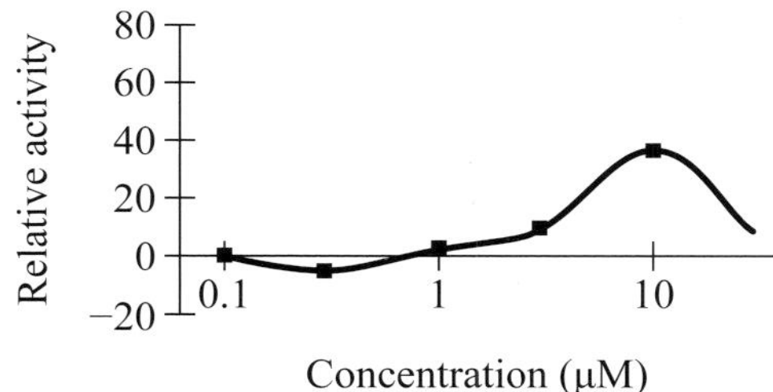

O **B.**

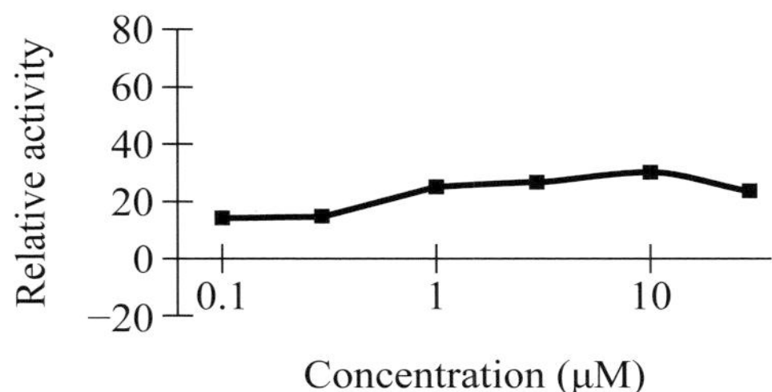

O **C.**

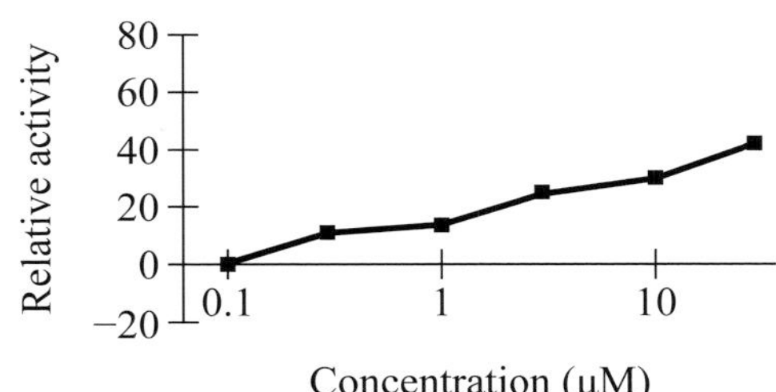

O **D.**

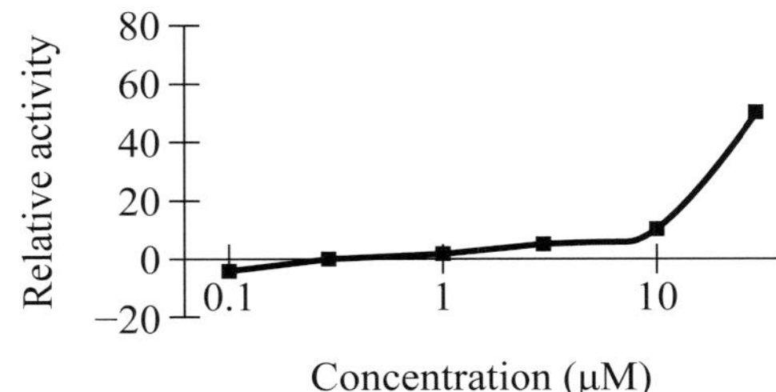

Question 28

Serine, an amino acid often found in the interior of the proteasome, is most likely to attack which of the following bonds?

```
         R   O       R   O
H        |   ||      |   ||
 >N — C — C — N — C — C — O — H
H     ↑  |  ↑     ↑  |  ↑  |
      |  H  |     |  H  |  H
      A     B     C     D
```

O **A.** A

O **B.** B

O **C.** C

O **D.** D

Question 29

Cisplatin, a transition metal compound used as an anti-cancer chemotherapeutic, is most likely to have which of the following geometries?

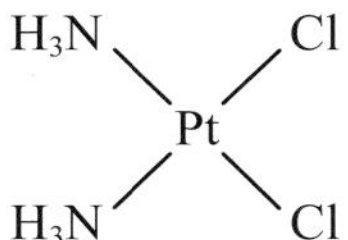

O **A.** Linear

O **B.** Trigonal planar

O **C.** Tetrahedral

O **D.** Square planar

STOP. If you finish before time is called, check your work. You may go back to any question in this test.

ANSWERS & EXPLANATIONS for Test 2B can be found on p. 240.

Oxygen Containing Reactions

TEST 3A

Time: 95 minutes
Questions 1–59

DIRECTIONS: Most of the questions in this test section are grouped with a passage. Read the passage, then select the best answer to each question. Some questions are independent of any passage and of one another. Select the best answer to each of these questions. If you are unsure of an answer, rule out incorrect choices and select from the remaining options. Indicate your selection beside the option you choose. A periodic table can be found on the last page of this book for you to use at any point during this test section.

Passage 1 (Questions 1-5)

Chlorinated organic compounds, or organohalogens, are widely used as precursors during organic synthesis or as synthetic targets on their own. These compounds display a wide range of applications including antibiotics, gas warfare agents, flame retardants, and polymerization agents. Surprisingly, organohalogens are not strictly found in industrial or laboratory settings. A member of a species of toxic mushroom, *Hypholoma elongatum*, which consumes fallen trees, biosynthesizes its own halogenated compound, (3,5-dichloro-4-methoxyphenyl) methanol, shown in Figure 1.

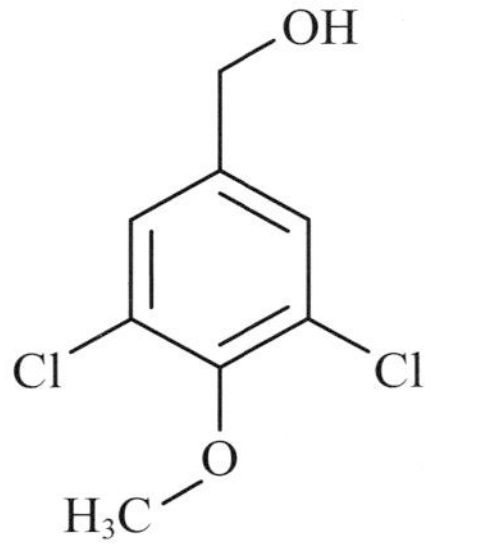

Figure 1 Structure of (3,5-dichloro-4-methoxyphenyl)-methanol

In a recent experiment, researchers extracted a sample of what they believed to be (3,5-dichloro-4-methoxyphenyl)-methanol from an *H. elongatum* specimen. To verify that the extracted product was truly (3,5-dichloro-4-methoxyphenyl)-methanol, the researchers subjected both a synthesized version of the same molecule and the naturally derived extract to gas chromatography-mass spectroscopic analysis. The researcher's synthesis utilized a facile "single pot" approach, outlined below, in Reaction 1.

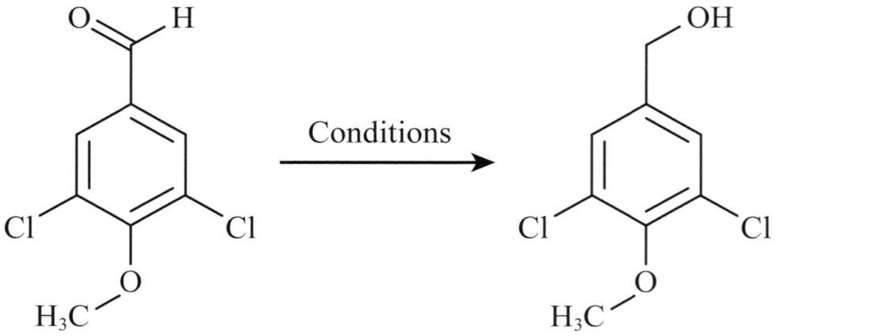

Compound 1 —Conditions→ (3,5-dichloro-4-methoxyphenyl)-methanol

Reaction 1

The GC trace of the original sample is shown in Figure 2.

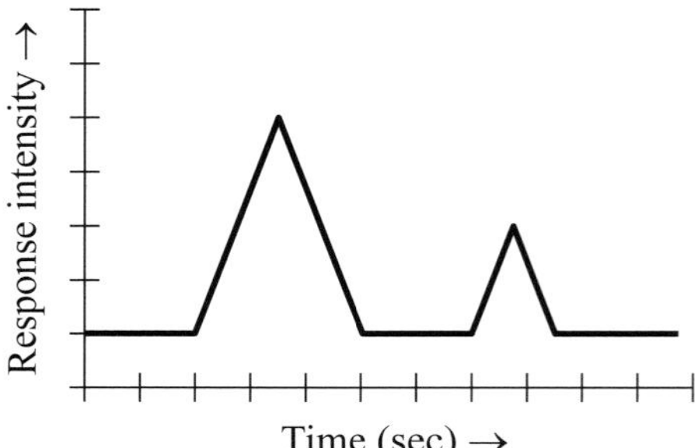

Figure 2 GC trace of original sample

Question 1

If the researchers wanted to cleave the methyl-oxygen bond of the methoxy ether of Compound 1, which of the following reagents would be most appropriate?

- **A.** Cl_2/NaOH(*aq*)
- **B.** HCl(*aq*)
- **C.** CH_3Cl(*l*)
- **D.** NaCl(*aq*)

Question 2

The conditions of Reaction 1 were most likely:

- **A.** methylmagnesium iodide in anhydrous ether.
- **B.** methylbromide in anhydrous ether.
- **C.** catalytic H_2SO_4 in methanol.
- **D.** sodium borohydride in ethanol.

Question 3

Compound 1 can be classified as an aryl-substituted:

- **A.** methan-1-one.
- **B.** methan-1-al.
- **C.** methan-3-al.
- **D.** propan-2-al.

Question 4

The compound below was obtained by subjecting a separate fungal extract to a solution of acidified acetone and molecular sieves.

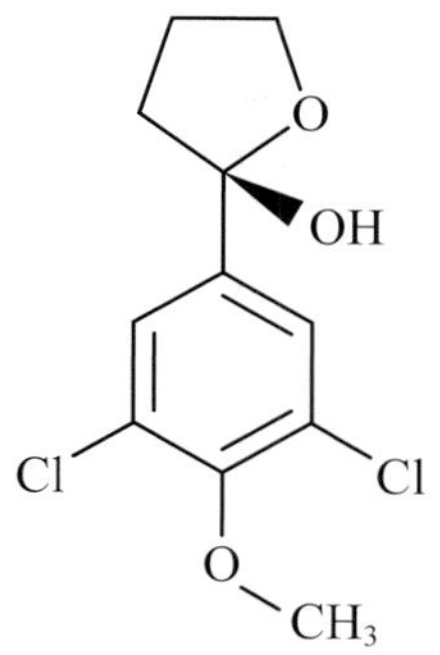

Which of these structures was most likely in the fungal extract?

- A. 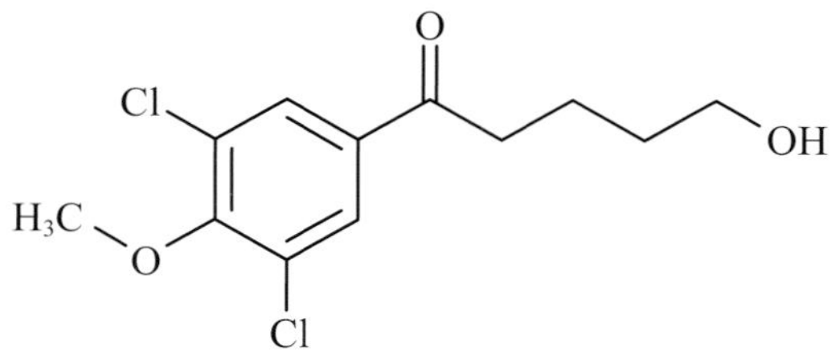
- B. 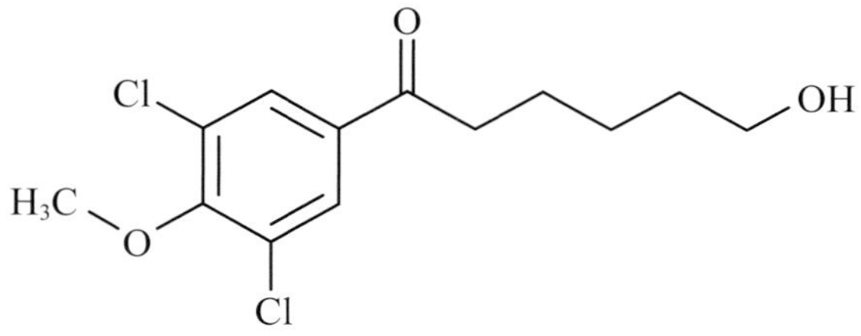
- C. 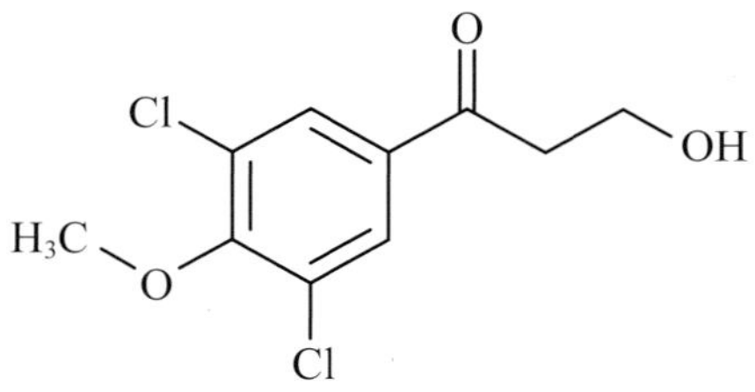
- D.

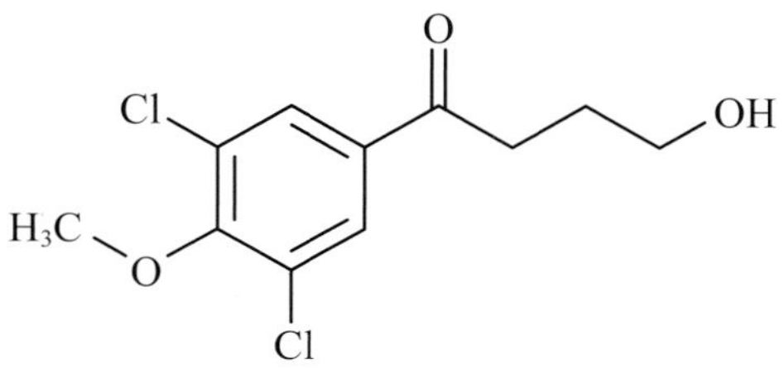

Question 5

Two derivatives of Compound 1 are shown below:

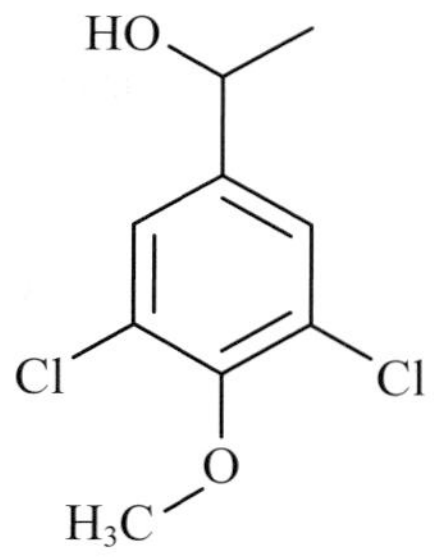

Compound 2 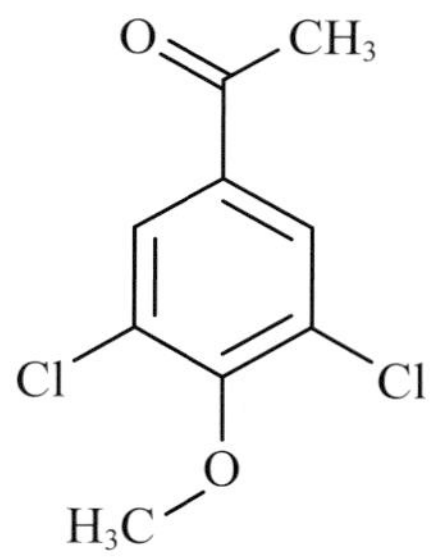 Compound 3

Which of the following relationships to Compound 1 are most likely true?

- A. Sodium borohydride can reduce Compound 3 but not Compound 1.
- B. Compound 1 and Compound 2 can both undergo alkylation in the presence of ethymagnesium bromide.
- C. Compound 2 has a greater boiling point than Compound 1.
- D. When exposed to an alcohol, dilute acid and a desiccating agent, Compound 3 can form hemiacetals, but Compound 1 cannot.

Passage 2 (Questions 6-10)

Neuraminidase (NA) is a key enzyme in the influenza virus life cycle. Hemagglutinin (HA), another influenza protein, is used by the virus for attachment and infection of new cells. HA has a strong affinity for the sialic acid residues present in glycoproteins on a cell's surface. As new viruses bud off an infected cell, HA on the viral capsids bind to the glycoproteins on the cell's surface. This prevents the viruses from infecting new cells. NA allows viral particles to detach themselves by cleaving terminal sialic acid residues from the glycoprotein. Sialic acid is a derivative of neuraminic acid, which is a monosaccharide. The structure of neuraminic acid is shown in Figure 1.

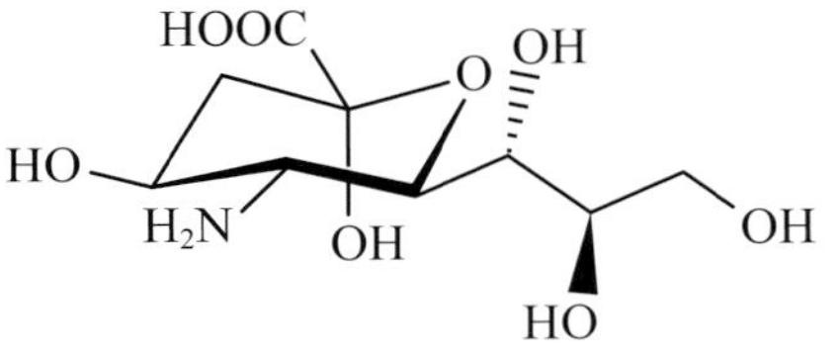

HOOC O OH HO H_2N OH OH HO

Figure 1 Neuraminic acid

NA is a common target for some antiviral medications. Oseltamivir and zanamivir are competitive inhibitors of NA that have been approved for treatment of influenza infection, also known as the flu. Studies have shown that oseltamivir treatment within 48 hours of symptom onset reduces the length and severity of the flu. Oseltamivir, which is synthesized from shikimic acid, is an inactive prodrug that is activated by catalyzed ester hydrolysis in the liver. The structures of shikimic acid and oseltamivir are shown in Figure 2.

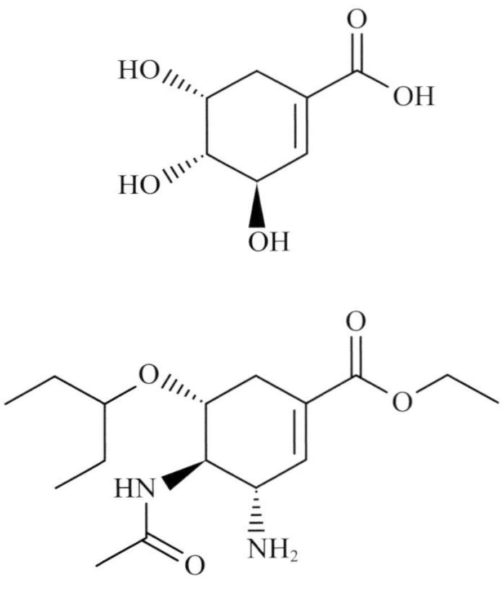

O HO OH HO OH

O O O HN NH_2 O

Figure 2 Shikimic acid (top) and oseltamivir (bottom)

Question 6

A student treats 5.5 moles of oseltamivir with 11 moles of $LiAlH_4$. What is the predominant structure obtained from the reaction?

- A. O O H HN O NH_2
- B. O O O HN O NH_2
- C. OH O OH HN O NH_2
- D. O O H H_2N NH_2

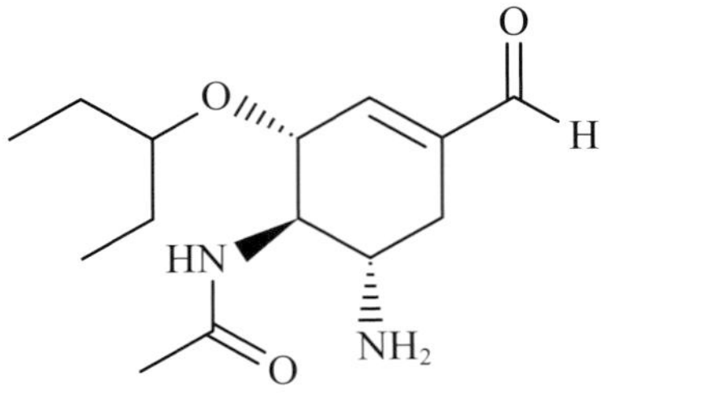

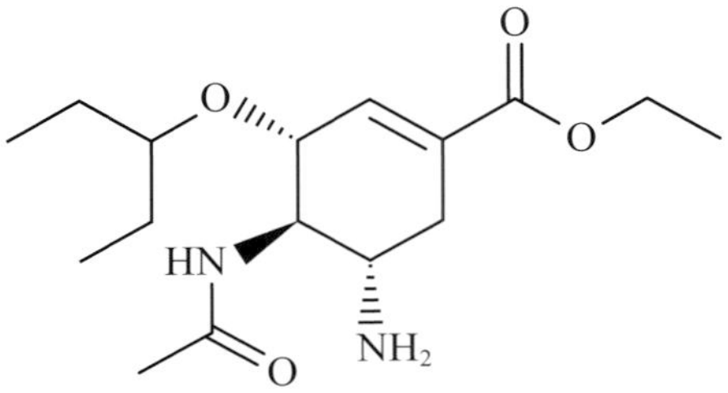

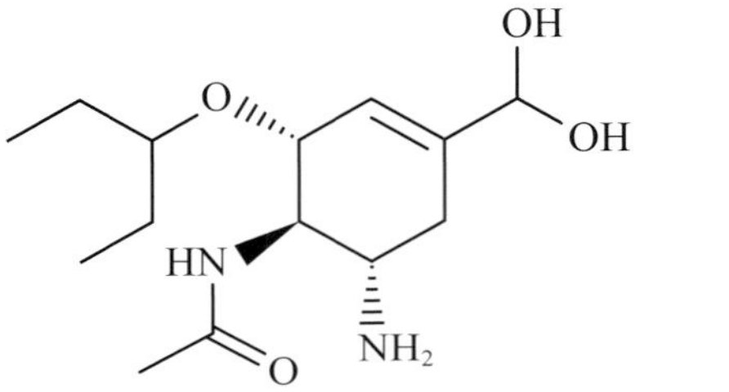

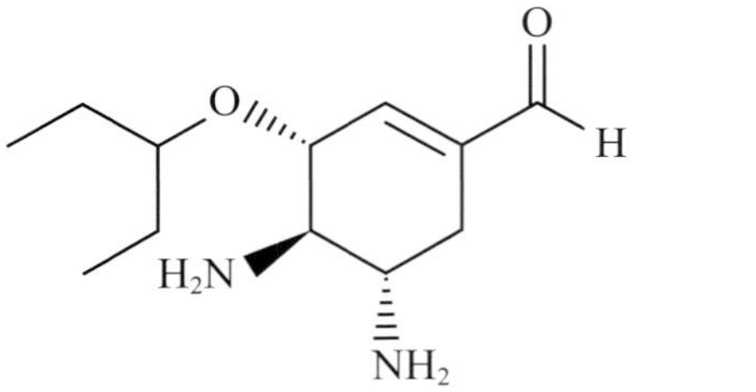

Question 7

Which new functional group is formed when oseltamivir is converted into its active form?

- A. An amide
- B. A carboxylic acid
- C. An amine
- D. An ester

Question 8

In the figure of oseltamivir below, which hydrogen is the most acidic?

- O **A.** Hydrogen 1
- O **B.** Hydrogen 2
- O **C.** Hydrogen 3
- O **D.** Hydrogen 4

Question 9

Which reagent could be used to make the esterification of shikimic acid require fewer moles of reactants?

- O **A.** $SOCl_2$
- O **B.** $NaBH_4$
- O **C.** $KMnO_4$
- O **D.** CH_3CH_2OH

Question 10

Which type of monosaccharide is neuraminic acid?

- O **A.** Aldohexose
- O **B.** Ketononose
- O **C.** Aldononose
- O **D.** Ketohexose

Passage 3 (Questions 11-14)

One of the most important classes of drugs in modern medicine are local anesthetics. These drugs reversibly block sodium channels responsible for the depolarization of nerve cells that transmit sensory information. When sodium channels are blocked, ionic sodium cannot enter the nerve cell during an event which would normally lead to a depolarization. As a result, action potentials are not propagated from the periphery to the central nervous system for processing. At an organismal level, the effects of these drugs are felt as transient numbness in the site of their administration.

The alkaloid cocaine is a naturally occurring local anesthetic. Due its addictive nature and toxic effects, drug chemists sought to identify its pharmacophore, or essential structural components that lead to its biological properties. Analysis revealed that the pharmacophore responsible for cocaine's anesthetic effects is a benzoate ester linked with a carbon chain to a tertiary amine, as shown in Figure 1. Subsequent drug designs replaced the ester with an amide functionality to connect the aromatic group to the carbon chain. These changes improved stability and reduced the risk of allergic reactions.

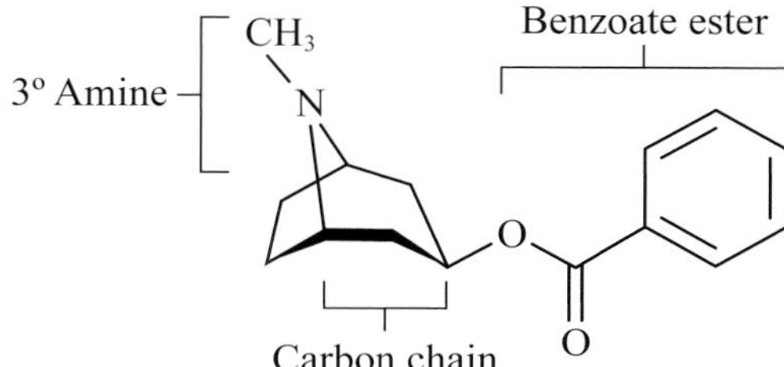

Figure 1 Anesthetic pharmacophore of cocaine

Based on the structure of cocaine, one of the first analogs to be developed was procaine. It can be synthesized according to the two routes shown below (Reactions 1 – 5).

H_2N Compound 1 + HO Compound 2 (N)

Reaction 1 NaOEt

H_2N Novocaine

Reaction 5 Reduction

O_2N Compound 4

O_2N *p*-nitrotoluene

Reaction 2 Oxidation

O_2N COOH 4-nitrobenzoic acid

Reaction 3 $SOCl_2$

O_2N Cl Compound 3

Reaction 4 HO NEt_2

Question 11

During Reaction 1, dilute acid would serve:

- A. as a suitable replacement for NaOEt because it would increase the electrophilicity of Compound 1.
- B. as an unsuitable replacement for NaOEt because it would change the solubility properties of Compound 1 and Compound 2.
- C. as an unsuitable replacement for NaOEt because it would increase the nucleophilicity of Compound 1.
- D. as a suitable replacement for NaOEt because it would create water as a leaving group.

Question 12

Which of the following reagents would best perform the oxidation shown in Reaction 2?

- A. Pyridinium chlorochromate and dichloromethane
- B. Sodium dichromate, water, and sulfuric acid
- C. Lithium aluminum hydride, and diethyl ether
- D. Ozone gas

Question 13

The reaction coordinate energy diagram of Reaction 1 in the absence of NaOEt is shown below:

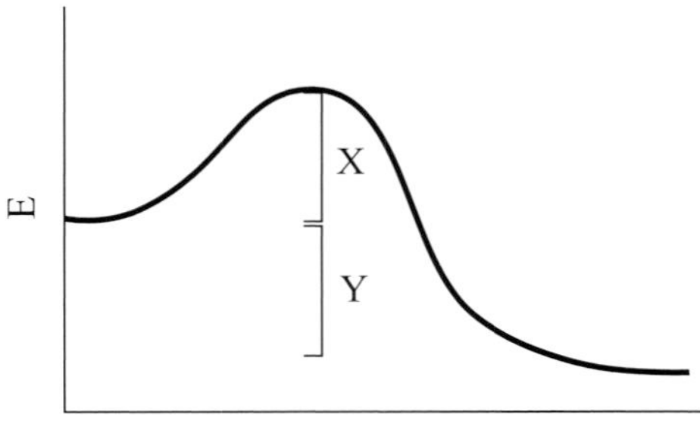

What effect does adding NaOEt have on this diagram?

- A. It decreases the value of X.
- B. It increases the value of Y.
- C. It decreases the value of X and increases the value of Y.
- D. It increases the value of X and decreases the value of Y.

Question 14

In a solution of sodium ethoxide, which of the following chemicals will most efficiently form Tetracaine (shown)?

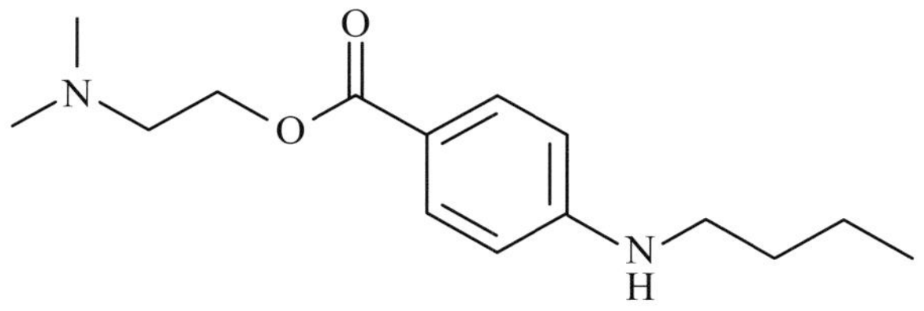

Tetracaine

O **A.**

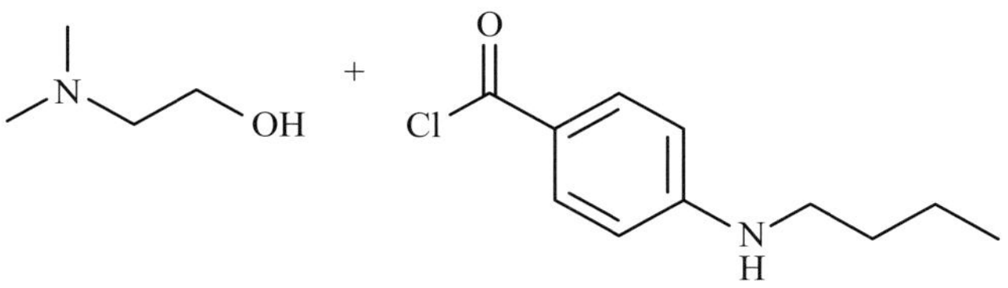

O **B.**

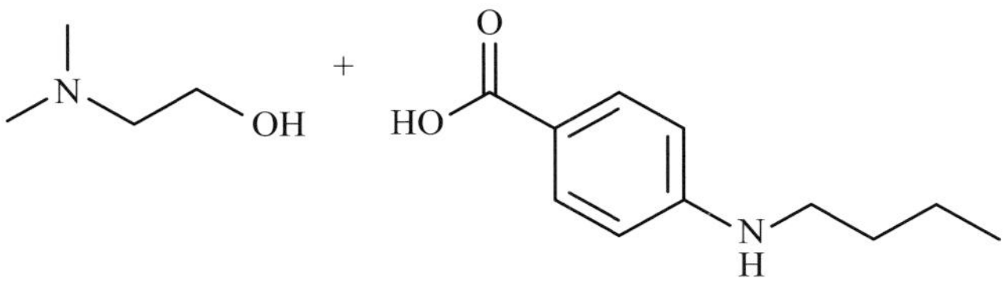

O **C.**

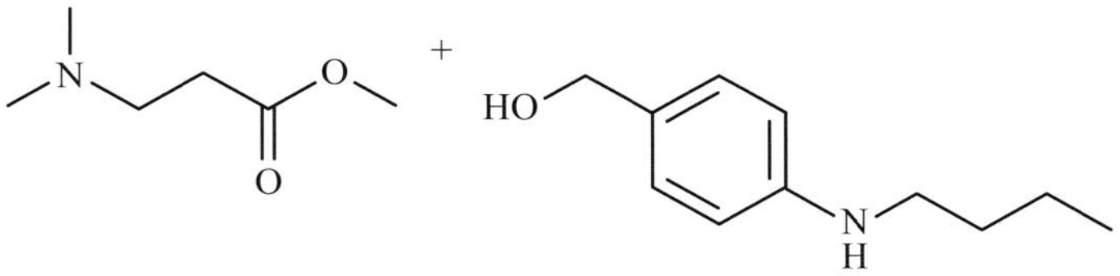

O **D.**

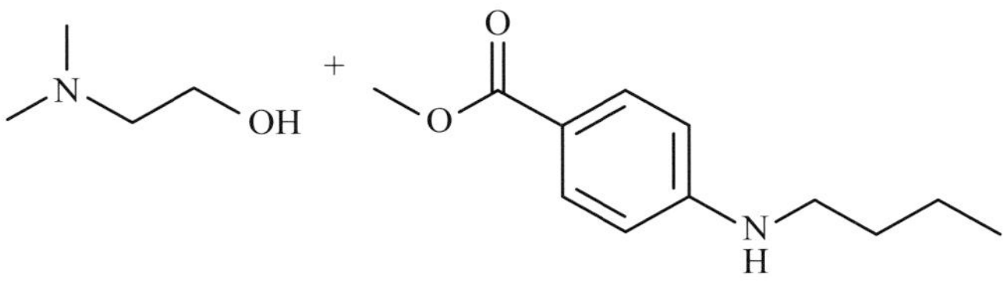

Questions 15 - 18 do not refer to a passage and are independent of each other.

Question 15

The nitrile group has a robust functionality in pharmaceutical compounds and is not readily broken down by the body. It can be introduced via sequential substitution reactions on an alcohol substrate, using a tosyl halide and a cyanide salt as shown below:

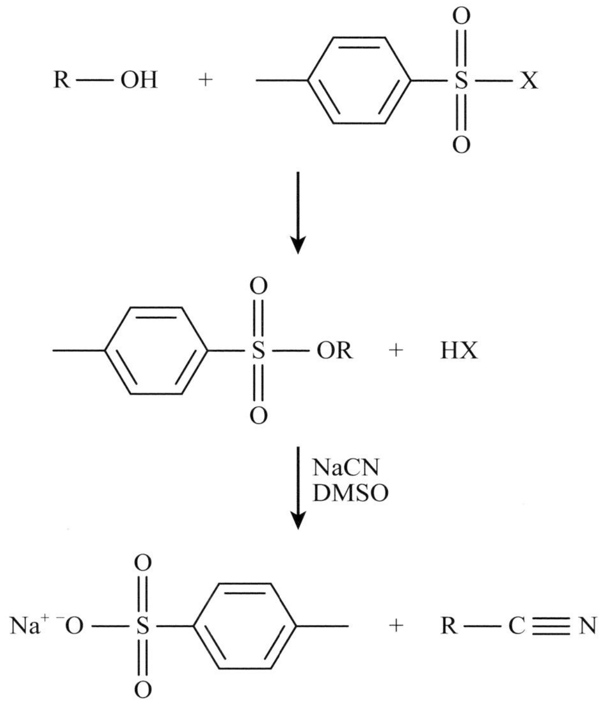

R—OH + $CH_3C_6H_4SO_2X$ → $CH_3C_6H_4SO_2OR$ + HX

NaCN, DMSO → $Na^+ \, ^-OSO_2C_6H_4CH_3$ + R—C≡N

Which halogen X would be LEAST effective for this reaction?

O **A.** F

O **B.** Cl

O **C.** Br

O **D.** I

Question 16

The creation of an alkyl chloride from a primary alcohol requires a two step process. Step 1 reacts an alcohol (ROH) with 4-Toluenesulfonyle chloride ($CH_3C_6H_3SO_2Cl$). This newly formed tosylate ($CH_3C_6H_3SO_2OR$) then undergoes an S_N2 reaction with a chloride ion. The purpose of step 1 is to:

O **A.** generate a stronger nucleophile capable of displacing the alcohol group.

O **B.** make the alcohol into a better leaving group.

O **C.** provide resonance to stabilize the intermediate of the S_N2 reaction.

O **D.** create a less sterically hindered molecule that can be attacked by the nucleophile in Step 2.

Question 17

An alkyl alcohol has all of the following properties EXCEPT:

- A. hydrogen bonding.
- B. an acidic hydrogen.
- C. resonance.
- D. polar bonds.

Question 18

Which of the following is an expected difference between propanoic acid and butanol?

- A. Butanol has a higher boiling point than propanoic acid.
- B. Propanoic acid is soluble in water and hexane while butanol is only slightly soluble in water.
- C. Butanol is more likely to react with a nucleophile than propanoic acid.
- D. Propanoic acid is unable to participate in hydrogen bonding.

Passage 4 (Questions 19-23)

1-methyl-4-phenyl-1,2,3,6-tetrahydropyridine (MPTP) is a potent pre-neurotoxin, metabolized by glial cells into the toxin 1-methyl-4-phenylpyridiunium (MPP+) by the enzyme monoamine oxidase-B. MPP+ is particularly toxic to neurons responsible for the production of the neurotransmitter dopamine, leading to the rapid onset of symptoms commonly seen in Parkinson's disease (PD). For this reason, MPTP is used in monkey and rodent models of Parkinson's disease.

The neurotoxicity of MPTP was discovered by accident, when an organic chemistry graduate student illicitly synthesized desmethylprodine (MPPP) via Reactions 1 and 2 and self-administered the synthetic opiate.

During the synthesis, the competing reaction of Reaction 2, Reaction 3 also occurred, contaminating the product and leaving him with irreversible Parkinsonian symptoms. Subsequent analysis of the contaminated product and *in vivo* animal models confirmed the neurotoxicity of MPTP.

Despite the utility of MPTP induced PD, there are key distinctions between the experimental model and the clinical disease. In MPTP induced PD, there is an absence of one of the key histological findings in clinical PD: Lewy bodies. Moreover, in clinical PD the neurodegeneration of nigral neurons and manifestation of Parkinsonian symptoms is gradual, whereas the MPTP induced models demonstrate a rapid onset of symptoms and nigral degeneration.

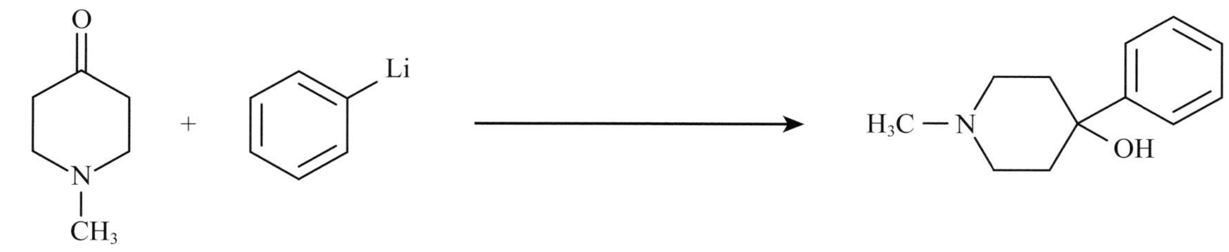

Compound 1 + Compound 2 → Compound 3

H_3C-N (piperidine with OH and phenyl)

Reaction 1

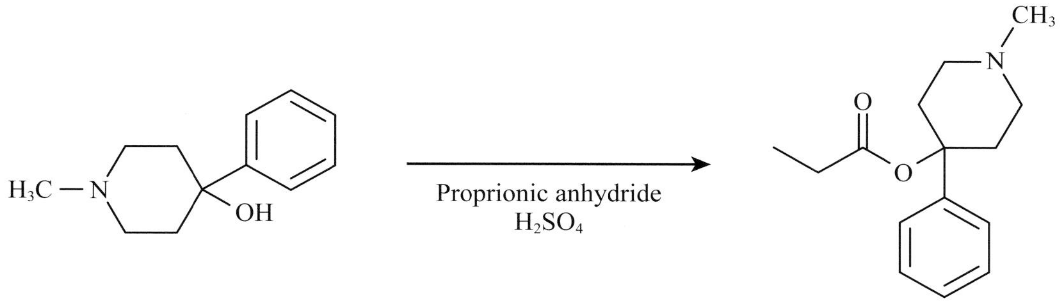

Compound 3 → MPPP

Proprionic anhydride
H_2SO_4

Reaction 2

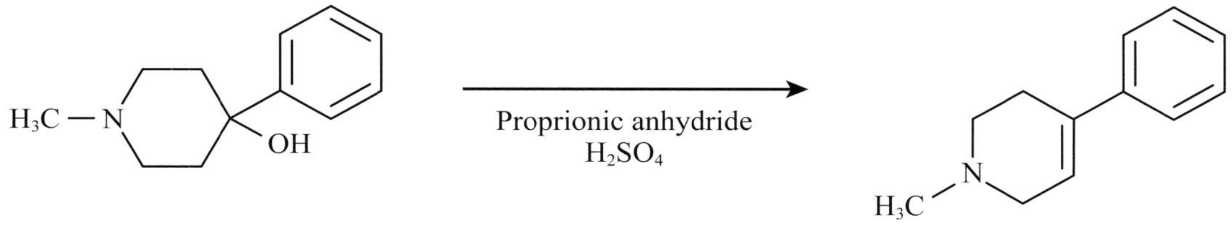

Compound 3 → MPTP

Proprionic anhydride
H_2SO_4

Reaction 3

Question 19

Which of the following is the LEAST suitable solvent in which to perform Reaction 1?

- O **A.** Benzene
- O **B.** Ethyl acetate
- O **C.** Hexane
- O **D.** Diethyl ether

Question 20

What is the systematic name of MPPP?

- O **A.** (4-Methyl-1-phenylpiperidin-1-yl) ethanoate
- O **B.** (1-Methyl-4-phenylpiperidin-4-yl) butanoate
- O **C.** (1-Methyl-4-phenylpiperidin-4-yl) ethanoate
- O **D.** (1-Methyl-4-phenylpiperidin-4-yl) propanoate

Question 21

The preparation of propionic anhydride from two equivalents of propionic acid requires:

- O **A.** an acid catalyst, high temperatures, and a desiccating agent.
- O **B.** a basic catalyst, high temperatures, and a desiccating agent.
- O **C.** an acid catalyst, low temperatures, and addition of water.
- O **D.** a basic catalyst, high temperatures, and the addition of water.

Question 22

Suppose 4-methyl-pentanoic anhydride is used instead of proprionic anhydride in Reaction 2, and the competing reaction is prevented. Which of the following structures is the most likely product?

- A.
- B.
- C.
- D.

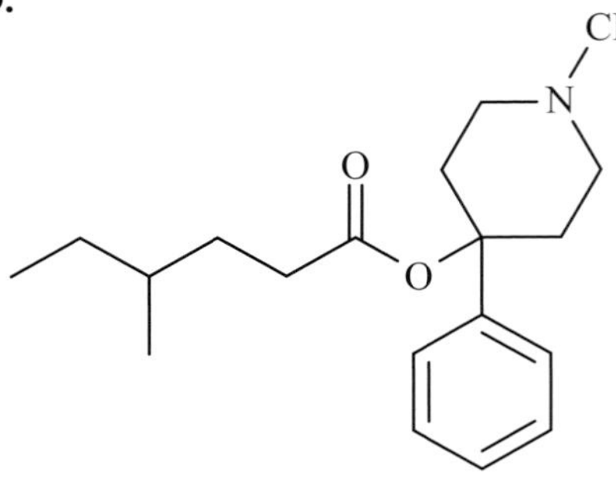

Question 23

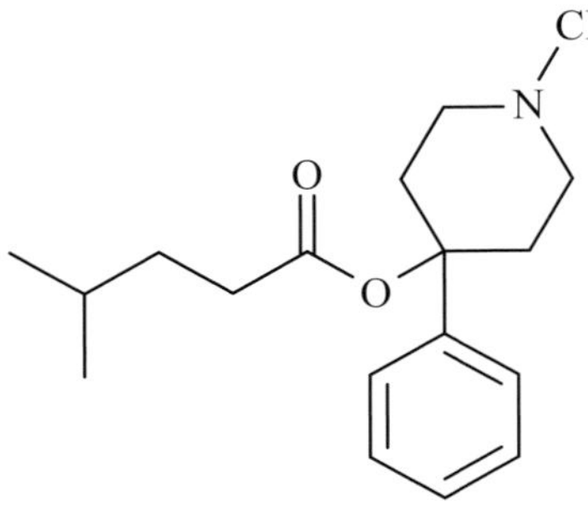

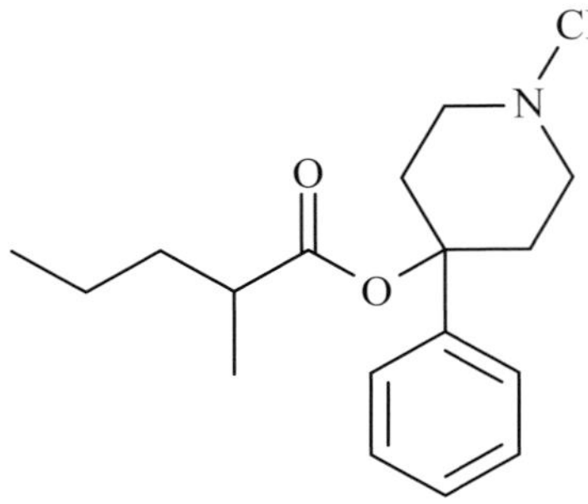

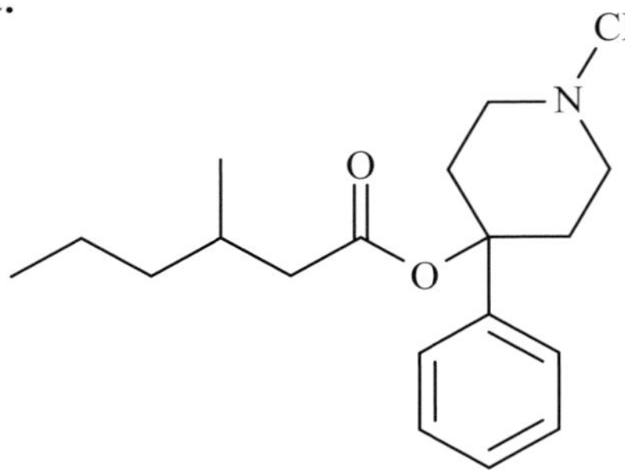

Reaction 3 can only compete with Reaction 2 when the temperature of the solution rises above 30°C. Which of the following reaction coordinate diagrams would be expected for Reactions 2 and 3?

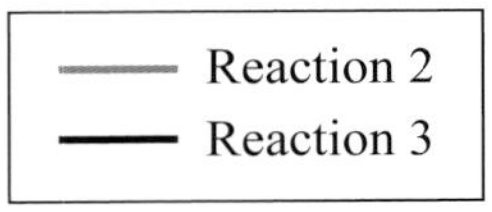

Reaction 2
Reaction 3

- A.

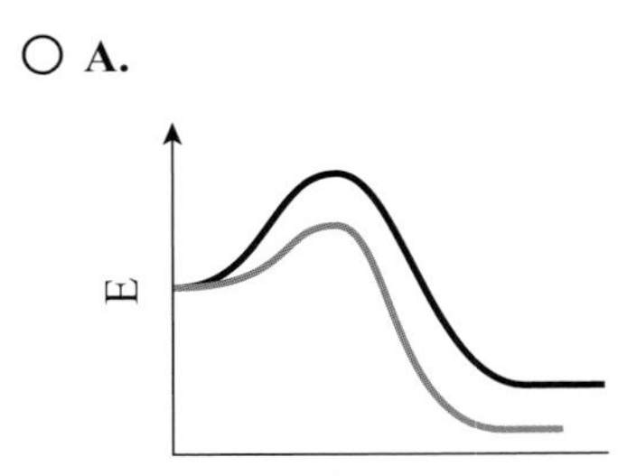

- B.

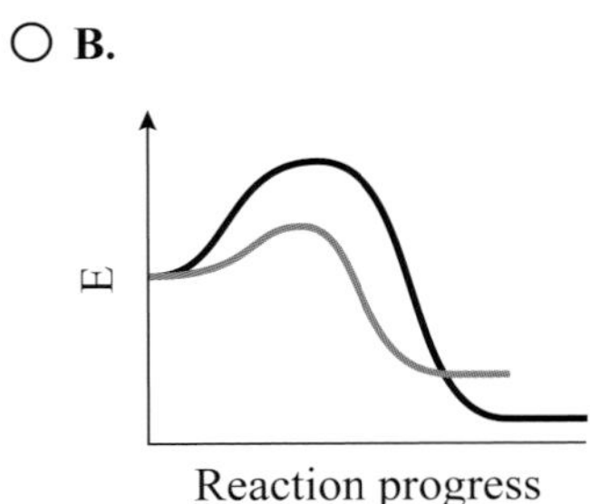

- C.

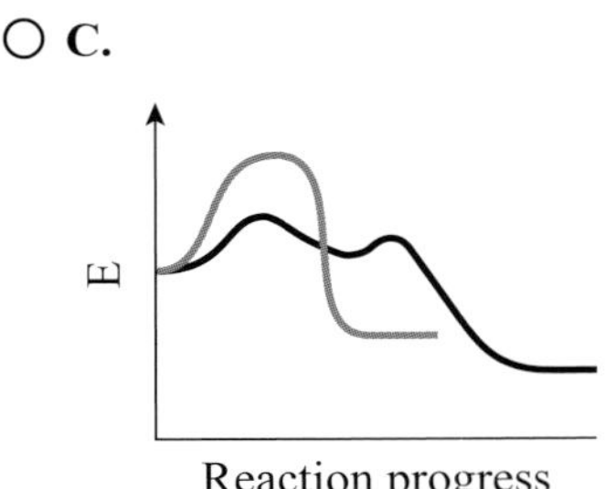

- D.

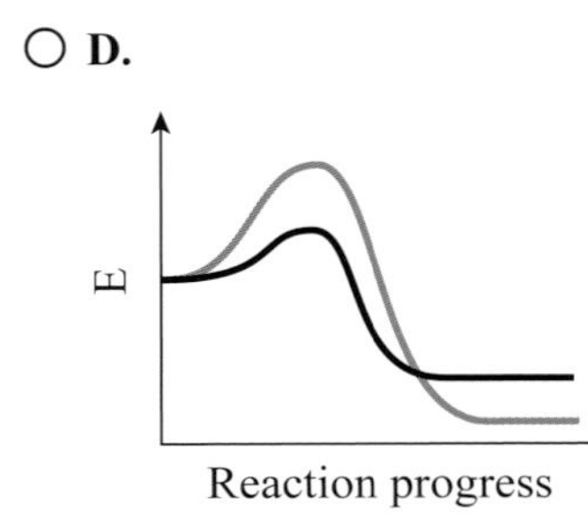

Passage 5 (Questions 24-27)

Artificial sweeteners are useful as sweetening agents in food for individuals who cannot tolerate traditional biogenic sugars, such as sucrose or fructose. In addition, even individuals who may tolerate traditional biogenic sugars, but who are attempting to reduce their body mass through restricting caloric intake, often elect to consume them. Artificial sweeteners are typically either completely devoid of nutritional content, or require such low concentrations to produce the desired flavor, that they have a negligible influence on the caloric content of the food.

Aspartame, a non-saccharide artificial sweetener, is 200 times sweeter than sucrose. It is an ingredient in a variety of edible goods, such as drinks, cereals, yogurts, chewing gum, and breath mints. Its synthesis (Reactions 1–5) relies on a unique property of the α-amino group on amino acids: α-amino groups increase the acidity of their neighboring carboxylic acids by approximately 2 pK_a units due to their electron withdrawing effect. This effect is exploited to perform the asymmetric ether hydrolysis shown in Reaction 3 without affecting the adjacent benzylic ester.

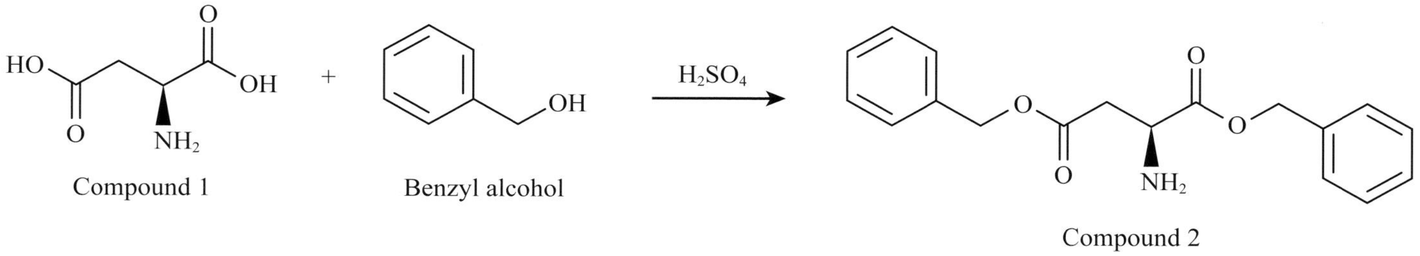

Compound 1 + Benzyl alcohol $\xrightarrow{H_2SO_4}$ Compound 2

Reaction 1

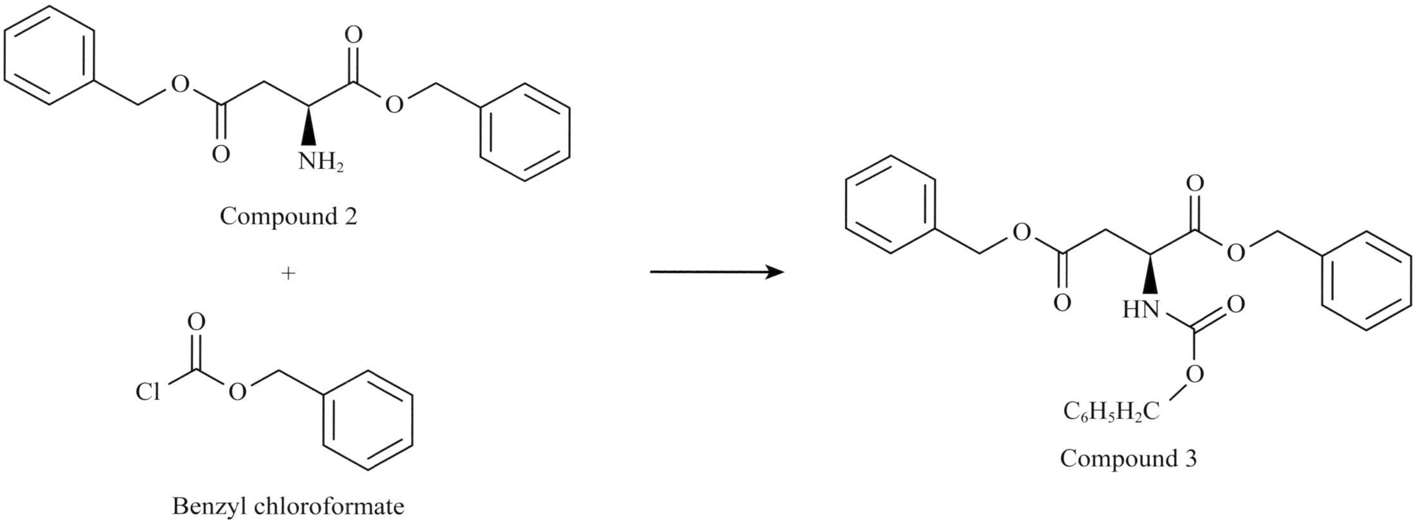

Compound 2 + Benzyl chloroformate ⟶ Compound 3

Reaction 2

Compound 3 $\xrightarrow{H_2O,\ \text{acetone, LiOH}}$ Compound 4

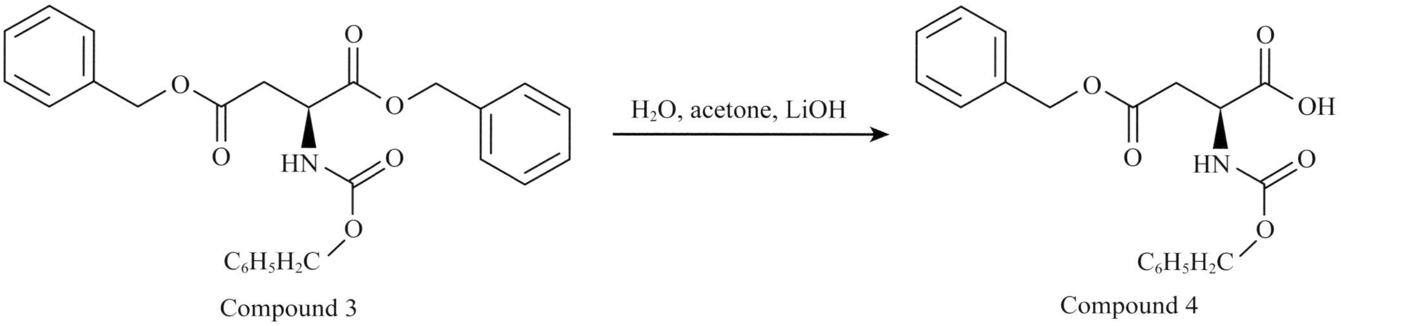

Reaction 3

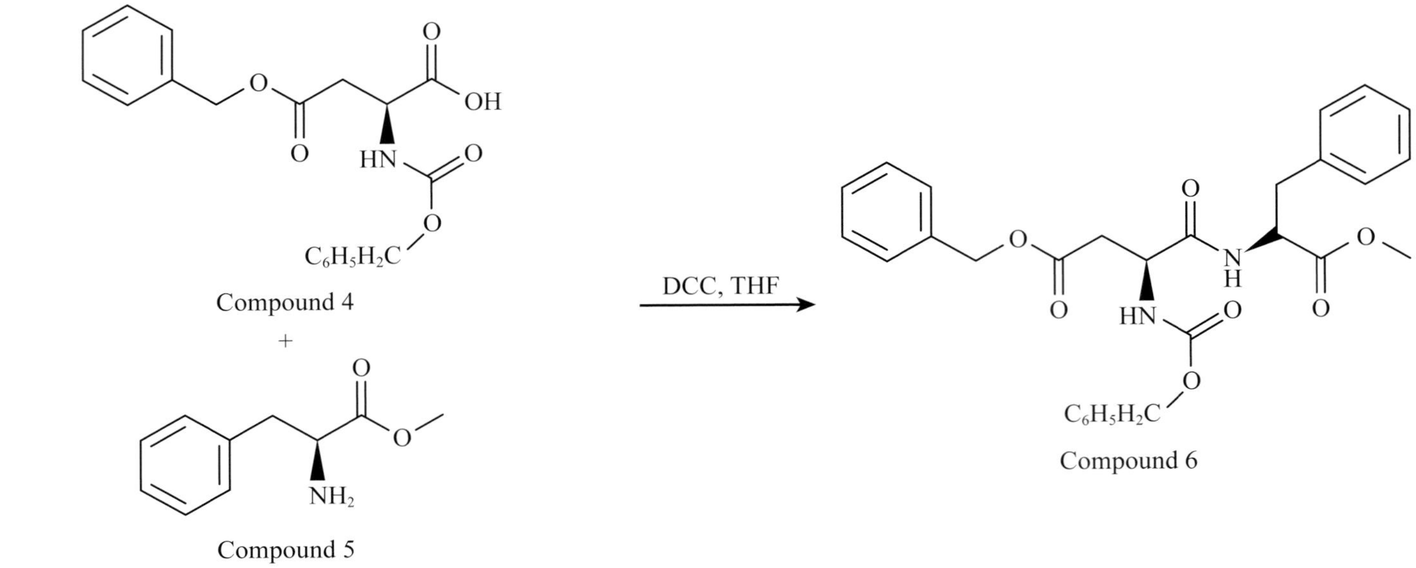

Compound 4

+

Compound 5

DCC, THF

Compound 6

Reaction 4

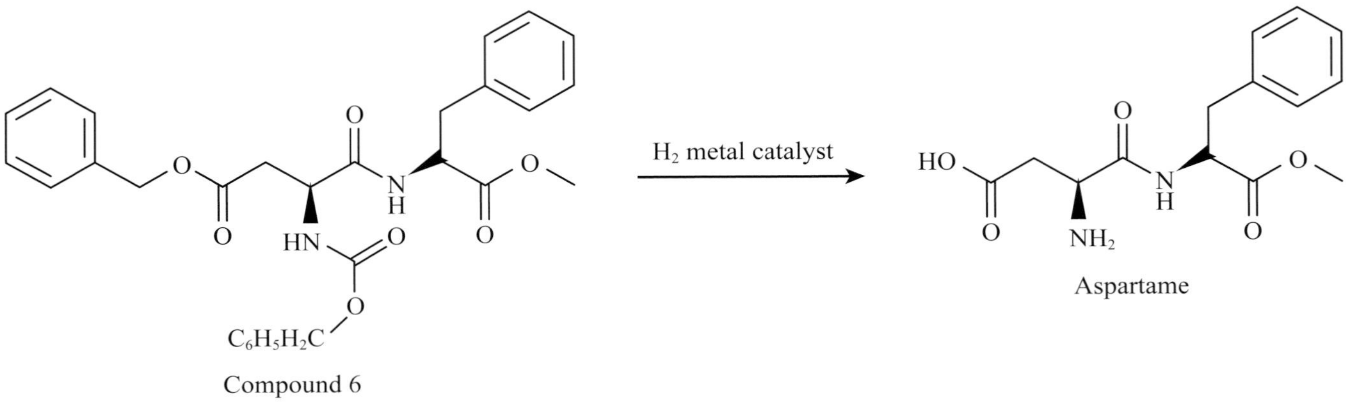

Compound 6

H_2 metal catalyst

Aspartame

Reaction 5

TEST 3A

Question 24

What synthetic obstacle, if any, would occur if amino protection with a large excess of benzyl chloroformate were performed on Compound 1 and then followed with an acid catalyzed esterification reaction in benzyl alcohol?

- A. Benzyl chloroformate would experience preferential nucleophilic attack by the hydroxyl groups of the carboxylic acid moieties, and the amino group would not undergo acylation.
- B. Compound 1 would form an ether which is too reactive for selective hydrolysis during Reaction 3.
- C. Compound 1 would form an anhydride which is too reactive for selective hydrolysis during Reaction 3.
- D. There would be no synthetic obstacle, and selective hydrolysis would remain viable during Reaction 3.

Question 25

Aspartame is best characterized as:

- A. a tripeptide of a methyl ester of phenylalanine, glutamic acid, and glycine.
- B. a dipeptide of a methyl ester of phenylalanine and aspartic acid.
- C. a dipeptide of a methyl ester of phenylalanine and glutamic acid.
- D. a tripeptide of a methyl ester of phenylalanine, aspartic acid, and glycine.

Question 26

The goal of Reaction 2 is to avoid which side product later during the synthesis of aspartame?

- A.
- B.
- C.
- D.

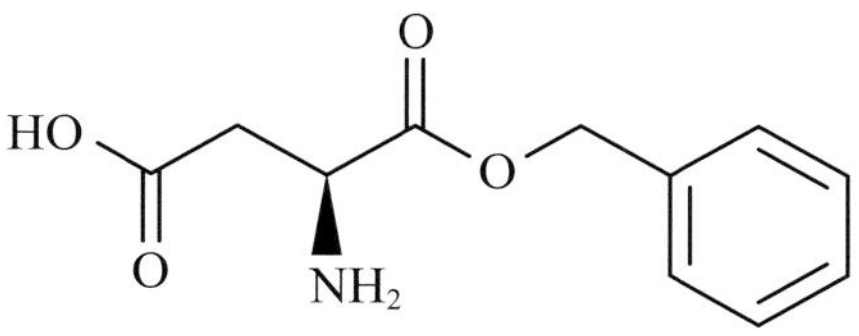

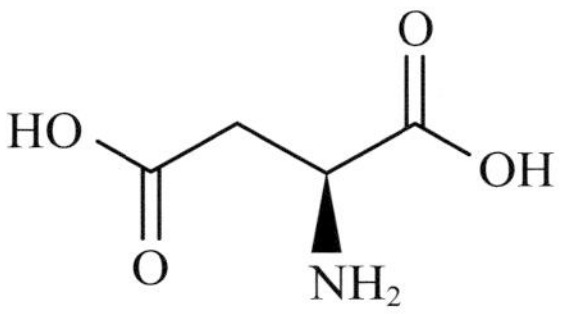

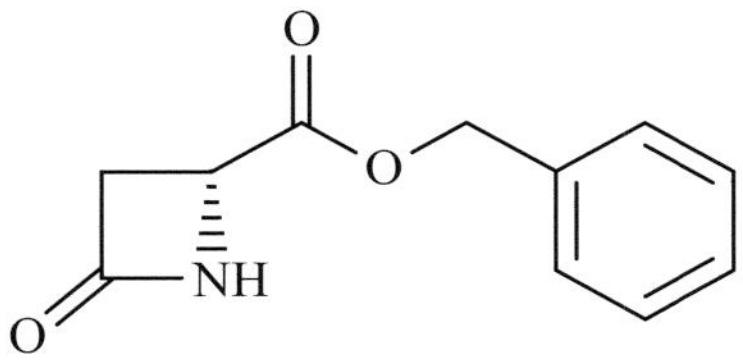

Question 27

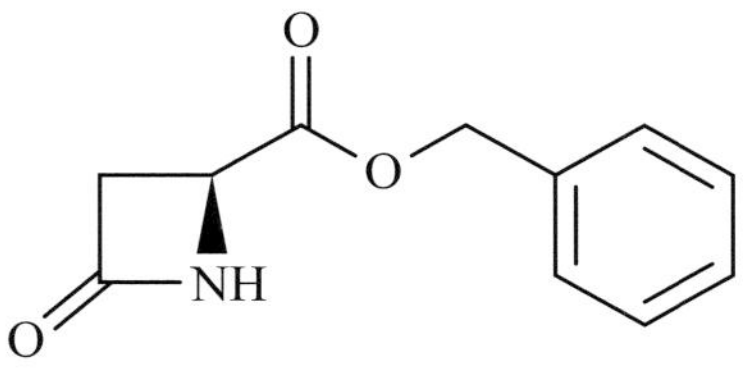

If aspartame were refluxed in an aqueous solution of concentrated sulfuric acid, which of the following products could be isolated?

I. methanol
II. phenylalanine
III. glutamic acid

- A. II and III only
- B. I and II only
- C. I and III only
- D. I, II, and III

Questions 28 - 31 do not refer to a passage and are independent of each other.

Question 28

The structure below was synthesized from an unknown compound and 4-toluenesulfonyl chloride. Which of the following is most likely the unknown compound?

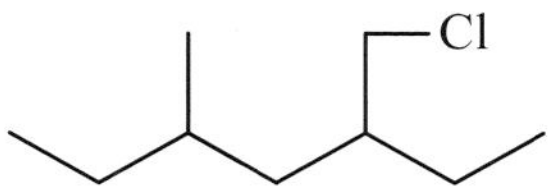

- A. 2-ethyl-4-methylhexan-1-ol
- B. 5-methyl-3-heptanol
- C. 2,4-diethyl-1-pentanol
- D. 5-ethyl-3-methyl-6-hexanol

Question 29

β-lactam antibiotic residues found in the aftermath of pasteurized milk present a public health issue. To combat this problem, researchers performed a study comparing different temperature and time cycles, and their effects on β-lactam degradation. What is the most probable reason β-lactam antibiotics degrade during the pasteurization process?

- A. Strain of the β-lactam ring makes it susceptible to heat.
- B. Cyclic esters of four or less atoms are susceptible to heat, which breaks the ring during the pasteurization process.
- C. The aromatic ring gains enough energy to break the stable bonds.
- D. Pasteurization lowers the temperature enough to cause the ring to become unstable.

Question 30

Which of the following is expected to have the highest boiling point?

- A. Acetic acid
- B. Ethanamide
- C. Ethanoyl chloride
- D. Methyl acetate

Question 31

A researcher unsuccessfully attempts to synthesize an ester by reacting 2,2-dimethylpropanoic acid with 1-ethylbutanol. Addition of which of the following would increase the likelihood of synthesizing an ester?

- A. 5,3-dimethylpentanoic acid instead of 2,2-dimethylpropanoic acid
- B. 1,1-dimethylbutanol instead of 1-ethylbutanol since it is better at stabilizing a carbocation
- C. 2,2-dimethylpropanamide instead of 2,2-dimethylpropanoic acid
- D. A catalytic amount of NaOH to increase the polarity of the carbonyl bond

TEST 3A

Passage 6 (Questions 32-35)

The Mannich reaction creates β-amino-carbonyl compounds via a one pot reaction between a 1° or 2° amine, formaldehyde, and a ketone. Mechanistically, the reaction can be considered as occurring in two steps. In the first step, a 1° or 2° amine is reacted with formaldehyde and dilute acid to produce and iminium salt.

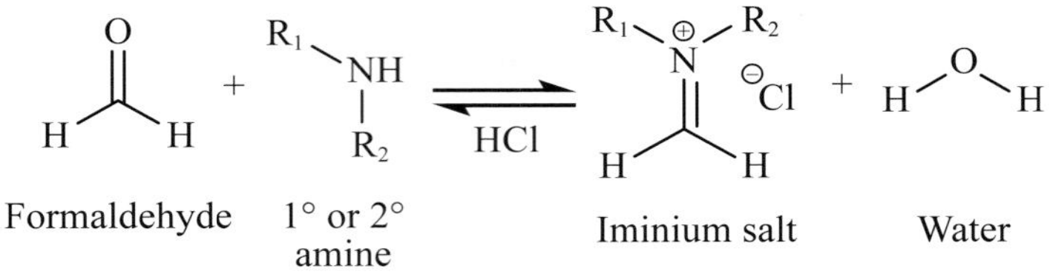

Formaldehyde + 1° or 2° amine ⇌ (HCl) Iminium salt + Water

Step 1

Subsequently, the iminium ion reacts with the ketone. Since the nucleophilicity of the enol tautomer's unsaturated bond is required for the second reaction, the dilute acid continues to play a catalytic role, facilitating the tautomerization reaction necessary for enol formation.

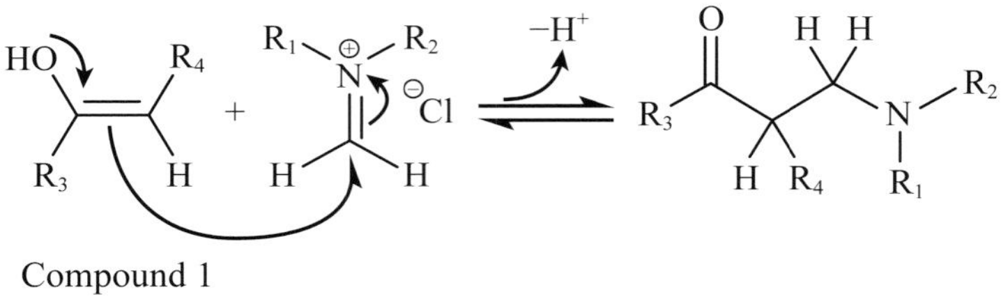

Compound 1 + iminium salt ⇌ ($-H^+$) product

Compound 1

Step 2

The Mannich reaction was utilized to produce tropinone, a synthetic precursor to atropine (Reaction 1).

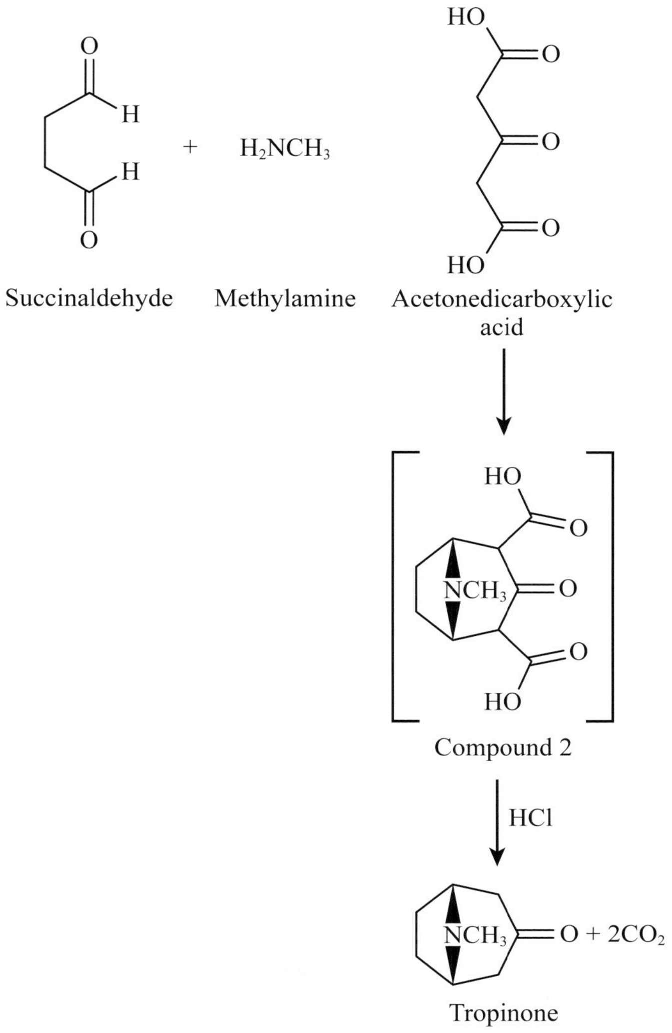

Succinaldehyde + H_2NCH_3 (Methylamine) + Acetonedicarboxylic acid → [Compound 2] → (HCl) → Tropinone + $2CO_2$

Reaction 1

Atropine is a widely prescribed antimuscarinic that is used to treat bradycardia and to induce dilation of the pupils. To synthesize atropine, first tropinone is reduced to tropine using metallic zinc and hydroiodic acid. Subsequently, tropine is reacted with tropic acid in the presence of an acid catalyst to produce atropine. The structures of tropine and tropic acid are shown in Figure 1.

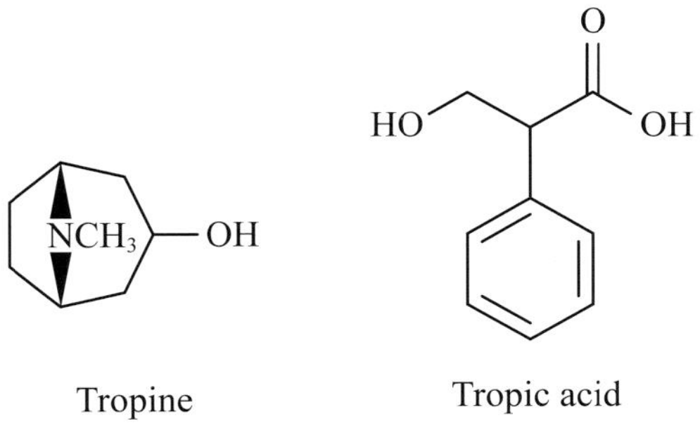

Tropine Tropic acid

Figure 1 Structures of tropine and tropic acid

Question 32

Which of the following compounds would most likely exist in equilibrium with Compound 1in an aqueous solution?

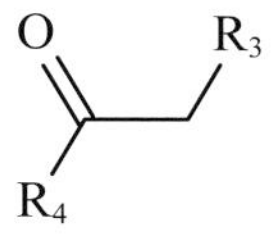

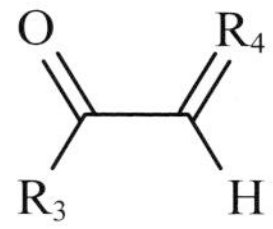

- A. $R_3C(=O)CH_2R_4$
- B. $R_4C(=O)CH_2R_3$
- C. $R_3C(=O)CH=C(H)R_4$
- D. $R_3CH(OH)CH_2R_4$

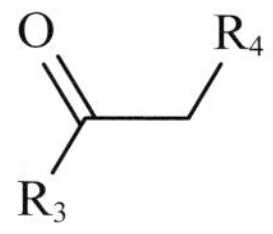

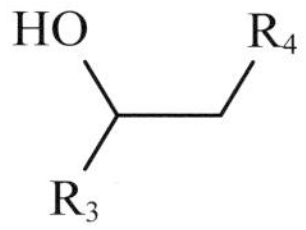

Question 33

All of the following occur during formation of the iminium salt in Step 1 EXCEPT:

- A. ejection of water as a leaving group.
- B. formation of a planar intermediate after nucleophilic attack.
- C. protonation of the carbonyl oxygen.
- D. formation of a hemiaminal after nucleophilic attack.

Question 34

Unlike other carboxylic acids, Compound 2 readily undergoes decarboxylation in the presence of dilute acid. Which of the following best explains this reactivity?

- A. Upon protonation of the carbonyl oxygen, resonance permits the delocalization of the resulting positive charge during decarboxylation.
- B. β-keto acids can form a stable five membered cyclic intermediate during decarboxylation.
- C. β-keto acids rely on resonance to stabilize the anionic intermediate during decarboxylation.
- D. γ-keto acids can form a stable six membered cyclic intermediate during decarboxylation.

Question 35

What is the structure of atropine?

- A.

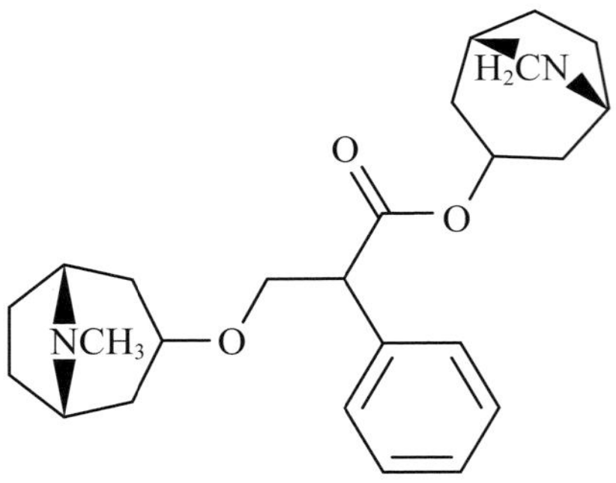

H_2CN O O NCH_3 O

- B.

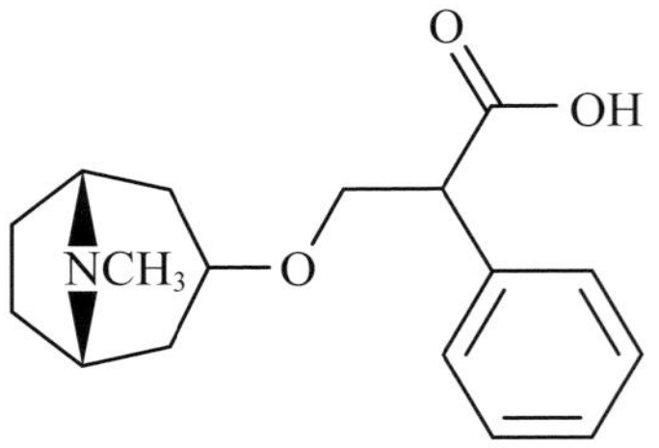

O OH NCH_3 O

- C.

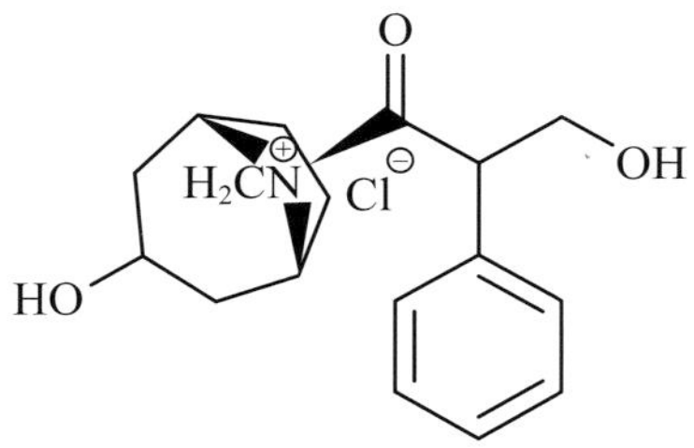

O H_2CN ⊕ $Cl^{\ominus}$ OH HO

- D.

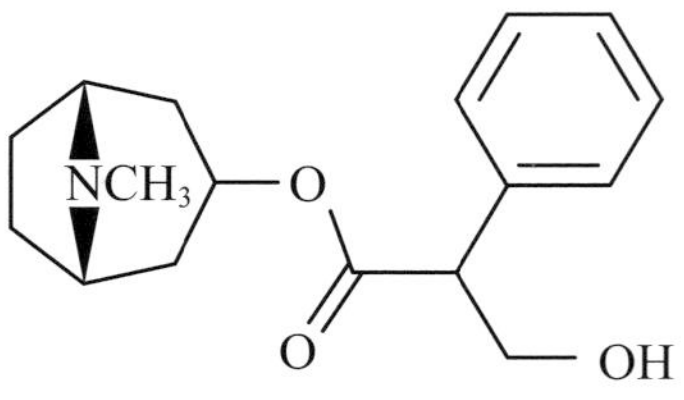

NCH_3 O O OH

Passage 7 (Questions 36-39)

Sucralose is a semi-synthetic derivative of table sugar, or sucrose, obtained by selective chlorination. It is unable to be metabolized and does not contribute calories to the body's nutrition. In addition, sucralose consumption does not lead to an increase in blood sugar, and is not cariogenic; microbiota of the oral cavity cannot metabolize it either. These properties make sucralose ideal for individuals pursuing weight loss regimes, or who have diabetes and wish to continue to eat sweetened foods.

In a taste discrimination test, sucralose was able to elicit a taste in greater than 50% of test subjects at one-six-hundredth the concentration that sucrose required. This vastly greater potency allows the cost of sucralose per unit of sweetness to be substantially lower than that of sucrose.

The synthesis of sucralose begins with the sequential protection of naturally obtained sucrose, through Reaction 1.

Selective deprotection carried out in Reaction 2 produces Compound 3, which is used in Reaction 3, a catalyzed isomerization reaction.

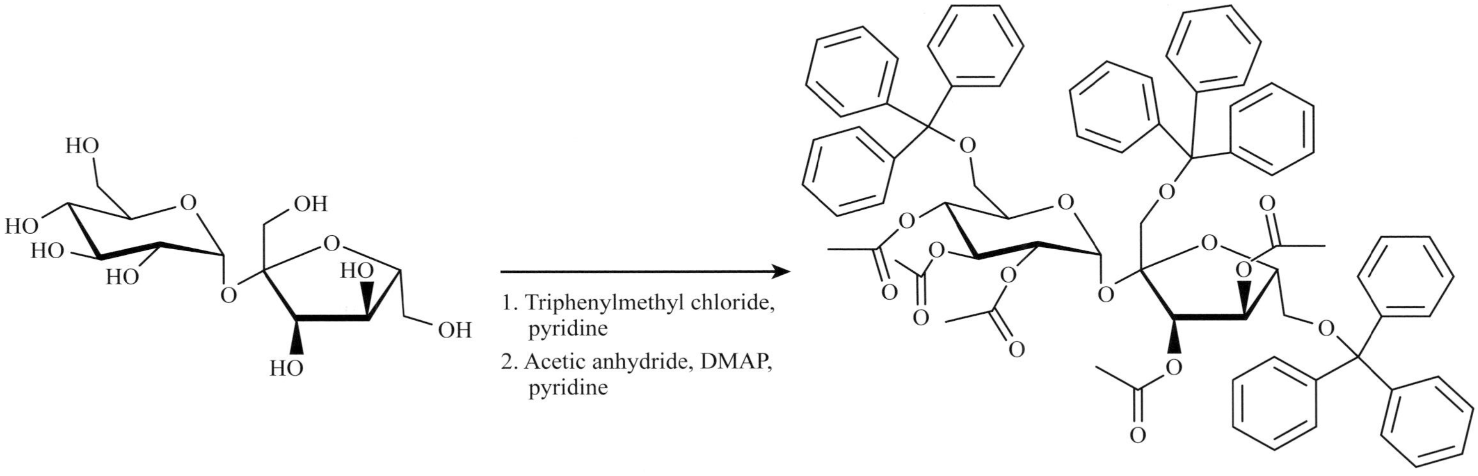

HO
HO
HO
HO
O
OH
O
HO
O
OH
HO

1. Triphenylmethyl chloride, pyridine
2. Acetic anhydride, DMAP, pyridine

Sucrose

Compound 2

Reaction 1

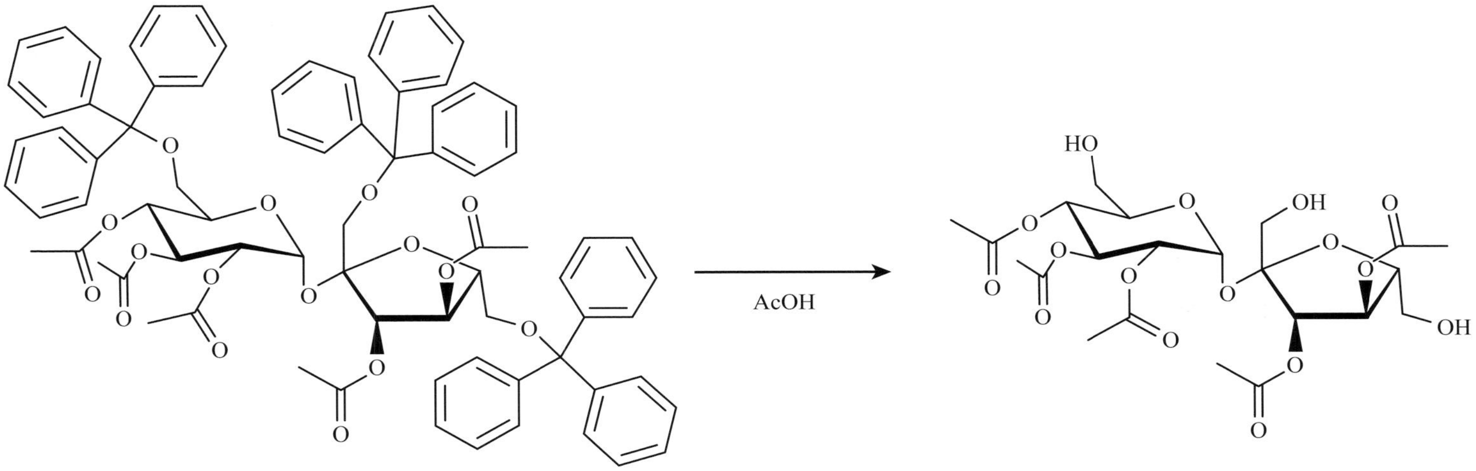

AcOH

Compound 2

Compound 3

Reaction 2

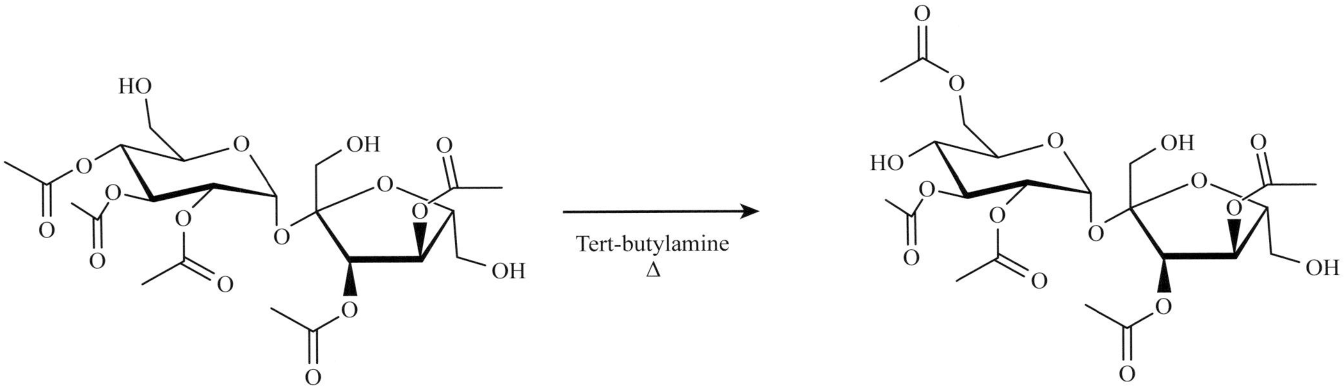

Tert-butylamine
Δ

Compound 3

Compound 4

Reaction 3

Chlorination and deprotection allows the product to be isolated, as shown in Figure 1.

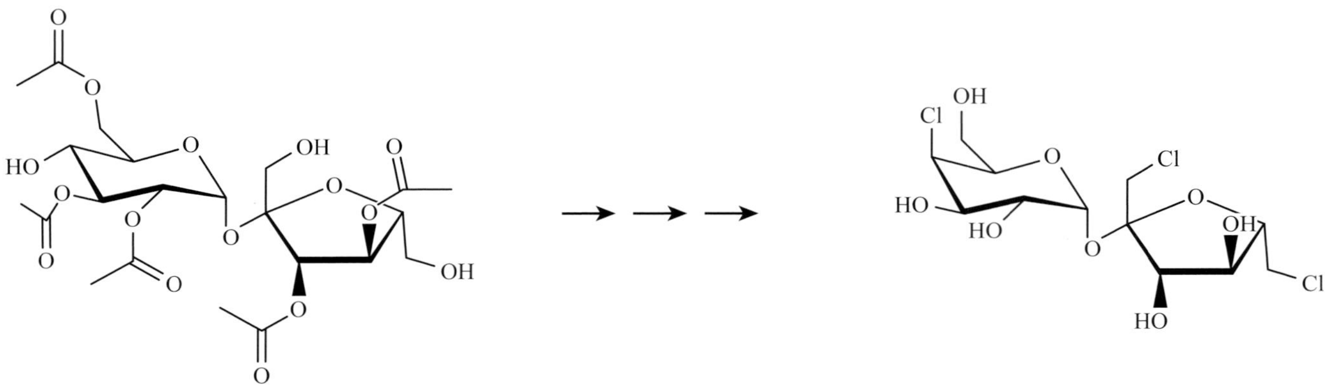

Compound 4

Sucralose

Figure 1 Structure of Sucralose

Question 36

The chlorination and deprotection shown in Figure 1 is best carried out with:

- A. thionyl chloride and hydrochloric acid.
- B. sulfuryl chloride and sulfuric acid.
- C. sodium chloride and sodium ethoxide.
- D. sulfuryl chloride and sodium hydroxide.

Question 37

Sucrose is best described as:

- A. a nonreducing disaccharide with an α-1,β-2 glycosidic linkage.
- B. a nonreducing disaccharide with an α-1,2 glycosidic linkage.
- C. a reducing disaccharide with an α-1,β-2 glycosidic linkage.
- D. a reducing disaccharide with an α-1,2 glycosidic linkage.

Question 38

If the isomerization reaction proceeds with an intermediate species that has a deprotonated hydroxyl group on the C6 residue of glucose, what else is most likely true of the reaction?

- A. a transiently lived 5 membered ring is formed during the transesterification.
- B. a transiently lived 6 membered ring is formed during the transesterification.
- C. a transiently lived 6 membered ring is formed during the C4 ester hydrolysis.
- D. a transiently lived 5 membered ring is formed during the C5 ester hydrolysis.

Question 39

Suppose the sequence of Reaction 1 were reversed, adding acetic anhydride and DMAP before adding triphenylmethyl chloride. What product(s) is/are expected?

○ A.

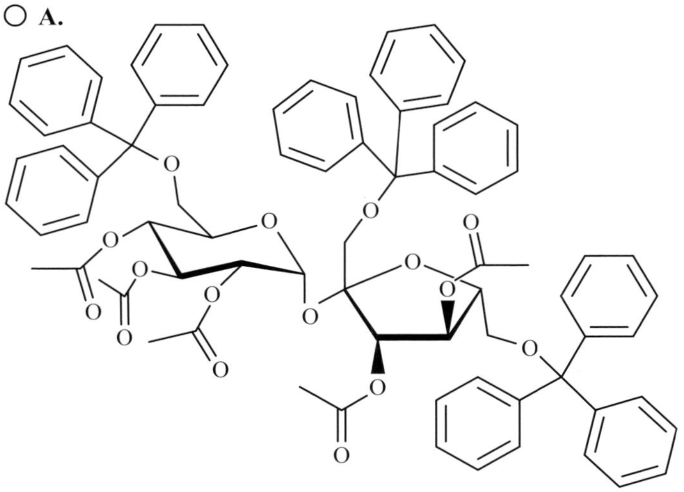

○ B.

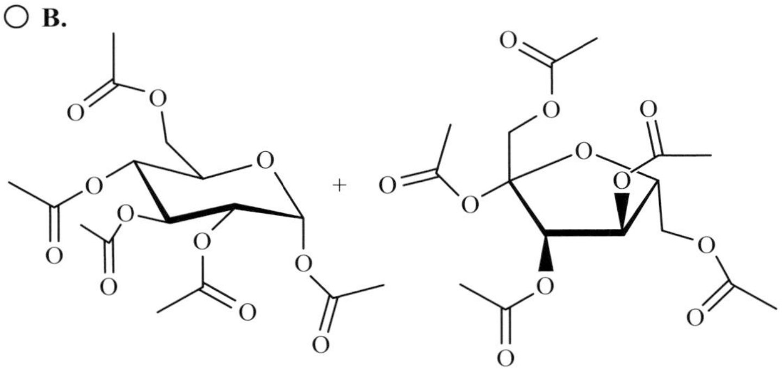

○ C.

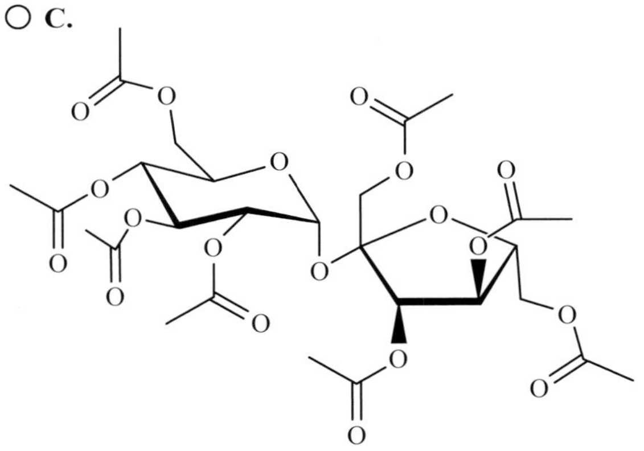

○ D.

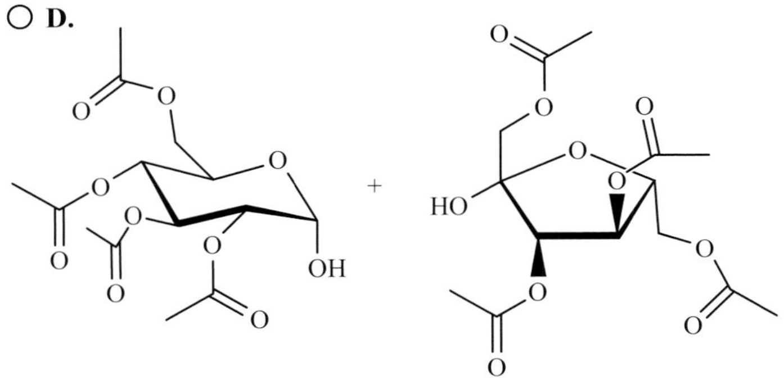

Passage 8 (Questions 40-43)

Heart failure describes conditions where the heart cannot adequately pump blood to perfuse the body's tissues. With poor output from the heart, low arterial blood pressure often occurs. To maintain homeostasis, low arterial blood pressure triggers the sympathetic nervous system, which induces vasoconstriction. In addition, the sympathetic stimulation signals for posterior pituitary secretion of antidiuretic hormone (ADH), leading to fluid retention. The net effect of these homeostatic reflexes, and those which follow, is to increase blood pressure and volume. As blood pressure and volume continue to increase throughout the vasculature, hydrostatic pressure dramatically rises in the capillaries, leading to the transport of fluid to the interstitial space, ultimately resulting in edema if not properly regulated.

Diuretics are a highly effective treatment modality for edema associated with heart failure. The diuretic spironolactone has been used for this purpose for over half of a century. It is synthesized from a commonly available precursor, DHEA, according to the Reactions 1-7.

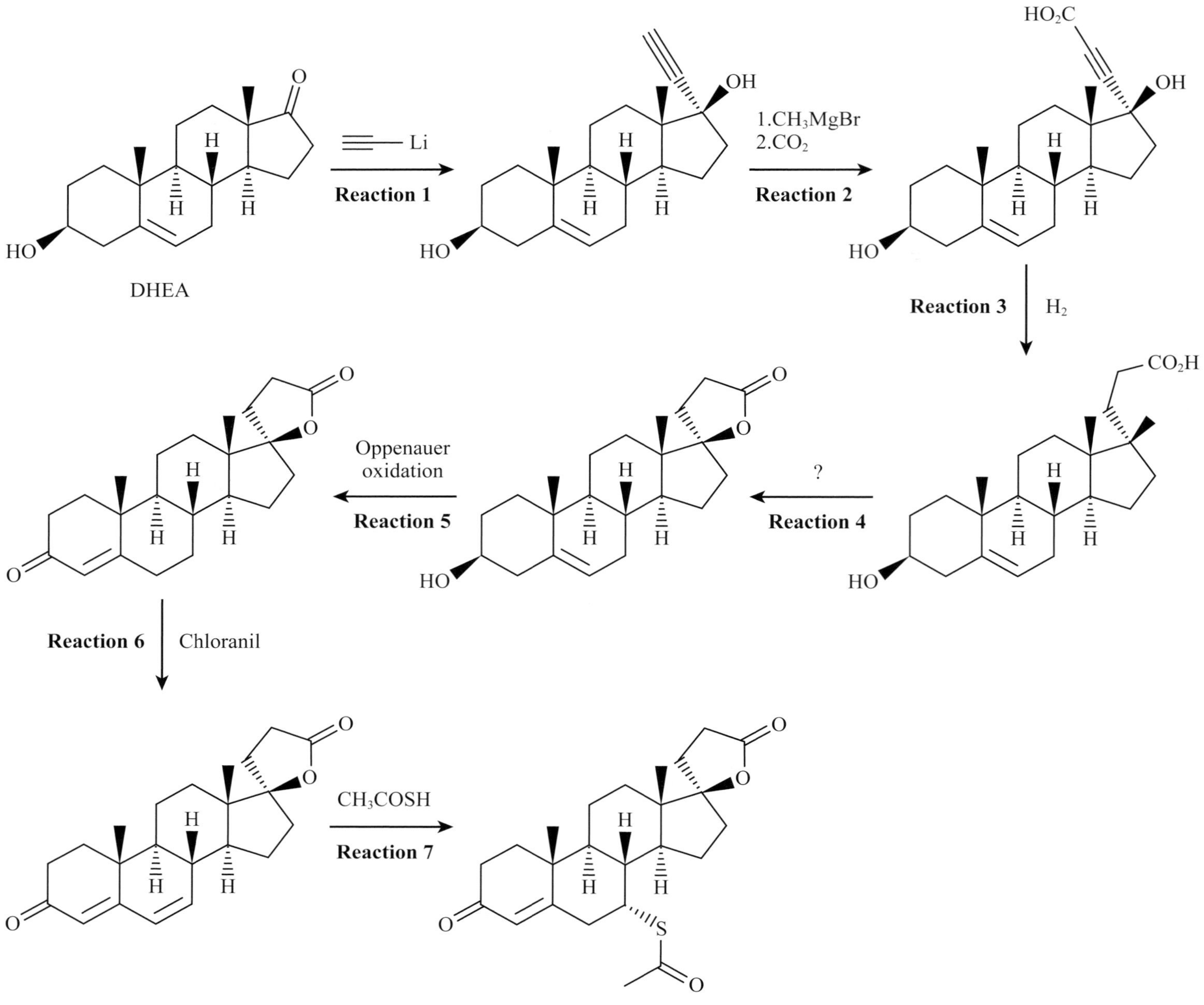

TEST 3A

HO DHEA → (≡—Li, Reaction 1) → HO, OH → (1. CH_3MgBr 2. CO_2, Reaction 2) → HO_2C, OH → (Reaction 3, H_2) → CO_2H → (?, Reaction 4) → lactone → (Oppenauer oxidation, Reaction 5) → O → (Reaction 6, Chloranil) → O → (CH_3COSH, Reaction 7) → Spironolactone

Question 40

The product of Reaction 2 could only be formed if:

- ○ **A.** a protic solvent was used and a dilute acid work-up step was performed.
- ○ **B.** an aprotic solvent was used and a dilute base work-up step was performed.
- ○ **C.** a protic solvent was used and a dilute base work-up step was performed.
- ○ **D.** an aprotic solvent was used and a dilute acid work-up step was performed.

Question 41

Which reagent would best facilitate lactone formation in Reaction 4?

- ○ **A.** Toluene sulfonic acid
- ○ **B.** Acetic acid
- ○ **C.** Sodium acetate
- ○ **D.** Butyric acid

Question 42

Substituted benzylidene derivatives of DHEA have been tested as potential anti-cancer agents. What is the structure of the derivative synthesized by the reaction below?

○ A.

○ B.

○ C.

○ D.

Question 43

Suppose spironolactone is reacted with sodium hydroxide in a heated glycerol solution. Which of the following products would most likely form?

○ A.

○ B.

○ C.

○ D.

TEST 3A

Questions 44 - 47 do not refer to a passage and are independent of each other.

Question 44

A student first reacts pentanal with $KMnO_4$ followed by two equivalents of $NaBH_4$. What is the resulting molecule?

- O **A.** Pentanal
- O **B.** Butanoic acid
- O **C.** Pentanol
- O **D.** Pentanoic acid

Question 45

Rank the following molecules in order of increasing boiling point:

I. Propanone
II. Propanol
III. Butanol

- O **A.** I < II < III
- O **B.** II < I < III
- O **C.** III < II < I
- O **D.** I < III < II

Question 46

Which of the following is the most likely product formed after the reaction of 2-methyl-propanoic acid and Cl_2 in basic conditions followed by acidic workup?

- O **A.** 2-methylpropanoyl chloride
- O **B.** 2-chloro-2-methylpropanoic acid
- O **C.** 2-chloropropanoic acid
- O **D.** 2-methyl-butanoic acid

Question 47

α-halogenation (shown) is a synthetic approach for the substitution of α-hydrogens with halogens that proceeds through an enolate intermediate, in base promoted conditions.

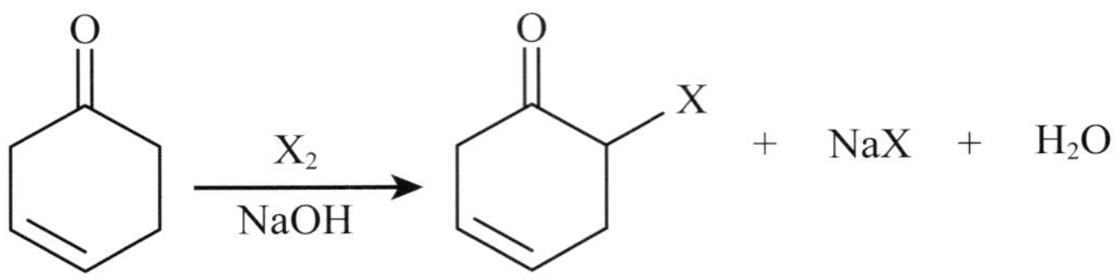

$$\xrightarrow[\text{NaOH}]{X_2} \quad + \ \text{NaX} \ + \ H_2O$$

What is true regarding this reaction?

- O **A.** The product is less likely to form an enolate, and mono-halogenation is expected.
- O **B.** The product is more likely to form an enolate, and poly-halogenation is expected.
- O **C.** The product is less likely to form an enolate, and poly-halogenation is expected.
- O **D.** The product is more likely to form an enolate, and mono-halogenation is expected.

Passage 9 (Questions 48-51)

Cardenolide glycosides (CGs) are a group of bioactive molecules synthesized in a range of plant and insect species. Structurally, they consist of a steroid component and a sugar component. The steroid has 23 carbons, with methyl groups at C10 and C13, and a butenolide group at C17. The sugar group is typically bound via an ether linkage to C3. The general steroidal motif of CGs and the structure of two well characterized CGs are shown in Figure 1.

General steroidal motif of CGs

Digoxin

Ouabain

Figure 1 Cardenolide glycosides

CGs act by stabilizing a transition state that occurs during the extrusion of intracellular sodium from cardiomyocytes by their Na^+/K^+ pumps. When the transition state is stabilized, the pump is inhibited and the intracellular concentration of sodium rises. Increased intracellular sodium concentrations slows the action of a Ca^{2+}/Na^+ pump responsible for the uptake of sodium and removal of calcium from the cytoplasm, leading to increased cytoplasmic calcium concentration. This cytoplasmic calcium is readily taken up by the sarcoplasmic reticulum, ultimately leading to a slower and more forceful contraction of the heart.

In therapeutic doses CGs and their synthetic derivatives are useful in the management of congestive heart failure. A comparison of the efficacies of CGs and some of their aglycones are shown in Figure 2.

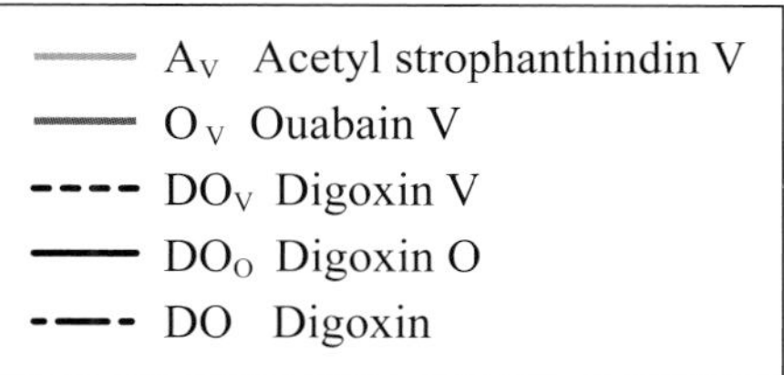

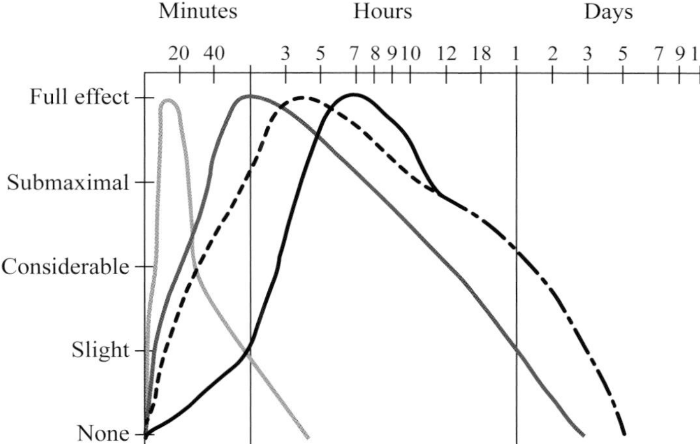

Figure 2 Efficacies of CGs

In pre-21st century medicine, digoxin was given as tinctures containing *Digitalis lanata* (DL) plant extracts. The strength was quantified using "cat units". A single cat unit was the lowest dose of the drug per kilogram of cat, which, when administered intravenously, was lethal to the cat.

Question 48

The glycosidic linkages in digoxin are:

- **A.** α-1,4′.
- **B.** β-1,4′.
- **C.** α-1,3′.
- **D.** β-1,3′.

Question 49

After refluxing digoxin in $H_2SO_4(aq)$ which of the following could most likely be isolated?

- A.

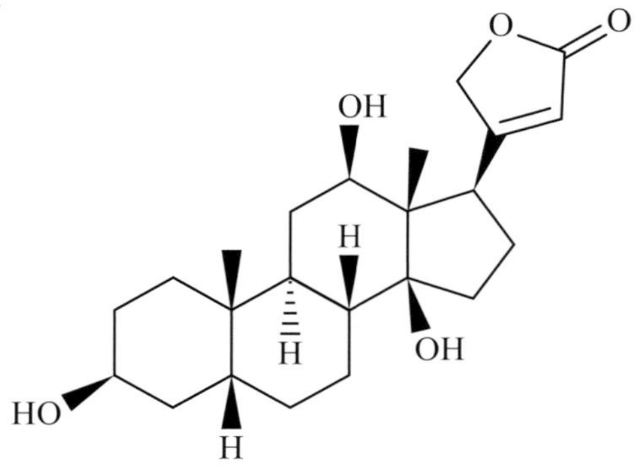

- B.

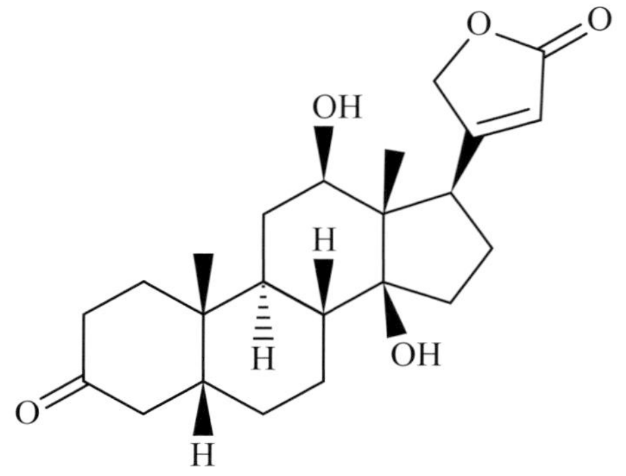

- C.

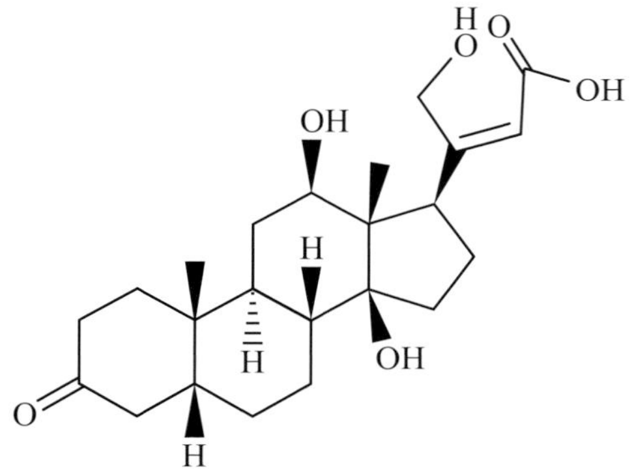

- D.

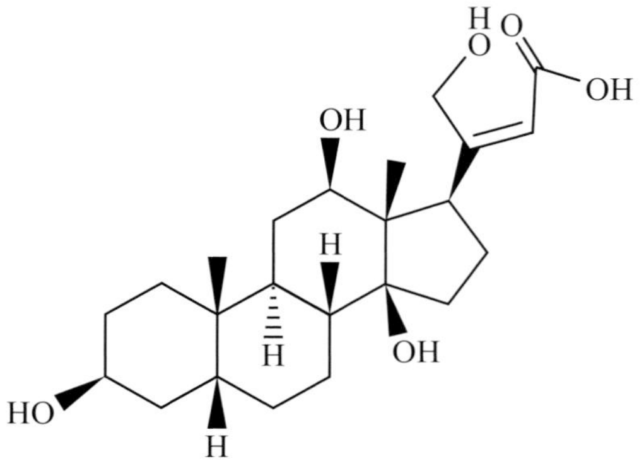

Question 50

Digoxin is mixed with catalytic HCl and ethanol. What next step should be performed to favor the formation of hemiacetal monosaccharides?

- **A.** Addition of water to the reaction vessel.
- **B.** Removal of water from the reaction vessel.
- **C.** Addition of methanol to the reaction vessel.
- **D.** Reducing the temperature of the reaction vessel.

Question 51

Digoxin contains all of the following functional groups EXCEPT a(n):

- **A.** lactone.
- **B.** polysaccharide.
- **C.** alcohol.
- **D.** lactam.

Passage 10 (Questions 52-56)

Mosquitos are blood parasites that primarily feed on a variety of vertebrate hosts. During feeding, their saliva causes vasodilation while inhibiting coagulation and platelet aggregation. Their saliva also contains a variety of other proteins and antigens, which trigger an immune response, often leading to the formation of a raised, swollen, and pruritic bump on the skin. Besides uncomfortable bites, mosquitos transmit many dangerous infections such as malaria, dengue fever, yellow fever, and West Nile virus.

To prevent mosquito bites, topical repellents such as diethyltoluamide (DEET) are used. Studies have provided evidence that DEET works by blocking mosquito olfactory receptors for 1-octen-3-ol. This molecule is released in human sweat and breath and attracts mosquitos. In addition, DEET also seems to act as a general repellent, even in the absence of body odor molecules such as 1-octen-3-ol. Both male and female mosquitos will actively avoid DEET if possible.

DEET is synthesized from *m*-toluic acid according to reaction 1.

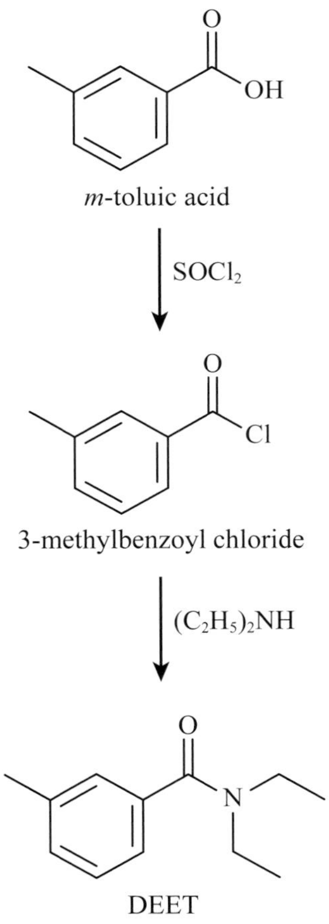

m-toluic acid

$SOCl_2$

3-methylbenzoyl chloride

$(C_2H_5)_2NH$

DEET

Reaction 1

The protective effects of DEET are concentration dependent. More concentrated solutions exert longer lasting and more repellent effects when applied to the skin.

Question 52

How many equivalents of HCl are produced during DEET synthesis?

- A. 3
- B. 2
- C. 1
- D. 0

Question 53

The first step in DEET synthesis does not produce a pure product. Which of the following is mostly present in addition to the product depicted in the first step of the reaction scheme?

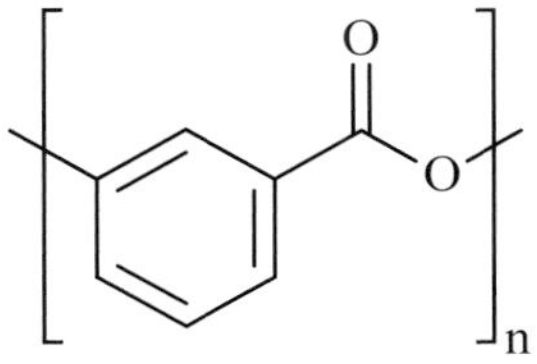

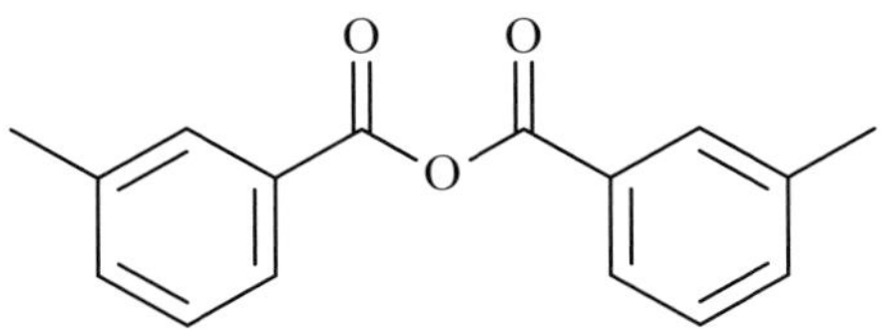

- A.
- B.
- C.
- D.

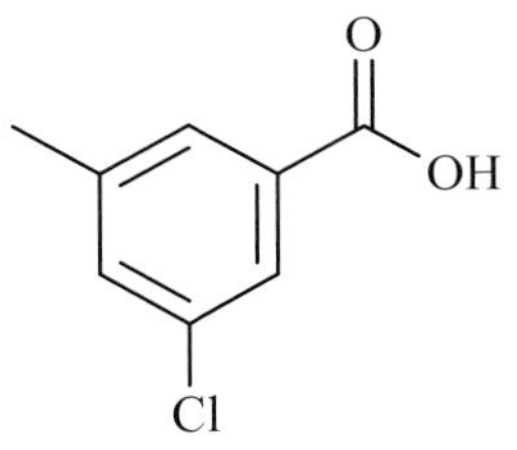

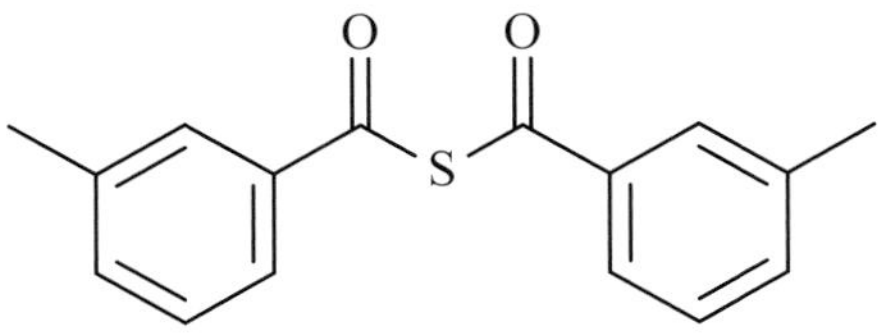

Question 54

Suppose DEET is heated in an HCl and water solution. Which product is NOT possible?

- O **A.** 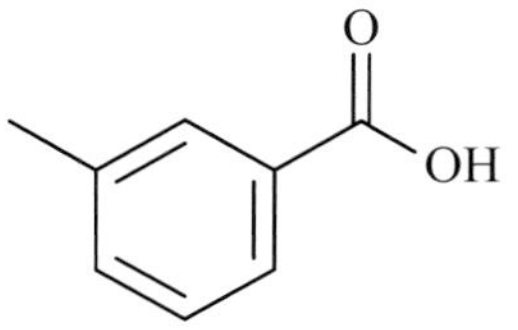
- O **B.** 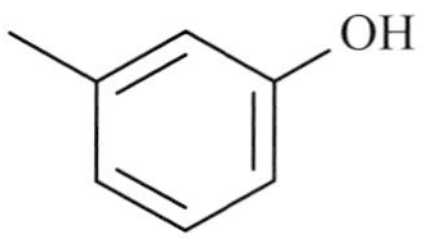
- O **C.** 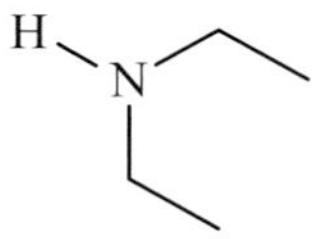
- O **D.**

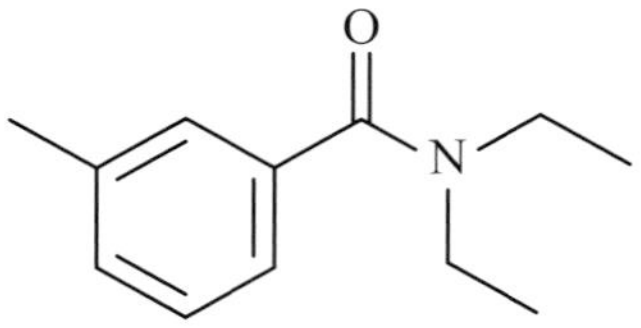

Question 55

Suppose that 1-(*m*-tolyl)ethan-1-one (shown below) is reacted with $(C_2H_5)_2NH$ and catalytic acid. The product is best described as an:

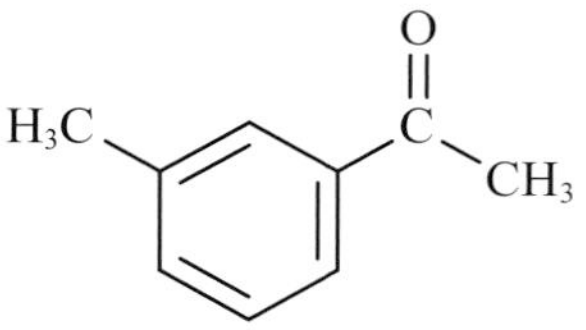

1-(*m*-tolyl)ethan-1-one

- O **A.** amine.
- O **B.** imine.
- O **C.** enamine.
- O **D.** amide.

Question 56

If the last step of Reaction 1 was contaminated by ethanol, which of the following would be expected?

- O **A.** The major product would contain an ester since ethanol is more reactive than an amine
- O **B.** DEET would still be the major product since amides are more reactive than esters.
- O **C.** The major product would contain an ester and an amide group.
- O **D.** There would be no significant change in the final product of the reaction.

Questions 57 - 59 do not refer to a passage and are independent of each other.

Question 57

All of the following are common oxidizing agents EXCEPT:

- O **A.** $KMnO_4$.
- O **B.** Na.
- O **C.** H_2O_2.
- O **D.** F_2.

Question 58

Which of the following compounds will react with CN at the fastest rate?

- O **A.**

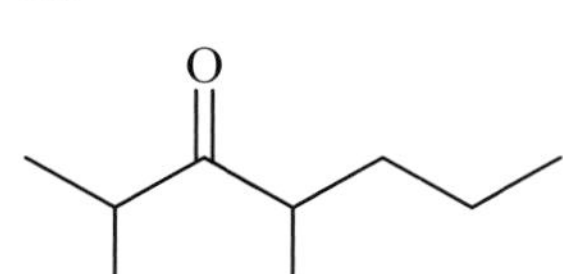

- O **B.** 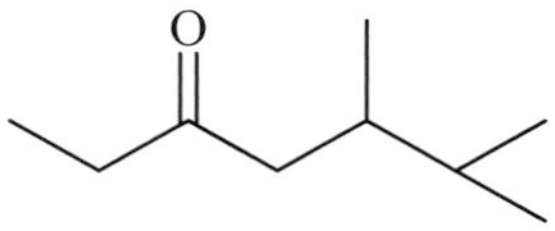
- O **C.**

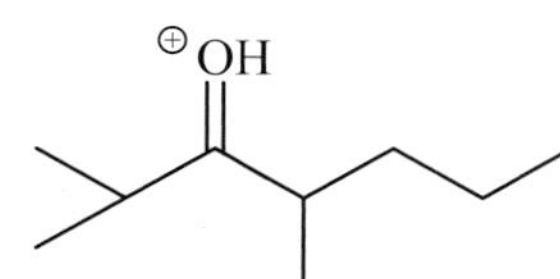

- O **D.**

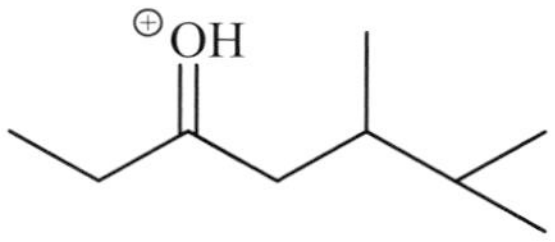

Question 59

Which of the following reagents will turn a primary alcohol into an aldehyde?

I. $KMnO_4$
II. PCC
III. CrO_3 in aqueous H_2SO_4

- O **A.** I only
- O **B.** II only
- O **C.** I and III only
- O **D.** II and III only

STOP. If you finish before time is called, check your work. You may go back to any question in this test.

ANSWERS & EXPLANATIONS for Test 3A can be found on p. 262.

Oxygen Containing Reactions

MINI-TEST 3B

Time: 45 minutes
Questions 1–29

DIRECTIONS: Most of the questions in this test section are grouped with a passage. Read the passage, then select the best answer to each question. Some questions are independent of any passage and of one another. Select the best answer to each of these questions. If you are unsure of an answer, rule out incorrect choices and select from the remaining options. Indicate your selection beside the option you choose. A periodic table can be found on the last page of this book for you to use at any point during this test section.

Passage 1 (Questions 1-6)

Bilharzia results from infection by parasitic flat-worms. The infection can be debilitating, starting with a painful rash where the larval stage of the parasite entered the skin. The acute phase of infection, characterized by a flu-like fever, occurs when the parasite travels through the blood stream to the species specific organs where they mature. Eggs laid in the bladder can lead to chronic inflammation and blood in the urine. Eventually, blockage of the ureters can lead to kidney failure.

The first line treatment of bilharzia is the anti-helminthic drug praziquantel (Figure 1).

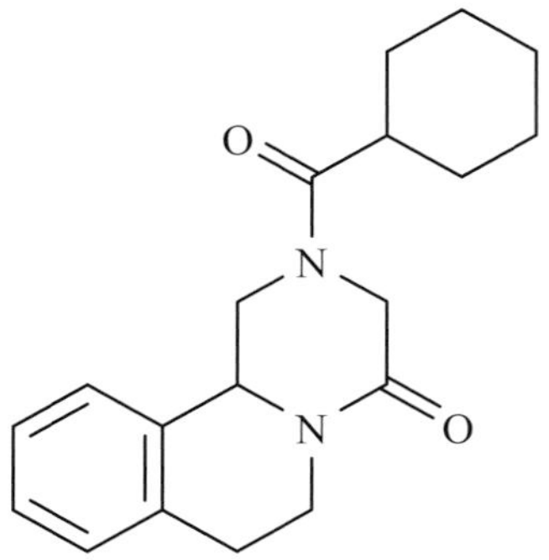

Figure 1 Structure of Praziquantel

In a new synthetic scheme, it can be formed using the multicomponent Ugi Reaction (Reaction 1) followed by a Pignet-Spengler cyclization. The Ugi reaction is unique in that it allows for the one pot synthesis of a bisamide from a ketone or aldehyde, carboxylic acid, isocyanide, and amine.

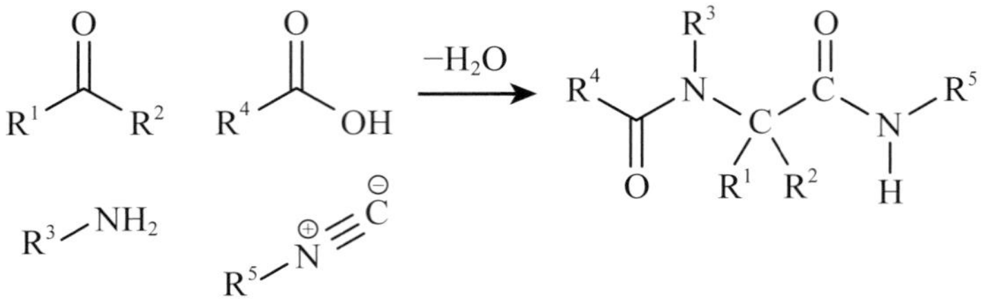

Reaction 1

Derivatives of the sesquiterpene lactone, artemisinin, have been used successfully to treat flat-worm infections as well. Artemisinin is isolated from extracts of *Artemesia annua*, or sweet wormwood, which is an herb used in traditional Chinese medicine. The endoperoxide bridge of the trioxane ring of artemisinin is relatively stable, allowing for its derivatization. The structures of artemisinin and some of its derivatives are shown in Figure 2.

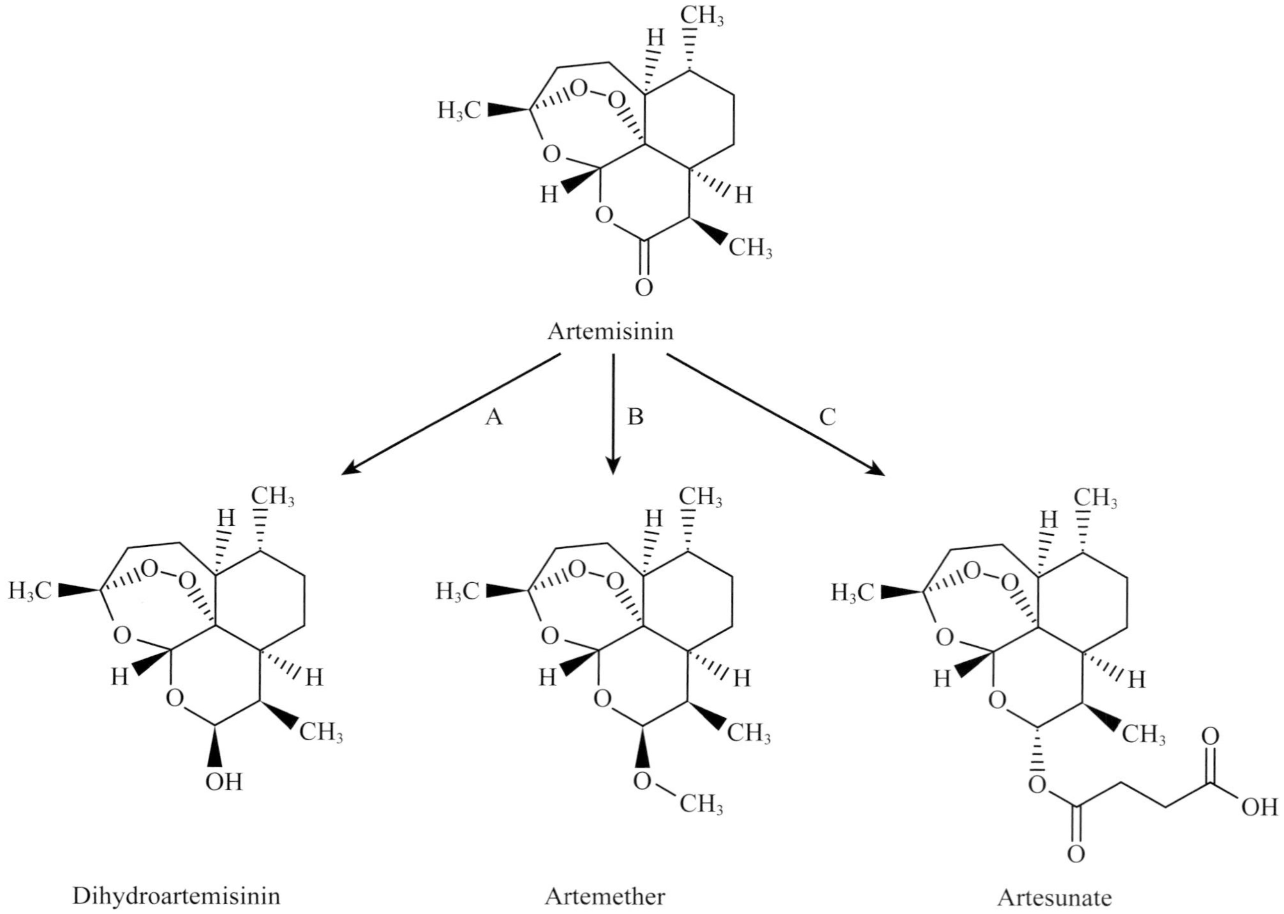

Artemisinin

A B C

Dihydroartemisinin Artemether Artesunate

Figure 2 Artemisinin and its derivatives

Question 1

The reagents below are used in an Ugi reaction during Praziquantel synthesis:

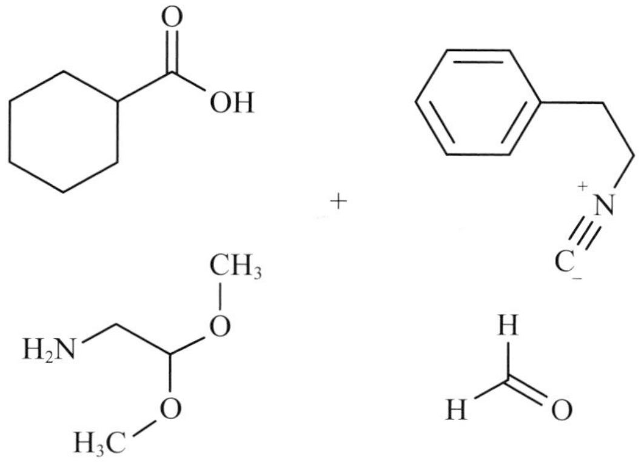

After the Ugi reaction, which of the following structures is most likely the intermediate product, prior to Pignet-Spengler cyclization?

- A. 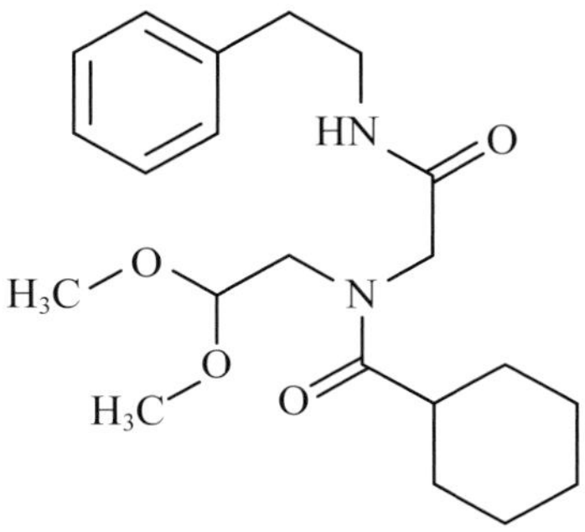
- B. 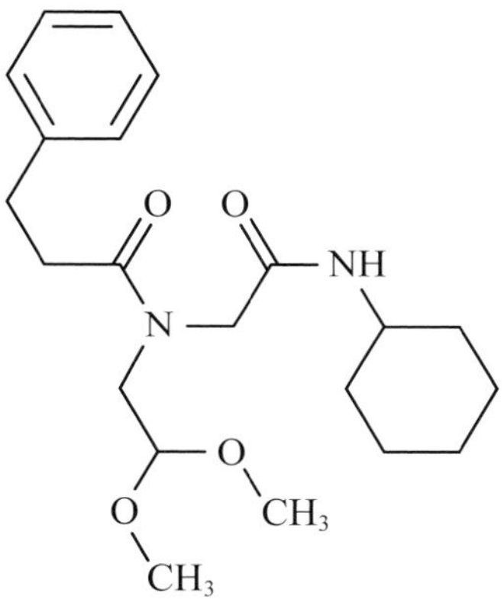
- C. 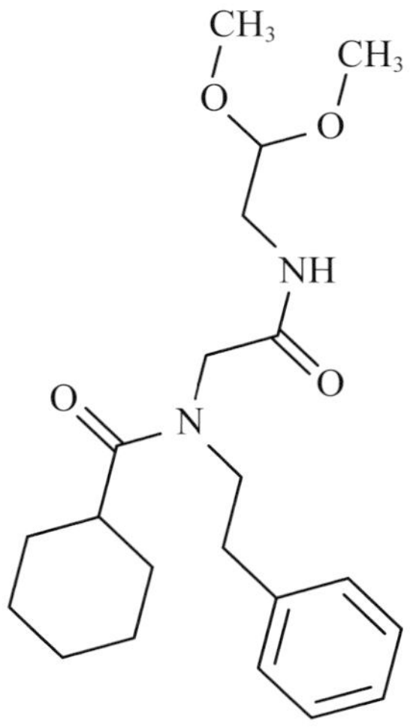
- D.

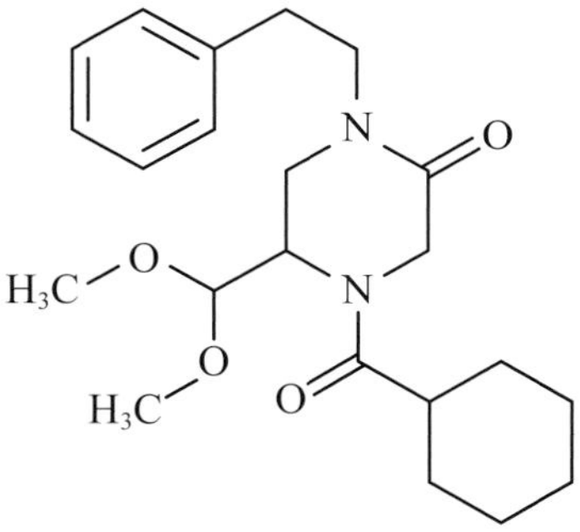

Question 2

The first step in converting artemisinin into artesunate is:

- A. oxidation via Reaction *A*.
- B. reduction via Reaction *A*.
- C. oxidation via Reaction *B*.
- D. reduction via Reaction *B*.

Question 3

Which of the following reagents would best convert dihydroartemisinin into artemether:

- A. acetic anhydride and pyridine.
- B. methanol, NaOH, and molecular sieves.
- C. methylmagnesium bromide and diethyl ether.
- D. methanol, HCl and molecular sieves.

Question 4

Which of the following molecules at position R4 would most likely have the fastest rate for the nucleophilic substitution reaction?

- A. $CH_2CH_2CH_3$
- B. $C(CH_3)_3$
- C. $CH(CH_3)_2$
- D. $C(CH_2CH_3)_3$

Question 5

Reaction *A* is best accomplished with:

- A. hydrochloric acid and water.
- B. hydrochloric acid and methanol.
- C. sodium borohydride and ethanol.
- D. sodium hydroxide and water.

Question 6

The first step in the Ugi reaction involves the condensation reaction shown below:

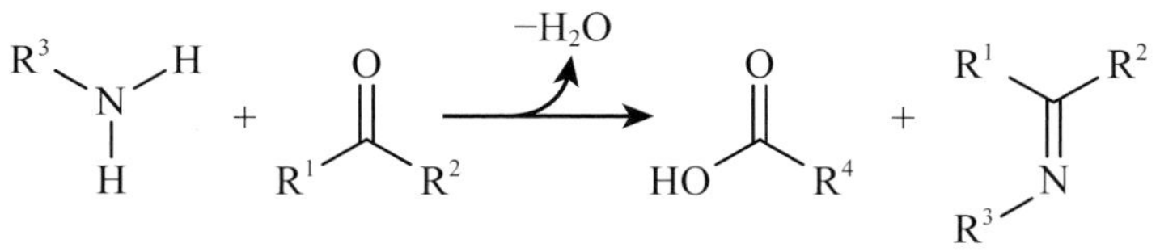

$-H_2O$

What new functional group is formed during this step?

- A. amine
- B. enamine
- C. imine
- D. amide

Passage 2 (Questions 7-11)

The Cannizzaro reaction takes advantage of a unique class of aldehydes, which lack a bond to a hydrogen atom in the α-position. These aldehydes demonstrate vigorous reactivity in the presence of an alkali metal base, undergoing disproportionation to yield equimolar concentrations of redox products, namely, a carboxylic acid and an alcohol.

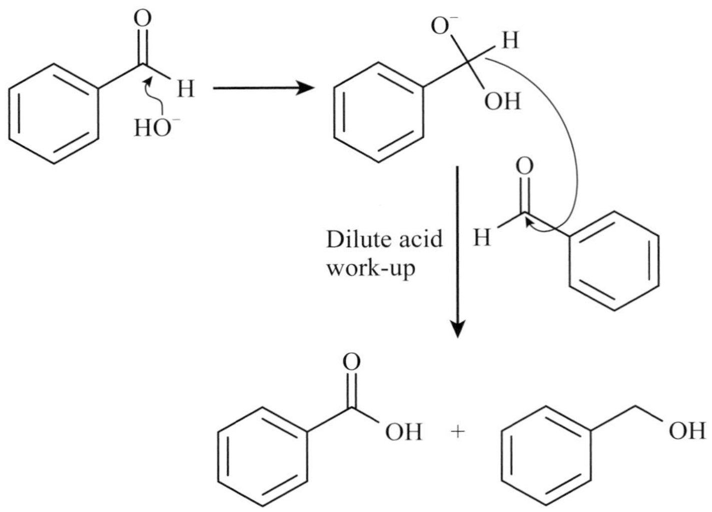

Dilute acid work-up

Reaction 1

The kinetics of this reaction are described by the rate law R = $k[RCHO]^2[OH^-]$. As the concentration of base becomes extremely high, an alternative reaction pathway becomes available, which utilizes a dianionic intermediate. The rate law of this second pathway is R = $k'[RCHO]^2[OH^-]^2$. The net reaction rate in the presence of highly concentrated strong base is the sum of the rates of the competing pathways:

$$R_{net} = k[RCHO]^2[OH^-] + k'[RCHO]^2[OH^-]^2.$$

This reaction has a theoretical yield of 50% for the alcohol product. To circumvent this synthetic obstacle, and prevent the undesired oxidation of valuable reagents, chemists introduce a sacrificial aldehyde, typically methanal, into the reaction. Methanal participates in a crossed Cannizzaro reaction with the target substrate, leading to the target's reduction, and undergoes oxidation to form a metal methanoate salt.

Question 7

Which statement supports that the hypothesis that the mechanism of reduction to the alcohol product is mediated via a hydride transfer from the reactant?

- **A.** When this reaction is performed in D_2O, the product alcohol contains a deuterated α-carbon.
- **B.** When this reaction is performed in D_2O, the product alcohol contains a deutarated hydroxyl group.
- **C.** When this reaction is performed in D_2O, half of the product alcohol contains a deuterated α-carbon.
- **D.** When this reaction is performed in D_2O, the product alcohol does not contain a deuterated α-carbon.

Question 8

Suppose cyclohexanecarboxaldehyde (shown) was used in Reaction 1 in place of benzaldehyde. What product(s) would be expected?

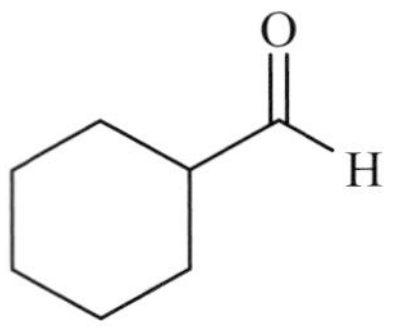

Cyclohexanecarboxaldehyde

- **A.** 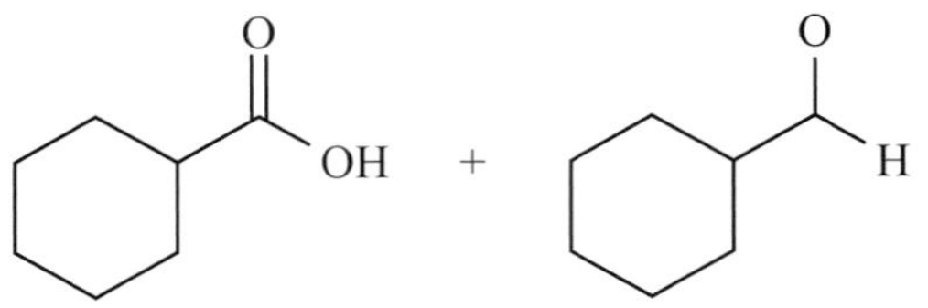
- **B.** 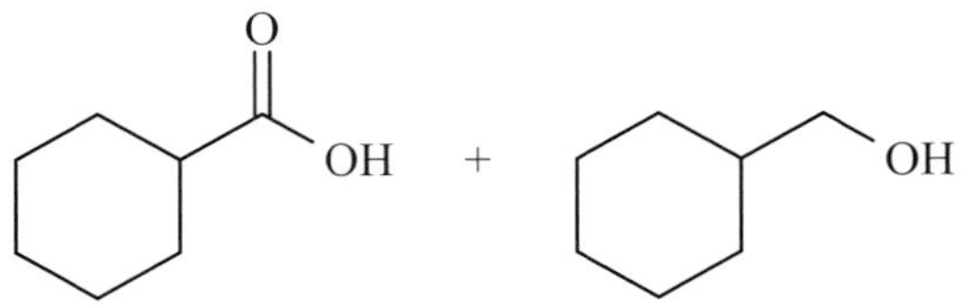
- **C.** 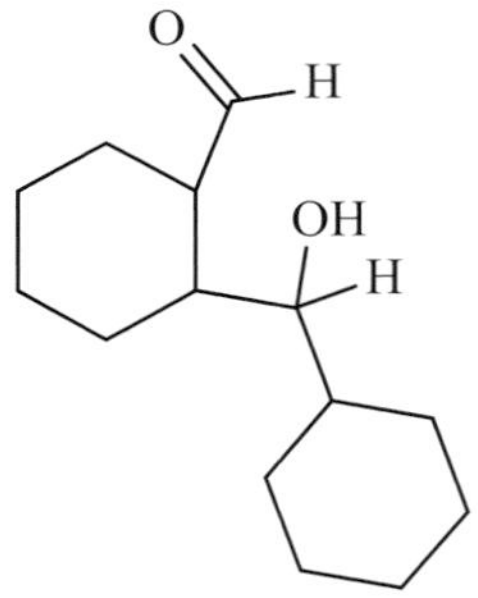
- **D.**

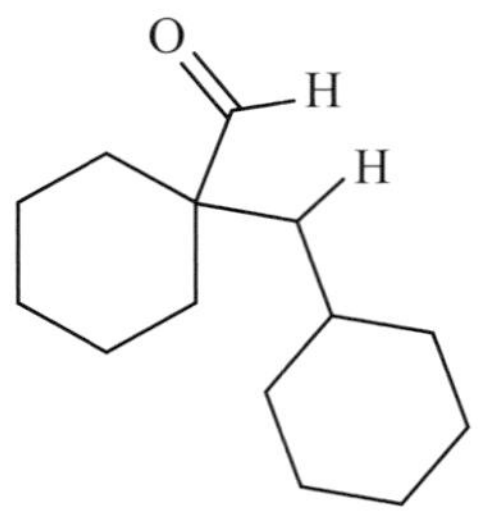

TEST 3B

Question 9

Which of the following would make the best sacrificial aldehyde for a crossed Cannizzaro reaction?

O **A.** Cl(Cl)C=C(Cl)C(=O)CH$_3$ [structure: Cl, Cl, Cl, O, CH$_3$]

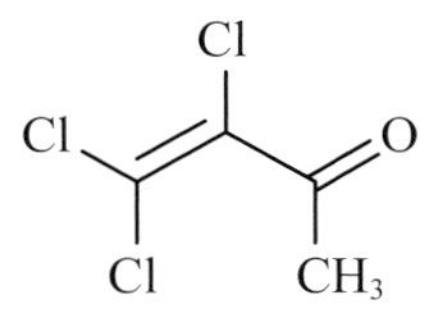

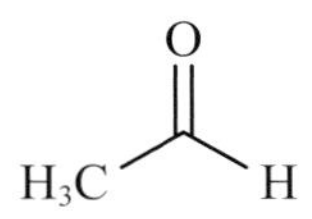

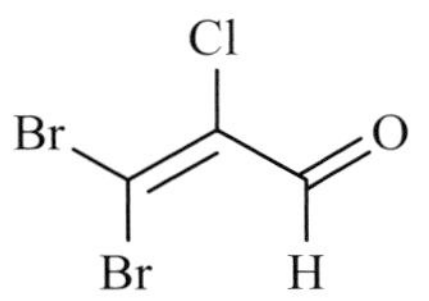

O **B.** H$_3$C–C(=O)–H

O **C.** Br(Br)C=C(Cl)C(=O)H [structure: Br, Br, Cl, O, H]

O **D.** Cl–C(=O)–H

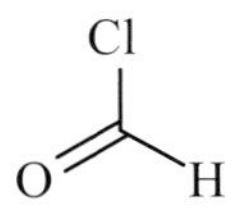

Question 10

When benzaldehyde and methanal undergo a crossed Cannizzaro reaction, which is this the oxidizing agent?

O **A.** Benzaldehyde is the oxidizing agent because its carbonyl carbon has a weaker δ+.

O **B.** Methanal is the oxidizing agent because it has a greater δ+.

O **C.** Benzaldehyde is the oxidizing agent because its carbonyl carbon has a greater δ+.

O **D.** Methanal is the oxidizing agent because it has a weaker δ+.

Question 11

What is true regarding the products of Reaction 1?

I. The alcohol boils at a lower temperature than the carboxylic acid.

II. As a result of resonance, the carboxylic acid cannot participate in hydrogen bonding.

III. The dilute acid work-up step reduces the solubility of one of the products in water.

O **A.** III only

O **B.** II only

O **C.** I and II only

O **D.** I and III only

Questions 12 - 15 do not refer to a passage and are independent of each other.

Question 12

Which of the following statements regarding the reaction of acetylacetone with potassium *tert*-butoxide to produce an enolate is NOT true?

O **A.** The reaction will produce a nucleophilic α-carbon.

O **B.** The reaction would proceed faster if a nitro group were attached to the α-carbon.

O **C.** The reaction would proceed faster if a methyl group were attached to the α-carbon.

O **D.** Removing one of the carbonyls would increase the pK_a of the α-carbon.

Question 13

Which compound can be reacted with a specific aldehyde or ketone to render a cyanohydrin compound?

O **A.** H_2O with catalytic H_2SO_4

O **B.** KCN

O **C.** $NaNH_2$

O **D.** HNO_3

Question 14

Which of the following will increase the rate of new carbon-carbon bond formation in the reaction of iodomethane with 2-pentanone?

O **A.** Using pentanal instead of 2-pentanone

O **B.** Adding catalytic H_2SO_4 to the reaction to protonate the α-carbon

O **C.** Using a better nucleophile like CH_3O^-

O **D.** Halogenating the 4-position prior to the reaction

Question 15

Which of the following reactants would most increase the likelihood of a substitution reaction occurring at the α-position of a ketone?

O **A.** A bulky nucleophile that will preferentially attack the less sterically hindered α-carbon.

O **B.** A strong base that is a poor nucleophile.

O **C.** A strong nucleophile that has less steric hindrance.

O **D.** A nucleophile that is stabilized by resonance.

Passage 3 (Questions 16-21)

Xylitol is a sugar alcohol used in the food industry to improve the taste and texture of processed foods. Its nutrition profile makes it desirable for individuals with metabolic disorders such as diabetes because it does not significantly affect blood sugar levels. In addition, xylitol is nonfermentable by the bacteria of the oral cavity. Since it has a similar shape to conventional sugars, it is still absorbed by these bacteria, but instead of being converted into energy and acidic products, it disrupts their growth and reproduction. Its sweetness also induces salivation, which assists in neutralizing the acidity of the mouth, and washes away food particles which may adhere to teeth.

In contrast, high fructose corn syrup (HFCS) is composed of glucose and fructose as well as glucose oligomers. Its nutrition profile makes it undesirable for diabetics as it can significantly affect blood sugar levels. HFCS is absorbed and metabolized by bacteria of the oral cavity, which release acidic products during metabolism. These acidic products can harm teeth, and there is a strong link between the consumption of foods rich in HFCS and tooth decay.

The structures of these molecules are shown in Figure 1.

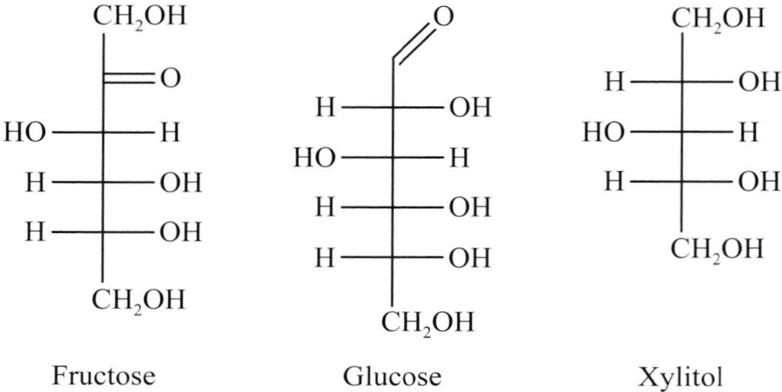

Figure 1 Structures of sugars and sugar alcohol

Question 16

Respectively, glucose and fructose are:

- **A.** a ketose and an aldose.
- **B.** both ketoses.
- **C.** an aldose and a ketose.
- **D.** both aldoses.

Question 17

Which of the following is a both an anomer and epimer of α-D-glucose, found in HFCS?

A. **B.**

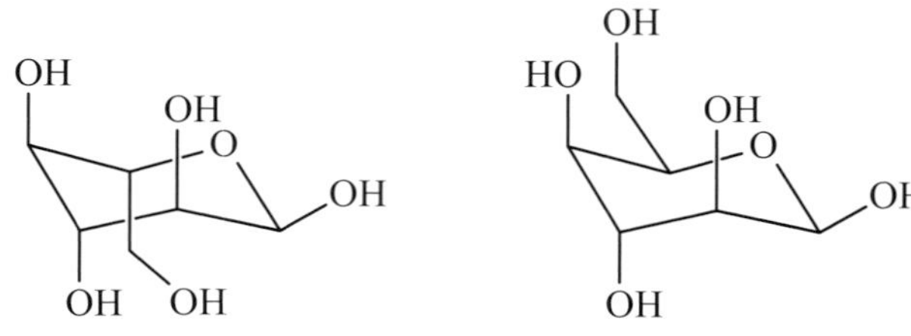

C. **D.**

Question 18

Sucrose (shown below) is a disaccharide formed of glucose and fructose. What is true of sucrose?

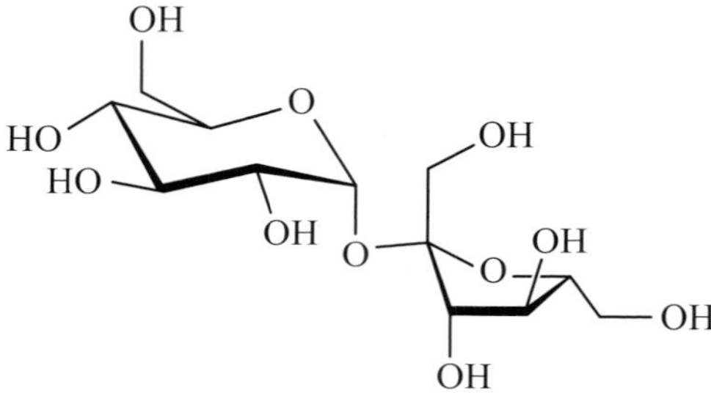

Sucrose

- **A.** It has a β-1, α-4 gycosidic bond.
- **B.** It has an α-1, β-2 glycosidic bond.
- **C.** It has an α-1, β-4 glycosidic bond.
- **D.** It has an α-1,2 glycosidic bond.

Question 19

Xylitol can be converted to the aldose xylose via:

- **A.** Oxidation of carbon 5.
- **B.** Reduction of carbon 1.
- **C.** Oxidation of carbon 2.
- **D.** Reduction of carbon 4.

Question 20

Sucralose is another sweet disaccharide which does not affect blood sugar levels. The second step in its synthesis requires acetylation (shown below). Which of the following reagents would best accomplish this reaction?

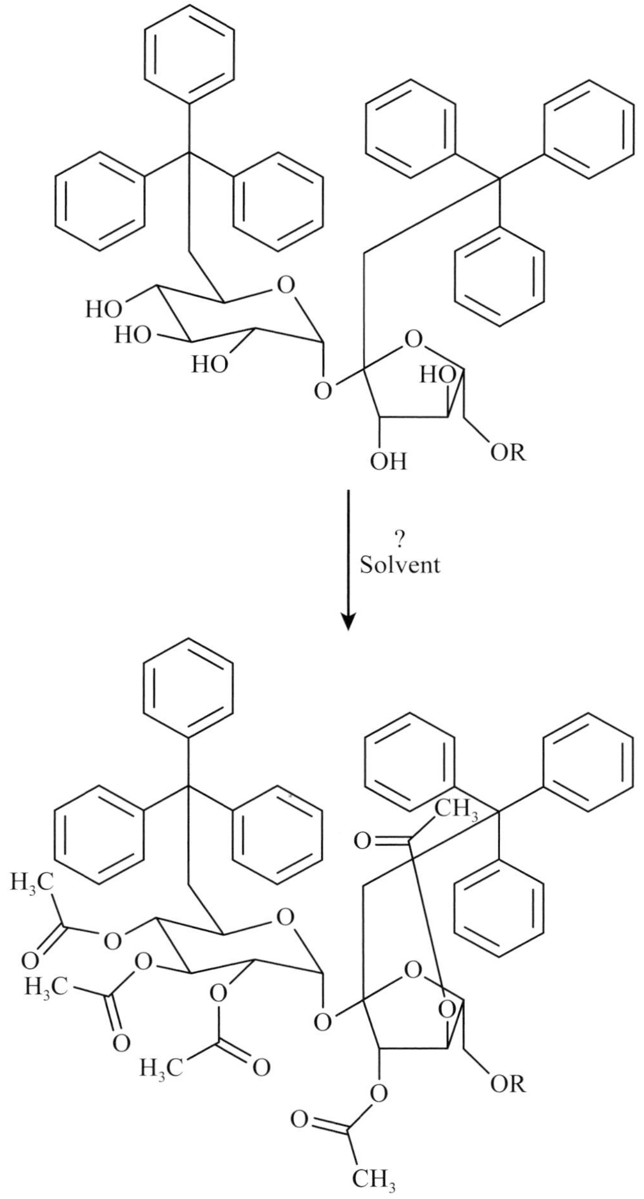

? Solvent

- O **A.** Acetone
- O **B.** Acetic acid
- O **C.** Sodium acetate
- O **D.** Acetic anhydride

Question 21

The process of converting D-glucose to a D-fructose is:

- O **A.** accomplished through resonance.
- O **B.** irreversible.
- O **C.** initiated by the deprotonation of an alcohol.
- O **D.** more likely in the presence of a bulky base.

Passage 4 (Questions 22-26)

Lipids, mainly in the form of triacylglycerides (TAGs), play a vital role in human energy storage. During periods of low nutritional intake, such as during fasting or between meals, lipases within adipocytes breakdown stored TAGs, liberating free fatty acids (FFAs) into systemic circulation. Specific transport proteins allow for their assimilation into the cell where they are converted into ATP through β-oxidation and the citric acid cycle.

Structurally, TAGs are composed of glycerol that is esterified with three fatty acids. The fatty acids may be unsaturated, such as erucic acid, or saturated, like stearic acid. The structures of these fatty acids are shown in Figure 1.

$CH_3(CH_2)_7CH{=}CH(CH_2)_{11}COOH$ — Erucic acid

$CH_3(CH_2)_{16}COOH$ — Stearic acid

Figure 1 Unsaturated and saturated FFAs

An important class of TAG derivatives are the phospholipids formed from a diacylglycerol (DAG) and a phosphoric acid ester. These molecules, such as the one shown below (Figure 2), play crucial roles in maintaining cell membrane architecture, and some function as signaling molecules.

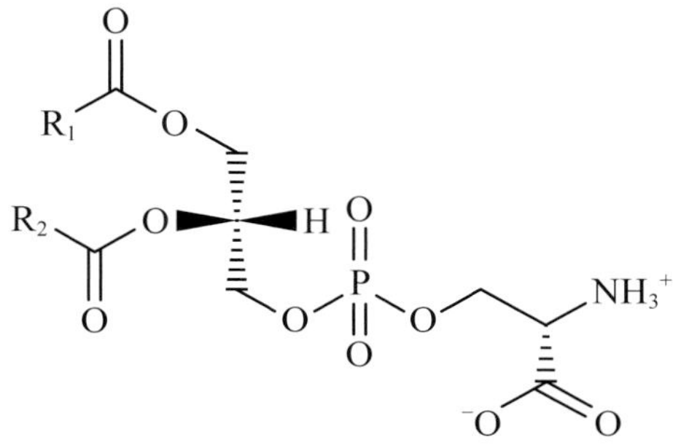

Figure 2 Structure of representative phospholipid

The amphipathic character of phospholipids allows them to form bilayered spheres in solution, composed of two hydrophilic surfaces with a hydrophobic region separating them. These phospholipid bilayers form the main structure of the cell membrane, causing it to be impermeable to most ions and proteins.

Question 22

Based on the structure of the representative phospholipid, which of the following structures accurately represent that of the non-esterified α-amino acid?

- O **A.** $PO_3^-OCH_2CNH_3^+COO^-$
- O **B.** $OOC^-CH_2CNH_3^+COO^-$
- O **C.** $HOCH_2PO_4OCH_2CNH_3^+COO^-$
- O **D.** $HOCH_2CNH_3^+COO^-$

Question 23

What is true after fully saturating the ω-9 bond in erucic acid?

- A. Its melting point increases.
- B. Its melting point decreases.
- C. A fatty acid is converted to a TAG.
- D. A TAG is converted to a fatty acid.

Question 24

Suppose the α-amino acid of the representative phospholipid is metabolized to form the unsaturated amine, shown below:

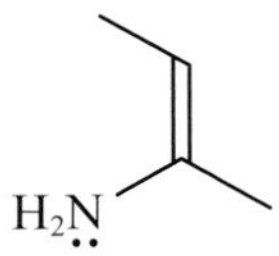

If this compound were mixed with (*S*)-1-deutero-1-bromopropane, which of the following is the most likely product?

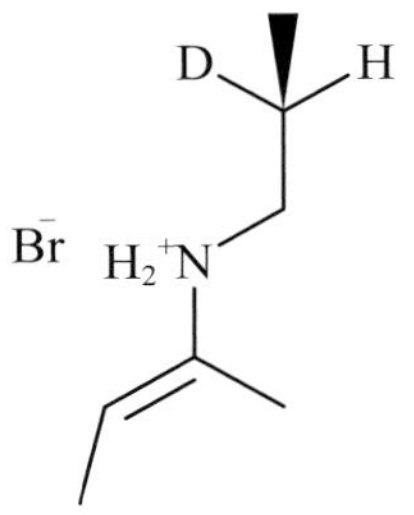

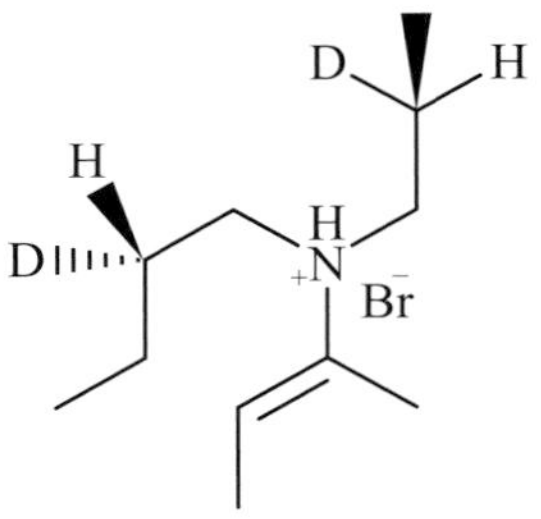

- A.
- B.
- C.
- D.

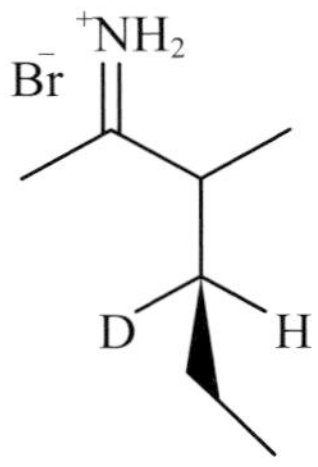

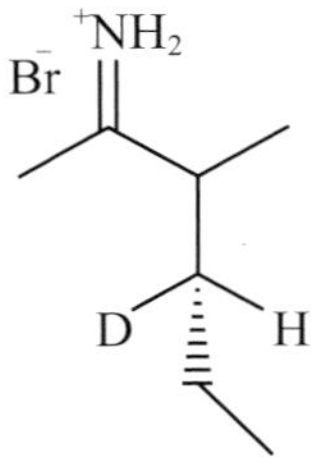

Question 25

If all three of a TAG's esters were composed of stearic acid, what is the product of its saponification with NaOH?

- A. $CH_3(CH_2)_{16}CH_2O^-Na^+$
- B. $CH_3(CH_2)_{16}COOH$
- C. $CH_3(CH_2)_{16}CH_2OH$
- D. $CH_3(CH_2)_{16}COO^-Na^+$

Question 26

If stearic acid is reacted with phenyllithium, what is the IUPAC name of the expected product?

- A. Phenyl octadecanoate
- B. Octadecanyl benzoate
- C. Lithium octadecanoate
- D. Phenoxyoctadecane

Questions 27 - 29 do not refer to a passage and are independent of each other.

Question 27

Sucrase is an enzyme found in the GI tract that this capable of breaking the sucrose into the individual monosaccharides. Which of the following is most likely true of sucrase?

- O **A.** A fever will most likely decrease its activity.
- O **B.** It catalyzes a dehydration reaction.
- O **C.** It breaks an ester bond.
- O **D.** It uses water to facilitate the digestion.

Question 28

The following aldehydes were used as substrates in four separate traditional Strecker amino acid syntheses.

I.

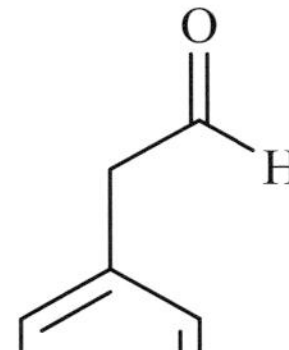

II.

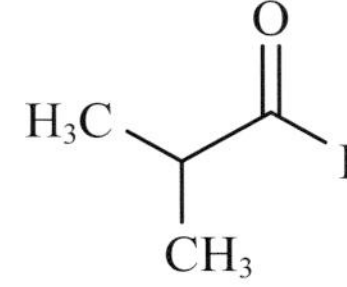

III.

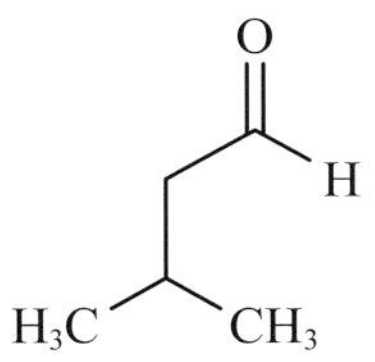

Which of the substrates will form an optically inactive aqueous solution during the H_2O/H^+ work-up step?

- O **A.** II only
- O **B.** I and II only
- O **C.** I and III only
- O **D.** I, II, and III

Question 29

Prunasin is a metabolite of amygdalin, a highly toxic chemical which was investigated as a potential anti-cancer compound. When refluxed in $H_2SO_4(aq)$, and then neutralized, prunasin releases glucose (1 equivalent), HCN (1 equivalent), and benzaldehyde (C_6H_5CHO, 1 equivalent). Which structure matches that of prunasin?

O **A.**

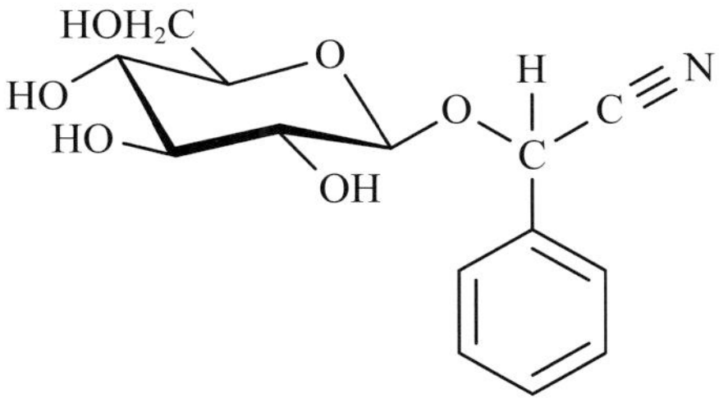

O **B.**

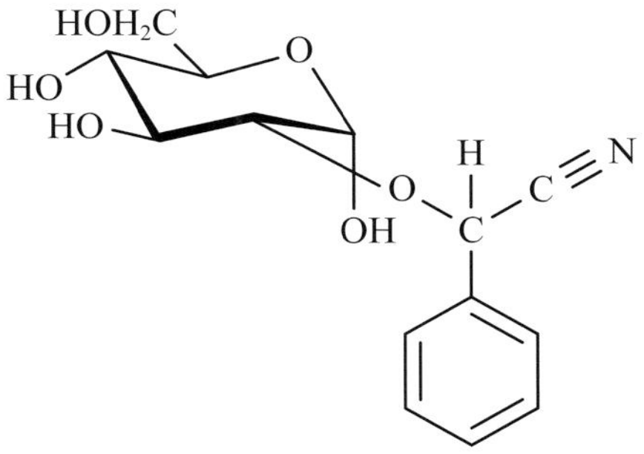

O **C.**

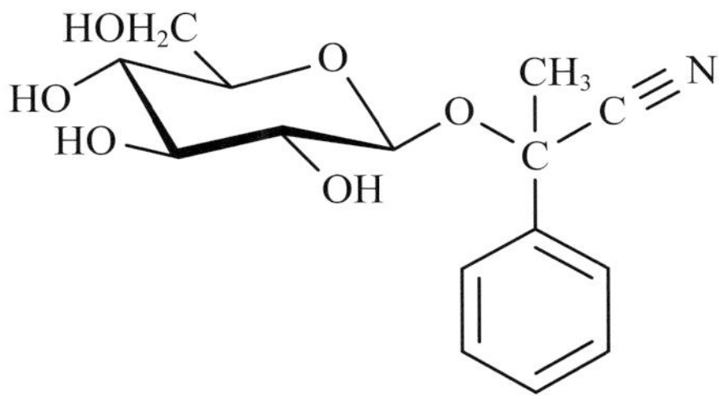

O **D.**

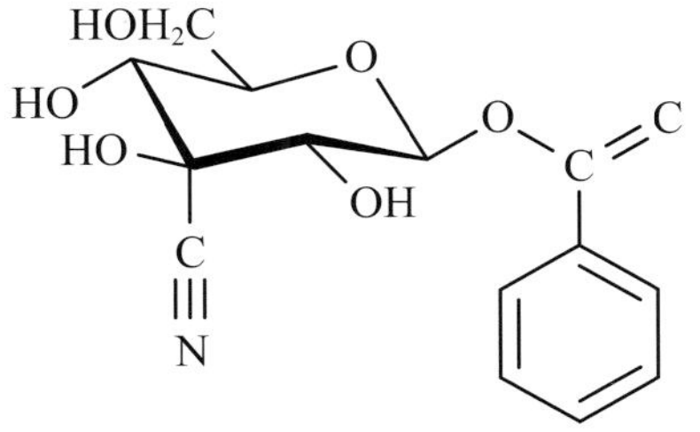

STOP. If you finish before time is called, check your work. You may go back to any question in this test.

ANSWERS & EXPLANATIONS for Test 3B can be found on p. 262.

Thermodynamics and Kinetics

TEST 4A

Time: 95 minutes
Questions 1–59

DIRECTIONS: Most of the questions in this test section are grouped with a passage. Read the passage, then select the best answer to each question. Some questions are independent of any passage and of one another. Select the best answer to each of these questions. If you are unsure of an answer, rule out incorrect choices and select from the remaining options. Indicate your selection beside the option you choose. A periodic table can be found on the last page of this book for you to use at any point during this test section.

Passage 1 (Questions 1-5)

Depurination , the release of purine bases from nucleic acids by the hydrolysis of N-glycosidic bonds, has stimulated considerable interest for a long time because of its close relationship with the mutation and repair of nucleic acids. At apurinic sites caused by depurination, the covalent structure of DNA becomes more susceptible to damage, which induces spontaneous mutagenesis, carcinogenesis and cellular aging. Depurination is believed to follow two pH dependent reaction pathways, as shown below in Figure 1.

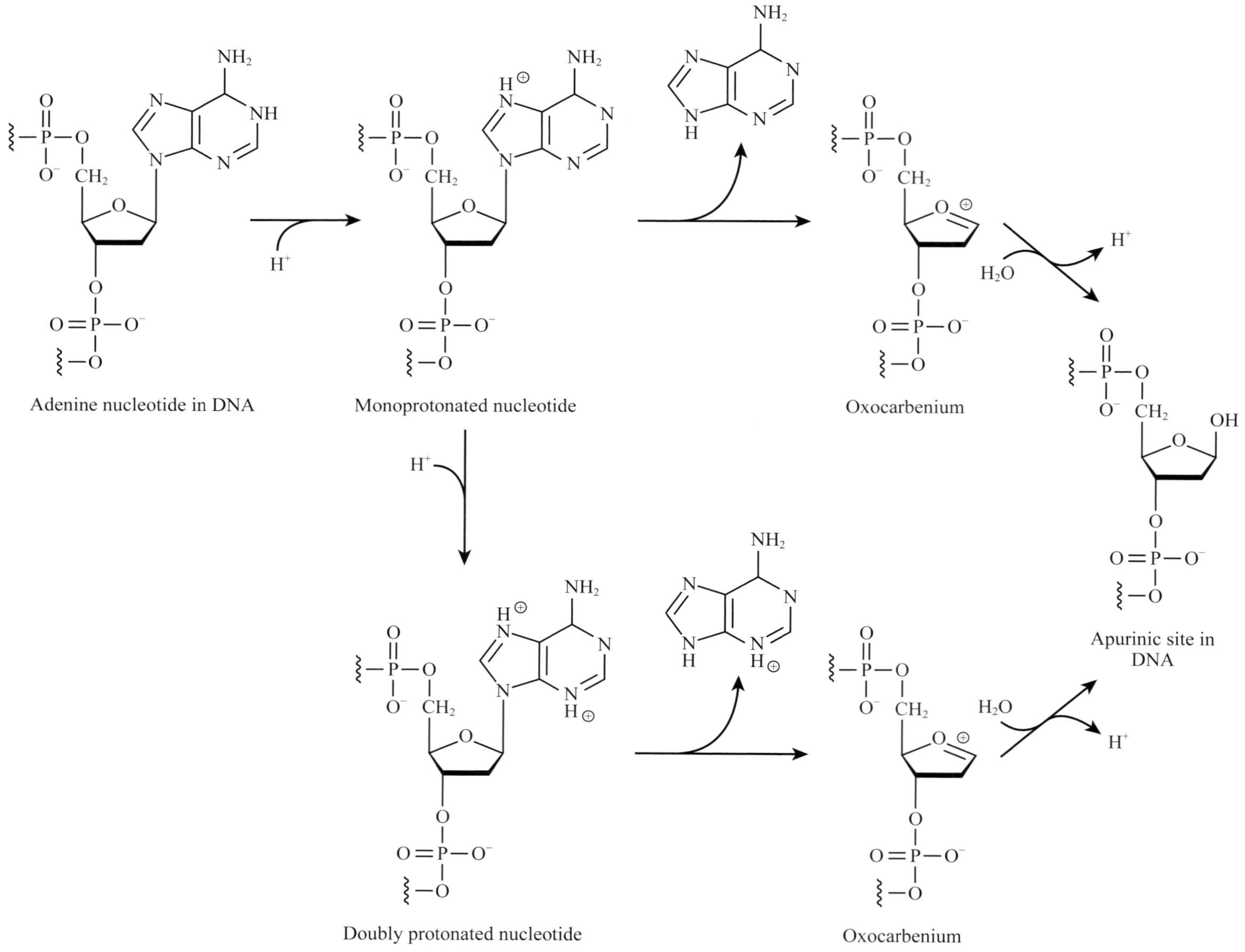

Figure 1 pH dependent reaction pathways of depurination

In an experiment, researchers designed and used a pool of 30-nucleotide-long oligodeoxynucleotides (ODNs) with various sequences for depurination to explore the relationship of pH, temperature, and salt concentration on the kinetics of the depurination reaction. After each reaction, the results were quantified using high performance liquid chromatography (HPLC) with uracil as the internal standard. It was observed that the acid-mediated depurination reaction followed first order kinetics, and its temperature dependence obeyed the Arrhenius Equation, shown below, where k is the observed rate constant, T is the absolute temperature, R is the gas constant 8.3 J/K · mol, A is a pre-exponential factor, and E_a is the activation energy of the reaction.

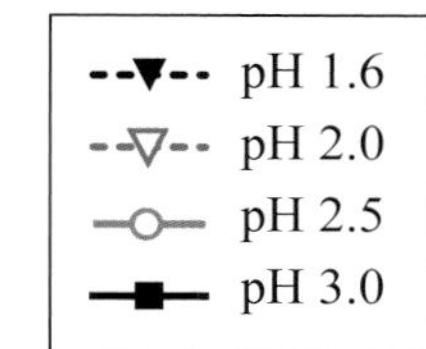

$$k = Ae^{-\frac{E_a}{RT}}$$

Arrhenius equation

The results of their tests are shown in Figures 2, 3, and 4.

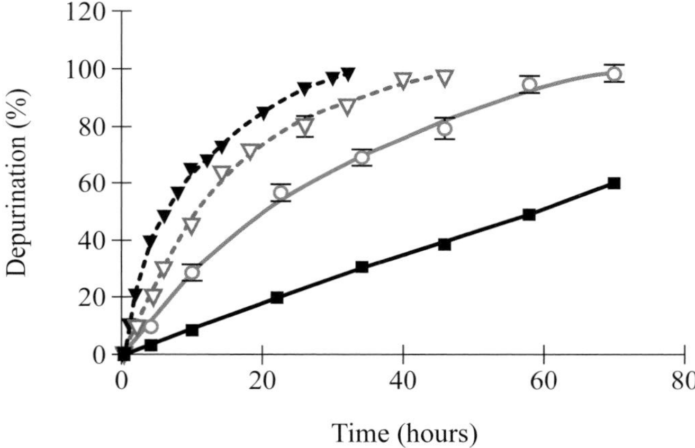

Figure 2 Time courses of non-enzymatic depurination with 50 μM of ODN

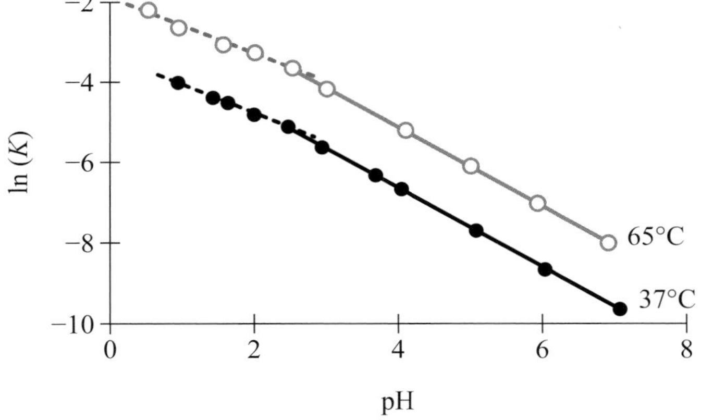

Figure 3 Rate constants as a function of pH for depurination

A.

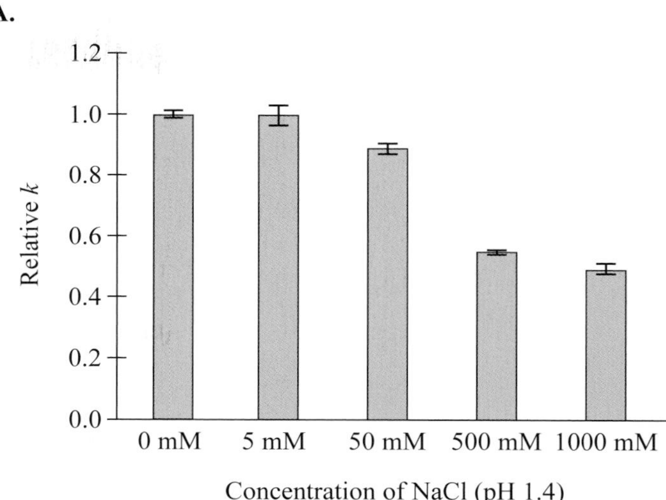

B.

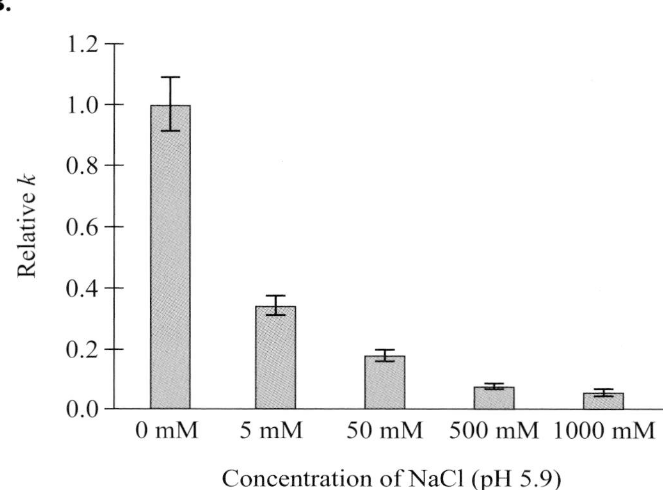

Figure 4 Effect of salt concentration on depurination rate: (A) strongly acidic conditions; (B) moderately acidic conditions

This passage was adapted from " Non-Enzymatic Depurination of Nucleic Acids: Factors and Mechanisms." An R, Jia Y, Wan B, Zhang Y, Dong P, et al. *PLoS ONE*. 2014. 9(12) doi:10.1371/journal.pone.0115950 for use under the terms of the Creative Commons CC BY 4.0 license (http://creativecommons.org/licenses/by/4.0/legalcode).

Question 1

What is the average rate of depurination in the trial performed at an $[H^+] = 10^{-3}$ M?

- ○ **A.** 2.3×10^{-4} μM/sec
- ○ **B.** 8.5×10^{-1} μM/sec
- ○ **C.** 5.7×10^{-1} μM/sec
- ○ **D.** 1.2×10^{-4} μM/sec

Question 2

Another published study claims that NaCl concentration has a negligible effect on the depurination rate constant. The researchers in that study:

- A. most likely only tested highly alkaline solutions.
- B. most likely only tested highly acidic solutions.
- C. most likely used a salt that releases a phosphate anion.
- D. most likely used a salt with which forms a divalent metal cation.

Question 3

If ln(k) of a depurination reaction were plotted on the y-axis against the reciprocal of the reaction's absolute temperature, which of the following is equivalent to the y-intercept value?

- A. $-E_a/R$
- B. $-\ln(A)$
- C. $\ln(A)$
- D. A

Question 4

Which of the following would most increase the rate of an acid-mediated depurination reaction?

- A. Increasing the pH of the reaction.
- B. Performing the reaction in an ice bath.
- C. Addition of an enzyme that lowers the activation energy required to doubly protonate a nucleotide.
- D. Addition of an enzyme that lowers the activation energy required to form an oxocarbenium ion.

Question 5

Similar to depurination, all of the following reactions have a total reaction order of 1 EXCEPT:

- A. the decomposition of $H_2O_2(l)$ into $O_2(g)$ and $H_2(g)$ at room temperature.
- B. the solvolysis of triphenylmethyl bromide in methanol.
- C. the bromination of iodomethane with NaBr(aq) in $H_2O(l)$.
- D. the α-decay of ^{238}U into ^{234}Th.

Passage 2 (Questions 6-9)

Cooling systems such as air conditioning or refrigeration play an indispensable role in industrial, clinical, and domestic settings. The vast majority of these systems utilize a refrigerant, which must satisfy a variety of thermodynamic properties such as a high enthalpy of vaporization and critical temperature, and a boiling point that is somewhat lower than the target temperature of the system.

Cooling systems work by pressurizing the gaseous refrigerant in a compressor, until it becomes a liquid at a lower temperature and higher pressure. The liquefied refrigerant releases its heat to the surroundings as it travels to a thermal expansion valve. Once it is cool enough, a small portion of the liquefied refrigerant is allowed to pass through the valve into a low pressure pipe of the system, where it rapidly evaporates, absorbing heat and cooling the contents of the system. The cold gaseous refrigerant is ultimately recovered by the compressor and another cycle starts. The relationship between pressure (P) and the change in enthalpy (ΔH) of a refrigerant during a refrigeration cycle is shown in the phase diagram in Figure 1.

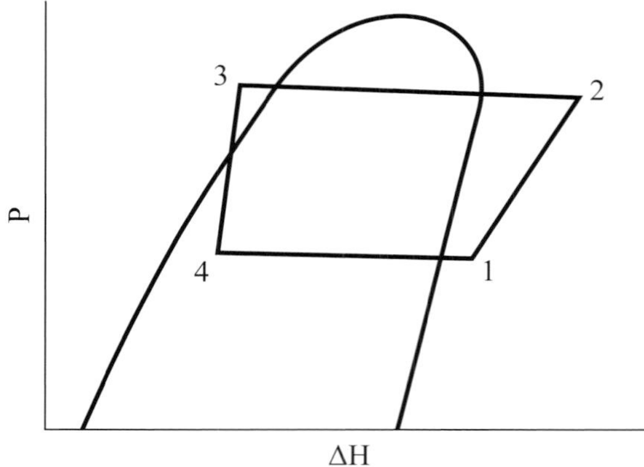

Figure 1 Phase diagram of refrigerant during refrigeration cycle

Early refrigerants were compounds that contained only carbon, fluorine, or chlorine. These compounds, named, "chlorofluorocarbons" (CFCs) are remarkably inert. Unlike other gases, CFCs experience virtually no atmospheric decomposition, until they rise to the stratosphere. The high energy photon environment of the stratosphere converts CFCs into radical decomposition products such as ·Cl. Radical decomposition products pose a significant threat to human health. They cleave stratospheric ozone into molecular oxygen.

$$\cdot Cl(g) + O_3(g) \rightarrow ClO\cdot(g) + O_2(g)$$

Step 1

$$ClO\cdot(g) + \cdot O(g) \rightarrow \cdot Cl(g) + O_2(g)$$

Step 2

$$O_3(g) + \cdot O(g) \rightarrow 2O_2(g)$$

Net Reaction

Since ozone absorbs many of the harmful UV rays emitted from the sun, individuals living in areas of ozone depletion suffer a greater risk of UV-light associated health conditions such as sunburns, eye damage, and skin cancer.

Question 6

During the cleavage of ozone, chlorine:

- O **A.** drives the net reaction by causing it to have a more negative change in enthalpy.
- O **B.** drives the net reaction by decreasing its activation energy.
- O **C.** drives the net reaction by causing it to have a more positive change in enthalpy.
- O **D.** drives the net reaction by causing it to have a more positive change in entropy.

Question 7

A gaseous refrigerant expands from 1000 cm^3 to 5000 cm^3 in a low pressure tube of 68 kPa. How much work has the gas performed?

- O **A.** 272×10^3 J
- O **B.** 272 J
- O **C.** 340 J
- O **D.** 340×10^3 J

Question 8

During the expansion of a refrigerant in a pipe:

I. $\Delta S > 0$
II. $\Delta G = 0$
III. $\Delta H > 0$

- O **A.** III only
- O **B.** I and II only
- O **C.** I and III only
- O **D.** I, II, and III

Question 9

Based on the figure below depicting a particular gaseous refrigerant as a function of volume and pressure, which of the following is NOT true?

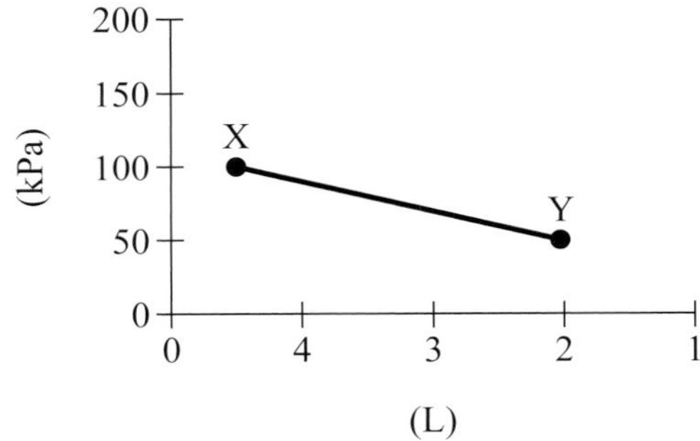

- O **A.** More than 100 J of work was performed on the gas.
- O **B.** Less than 200 J of work was performed on the gas.
- O **C.** It can be accomplished isothermally by releasing 75% of the gas in the pipe.
- O **D.** It can be accomplished isothermally by releasing 50% of the gas in the pipe.

Questions 10 - 13 do not refer to a passage and are independent of each other.

Question 10

What are the units of k in a third order reaction?

- O **A.** s^{-1}
- O **B.** $M^{-2} \cdot s^{-1}$
- O **C.** $M^{-1} \cdot s^{-1}$
- O **D.** $M \cdot s^{-1}$

Question 11

A nucleophilic substitution reaction that always proceeds with inversion of stereochemistry is best defined by which of the following kinetic parameters?

O **A.**

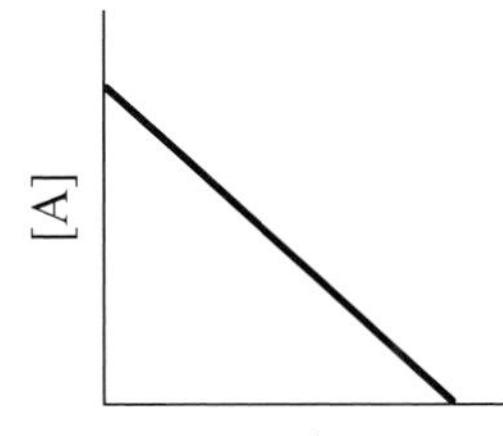

O **B.**

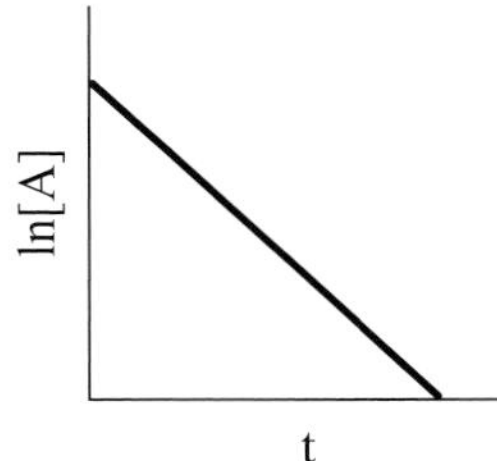

O **C.**

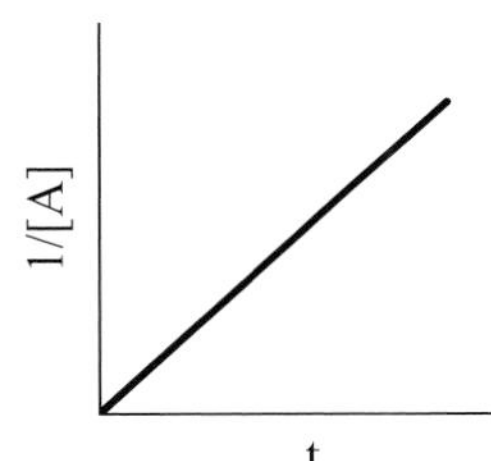

O **D.**

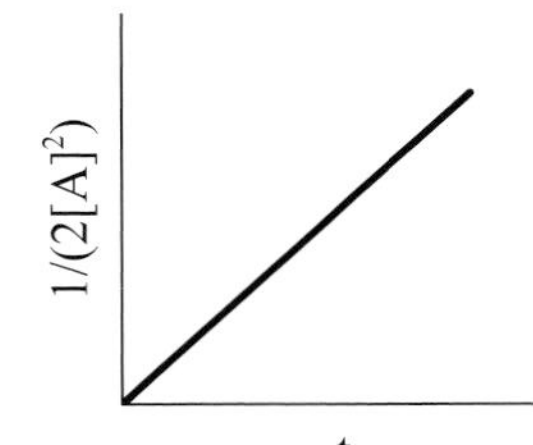

Question 12

A research group is developing a drug but is having difficulties isolating a pure final product. The samples are continuously contaminated by a less stable product. How can the purity of the sample be increased?

- A. Increase temperature
- B. Decrease temperature
- C. Add a catalyst
- D. Increase concentration of reactants

Question 13

A researcher performed the reactions shown below and used the data to determine the rate law of the reaction (Rate = $[Ca^{2+}]]^x[Citrate]^y$). What are the values of x and y, respectively?

Trial	Initial $[Ca^{2+}]$	Initial [Citrate]	Rate
1	0.2 M	0.5 M	3.42 Mol $L^{-1}s^{-1}$
2	0.2 M	2.0 M	13.92 Mol $L^{-1}s^{-1}$
3	0.4 M	4.0 M	26.8 Mol $L^{-1}s^{-1}$

- A. 1, 1
- B. 1, 2
- C. 0, 1
- D. 0, 2

TEST 4A

Passage 3 (Questions 14-17)

Ionic liquids (ILs), such as [DEEA][Pro] (Figure 1), are molten salts with melting points below 100°C. ILs have unique physicochemical properties such as broad liquid temperature ranges, negligible vapor pressures, wide electrochemical windows, high thermal stabilities, and high specific solvent abilities. The thermo-physical properties of ILs can be tuned by appropriate selection of cation and anion. As a result, ILs can be made biocompatible. These thermodynamic properties are useful in characterizing the solvation behavior of vitamins and to further understand solute-solute and solute-solvent interactions.

Ascorbic acid (vitamin C), one of the most important vitamins for human health and nutrition, is found in fruits and vegetables. It is a sugar acid, has antioxidant properties, and can prevent or treat the common cold and scurvy. It also acts as a cofactor and thus maintains the activity of various enzymes. The degradation of ascorbic acid (AA) is very important and is considered to be the major cause of color and quality change during storage or processing of food materials. ILs are a potential way to characterize the solubility of AA in stored food.

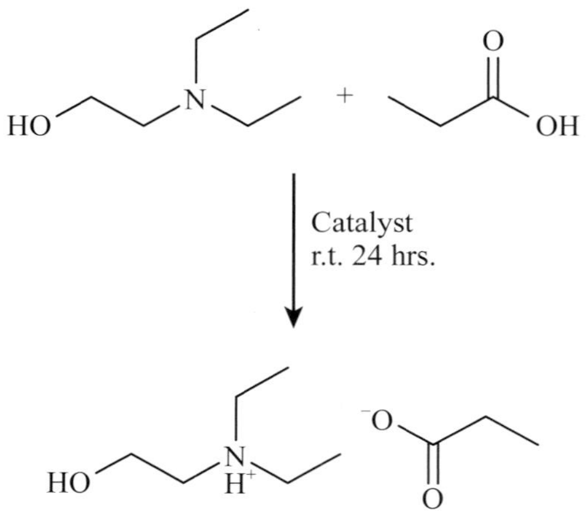

HO N + O OH

Catalyst
r.t. 24 hrs.

HO N H+ O- O

Figure 1 Synthesis of diethylethanolammonium propanoate [DEEA][Pro]

Thermal expansion coefficients predict the solubility of compounds in ILs at various temperatures. The thermal expansion coefficient ($\partial V_2°/\partial T$) and its second derivative ($\partial^2 V_2°/\partial T^2$) describe the attractive forces between ILs and the solute, such as AA, and the energy change of the solvent, such as [DEEA][Pro], as its lattice structure is disrupted during solvation (Table 1).

Table 1 Partial Molar Expansion Coefficients ($\partial V_2°/\partial T$) and ($\partial^2 V_2°/\partial T^2$) of Ascorbic Acid in Aqueous [DEEA][Pro] Solutions at Various Temperatures

m_s/mol · kg^{-1}	$(\partial V_2^{\infty}/\partial T)p \cdot 10^6$								$(\partial^2 V_2^{\infty}/\partial T^2)p \cdot 10^6$
	$m^3 \cdot mol^{-1} \cdot K^{-1}$								$m^3 \cdot mol^{-1} \cdot K^{-2}$
	T/K								
	293.15	298.15	303.15	308.15	313.15	318.15	323.15	328.15	
0.00	0.129	0.123	0.118	0.112	0.106	0.101	0.095	0.089	−0.001
0.10	0.176	0.166	0.155	0.145	0.135	0.124	0.114	0.104	−0.002

This passage is adapted from "Thermodynamic and Ultrasonic Properties of Ascorbic Acid in Aqueous Protic Ionic Liquid Solutions." Singh V, Sharma G, and Gardas R. *PLoS ONE.* 2015. doi:10.1371/journal.pone.0126091 for use under the terms of the Creative Commons CC BY 4.0 license (http://creativecommons.org/licenses/by/4.0/legalcode).

Question 14

Increasing the temperature of Reaction 1 will increase the reaction rate by:

O **A.** increasing the energy of the transition state.

O **B.** lowering the activation energy of the reaction.

O **C.** decreasing the energy level of the final product by making it more stable.

O **D.** providing more molecules with sufficient kinetic energy to complete the reaction.

Question 15

Which of the following statements best describes the entropy change as AA is solvated in [DEEA][Pro]?

O **A.** The entropy of the solution increases.

O **B.** The entropy of the solution decreases.

O **C.** The entropy of the solution does not change.

O **D.** The entropy of the solution decreases then increases.

Question 16

Within the beaker containing the ionic liquid and AA, the transfer of heat throughout the solution produces the various temperatures shown in Table 1 and most likely occurs by:

I. conduction.
II. convection.
III. radiation.

O **A.** I only

O **B.** II only

O **C.** I and III only

O **D.** II and III only

Question 17

The results shown in Table 1 suggest that:

O **A.** increasing temperature decreases the attractive forces between AA and [DEEA][Pro], and increases the ordered arrangement of [DEEA][Pro] molecules.

O **B.** decreasing temperature decreases the attractive forces between AA and [DEEA][Pro], and increases the ordered arrangement of [DEEA][Pro] molecules.

O **C.** increasing temperature decreases the attractive forces between AA and [DEEA][Pro], and decreases the ordered arrangement of [DEEA][Pro] molecules.

O **D.** decreasing temperature decreases the attractive forces between AA and [DEEA][Pro], and decreases the ordered arrangement of [DEEA][Pro] molecules.

Passage 4 (Questions 18-21)

Patchouli alcohol (PA, Figure 1) is a sesquiterpene with a tricyclic structure, and has been extracted from a whole plant of traditional Chinese medicine called Guang-huo-xiang. In traditional Chinese medicine, PA has been used to treat cold symptoms, nausea, and diarrhea. However, Patchouli alcohol easily evaporates, even at room temperature, due to its volatile nature, which can decrease the bioactivity in the processing and storage of the chemical.

Cyclodextrins (CDs) are a group of cyclic oligosaccharides consisting of 6 to 8 units of 1,4-α or 1,4-β-linked glucose units. The spaces of these macromolecules are expressed as circular table shape with different diameters. The property of the inner cavity is hydrophobic, while the outer side is hydrophilic. In this research, Patchouli alcohol and β-CD (Figure 1) were prepared to form an inclusion complex with a saturated aqueous solution method, which was designed to improve the solubility and stability of PA.

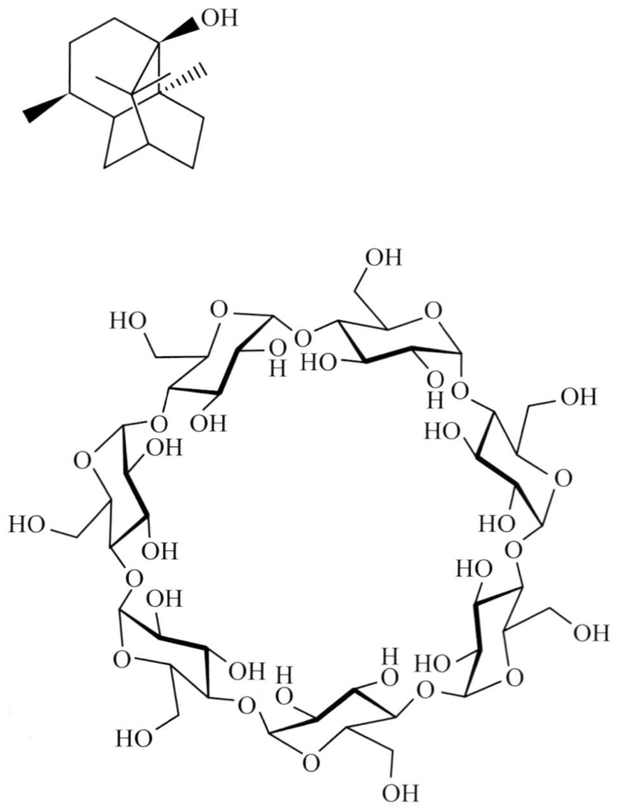

Figure 1 Chemical structures of (A) PA and (B) β-cyclodextrin

In order to investigate and confirm the inclusion behavior of guest patchouli alcohol (PA) into host (β-CD), scientists modeled change in Gibbs free energy that resulted from the binding of these chemicals. The binding energy ($\Delta_b G°$) was calculated according to Equation 1:

$$\Delta_b G° = E_{complex} - E_{\beta\text{-CD}} - E_{PA}$$

Equation 1

Solubility phase analysis was performed to detect the solubilizing ability of β-CD to PA and the inclusion stability constant of PA/CD complex inclusion. Figure 2 shows the solubility phase diagrams of PA-β-CD inclusion in two different temperatures (25, 35°C).

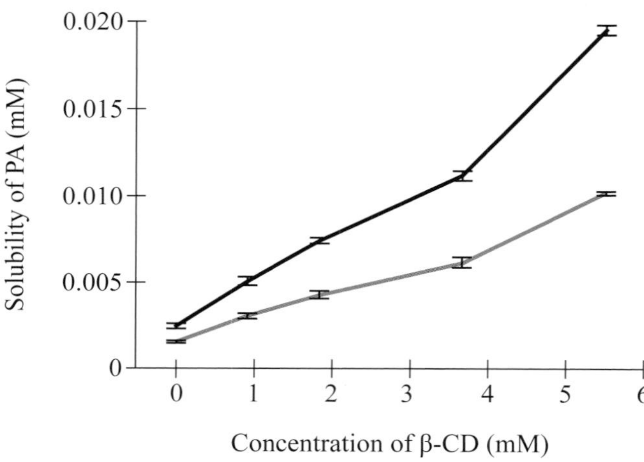

Figure 2 Phase solubility diagram of PA and β-CD at 25, 35°C

This passage is adapted from "Investigation of Inclusion Complex Patchouli Alcohol with β-Cyclodextrin." Xu F, Yang Q, Wu L, Qi R, Wu Y, et al. *PLoS ONE.* 2017. doi:10.1371/journal.pone.0169578 for use under the terms of the Creative Commons CC BY 4.0 license (http://creativecommons.org/licenses/by/4.0/legalcode).

Question 18

Which of the following changes would likely improve the processing and storage of PA?

I. Low temperature
II. High atmospheric pressure
III. Large surface area

- A. I only
- B. I and II only
- C. II and III only
- D. I, II, and III

Question 19

Modeling the interaction between β-CD and PA produced the energy values shown below. The $\Delta G_b°$ is most likely to be:

$E_{complex}$ (kcal/mol)	$E_{\beta\text{-CD}}$ (kcal/mol)	E_{PA} (kcal/mol)
−781.2432	−743.7955	−26.6304

- A. −11 kcal/mol and spontaneous.
- B. −11 kcal/mol and non-spontaneous.
- C. −1552 kcal/mol and spontaneous.
- D. −1552 kcal/mol and non-spontaneous.

Question 20

The binding of PA to β-CD is defined by the elementary reaction shown below. Which of the following statements best describes the order of the reaction?

$$\text{PA} + \beta\text{-CD} \rightleftharpoons \beta\text{-CD-PA}$$

- A. The order of the reaction with respect to β-CD is two.
- B. The order of the reaction with respect to the reactants is one.
- C. The overall order of the reaction is two.
- D. The overall order of the reaction must be experimentally determined.

Question 21

A scientist compared the solubility of PA in a 10 mL solution of water and β-CD under neutral pH, acidic, or basic conditions, and recorded the values shown in the table below.

Condition	Solubility	Solubility time
Neutral pH	13.7 μg/mL	12 seconds
Acidic pH	17.4 μg/mL	9 seconds
Basic pH	11.1 μg/mL	17 seconds

Which of the following statements best describes the results of the experiment?

- A. The addition of an acid lowered the $\Delta G^{\ddagger}$ of the reaction.
- B. The addition of a base lowered the ΔG of the reaction.
- C. The highest $\Delta G^{\ddagger}$ was found in the neutral pH condition.
- D. The highest ΔG was found in the basic condition.

Passage 5 (Questions 22-25)

Intumescent materials undergo rapid expansion in the presence of heat, and this expansion can be mediated through both physical and chemical reactions. Industry relies on intumescent materials as flame retardants. In particular, they are positioned around wall-bound pipes, and in the event of a fire, expand. During their expansion they seal the pipe they surround, and prevent the formation of apertures which could facilitate the spread of the fire. A list of chemically activated intumescents and their properties are provided in Table 1.

Table 1 Intumescents and Associated Properties

Material	Active temperature (°C)	Expansion (% original size)	Initial density (g/m^3)
LLC	160	5000	6.3
SSC	300	1000	5.0
KKC	200	3000	7.1

Intumescence can be robustly demonstrated by burning a mixture of glucose and sodium bicarbonate. The resulting incomplete combustion leaves many organic residues, including elemental carbon. This forms a winding, snake-like object of low density because of the CO_2 gas bubbles trapped within the solid.

Sodium bicarbonate liberates CO_2 via thermal decomposition.

$$2Na_2CO_3(s) \rightleftharpoons Na_2CO_3(s) + CO_2(g) + H_2O(g)$$

Reaction 1

Glucose decomposes to elemental carbon, in the absence of oxygen, with the application of heat.

$$C_6H_{12}O_6(s) \rightarrow 6C(s) + 6H_2O(l)$$

Reaction 2

Reaction 2 typically requires a fuel source that burns intensely because of the high activation energy necessary to break carbon-carbon bonds. The thermochemical data in Table 2 lists some properties of materials at 25°C and 1 atmosphere of pressure.

Table 2 Thermochemical Properties of Selected Materials

Species	Phase	Molecular formula	$\Delta H_f°$ (kJ/mol)
Ethanol	Liquid	CH_3CH_2OH	−277.0
Glucose	Solid	$C_6H_{12}O_6$	−1271.0
Water	Liquid	H_2O	−285.8
Butane	Liquid	$CH_3CH_2CH_2CH_3$	−125.5
Carbon dioxide	Gas	CO_2	−393.5
Benzene	Liquid	C_6H_6	48.9

Question 22

What is the heat of reaction for Reaction 2?

- O **A.** −985.2 kJ/mol
- O **B.** 985.2 kJ/mol
- O **C.** −443.8 kJ/mol
- O **D.** 443.8 kJ/mol

Question 23

Reaction 1 rests at equilibrium in a sealed vessel. Which of the following changes favor the formation of sodium bicarbonate?

I. Addition of $CO_2(g)$
II. Addition of $H_2O(g)$
III. Addition of helium gas

- O **A.** I and II only
- O **B.** I and III only
- O **C.** II and III only
- O **D.** I, II, and III

Question 24

Which of the following lists the activation energy of the expansion reaction for the various intumescents in increasing order?

- O **A.** LLC, SSC, KKC
- O **B.** SSC, KKC, LLC
- O **C.** LLC, KKC, SSC
- O **D.** KKC, SSC, LLC

Question 25

Addition of a catalyst to Reaction 1:

- O **A.** increases the value of K_{eq} because $E_{a\ forwards}$ has decreased.
- O **B.** decreases the value of K_{eq} because $E_{a\ backwards}$ has decreased.
- O **C.** does not have an effect on K_{eq} while $E_{a\ forwards}$ has decreased.
- O **D.** increases the value of K_{eq} while $E_{a\ backwards}$ has decreased.

Questions 26 - 29 do not refer to a passage and are independent of each other.

Question 26

A researcher performed several trials of a multi-step reaction and determined the rate law to be first order with respect to [A], second order with respect to [B], and zero order with respect to [C]. Which of the following is most likely true of this reaction?

- O **A.** The addition of a catalyst would increase the rate of the reaction by stabilizing the products.
- O **B.** The rate is determined by [B] since it is second order while the reaction is first order with respect to [A].
- O **C.** The reaction is second order overall since the largest effect on the rate is [B] which is second order.
- O **D.** The slowest step of the reaction does not involve molecule C.

Question 27

The transition state for a reactions is:

- O **A.** a high energy intermediate compound that is capable of being isolated.
- O **B.** stabilized when the reaction is heated, which accounts for the increase in reaction rate.
- O **C.** a low energy complex that requires a sufficient activation energy to be formed and for the reaction to proceed.
- O **D.** a compound which is capable of giving rise to the reactants or products of a reaction.

Question 28

Two metabolic reactions are compared for certain parameters in a laboratory. Reaction A has a ΔG of -120 kJ/mol while reaction B has a ΔG of -67.2 kJ/mol. Which reaction will proceed faster under standard temperature and pressure?

- ○ **A.** Reaction A.
- ○ **B.** Reaction B.
- ○ **C.** They will proceed at the same rate.
- ○ **D.** Not enough information.

Question 29

Xylitol is reduced from xylose using hydrogen and the metal catalyst, Raney Ni.

OH OH OH OH O

Xylose

H_2, Raney Ni
27 atm

HO OH OH OH OH

Xylitol

All of the following are true of Raney Ni EXCEPT?

- ○ **A.** Raney Ni reduces the activation energy of the reaction.
- ○ **B.** Increasing the concentration of Raney Ni increases the rate of reaction.
- ○ **C.** Raney Ni is not consumed during this reaction.
- ○ **D.** Raney Ni has no effect on the free energy change of this reaction.

Passage 6 (Questions 30-35)

When characterizing novel proteins, it is vital to understand the thermodynamics of the proteins' folding. Knowing the thermodynamics of protein folding leads to a greater understanding of protein stability and allows for the design of novel proteins with unique functions. Protein folding is a reversible reaction; an equilibrium exists between the protein's folded and unfolded forms.

Standard Gibbs free energy change ($\Delta G°$) is an important thermodynamic parameter that predicts the stability of protein folding. Researchers can determine the Gibbs free energy change of protein folding by taking advantage of the variable fluorescence of tryptophan in nonpolar and polar environments. Tryptophan's fluorescence is less intense in polar environments than in nonpolar environments, such as those found in the core of proteins. Researchers measure tryptophan fluorescence in the presence of varying concentrations of urea, a denaturant, to infer the relative concentration of folded and unfolded protein. A typical graph of fluorescence at various urea concentrations is shown in Figure 1. The steep transition region represents an experimentally discernable equilibrium between the folded and unfolded states, while the leftmost and rightmost horizontal regions do not have experimentally discernable equilibria between the folded and unfolded states.

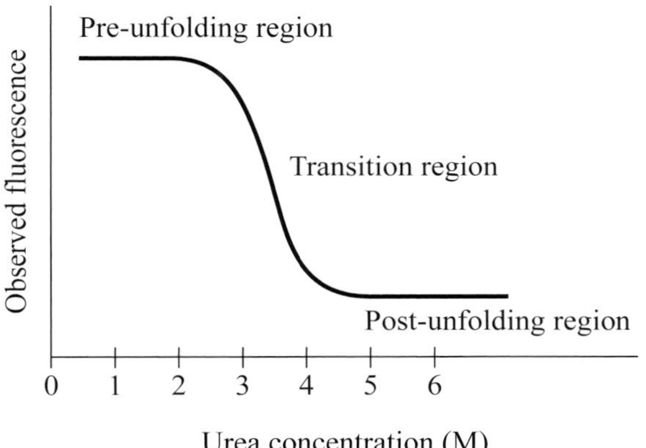

Figure 1 Tryptophan fluorescence as a function of urea concentration

The data from the transition region are used to determine the equilibrium constant and the Gibbs free energy (ΔG) of the unfolding reaction at each urea concentration. ΔG is plotted against urea concentration, and a linear regression is used to determine the ΔG when there is no urea present in the solution. Researchers applied the technique to protein Y, a 50 kDa monomer, and found the ΔG of folding is -14 kJ/mol. A graph of Gibbs free energy plotted against urea concentration for protein Y is shown in Figure 2. Using separate calorimetric methods, researchers determined that the standard enthalpy of folding of protein Y to be -20 kJ/mol.

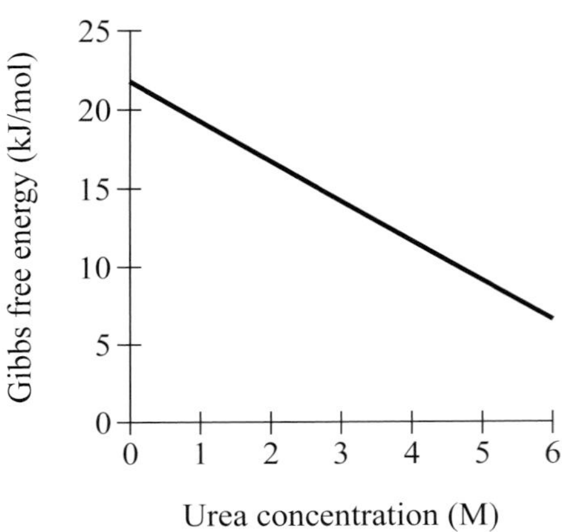

Figure 2 Gibbs free energy as a function of urea concentration for protein Y

Question 30

Which of the following choices is true of the reaction by which protein Y is folded?

I. The process is exothermic.
II. The process is exergonic.
III. The process is second order.

- **A.** I only
- **B.** II only
- **C.** I and II only
- **D.** I, II, and III

Question 31

In an open beaker, aqueous urea undergoes solvolysis in water to form ammonia and gaseous carbon dioxide. Which statement is NOT true about the reaction?

- **A.** An equilibrium will be established with equal concentrations of urea and ammonia.
- **B.** Urea is the limiting reagent.
- **C.** The solution will become basic.
- **D.** Ammonia is a nucleophile.

Question 32

What is the standard Gibbs free energy change of folding for protein Y in pure water?

- **A.** 7 kJ/mol
- **B.** 22 kJ/mol
- **C.** −7 kJ/mol
- **D.** −22 kJ/mol

Question 33

If the experiments on protein Y were conducted at 25°C, what is the change in entropy?

- **A.** −240 J/K · mol
- **B.** −20.1 J/K · mol
- **C.** 20.1 J/K · mol
- **D.** 240 J/K · mol

Question 34

Which of the following would provide the best negative control for the experiment described in the passage?

- **A.** A solution with urea and no protein
- **B.** A solution with both protein and urea
- **C.** A solution with protein and no urea
- **D.** A negative control is not needed because the reaction is in equilibrium

Question 35

A researcher running the experiment calibrated the digital thermometer and fluorometer incorrectly. The fluorometer readings were shifted up ten fluorescence intensity units and the temperature was measured at 50°C when the actual temperature was 25°C. Which of the following options are true?

I. The incorrect calibration introduces bias in the fluorescence data
II. The incorrect calibration affects accuracy in the fluorescence data
III. When calculated from K_{eq}, the Gibbs free energy at each urea concentration will be doubled

- **A.** I only
- **B.** II only
- **C.** I and II only
- **D.** I, II and III

Passage 7 (Questions 36-39)

The digestion of food in the body can be understood as a thermochemical process. In particular, the chemical changes that occur when carbohydrates or fats undergo oxidation during cellular respiration are identical to the chemical changes these materials undergo when they are burnt in the presence of oxygen. When a material is completely burned in the presence of oxygen, it is said to have combusted and follows Reaction 1 below.

$$\text{Fuel}(s/l/g) + O_2(g) \rightarrow H_2O(l) + CO_2(g)$$

Reaction 1

The energy released during these processes can be calculated with a bomb calorimeter. A bomb calorimeter consists of a tightly sealed steel vessel that is pressurized with 20 atm of oxygen. The material to be analyzed is placed in the vessel. The vessel is sealed and submerged in a thermally insulated water-bath, containing a known mass of water (m_w). An internal circuit initiates the oxidation reaction by heating a pre-weighed iron fuse. After the reaction, the temperature change of the water (ΔT), specific heat of water (c_w), heat capacity of the bomb calorimeter (C_v), standard combustion heat of iron (H_{Fe}), and the mass of the iron fuse (m_{Fe}) can be used to calculate the energy released during the combustion according to Equation 1.

$$q = \Delta T(m_w c_w - C_v) - H_{Fe} m_{Fe}$$

Equation 1

A study was conducted to investigate the nutritional value of a common saturated fatty acid, $CH_3(CH_2)_{16}COOH$, found in dairy butter, by utilizing a bomb calorimeter. Figure 1 shows temperature measurements of the water during the course of the experiment.

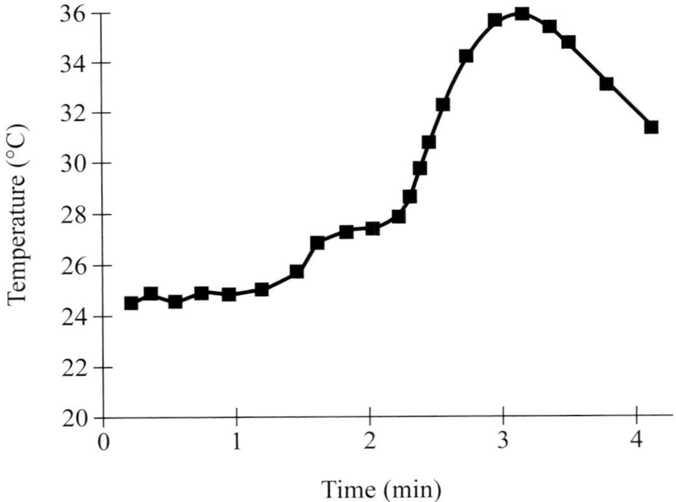

Figure 1 Temperature measurements during combustion

Question 36

What assumptions must be true for Equation 1 to be valid?

I. The mass of the analyte is known.

II. The saturation vapor pressure of water has been reached in the calorimeter before the reaction begins and remains saturated during the course of the reaction.

III. The iron fuse is completely oxidized during the reaction.

- **A.** I only
- **B.** III only
- **C.** II and III only
- **D.** I, II, and III

Question 37

Which value of ΔT should be used to determine the energy released during the experiment described in the passage?

- **A.** 11°C
- **B.** –11°C
- **C.** 7°C
- **D.** –7°C

Question 38

Several hours after the experiment is performed, the water bath is observed to be at room temperature. The change in internal energy of the system:

- **A.** is greater than zero, because energy was gained from the surroundings during the oxidation reaction.
- **B.** is zero because no energy was exchanged with the surroundings.
- **C.** is zero because no PV work was performed.
- **D.** is less than 0 because energy was exchanged with the surroundings.

Question 39

In what order did energy change form during the ignition of the fuse as described in the passage?

- **A.** Thermal, electrical, chemical, thermal
- **B.** Electrical, thermal, chemical, thermal
- **C.** Electrical, chemical, thermal,
- **D.** Chemical, thermal

Questions 40 - 43 do not refer to a passage and are independent of each other.

Question 40

The order of the reaction with respect to molecular oxygen in the following elementary equation is:

$$2SO_2(g) + O_2(g) \leftrightarrow 2SO_3(g)$$

- O **A.** zero.
- O **B.** one.
- O **C.** two.
- O **D.** three.

Question 41

Decreasing the temperature of the reaction that converts pyruvate to lactic acid is LEAST likely to:

- O **A.** decrease the concentration lactic acid.
- O **B.** increase the concentration of pyruvate.
- O **C.** decrease the rate of the reaction.
- O **D.** increase the rate of the reaction.

Question 42

Hydrogen peroxide also decomposes, releasing oxygen, as shown in the reaction below.

$$2H_2O_2(aq) \rightarrow 2H_2O(l) + O_2(g)$$

Addition of the enzyme, catalase, to a solution of hydrogen peroxide is expected to:

I. increase the rate of this decomposition reaction relative to this reaction being performed without catalase.

II. allow this decomposition reaction to proceed at a lower temperature relative to this reaction being performed without catalase.

III. favor the products of this reaction at equilibrium relative to this reaction being performed without catalase.

- O **A.** I only
- O **B.** III only
- O **C.** I and II only
- O **D.** I, II and III

Question 43

Since there are 3 hydrogen bonds between cytosine and guanine DNA bases compared to 2 between adenine and thymine base pairs, how does denaturation of similar length DNA strands, one of which has a higher C/G constant, compare in terms of enthalpy and entropy?

- O **A.** Denaturation of the strand with higher C/G constant content will have a greater enthalpic change and greater entropic change.
- O **B.** Denaturation of the strand with higher C/G constant content will have a greater enthalpic change and a similar entropic change.
- O **C.** Denaturation of the strand with higher C/G constant content will have a lower enthalpic change and greater entropic change.
- O **D.** Denaturation of the strand with higher C/G constant content will have a lower enthalpic change and lower entropic change.

Passage 8 (Questions 44-48)

Heat shock protein 90 (Hsp90) is a component of the cellular chaperone machinery. Two groups of natural product inhibitors of Hsp90, based on geldanamycin and radicicol, have been discovered that bind to the N-terminal domain ATP-binding pocket. Experience with the natural products generated interest in alternative chemotypes, and the first synthetic inhibitors (ICPDs) that bind the ATP-binding site at the NH_2 terminus of Hsp90 have been designed based on a purine scaffold. Despite these achievements, full thermodynamic description of the ligand binding to Hsp90 is rather fragmented despite its importance for structure-based drug development.

The energetics of ICPD47 compound binding to Hsp90 was measured using a calorimeter in two unique buffer solutions and over a wide range of pH values. The observed enthalpy of binding is shown in Figure 1.

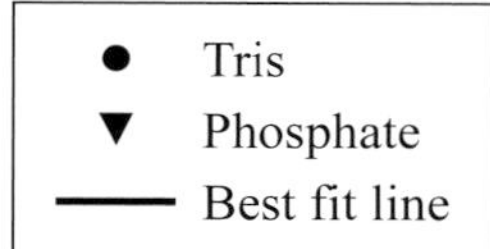

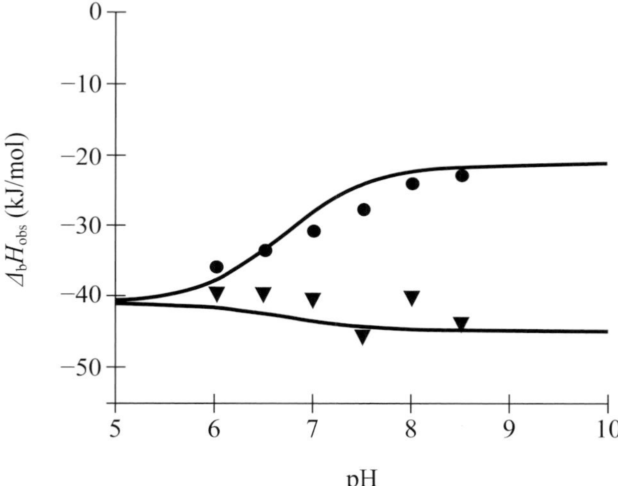

Figure 1 The pH and buffer effects of ICPD inhibitor binding to Hsp90

After characterizing the enthalpy changes associated with ICPD47 binding, scientists measured the thermodynamic properties of other ICPD inhibitors to various isoforms of HSP90, as shown in Figure 2.

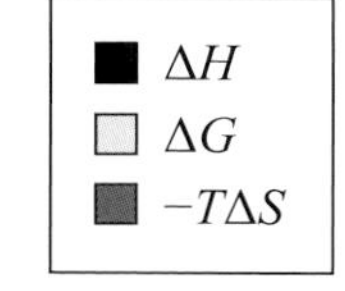

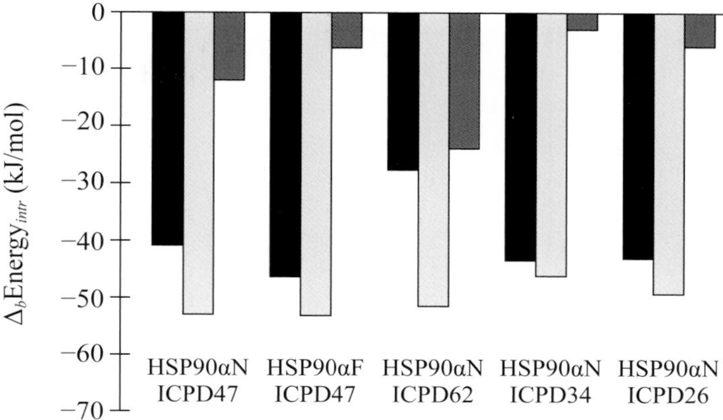

Figure 2 Relative contributions of various thermodynamic properties of ICPD compound to Hsp90 at 37°C

This passage is adapted from "Thermodynamics of Aryl-Dihydroxyphenyl-Thiadiazole Binding to Human Hsp90." Kazlauskaz E, Petrikaite V, Michailoviene V, Revuckiene J, Matuliene J, et al. *PLoS ONE*. 2012. 7(5) doi:10.1371/journal.pone.0036899 for use under the terms of the Creative Commons CC BY 3.0 license (http://creativecommons.org/licenses/by/3.0/legalcode).

Question 44

Which of the following statements best describes the results shown in Figure 1?

- O **A.** As the pH increases, the entropy of ICPD47 binding to Hsp90 increases.
- O **B.** As pH decreases, the binding of ICPD47 to Hsp90 becomes more exothermic.
- O **C.** As pH increases, the binding of ICPD47 to Hsp90 becomes more endothermic.
- O **D.** As pH decreases, the entropy of ICPD47 binding to Hsp90 increases and the reaction becomes more exothermic.

Question 45

How does the entropy change when geldanamycin binds the ATP-binding pocket of Hsp90?

- O **A.** The entropy of the reaction increases and the entropy of the universe increases.
- O **B.** The entropy of the reaction decreases and the entropy of the universe increases.
- O **C.** The entropy of the reaction increases and the entropy of the universe decreases.
- O **D.** The entropy of the reaction decreases and the entropy of the universe decreases.

Question 46

The binding of ICPD26 is likely to be driven by:

- O **A.** enthalpy more than entropy.
- O **B.** entropy more than enthalpy.
- O **C.** entropy and enthalpy equally.
- O **D.** neither entropy nor enthalpy.

Question 47

A scientist attempts to replicate the findings shown in Figure 2 with a known inhibitor of Hsp90, radicicol (shown below), in a solution with a pH of 12 and finds that the enthalpy change is greater than that of the ICPD compounds, even when controlling for drug and protein concentration. Which of the following statements is a possible explanation for the findings?

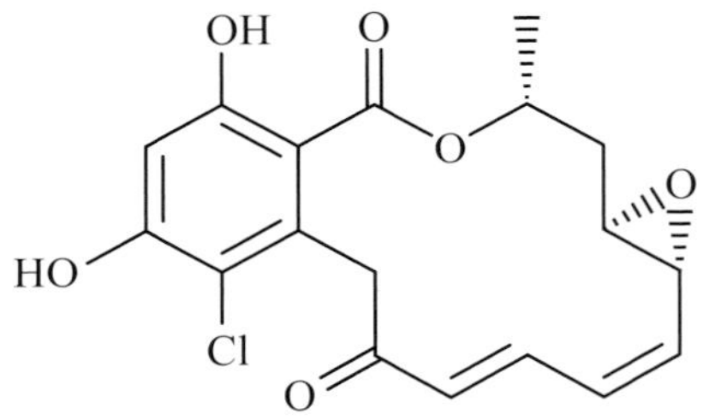

- O **A.** Radicicol dissociates in water to increase the entropy change of the reaction.
- O **B.** The binding of radicicol requires an initial addition of heat to overcome the repulsive forces between Hsp90 and radicicol.
- O **C.** The high concentration of hydroxide cleaves the epoxide ring, releasing additional heat.
- O **D.** The reaction between radicicol and Hsp90 is spontaneous, while the reaction between the ICPD compounds and Hsp90 is not.

Question 48

Instead of using a calorimeter to conduct the experiment, a scientist conducts the reaction in a sealed chamber with a moveable piston. Over the course of experiment one, the piston is most likely to:

- O **A.** remain stationary.
- O **B.** rise then fall back to the starting position.
- O **C.** fall then rise back to the starting position.
- O **D.** continue rising.

Passage 9 (Questions 49-52)

The enzyme heparanase and its substrate, heparin sulfate (HS), play key roles during sepsis. Heparanase acts on HS liberating HS-fragments, triggering the pro-inflammatory response.

Researchers interested in anti-inflammatory agents designed a synthetic peptide (Compound 1, Figure 1). Its interaction with HS fragments was measured using isothermal calorimetric titration.

Figure 1 Structure of synthetic peptide, Compound 1

Isothermal calorimetric titrations (ICTs) measure the power required to maintain the same temperature in an experimental cell and a reference cell. Before adding materials to the experimental cell, the same power is applied to each cell and is continuously applied to the reference cell during the experiment. Depending on the type of reaction, the power applied to the experimental cell will vary to maintain isothermality with the reference cell: exothermic reactions decrease its power requirements, and endothermic reactions increase them. The experimental cell contained HS fragments (L) at 37°C. Fixed volumes of a solution containing Compound 1 (M) at 37°C were added until the only change in solution temperature was due to solvation effects, and not macromolecule—ligand binding processes, as shown in Reaction 1.

$$M + L \leftrightarrow ML$$

Reaction 1

The first enthalpic measurements obtained represent the ΔH of this macromolecule—ligand binding process at body temperature, as all added peptide initially reacts with the excess ligand. Thermodynamic information from the ICT is shown in Table 1 and Figure 2.

Table 1 Thermodynamic Parameters of Compound 1 Binding to HS Fragments

Trial	N (w/w ratio)	K_a (M^{-1})	K_D (M)	cal/(mol · K)
1	0.511	1.93×10^6	5.18×10^{-7}	4.46
2	0.475	1.52×10^7	6.57×10^{-8}	6.42
3	0.547	1.55×10^7	6.45×10^{-8}	10.80
4	0.534	1.20×10^7	8.33×10^{-8}	6.77

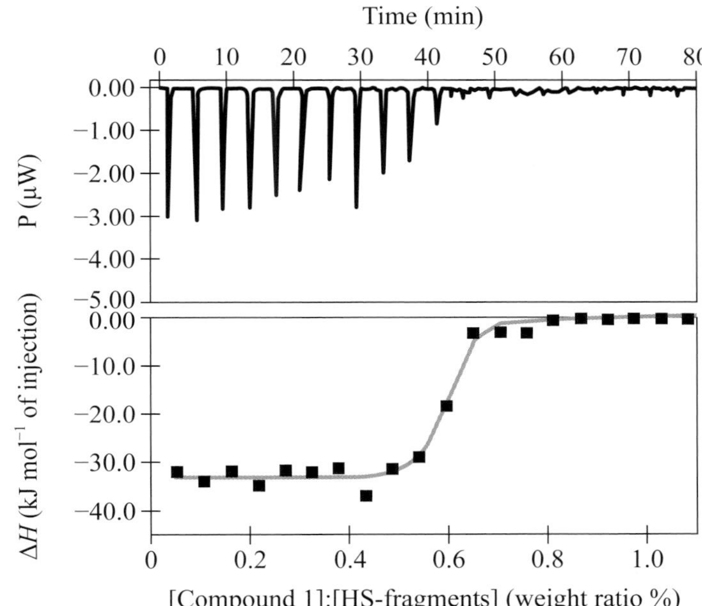

Figure 2 Power applied to experimental cell (top) and enthalpy change of Reaction 1 (bottom)

The dissociation constant K_D of this reaction is the reciprocal of the association constant K_a = [ML]/[M][L]. The free energy change of this reaction is given in Equation 1.

$$\Delta G = RT\ln(K_D) = \Delta H - T\Delta S$$

Equation 1

It was observed that the interaction between Compound 1 and HS-fragments is a result of coulomb binding of the positive peptide charges with the negatively charged sulfate groups from HS-fragments at physiological pH.

This passage was adapted from "The Synthetic Antimicrobial Peptide 19-2.5 Interacts with Heparanase and Heparan Sulfate in Murine and Human Sepsis." Martin L, De Santis R, Koczera P, Simons N, Haase H, Heinbockel L, et al. *PLoS ONE*. 2015. 10(11) doi:10.1371/journal.pone.0143583 for use under the terms of the Creative Commons CC BY 4.0 Attribution license (http://creativecommons.org/licenses/by/4.0/legalcode).

Question 49

What is the free energy change associated with the interaction of HS fragments and the synthetic peptide during Trial 1? (Note: 4.2 J = 1 cal)

- A. −192.7 cal/mol
- B. −9002 cal/mol
- C. −1415 cal/mol
- D. −7784 cal/mol

Question 50

If the solution that contained Compound 1 had a lower temperature than the experimental cell prior to its addition:

- A. the ICT apparatus would apply less power to the experimental cell.
- B. the measured value for ΔH would have a greater magnitude.
- C. there would be no change in the measured value of ΔH.
- D. the measured value for ΔH would have a lower magnitude.

Question 51

Which of the following expressions is equivalent to the free energy change associated with the interaction of HS fragments and the synthetic peptide?

- A. $1/RT\ln(K_a)$
- B. $-RT\ln(K_a)$
- C. $RT\ln(K_a)$
- D. RTe^{Ka}

Question 52

Suppose two experimental cells, X and Y, are connected to the same reference cell, and all cells contain the same mass of liquid. The reference cell and X contain mercury, but Y contains benzene. If X is in thermal equilibrium with the reference cell, and Y is in thermal equilibrium with the reference cell, what is true? (Note: $c_{Hg} = 0.14$ J/g • °C and $c_{benzene} = 1.8$ J/g • °C)

- A. For a given application of power, Y's temperature will increase more than X's.
- B. The particles in X and Y have the same average kinetic energy.
- C. The particles in X and Y do not necessarily share the same temperature.
- D. The particles in X and the reference cell share the same temperature and average kinetic energy; those in Y only share the same temperature with X and the reference cell.

Passage 10 (Questions 53-56)

Hypoxia, the deprivation of oxygen, can be lethal to cells. Without adequate oxygen, cellular respiration cannot occur, and intracellular pH falls inactivating and denaturing life sustaining enzymes and proteins. Neuronal and glial cells die via a different mechanism due to their inability to perform anaerobic respiration. Excess extracellular glutamate triggers the influx of ionic calcium, which leads to the release of ATP into the extracellular environment. This extracellular ATP activates apoptotic and necrotic cascade pathways. Hypoxia is extremely lethal to brain cells and kills them within minutes.

For individuals who are at risk of being trapped in low oxygen environments, such as miners, astronauts, and submariners, oxygen "candles" can be lit to temporarily protect them from hypoxic conditions until oxygen supply is restored to normal or help arrives.

Oxygen candles consist of a mix of sodium chlorate and iron filaments, along with a binding agent. Ignition with the use of a spark plug serves to initiate the decomposition shown in Reaction 1.

$$NaClO_3(s) \rightarrow NaCl(s) + \frac{3}{2}O_2(g) \quad \Delta H° = -45.76 \text{ kJ/mol}$$

Reaction 1

The oxygen gas and heat produced during this reaction oxidize the iron filaments through Reaction 2, releasing even more heat, necessary to propagate Reaction 1. An excess quantity of $NaClO_3$ within the candle ensures adequate oxygen production despite Reaction 2 consuming some oxygen.

$$4Fe(s) + 3O_2(g) \rightarrow 2Fe_2O_3(s)$$

Reaction 2

Question 53

Based on the thermochemical equations below, what is the heat of reaction of Reaction 2?

$$2Fe(s) + 6H_2O(l) \rightarrow 2Fe(OH)_3(s) + 3H_2(g) \quad \Delta H = 321.0 \text{ kJ/mol}$$
$$2H_2O(l) \rightarrow 2H_2(g) + O_2(g) \quad \Delta H = 571.7 \text{ kJ/mol}$$
$$Fe_2O_3(s) + 3H_2O(l) \rightarrow 2Fe(OH)_3(s) \quad \Delta H = 288.6 \text{ kJ/mol}$$

- A. 2934.3 kJ/mol
- B. 1779.9 kJ/mol
- C. –1648.2 kJ/mol
- D. –493.8 kJ/mol

TEST 4A

Question 54

The formation of salt from its constituent elements is highly exothermic, as shown.

$$2Na(s) + Cl_2(g) \rightarrow 2\ NaCl(s) \quad \Delta H_f^\circ = -411\ kJ/mol$$

What is ΔH° of the proposed reaction:

$$2Na(s) + Cl_2(g) + 3O_2(g) \rightarrow 2NaClO_3(s)?$$

- O **A.** –365.2 kJ/mol
- O **B.** –319.5 kJ/mol
- O **C.** –456.8 kJ/mol
- O **D.** –502.5 kJ/mol

Question 55

After lighting an oxygen candle in a sealed mine, the surrounding air is observed to be warmer. This observation:

- O **A.** demonstrates the first law of thermodynamics, as the energy of the candle-mine system becomes more spread throughout the system.
- O **B.** demonstrates the third law of thermodynamics, as the energy of the candle-mine system is constant, despite less energy being in the candle.
- O **C.** demonstrates the second law of thermodynamics, as the energy of the candle-mine system becomes more spread throughout the system.
- O **D.** demonstrates the zeroth law of thermodynamics, as the energy of the candle-mine system is constant, despite less energy being in the candle.

Question 56

Which of the following statements best describe Reaction 1?

- O **A.** Reaction 1 is only spontaneous at high temperatures because of its positive change in enthalpy.
- O **B.** Reaction 1 is only spontaneous at low temperatures because of its negative change in enthalpy.
- O **C.** Reaction 1 is spontaneous at all temperatures despite its negative change in entropy because it has a negative change in enthalpy.
- O **D.** Reaction 1 is spontaneous at all temperatures because it has a negative change in enthalpy and a positive change in entropy.

Questions 57 - 59 do not refer to a passage and are independent of each other.

Question 57

Breathing into a paper bag treats psychologically induced hyperventilation. If the bag's initial volume was 0.1 L, and its final volume is 2.4 L, how much work was done on the bag? (Note: 1 atm = 10^5 Pa)

- O **A.** 2.3×10^5 J
- O **B.** 2.3 J
- O **C.** 230 J
- O **D.** 2.4 J

Question 58

Which of the following is the change in enthalpy for the simple reaction shown below?

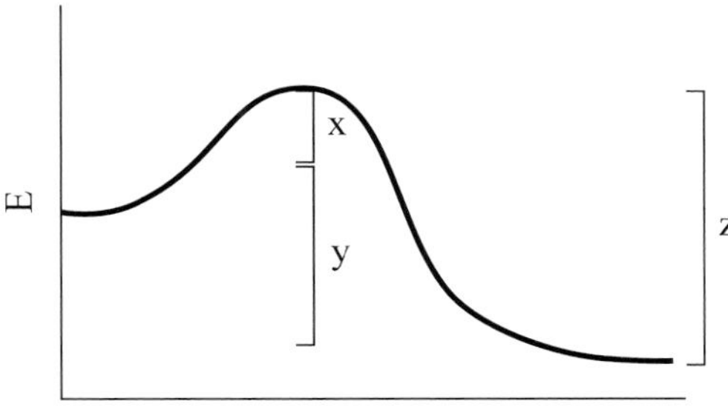

- O **A.** Z – Y
- O **B.** Z – X
- O **C.** X + Y
- O **D.** X/2 + Y

Question 59

Which step during the formation of a macromolecule-ligand complex is an example of the second law of thermodynamics?

- O **A.** Two separate molecules come together to form a single larger complex.
- O **B.** The size of the aqueous solvation layer on each of the two molecules increases when they combine to form a single complex.
- O **C.** The size of the aqueous solvation layer on each of the two molecules decreases when they combine to form a single complex.
- O **D.** A single larger complex is broken into two separate smaller molecules.

STOP. If you finish before time is called, check your work. You may go back to any question in this test.

ANSWERS & EXPLANATIONS for Test 4A can be found on p. 286.

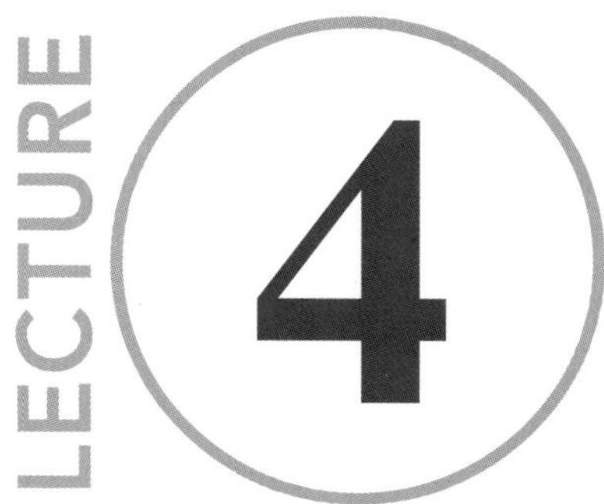

Thermodynamics and Kinetics

TEST 4B

Time: 45 minutes
Questions 1–29

DIRECTIONS: Most of the questions in this test section are grouped with a passage. Read the passage, then select the best answer to each question. Some questions are independent of any passage and of one another. Select the best answer to each of these questions. If you are unsure of an answer, rule out incorrect choices and select from the remaining options. Indicate your selection beside the option you choose. A periodic table can be found on the last page of this book for you to use at any point during this test section.

Passage 1 (Questions 1-4)

DNA is continuously damaged by reactive oxygen species (ROS) generated by UV light, ionizing radiation, and during metabolism. These changes are linked to various health issues, including melanoma. Among the various products of oxidative stress, 7,8-dihydro-8-oxoguanosine (oxoG) is the most commonly found. It causes pre-mutagenic DNA lesions since oxoG is able to mispair with adenine, generating G/C to T/A transversion mutations. As is the case of most oxidized bases, oxoG is primarily removed in the base excision repair (BER) pathway. This pathway is initiated by the recognition of the modified bases by specific DNA glycosylases. In human cells, 8-oxoguanine DNA glycosylase HOGG1 accomplishes the excision of oxoG residues. HOGG1 is a bifunctional enzyme, possessing DNA glycosylase activity (step 1, hydrolysis of the N-glycosidic bond of the damaged nucleotide resulting in formation of the abasic product) and AP lyase activity (step 2, elimination of the 39-phosphate) shown in Figure 1, with a greater impact on hydrolysis of the N-glycosidic bond.

Researchers performed experiments to characterize the thermodynamic and kinetic properties of the hydrolysis and elimination reactions. Based on their findings, the hydrolysis of the N-glycosidic bond was determined to behave according to second-order kinetics. Thermodynamic properties are shown in Table 1.

Table 1 Thermodynamic Properties of Step 1 and 2

Step	ΔG (kcal/mol)	ΔH (kcal/mol)	ΔS (cal/K · mol)	ΔG of uncatalyzed transition state
1	−6.4	−2.8	11.2	19.6
2	−0.2	2.1	7.7	21.0

This passage was adapted from "Thermodynamics of the DNA Damage Repair Steps of Human 8-Oxoguanine DNA Glycosylase." Kuznetsov NA, Kuznetsova AA, Vorobjev YN, Krasnoperov LN and Fedorova OS. *PLoS ONE*. 2014. 9(6) doi:10.1371/journal.pone.0098495 for use under the terms of the Creative Commons CC BY 4.0 license (http://creativecommons.org/licenses/by/4.0/legalcode).

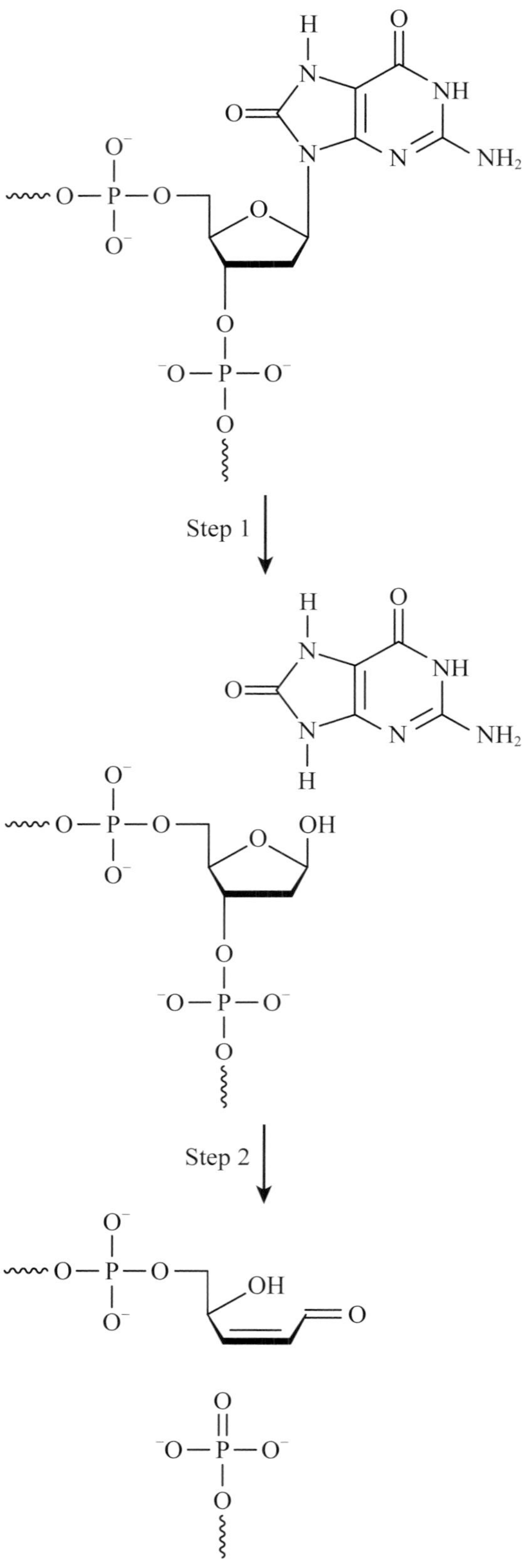

Step 1

Step 2

Figure 1 Steps 1 and 2 catalyzed by HOGG1

TEST 4B

Question 1

Which of the following processes does NOT contribute to the ΔH of step 1?

- A. The energy absorbed when the C–N bond is broken.
- B. The energy released when the C–O bond is formed.
- C. The energy released when the N–H bond is formed.
- D. The energy released when the O–H bond is formed.

Question 2

Based on the passage, which of the following statements best describes the effect that HOGG1 has on steps 1 and 2 in Figure 1?

- A. HOGG1 has a greater effect on the equilibrium of step 1 than that of 2.
- B. HOGG1 has a greater effect on the equilibrium of step 2 than that of 1.
- C. HOGG1 has a greater effect on the speed of step 1 than that of 2.
- D. HOGG1 has a greater effect on the speed of step 2 than that of 1.

Question 3

What is the closest value to the temperature at which the studies on step 1 were performed?

- A. 100 K
- B. 273 K
- C. 320 K
- D. 400 K

Question 4

Which of the following statements is true about the thermodynamics of steps 1 and 2?

- A. Step 1 is never spontaneous.
- B. Step 1 is only spontaneous at high temperatures.
- C. Step 2 is only spontaneous at high temperatures.
- D. Step 2 is not spontaneous at all temperatures.

Passage 2 (Questions 5-9)

Thermoregulatory responses are a key class of homeostatic reflexes, which are necessary for survival and health. If the body's temperature falls below 37°C, shivering, hyperventilation, vasoconstriction of cutaneous blood vessels, and blood diversion from the extremities result. If the body's temperature exceeds that threshold, sweating and vasodilation of cutaneous blood vessels occur. When these compensatory mechanisms fail to return the body to 37°C, hypo and hyperthermia can occur.

To survive harsh environmental conditions, humans build insulated homes. The ability of materials to insulate can be described by their R-value. R-values can be calculated using the equation $R = \frac{\Delta T}{Q_a}$, where ΔT is the temperature difference between different sides of the material, and Q_a is the heat transferred through the material per unit area of material as a result of the temperature difference. Q_a is described in W/m^2.

Some common R-values are listed in the table below:

Table 1 R-values of Common Materials

Material	R-value
Wood	1.25
Brick	0.11
Drywall	1.00
Sand and gravel	0.59

Insulated homes protect their occupants from the intense heat of the sun. This heat can be approximated with the Stefan-Boltzman equation, $P = 4\sigma\pi r^2 T^4$, where P is the power the sun radiates, σ is the Stefan-Boltzman constant, which is equal to 5.67×10^{-8} W m^{-2} K^{-4}, r is the radius of the sun, and T is the temperature of the sun.

During brick manufacturing, bricks are made lightweight by incorporating hydrogen bubbles inside of them through Reaction 1. This production increases their R-value.

$$2Al(s) + 3H_2SO_4(aq) \rightleftharpoons Al_2(SO_4)_3(aq) + 3H_2(g)$$

Reaction 1

Question 5

A distant star is twice the temperature and half the radius of the sun. It radiates:

- A. the same amount of heat as the sun per minute.
- B. 64 times the heat of the sun per minute.
- C. 16 times the heat of the sun per minute.
- D. 4 times the heat of the sun per minute.

Question 6

Compared to wood, brick:

- A. transfers heat via conduction less effectively.
- B. transfers heat via convection less effectively.
- C. transfers heat via conduction more effectively.
- D. transfers heat via convection more effectively.

Question 7

The first step in synthetic drywall production is the following reaction:

$$CaCO_3(s) + SO_2(g) \rightarrow CaSO_3(s) + CO_2(g)$$

What is the equilibrium constant?

- A. $K = \frac{[CaSO_3][CO_2]}{[CaCO_3][SO_2]}$
- B. $K = \frac{[CO_2]}{[CaCO_3][SO_2]}$
- C. $K = \frac{[SO_2]}{[CO_2]}$
- D. $K = \frac{[CO_2]}{[SO_2]}$

Question 8

When Reaction 1 starts producing hydrogen gas, what is true?

- A. $K_{eq} > Q$
- B. $K_{eq} = Q$
- C. $K_{eq} < Q$
- D. $K_{eq} = 1$

Question 9

An energy coordinate diagram of Reaction 1 is shown. The arrow indicates:

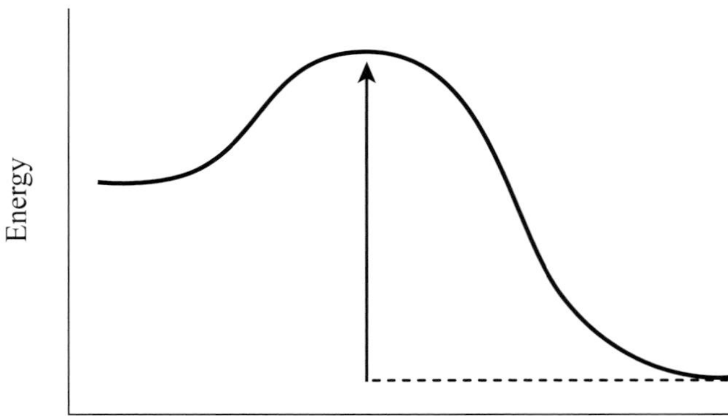

- A. $\Delta H_{forwards}$.
- B. $E_{a\ forwards}$.
- C. $E_{a\ reverse}$.
- D. $\Delta H_{reverse}$.

Passage 3 (Questions 10-13)

Phosgene is a valuable reagent in organic synthesis and can be used to couple bisphenol A (BPA) during polymerization reactions, which give rise to thermoplastic materials. Despite its utility, phosgene is an immensely toxic gas, with a lethal human dose at the 3 ppm level. Its toxicity stems from its ability to rapidly denature the proteins of the pulmonary alveoli when it is inhaled. In particular, phosgene undergoes nucleophilic attack by the protein's amino groups and forms urea-like linkages (Figure 1). When phosgene is required in a reaction, it is usually carefully manufactured at the reaction site, in order to avoid any accidents which may occur during transportation.

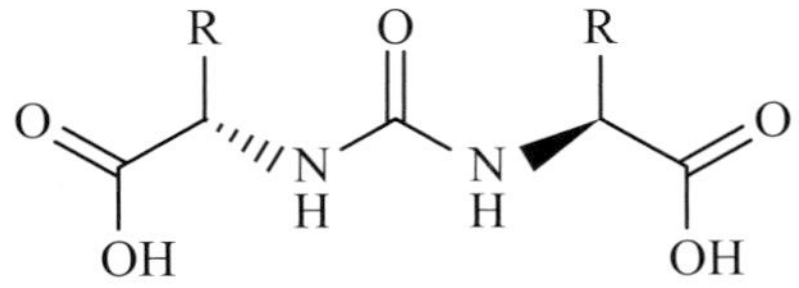

Figure 1 Urea-like linkage of generic amino acids after exposure to phosgene

Phosgene is manufactured by mixing carbon monoxide and chlorine gas in the presence of a high surface area carbon catalyst. Its net reaction is shown in Reaction 1.

$$CO(g) + Cl_2(g) \rightleftharpoons COCl_2(g)\ (\Delta H_{reaction} = -107.6\text{ kJ/mol})$$

Reaction 1

Its formation is believed to proceed sequentially, following the steps below:

$$Cl_2(g) \leftrightarrow 2Cl(g)$$

Step 1

$$Cl(g) + CO(g) \leftrightarrow COCl(g)$$

Step 2

$$COCl(g) + Cl_2(g) \leftrightarrow COCl_2(g) + Cl(g)$$

Step 3

The overall order of the reaction of phosgene formation from these precursors is a non-integer value. Below is the experimentally determined rate law:

$$\frac{\Delta[COCl_2]}{\Delta t} = k[Cl_2]^{3/2}[CO]$$

Equation 1

Question 10

What effect would doubling the concentration of $Cl_2(g)$ have on the rate of this reaction?

- A. It would increase the rate by a factor of 2.
- B. It would increase the rate by a factor of $2\sqrt{2}$.
- C. It would increase the rate by a factor of $3\sqrt{2}$.
- D. It would increase the rate by a factor of $2\sqrt{3}$.

Question 11

During phosgene synthesis, the volume of the reaction vessel was quadrupled while the temperature remained constant. The value of K_{eq}:

- O **A.** was reduced by a factor of 2.
- O **B.** was reduced by a factor of 4.
- O **C.** was reduced by a factor of 16.
- O **D.** stayed the same.

Question 12

The reaction coordinate energy diagram for the formation of phosgene is shown below. After removal of the high surface area carbon, which of the following best predicts the new reaction diagram?

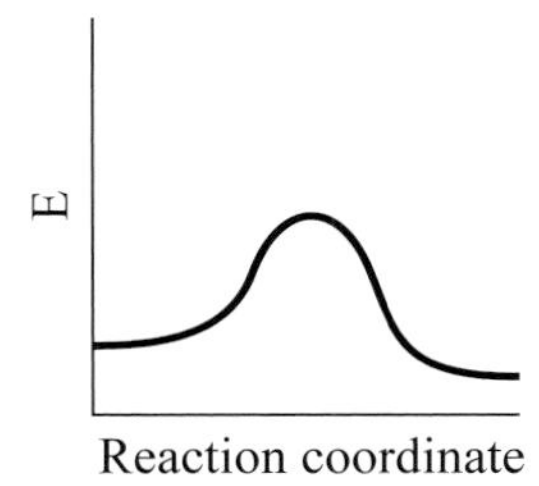

O **A.**

O **B.**

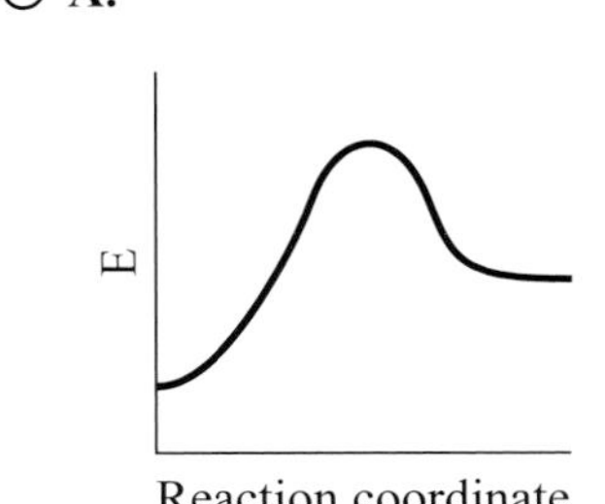

E

Reaction coordinate

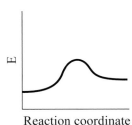

O **C.**

O **D.**

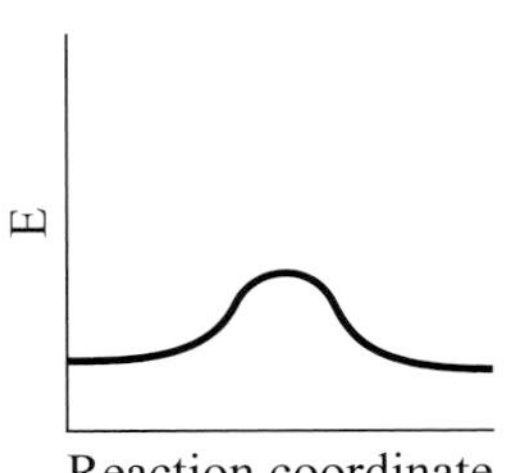

E

Reaction coordinate

Question 13

Heating the vessel in which Reaction 1 occurs is expected:

- O **A.** to increase the value of K_{eq}, increasing the equilibrium concentration of products.
- O **B.** to decrease the value of K_{eq}, increasing the equilibrium concentration of products.
- O **C.** to increase the value of K_{eq}, increasing the equilibrium concentration of reactants.
- O **D.** to decrease the value of K_{eq}, increasing the equilibrium concentration of reactants.

Questions 14 - 17 do not refer to a passage and are independent of each other.

Question 14

Which of the following correctly depicts the entropy of a solid as it is converted from a solid to liquid to gas via heat?

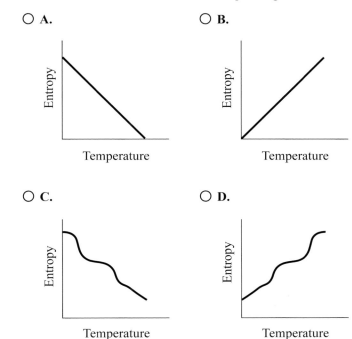

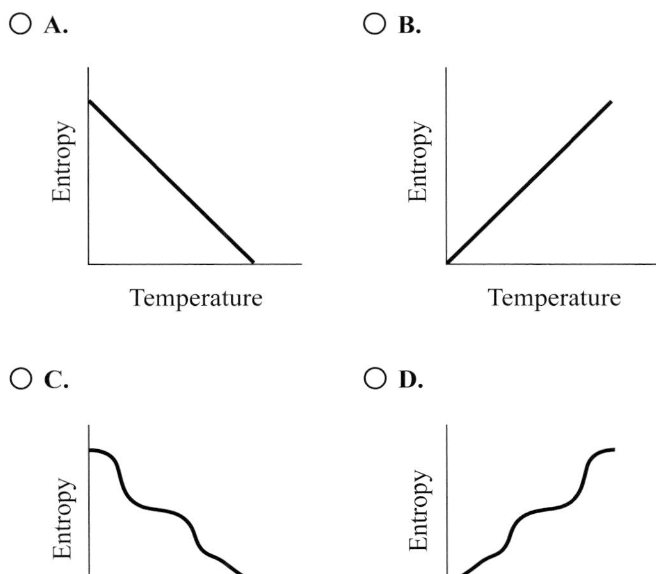

Question 15

NH_4NO_3 dissolves in aqueous solutions with $\Delta H_{solution} = 26.4$ kJ/mol. To occur at 25°C, this reaction must exceed what minimum change in entropy?

- O **A.** –0.09 kJ/K · mol
- O **B.** 0.09 kJ/K · mol
- O **C.** –1.1 kJ/K · mol
- O **D.** 1.1 kJ/K · mol

Question 16

Lactic acid metabolism can be described by Reaction 1, and glucose metabolism can be described by Reaction 2:

$$C_3H_6O_3(s) + 3O_2(g) \rightarrow 3CO_2(g) + 3H_2O(l)\ \Delta H = -1344 \text{ kJ/mol}$$

Reaction 1

$$C_6H_{12}O_6(s) + 6O_2(g) \rightarrow 6CO_2(g) + 6H_2O(l)\ \Delta H = -2808 \text{ kJ/mol}$$

Reaction 2

What energy is released during anaerobic respiration, i.e.

$$C_6H_{12}O_6(s) \rightarrow 2C_3H_6O_3(s)?$$

- O **A.** −1464 kJ/mol
- O **B.** −120 kJ/mol
- O **C.** −5496 kJ/mol
- O **D.** −4152 kJ/mol

Question 17

H. pylori produce an enzyme, called urease, that is capable of hydrolyzing urea $(NH_2)_2CO$, to form carbon dioxide and ammonia. What is the approximate ΔH of this reaction? (bond energies in kJ/mol: N–H = 391; N–C = 305; O–H = 463; C–O = 146; C=O = 799)

- O **A.** −45 kJ
- O **B.** 45 kJ
- O **C.** 1128 kJ
- O **D.** −1128 kJ

TEST 4B

Passage 4 (Questions 18-21)

Cellular metabolism involves the joint activity of hundreds of enzyme-catalyzed biochemical reactions. A system-wide understanding of cellular metabolism requires the quantification of substrate flux through these reactions and the concentrations of the corresponding metabolites. For steady-state systems, substantial insight into metabolic reaction rates can be achieved through constraints imposed by the law of mass balance under a steady-state assumption: for each internal metabolite, total influx must equal total efflux. An alternative approach involves genome-scale modeling of metabolite concentrations by accounting for thermodynamic considerations. These methods capitalize on the fact that the net flux direction depends on the thermodynamic driving force, $\Delta G'$, which is calculated according to Equation 1:

$$\Delta G' = \Delta G'^{\circ} + RT \ln Q$$

Equation 1

As the cytoplasm is a dilute aqueous solution, the chemical activity of various glycolysis intermediates is approximately equal to their absolute concentrations. Some glycolytic substrates include glucose and glycogen, the storage form of glucose, while two important enzymes are hexokinase and aldolase. Modeling the flux through metabolic pathways often involves an understanding of both the enzyme levels and metabolite concentrations, as shown in Equation 2. Equation 2 approximates the minimal enzyme level (E) required for maintaining a given net reaction rate (v) and the associated thermodynamic driving force ($-\Delta G'$). The kinetic effect of substrate and product concentrations is denoted by w^+.

$$E = \frac{v}{w^+(1 - e^{\frac{\Delta G'}{RT}})}$$

Equation 2

This passage is adapted from "Steady-State Metabolite Concentrations Reflect a Balance between Maximizing Enzyme Efficiency and Minimizing Total Metabolite Load." Tepper N, Noor E, Amador-Noguez D, Haraldsdottir H, Milo R, et al. *PLoS ONE*. 2013. doi:10.1371/journal.pone.0075370 for use under the terms of the Creative Commons CC BY 4.0 license (http://creativecommons.org/licenses/by/4.0/legalcode).

Question 18

A scientist modeled the flux through glycolysis at 39°C and 37°C in order to predict the rate of transcription of glycolytic genes during extended exercise and rest, respectively. Which of the following statements most likely describes the results of the experiment ?

- O **A.** A higher concentration of glucose is present in cells during exercise versus rest.
- O **B.** A higher concentration of hexokinase is present in cells during exercise versus rest.
- O **C.** A higher concentration of glycogen is present in cells during exercise versus rest.
- O **D.** A lower concentration of aldolase is present in cells during exercise versus rest.

Question 19

The conversion between $dADP^{2-}$ and $dATP^{3-}$ is shown in the reaction below and is part of glycolysis. This reaction is most likely to be:

$$ATP^{3-} + dADP^{2-} \rightleftharpoons ADP^{2-} + \frac{1}{2}dATP^{3-} + \frac{1}{2}dAMP^{-}$$

$$\Delta G° = 22.8 \text{ kJ/mol}$$

- ○ **A.** spontaneous and thermodynamically favorable.
- ○ **B.** spontaneous and thermodynamically unfavorable.
- ○ **C.** non-spontaneous and thermodynamically favorable.
- ○ **D.** non-spontaneous and thermodynamically unfavorable.

Question 20

The first step of glycolysis occurs by the reaction shown below.

$$\text{Glucose} + \text{ATP} \rightleftharpoons \text{Glucose-6-P} + \text{ADP}$$

The reaction quotient of the initial reaction is most likely:

- ○ **A.** $Q = \frac{[\text{Glucose}][\text{ATP}]}{[\text{G6P}][\text{ADP}]}$
- ○ **B.** $K = \frac{[\text{G6P}][\text{ADP}]}{[\text{Glucose}][\text{ATP}]}$
- ○ **C.** $K = \frac{[\text{G6P}][\text{ATP}]}{[\text{Glucose}][\text{ADP}]}$
- ○ **D.** $Q = \frac{[\text{G6P}][\text{ADP}]}{[\text{Glucose}][\text{ATP}]}$

Question 21

As glucose is converted to pyruvate, a three-carbon compound, which of the following statements is (are) likely to be true?

I. The entropy of the universe increases.
II. The entropy of the overall reaction decreases.
III. The entropy is increased by enzyme catalysis.

- ○ **A.** I only
- ○ **B.** II only
- ○ **C.** I and III only
- ○ **D.** I, II, and III

Passage 5 (Questions 22-26)

Significant effort has been devoted to develop drugs that bind to their targets with high affinity and sufficient selectivity. The binding affinity is equal to the change in Gibbs free energy of binding (ΔG). Optimization of the enthalpic and entropic contributions to binding is fundamental to improving the affinity of small molecule inhibitors in drug development.

Thermodynamics has found increasing use in drug design and development when targeting the inhibition of carbonic anhydrases (CAs). Abnormal activities of CAs are often associated with different human diseases, such as glaucoma, epilepsy, Alzheimer's and Parkinson's diseases, obesity, and cancer. The most studied class of CA inhibitors is the aromatic sulfonamides, a few of which are shown in Figure 1.

1a

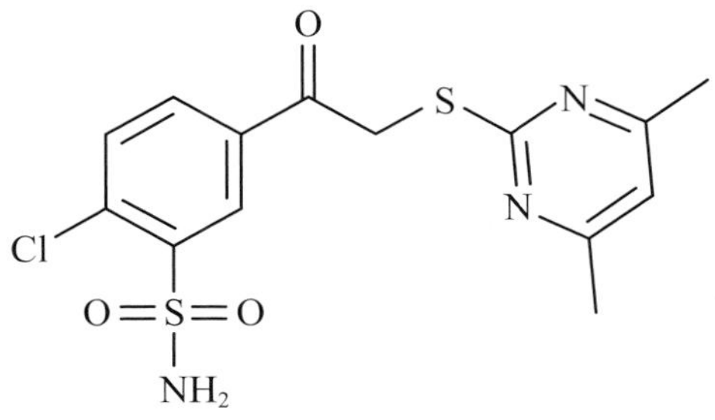

1b

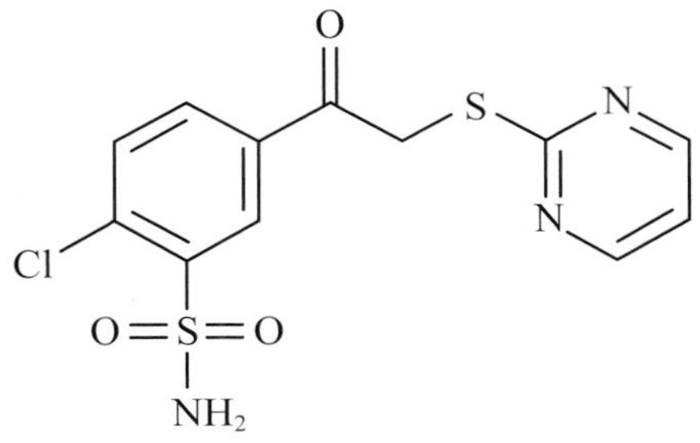

2a

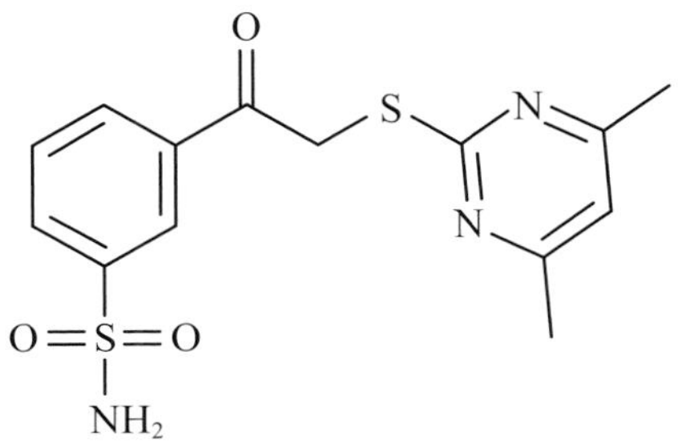

2b

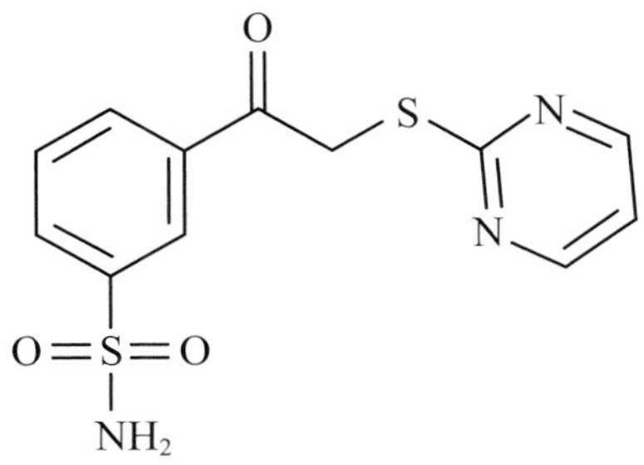

Figure 1 Structures of tested compounds

In this study, the structure-thermodynamic profiles of CA inhibitors binding were investigated. The underlying contributions of ΔH and $T\Delta S$ to the ΔG have been shown to be important parameters to integrate into rational drug design programs targeted at CAs. It is important to note that only the deprotonated form of the sulfonamide binds to the CA active site. Since the modification of functional groups is the basis of medicinal chemistry in rational drug development and is essential to optimization of promising lead candidates, it is of fundamental importance to calculate the intrinsic parameters that can be used to estimate the effect of the addition or replacement of functional groups. The thermodynamic profile of several CA inhibitors is shown in Table 1.

Table 1 Thermodynamic Profile of Aromatic Sulfonamides 1a, 1b, 2a, and 2b Binding to CA I

CA I	1a	1b	2a	2b
ΔH	−18.1 kcal/mol	−16.6 kcal/mol	−33.2 kcal/mol	−31.7 kcal/mol
$T\Delta S$	17.7 kcal/mol	16.5 kcal/mol	3.7 kcal/mol	3.7 kcal/mol

This passage was adapted from "Intrinsic Thermodynamics and Structure Correlation of Benzosulfonamides with a Pyrimidine Moiety Binding to Carbonic Anhydrases I, II, VII, XII, and XIII." Kisonaite M, Zubriene A, Capkausaite E, Smirnov A, Smirnoviene J et al. *PLoS ONE*. 2014. 9(12) doi:10.1371/journal.pone.0114106 for use under the terms of the Creative Commons CC BY 4.0 license (http://creativecommons.org/licenses/by/4.0/legalcode).

Question 22

The experiment summarized in Table 1 was conducted at room temperature. If a similar, *in vivo* experiment was performed, which of the following differences would be expected?

- **A.** Enthalpy plays a larger role in binding affinity due to the higher temperature in the body.
- **B.** Entropy plays a larger role in binding affinity due to the higher temperature in the body.
- **C.** Enthalpy plays a larger role in binding affinity due to the lower temperature in the body.
- **D.** Entropy plays a larger role in binding affinity due to the lower temperature in the body.

Question 23

What is the Gibbs free energy of binding for the binding of 1a to CA I?

- **A.** − 320 kcal/mol
- **B.** −0.4 kcal/mol
- **C.** −35.8 kcal/mol
- **D.** 35.8 kcal/mol

Question 24

What conditions would most strongly improve binding affinity of 1b to the CA I active site?

- **A.** Low pH and low temperature
- **B.** Low pH and high temperature
- **C.** High pH and low temperature
- **D.** High pH and high temperature

Question 25

Which of the following conclusions can be drawn based on a comparison of the characteristics of 1b and 2b in Figure 2?

- **A.** The difference in energy between the bonds broken and formed when 1b binds to CA I is smaller than the difference between those of 2b and CA I.
- **B.** Binding of 1b to CA I occurs faster than binding of 2b to CA I.
- **C.** Binding of 1b to CA I is spontaneous regardless of temperature, while binding of 2b to CA I only occurs spontaneously in relatively lower temperature.
- **D.** Binding of 1b to CA I occurs slower than binding of 2b to CA I.

Question 26

Which of the following is true regarding the impact of temperature on inhibitor binding to CA I?

- **A.** 2a would exhibit more consistent pharmacologic behavior during a fever than 1a.
- **B.** 1a would exhibit more consistent pharmacologic behavior during a fever than 2a.
- **C.** 2a binds more favorably in lower temperature than in higher temperature.
- **D.** 1a binds more favorably in lower temperature than in higher temperature.

Questions 27 - 29 do not refer to a passage and are independent of each other.

Question 27

Which of the following correctly describes the enthalpy ($\Delta H°$) of the following reaction?

$$\text{Glucose} + O_2 \rightarrow CO_2 + H_2O$$

Molecule	$\Delta H°_f$
Glucose	–1275.0 kJ/mol
O_2	0.0 kJ/mol
CO_2	–393.5 kJ/mol
H_2O	–285.8 kJ/mol

- **A.** $\Delta H° = -2801$ kJ, exothermic
- **B.** $\Delta H° = 596$ kJ, endothermic
- **C.** $\Delta H° = -1954$ kJ, exothermic
- **D.** $\Delta H° = 596$ kJ, exothermic

Question 28

An enzyme:

- **A.** increases $\Delta G°_{rxn}$.
- **B.** decreases $\Delta G°_{rxn}$.
- **C.** increases $\Delta G^{‡}$.
- **D.** decreases $\Delta G^{‡}$.

Question 29

Which of the following expressions best describes the initial rate of the reaction shown below?

$$CO_2(g) + NaOH(aq) \leftrightarrow NaHCO_3(aq)$$

- **A.** $K_{eq} = [NaHCO_3(aq)]/[NaOH(aq)]$
- **B.** $Q = [NaHCO_3(aq)]/[NaOH(aq)]$
- **C.** $K_{eq} = [CO_2(g)][NaOH(aq)]/ = [NaHCO_3(aq)]$
- **D.** $Q = [CO_2(g)][NaOH(aq)]/ = [NaHCO_3(aq)]$

STOP. If you finish before time is called, check your work. You may go back to any question in this test.

ANSWERS & EXPLANATIONS for Test 4B can be found on p. 286.

Phases

TEST 5A

Time: 95 minutes
Questions 1–59

DIRECTIONS: Most of the questions in this test section are grouped with a passage. Read the passage, then select the best answer to each question. Some questions are independent of any passage and of one another. Select the best answer to each of these questions. If you are unsure of an answer, rule out incorrect choices and select from the remaining options. Indicate your selection beside the option you choose. A periodic table can be found on the last page of this book for you to use at any point during this test section.

Passage 1 (Questions 1-5)

Altitude sickness can result in headaches, fatigue, dizziness, and possibly confusion in more severe cases. The risk of developing altitude sickness is independent of a person's conditioning as even world-class athletes are prone to developing altitude sickness. The rate of ascent is positively correlated with the risk of developing altitude sickness.

The percentage of oxygen and CO_2 in the atmosphere remains relatively constant despite changes in elevation (21% and 0.04% respectively). To study the effects of altitude, volunteers were placed in a hypobaric chamber, which can simulate the atmospheric pressure experienced at specific elevations. Researchers acquired samples of venous blood returning to the lungs from these volunteers at specific simulated elevations. The results of this study are shown in Figure 1.

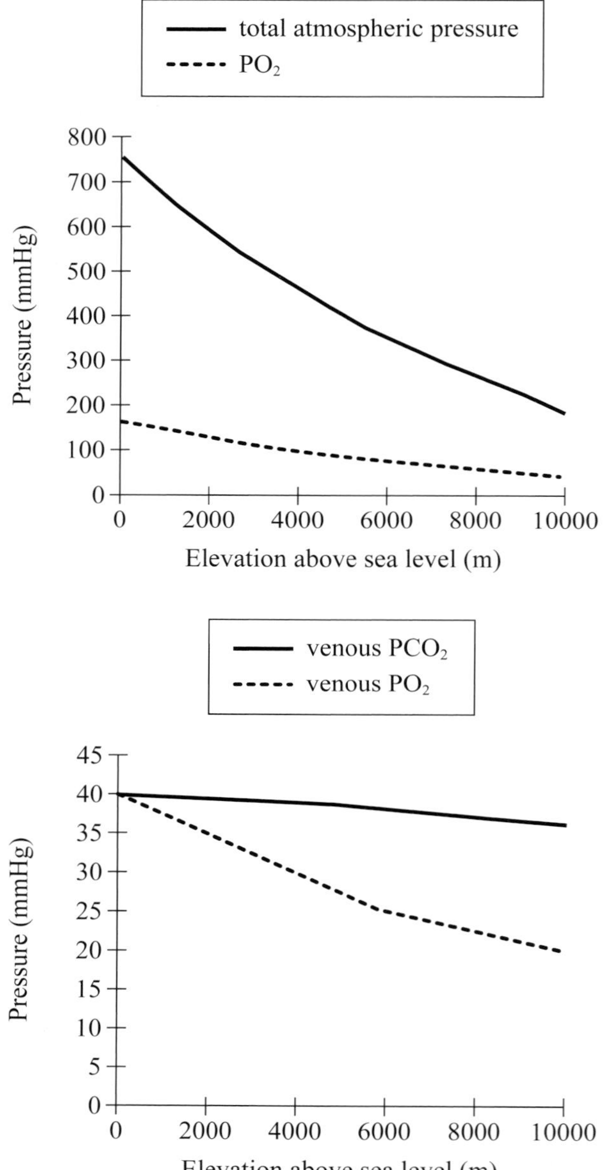

Figure 1 The effect of elevation change on atmospheric pressure and partial pressure of O_2 and CO_2 gasses

The lungs utilize partial pressure differences between the atmosphere and the capillaries to facilitate the exchange of O_2 into the capillaries and CO_2 in the opposite direction. Equation 1 can be used to calculate the rate of diffusion across a membrane, where R is the rate of diffusion, A is the area of the membrane, T is the thickness, D_k is a diffusion constant, and ΔP is the difference in pressure across the membrane. The diffusion constant is directly related to the temperature of the substance and inversely related to the density.

$$R = \frac{A}{T} D_k (\Delta P)$$

Equation 1

Researchers created a model of the alveoli consisting of two closed, fixed-volume chambers (five liters each) separated by a semi-permeable membrane. After filling each chamber independently, a divider is removed, and gas molecules are free to move between the two chambers through the membrane. The time needed for the system to reach equilibrium is used to calculate the rate of diffusion through the membrane.

Question 1

Climbers can compensate for the change in altitude by increasing their breathing rate. At a certain elevation, this short-term compensation is insufficient because:

- **A.** the partial pressure of CO_2 in the alveoli is too high, which prevents CO_2 from diffusing out of the capillaries.
- **B.** the decreased partial pressure of O_2 in the venous blood lowers the diffusion rate of oxygen into the capillaries.
- **C.** the mole fraction of O_2 in the air is too low at high altitudes.
- **D.** the partial pressure of O_2 in the air and blood are too similar.

Question 2

Which of the following would most likely compromise the reliability of the results obtained from the two-chamber model described in the passage?

- **A.** Performing the experimental trials at a temperature of 300 K rather than 273 K
- **B.** Replicating previous trials by maintaining the same ratio of pressure in the two chambers used in the original trial
- **C.** Not removing all of the gas from the chambers of a previously completed experiment
- **D.** Using nitrogen instead of oxygen as the gas in the chambers

Question 3

After the two chambers reach equilibrium, a researcher increases the temperature of the system. This will most likely result in:

- A. the volume of individual gas molecules having a significant effect on the total volume because of the higher average energy.
- B. an increase in the average velocity of the gas molecules.
- C. a decrease in the pressure exerted on the walls of the chambers.
- D. an increase in the intermolecular forces between individual gas molecules.

Question 4

Based on the data in Figure 1, what is the partial pressure of nitrogen in the atmosphere at sea level assuming it makes up 78% of the atmosphere?

- A. 120 mmHg
- B. 270 mmHg
- C. 610 mmHg
- D. 940 mmHg

Question 5

Using the model depicted in the passage at standard temperature and pressure, a scientist fills Chamber A with 1 L of F_2 (38 g/mol) and Chamber B with 4 L of water vapor (18 g/mol). What is the approximate ratio of gas molecules added to Chamber A compared to Chamber B?

- A. 1:1
- B. 1:2
- C. 1:4
- D. 1:8

Passage 2 (Questions 6-9)

During the explosion of a grenade, gas with a high pressure and temperature is rapidly formed and released, violently displacing air as it travels outwards in a spherical shape. The ensuing shock wave is characterized by the overpressure (OP) it generates. The OP refers to the pressure generated by an explosion that exceeds atmospheric pressure. During the rapid change in pressure that gives rise to the OP, bodily structures open to the atmosphere, such as the ears and lungs are particularly vulnerable to severe, possibly lethal damage, as shown in Table 1.

Table 1 OP and Damage to Bodily Structures

Overpressure (kPA)	Damage
6.9	Threshold of ear drum rupture
103.4	Threshold of lung damage
310.2	Ear drum rupture in 99% of population
448.0	Death of 99% of population

In addition, after the shockwave has left, the vacuum generated by the expelled air is quickly filled, generating an additional pressure change and creating powerful winds that can further cause bodily harm. The duration of the OP is correlated with the likelihood of survival of the blast victim, as shown in Figure 1.

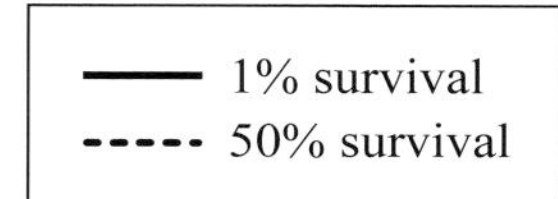

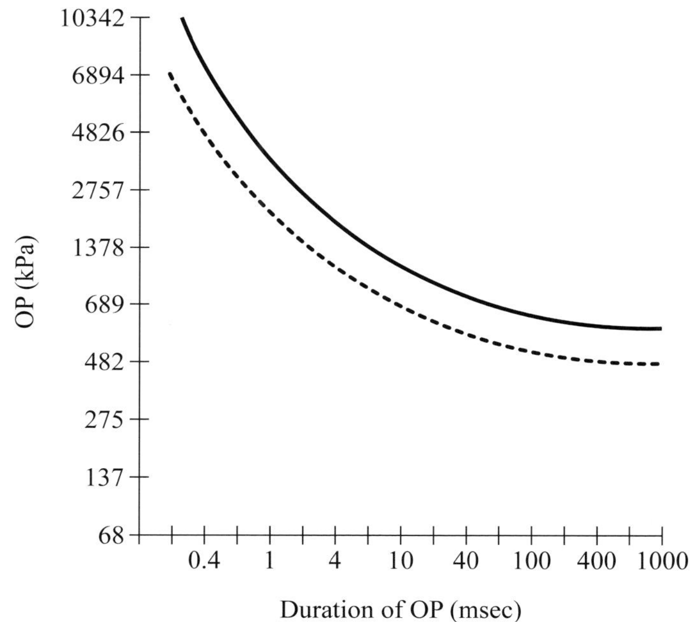

Figure 1 Survival curve

TEST 5A

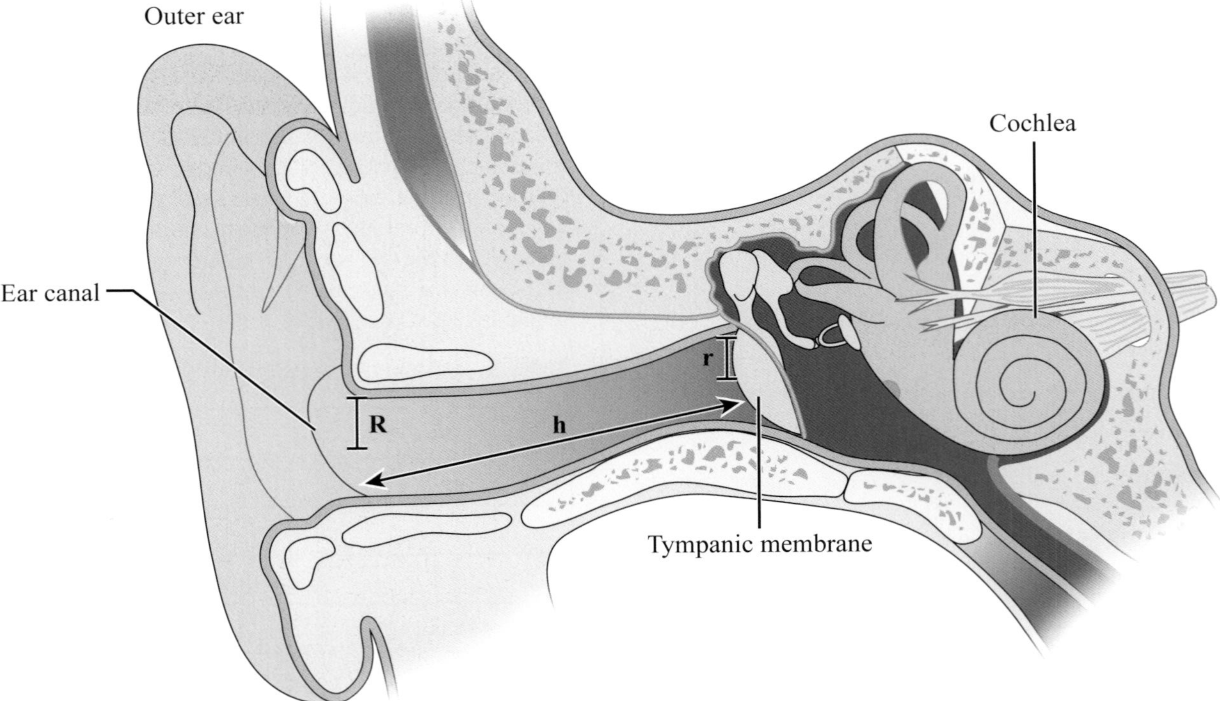

Figure 2 Computational model of inner ear

For biomechanical analysis, the ear canal can be modeled as a frustum, or topless cone, and gas behavior can be assumed to be ideal (Figure 2).

The ear canal's volume (V) is related to its small and large radii (r and R) and height (h) through the relationship in Equation 1.

$$V = \pi \frac{h}{3}(R^2 + Rr + r^2)$$

Equation 1

Question 6

In the computational model, doubling the larger radius has what effect on the number of gas particles contained in the ear canal?

- **A.** It causes the ear canal to contain a greater number of gas particles as compared to doubling the smaller radius.
- **B.** It causes the ear canal to contain a smaller number of gas particles as compared to doubling the smaller radius.
- **C.** It has an identical effect to doubling the smaller radius with respect to how many gas particles can be contained in the ear canal.
- **D.** It will cause no change in the number of gas particles that can be contained in the ear canal.

Question 7

At 0°C, what is the molar volume of air which is lethal to 50% of blast victims after 1 second of exposure? (Note 1 atm = 10^5 Pa)

- **A.** 0.78 L
- **B.** 3.8 L
- **C.** 4.6 L
- **D.** 3849 L

Question 8

The explosive yield of trinitrotoluene (TNT) is used to quantify the power of other weapons. It decomposes and burns according to the reaction shown below.

$2C_7H_5N_3O_6(s) + 7O_2(g) \rightarrow 3N_2(g) + 5H_2O(g) + 7CO(g) + 7CO_2(g)$

If a sealed container of TNT and stoichiometric oxygen completely reacted and did not burst, after returning to its starting temperature, by approximately what factor has the pressure inside the container changed?

- O **A.** It has increased by a factor of 2.5.
- O **B.** It has increased by a factor of 3.
- O **C.** It has increased by a factor of 15.
- O **D.** It has increased by a factor of 22.

Question 9

A pneumothorax, shown below, occurs when air occupies the pleural space and can be a consequence of blast injury.

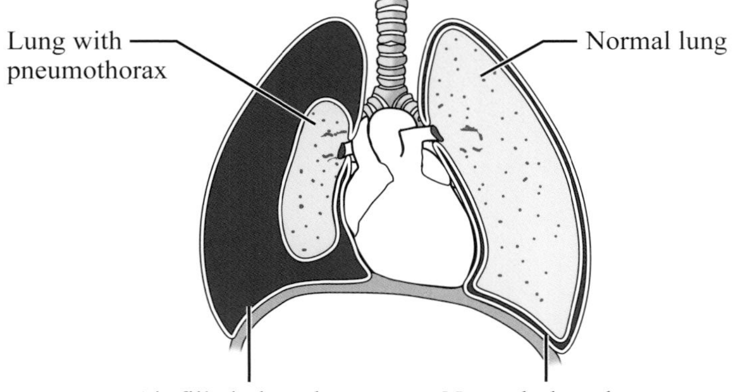

Which of the following statements most likely characterize the breathing mechanics of a patient with a pneumothorax?

- O **A.** The initiation of inhalation is difficult, but continuing to fill the lung with air becomes easier as more air is inhaled.
- O **B.** The initiation of inhalation is difficult, but continuing to fill the lung with air becomes even more difficult as more air is inhaled.
- O **C.** There is no difference between breathing with a pneumothorax or with a healthy lung.
- O **D.** Both exhalation and inhalation are more difficult with a pneumothorax.

Questions 10 - 13 do not refer to a passage and are independent of each other.

Question 10

The densities of commonly inhaled medical gases are shown in the table below. If all gases were combined and maintained at 0°C, which of the following best describes the mixture?

Gas	Mean (kg/m^3)
Nitrogen	1.02
Oxygen	1.23
Halothane	6.48
Sevoflurane	6.12
Desflurane	5.44

- O **A.** The gases will be evenly dispersed throughout the volume of the containers.
- O **B.** The gases will be initially evenly dispersed, then separate with sevoflurane at the top of the container and oxygen at the bottom of the container.
- O **C.** The gases will be initially evenly dispersed, then separate with halothane at the bottom of the container and nitrogen at the top of the container.
- O **D.** The gases will never be evenly dispersed, as they will separate with desflurane at the bottom of the container and nitrogen at the top of the container.

Question 11

The structure of a gaseous inhaled anesthetic, isoflurane, is shown below. Which of the following interactions is LEAST likely to occur between isoflurane molecules if they acted in an ideal manner?

Cl F
F O F
F
F

I. Hydrogen bonding
II. Ionic bonding
III. Electrostatic interactions

- O **A.** I only
- O **B.** I and II only
- O **C.** II and III only
- O **D.** I, II, and III

Question 12

Supplemental oxygen is often administered at a constant pressure and at a volumetric flow rate of 1 L/min. Increasing the temperature of the oxygen is likely to:

- O **A.** increase the pressure of the administered gas in the trachea.
- O **B.** decrease the pressure of the administered gas in the trachea.
- O **C.** initially increase then decrease the pressure of the administered gas in the trachea.
- O **D.** have no effect on the pressure of the gas in the trachea.

Question 13

As a patient inhales, which of the following statements best describes the movement of air?

- O **A.** The expansion of the lungs decreases the intrathoracic pressure, allowing room air to flow into the lungs.
- O **B.** The expansion of the lungs increases the intrathoracic pressure, allowing room air to flow into the lungs.
- O **C.** The deflation of the lungs decreases the intrathoracic pressure, allowing room air to flow into the lungs.
- O **D.** The deflation of the lungs increases the intrathoracic pressure, allowing room air to flow into the lungs.

Passage 3 (Questions 14-17)

Movement of air particles into and out of the lungs can be explained using Boyle's law, which relates the constant relationship, K, between the pressure P and volume V of an enclosed gas at constant temperature, as shown in Equation 1.

$$PV = \mathrm{K}$$

Equation 1

Inspiration is mediated through lung volume expansion via diaphragmatic contraction. This increase in lung volume transiently reduces intrapulmonary pressure, until air from the atmosphere fills the lungs, restoring the differential pressure to zero.

Expiration is mediated through lung volume reduction; relaxation of the diaphragm allows the elastic recoil of the lungs to reduce lung volume, transiently raising intrapulmonary pressure, ejecting air from the lungs, and restoring the differential pressure to zero.

In an experimental demonstration of Boyle's law, students filled a small spherical balloon with air and placed it into a large modified syringe. Depression or retraction of the plunger changed the pressure surrounding the balloon and was measured by the distance, h, from the plunger to the syringe end (Figure 1).

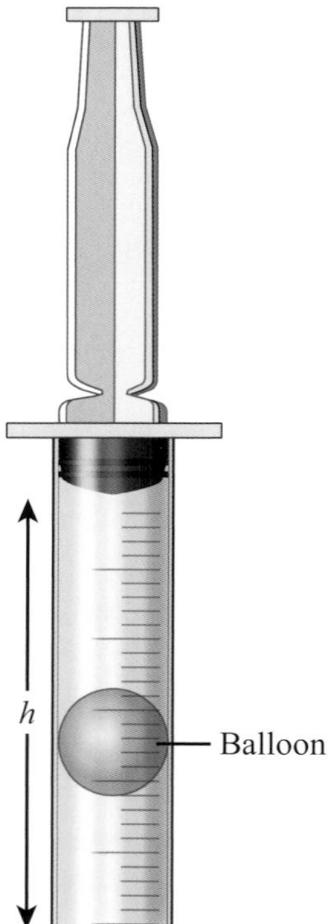

Figure 1 Experimental design

Question 14

The students observed a mathematical relationship between h, the balloon volume V_b, and a conversion factor β. Which of the following most likely describes this relationship?

- A. $\beta V_b = h$
- B. $\sqrt{V_b \beta} = h$
- C. $\beta \frac{1}{V_b} = h$
- D. $\beta V_b^2 = h$

Question 15

If the experiment were repeated with the balloon filled with helium instead of air, which of the following would most likely be observed?

- A. During depression of the syringe, the balloon would not contract as substantially as in the original experiment.
- B. During retraction of the syringe, the balloon would not expand as substantially as in the original experiment.
- C. The balloon would expand and contract identically during retraction and depression of the syringe, respectively, compared the original experiment.
- D. The balloon would contract less during depression of the syringe, but expand more during retraction of the syringe, compared to the original experiment.

Question 16

The air in the balloon is composed of 25% oxygen and 75% nitrogen by mass. If the balloon has an internal pressure of 1 atm, what is the partial pressure of oxygen in the balloon?

- A. 0.25 atm
- B. 0.12 atm
- C. 0.22 atm
- D. 0.75 atm

Question 17

Suppose a weight of mass, m, depressed a massless modified syringe from a height h to h/2. If the plunger has a surface area, A, how should Equation 1 be rearranged to solve for the mass of the weight, assuming the final syringe pressure was P and its initial volume was V?

- A. $\frac{2K}{AV_g}$
- B. $\frac{KA}{V_g}$
- C. $\frac{KA}{V}$
- D. $\frac{2KA}{V_g}$

TEST 5A

Passage 4 (Questions 18-21)

Inspiration is mediated by contraction of the diaphragm, which increases lung volume. According to the ideal gas law, the pressure P, volume V, number of particles n, and temperature T of a gaseous sample have a constant relationship to each other. This relationship requires that an increase in lung volume be accompanied by the generation of a negative intrapulmonary pressure relative to the atmosphere, as implied by Equation 1.

$$\frac{PV}{nT} = \mathrm{R}$$

Equation 1

The negative intrapulmonary pressure only lasts transiently as it is quickly relieved by the rapid migration of atmospheric air particles into the lungs. During expiration, the opposite process occurs. The diaphragm relaxes, and the elastic recoil of the lungs decreases their volume. This reduction in volume is accompanied by the generation of positive intrapulmonary pressure relative to the atmosphere, forcing air out of the lungs. The volume of air capable of being expired from the lungs is a diagnostic parameter known as vital capacity (VC). Fairly accurate VC measurements can be performed by using an instrument that traps gas through the displacement of water.

A rectangular trough was filled with 3 L of 25°C water. A graduated cylinder, also filled with water, was rapidly inverted over the water-filled trough so that fluid did not leave the cylinder. Its bottom face was just barely submerged, and the cylinder was clamped in place. A plastic hose was inserted just under the volumetric cylinder, and its end extended beyond the trough. The volume of water displaced in the cylinder by the gas exhaled into the hose provided measurements of lung volume. A diagram of this apparatus can be seen in Figure 1.

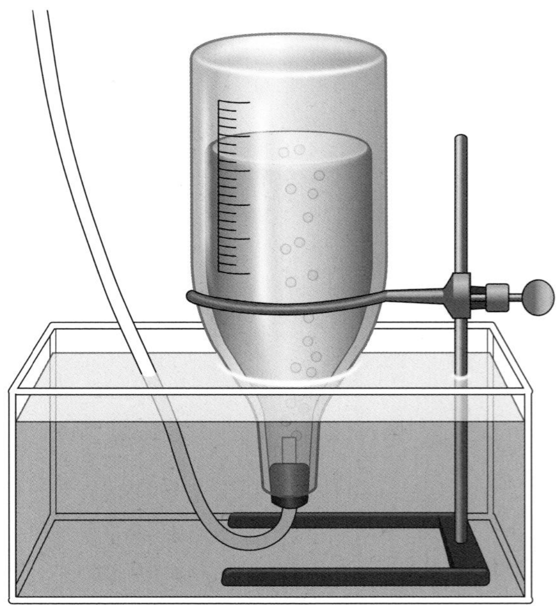

Figure 1 VC measurement apparatus

The VCs for a single participant as measured by the apparatus described above are displayed in Table 1.

Table 1 VC Measurements

Trial	Volume (L)
1	3.2
2	4.3
3	4.5
4	4.4

Question 18

If the participant repeated this experiment in a trough filled with dry ice and acetone at −78°C, his average VC as measure by the apparatus would most likely be:

- **A.** 1.9 L.
- **B.** 2.9 L.
- **C.** 4.4 L.
- **D.** 6.6 L.

Question 19

Halfway through a measurement, a hole opens at the base of the inverted graduated cylinder. If the participant stopped exhaling, the water level in the cylinder:

- **A.** falls until it is equal in height to the water in the trough.
- **B.** falls, but remains greater than the height of the water in the trough.
- **C.** remains at the height it was at when the participant stopped exhaling.
- **D.** falls as water exits the opening of the hose.

Question 20

VCs may decrease with cold air. If air is 80% nitrogen by volume, how many atoms of nitrogen are present in 1 L of 0°C air?

- **A.** $(0.8 \times 6.022 \times 10^{23})/22.4$ atoms
- **B.** $0.8 \times 6.022 \times 10^{23} \times 22.4$ atoms
- **C.** $(0.8 \times 6.022 \times 10^{23} \times 2)/22.4$ atoms
- **D.** $0.8 \times 6.022 \times 10^{23} \times 2 \times 22.4$ atoms

Question 21

6.27 kJ of energy is directly added to the water in the trough. What temperature change does the water experience?

$\left(\text{Note } C_{H_2O} = 4.18\frac{\mathrm{J}}{\mathrm{g \cdot K}}\right)$

- **A.** 8.7°C
- **B.** 2.0°C
- **C.** 5.0×10^{-1} °C
- **D.** 5.0×10^{-4} °C

TEST 5A

Passage 5 (Questions 22-25)

The form and function of the human respiratory system ensures efficient gas exchange with the environment. During expiration, hot, humid air that is rich in carbon dioxide (CO_2) and depleted of oxygen is vented away from the body. During inspiration, air from the immediate surroundings of the face is inhaled in a diffuse manner from all directions.

When a facepiece respirator (FFR) covers the mouth and nostrils, air exchange is altered, and the physiological dead space is extended. It is not surprising that FFRs are known to adversely affect the comfort of the wearer in terms of lowered thermal comfort and elevated CO_2 levels. The elevated CO_2 levels originate from the CO_2-rich expired air that is around one-hundred times higher in CO_2 concentration than that of atmospheric air, and remains trapped in the FFR. This elevated CO_2 concentration is potentially hazardous: increased CO_2 levels have been linked to changes in visual performance, altered exercise endurance, headaches, shortness of breath, decreased reasoning and alertness, and increased irritability.

In order to reduce the CO_2 levels in the dead space to near-ambient levels, an active venting system (AVS) was developed that aims to mimic and restore the functionality of the human respiratory system even when a FFR is covering the mouth and nostrils. The AVS comprises a housing for a one-way valve, a blower and battery that can be attached to the FFR with negligible mechanical deformation of the filter. The blower illustrated in Figure 1 vents the air out from the FFR and reduces the CO_2 concentration inside the dead space, as shown in Figure 2.

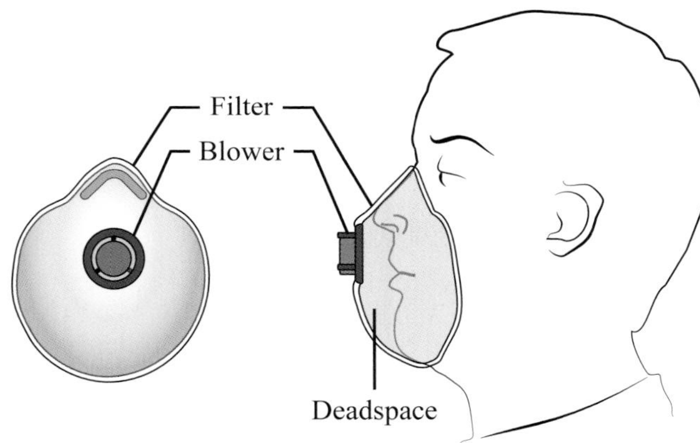

Figure 1 AVS attached to FFR

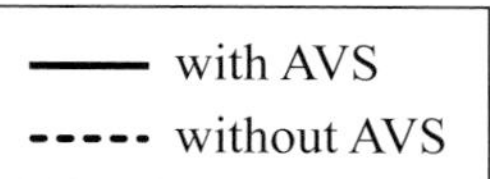

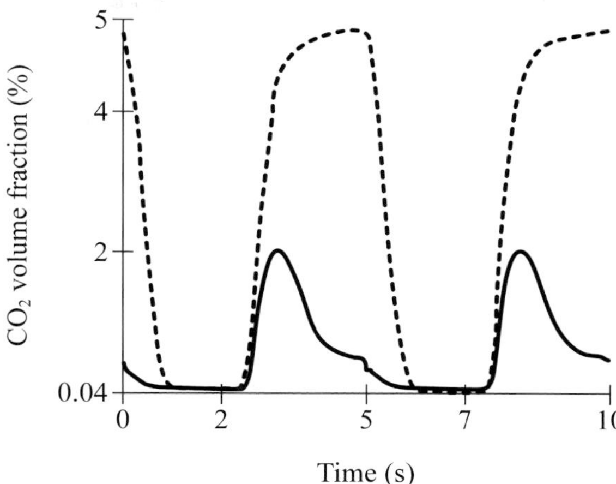

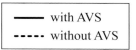

Figure 2 Average volume fraction (%) of CO_2 in the dead space of a FFR

This passage was adapted from "Reduction of Carbon Dioxide in Filtering Facepiece Respirators with an Active-Venting System: A Computational Study." Birgersson E, Tang EH, Lee WLJ, Sak KJ. *PLoS ONE*. 2015. 10(6) doi:10.1371/journal.pone.0130306 for use under the terms of the Creative Commons CC BY 4.0 license (http://creativecommons.org/licenses/by/4.0/legalcode).

Question 22

At the end of exhalation, the AVS has reduced the partial pressure of CO_2 in the FFR by what percent?

- O **A.** 2%
- O **B.** 3%
- O **C.** 40%
- O **D.** 60%

Question 23

Boltzmann's constant is useful for describing the microscopic behavior of CO_2 particles. Which of the following are required to calculate Boltzmann's constant?

I. Absolute temperature of a sample CO_2
II. Pressure of a sample of CO_2
III. Mass of a sample of CO_2

- O **A.** I and II only
- O **B.** I and III only
- O **C.** II and III only
- O **D.** I, II, and III

Question 24

The pump of the FFR was used to empty an air filled flask pressurized to 1 atm and attached to a mercury filled manometer as shown below.

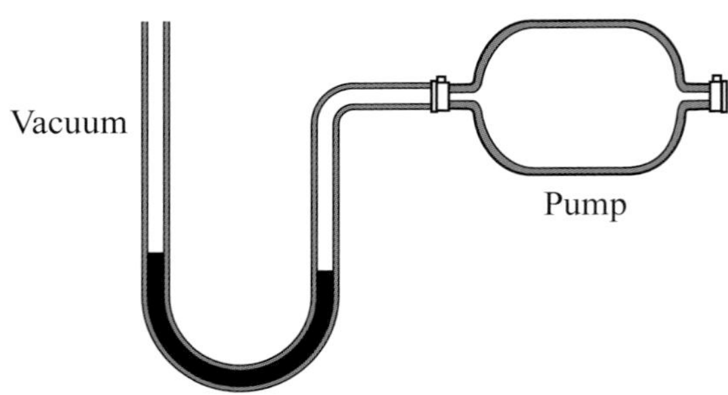

If the left side of the column fell 76 mm, what percentage of the particles in the flask was removed? (Note $\rho_{Hg} = 13.5$ g/mL and $R = 8.2 \times 10^{-2}$ L · atm/K · mol)

- A. 10%
- B. 60%
- C. 76%
- D. 90%

Question 25

Other proposed methods of carbon dioxide removal require the use of fabrics impregnated with calcium hydroxide. Calcium hydroxide captures carbon dioxide according to the reaction shown:

$$Ca(OH)_2(s) + CO_2(aq) \rightarrow H_2O(l) + CaCO_3(s)$$

How much calcium hydroxide is required to trap 5 L of CO_2 exhaled at 273 K?

- A. 10.2 g
- B. 12.7 g
- C. 16.5 g
- D. 19.4 g

TEST 5A

Questions 26 - 29 do not refer to a passage and are independent of each other.

Question 26

During this experiment, air was assumed to behave as an ideal gas. Which of the following graphs demonstrates an ideal gas's behavior?

A.

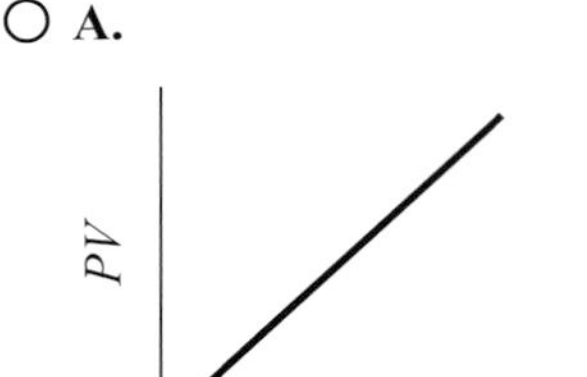

B.

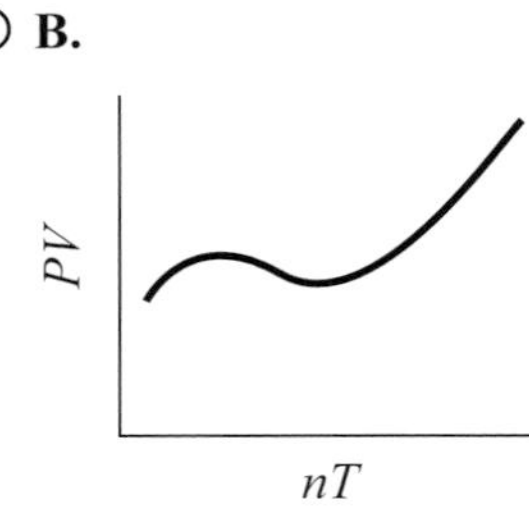

C.

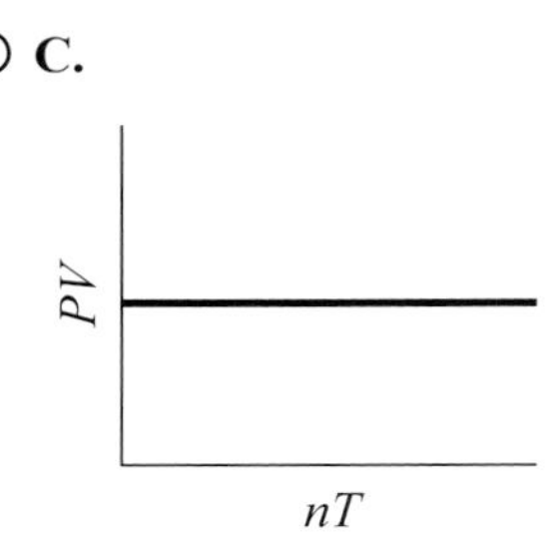

D.

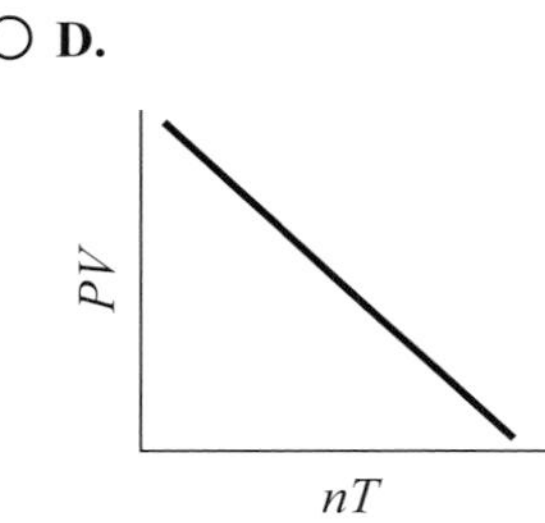

Question 27

The pressure of one mole of air in a pair of stationary lungs with a volume of 3 L is:

- A. greatest when it first enters the lungs at 20°C.
- B. greatest at 25°C.
- C. greatest when the air reaches body temperature (37°C).
- D. the same at all temperatures.

Question 28

Lactic acid is produced by skeletal muscle cells during strenuous exercise. If 0.026 g of lactic acid is vaporized in a 200 mL beaker at 150°C and the final pressure inside the beaker is 0.5 atm, what is the molecular mass of lactic acid. (Note R = 0.82 L · atm/mol · K)

- A. 32 g/mol
- B. 90 g/mol
- C. 52 g/mol
- D. 71 g/mol

Question 29

Which of the following characteristics is not a defining feature for an ideal gas?

- A. Molecules undergo elastic collisions.
- B. Molecules exert very little force on each other.
- C. Molecules have zero volume.
- D. The kinetic energy is proportional to the temperature.

Passage 6 (Questions 30-34)

For those with respiratory illnesses, such as chronic obstructive pulmonary disease, excessive atmospheric water vapor can lead to severe discomfort and difficulty breathing. Water vapor condenses fairly easily. As such, its behavior indicates that the Kinetic Molecular Theory of Gases fails as a descriptive tool since it ignores molecular volume and intermolecular forces, which are non-negligible parameters. To more accurately describe water vapor and other non-ideal gases, the van der Waals equation (Equation 1) is used, where a and b are constants that are characteristic to the non-ideal gaseous species.

$$\left[P + \frac{n^2 a}{v^2}\right](V - nb) = nRT$$

Equation 1

The van der Waals constant, a, for many gases can be found by measuring the volume that a given amount of gas occupies at a specific temperature and pressure. One technique for accomplishing this is to vaporize the gas in a hot water bath and indirectly measure the mass of the gas produced. To accomplish this, the mass of the modified flask connected to a capillary tube with a tight connection of flexible plastic tubing was recorded (Figure 1).

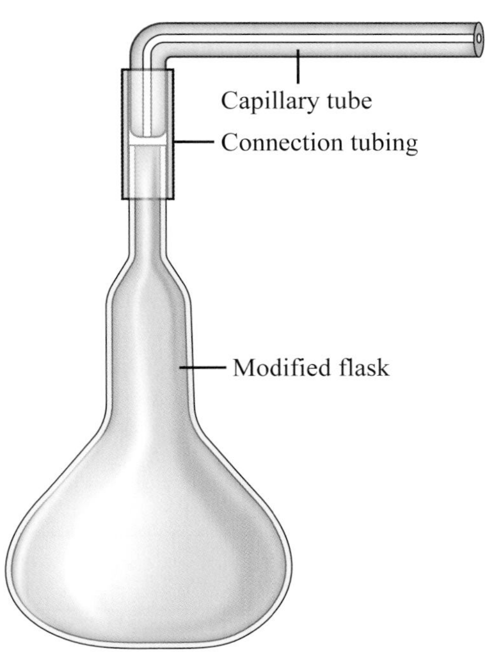

Figure 1 Glassware used to determine van der Waals constant

A volatile liquid was added to the flask and sealed under the capillary tube. The flask was heated for ten minutes in a boiling water bath. After cooling to room temperature and being reweighed, the mass of the gas was calculated as the differences in the masses of the flask before and after the heating procedure. The pressure of the gas was assumed to be equal to the ambient pressure during the time of the experiment. The volume of the flask was calculated by determining the mass of water required to fill the flask, and multiplying this value by ρ_{H_2O}.

Question 30

Which arrangement of the terms in Equation 1 provides the constant which corrects for intermolecular forces?

- A. $\dfrac{V\left[\dfrac{P + n^2 a}{v^2}\right] - nRT}{np + \dfrac{n^3 a}{v^2}}$
- B. $\left[\dfrac{nRT}{V - nb} - P\right]\dfrac{V^2}{n^2}$
- C. $\dfrac{\left[\dfrac{P + n^2 a}{V^2}\right](V - nb)}{nR}$
- D. $\left[\dfrac{nRT}{V - nb} - P\right]\dfrac{n^2}{V^2}$

Question 31

What assumption is necessary for the results of this experiment to be valid?

- A. Water used to measure the flask's volume remains in the flask throughout the course of the experiment.
- B. The volume that each gas particle occupies in the flask is negligible.
- C. After being removed from the hot water bath, air enters the flask at a negligible rate.
- D. Air does not escape the flask during the vaporization of the volatile liquid.

Question 32

Why was boiling water used to heat the gas?

- A. Boiling water is an effective medium of thermal energy transfer.
- B. The temperature of boiling water continuously rises as it is heated, and can rapidly vaporize the liquid sample.
- C. A flask in boiling water represents an isothermal system.
- D. A flask in boiling water represents an isobaric system.

Question 33

What are the units of b?

- A. L/mol
- B. mol/L
- C. mol
- D. $L^2 \cdot atm/mol^2$

Question 34

Ambient pressure during the experiment was measured with a mercury barometer. Which equation provides the height of the mercury in the evacuated column?

- A. $\frac{P_{atm}}{\rho_{Hg} g}$
- B. $\frac{P_{atm} g}{\rho_{Hg}}$
- C. $\frac{P_{atm} \rho_{Hg}}{g}$
- D. $\frac{P_{atm}}{\rho_{Hg} g^2}$

TEST 5A

Passage 7 (Questions 35-38)

The most common form of sleep disordered breathing is obstructive sleep apnea (OSA). OSA is associated with the transient collapse of the soft tissue of the upper airway as the cause of breathing cessation or reduction. The standard first-line treatment for OSA is continuous positive airway pressure (CPAP). CPAP is fan-generated air pressure delivered via a nasal mask and titrated to offset negative intrathoracic pressures produced during inhalation. As such, CPAP provides the air pressure necessary to the keep the upper airway open.

OSA causes dramatically decreased rapid eye movement (REM) sleep, and CPAP usage can usually reverse this effect of OSA. In healthy adults, REM sleep occupies 20–25% of total sleep time and is associated with many physiologic changes including corneal thickening. One hypothesis proposes that eye movements in REM sleep help corneal oxygenation because thermal circulation of the aqueous humor is needed for adequate corneal respiration.

Healthy human corneal thickness is around 500 microns, but the cornea can swell under conditions of inadequate oxygen perfusion. This kind of corneal swelling is common, especially for those who wear contact lenses when the contacts have a low oxygen diffusion flux, J, as described by Fick's law:

$$J = D\left(\frac{\Delta[x]}{\delta}\right)$$

Equation 1

where $\Delta[x]$ is the difference between the atmospheric and ocular oxygen concentrations, δ is the thickness of the lens, and D is the diffusion coefficient.

A study was performed to assess whether CPAP has an indirect effect on corneal thickness. The findings are summarized in Table 1.

Table 1 Corneal Thickness Before and After Sleep, with and without CPAP Administration

Group	Pre-sleep left cornea (μm)	Post-sleep left cornea (μm)	Pre-sleep right cornea (μm)	Post-sleep right cornea (μm)
Without CPAP	537.5	553.5	538.0	559.0
With CPAP	544.8	545.2	545.7	551.4

CPAP pressure is measured in cmH_2O. This unit corresponds to the pressure exerted by a column of water 1 cm high. Standard therapeutic settings are 5−10 cmH_2O beyond atmospheric pressure. Depending on the need, the air may be humidified, and different concentrations of oxygen may be delivered as well. The pressure of these devices can be measured using a cylindrical water column manometer.

This passage was adapted from "The Relationship between CPAP Usage and Corneal Thickness." Gelir E, Budak M, Ardic S. *PLoS ONE.* 2014. 9(1) doi:10.1371/ journal. pone.0087274 for use under the terms of the Creative Commons CC BY 4.0 Attribution license (http://creativecommons.org/licenses/by/4.0/legalcode).

Question 35

Water is present in a humidified CPAP tube. As it condenses, the temperature of the tube:

- O **A.** decreases because condensation is an endothermic process.
- O **B.** increases because condensation is an endothermic process.
- O **C.** increases because condensation is an exothermic process.
- O **D.** decreases because condensation is an exothermic process.

Question 36

Who is expected to have the most and least swollen cornea, respectively?

- O **A.** A driver in a car at sea level and a pilot in a plane pressurized to 1 atm
- O **B.** A submarine operator 300 m below sea level and a climber 550 m above sea level
- O **C.** A pilot in a plane pressurized to 1 atm and a driver in a car at sea level
- O **D.** A climber 5500 m above sea level and a submarine operator 300 m below sea level

Question 37

If the delivered air is 35% oxygen, what volume will one mole of it occupy at 1 atm and 0°C?

- O **A.** 3.5 L
- O **B.** 7.8 L
- O **C.** 11.2 L
- O **D.** 22.4 L

Question 38

The following product and biometric data was obtained during contact lens testing:

Lens model	Lens thickness (mm)
1	2.7
2	6.2

Patient	Right corneal thickness before use (μm)	Right corneal thickness after use (μm)
X	533.1	550.3
Y	510.0	512.2

Which patient wore which lens?

- O **A.** X wore 2, and Y wore 2.
- O **B.** X wore 1, and Y wore 2.
- O **C.** Y wore 1, and X wore 2.
- O **D.** There is not enough information to determine which lens each patient wore.

Passage 8 (Questions 39-42)

The presence of excess gas in the stomach and viscera can lead to discomfort and bloating. The gas can enter the body through swallowed air, arise as the metabolic waste of endogenous bacteria, or through consuming $CaCO_3$ for the treatment of heart burn. The rate at which gas can leave the body is dependent on how rapidly it can bubble out of solution. Bubble formation is dependent on the work required to form a bubble as described in Equation 1, where $P' - P$ is the pressure difference across the interface, γ_{lv} is the liquid-vapor surface tension, and θ is the contact angle.

$$W = \frac{16\pi\gamma_{lv}^3}{(P' - P)}\left(\frac{(1-\cos\theta)^2(2+\cos\theta)}{4}\right)$$

Equation 1

The contact angle is determined by placing a drop of the solution in question on a polycarbonate surface and measuring the angle that the meniscus forms on contact (Figure 1).

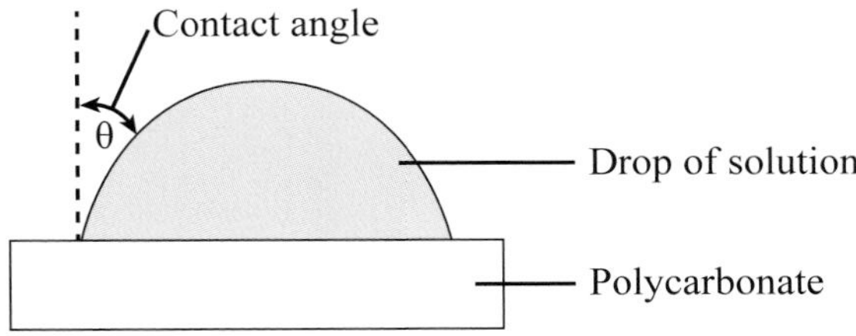

Figure 1 Method of determining contact angle

Reducing the surface tension of a solution facilitates the formation of bubbles. This process is utilized clinically by administering surfactants, such as simethicone (Figure 2), to reduce the surface tension of luminal fluid. When the luminal fluid has a lower surface tension, it is easier for gas to bubble and escape, which relieves the discomfort and bloating associated with gas accumulation.

$$H_3C-\underset{CH_3}{\overset{CH_3}{Si}}\left[-O-\underset{CH_3}{\overset{CH_3}{Si}}-\right]_n CH_3 + SiO_2$$

Figure 2 Structure of simethicone

Question 39

$CaCO_3$ is used to neutralize a 1 L aqueous solution of HCl with a pH of 6. What volume of CO_2 is released at STP?

- O **A.** 1×10^{-5} L
- O **B.** 4×10^{-5} L
- O **C.** 1×10^{-6} L
- O **D.** 4×10^{-4} L

Question 40

Which conditions would be most favorable to determine butanol's contact angle?

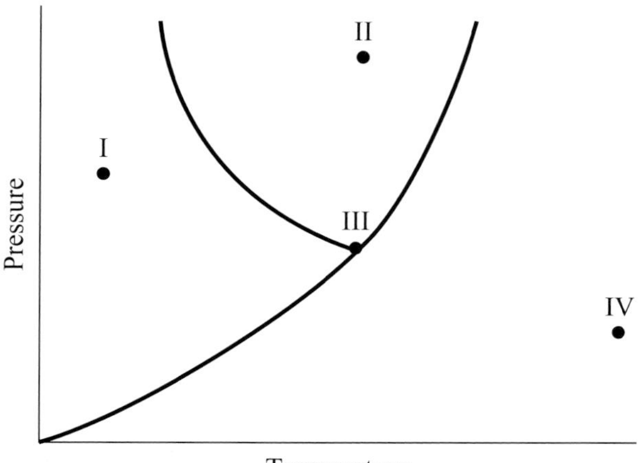

- O **A.** I
- O **B.** II
- O **C.** III
- O **D.** IV

Question 41

Trimethylsilanol (shown) is an organosilicon like simethicone. It is expected to:

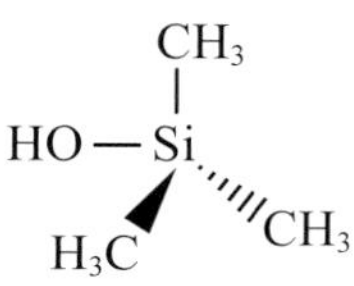

Trimethylsilanol

- O **A.** have a lower boiling point than *t*-Butyl alcohol.
- O **B.** have a greater vapor pressure than *t*-Butyl alcohol.
- O **C.** have a lower vapor pressure than *t*-Butyl alcohol.
- O **D.** have a greater number of chiral centers than *t*-Butyl alcohol.

Question 42

In tonic water, the vapor pressure of water and carbon dioxide is 289.1 mmHg and 1875 mmHg respectively. If a can of tonic water is to be sealed, what pressure must the lid be able to support?

- O **A.** 1585.9 mmHg
- O **B.** 542062.5 mmHg
- O **C.** 2164.1 mmHg
- O **D.** 2000 mmHg

Questions 43 - 46 do not refer to a passage and are independent of each other.

Question 43

A climber brings a rigid tank that was filled with oxygen under high pressure to maximize the amount of oxygen it could store. As the climber ascends, the temperature of the gas decreases. Which of the following is most likely to occur?

- O **A.** The amount of oxygen in the containers will increase.
- O **B.** The intermolecular forces between gas molecules will increase.
- O **C.** The tanks will significantly expand.
- O **D.** The gas molecules will move faster.

Question 44

What is the minimal mass of phosgene ($COCl_2$) needed to evaporate at STP in a 22×10^3 L room to produce a lethal dose for a human (LD = 3 ppm)?

- O **A.** $22 \times 99 \times 3 \times 10^{-3}$ g
- O **B.** $22 \times 22.4 \times 3 \times 99 \times 10^{-3}$ g
- O **C.** $22 \times 22.4 \times 3 \times 99 \times 10^{3}$ g
- O **D.** $22 \times 22.4 \times 3 \times \frac{1}{99} \times 10^{-3}$ g

Question 45

Saliva typically contains many non-volatile solutes, such as proteins, dissolved in water. If a beaker with a saliva sample is left in a closed environment with a beaker of pure water, which of the following is true once the system reaches equilibrium?

- O **A.** The pure water beaker will contain all of the water.
- O **B.** The saliva beaker will contain all of the water.
- O **C.** The amount of water in each beaker will not change.
- O **D.** Both beakers will contain the same amount of water regardless of how much with which they started.

Question 46

An aerosolized breathing treatment is packaged in very compliant plastic containers for easy transport to developing countries in the Saharan desert. The packaging is designed to not melt with the large increase in temperature. Which of the following changes is expected?

- O **A.** Increase in volume
- O **B.** Decrease in volume
- O **C.** Increase in pressure
- O **D.** Decrease in pressure

Passage 9 (Questions 47-52)

Volatile organic compounds (VOCs) are a large and highly diverse group of carbon-based molecules, generally related by their volatility at ambient temperature. The diagnostic potential of VOCs in biological specimens has begun to receive considerable attention, and correlations between the VOC metabolome and various diseases are emerging. Specialized sampling methods, such as solid-phase microextraction (SPME), have greatly facilitated the isolation of VOCs from biological specimens. Pioneering human fecal VOC metabolomic investigations have utilized a single SPME fiber type for analyte extraction and analysis. The first step involves the extraction of liquid phase VOCs through partitioning into a polymeric coating adhered to a solid silica fiber. This is followed by desorption of the VOCs by conversion of VOCs to gaseous phase. The VOCs are then separated by gas-liquid partition chromatography, which separates out VOCs by vapor pressure of a sample at given conditions. The VOCs are finally detected by mass spectrometry.

While the polarity of the analyte of interest is typically used to guide the selection of a particular SPME fiber, metabolomic analyses generally strive to isolate and identify chemically diverse types of analyte molecules. Thus, a single SPME fiber coating may be insufficient for a comprehensive analysis of the complex analyte mixtures typically present in biological samples. Researchers compared single and multiple fiber extraction in terms of the diversity of metabolites present in the isolate. The results are presented in Table 1.

Table 1 Percentage of VOCs with Varying Number of Fibers

Number of unique fibers	Percentage of VOCs isolated
1	63
2	78
3	89
4	93
5	96

This passage was adapted from "Solid-Phase Microextraction and the Human Fecal Metabolome." Dixon E, Clubb C, Pittman S, Ammann Z, Rasheed Z et al. *PLoS ONE*. 2011. 6(4) doi:10.1371/journal.pone.0018471 for use under the terms of the Creative Commons CC BY 3.0 license (http://creativecommons.org/licenses/by/3.0/legalcode).

Question 47

Which of the following statements is true regarding how the VOCs change after the desorption process is complete?

- **A.** The VOCs take up less volume.
- **B.** The VOCs have lower heat capacity.
- **C.** The VOCs are experiencing stronger intermolecular forces.
- **D.** The VOCs can undergo deposition.

Question 48

Which of the following changes to the experiment would reduce the ability to desorb a large diversity of VOCs from the fibers?

I. Increasing the pressure of the desorption chamber
II. Increasing the temperature of the desorption chamber
III. Reducing the number of unique fibers

- **A.** I only
- **B.** II only
- **C.** I and III only
- **D.** II and III only

Question 49

During the extraction of VOCs from the sample by fibers, the sample can be subjected to high pressure. What is the most likely reason for this?

- **A.** To increase the heat capacity of the VOCs
- **B.** To prevent sublimation of the VOCs
- **C.** To maintain the solid phase of the fibers
- **D.** To prevent evaporation of the VOCs

Question 50

Helium is often used as a carrier gas during gas-liquid partition chromatography. What is the most likely reason that helium is used over other gases?

- **A.** Helium has a fairly small molecular weight.
- **B.** Helium is an inert, nonreactive gas.
- **C.** Helium nuclei form alpha particles.
- **D.** Helium does not form diatomic molecules.

Question 51

Suppose a mixture of VOCs obtained following desorption behaves more like a real than ideal gas. Which of the following is true when comparing this sample to a more ideally behaving sample?

- A. It has less volume and higher pressure.
- B. It has less volume and lower pressure.
- C. It has more volume and higher pressure.
- D. It has more volume and lower pressure.

Question 52

Compound A ($C_{12}H_{10}O$), B ($C_{10}H_7OH$), and C (C_3H_5NO) are a few examples of common VOCs. Which compound has the highest density in gaseous phase assuming the same number of molecules are in the containers at equal temperature and pressure conditions?

- A. Compound A
- B. Compound B
- C. Compound C
- D. All three compounds have the same density.

Passage 10 (Questions 53-56)

Dry ice is the common name for the solid form of carbon dioxide. It is a particularly descriptive name because, unlike conventional ice composed of solid water, it sublimates at ambient conditions, directly entering the gas phase and never existing in liquid form. These properties make dry ice particularly useful for transporting perishable materials that must be kept cold, as its sublimation temperature at atmospheric pressure is −78.5°C, and its enthalpy of sublimation is 571 kJ kg^{-1}.

Dry ice is manufactured from carbon dioxide gas, often harvested from industrial sites. The gas is subjected to pressurization and refrigeration until it reaches a liquid form. At this point, the pressure is rapidly reduced to induce vaporization. Although some of the starting material is lost during this phase of manufacturing, the highly endothermic nature of the vaporization process forces the remaining liquid to solidify. Dry ice's temperature and pressure dependent properties are shown in Figure 1.

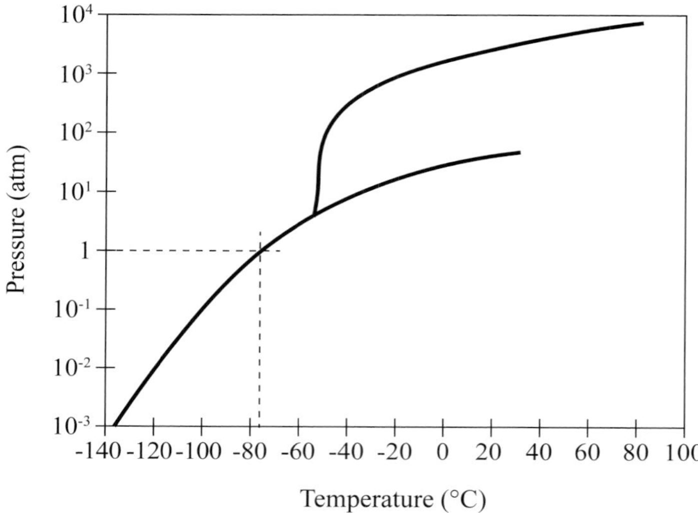

Figure 1 Phase diagram of dry ice

In an experiment, dry ice was placed in a cylindrical piston chamber of radius *R*, sides of negligible thickness, and height *h*. The mass of the piston, which was used to seal the chamber, was small enough to be considered negligible as well.

After adding the dry ice, the system was sealed with a piston, and various quantities of weights with mass *m* were added on top of the piston. Once thermal equilibrium with the surroundings was achieved, the depression of the piston was recorded after it stabilized, as a function of the total weight depressing it. A schematic of this experiment is shown in Figure 2.

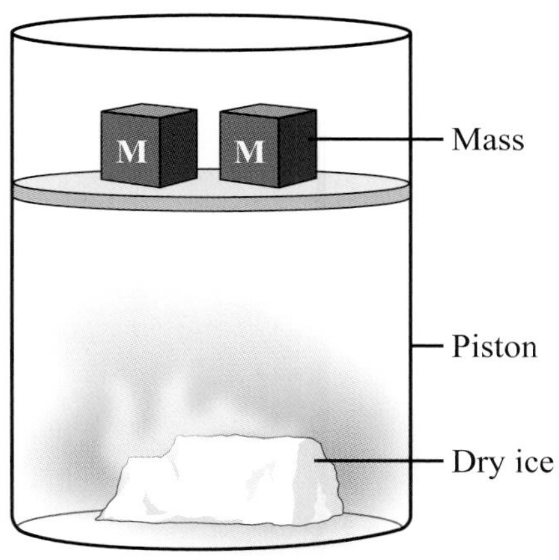

Figure 2 Schematic of experimental design

The volume of a cylinder is described by Equation 1.

$$V = \pi r^2 h$$

Equation 1

Question 53

Which of the following graphs best illustrates the relationship between m and h?

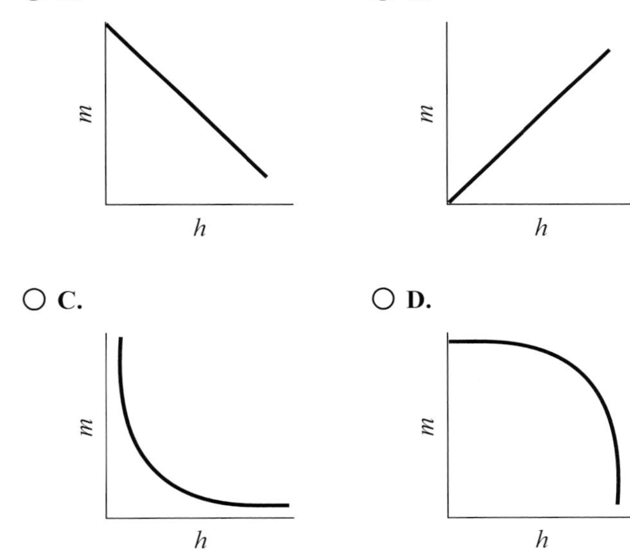

Question 54

Which of the following does NOT describe carbon dioxide's phase behavior?

- **A.** At −57°C and 5.1 atm, CO_2 exists in equilibrium between the solid, liquid, and gas phases.
- **B.** At 31°C and 72.8 atm, CO_2 exists as neither a liquid nor a gas.
- **C.** At −60.5°C and 10 atm, CO_2 exists as a solid.
- **D.** At −48.1°C and 10 atm, CO_2 will not freeze.

Question 55

What expression will solve for the mass of dry ice added to the piston chamber if only one weight is placed on top of the piston and the entire mass of dry ice sublimates?
(Note: $MWCO_2$ = molecular mass of CO_2)

- **A.** $\left(\frac{mgh}{RT}\right) \times MW_{CO_2}$
- **B.** $mghRT \times MW_{CO_2}$
- **C.** $\frac{mgh}{(RT \times MW_{CO_2})}$
- **D.** $\frac{mg}{(hRT \times MW_{CO_2})}$

Question 56

What is true during dry ice manufacturing when the carbon dioxide liquid enters the gas phase?

- **A.** $\Delta H > 0$ and $\Delta S < 0$
- **B.** $\Delta H > 0$ and $\Delta S > 0$
- **C.** $\Delta H < 0$ and $\Delta S < 0$
- **D.** $\Delta H < 0$ and $\Delta S > 0$

Questions 57 - 59 do not refer to a passage and are independent of each other.

Question 57

Air is normally 80% nitrogen and 20% oxygen. If on a humid day, water vapor comprises 5% of air, the new partial pressure of oxygen will be:

- O **A.** 95.0% of its initial partial pressure.
- O **B.** 97.5% of its initial partial pressure.
- O **C.** 75.0% of its initial partial pressure.
- O **D.** unchanged from its initial partial pressure.

Question 58

Which of the following are possible units for the universal gas constant R?

- O **A.** $L \cdot atm \cdot mol^{-1} \cdot K^{-1}$
- O **B.** $L^{-1} \cdot atm \cdot mol^{-1} \cdot K^{-1}$
- O **C.** $L^{-1} \cdot atm^{-1} \cdot mol \cdot K$
- O **D.** $L \cdot atm \cdot mol^{-1}$

Question 59

Assuming He behaves like an ideal gas, how many liters do 4 moles of He occupy at STP?

- O **A.** 9.0 L
- O **B.** 22.4 L
- O **C.** 89.6 L
- O **D.** 97.8 L

TEST 5A

STOP. If you finish before time is called, check your work. You may go back to any question in this test.

ANSWERS & EXPLANATIONS for Test 5A can be found on p. 308.

Phases

MINI-TEST 5B

Time: 45 minutes
Questions 1–29

DIRECTIONS: Most of the questions in this test section are grouped with a passage. Read the passage, then select the best answer to each question. Some questions are independent of any passage and of one another. Select the best answer to each of these questions. If you are unsure of an answer, rule out incorrect choices and select from the remaining options. Indicate your selection beside the option you choose. A periodic table can be found on the last page of this book for you to use at any point during this test section.

Passage 1 (Questions 1-5)

The average human body is approximately 55-75% water by weight. Proper homeostatic management of body hydration is crucial for survival because water is the medium in which virtually the body's entire metabolism occurs. In addition, water, in the form of sweat, plays an equally vital role in thermoregulation.

Water's performance as an effective cooling agent in sweat stems from both its high specific heat capacity ($C_{H_2O} = 4.18$ J/K · g) and its enthalpy of vaporization (ΔH_{vap} = 40.7 kJ/mol). Environmental factors that prevent the vaporization of sweat, such as an elevated atmospheric partial pressure of water, commonly referred to as humidity, are associated with an increased risk of hyperthermia and its sequelae: heat stroke, organ failure, and death. Once humidity reaches the saturation vapor pressure of water on the surface of the skin, it is impossible for sweat to evaporate. The temperature dependence of saturation vapor pressure is shown in Figure 1.

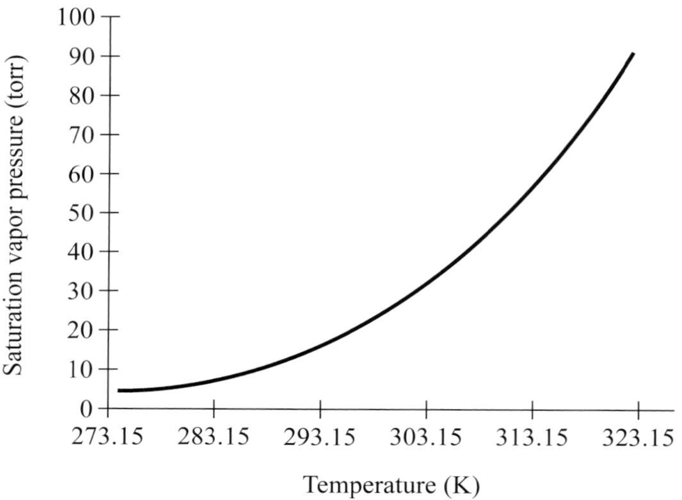

Figure 1 Temperature dependence of saturation vapor pressure

Evaporative heat loss from the skin to the environment (E) is governed not only by the difference in water vapor pressure between the surface of the skin and the atmosphere (ΔP), but is also influenced by the effective radiating surface area of the skin (A). These parameters obey the relationship $\frac{E}{(A \cdot \Delta P)} = h_e$ where h_e, the coefficient of evaporative heat transfer, is constant.

If sweat cannot evaporate, and the body's temperature continues to rise, vital cellular enzymes will cease to function effectively. Further temperature increases may even denature these enzymes altogether, causing severe dysfunction of the heart and brain. Figure 2 shows the temperature dependence of a certain cardiac enzyme.

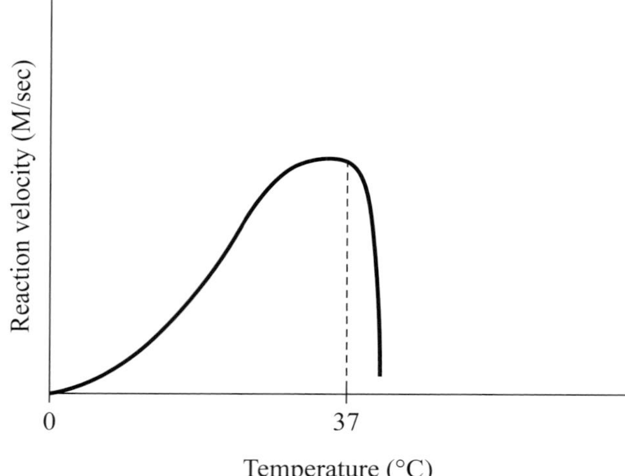

Figure 2 Effect of temperature on enzyme function

Question 1

If an athlete trains without a shirt and increases the effective radiating surface area by half of its original value, the evaporative heat loss will:

- O **A.** increase by 50%.
- O **B.** increase by 66%.
- O **C.** increase by 150%.
- O **D.** decrease by 150%.

Question 2

Suppose sweat has reached thermal equilibrium with skin at 40°C. What vapor pressure of atmospheric moisture will prevent evaporative heat loss?

- O **A.** 20 torr
- O **B.** 30 torr
- O **C.** 55 torr
- O **D.** 92 torr

Question 3

Vaporizing 1 g of boiling water compared to bringing 1 g of 0°C water to 100°C requires approximately:

- O **A.** 5 times more energy.
- O **B.** 10 times more energy.
- O **C.** 100 times more energy.
- O **D.** half as much energy.

Question 4

Which of the following is true when equilibrium is reached between sweat on the skin and atmospheric moisture?

- **A.** No water can condense on the skin.
- **B.** No water can vaporize from the skin.
- **C.** Water can vaporize from the skin.
- **D.** No water can condense or vaporize from the skin.

Question 5

In a separate study, different fabrics were wrapped around participants' skin. After spending 12 hours in the same room, the fabrics were removed and sweat production was recorded in the table below:

Fabric polymer	Sweat (mL)
W	3.0
X	1.0
Y	0.3
Z	5.0

Based on the passage, which hypothesis is most likely correct?

- **A.** Fabric W is the least permeable to gases and fabric Y is the most permeable to gases.
- **B.** Fabric Z is the most permeable to gases and fabric Y is the least permeable to gases.
- **C.** Fabric Y is the most permeable to gases and fabric Z is the least permeable to gases.
- **D.** Fabric X is most permeable to gases.

Passage 2 (Questions 6-11)

An experiment was conducted to investigate the thermochemical properties of inert elemental solids with regard to their heat absorption characteristics. For this purpose, 0.1 moles of various elements were heated and placed in a sealed and thermally insulated solution of deionized water. The temperature change of the solution ΔT_s and that of the various elements ΔT_e, along with the specific heat capacity of the water solution c_s, and the mass of the water solution m_s were used to calculate the specific heat of each element. Some data from this experiment is shown in Table 1.

Table 1 Thermochemical and Physical Properties of Elemental Solids

Element	Specific Heat (J/g · K)	Density (g/cm^3)
Al	0.904	2.7
Si	0.710	2.3
Fe	0.449	7.9
Co	0.421	8.9
Ni	0.445	8.9
Cu	0.384	8.9

In pre-modern times, early chemists realized that, for many elements, the specific heat could be approximated with a constant, K, divided by the molecular weight, M, of the element.

$$M = \frac{K}{c}$$

Equation 1

Equation 1 is not valid for all cases. For elements under cryogenic settings, the quantum mechanical behavior of energy storage introduces errors into this equation, rendering it invalid.

Question 6

Which graph best illustrates the approximate relationship between M and c?

A.

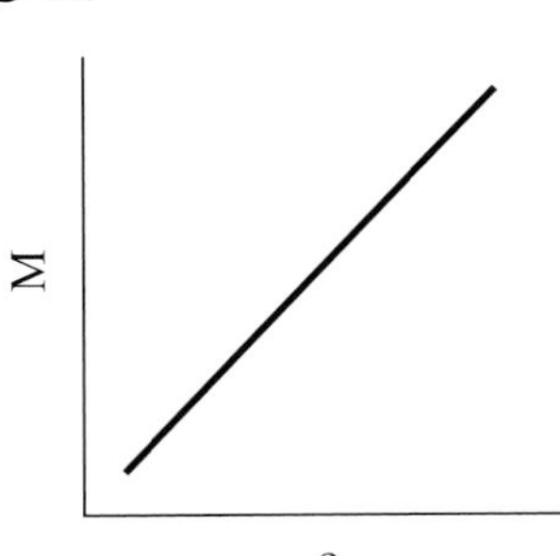

B.

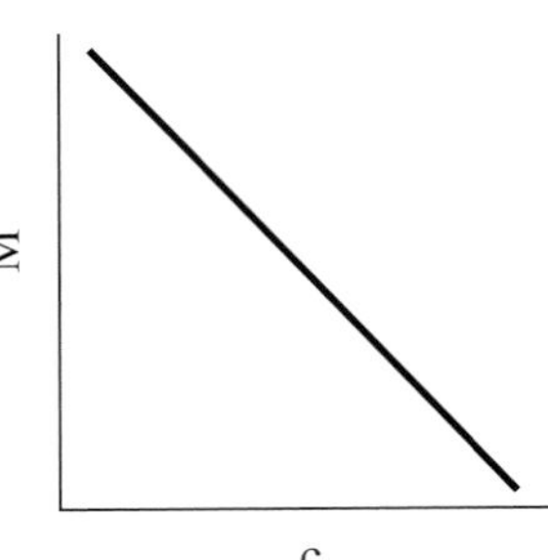

C.

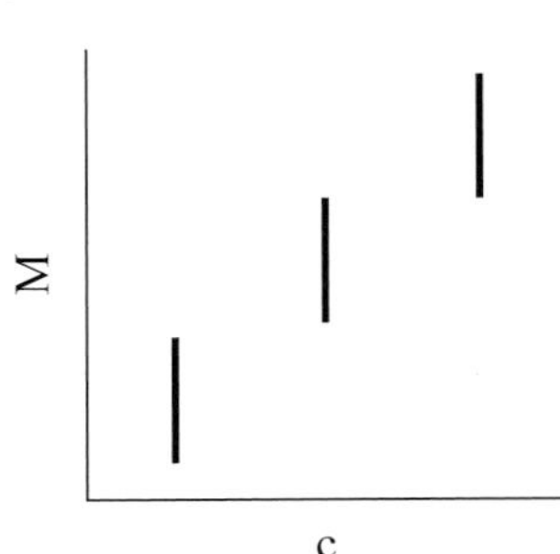

D.

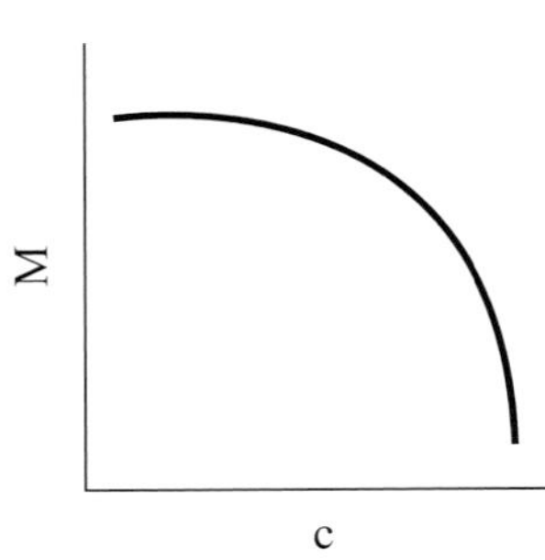

Question 7

What was the goal of the experiment described in the passage?

- **A.** To evaluate water's capacity to resist changes in temperature
- **B.** To apply the conservation of energy in order to calculate the specific heat capacity of metals
- **C.** To calculate a constant that relates specific heat capacity to molecular weight
- **D.** To study the relationship between density and specific heat capacity

Question 8

Ethanol's specific heat capacity is about half the specific heat of water. If the experiment described in this passage were repeated with ethanol instead of water, what would be observed?

- **A.** The magnitude of ΔT_s would increase and the magnitude of ΔT_e would increase.
- **B.** The magnitude of ΔT_s would decrease and the magnitude of ΔT_e would decrease.
- **C.** The magnitude of ΔT_s would increase and the magnitude of ΔT_e would decrease.
- **D.** The magnitude of ΔT_s would decrease and the magnitude of ΔT_e would increase.

Question 9

How should the variables described in the passage be arranged to solve for the specific heat capacity of a metal sample?

- **A.** $\frac{10 m_s c_s \Delta T_s}{M \Delta T_e}$
- **B.** $m_s c_s \Delta T_s$
- **C.** $\frac{10 m_s c_s \Delta T_e}{M \Delta T_s}$
- **D.** $10 M c_s \Delta T_s$

Question 10

After addition of a nickel sample, a 25°C 100 g water solution boiled. All of the following are true EXCEPT: (Note $c_w = 4.2$ J/g • K)

- **A.** the vapor pressure of the solution was at least equal to atmospheric pressure.
- **B.** 31.5 kJ of energy was gained by the water.
- **C.** addition of a hotter piece of nickel would not result in a greater temperature change for the water solution.
- **D.** at thermal equilibrium, the average velocity of the nickel sample is the same as the average velocity of the water solution.

Question 11

Identical masses of Al and Ni were heated to the same temperature and added to identical solutions of water. The solution which received the Al sample experienced a change in temperature that was:

- **A.** double that of the solution which received the Ni.
- **B.** half that of the solution which received the Ni.
- **C.** the same as that of the solution which received the Ni.
- **D.** a quarter that of the solution which received the Ni.

Questions 12 - 15 do not refer to a passage and are independent of each other.

Question 12

A mercury thermometer obeys similar principles as a mercury barometer. Which of the following explains this phenomenon?

- **A.** Mercury has a melting point of −39°C.
- **B.** Mercury has a boiling point of 357°C.
- **C.** Boyle's law dictates the barometer, and Charles' law dictates the thermometer.
- **D.** Charles' law dictates the barometer, and Boyle's law dictates the thermometer.

Question 13

Which of the following gases deviates most from ideal behavior?

Gas	*a*	*b*
Ammonia (NH_3)	4.2	0.04
Bromine (Br_2)	9.6	0.06
Neon (Ne)	0.2	0.02
Water (H_2O)	5.5	0.03

- **A.** Ammonia
- **B.** Bromine
- **C.** Neon
- **D.** Water

Question 14

Increasing the temperature of a sealed sample of $CO_2(g)$ by 5°C requires:

- **A.** the most energy if its pressure remains constant, but its volume can change.
- **B.** the most energy if its volume remains constant, but its pressure can change.
- **C.** an equal amount of energy whether the energy is added under isobaric or isovolumetric conditions.
- **D.** the most energy if neither its pressure nor volume can change.

Question 15

A warm water bath is often used to thaw frozen blood prior to transfusion. How much heat is required to thaw a 0.5 kg unit of blood from 0°C to 25°C? (Blood has a heat capacity of 3600 J/kg/°C)

- **A.** 12.5 kJ
- **B.** 45 kJ
- **C.** 90 kJ
- **D.** 1800 J

Passage 3 (Questions 16-20)

Microwave ovens heat food via dielectric heating. The electromagnetic waves they emit pass over food and cause polar molecules to rotate as they attempt to align with the alternating electric field of the microwaves. This rotation increases the kinetic energy of the molecules that compose the food and is more pronounced in molecules with stronger dipole moments.

In addition to heating food, microwave ovens can be used to sterilize materials through the production of steam. Recently this approach has been suggested as a way to recycle filtering face-piece respirators (FFR) for home and healthcare environments during an influenza pandemic. Without sterilization, reuse of FFRs may result in a risk of viral transmission by touching a contaminated surface of the respirator followed by contact with the eyes, nose, or mouth.

Steam production is conveniently accomplished with off-the-shelf microwave steam bags (MSBs). Because these bags are sealed, except for a small exhaust port in the side, the water inside can easily overcome the heat of vaporization, which is 40.0 kJ/mol. Once supplied with water, sealed, and exposed to microwave radiation, the MSBs produce steam (Figure 1).

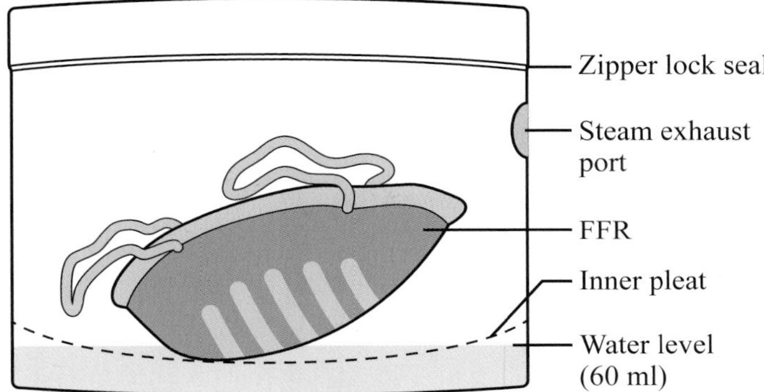

Figure 1 Microwave steam bag

In an experiment, researchers contaminated FFRs with the MS2 virus and sterilized the FFRs using MSBs. The results are in Table 1.

Table 1 Decontamination Efficacy of the Microwave Steam Bags

	FFR model	MS2 from load controls $\log_{10}$ (pfu/ FFR)	MS2 from stream treated FFR $\log_{10}$ (pfu/ FFR)	Difference (load vs. treated) $\log_{10}$ (pfu/ FFR)	Reduction (%)
MSB X	1870	7.57	4.47	3.10	99.90
	KC	7.09	3.85	3.25	99.93
	Moldex	9.96	5.32	4.64	99.99
MSB Y	1870	6.93	3.69	3.24	99.94
	KC	8.15	4.70	3.45	99.93
	Moldex	7.04	3.93	3.11	99.86

This passage was adapted from "Evaluation of Microwave Steam Bags for the Decontamination of Filtering Facepiece Respirators." Fisher E, Williams J, Shaffer R. *PLoS ONE*. 2011. 6(4) doi:10.1371/journal.pone.0018585 for use under the terms of the Creative Commons CC BY 3.0 Attribution license (http://creativecommons.org/licenses/by/3.0/legalcode).

Question 16

How much energy is required to create steam using a room temperature MSB as described in the passage?

(Note: $C_{H_2O} = 4.1\ \text{J g}^{-1}\ ^\circ\text{C}^{-1}$)

- O **A.** 18.5 kJ
- O **B.** 181×10^2 kJ
- O **C.** 151.6 kJ
- O **D.** 133.2 kJ

Question 17

What change to the experimental procedure would increase the temperature of the liquid water during the sterilization procedure?

I. Saturate the water with sodium chloride.
II. Expand the bag to increase its surface area.
III. Seal the exhaust port.

- O **A.** III only
- O **B.** I and II only
- O **C.** I and III only
- O **D.** I, II, III

Question 18

What was the primary goal of the experiment in the passage?

- O **A.** To calculate the energy necessary to vaporize water in a microwave.
- O **B.** To evaluate the heat capacity of different masks.
- O **C.** To determine which FFR can be best sterilized with conductive heating.
- O **D.** To determine which FFR can be best sterilized with convection heating.

Question 19

The KC FFR has a specific heat of $2\ \text{J g}^{-1}\ \text{K}^{-1}$. If the Moldex FFR has twice the mass of the KC FFR, but absorbs the same amount of energy when water boils from room temperature, what is its specific heat?

- O **A.** $1\ \text{J g}^{-1}\ \text{K}^{-1}$
- O **B.** $2\ \text{J g}^{-1}\ \text{K}^{-1}$
- O **C.** $4\ \text{J g}^{-1}\ \text{K}^{-1}$
- O **D.** $6\ \text{J g}^{-1}\ \text{K}^{-1}$

Question 20

Four MSBs were filled, and heated on a tray with the following materials:

Substance	Specific heat J/g · K
Olive oil	1.97
Ethanol	2.46
Benzene	1.74
Water	4.18

In what order will they reach 70°C ?

- O **A.** Water, Ethanol, Olive Oil, Benzene
- O **B.** Benzene, Olive Oil, Ethanol, Water
- O **C.** Benzene, Ethanol, Olive Oil, Water
- O **D.** Water, Olive Oil, Ethanol, Benzene

Passage 4 (Questions 21-26)

In recent decades, routine screening has helped to significantly reduce the incidence and deaths from invasive carcinoma (IC) of the uterine cervix in the USA. Nonetheless, current technology is unable to distinguish between early and more advanced stages of IC, or other disease status indicators, such as nodal involvement.

In a recent experiment, differential scanning calorimetry (DSC) was used for the characterization of plasma in patients with cervical disease. DSC is commonly used to measure the denaturation profiles of biomolecules, known as thermograms, by directly monitoring the change in heat capacity associated with molecular events as a function of temperature. This is accomplished by comparing the energy, q_s, required to raise the sample to a specific temperature, to the energy, q_r, required to raise a reference medium, made of the solvent solution, to the same temperature. The excess heat capacity C_p^{ex} can be derived from the energy difference, Δq, observed at each temperature, where $\Delta q = q_s - q_r$.

The differential scanning calorimeter used in this experiment operated with a power source of 100 V and heated both the reference medium and the sample with two separate resistors of equivalent resistance, as shown in Figure 1. Each cell contained 50 mL of solution.

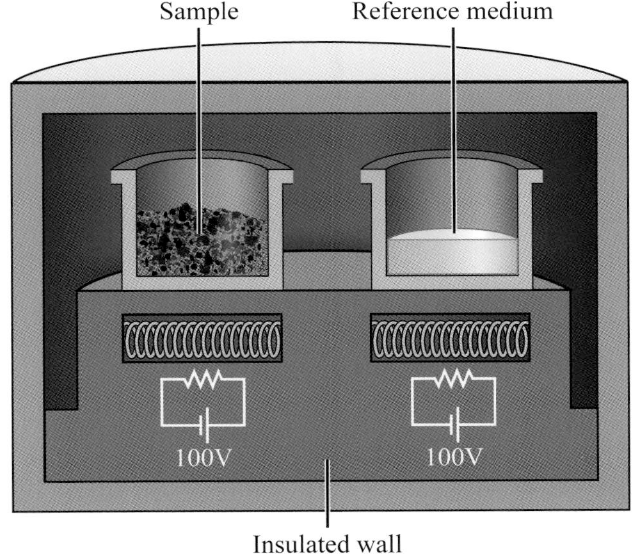

Figure 1 Schematic of the differential scanning calorimeter used in the experiment

The thermogram of plasma from healthy individuals reflected the weighted sum of the denaturation profiles of the most abundant plasma proteins; however, thermograms from individuals with various conditions or diseases are significantly changed, as shown in Figure 2. It is believed these changes reflect the presence of biomarkers that modify or interact with plasma proteins, thereby affecting their denaturation properties.

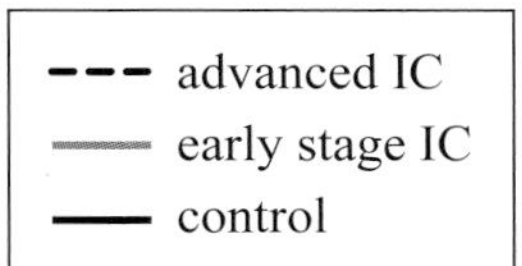

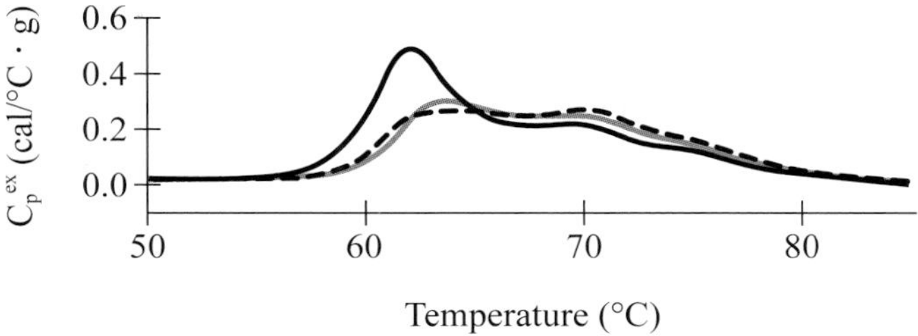

Figure 2 Thermogram of plasma from control and patients with IC

This passage was adapted from "Detection of Cervical Cancer Biomarker Patterns in Blood Plasma and Urine by Differential Scanning Calorimetry and Mass Spectrometry." Garbett NC, Merchant ML, Helm CW, Jenson AB, Klein JB, et al. *PLoS ONE*. 2014. 9(1) doi:10.1371/journal.pone.0084710 for use under the terms of the Creative Commons CC BY 4.0 license (http://creativecommons.org/licenses/by/4.0/legalcode).

Question 21

To provide accurate measurements, the reference medium will:

- A. have a specific heat capacity which is greater than that of the sample solution.
- B. contain the same solutes in the same concentration as in the sample solution.
- C. contain the same mass of solvent as does the sample solution.
- D. have a specific heat capacity which is less than that of the sample solution.

Question 22

If the differential scanning calorimeter heated a sample solution 1°C/min, what is the resistance of its resistor? (Note: $\rho_{solution}$ 1.0 g/mL and $c_{solution} = 4.1$ J/g · K)

- A. 29.3 Ω
- B. 2926 Ω
- C. 48.9 Ω
- D. 2232 Ω

Question 23

If DSC were performed by cooling the sample solution from 55°C to 50°C, which of the following best illustrates the cooling rate of the sample solution relative to the reference medium? (Note: → = direction of sweep)

- A.

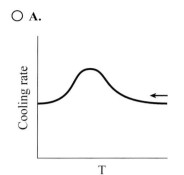

- B.

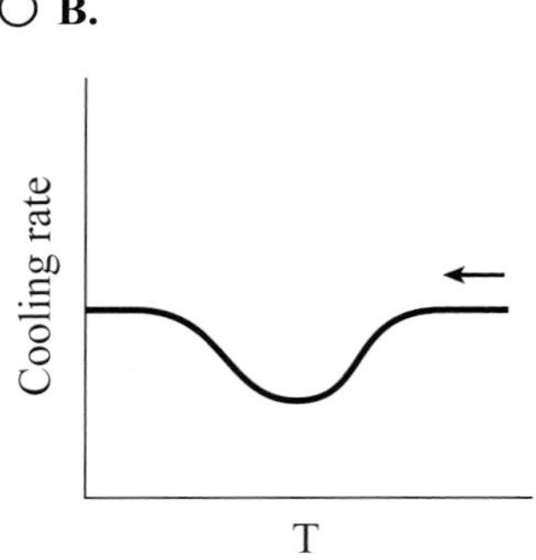

- C.

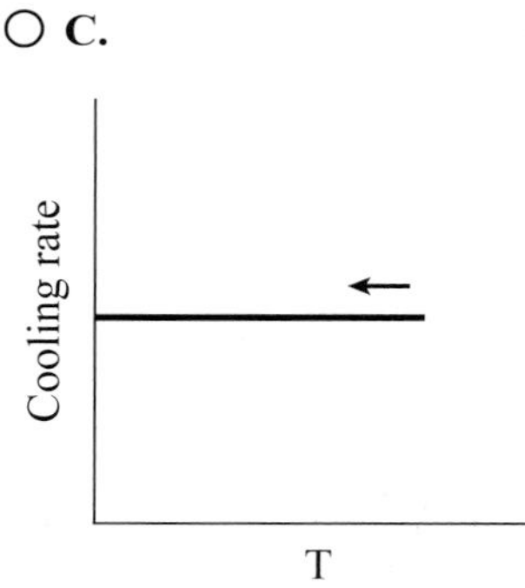

- D.

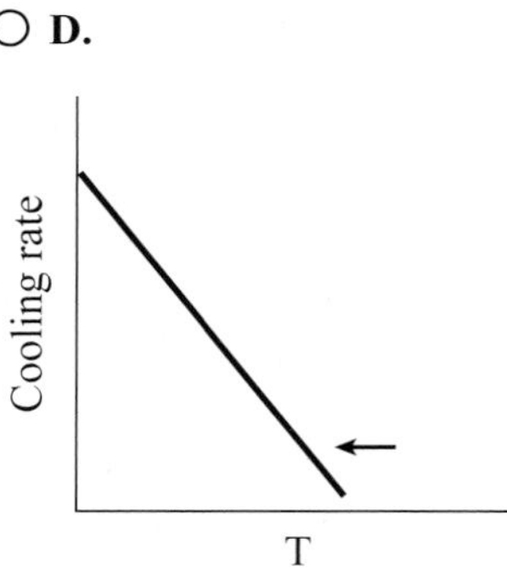

Question 24

If the reference medium was buffered, and contained a concentrated non-volatile solute, relative to the pure solvent, the reference medium:

- **A.** will exhibit a greater vapor pressure.
- **B.** will exhibit a smaller vapor pressure.
- **C.** will exhibit the same vapor pressure.
- **D.** will exhibit a greater or smaller vapor pressure depending on the concentration of the solute.

Question 25

What is the value of Δq during the DSC trial of the advanced IC serum between 50°C and 55°C? (Note: $\rho_{solution}$ 1.0 g/mL and $C_{solution}$ = 4.1 J/g · K)

- **A.** 1025 J
- **B.** −1025 J
- **C.** 1000 J
- **D.** 0 J

Question 26

Water accounts for 93% of serum volume, and its phase diagram is shown below:

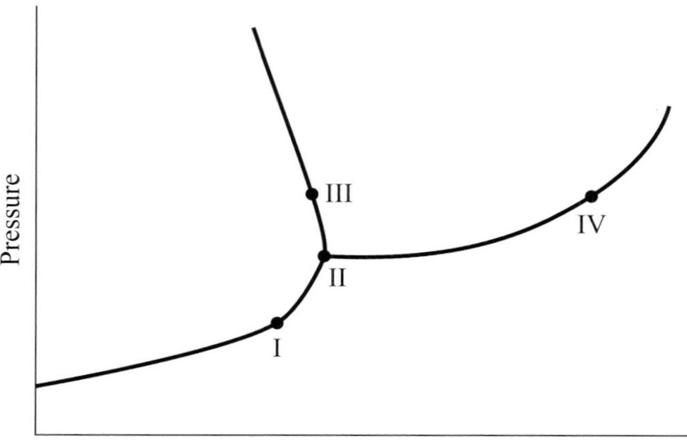

At what point will water sublimate?

- **A.** I
- **B.** II
- **C.** III
- **D.** IV

Questions 27 - 29 do not refer to a passage and are independent of each other.

Question 27

How much more work is required to expand a spherical balloon's radius from four-times its relaxed length r_o to five-times its relaxed length, with a constant filling pressure of 1.022 atm? (Note: $V_{sphere} = \frac{4}{3}\pi r^3$; 1 atm = 10^5 Pa; r_o = 5 cm)

- A. $\frac{1.022 \times 10^5 \times 4 \times (20^3 - 25^3) \times \pi}{3}$ J
- B. $\frac{1.022 \times 4 \times (20^3 - 25^3) \times \pi}{3}$ J
- C. $\frac{1.022 \times 10^3 \times 4 \times (20^3 - 25^3) \times \pi}{3}$ J
- D. $\frac{1.022 \times 4 \times (20^3 - 25^3) \times \pi}{3}$ J

Question 28

Which of the following does NOT correctly describe a phase transition?

- A. Sublimation is the transition from a solid to liquid.
- B. Vaporization is the transition from a liquid to a gas.
- C. Condensation is the transition from a gas to a liquid.
- D. Deposition is the transition from a gas to a solid.

Question 29

What transition in Figure 1 corresponds to the evaporation of liquid refrigerant?

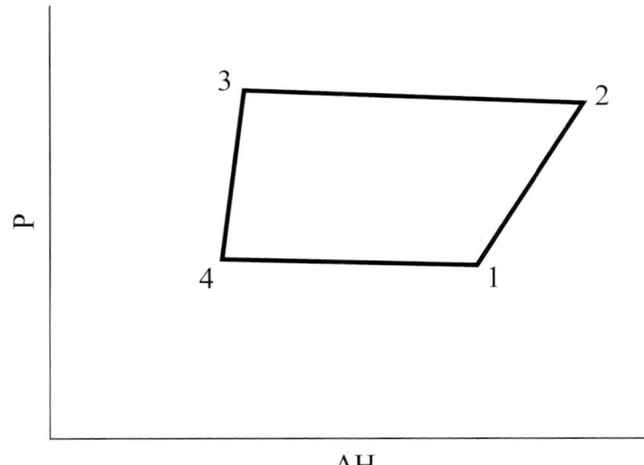

- A. 3 to 2
- B. 2 to 3
- C. 4 to 1
- D. 1 to 4

STOP. If you finish before time is called, check your work. You may go back to any question in this test.

ANSWERS & EXPLANATIONS for Test 5B can be found on p. 308.

Solutions and Electrochemistry

TEST 6A

Time: 95 minutes
Questions 1–59

DIRECTIONS: Most of the questions in this test section are grouped with a passage. Read the passage, then select the best answer to each question. Some questions are independent of any passage and of one another. Select the best answer to each of these questions. If you are unsure of an answer, rule out incorrect choices and select from the remaining options. Indicate your selection beside the option you choose. A periodic table can be found on the last page of this book for you to use at any point during this test section.

Passage 1 (Questions 1-5)

Nephrolithiasis, also called a kidney stone, is a common occurrence in the United States that can cause severe pain as the stones become lodged in parts of the ureters with a smaller diameter. Calcium oxalate (CaC_2O_4) is the most common precipitate found in uncomplicated cases. Risk factors for kidney stone formation include consistently low water intake, a high-sodium diet high, as well as certain genetic factors. The formation of calcium oxalate stones occurs via Reaction 1.

$$CaC_2O_4(s) \rightarrow Ca^{2+}(aq) + C^2O_4^{2-}(aq) \qquad K_{sp} = 1.5 \times 10^{-8}$$

Reaction 1

A higher rate of nephrolithiasis in the southern United States is often attributed to the increased risk of chronic dehydration. Another hypothesis proposes that the cause is large consumption of tea, particularly black iced tea without milk. This hypothesis stems from the observation that tea leaves contain a high amount of oxalate. To assess whether oxalate is efficiently extracted from the leaves, oxalate concentration of four different preparations of tea was measured using ion chromatography, which is able to determine the concentration of charged, water-soluble compounds. The results are shown in Figure 1.

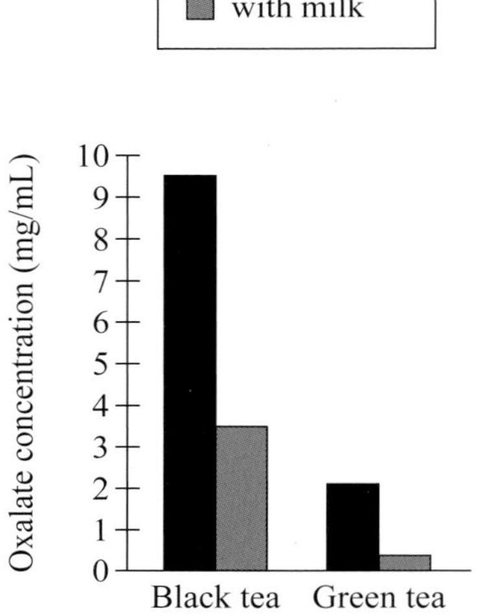

Figure 1 Oxalate concentration in four preparations of tea

The pH of urine can also affect the formation of kidney stones. The solubility of several compounds at varying pH values was determined and is displayed in Figure 2.

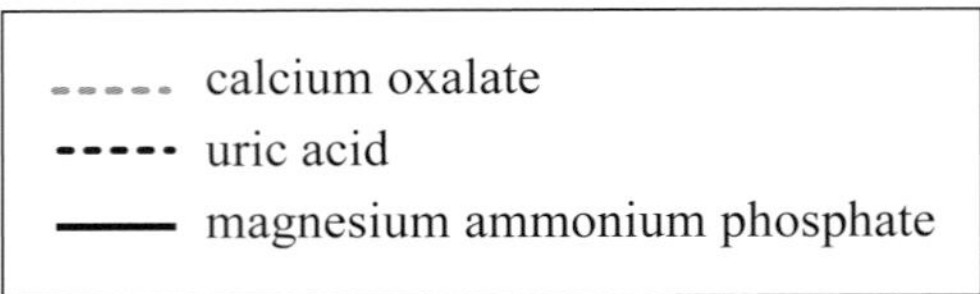

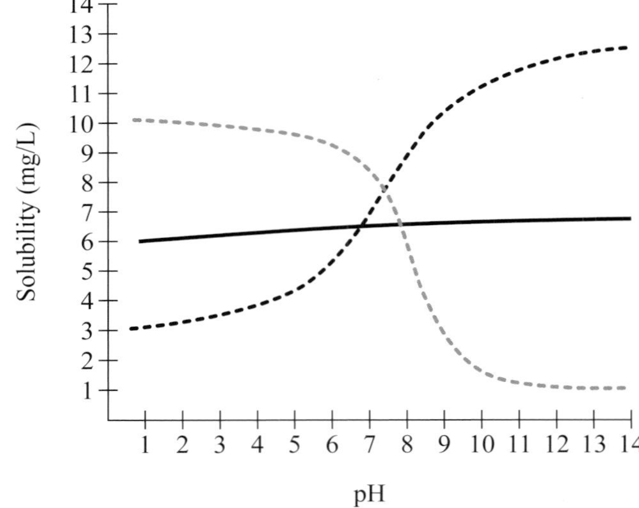

Figure 2 Solubility of several compounds and the effect of pH

Question 1

Which of the following ions could combine with calcium ions in the urine to form kidney stones?

- O **A.** Hydronium
- O **B.** Phosphate
- O **C.** Ammonium
- O **D.** Chloride

Question 2

Which of the following occurs when calcium oxalate stones are formed?

- O **A.** Dipole-dipole bonds are broken between water molecules and calcium ions.
- O **B.** Calcium covalently bonds with oxalate ions dissolved in the urine.
- O **C.** The K_{sp} for Reaction 1 decreases which causes the reaction to shift to the right.
- O **D.** Hydrogen bonds between water molecules are replaced by new bonds between H_2O and oxalate ions.

Question 3

Certain bacterial species have the protein urease that can lower the concentration of hydrogen ions in the urine. Based on the data in Figure 1, which of the following would most likely occur?

- O **A.** Phosphate ion concentration increases
- O **B.** Number of calcium oxalate stones increase
- O **C.** Uric acid solubility decreases
- O **D.** Precipitation of magnesium ammonium phosphate increases

Question 4

A patient comes to the hospital with severe dehydration. The risk of kidney stone formation would be increased by giving the patient:

- O **A.** IV fluid of 0.9% NaCl.
- O **B.** a sports drink containing NaCl, KCl, and $CaCl_2$.
- O **C.** tap water with high levels of precipitated $CaCO_3$.
- O **D.** green tea with milk.

Question 5

Which of the following best describes the orientation of the oxygen atoms in the water molecules used as a solvent for Reaction 1?

- O **A.** Towards calcium ions
- O **B.** Towards oxalate ions
- O **C.** Away from calcium oxalate
- O **D.** Towards other oxygen atoms of neighboring water molecules

Passage 2 (Questions 6-9)

Meningeal inflammation, including the presence of semi-organized tertiary lymphoid tissue, has been associated with cortical pathology at autopsy in secondary progressive multiple sclerosis (SPMS). Accessible and robust biochemical markers of cortical inflammation for use in SPMS clinical trials are needed. Increased levels of chemokines in the cerebrospinal fluid (CSF) can report on inflammatory processes occurring in the cerebral cortex of MS patients. A multiplexed chemokine array that included BAFF, a high sensitivity CXCL13 assay and composite chemokine scores were developed to explore differences in lymphoid (CXCL12, CXCL13, CCL19 and CCL21) and inflammatory (CCL2, CXCL9, CXCL10 and CXCL11) chemokines in a small pilot study. Paired CSF and serum samples were obtained from healthy controls ($n = 12$), relapsing-remitting MS (RRMS) ($n = 21$) and SPMS ($n = 12$). A subset of the RRMS patients ($n = 9$) was assessed upon disease exacerbation and 1 month later following intravenous methylprednisolone. SPMS patients were sampled twice to ascertain stability. Both lymphoid and inflammatory chemokines were elevated in RRMS and SPMS with the highest levels found in the active RRMS group. Inflammatory and lymphoid chemokine signatures were defined and generally correlated with each other. This small exploratory clinical study shows the feasibility of measuring complex and potentially more robust chemokine signatures in the CSF of MS patients during clinical trials. No differences were found between stable RRMS and SPMS. Future trials with larger patient cohorts with this chemokine array are needed to further characterize the differences, or the lack thereof, between stable RRMS and SPMS.

This passage was adapted from "Feasibility of the Use of Combinatorial Chemokine Arrays to Study Blood and CSF in Multiple Sclerosis." Edwards KR, Goyal J, Plavina T, Czerkowicz J, Goelz S, et al. *PLoS ONE*. 2013. 8(11) doi:10.1371/journal.pone.0081007 for use under the terms of the Creative Commons CC BY 3.0 license (http://creativecommons.org/licenses/by/3.0/legalcode).

Question 6

Inorganic phosphate concentration in the CSF has been used as a surrogate for blood brain barrier function. Which of the following ions is being measured?

- O **A.** PO_3^{2-}
- O **B.** PO_3^{3-}
- O **C.** PO_4^{2-}
- O **D.** PO_4^{3-}

Question 7

CXL13 is a protein ligand used for cell signaling. Which of the following amino acids on the surface of the protein would be expected to undergo stronger dipole interactions?

- O **A.** Ala
- O **B.** Gln
- O **C.** Phe
- O **D.** Tyr

Question 8

Methylprednisolone is a steroid that is not soluble in the aqueous fluids in the body. By which force is methylprednisolone transported through the blood by carrier proteins?

- O **A.** Ionic bonds
- O **B.** Hydrogen bonds
- O **C.** Dipole interactions
- O **D.** Van der Waal's forces

Question 9

Multiple sclerosis is caused by destruction of myelin along the axons of motor neurons. Which of the following depicts the electromotive force down the length of the axon in the absence of myelin?

O **A.**

Cell body −70 −70 −70 −70 −70 Axon terminal

O **B.**

Cell body −70 −70 40 40 40 Axon terminal

O **C.**

Cell body 40 −70 −70 −70 −70 Axon terminal

O **D.**

Cell body 40 40 40 40 40 Axon terminal

Questions 10 - 13 do not refer to a passage and are independent of each other.

Question 10

A high concentration of citrate in beverages lowers the likelihood of developing large calcium oxalate crystals. This is best explained by the fact that:

- O **A.** citric acid dissociates into citrate and hydrogen ions raising the pH.
- O **B.** citrate forms a complex ion with oxalate, which decreases the concentration of oxalate and increases the solubility of calcium oxalate.
- O **C.** citrate decreases the mass of calcium.
- O **D.** calcium complexes with citrate but remains dissolved in solution.

Question 11

What expression provides the solubility product constant of $ZnCl_2$?

- O **A.** $[Zn^{2+}][Cl^-]^4$
- O **B.** $[Zn^{2+}]^2[Cl^-]^2$
- O **C.** $[Zn^{2+}]^2[Cl^-]$
- O **D.** $[Zn^{2+}][Cl^-]^2$

Question 12

Which of the following additions to a mixture of solid anhydrous calcium sulfate and water will allow more anhydrous calcium sulfate to dissolve?

I. Addition of 1 g of barium nitrate
II. Addition of 1 g of sodium sulfate
III. Raising the temperature of the mixture
IV. Adding 25% more water to the mixture

- O **A.** I, II, III, and IV
- O **B.** I, III, and IV only
- O **C.** II, III, and IV only
- O **D.** I and III only

Question 13

The solubility, S, of H_2U is defined as the total analytical concentration of H_2U or $S = [H_2U] + [UH^-]$. Which of the following expressions provides the solubility of H_2U?

- O **A.** $\left(\frac{K_{sp}}{K_D}\right)\left(\frac{K_D}{10^{-pH}}+1\right)$
- O **B.** $\left(\frac{K_D}{K_{sp}}\right)\left(\frac{K_D}{10^{-pH}}+1\right)$
- O **C.** $\left(\frac{K_{sp}}{K_D}\right)\left(\frac{K_D}{10^{-pH}}-1\right)$
- O **D.** $\left(\frac{K_D}{K_{sp}}\right)\left(\frac{K_D}{10^{-pH}}-1\right)$

Passage 3 (Questions 14-17)

Bacteria can adapt to new stressful environments by morphological adjustment, genetic mutation, or metabolic alteration. These adaptations give rise to drug resistant bacterial species which can cause poorly treatable life-threatening infections. In a study, researchers sought to explore how well bacteria could adapt to challenging uncommon industrial environments.

The researchers introduced the bacteria into the electrolyte of a battery, consisting of $LiMn_2O_4$ (LMO) and zinc metal electrodes, in an aqueous electrolyte containing 0.1 M LiCl and 0.1 M $ZnCl_2$, pH adjusted to 4.0. The bacteria were challenged to survive numerous discharge/recharge cycles. After acclimating to the cell, the surviving bacteria were challenged in a similar electrolyte solution. The results of this phase of the study are shown below in Figure 1.

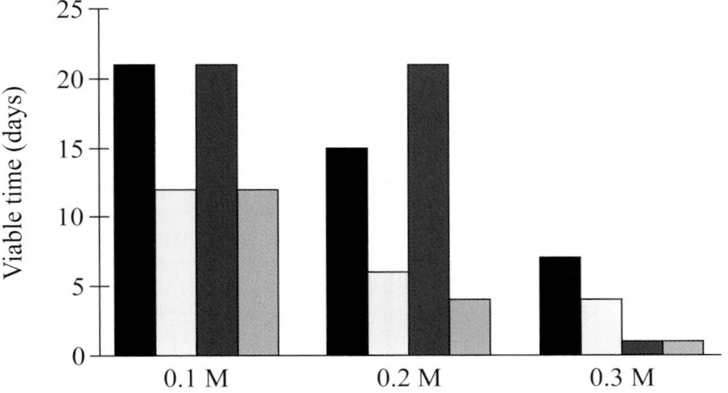

Figure 1 Viability of bacteria during osmotic challenge

The environmental stress encountered by the bacteria placed inside the battery include (1) ion shuttle: During discharge, Zn atoms lose electrons, become Zn^{2+}, hydrate into the electrolyte, and move to the LMO cathode. Hydrated Li^+ ions move to the cathode, obtain electrons and intercalate into the LMO matrix. Cl^- ions also move together with cations during both charge and discharge. (2) pH gradient: Due to the ion shuttling, a large pH gradient inside the battery exists while it is running. The pH gradients are approximately 3 at the anode, 9 at the cathode, and between 6 and 7 at the center of the wells. (3) Electric field: When direct current is applied to a pair of electrodes, an electric field inside the battery is generated. It induces a transmembrane potential inside the bacteria placed in the electrolyte, changing bacterial cell shape and surface hydrophobicity, the orientation of membrane lipids, net surface charge, DNA and protein synthesis, and bacterial activity and metabolism.

This passage was adapted from "Bacterial Acclimation Inside an Aqueous Battery." Dong D, Chen B, Chen P. *PLoS ONE*. 2015. 10(6) doi:10.1371/journal.pone.0129130 for use under the terms of the Creative Commons CC BY 4.0 Attribution license (http://creativecommons.org/licenses/by/4.0/legalcode)

Question 14

What is the concentration of OH^- in the cell described in the passage?

- A. 10^{-8}
- B. 10^{-10}
- C. 10^{-12}
- D. $10^{-8.5}$

Question 15

Which side reaction is most likely occurring at the anode?

- A. $2H_2O(l) \rightarrow 2H_2(g) + O_2(g)$
- B. $4\ OH^-(aq) \rightarrow O_2(g) + 2H2O(l) + 4e^-$
- C. $2H_2O(l) \rightarrow O_2(g) + 4H^+(aq) + 4e^-$
- D. $2H^+(aq) + 2e^- \rightarrow H_2(g)$

Question 16

Phosphatidylethanolamines (shown) are a class of membrane lipids found in the membrane of *E. coli*. When the cell is running, which of the following is true?

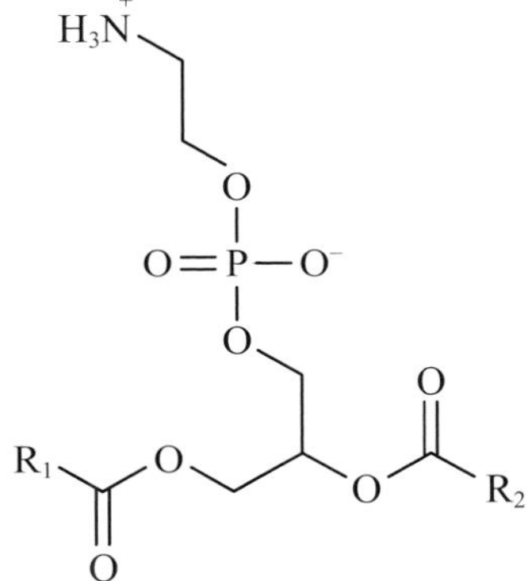

General structure of phosphatidylethanolamines

- A. The phosphate group of the lipid is oriented towards the LMO.
- B. The amino group of the lipid is oriented towards the LMO.
- C. The lipid molecule has a net charge of zero, and is not subject to influence by an electrical field.
- D. The lipid molecule continuously rotates to align with the electric field.

Question 17

What hypothesis is best supported by this experiment?

- A. Acclimated *E. coli* can survive osmotic challenges better than acclimated *B. subtilis*.
- B. *B. subtilis* can survive higher molarity electrolyte solutions than *E. coli*.
- C. Bacteria can only acclimate to a certain concentration threshold, at which point they are no longer viable.
- D. Acclimated *E. coli* is better capable of surviving the most lethal electrolyte concentration of the study than *B. subtilis*.

Passage 4 (Questions 18-21)

The term "chalk" refers to a variety of brittle solids, many of which are metal carbonate salts, exploited for several purposes. "Natural" chalk, calcium carbonate, is derived from the shells of aquatic organisms. Its basic properties allow it to be used as an antacid, alleviating symptoms of heart burn, and to deacidify soil for agricultural applications.

Natural chalk's third row analog, magnesium carbonate, is remarkably hygroscopic. In addition to its medical use as a potent laxative, magnesium carbonate can remove water from the hands and feet, improving athletic performance in sports such as weight lifting, gymnastics and rock climbing.

Curiously, classroom chalk is actually not made of a metal carbonate salt whatsoever. It is instead composed of gypsum, or calcium sulfate dihydrate. Upon dehydration followed by rehydration, gypsum becomes pliable and then forms a rigid solid. This chemical behavior makes it useful in orthopedic casts, which can be molded to immobilize broken bones. Casts are often made of gauze impregnated with dehydrated calcium sulfate. Hydration of gypsum proceeds through Reaction 1.

$$CaSO_4{\bullet}\tfrac{1}{2}H_2O(s) + \tfrac{3}{2}H_2O(l) \rightarrow CaSO_4{\bullet}2H_2O(s)$$

Reaction 1

The solubility properties of many chalks are shown in Table 1 below.

Table 1 Solubility Product Constants of Selected Chalks

Chalk	K_{sp}
Calcium carbonate	3.3×10^{-9}
Magnesium carbonate	$1 \times 10^{-7.8}$
Calcium sulfate dihydrate	3.1×10^{-5}
Calcium sulfate anhydrous	4.9×10^{-5}
Barium sulfate	1.1×10^{-10}

Question 18

If each chalk were added to pure water, which chalk-water mixture would have the greatest concentration of dissolved chalk?

- A. Barium sulfate
- B. Calcium sulfate anhydrous
- C. Calcium sulfate dihydrate
- D. Magnesium carbonate

Question 19

What is the ratio of the solubility of calcium sulfate dihydrate to barium sulfate?

- A. $2.8 \times 10^{5/2}$:1
- B. $1.6 \times 10^{5/2}$:1
- C. 2.8×10^{5}:1
- D. 1.6×10^{5}:1

TEST 6A

Question 20

Suppose a 50 mL solution of 1 M calcium acetate were mixed with a 3 M solution of ammonium carbonate until a precipitate no longer formed. What is the final volume of this solution?

- A. 16.6 mL
- B. 74.2 mL
- C. 66.6 mL
- D. 83.3 mL

Question 21

A copper wire was immersed in a solution containing solid silver carbonate. No reaction occurred until nitric acid was added, causing silver to plate on the copper wire. Based on these findings, which of the following statements is most likely true?

- A. Nitric acid acts as a Lewis acid catalyst.
- B. Immersion of a silver wire in a solution containing copper sulfate would cause copper to plate on the silver wire, after nitric acid had been added.
- C. Immersion of a silver wire in a solution containing copper sulfate would cause copper to plate on the silver wire, without requiring the addition of nitric acid.
- D. Bubbles were observed forming on the solid silver carbonate during this experiment.

Passage 5 (Questions 22-25)

Enamel is a unique bodily tissue, containing no blood supply. In addition, it is a largely inorganic structure, primarily composed of the mineral hydroxyapatite. The very low solubility of hydroxyapatite allows for the remineralization of enamel to compensate for losses due to chemical or mechanical causes, such as consuming sweets or bruxism.

Hydroxyapatite demineralizes and remineralizes according to the equilibrium shown in Reaction 1.

$$Ca_{10}(PO_4)_6(OH)_2(s) \leftrightarrow 10Ca^{2+}(aq) + 6PO_4^{3-}(aq) + 2OH^-(aq)$$
$$K_{sp} = 2.34 \times 10^{-59}$$

Reaction 1

When remineralization occurs at a slower rate than demineralization, enamel is lost. If too much enamel is lost, dental caries, or cavities, may form, allowing bacteria to infiltrate the softer living tissues of the tooth, resulting in pain and possibly dangerous infections.

A standard treatment for dental caries is removing the decayed material and filling it. Although modern polymers which match the color of the tooth exist, silver amalgam is cheaper and often the filling of choice for many patients.

Some patients with silver amalgam report experiencing pain if they accidentally put aluminum foil in their mouth. This pain results from the current generated through the coupled Reactions 2 and 3, occurring in the mouth at the oxidized surface of the silver amalgam as it reacts with the aluminum foil.

$$Al(s) \rightarrow Al^{3+}(aq) + 3e^-$$

Reaction 2

$$Ag_2O(s) + 2e^- \rightarrow 2Ag(s) + O^{2-}(g)$$

Reaction 3

Question 22

For every nanogram of aluminum which is oxidized, how many nanograms of the elemental silver are formed?

- A. 8.0 ng
- B. 1.3 ng
- C. 1.0 ng
- D. 12.0 ng

Question 23

Which of the following expressions provides the molar solubility of hydroxyapatite?

- A. $\sqrt[18]{\dfrac{2.34\times10^{-59}}{10^{10}\times6^{6}\times4}}$
- B. $\sqrt[18]{\dfrac{2.34\times10^{-59}}{5^{10}\times3^{6}}}$
- C. $2\times\sqrt[18]{\dfrac{2.34\times10^{-59}}{5^{10}\times3^{6}}}$
- D. $3\times\sqrt[18]{\dfrac{2.34\times10^{-59}}{10^{10}\times6^{6}\times4}}$

Question 24

During Reactions 2 and 3, saliva acts:

- A. analogously to the wire in an electrochemical cell.
- B. analogously to the anode in an electrochemical cell.
- C. analogously to the salt bridge in an electrochemical cell.
- D. analogously to the cathode in an electrochemical cell.

Question 25

For every decrease in a pH unit, the solubility of hydroxyapatite increases by a factor of ten. Based on this information, which of the following graphs best illustrate the solubility of hydroxyapatite?

A.

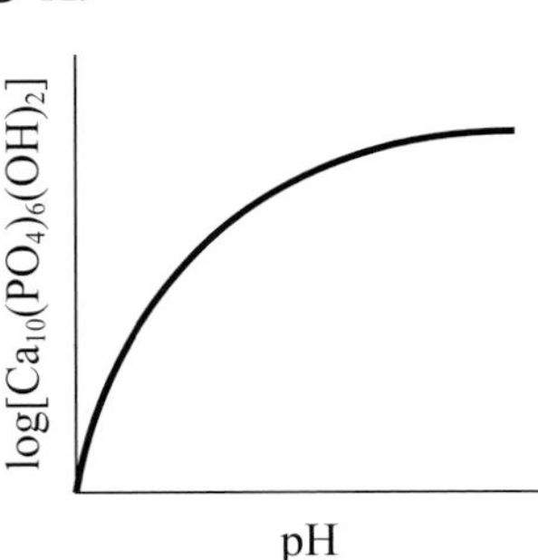

B.

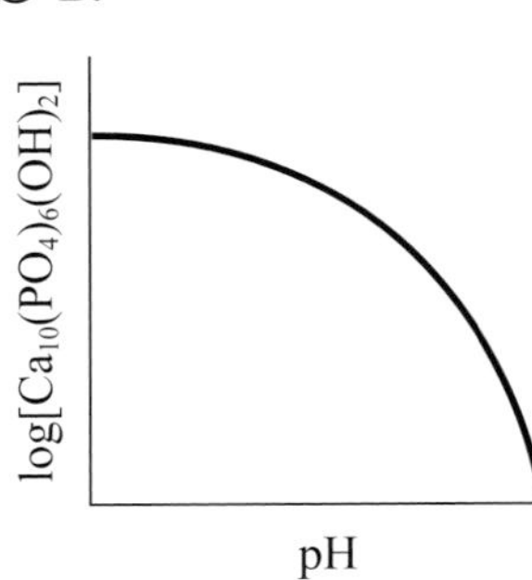

C.

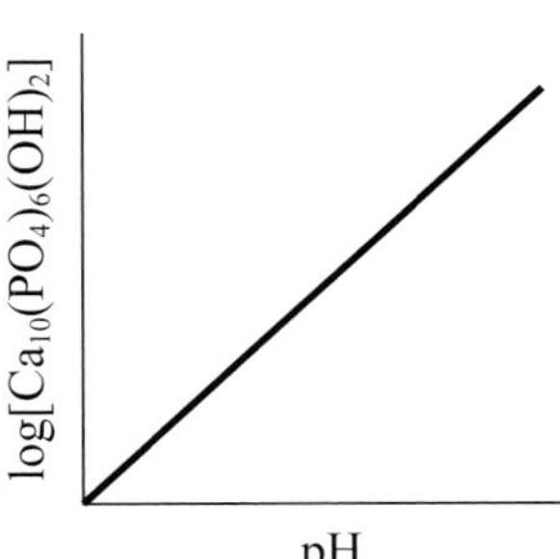

D.

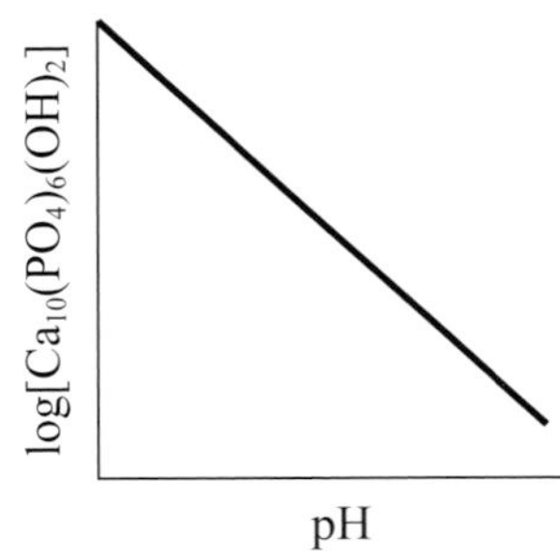

Questions 26 - 29 do not refer to a passage and are independent of each other.

Question 26

Guanine is likely to be most soluble in:

- A. H_2O.
- B. EtOH.
- C. methane.
- D. nonane.

Question 27

Iron(III) hydroxide is fairly insoluble with a K_{sp} of 2.8×10^{-39}. At room temperature, how much less soluble is iron(III) hydroxide in an aqueous solution with a pH of 8, compared to neutral water?

- A. 10 times less soluble
- B. 100 times less soluble
- C. 1000 times less soluble
- D. 10,000 times less soluble

Question 28

The electrolyte of lead battery is a solution of 30% sulfuric acid by mass. What is the molarity of a 1 L solution of this electrolyte? (Note: $\rho_{solution} = 1$ g/mL)

- A. 3 M
- B. 2.5 M
- C. 4 M
- D. 3.5 M

Question 29

To prepare a solution of bicarbonate to infuse into the acidotic blood of a patient, a physician dissolves sodium bicarbonate into a solution of 1 M water. Which of the following can be used to solve for the solubility product?

- A. $K_{sp} = [Na^+][HCO_3^-]$
- B. $K_{sp} = [Na^+]^2[HCO_3^-]$
- C. $K_{sp} = \dfrac{[Na^+][HCO_3^-]}{[NaHCO_3]}$
- D. $K_{sp} = \dfrac{[Na^+]^2[HCO_3^-]}{[H_2O]}$

Passage 6 (Questions 30-33)

Diabetes describes a group of metabolic disorders that result in abnormally high concentrations of blood glucose. If unmanaged, diabetes can prove to be a lethal condition due to complications arising from hyperglycemia such as stroke, cardiovascular disease, coma, blindness, kidney failure, and ulcers of the lower extremities. Due to the lower pH of the urine of a patient with diabetes, products from purine metabolism such as adenine, xanthine, and uric acid (H_2U) can precipitate in the forms of kidney stones.

The dissociation of H_2U in aqueous solution follows Reaction 1, and is governed by the equilibrium Equations 1 and 2.

$$H_2U(s) \leftrightarrow H^+(aq) + UH^-(aq)$$

Reaction 1

$$K_D = [H^+][UH^-]/[H_2U]$$

Equation 1

$$K_{sp} = [H^+][UH^-]$$

Equation 2

As such, management of diabetes includes vigilant monitoring of blood sugar concentrations with test strips, and correcting deviations below or above healthy levels with the administration of subcutaneous insulin, or consumption of carbohydrates.

Diabetes tests strips rely on sequential electrochemical reactions. Reaction 2 occurs first, on a solid state catalyst of glucose oxidase.

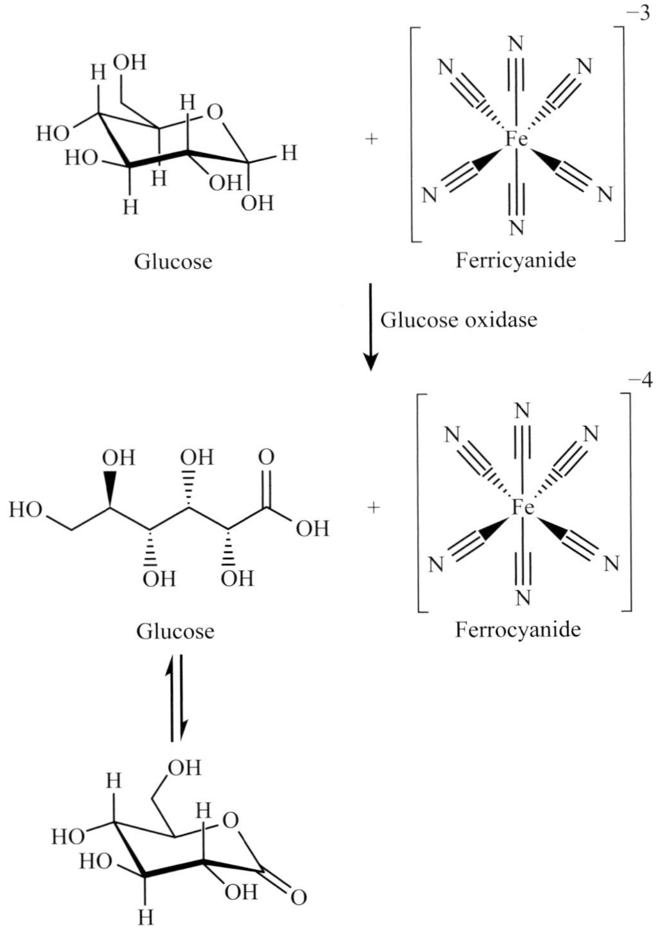

Glucose + Ferricyanide (-3) —Glucose oxidase→ Glucose + Ferrocyanide (-4)

Reaction 2

Subsequently, the ferrocyanide formed in Reaction 2 is reverted to ferricyanide by an electrode in the test strip, producing a current via Reaction 3.

$$[Fe(CN)_6]^{-4} + \text{Electrode} \rightarrow \text{Electrode}^- + [Fe(CN)_6]^{-3}$$

Reaction 3

The magnitude of the current is related to the glucose in the patient's blood sample, and a detector provides the patient's blood glucose concentration.

Question 30

The standard one electron oxidation potentials of several proposed electrodes are shown below, alongside that of ferricyanide.

Material	$\varepsilon^\circ_{oxidation}$ (V)
Electrode X	0.37
Electrode Y	0.25
Electrode Z	0.65
Ferrocyanide	0.37

Which of the following electrode materials would be suitable for a blood glucose test strip?

- O **A.** Electrode Y and electrode X
- O **B.** Electrode Z and electrode X
- O **C.** Electrode Y
- O **D.** Electrode Z

Question 31

According to the Valence Shell Electron Pair Repulsion Theory, what is the molecular shape of the ferricyanide complex?

- O **A.** Trigonal bipyrimadal
- O **B.** Octahedral
- O **C.** Square planar
- O **D.** T-shaped

Question 32

Suppose a hypoglycemic patient with a blood sugar concentration of 50 mg/dL is to consume glucose in order restore their blood sugar to a normal concentration of 100 mg/dL. If the patient's blood volume is 5 L, it is necessary to consume what mass of glucose?

- A. 1 g
- B. 0.5 g
- C. 5 g
- D. 2.5 g

Question 33

During Reaction 2 and Reaction 3, the cyanide containing complex reacts:

- A. at the cathodic terminal of the solid state catalyst, and at the anodic terminal of the electrode, respectively.
- B. at the anodic terminal of the solid state catalyst, and at the cathodic terminal of the electrode, respectively.
- C. at the cathodic terminal of the solid state catalyst, and at the cathodic terminal of the electrode, respectively.
- D. at the anodic terminal of the solid state catalyst, and at the anodic terminal of the electrode, respectively.

Passage 7 (Questions 34-37)

Disinfectants are substances that destroy microbial life. For example, ethanol is a common disinfectant used in laboratory settings to sterilize cell culture hoods. Ethanol denatures proteins and disrupts the phospholipids in cell membranes, which kills bacteria. Sterilization prevents bacteria from contaminating laboratory results.

In residential pools, hypochlorite (ClO^-) is used as a disinfectant to keep the water clean, killing and preventing the growth of dangerous bacteria and algae. Hypochlorite is a strong oxidant that denatures proteins and breaks apart other organic compounds, thus killing any microbial life. Hypochlorite is added to pools in the form of calcium hypochlorite, $Ca(ClO)_2$. The reduction half-reaction of hypochlorite in water is shown in Reaction 1.

$$ClO^- + H_2O + 2e^- \rightarrow Cl^- + 2OH^-$$

Reaction 1

Calcium hypochlorite has a solubility of 0.21 g/mL. To protect the concentration of hypochlorite, chlorine-based pools are kept at a slightly basic pH between 7.4 and 7.6 and cyanuric acid is added to stabilize the hypochlorite, which breaks down in the presence of sunlight.

Ionic copper can also be used to disinfect pools. In a copper ion disinfectant system, a low voltage is applied across a solid copper bar to release copper ions and form hydrogen gas. The standard reduction potentials of copper are shown in Reaction 2 and Reaction 3, and reduction potential of hydrogen is shown in Reaction 4.

$$Cu^+(aq) + e^- \rightarrow Cu(s) \qquad E° = +0.521\text{ V}$$

Reaction 2

$$Cu^{2+}(aq) + 2e^- \rightarrow Cu(s) \qquad E° = +0.337\text{ V}$$

Reaction 3

$$2H^+(aq) + 2e^- \rightarrow H_2(g) \qquad E° = 0.00\text{ V}$$

Reaction 4

Question 34

What is the solubility product constant of calcium hypochlorite?

- A. 12.67
- B. 3.17
- C. 9.26×10^{-3}
- D. 3.70×10^{-2}

TEST 6A

Question 35

A 500 g bar of copper is used in a pool disinfected by copper ions. A 1 A current is run over the copper bar at 0.5 V. For how long will the bar last? (F = 96,485 C/mol e^-)

- O **A.** 3.0×10^6 seconds
- O **B.** 1.5×10^6 seconds
- O **C.** 1.3×10^5 seconds
- O **D.** 2.6×10^5 seconds

Question 36

Hypochlorous acid may be formed from chlorine gas in the following half-reaction:

$$Cl_2(g) + 2H_2O \rightarrow 2HClO + 2H^+ + 2e^- \qquad E° = -1.62 \text{ V}$$

A scientist uses a copper electrode submerged in an aqueous solution of $Cu(NO_3)_2$ and a chlorine-gas electrode submerged in aqueous hypochlorous acid in a galvanic cell in an attempt to form more hypochlorous acid. Which of the following are true about this reaction?

I. No reaction occurs
II. Hypochlorous acid is formed
III. Copper is the anode

- O **A.** I only
- O **B.** II only
- O **C.** III only
- O **D.** II and III only

Question 37

Hypochlorous acid (HClO) is a weak acid. Calcium hypochlorite would be the most soluble in a solution with a pH of:

- O **A.** 2.
- O **B.** 7.5.
- O **C.** 12.
- O **D.** pH has no effect.

Questions 38 - 41 do not refer to a passage and are independent of each other.

Question 38

Which of the following statements about dipole-dipole interactions is true?

- O **A.** Dipole-dipole interactions are intramolecular forces between neighboring molecules.
- O **B.** They occur between atoms of the same molecule that have largely different electronegativities.
- O **C.** Hydrogen bonding is a type of dipole-dipole interaction.
- O **D.** To lower the energy of the system, neighboring molecules are oriented so similar charges are next to each other.

Question 39

$Sr(OH)_2$ is a slightly soluble compound in water. Which of the following will increase the amount of $Sr(OH)_2$ dissolved in a saturated solution?

- O **A.** Adding SrCl to the solution
- O **B.** Increasing the pressure
- O **C.** Stirring the solution overnight
- O **D.** Decreasing the pH

Question 40

A student mixes 150 g of sodium chloride into 750 mL of water. What is the mole fraction of sodium chloride it fully dissolves?

- O **A.** 0.011
- O **B.** 0.033
- O **C.** 0.058
- O **D.** 0.116

Question 41

The reduction potentials of several biologically important metals are shown in the table below. Which of the species is likely to serve as the strongest reducing agent?

Half Reaction	$E°$ (V)
$Fe^{3+} + e^- \rightarrow Fe^{2+}$	0.77
$Cu^{2+} + 2e^- \rightarrow Cu$	0.34
$Fe^{2+} + 2e^- \rightarrow Fe$	−0.44
$Zn^{2+} + 2e^- \rightarrow Zn$	−0.76

- O **A.** Fe^{3+}
- O **B.** Cu^{2+}
- O **C.** Fe^{2+}
- O **D.** Zn^{2+}

Passage 8 (Questions 42-47)

Sodium dodecyl sulfate polyacrylamide gel electrophoresis (SDS-PAGE) is used to separate proteins based on size, and requires the maintenance of a direct current (DC) or steady electric field in an electrolyte. This is traditionally accomplished through Faradaic reactions occurring at the interface where each electrode contacts the electrolyte. In most cases, the overall electrochemical reaction is the electrolysis of water, which consists of two half reactions and occurs at 1.2 V:

$$2H_2O \rightarrow O_2 + 4H^+ + 4e^-$$

Reaction 1

$$4H_2O + 4e^- \rightarrow 2H_2 + 4OH^-$$

Reaction 2

These products are all undesirable. The gases produced effectively reduce the active electrode area, and the acid and base can negatively impact the molecules being separated, particularly when electrophoresis of proteins in their native structure is intended. To protect water from electrolysis, and still maintain a potential difference across the terminals of the gel, it is possible to oxidize and reduce material that remains attached to or within the electrodes.

A conductive polymer, poly(3,4-ethylenedioxythiophene) (PEDOT) and sodium poly(styrenesulfonate) (PSS), were drop cast over Pt wire on a glass side and used as electrodes in place of naked Pt wire in a standard PAGE configuration (Figure 1).

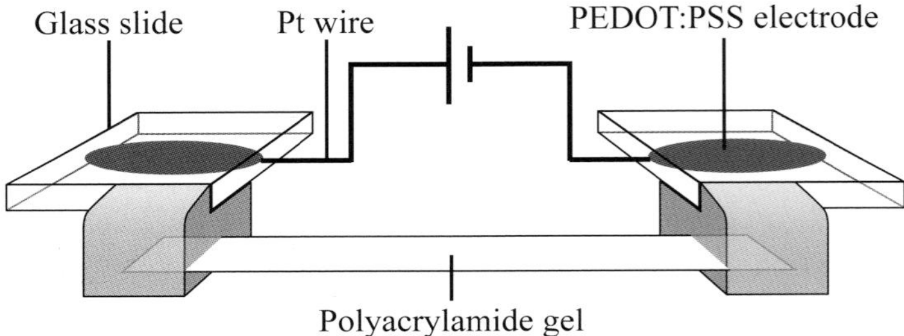

Figure 1 PAGE configuration with PEDOT:PSS electrode

The negatively-charged PSS acts as the counter ion when PEDOT is oxidized.

$$PEDOT^\circ + M^+\,PSS^- \rightarrow PEDOT^+\,PSS^- + M^+ + e^-$$

Reaction 3

The protective effects of this configuration were measured based on the current obtained at 1 V, and were compared to the performance of a naked Pt wire. The results are shown in Figure 2.

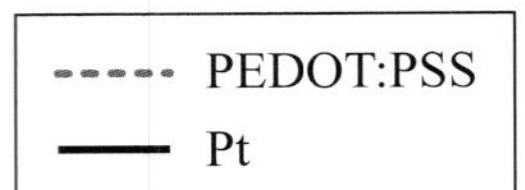

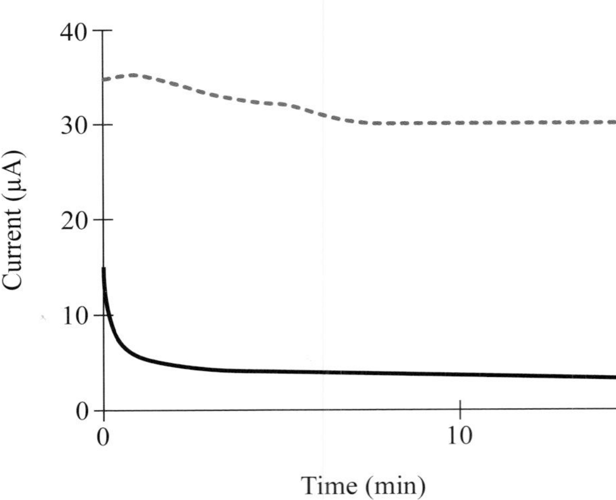

Figure 2 Current vs. time in different PAGE configurations

This passage was adapted from "Conducting Polymer Electrodes for Gel Electrophoresis." Bengtsson K, Nilsson S, Robinson N. *PLoS ONE.* 2014. 9(2) doi:10.1371/journal.pone.0089416 for use under the terms of the Creative Commons CC BY 4.0 Attribution license (http://creativecommons.org/licenses/by/4.0/legalcode).

Question 42

Reactions 1, 2, and 3 are, respectively:

- O **A.** oxidation, reduction, and reduction reactions.
- O **B.** reduction, oxidation, and oxidation reactions.
- O **C.** reduction, oxidation, and reduction reactions.
- O **D.** oxidation, reduction, and oxidation reactions.

Question 43

To maximize the life of the electrodes, Reaction 2 should be performed on:

- O **A.** the cathode material.
- O **B.** the anode material.
- O **C.** both cathode and anode materials.
- O **D.** neither cathode nor anode materials.

Question 44

Between minutes 8 and 10, how many moles of $PEDOT^+$ were produced? (Faraday's constant $= 9.6 \cdot 10^4$ C × mol^{-1})

- O **A.** 3.75×10^{-3} moles
- O **B.** 6.25×10^{-5} moles
- O **C.** 1.88×10^{-5} moles
- O **D.** 3.75×10^{-5} moles

TEST 6A

Question 45

3.0 g of TRIS (MW = 121.14 g × mol^{-1}) is mixed in half a liter of water to prepare a buffer for PAGE. What is the concentration of this solution?

- A. 0.1 M
- B. 0.0125 M
- C. 0.025 M
- D. 0.05 M

Question 46

During SDS-PAGE, SDS (shown) denatures proteins, and causes them to migrate to the:

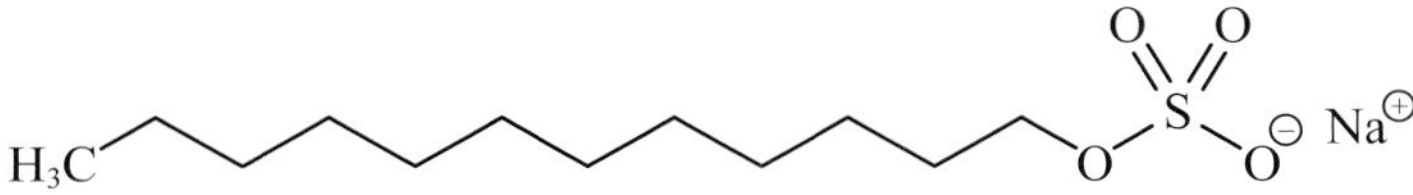

- A. area in the gel matrix where pH < pI.
- B. area in the gel matrix where pH = pI.
- C. cathode.
- D. anode.

Question 47

If a protein is to dissolve in solution, what must be true?

I. $\Delta S > 0$
II. $\Delta H < 0$
III. $\Delta G < 0$
IV. $\Delta H > 0$

- A. I only
- B. I and III only
- C. I, II, and III only
- D. I, III, and IV only

Passage 9 (Questions 48-51)

Ferrous corrosion, commonly referred to as rust, is the result of an electrochemical reaction that takes place on iron surfaces. The first step of ferrous corrosion is the autoioniziation of water.

$$H_2O \leftrightarrow H^+ + OH^-$$

Reaction 1

Next, at sites of distortion in the crystal lattice, iron undergoes oxidation, forming water according to Reaction 2.

$$2Fe(s) + 4H^+(aq) + O_2(aq) \rightarrow 2Fe^{2+}(aq) + 2H_2O(l)$$

Reaction 2

Rust forms when iron(II) reacts with hydroxide in solution.

$$Fe^{2+}(aq) + 2OH^-(aq) \rightarrow Fe(OH)_2(s)$$

Reaction 3

Rust is typically removed with the application of oxalic acid. Oxalic acid acts by forming water, and removing iron(II) from the metal surface via chelation with the oxalate anion. The chelated product can be recrystallized as an octahedral dihydrate salt. Another approach is to construct an electrolytic cell with a "sacrificial" metal (SM) electrode. During the electrolysis, the SM is rusted via oxidation, and the rusted material is cleaned via the reduction of iron back to its elemental form. A schematic is shown in Figure 1 below:

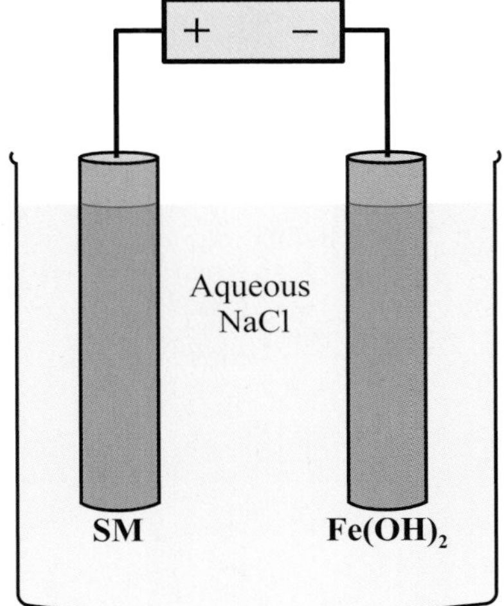

Figure 1 Electrolytic cell

Question 48

What reaction occurs at the cathode?

- A. $M^{2+} + 2e \rightarrow M$
- B. $M \rightarrow M^{2+} + 2e^-$
- C. $Fe + 2OH^- \rightarrow Fe(OH)_2 + 2e^-$
- D. $Fe(OH)_2 + 2e^- \rightarrow Fe + 2OH^-$

TEST 6A

Question 49

Replacing NaCl with which chemical would most decrease the rate of rust removal?

- A. Potassium bromide
- B. Acetic acid
- C. Hydrochloric acid
- D. Glucose

Question 50

Iron is added to two containers of water at the same temperature, and the second container is located 7000 m higher than the first container. The second container will:

- A. rust iron slower than the first container.
- B. rust iron faster than the first container.
- C. have no detectable change in the rate of rust formation compared to the first container.
- D. not enough information provided.

Question 51

If 5 grams of rust are removed in 8 hours, what average current passed through the cell? (Note: $F = 9.5 \times 10^4\ C\ mol^{-1}$)

- A. $\left(\frac{5 \times 9.5 \times 10^4}{90 \times 8 \times 60 \times 60}\right)$amps
- B. $\left(\frac{5 \times 2 \times 9.5 \times 10^4}{90 \times 8 \times 60 \times 60}\right)$amps
- C. $\left(\frac{5 \times 2 \times 9.5 \times 10^4}{90 \times 8}\right)$amps
- D. $\left(\frac{5 \times 2 \times 9.5 \times 10^4 \times 90}{8 \times 60 \times 60}\right)$amps

Passage 10 (Questions 52-56)

Potassium permanganate, $KMnO_4$, is a powerful oxidizing agent used in a variety of synthetic and analytical chemical procedures. It is particularly suited for the quantitative analysis of ferrous iron, Fe^{2+}, content in oral supplements, such as those used in the treatment of iron deficiency anemia. In acidic media with dissolved ferrous iron, the permanganate anion is reduced through Reaction 1. Concurrently, ferrous iron is oxidized to the ferric state through Reaction 2.

$$8H^+(aq) + MnO_4^- + 5e^- \rightarrow Mn^{2+}(aq) + 4H_2O(l)$$

Reaction 1

$$Fe^{2+}(aq) \rightarrow Fe^{3+}(aq) + e^-$$

Reaction 2

The permanganate anion has a deep violet color in solution, and Mn^{2+} is colorless. During a redox titration of ferrous iron, the first sustained appearance of a pale violet or pink color indicates that all of the ferrous iron has been oxidized.

Researchers sought to determine the percent by mass of ferrous iron in an oral iron supplement. They dissolved a 2.8 g tablet in 50 mL of 1 M H_2SO_4 solution, and titrated it with a standardized 0.1 M solution of $KMnO_4$. During the course of the experiment, the solution turned yellow before reaching the end point, so the researchers added a few drops of concentrated H_3PO_4 to make the solution clear again.

The solubility and optical properties of some reagents relevant to this experiment are shown in Table 1.

Table 1 Properties of Selected Reagents

Chemical	Solubility (K_{sp})	Color
$KMnO_4$	1.6×10^{-1}	violet
$Fe(OH)_3$	4×10^{-38}	yellow

Question 52

Phosphoric acid most likely:

- A. forms soluble complexes with Fe^{2+}.
- B. forms soluble complexes with Fe^{3+}.
- C. forms insoluble complexes with Fe^{2+}.
- D. forms insoluble complexes with Fe^{3+}.

Question 53

What is the net ionic equation that describes the reaction of the permanganate anion with ferrous iron?

- A. $MnO_4^-(aq) + 4Fe^{2+}(aq) \rightarrow Mn^{2+}(aq) + 4FeO(s)$
- B. $8H^+(aq) + MnO_4^-(aq) + 4Fe^{2+}(aq) \rightarrow Mn^{2+}(aq) + 4H_2O(l) + 4Fe^{3+}(aq)$
- C. $8H^+(aq) + MnO_4^-(aq) + 5Fe^{2+}(aq) \rightarrow Mn^{2+}(aq) + 4H_2O(l) + 5Fe^{3+}(aq)$
- D. $Fe^{2+}(aq) \rightarrow Fe^{3+}(aq) + e^-$

Question 54

If 50 mL of solution were required to reach the end point when analyzing the tablet, what is its mass percent of iron?

- A. 10%
- B. 40%
- C. 50%
- D. 30%

Question 55

In the absence of phosphoric acid, ferric iron behaves as:

- A. a Lewis base in aqueous solutions.
- B. a Lewis acid in aqueous solutions.
- C. a Brønsted-Lowry acid in aqueous solutions.
- D. a Brønsted-Lowry base in aqueous solutions.

Question 56

A cell was constructed using reagents from Reaction 1 and 2 (shown below).

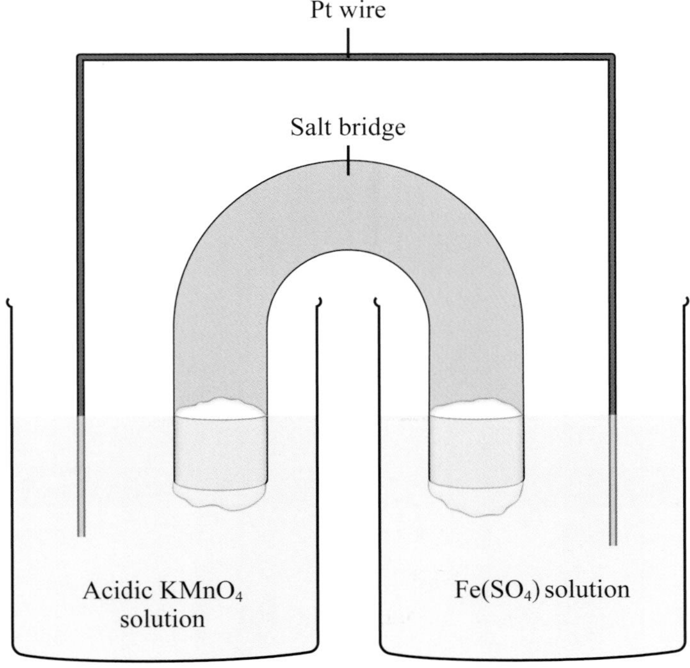

When the cell runs:

- A. elemental iron forms on the platinum wire.
- B. the pH decreases in the $KMnO_4$ containing half-cell.
- C. the $KMnO_4$ containing half-cell gradually becomes more violet.
- D. the pH increases in the $KMnO_4$ containing half-cell.

Questions 57 - 59 do not refer to a passage and are independent of each other.

Question 57

The oxidation potentials of the four DNA bases are shown in the table below. Which DNA base is LEAST likely to undergo reduction?

DNA base	Oxidation potential (V)
G	1.29
A	1.42
C	1.6
T	1.7

- A. Adenine
- B. Cytosine
- C. Guanine
- D. Thymine

Question 58

Which of the following is true regarding a galvanic cell but not an electrolytic cell?

I. Reduction occurs at the cathode
II. The cathode has a positive charge
III. An outside voltage source is required

- A. II only
- B. III only
- C. I and II only
- D. I and III only

Question 59

What is true in the cell below?

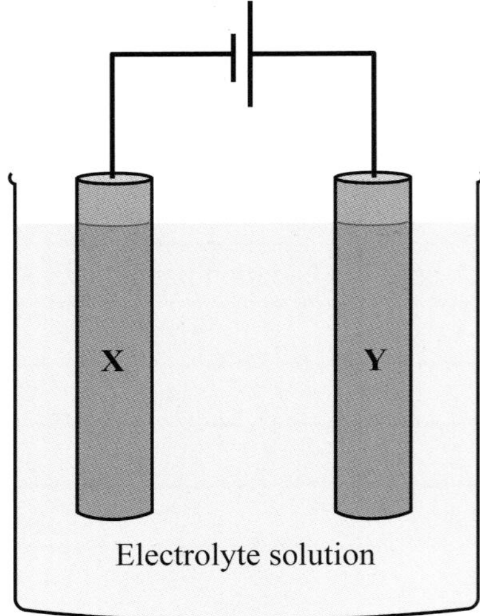

I. Electrons flow into electrode Y.

II. Conventional current flows from electrode X to electrode Y.

III. Electrons flow into electrode X.

IV. Electrode X is the anode.

- ○ **A.** I, II, and IV only
- ○ **B.** I and II only
- ○ **C.** I and IV only
- ○ **D.** III only

STOP. If you finish before time is called, check your work. You may go back to any question in this test.

ANSWERS & EXPLANATIONS for Test 6A can be found on p. 334.

Solutions and Electrochemistry

MINI-TEST 6B

Time: 45 minutes
Questions 1–29

DIRECTIONS: Most of the questions in this test section are grouped with a passage. Read the passage, then select the best answer to each question. Some questions are independent of any passage and of one another. Select the best answer to each of these questions. If you are unsure of an answer, rule out incorrect choices and select from the remaining options. Indicate your selection beside the option you choose. A periodic table can be found on the last page of this book for you to use at any point during this test section.

Passage 1 (Questions 1-4)

Environmental agents, such as UV-light or free radicals, often oxidize DNA bases. Guanine can be oxidized to form several oxidation products. Guanine-rich sequences exist in many important genomic regions, such as telomeres, and these sequences can fold into quadruplex structures in the presence of suitable metal ions.

Scientists proposed a mechanism regulating oxidation in single-stranded or quadruplex DNA, as shown in Figure 1. In the proposed pathways, one-electron oxidation of guanine generates a guanine radical cation ($G^{\bullet+}$), and ($G^{\bullet+}$) is subsequently modified in two competitive pathways. In single-stranded DNA, ($G^{\bullet+}$) is deprotonated at the N1 position and the neutral guanine radical $G(-H)^{\bullet}$] is formed (Pathway 1). Thereafter, the formation of peroxide and the nucleophilic addition of water induce a subsequent rearrangement, leading to the formation of Iz. The hydrogen bond between the N1 proton of ($G^{\bullet+}$) and the O6 of its neighbor guanine forms in quadruplex DNA (Pathway 2), blocking Pathway 1. In this case, the 8-hydroxy-7,8-dihydroguanyl radical is formed and subsequently oxidized to 8oxoG in quadruplex DNA. Both pathways are shown in Figure 1.

This passage is adapted from "Analysis of Guanine Oxidation Products in Double-Stranded DNA and Proposed Guanine Oxidation Pathways in Single-Stranded, Double-Stranded or Quadruplex DNA." Morikawa M, Kino K, Oyoshi T, Suzuki M, Kobayashi T, et al. *Biomolecules*. 2014. doi:10.3390/biom4010140 for use under the terms of the Creative Commons CC BY 4.0 license (http://creativecommons.org/licenses/by/4.0/legalcode).

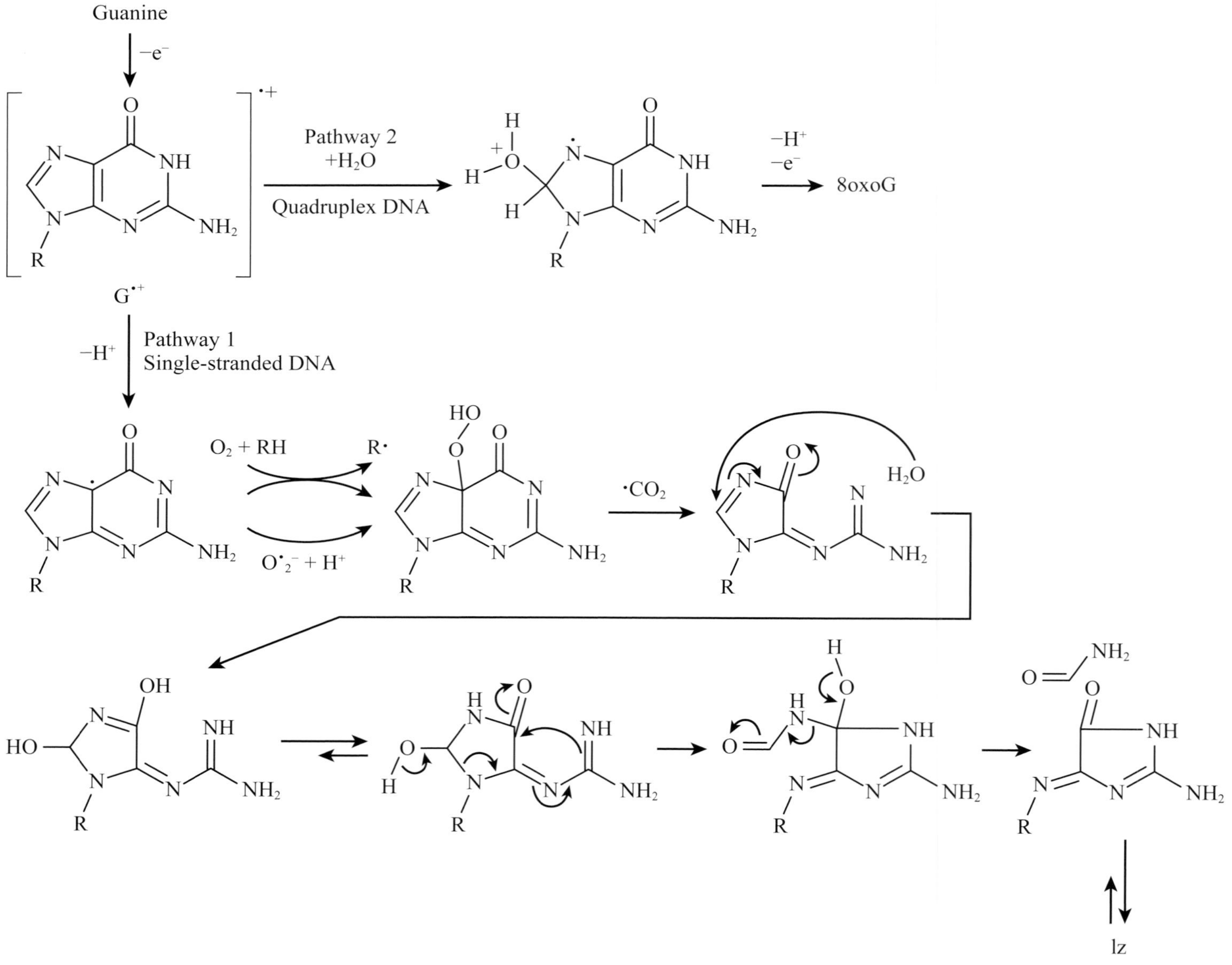

Figure 1 Pathways 1 and 2

Question 1

2.5 mol of $(G^{\bullet +})$ are formed in a 2 L solution of water after oxidation of G. The molality of the solution is most likely:

- O **A.** 0.75 molal.
- O **B.** 1.25 molal.
- O **C.** 2.5 molal.
- O **D.** 5 molal.

Question 2

In a separate reaction, scientists reacted guanine with Cr(IV) and observed the formation of $(G^{\bullet +})$ and $[G(-H)^{\bullet}]$, similar to Pathway 1. In this reaction, Cr(IV) serves as:

- O **A.** a Brønsted acid.
- O **B.** a Brønsted base.
- O **C.** an oxidizing agent.
- O **D.** a reducing agent.

Question 3

To monitor the progress of the reactions in Pathway 2, scientists placed a thermometer in the water bath surrounding the reaction container. Which of the following graphs best depicts the change in temperature throughout the reaction?

O **A.**

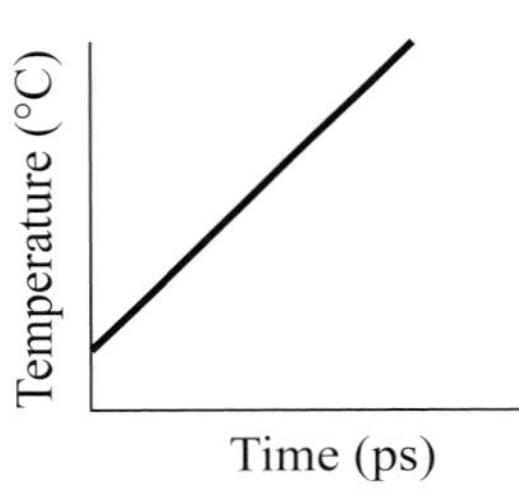

O **B.**

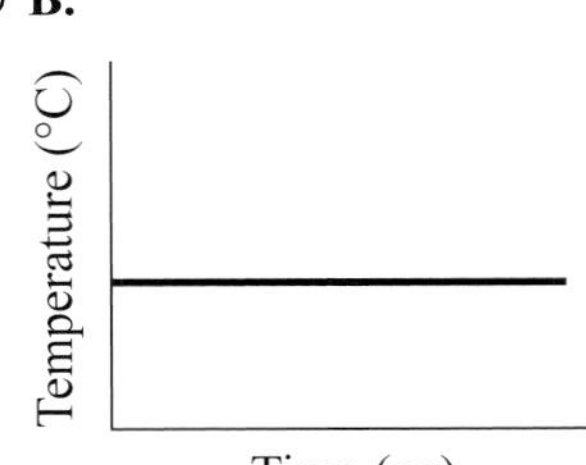

O **C.**

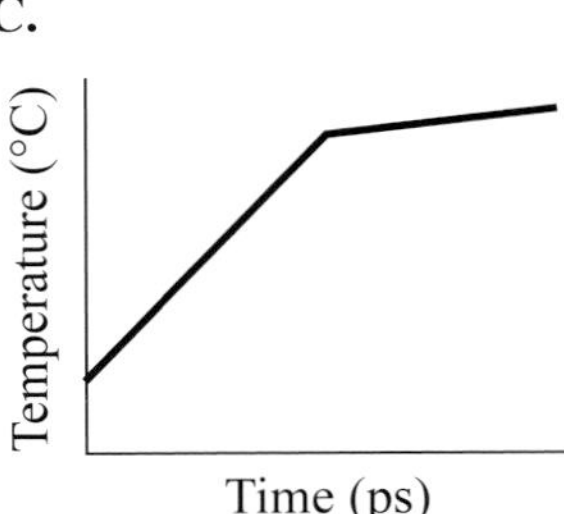

O **D.**

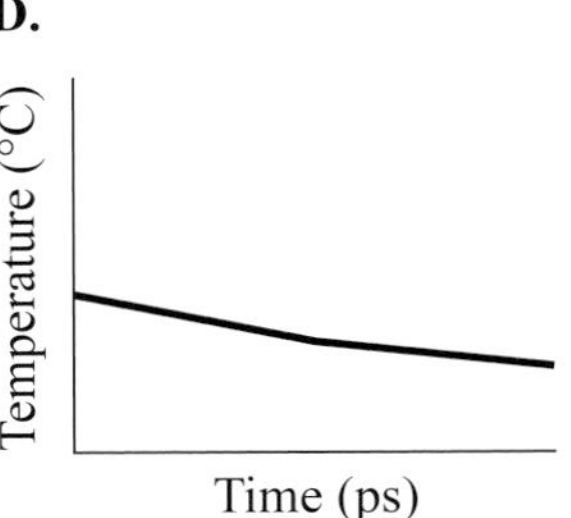

Question 4

The deprotonation of $(G^{\bullet +})$ in single-stranded, double-stranded and quadruplex DNA is represented in the equation below. Which of the following equations best defines the equilibrium constant:

$$H_2O + G^{+} \underset{}{\overset{K_s}{\rightleftharpoons}} H_3O^{+} + G(-H)$$

- O **A.** $K_s = \dfrac{[H^{+}][G(-H)]}{[G^{+}]}$
- O **B.** $K_s = \dfrac{[H_3O^{+}][G(-H)]}{[G]}$
- O **C.** $K_s = \dfrac{[H^{+}][G^{+}]}{[G(-H)]}$
- O **D.** $K_s = \dfrac{[H^{+}][G(-H)]}{[G^{+}][H_2O]}$

Passage 2 (Questions 5-9)

Insoluble precipitates of biologically available ions can form in the kidney and become trapped in the ureter. The formation of these kidney stones can be understood in terms of the solubility product constant (K_{sp}) of the stones, which relates the maximum concentration of ions able to remain in solution after a precipitate has formed. Processes which lead to more concentrated urine, such as poor fluid intake, are expected to increase the risk of kidney stone formation.

The K_{sp} of some materials can be determined experimentally with the use of a concentration cell. In one analysis, the K_{sp} of lead iodide was determined using this technique. The anodic portion of the cell was filled with a saturated lead iodide solution, and the cathodic portion was filled with a 5 M lead nitrate solution. The half-cell solutions were connected with a salt bridge made of cotton dipped in a potassium nitrate solution, in a glass u-shaped tube. Both electrodes were made of lead, connected with copper wire, and a voltmeter was placed across the wire. A schematic of the experimental setup is shown in Figure 1.

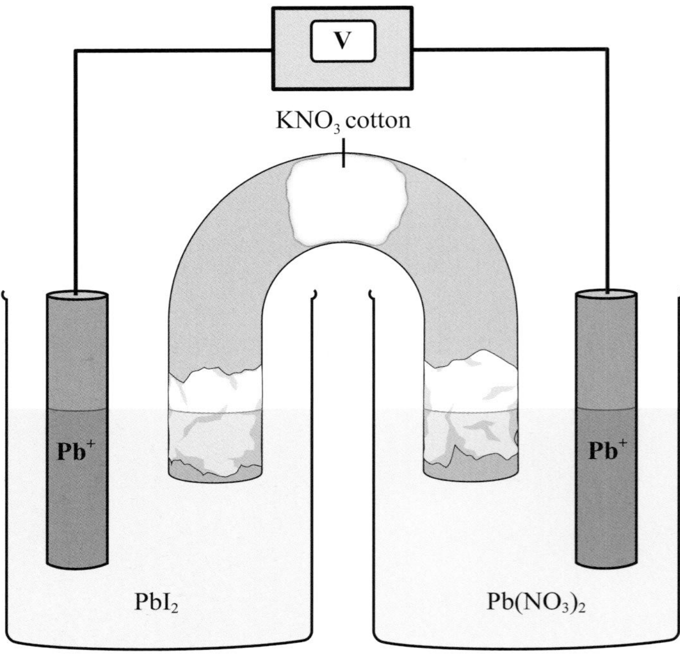

Figure 1 Experimental setup of concentration cell

After determining the initial voltage of the cell, the Nernst equation, $E_{cell}^{\circ} = E_{cell}^{\circ} - \left(\frac{RT}{nF}\right)\ln\left(\frac{Pb_{anode}^{2+}}{Pb_{cathode}^{2+}}\right)$ could be used to determine the K_{sp} of lead iodide.

Question 5

Which of the following solutions should be used in the lead-nitrate half-cell, as described in the passage?

- **A.** 200 g of water mixed with 165.6 g of $Pb(NO_3)_2$
- **B.** 100 g of water mixed with 331.2 g of $Pb(NO_3)_2$
- **C.** 200 g of water mixed with 331.2 g of $Pb(NO_3)_2$
- **D.** 100 g of water mixed with 152.6 g of $Pb(NO_3)_2$

Question 6

How should the Nernst equation be rearranged to most conveniently use the values from the experiment in the passage to calculate the K_{sp} of lead iodide?

- **A.** $4\left(\left(\frac{(E_{cell}^{\circ} - E_{cell})nF}{RT}\right)[Pb_{cathode}^{2+}]\right)^2$
- **B.** $9\left(e^{\left(\frac{(E_{cell}^{\circ} - E_{cell})nF}{RT}\right)}[Pb_{cathode}^{2+}]\right)^4$
- **C.** $4\left(e^{\left(\frac{(E_{cell}^{\circ} - E_{cell})nF}{RT}\right)}[Pb_{cathode}^{2+}]\right)^2$
- **D.** $9\left(e^{\left(\frac{(E_{cell}^{\circ} - E_{cell})RT}{nF}\right)}[Pb_{cathode}^{2+}]\right)^4$

Question 7

Which of the following does NOT occur when the cell produces a current?

I. Electrons flow from the lead iodide half-cell to the lead nitrate half-cell.
II. Electrons flow from the lead nitrate half-cell to the lead iodide half-cell.
III. The voltage of the cell increases until the concentration of lead ions in each half-cell is equal.
IV. The cathodic electrode increases in mass by the same amount that the anodic electrode decreases in mass.

- **A.** II only
- **B.** II and IV only
- **C.** II, and III only
- **D.** I, III, and IV only

Question 8

After running for several hours, the cell was disconnected, and its half-cells were allowed to evaporate. New white crystals were found in the lead iodide half-cell. What is the most likely identity of these crystals?

- **A.** $Pb(NO_3)_2$
- **B.** KNO_3
- **C.** PbI_2
- **D.** $PbCl_2$

Question 9

Which salt bridge electrolyte would be least appropriate for the cell described in the passage?

- **A.** Sodium acetate
- **B.** Sodium nitrate
- **C.** Sodium perchlorate
- **D.** Sodium chloride

Questions 10 - 13 do not refer to a passage and are independent of each other.

Question 10

If the salt bridge were removed from a galvanic cell:

- A. the current would drop because of a greater resistance, but it would still run.
- B. copper wire could be used to connect the half-cell solutions, and it would continue to run.
- C. it would quickly stop as its EMF drops to zero, and prevents further movement of electrons.
- D. it would quickly stop as the increasing electrostatic potential difference prevents further movement of electrons.

Question 11

The reduction potential of the four DNA bases is shown in the table below. Which of the bases is most likely to lose an electron in a chemical reaction?

DNA base	Oxidation potential (V)
G	−1.29
A	−1.42
C	−1.60
T	−1.70

- A. A
- B. T
- C. G
- D. C

Question 12

Which solution would likely be the best conductor of electricity?

- A. 1 M $Ca(NO_3)_2$
- B. 2 M $NaNO_3$
- C. 1 M $Ca_3(PO_4)_2$
- D. 2 M Na_3PO_4

Question 13

Copper-bound proteins participate in one electron transfers in the electron transport chain of mitochondria in a reaction that involves the transition from Cu^+ to Cu^{2+}. Which of the following statements best describes the reaction involving Cu?

- A. Cu^+ is oxidized to Cu^{2+} by a one-electron transfer.
- B. Cu^+ is oxidized to Cu^{2+} by a two-electron transfer.
- C. Cu^+ is reduced to Cu^{2+} by a one-electron transfer.
- D. Cu^+ is reduced to Cu^{2+} by a two-electron transfer.

Passage 3 (Questions 14-17)

Acidthiobacillus ferooxidans is a species of acidophilic and chemoheterotrophic bacteria. *A. ferooxidans* is used extensively in hydrometallurgical processes which isolate copper from its ores, such as chalcopyrite ($CuFeS_2$) or covellite (CuS). The bacterially mediated leaching of ore from chalcopyrite proceeds via Reaction 1.

$$4CuFeS_2(s) + 11O_2(aq) + 6H_2O(l) \xrightarrow{A.ferooxidans} 4CuSO_4(aq) + 4Fe(OH)_3(s) + 4S(s)$$

Reaction 1

The sulfur produced in Reaction 1 is further metabolized by the bacteria through Reaction 2.

$$2S(s) + 3O_2(g) + 2H_2O(l) \xrightarrow{A.ferooxidans} 2H_2SO_4(aq)$$

Reaction 2

After removing the solid components from Reaction 1, copper can be precipitated through its reduction with elemental iron.

$$CuSO_4 + Fe \rightarrow FeSO_4 + Cu$$

Reaction 3

The copper formed via Reaction 3 is known as "blister copper." Although it is nearly 99% pure, due to the sensitivity of electrical conductivity to even trace impurities, a final electrolysis step is performed to further refine the material. The blister copper is formed into an electrode, as is high purity copper. A battery is connected to each, and they are immersed in a copper sulfate solution. The potential difference across the cell is just sufficient for electron transfer from the copper anode to the copper cathode. Activation of the battery causes the blister copper electrode to shrink and the high purity electrode to grow in size. Impurities from the blister copper form a sludge beneath it (Figure 1).

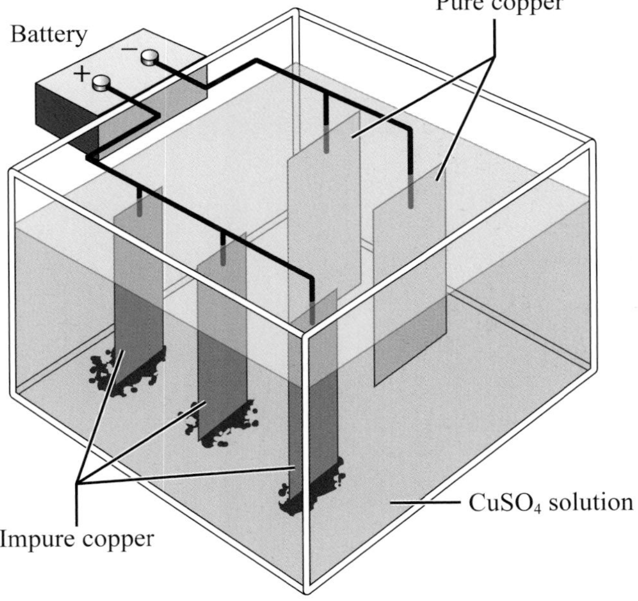

Figure 1 Electrolytic cell used during the purification of blister copper

The impurities that will comprise this sludge can be predicted based on the characteristics of the ore, and on the standard reduction table, shown on the next page.

Table 1 Standard Reductions of Selected Metal Species

Reduction half-reaction	$E°$ (V)
$Zn^{2+}(aq) + 2e^- \rightarrow Zn(s)$	−0.763
$Cu^{2+}(aq) + 2e^- \rightarrow Cu(s)$	+0.337
$Fe^{2+}(aq) + 2e^- \rightarrow Fe(s)$	−0.44
$Sn^{4+}(aq) + 2e^- \rightarrow Sn^{2+}(aq)$	+0.15
$Ag^{+}(aq) + e^- \rightarrow Ag(s)$	+0.799
$Au^{3+}(aq) + 3e^- \rightarrow Au(s)$	+1.50
$Hg^{2+}(aq) + 2e^- \rightarrow Hg(l)$	+0.855

Question 14

Which material, used in place of iron, could precipitate copper in Reaction 3?

- A. Au(s)
- B. $Sn^{2+}(aq)$
- C. Cu(s)
- D. Hg(l)

Question 15

As the cell shown in Figure 1 runs:

- A. the concentration of copper(II) ion in solution gradually falls.
- B. the concentration of copper(II) ion in solution gradually increases.
- C. the concentration of copper(II) ion in solution locally falls near the anode, and locally increases near the cathode.
- D. the concentration of copper(II) ion in solution stays the same.

Question 16

Which of the following changes would most increase the rate at which copper is purified in the electrolytic cell? ($\rho_{Cu} = 1.7 \times 10^{-8}$ m · Ω and $\rho_{Pt} = 1.0 \times 10^{-7}$ m · Ω)

- A. Decreasing the radius of the wire which connects the electrodes to the battery.
- B. Increasing the radius of the wire which connects the electrodes to the battery by 50%.
- C. Using an identical platinum wire to connect the electrodes instead of a copper wire.
- D. Inserting another wire identical to the first into the circuit, to connect the electrodes with two wires instead of one.

Question 17

A similar cell to that shown in Figure 1 was constructed, except the external voltage source was removed, and Zn electrodes were used instead of the blister copper electrodes. Will an oxidation-reduction reaction spontaneously occur?

- A. No; $E°_{cell} = +1.1$ V
- B. No; $E°_{cell} = -0.43$ V
- C. Yes; $E°_{cell} = +1.1$ V
- D. Yes; $E°_{cell} = -0.43$ V

Passage 4 (Questions 18-22)

Cellular metabolism exploits the oxidation of glucose to power the synthesis of adenosine-triphosphate (ATP). During the process, electrons are transported through four membrane-bound complexes, culminating in the reduction of molecular oxygen into water. The energy liberated through these electron transfer events establishes an electrochemical proton gradient across the inner mitochondrial membrane space. The eventual return of these hydrogen ions to the mitochondrial matrix activates the enzyme ATP-synthase, allowing for the synthesis of new ATP molecules.

An electrochemical cell was designed based on the biology of cellular metabolism. Relying on high density enzyme and electron transport mediators at each terminal, as well as a proton-permeable electrolyte, this cell (Figure 1) generates electricity through the oxidation of glucose to gluconolactone.

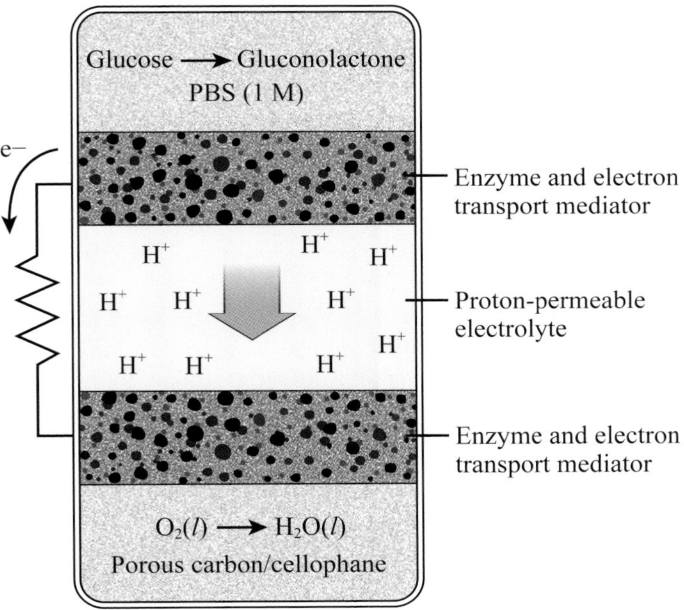

Figure 1 Electrochemical cell

The anode requires a highly concentrated (1 M) phosphate buffer solution (PBS). The cathode is unique, reducing molecular oxygen obtained through diffusion from air. It is composed of porous carbon and cellophane. These materials assist in the maintenance of ideal humidity during Reaction 1.

Glucose $\xrightarrow{(\frac{1}{2})O_2 \quad H_2O}$ Gluconolactone

Reaction 1

The Nernst equation describes the concentration-dependent behavior of the reduction potential (E_{red}) generated within each half-cell or in the full-cell, as shown in Equations 1 and 2 respectively. Faraday's constant (F), and the number of moles of electrons transported during each half-reaction or the full reaction (z), the ratio of oxidant to reductant ([Ox]/[Red]), or the reaction quotient (Q_r) are also required to calculate the reduction potential.

$$E_{red} = E^{\circ}_{red} + \left(\frac{RT}{ZF}\right)\ln\left(\frac{[Ox]}{[Red]}\right)$$

Equation 1

$$E_{red} = E^{\circ}_{red} - \left(\frac{RT}{ZF}\right)\ln(Q_r)$$

Equation 2

Question 18

What integer value should be used for Z when calculating the reduction potential in the glucose-containing half-cell?

- **A.** 2
- **B.** 4
- **C.** 3
- **D.** 1

Question 19

The scientists of this study compared the performance of their cell to that of a zinc-copper battery with the net reaction shown:

$$Zn + Cu^{2+}(aq) \rightarrow Cu + Zn^{2+}(aq)$$

The graph below was drawn from its performance:

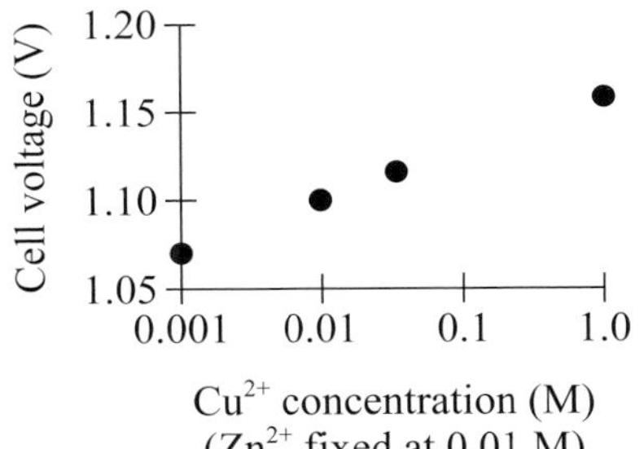

What is the value of E°_{cell} in this battery?

- **A.** 1.15 V
- **B.** 1.12 V
- **C.** 1.10 V
- **D.** 1.05 V

Question 20

How will removal of the catalyst in each half-cell affect $E°$?

- A. $E°$ will increase.
- B. $E°$ will decrease.
- C. $E°$ will remain unchanged.
- D. $E°$ may increase or decrease, but will not remain unchanged.

Question 21

How much glucose must be dissolved in 50 mL of buffer to produce a 1 M solution?

- A. 6.7 g
- B. 0.9 g
- C. 9 g
- D. 8 g

Question 22

If 1.7 g of gluconolactone is formed over 10 hours of continuous operation and the cell maintains a voltage of 0.5 V, what is the power output of the cell? (Note: $F = 96.5 \times 10^3$ $C \cdot mol^{-1}$)

- A. 27 mW
- B. 6.7 mW
- C. 95 mW
- D. 52 mW

Passage 5 (Questions 23-26)

Lead-storage batteries rely on coupled sulfation reactions which act on metallic lead and lead dioxide in acidic media. The terminals are separated from one another with a membrane, permissive to ion-transport. Metallic lead comprises the anode and undergoes Reaction 1:

$$Pb°(s) + HSO_4^-(aq) \rightarrow PbSO_4(s) + H^+(aq) + 2e^-$$

Reaction 1

Lead dioxide comprises the cathode and undergoes Reaction 2:

$$PbO_2(s) + HSO_4^-(aq) + 3H^+(aq) + 2e^- \rightarrow PbSO_4(s) + 2H_2O(l)$$

Reaction 2

Typically, a single lead-storage battery consists of numerous electrochemical cells connected in series. These batteries have a number of properties which make them useful as back-up power sources in settings where power-outages could be catastrophic, such as hospitals or communication systems.

Lead-storage batteries are rechargeable by connection of an external voltage source. The external voltage causes Reactions 1 and 2 to go in reverse, regenerating the species necessary to perform electrical work. In addition, lead storage batteries have very high surge currents. These high surge currents are necessary to start vehicle start-up engines. As a result, lead storage batteries are used in a variety of motorized vehicles such as cars, wheelchairs, and scooters.

Despite their utility, lead-storage batteries are not infinitely rechargeable. Overtime, not all of the lead sulfate, formed after a full discharge, can be converted back to lead dioxide and metallic lead. The excess lead sulfate eventually forms a hard stable white crust which significantly impairs battery performance.

Question 23

What is true after the full discharge of a lead-storage battery?

I. The cathode is covered in lead sulfate.
II. The anode is covered in lead sulfate.
III. $\Delta G_{reaction}$ equals 0 kJ/mol.
IV. The pH of the solution decreases.

- A. III only
- B. I and II only
- C. I, II, and IV only
- D. I, II, and III only

Question 24

Overcharging the battery can lead to explosions as water is split into hydrogen and oxygen gas according the reactions below:

$$2H_2O(l) \rightarrow O_2(g) + 4H^+(aq) + 4e^-$$

$$4H^+(aq) + 4e^- \rightarrow 2H_2(g)$$

When water splits due to overcharging, which of the following does NOT occur?

- **A.** Twice the volume of hydrogen gas to oxygen gas is produced.
- **B.** Hydrogen gas forms on the metallic lead terminal.
- **C.** Oxygen gas evolves at the anode.
- **D.** $\Delta S_{reaction} > 0$

Question 25

What is the solubility of $Pb(NO_3)_2$ in a 0.5 M Na_2SO_4 solution? ($K_{sp} = 2.13 \times 10^{-8}$)

- **A.** 1.07×10^{-10} M
- **B.** 1.07×10^{-8} M
- **C.** 4.26×10^{-8} M
- **D.** 4.26×10^{-9} M

Question 26

A lead concentration cell was constructed as shown:

$Pb°(s)$ | $Pb^{2+}(aq$, 0.5 M), $NO_3^{1-}(aq$, 1.0 M) || $Pb^{2+}(aq$, 3.0 M), $NO_3^{1-}(aq$, 6.0 M) | $Pb°(s)$

Which cell below will have the same emf as this cell?

- **A.** $Pb°(s)$ | $Pb^{2+}(aq$, 1.5 M), $NO_3^{1-}(aq$, 3.0 M) || $Pb^{2+}(aq$, 4.0 M), $NO_3^{1-}(aq$, 8.0 M) | $Pb°(s)$
- **B.** $Pb°(s)$ | $Pb^{2+}(aq$, 0.2 M), $NO_3^{1-}(aq$, 0.4 M) || $Pb^{2+}(aq$, 2.8 M), $NO_3^{1-}(aq$, 5.6 M) | $Pb°(s)$
- **C.** $Pb°(s)$ | $Pb^{2+}(aq$, 1.0 M), $NO_3^{1-}(aq$, 2.0 M) || $Pb^{2+}(aq$, 6.0 M), $NO_3^{1-}(aq$, 12.0 M) | $Pb°(s)$
- **D.** $Pb°(s)$ | $Pb^{2+}(aq$, 5.0 M), $NO_3^{1-}(aq$, 10.0 M) || $Pb^{2+}(aq$, 5.0 M), $NO_3^{1-}(aq$, 10.0 M) | $Pb°(s)$

Questions 27 - 29 do not refer to a passage and are independent of each other.

Question 27

Which of the following statements best describes the reactions occurring at the anode and cathode of the battery in a cardiac pacemaker?

- **A.** Oxidation at the anode and reduction at the cathode
- **B.** Oxidation at the anode and oxidation at the cathode
- **C.** Reduction at the anode and oxidation at the cathode
- **D.** Reduction at the anode and reduction at the cathode

Question 28

Lithium batteries are popular in electronic devices because they provide rechargeable power that is safe and controlled. On the other hand, nickel cadmium batteries:

- **A.** are not rechargeable.
- **B.** are not caustic.
- **C.** function without a redox reaction.
- **D.** have a "memory effect" that necessitates full use of the battery before recharge.

Question 29

Bleach is a solution that often includes hypochlorite salts. Which of the following is the molecular structure of hypochlorite?

- **A.** ClO^-
- **B.** ClO^{2-}
- **C.** ClO^{3-}
- **D.** ClO^{4-}

STOP. If you finish before time is called, check your work. You may go back to any question in this test.

TEST 6B

ANSWERS & EXPLANATIONS for Test 6B can be found on p. 334.

Acids and Bases

TEST 7A

Time: 95 minutes
Questions 1–59

DIRECTIONS: Most of the questions in this test section are grouped with a passage. Read the passage, then select the best answer to each question. Some questions are independent of any passage and of one another. Select the best answer to each of these questions. If you are unsure of an answer, rule out incorrect choices and select from the remaining options. Indicate your selection beside the option you choose. A periodic table can be found on the last page of this book for you to use at any point during this test section.

Passage 1 (Questions 1-5)

Triglycerides, or fatty acid esters of glycerol, are crucial for maintaining the body's energy balance. They are released during times of reduced nutrition, and carried by lipoproteins in the blood where they can fuel cellular metabolism. When blood concentrations of triglycerides exceed normal levels, they are associated with an increased risk or heart disease, and may be a sign of other underlying pathology such as kidney disease or hypothyroidism.

As a result, methods to quantify the concentration of triglycerides in the blood by converting them to their component fatty acids is useful for both research and clinical applications. One of the simplest ways to perform this analysis is to extract the triglycerides from blood with an alcohol-ether mixture, saponify them, convert the saponaceous product into free fatty acids, and then titrate the free fatty acids with phenolphthalein as an indicator. A schematic of this process is shown in Figure 1.

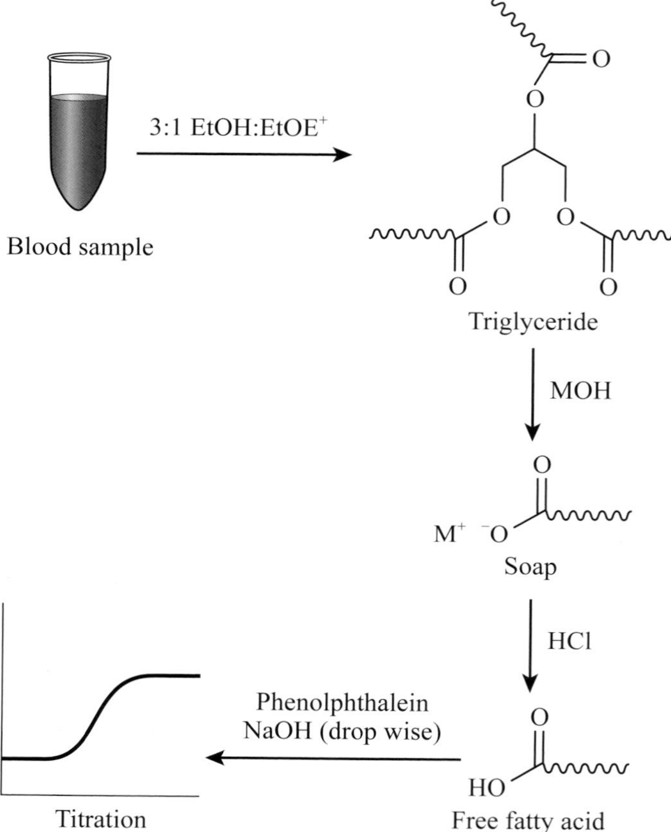

Figure 1 Procedure used to quantify blood triglyceride concentration

In a variation of this procedure, the acidic work-up of the saponaceous product is omitted, and the titration is performed with dilute acid. Figure 2 shows the results obtained from a titration performed using this method.

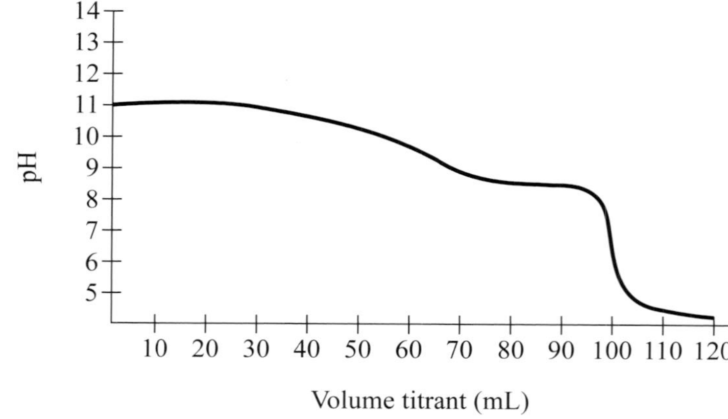

Figure 2 Titration of saponaceous product extracted from 100 cm^3 of blood ([HCl] = 0.1 M)

Question 1

Which of the following statements most likely describes why phenolphthalein was used as an indicator in the first method?

- **A.** When a solution changes from neutral to alkaline, it becomes colored.
- **B.** When a solution changes from neutral to acidic, it becomes colored.
- **C.** When a solution changes from alkaline to neutral, it becomes colored.
- **D.** When a solution changes from acidic to neutral, it becomes colored.

Question 2

The indicator o-cresophthalein was considered for this study. It becomes purple when its conjugate base form comprises at least 10% of the concentration of its acid form. If the pK_b of o-cresophthalein is 4.39, at what pH does it become purple?

- **A.** 3.39
- **B.** 10.61
- **C.** 8.61
- **D.** 4.39

Question 3

Suppose the soap formed in this experiment was dissolved until saturation in water and titrated with HCl. Which of the following is LEAST expected to occur?

- **A.** At the equivalence point, a larger mass of precipitate will have formed in the solution.
- **B.** At the equivalence point, a smaller mass of precipitate will have formed in the solution.
- **C.** At the equivalence point, there will be no change in the mass of the precipitate in the solution.
- **D.** At the half-equivalent point the precipitate will have completely dissolved into the solution.

Question 4

Suppose stearic acid, $CH_3(CH_2)_{16}COOH$, was formed from sodium stearate during this procedure. What is the value of the pK_b of sodium stearate if the solution has a pH of x?

○ **A.** $-\log\left(\dfrac{[CH_3(CH_2)_{16}COOH]}{[CH_3(CH_2)_{16}COO^-][H^+]}\right)$

○ **B.** $-\log\left(\dfrac{[CH_3(CH_2)_{16}COOH][10^{-x}]}{[CH_3(CH_2)_{16}COO^-]}\right)$

○ **C.** $-\log\dfrac{[CH_3(CH_2)_{16}COOH][10^{14-x}]}{[CH_3(CH_2)_{16}COO^-]}$

○ **D.** $-\log\dfrac{[CH_3(CH_2)_{16}COOH][10^{x-14}]}{[CH_3(CH_2)_{16}COO^-]}$

Question 5

What was the triglyceride concentration of the blood sample which was titrated in Figure 2?

○ **A.** 1.0×10^{-3} M

○ **B.** 1.0×10^{-4} M

○ **C.** 3.3×10^{-4} M

○ **D.** 3.3×10^{-3} M

Passage 2 (Questions 6-10)

Phenolphthalein (Figure 1) is amphoteric, existing in various pH dependent forms. In strongly acidic solution it exists as a cation, and the solution appears orange. In weakly alkaline solutions it adopts a vibrant fuchsia color, following deprotonation and planarization of its pi systems. This color will slowly fade as the alkalinity of the solution is increased, and approaches 13.0.

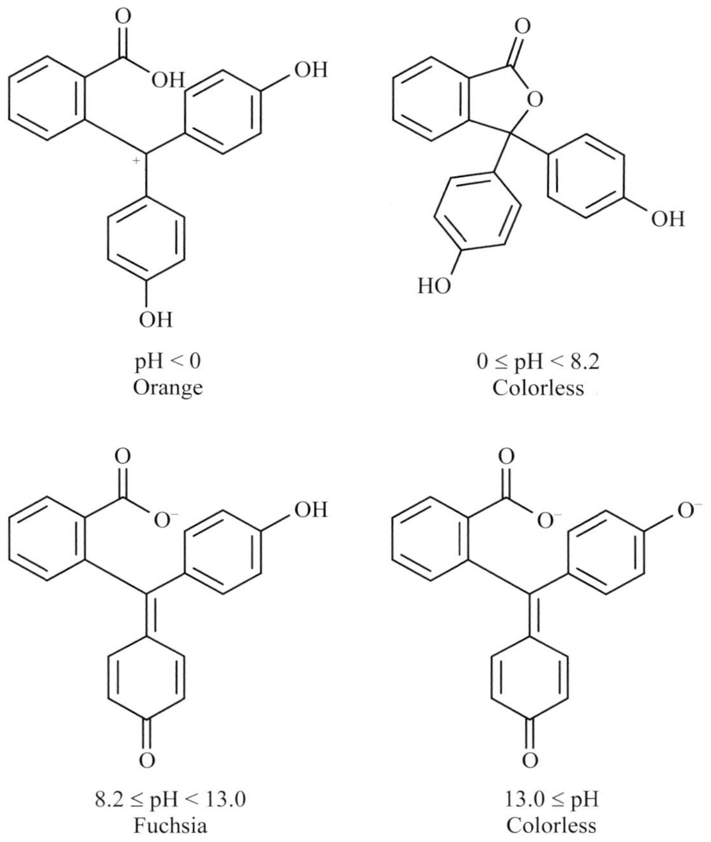

$pH < 0$
Orange

$0 \leq pH < 8.2$
Colorless

$8.2 \leq pH < 13.0$
Fuchsia

$13.0 \leq pH$
Colorless

Figure 1 pH dependent forms of phenolphthalein

For this reason, it is useful in a variety of laboratory settings, often as an indicator in acid-base titrations. The utility of this indicator stems from the sensitivity of the equivalence point to minute changes in acidity. At the equivalence point in a bufferless solution, infinitesimal changes in the hydronium concentration can lead to dramatic changes in pH. Less than a drop of titrant is usually required to change the color of the solution once it has reached the equivalence point.

In an experiment, researchers wished to determine the molar mass of an unknown monoprotic organic acid. After weighing the acid and dissolving it in 100 mL of water, a few drops of phenolphthalein were added to the solution. Next, 0.08 M sodium hydroxide was added drop by drop with a burette until the endpoint was reached. The data from numerous trials is summarized below in Table 1.

Table 1 Results from Titration of Unknown Acid

Trial no.	Mass (g)	Volume titrant (mL)
1	2.0	122
2	2.5	153
3	2.3	140
4	2.1	128

An additional trial was performed, but removed from the study results, when researchers realized that the organic acid which they used had been contaminated with crystals from a triprotic acid. The titration from this trial is shown below in Figure 2.

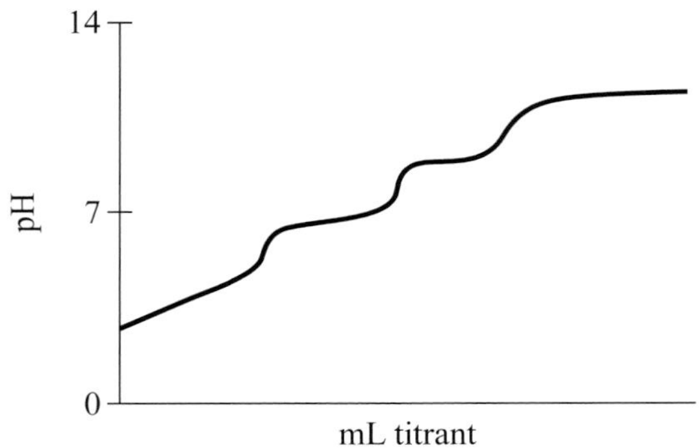

Figure 2 Titration from contaminated sample

Question 6

When the solution described in the passage just turns fuchsia, what is the concentration of OH^-?

- O **A.** $10^{5.8}$ M
- O **B.** $10^{8.2}$ M
- O **C.** $10^{-5.8}$ M
- O **D.** $10^{-8.2}$ M

Question 7

If the acid in trial number 3 were diprotic, what would its molar mass be?

- O **A.** 102.675 g/mol
- O **B.** 205.35 g/mol
- O **C.** 410.7 g/mol
- O **D.** 821.4 g/mol

Question 8

Which evidence most contradicts the hypothesis that after planarization, phenolphthalein reflects colored light?

- O **A.** At a pH less than 0, phenolphthalein reflects colored light.
- O **B.** At a pH less than 13.0 but greater than 8.2, phenolphthalein reflects colored light.
- O **C.** At a pH greater than 13, phenolphthalein does not reflect colored light.
- O **D.** At a pH greater than or equal to 0 but less than 8.2, phenolphthalein does not reflect colored light.

Question 9

The pK_a of the lactone form of phenolphthalein is 9.3. If a solution of phenolphthalein has just turned fuchsia with the addition of base, what is the ratio of the colored form to the lactone form?

- O **A.** 2:25
- O **B.** 1:10
- O **C.** 3:7
- O **D.** 1:100

Question 10

What is the pK_{a3} of the crystal contaminant?

- O **A.** 9.5
- O **B.** 6.0
- O **C.** 7.1
- O **D.** 4.3

Passage 3 (Questions 11-14)

The mechanism by which the pancreas secretes high HCO_3^- has not been fully resolved. This alkaline secretion, formed in pancreatic ducts, can be achieved by transporting HCO_3^- from serosa to mucosa or by moving H^+ in the opposite direction. Researchers sought to determine whether H^+K^+-ATPases are expressed and functional in human pancreatic ducts and whether proton pump inhibitors (PPIs) have effect on them. A PPI called omeprazole is shown below in Figure 1.

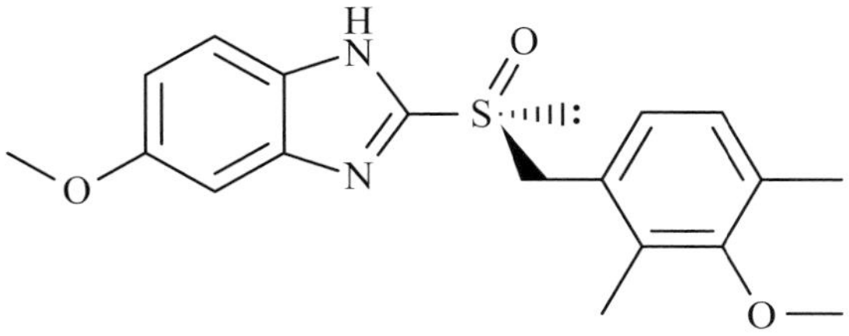

(*S*)-(−)-omeprazole (esomeprazole)

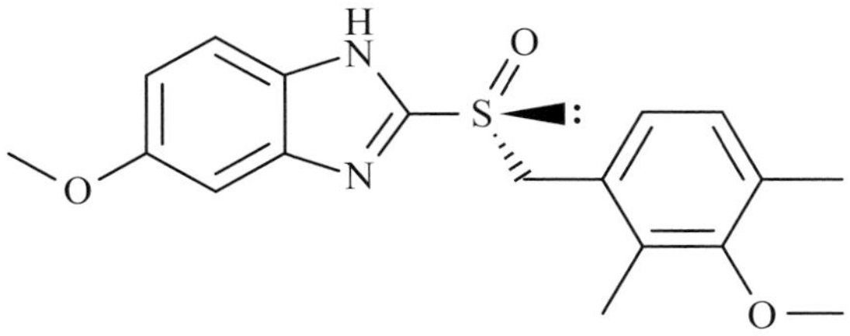

(*R*)-(−)-omeprazole

Figure 1 Omeprazole

Researchers showed that the gastric HKα1 and HKβ subunits (ATP4A; ATP4B) and non-gastric HKα2 subunits (ATP12A) of H^+K^+-ATPases are expressed in human pancreatic cells. Pumps have similar localizations in duct cell monolayers (Capan-1 cell line) and human pancreas, and notably the gastric pumps are localized on the luminal membranes. In Capan-1 cells, PPIs inhibited recovery of intracellular pH from acidosis. Furthermore, in rats treated with PPIs, pancreatic secretion was inhibited but concentrations of major ions in secretion follow similar excretory curves in control and PPI treated animals. In addition to HCO_3^-, the pancreas also secretes K^+.

This passage was adapted from "Proton Pump Inhibitors Inhibit Pancreatic Secretion: Role of Gastric and Non-Gastric H+/K+-ATPases." Wang J, Barbuskaite D, Tozzi M, Giannuzzo A, Sørensen CE, et al. *PLoS ONE.* 2015. 10(5) doi:10.1371/journal.pone.0126432 for use under the terms of the Creative Commons CC BY 4.0 license (http://creativecommons.org/licenses/by/4.0/legalcode).

Question 11

Which of the following correctly describes (R)-(+)-omeprazole?

- **A.** It has an acidic sulfur atom.
- **B.** It has a acidic carbon atom.
- **C.** It has an acidic oxygen atom.
- **D.** It has a basic oxygen atom.

Question 12

The principle acid found in the stomach is a:

- **A.** strong Brønsted acid.
- **B.** strong Lewis acid.
- **C.** weak Brønsted acid.
- **D.** weak Lewis acid.

Question 13

In the absence of a PPI, the pancreas produces:

- **A.** an acid.
- **B.** a salt.
- **C.** the salt of a weak base.
- **D.** the salt of a weak acid.

Question 14

An extension of the experiment described in the passage was undertaken to determine the effect of PPI's on the glomerulus. Which of the following would be the best experimental design?

- **A.** Injection of PPI into the efferent arteriole and measurement of HCl in the urine
- **B.** Injection of PPI into the efferent arteriole and measurement of NH_4^+ in the urine
- **C.** Injection of PPI into the afferent arteriole and measurement of HCl in the urine
- **D.** Injection of PPI into the afferent arteriole and measurement of NH_4^+ in the urine

Questions 15 - 18 do not refer to a passage and are independent of each other.

Question 15

Iron(III) chloride is another powerful mineral acid used in industry. It reacts with water according to the reaction below:

$$2FeCl_3(s) + 3H_2O(l) \rightarrow Fe_2O_3(s) + 6HCl(aq)$$

Iron(III) chloride is best described as:

- **A.** a Lewis acid.
- **B.** an Arrhenius acid.
- **C.** a Brønstead-Lowry acid.
- **D.** a Lewis base.

Question 16

Which of the following antacids is least soluble in neutral water?

Antacid	K_{sp}
$Mg(OH)_2$	1.5×10^{-11}
$CaCO_3$	3.3×10^{-9}
$MgCO_3$	$1 \times 10^{-7.8}$
$Al(OH)_3$	3×10^{-34}

- **A.** $Mg(OH)_2$
- **B.** $CaCO_3$
- **C.** $MgCO_3$
- **D.** $Al(OH)_3$

Question 17

The bicarbonate anion is made through the acidification of the carbonate anion. It obeys the following equilibrium in the blood:

$$HCO_3^-(aq) + H^+(aq) \rightleftharpoons H_2CO_3(aq) \rightleftharpoons H_2O(l) + CO_2(g)$$

Hyperventilating is expected to make the blood's pH:

- **A.** increase because the blood is more acidic.
- **B.** decrease because the blood is more basic.
- **C.** increase because the blood is more basic.
- **D.** decrease because the blood is more acidic.

Question 18

The buffering of blood is essential for equilibrium. Which of the following acids would be most appropriate as part of the buffer?

Acid	K_a
Hydrocyanic acid	4.0×10^{-10}
Carbonic acid	4.2×10^{-7}
Hypochlorous acid	3.5×10^{-8}
Dihydrogen phosphate acid	6.2×10^{-8}

- **A.** Hydrocyanic acid
- **B.** Carbonic acid
- **C.** Hypochlorous acid
- **D.** Dihydrogen phosphate acid

Passage 4 (Questions 19-22)

During an influenza pandemic, the risk of serious infection is exacerbated when care for the sick is provided by elderly individuals, or when the infected person lives with young children.

While numerous commercial virucidal agents are currently available, they may become scarce during pandemics and are often unavailable in low-income settings. Moreover, people are often unaware of these sophisticated agents, and instead clean with simple household supplies.

Researchers were curious about the anti-influenza properties simple household cleaning supplies may have, and assessed the effects of three common agents: 10% malt vinegar, bleach (BL), and generic dish-soap.

Vinegar is acetic acid (pK_a = 4.7), which weakly dissociates in water. Its antiviral properties stem from the low pH-dependent denaturation of flu-virus hemagglutinin protein.

$$CH_3COOH(aq) + H_2O(l) \rightleftharpoons CH_3COO^-(aq) + H_3O^+(aq)$$

Reaction 1

Bleach is an aqueous solution of NaClO and NaOH. The ClO^- anion acts as a powerful oxidizer and disinfectant. NaOH is added to prevent the formation of HClO in solution.

$$NaClO(aq) + H_2O(l) \rightleftharpoons HClO(aq) + NaOH(aq)$$

Reaction 2

Dish soap is composed of salts derived from fatty acids. They can disrupt the protein structure of some viruses by changing the polarity of the liquid medium, and in the case of some enveloped viruses, dissolve their envelope.

Solutions of each and a solution of pure water were maintained at 55°C, a "hand-hot" temperature, and an equal quantity of flu virus was added to each solution. Samples were assayed either immediately as a measure of rapid inactivation, or after 60 minutes to simulate prolonged contact. Plaque assays were used to assess the viability of the virus at set time points post incubation. These viabilities were compared to the viability of the input virus (V), cultured directly without being exposed to heated water (Figure 1).

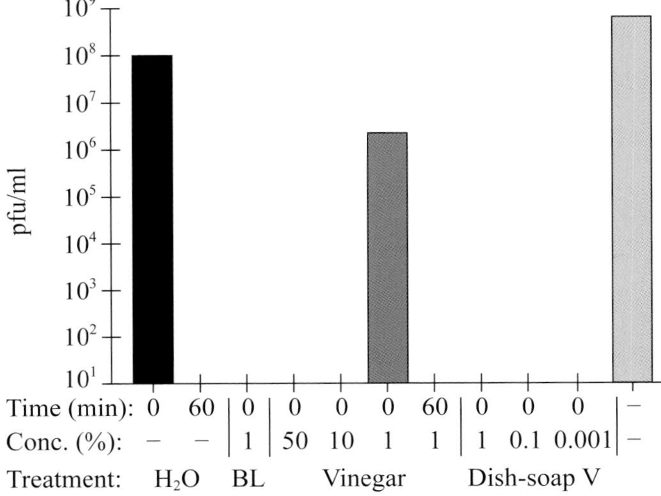

Figure 1 Virucidal properties of household cleaners

This passage was adapted from "Effectiveness of Common Household Cleaning Agents in Reducing the Viability of Human Influenza A/H1N1." Greatorex J, Page R, Curran M, Digard P, Enstone J, et al. *PLoS ONE*. 2010. 5(2) doi:10.1371/journal.pone.0008987 for use under the terms of the Creative Commons CC BY 3.0 Attribution license (http://creativecommons.org/licenses/by/3.0/legalcode).

Question 19

Before addition of the virus, the pH of the pure water in the experiment is:

- A. < 1.
- B. = 7.
- C. = 14.
- D. < 7.

Question 20

In Reaction 1, water acts as a:

- A. base.
- B. conjugate acid.
- C. acid.
- D. conjugate base.

Question 21

Based on the study, short (< 1 min) applications of dilute (1%) weak acids:

- A. can be relied on to fully inactivate flu viruses on contaminated surfaces.
- B. cannot be relied on to inactivate flu viruses on contaminated surfaces.
- C. is more effective at inactivating flu viruses than immersing the surface in hot water for an hour.
- D. is more effective at inactivating flu viruses than short (< 1 min) immersions of the surface in hot water.

Question 22

If trifluoroacetic acid is used instead of vinegar, it will:

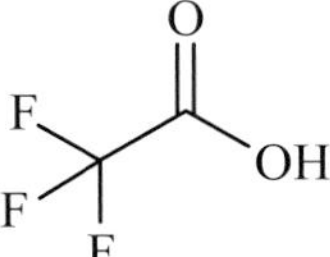

Trifluoroacetic acid

- A. inactivate fewer viruses since the conjugate base is more stable.
- B. inactivate more viruses since the O–H bond is stronger.
- C. inactivate fewer viruses since the O–H bond is weaker.
- D. inactivate more viruses since the conjugate base is more stable.

Passage 5 (Questions 23-27)

Hydrofluoric acid (HF) is a powerful mineral acid. It is used in industry to etch glass, remove rust, and as a catalyst in oil refinement. It is widely available for domestic use, and accidental spills or leaks lead to severe burns.

Like other acids, hydrofluoric acid causes primary burns through hydrolysis and pH dependent conformational changes of tissue proteins. These biochemical reactions manifest themselves as typical burn symptoms: redness, blistering, necrosis, and eschar formation.

Unlike other acids, hydrofluoric acid can cause systemic toxicity due to its ability to penetrate the skin. Skin penetration is so rapid that many times patients do not even feel pain until several hours after exposure. The fluoride anions form insoluble precipitates with bivalent cations in the blood such as magnesium or calcium. Changes in the blood concentration of these vital cations leads to enzymatic and cellular dysfunction, culminating in wide-spread cellular death. Depending on the magnitude of the exposure, hypocalcaemia and hypomagnesemia can even result, leading to neuromuscular and respiratory complications. Finally, fluoride disables the Na^+/K^+ pump and permits the escape of potassium from the cell. At nerve terminals these ionic changes lead to tremendous pain. Below, in Table 1, is a list of the solubility product constants of various fluoride salts, which can form in the body following hydrofluoric acid exposure.

Table 1 Solubility Product Constant of Selected Fluoride Salts

Chemical	K_{sp}
CaF_2	3.9×10^{-11}
MgF_2	5.16×10^{-11}
FeF_2	2.7×10^{-8}
ZnF_2	3.04×10^{-2}

Successful treatment of hydrofluoric acid burns involves initial decontamination of the affected site, management of the primary burn, and neutralization of any systemic fluoride ions. Typically, this is accomplished with the use of calcium gluconate ($CaGlu_2$, Figure 1) applied to the skin, injected, and via intravenous delivery.

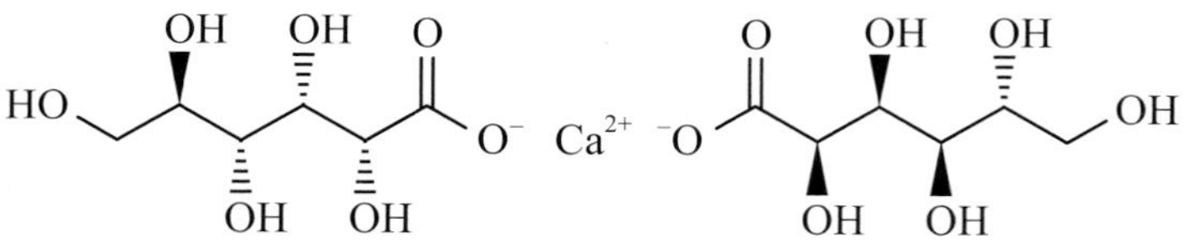

Figure 1 Structure of calcium gluconate

Question 23

Equal exposure to which acid solution is expected to cause the most severe primary burn?

- A. 1 M HF
- B. 1 M HCl
- C. 1 M HBr
- D. 1 M HI

Question 24

What is the concentration of $Ca^{2+}(aq)$ in a saturated calcium fluoride solution?

- A. 5.42×10^{-5} M
- B. $9.91 \times 10^{-3.66}$ M
- C. $9.91 \times 10^{-4.66}$ M
- D. $3.15 \times 10^{-3.66}$ M

Question 25

Suppose a solution of HF were reacted with calcium gluconate until all fluoride ions were precipitated. What is true?

I. The pH of the solution is less than 7.
II. The mole ratio of CaGlu to HF is about 2:1.
III. The mole ratio of CaGlu to HF is about 1:2.
IV. The pH of solution is greater than 7.

- A. I and II only
- B. I and III only
- C. II and IV only
- D. III and IV only

Question 26

If the percent disassociation of a 0.1 M solution of HF is 8%, what is the pK_a of HF?

- A. 1.2
- B. 5.2
- C. 4.5
- D. 3.2

Question 27

At what point during the titration of HF with NaOH is the solution neutral?

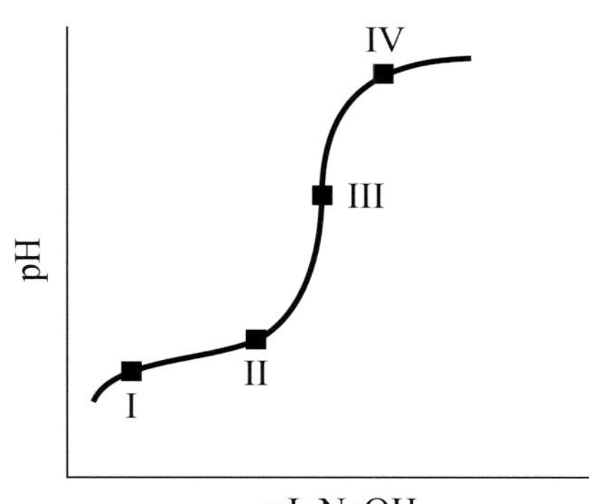

- A. I
- B. II
- C. III
- D. IV

Questions 28 - 31 do not refer to a passage and are independent of each other.

Question 28

What is the pH of the 10% vinegar solution (pK_a= 4.7)?

- A. 4.6
- B. 3.5
- C. 1.9
- D. 6.2

Question 29

The strength of an acid determines its effect on pH. How does a strong acid compare to a weak acid?

- A. A strong acid has a higher K_a and a lower pK_a than a weak acid.
- B. A strong acid has a lower K_a and a lower pK_a than a weak acid.
- C. A strong acid has a higher K_a and a higher pK_a than a weak acid.
- D. A strong acid has a lower K_a and a higher pK_a than a weak acid.

Question 30

$LiCO_3$ is used in the treatment of bipolar disorder. $LiCO_3$ is:

- A. slightly basic.
- B. neutral.
- C. slightly acidic.
- D. very acidic.

Question 31

Buffer solutions are used to analyze the properties of some drugs. All of the following combinations could make buffer solutions EXCEPT:

- A. NH_3 and $(NH_4)_2SO_4$.
- B. NaCl and HCl.
- C. $NaCH_4COO$ and CH_3COOH.
- D. $NaNO_2$ and HNO_2.

Passage 6 (Questions 32-35)

Heart burn is a painful condition caused by the escape of stomach acid into the esophagus. It is typically precipitated by changes in the lower esophageal sphincter (LES). In healthy adults, the LES prevents acid from entering the esophagus. If it is partially open, then stomach acid may travel through it and damage the sensitive esophageal tissue.

A common treatment for heartburn is the administration of oral antacids. Antacids are drugs, typically available over the counter, that neutralize stomach acid. A common ingredient in many of these drugs is $CaCO_3$. It rapidly dissolves in the strong acid of the stomach.

$$CaCO_3(s) + 2HCl(aq) \rightarrow CaCl_2(aq) + H_2O(l) + CO_2(g)$$

Reaction 1

The neutralizing capability of a series of antacids was tested by placing an inverted burette over pre-weighed antacid tablets in a wide mouth beaker. The beaker contained 300 mL of deionized (DI) water. A vacuum was applied to the burette to draw the DI water into it. Air was allowed back into the burette to lower the DI water height to the 75 mL mark, the highest mark on the burette (see Figure 1). Afterwards, concentrated HCl was added to the wide mouth beaker, to make a 1 M solution. After the antacid tablet was completely reacted, the water level was read. The difference between the two readings indicated the amount of carbon dioxide gas produced.

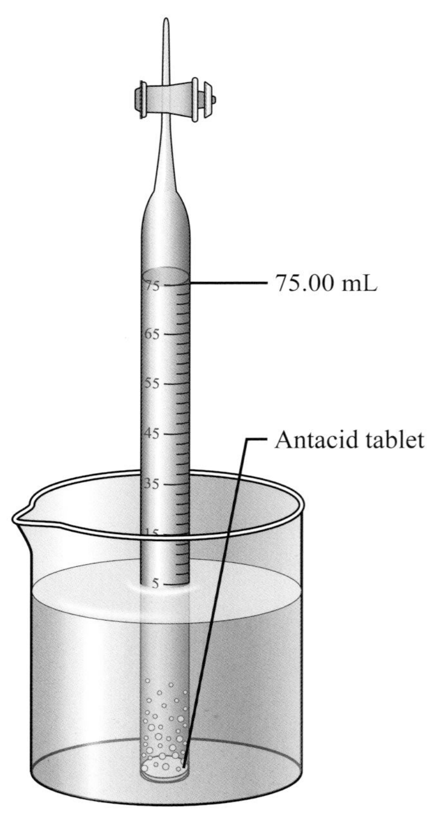

Figure 1 Burette setup

Question 32

The strength of the antacids' neutralizing capacity was quantified as an intensive property that increased with increasing antacid strength. Which of these units was most likely used?

- **A.** Mass of antacid tablet/L of CO_2 released
- **B.** Volume of CO_2 released/mass of antacid tablet
- **C.** Moles of CO_2 gas released
- **D.** pH of water solution final – pH of solution initial

Question 33

How much 12 M HCl must be added to the solution as described in the passage?

- **A.** 2.47 mL
- **B.** 2.50 mL
- **C.** 2.25 mL
- **D.** 1.53 mL

Question 34

Precipitated milk of magnesia, $Mg(OH)_2(s)$, was also tested in this study. Compared to pure $CaCO_3(s)$:

- **A.** equivalent molar masses of $Mg(OH)_2(s)$ will produce more carbon dioxide gas because the OH^- anion is a stronger base than the CO_3^{2-} anion.
- **B.** equivalent molar masses of $Mg(OH)_2(s)$ will produce less carbon dioxide gas because the OH^- anion is a weaker base than the CO_3^{2-} anion.
- **C.** equivalent molar masses of $Mg(OH)_2(s)$ will produce more carbon dioxide gas because the OH^- anion shifts the water-carbonic acid equilibrium to favor the production of carbon dioxide gas.
- **D.** equivalent molar masses $Mg(OH)_2(s)$ will produce less carbon dioxide gas because the OH^- anion reacts to form water in the presence of acid.

Question 35

Suppose 75 mL of water were displaced during the experiment, and, after acidification, the solution had a total volume of 310 mL. What is the new pH of the solution?

- **A.** $\log\left[\dfrac{(0.300\times10^{-1})-\left(\dfrac{2\times0.75}{8.31\times298}\right)}{0.300}\right]$
- **B.** $-\log\left[\dfrac{(300\times10^{-1})-\left(\dfrac{2\times75}{8.31\times25}\right)}{300}\right]$
- **C.** $-\log\left[\dfrac{(0.300\times10^{-1})-\left(\dfrac{2\times0.75}{8.31\times298}\right)}{0.300}\right]$
- **D.** $-\log\left[\dfrac{(0.300\times10^{-1})-\left(\dfrac{0.75}{8.31\times298}\right)}{0.300}\right]$

Passage 7 (Questions 36-39)

Hypercapnic respiratory failure, or the accumulation of excess carbon dioxide due to blocked respiration , is a complex condition associated with the malfunction of various organ systems crucial for many physiological processes, leading to an acid-base imbalance. Carbon dioxide is not the only independent variable that may cause alterations in acid-base balance. Total serum protein, albumin in particular, plays an important role, as does the strong ion difference (SID), or the difference between the strong positive ions in plasma and the strong negative ions, represented below:

$$SID = [Na^+ + K^+ + Ca^{2+} + Mg^{2+}] - [Cl^- + Lac^-]$$

Equation 1

In healthy adults, where blood pH is 7.4, body temp is 37°C and $PaCO_2$ = 40 mmHg, the ideal value of SID is 42 mmol/L. An increased SID correlates with alkalosis; a reduced SID is associated with acidosis. Altering SID shifts the water dissociation equilibrium, creating more or less H^+ with a concomitant change in $[H^+]$ and a change in pH.

For a given increase in CO_2, the only way to minimize the resulting acidemia is to produce compensatory metabolic alkalosis, which is obtained through complex urinary ion excretion mechanisms. Fluid homeostasis depends on the correct relationship between lung and kidney activities because they regulate most of the CO_2 and H^+ concentrations in extracellular fluid. However, in settings of low PaO_2 and high $PaCO_2$ patients, fluid homeostasis is disturbed, with avid retention of sodium and water.

Ventilation therapy is the firsthand treatment for hypercapnia (elevated blood CO_2). Noninvasive ventilation (NIV) was provided to a panel of hypercapnic patients, and their clinical parameters were evaluated over a period of 24 hours, shown in Table 1 below.

Table 1 Clinical Parameters of NIV Treatment for Hypercapnic Patients

Variables	1 h	2 h	6 h	24 h	p-value*
Heart rate (beats/min)	113.4 ± 14.7	111.3 ± 14.8**	106.9 ± 16.8**	100.3 ± 17.8**	< 0.001
Respiratory rate (breaths/min)	29.6 ± 4.9	28.5 ± 4.7**	26.0 ± 5.0**	22.6 ± 4.4**	< 0.001
pH	7.26 ± 0.07	7.38 ± 0.07**	7.31 ± 0.07**	7.35 ± 0.06**	< 0.001
PaO_2 (mmHg)	59.3 ± 8.9	61.8 ± 9.3*	64.3 ± 10.0**	66.5 ± 10.1*	< 0.001
$PaCO_2$ (mmHg)	68.0 ± 12.2	66.5 ± 12.2*	62.7 ± 12.5**	59.5 ± 11.7**	< 0.001
Lactate (mmol/L)	2.9 ± 0.6	2.6 ± 0.7**	2.1 ± 0.8**	1.4 ± 0.8**	< 0.001

* = $p < 0.01$, ** = $p < 0.001$

This passage was adapted from "Mixed Acid-Base Disorders, Hydroelectrolyte Imbalance and Lactate Production in Hypercapnic Respiratory Failure: The Role of Noninvasive Ventilation." Terzano C, Di Stefano F, Conti V, Di Nicola M, Paone G, et al. *PLoS ONE*. 2012. 7(4) doi: 10.1371/journal.pone.0035245 for use under the terms of the Creative Commons CC BY 3.0 license (http://creativecommons.org/licenses/by/3.0/legalcode).

Question 36

What happens to the water dissociation equilibrium when a large influx of chloride enters the bloodstream?

- **A.** Increased K_w, higher $[H^+]$ and higher $[OH^-]$
- **B.** Increased K_w, lower $[H^+]$ and lower $[OH^-]$
- **C.** Decreased K_w, higher $[H^+]$ and higher $[OH^-]$
- **D.** Decreased K_w, higher $[H^+]$ and lower $[OH^-]$

Question 37

Ventilators are assisted breathing devices that help restore blood pH balance. What is the mean effect of 24 hour NIV treatment on blood pH in terms of $[H^+]$ change?

- **A.** Increases by 2×10^{-8}
- **B.** Decreases by 5×10^{-8}
- **C.** Increases by 6×10^{-7}
- **D.** Decreases by 5×10^{-7}

Question 38

Which of the following salts would NOT restore blood pH equilibrium in a patient with metabolic acidosis?

- O **A.** Sodium bicarbonate
- O **B.** Ammonium chloride
- O **C.** Sodium acetate
- O **D.** Potassium bicarbonate

Question 39

What hypothesis summarizes the relationship between pH and other clinical parameters during NIV?

- O **A.** Blood pH is strictly determined by $PaCO_2$ levels.
- O **B.** Blood pH is proportional to lactate concentration.
- O **C.** Blood pH may be influenced by different parameters in the short term and the long term.
- O **D.** Blood pH is independent of all the other clinical parameters.

Passage 8 (Questions 40-43)

During drug development drugs oftentimes demonstrate inadequate performance in key biochemical and pharmaceutical parameters, such as solubility, bodily uptake, and shelf and temperature stability. To improve these characteristics, drugs can be converted into their acidic or basic forms, and paired with an appropriate counterion.

An important factor to consider during counterion selection is the common ion effect. The common ion effect describes a process where the solubility of an ionic precipitate is diminished, as a result of one species of the precipitate's ionic pair already being dissolved in solution. For example, the hydrochoric salt of the tetracycline class antibiotic, doxycycline, is reduced 4 fold in 0.1 M HCl solution compared to neutral solution. Since under normal conditions, the stomach contains approximately 0.1 M HCl, the common ion effect should not be ignored—especially when developing chloride salts intended for oral delivery.

Another effect drug designers consider is the microenvironment which will surround the drug. When a drug particle dissolves, a steady state boundary layer of highly concentrated drug ion and counterions surrounds the particle (Figure 1).

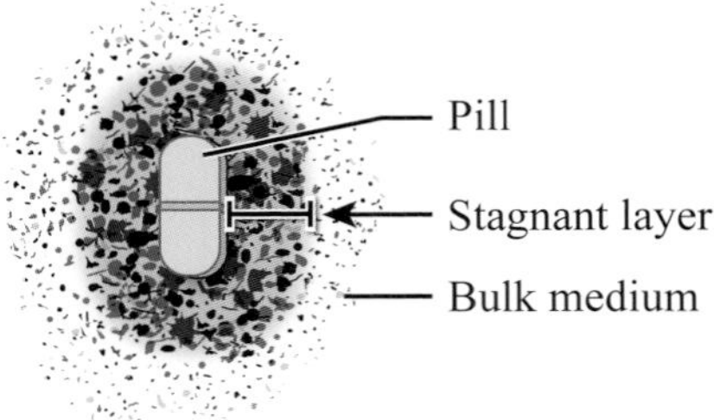

Figure 1 Schematic of stagnant layer

This layer has a pH which is very close to a saturated solution of the salt, but often different from the surrounding system. The thickness of this stagnant layer (h) affects the rate of diffusion of the drug into the bulk medium according to Noyes-Whitney equation (Equation 1), where D is the diffusion coefficient, A is the effective surface area of the drug, C_s is the solubility of the drug, and C_b is the concentration of drug dissolved in the bulk medium.

$$R = \frac{DA(C_s - C_b)}{h}$$

Equation 1

Question 40

Which of the following is most likely the salification product of hydrochloric acid and doxycycline?

- A. 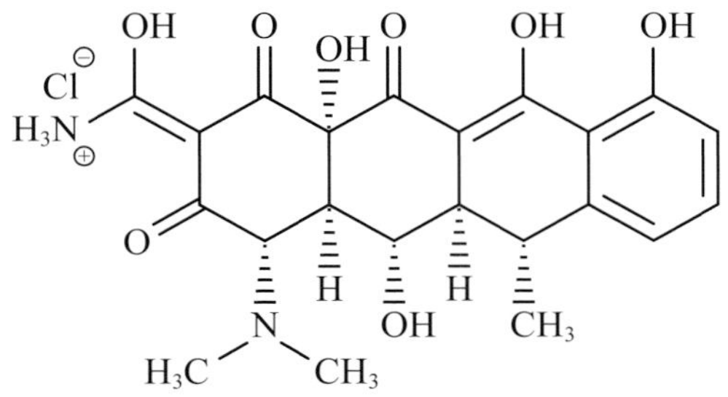
- B. 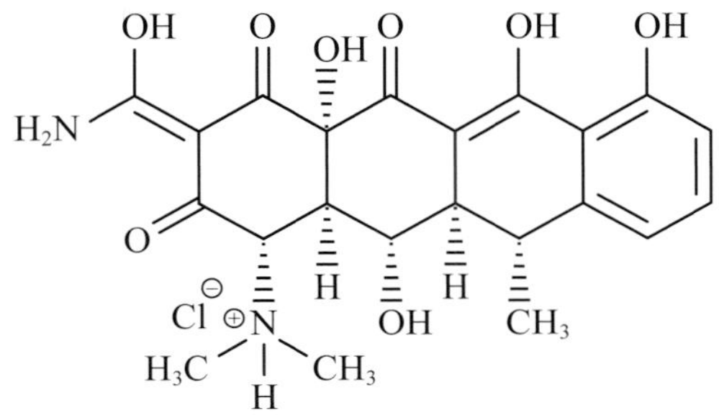
- C. 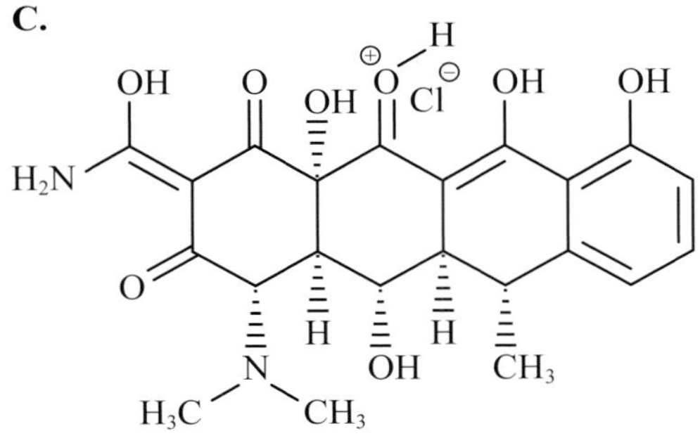
- D.

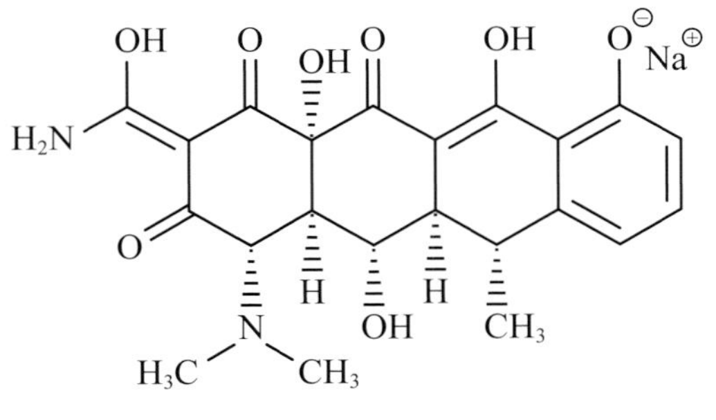

Question 41

Doxycycline · HCl has a pK_a of 3.1. After dissolving in the stomach, what is the ratio of the concentration of free base to the salt form of the drug?

- A. 1:1
- B. 0.12:1
- C. 0.01:1
- D. 0.08:1

Question 42

Which of the following will most increase the rate of diffusion of a spherically shaped drug, just placed at the bottom of a solution of deionized water (Note: Surface area of a sphere = $4\pi r^2$)?

- A. Addition of a chemical that reduces the stagnant layer by a factor of 2.
- B. Cutting the sphere in half to increase its surface area.
- C. Lowering the temperature of the solution
- D. Removing half of the solution, but keeping the spherically shaped drug undisturbed.

Question 43

How much more acidic is stomach acid than neutral water?

- A. Six times more acidic.
- B. One-hundred thousand times more acidic.
- C. One million times more acidic.
- D. Ten million times more acidic.

Questions 44 - 47 do not refer to a passage and are independent of each other.

Question 44

Proline has a pI of 6.4. Which of the following acid dissociation constants most likely describe proline?

- O **A.** $pK_{a1} = 1.9$ and $pK_{a2} = 10.9$
- O **B.** $pK_{a1} = 2.2$ and $pK_{a2} = 4.2$
- O **C.** $pK_{a1} = 10.9$ and $pK_{a2} = 1.9$
- O **D.** $pK_{a1} = 2.0$ and $pK_{a2} = 8.4$

Question 45

The titration curve of lactic acid titrated with ammonia is shown below. Addition of bicarbonate to the titration would most likely:

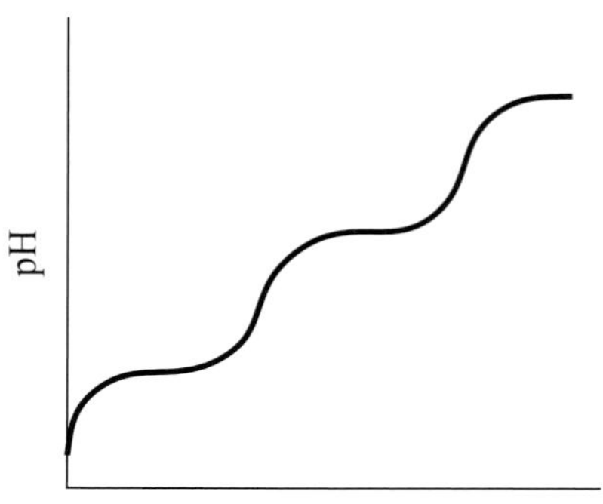

- O **A.** shift the titration curve to the left.
- O **B.** shift the titration curve to the right.
- O **C.** shift the titration curve up.
- O **D.** shift the titration curve down.

Question 46

Ingestion of a strong base, such as those found in cleaning supplies, can be lethal. However, attempts to reverse the basicity after ingestion are often more lethal. Which of the following principles of neutralization reactions may account for this?

- O **A.** The reactions are endothermic
- O **B.** The reactions are exothermic
- O **C.** The reactions are endergonic
- O **D.** The reactions are exergonic

Question 47

Phosphate salts are used as physiologic buffers. Which of the following correctly depicts the effect of a phosphate salt on blood pH?

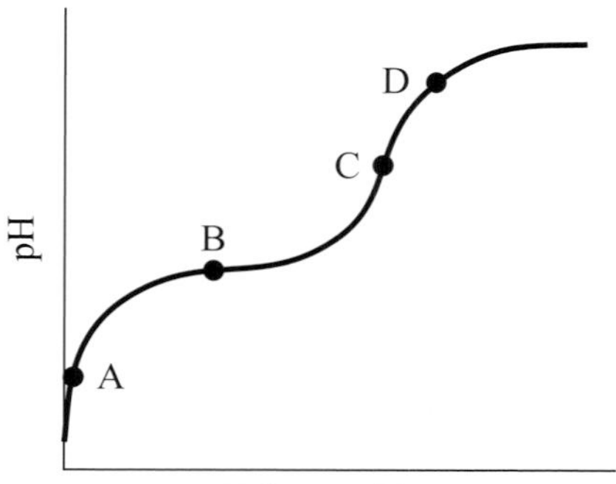

- O **A.** Point A
- O **B.** Point B
- O **C.** Point C
- O **D.** Point D

Passage 9 (Questions 48-51)

In order to maintain energy demand, tumor cells switch their metabolism to glycolysis, resulting in increased glucose consumption and pronounced lactic acid production. pH values in solid tumors are in the range of 6.5 to 6.8, and this acidic environment is important for tumor promotion and resistance to chemotherapeutics. This acidosis-induced stimulation of P-glycoprotein-dependent chemoresistance depends on MAP kinases. However, it is unclear whether these kinases are activated as extracellular pH-reduction occurs.

Scientists measured the intracellular pH of a cancer cell line at a normal extracellular pH (7.4), as well as under acidic conditions (Figure 1). In addition, they exposed the cancer cell line to 200 mM DIDS, which inhibits bicarbonate transport, or incubated the cells with 40 mM lactate to further elucidate the change in intracellular pH that may be occurring due to changes in the extracellular environment (Figure 1).

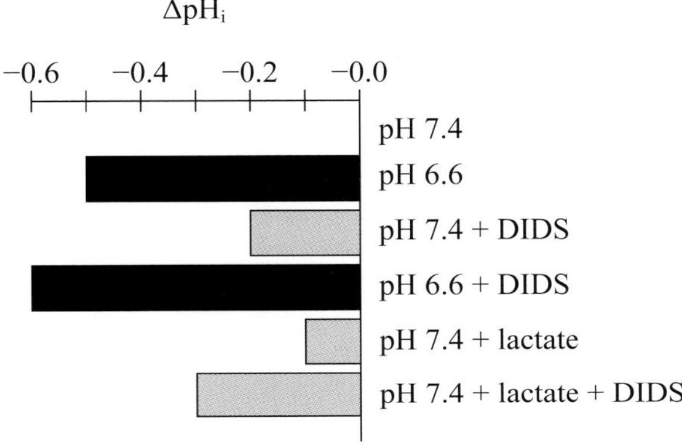

Figure 1 Impact of extracellular pH and bicarbonate transport inhibition on the intracellular pH of cancer cells

As increased phosphorylation could be either the result of increased kinase activity or of a reduced phosphatase rate, the impact of changing pH on the levels of an activated kinase, pMKK3, were measured by western blot. The results of the study are shown in Figure 2.

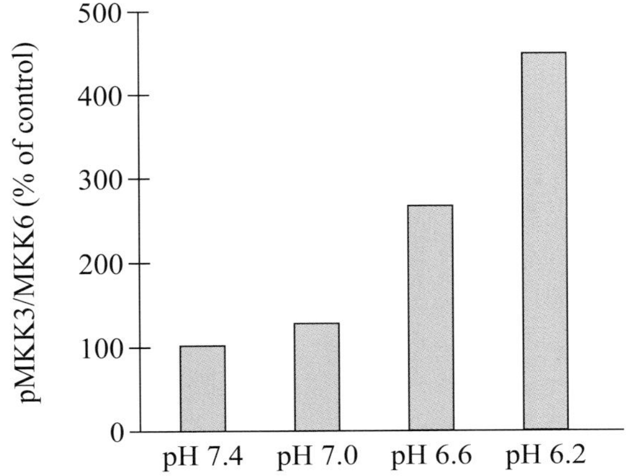

Figure 2 Effect of pH on the phosphorylation status of MKK3

This passage is adapted from "Acidic Environment Leads to ROS-Induced MAPK Signaling in Cancer Cells." Riemann A, Schneider B, Ihling A, Nowak M, Sauvant C, et al. *PLoS ONE.* 2011. 6(7) doi:10.1371/journal.pone.0022445 for use under the terms of the Creative Commons CC BY 3.0 license (http://creativecommons.org/licenses/by/3.0/legalcode).

Question 48

Addition of DIDS to the medium of a dish containing cancer cell lines at a normal physiologic pH most likely results in which of the following increases in the intracellular proton concentration?

- **A.** 4×10^{-4} M
- **B.** 1×10^{-4} M
- **C.** 7×10^{-7} M
- **D.** 2×10^{-8} M

Question 49

Inhibition of bicarbonate transport most likely results in:

- **A.** an increased pH in the cell culture dish.
- **B.** an increased pH in the cytosol of the cancer cell.
- **C.** an increased concentration of protons in the cell culture dish.
- **D.** a decreased concentration of protons in the cytosol of the cancer cell.

Question 50

Which of the following statements best describes the results shown in Figure 2?

- **A.** Increasing proton concentration allows for increased allosteric activation of a kinase.
- **B.** Increasing proton concentration allows for decreased allosteric activation of a kinase.
- **C.** Decreasing proton concentration allows for decreased allosteric activation of a phosphatase.
- **D.** Decreasing proton concentration allows for increased allosteric activation of a phosphorylase.

Question 51

When lactate was added to the cell culture dish, some of the lactate was observed to turn into lactic acid. Lactic acid was generated when:

- **A.** lactate served as a nucleophile to remove a hydrogen from H_3O^+.
- **B.** lactate served as an electrophile to remove a hydrogen from H_3O^+.
- **C.** lactate served as a nucleophile to remove a hydrogen from HCO_3^-.
- **D.** lactate served as an electrophile to remove a hydrogen from HCO_3^-.

Passage 10 (Questions 52-56)

Local infections and burn wound sepsis are key concerns in the treatment of thermally injured patients. Burn wounds are readily colonized with a range of pathogenic micro-organisms, vastly increasing the risks of systemic infection and graft failure. As a result, systemic sepsis from invasive infection remains the leading cause of death among those with burn wounds.

Owing to the reducing efficacy of antibiotics against a large number of nosocomial pathogens, the high doses required to treat organisms growing in sessile biofilms, and the realization that routine use of antibiotics does not prevent bacterial colonization, there is much interest in the use of novel biocide applications to prevent or reduce microbial contamination and bacterial loads in burns and wounds.

Acetic acid (AA), was evaluated for its capacity to both prevent biofilm formation and to eradicate pre-formed biofilms. To do so, its concentration was gradually increased in an inoculated broth culture and the effects it had on bacterial growth were recorded. To evaluate its biofilm eradication properties, a biofilm coated peg was incubated at 33°C in a range of AA solutions. After exposing the peg to a culture broth and incubating it over night, the turbidity of the resulting culture was quantified by its optical density. The results are shown in Figures 1 and 2. The physical characteristics of AA are shown in Table 1.

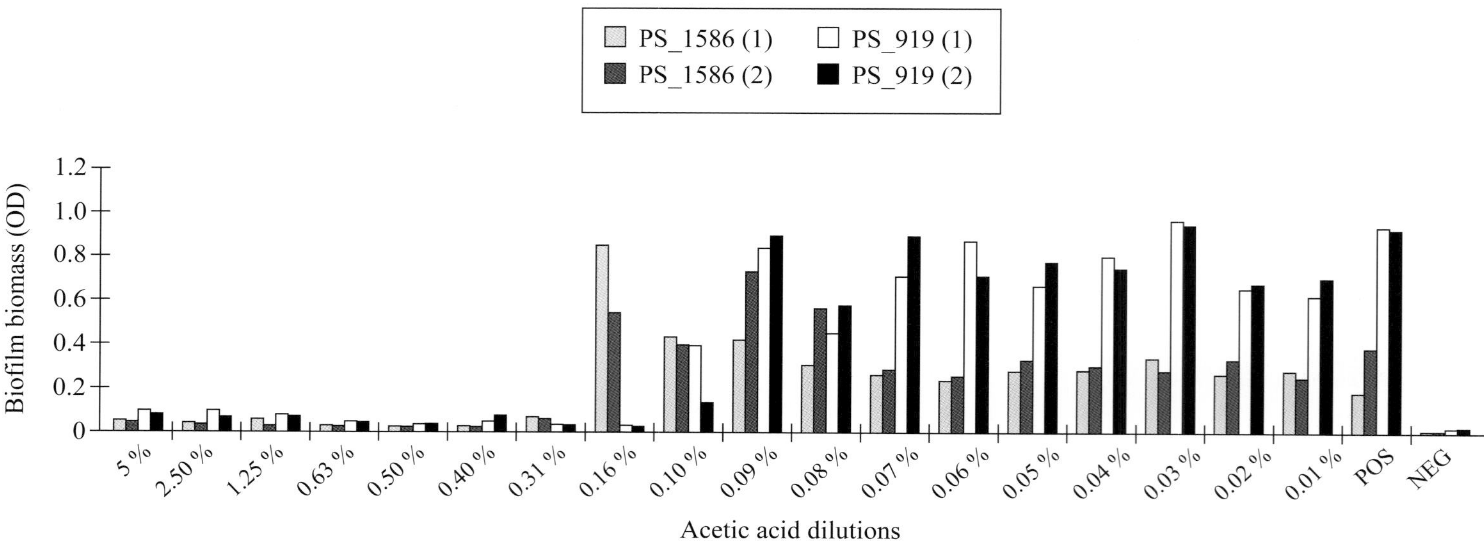

Figure 1 Biofilm inhibition as function of AA concentration (vol AA/vol solution)

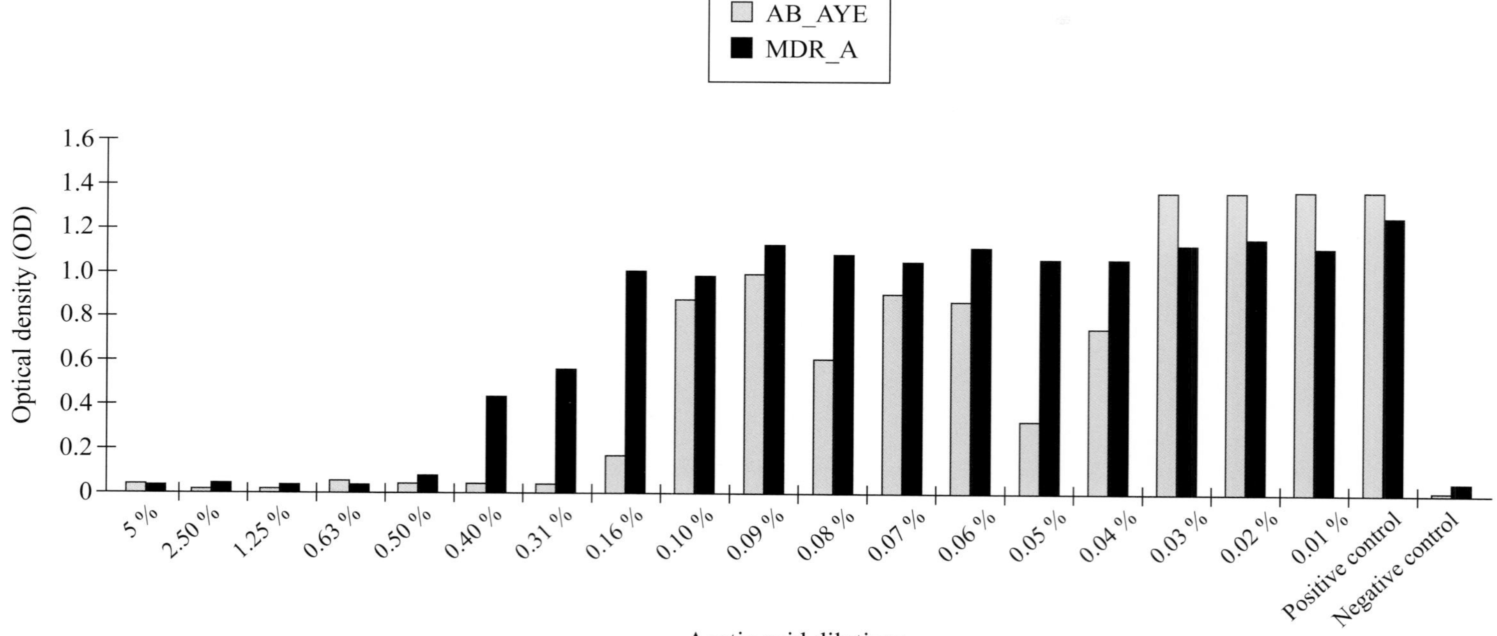

Figure 2 Biofilm eradication as function of AA concentration (vol AA/vol solution)

Table 1 AA Physical Characteristics

Structure	$H_3C-C(=O)-O-H$
pK_a	4.75
M_W (g/mol)	60.05
ρ (g/cm^3)	1.05
T_b (°C)	118

This passage was adapted from "The Antibacterial Activity of Acetic Acid against Biofilm-Producing Pathogens of Relevance to Burns Patients." Halstead FD, Rauf M, Moiemen NS, Bamford A, Wearn CM, Fraise AP, et al. *PLoS ONE.* 2015. 10(9): doi:10.1371/journal.pone.0136190 for use under the terms of the Creative Commons CC BY 4.0 license (http://creativecommons.org/licenses/by/4.0/legalcode).

Question 52

What is the pH of a 4 M solution of acetic acid at room temperature?

- O **A.** 3.7
- O **B.** 2.1
- O **C.** 1.3
- O **D.** 8.2

Question 53

Which of the following broth solutions would most favor the growth of PS_1586?

- O **A.** 16.8 g of AA mixed with 100 mL of broth
- O **B.** 16.8 g of AA mixed with 84 mL of broth
- O **C.** 16 g of AA mixed with 84 mL of broth
- O **D.** 15.2 g of AA mixed with 84 mL of broth

Question 54

If 1 mole of calcium acetate were dissolved in a 2000 mL 1 M acetic acid solution, what would be the new pH of the solution?

- O **A.** 6.1
- O **B.** 4.7
- O **C.** 4.4
- O **D.** 3.7

Question 55

What was the purpose of the negative control used in this experiment?

- O **A.** To determine if any bacteria other than what was inoculated into the broth could be responding to the gradually increased pH of the broth solution
- O **B.** To determine the growth characteristics of bacteria before the pH of their environment was increased
- O **C.** To determine the growth characteristics of bacteria before the pH of their environment was reduced
- O **D.** To determine if any bacteria other than what was inoculated into the broth could be responding to the gradually reduced pH of the broth solution

Question 56

Which of the following conclusions is best supported by the finding that hydrochloric acid solutions with the same pH as the AA solutions tested in this experiment are less active against bacteria?

- O **A.** The lower osmolarity of the acetic acid solutions lead to more cytolysis relative to the HCl solution.
- O **B.** The acid form of acetic acid can cross the bacterial cell membrane and damage internal cellular structures.
- O **C.** The protons released by HCl are held in closer proximity to the highly electronegative chloride anion, which prevents them from attacking cellular structures.
- O **D.** The deprotonated form of acetic acid can cross the bacterial cell membrane and damage internal cellular structures.

Questions 57 - 59 do not refer to a passage and are independent of each other.

Question 57

Research has shown that the tumor microenvironment has a high concentration of carbonic acid. Bicarbonate is the:

- A. conjugate acid of HCO_3^-.
- B. conjugate base of HCO_3^-.
- C. conjugate acid of H_2CO_3.
- D. conjugate base of H_2CO_3.

Question 58

The titration of acetic acid with pyridine, C_5H_5N, is shown below. Substitution of acetic acid for hydrobromic acid would be most likely to:

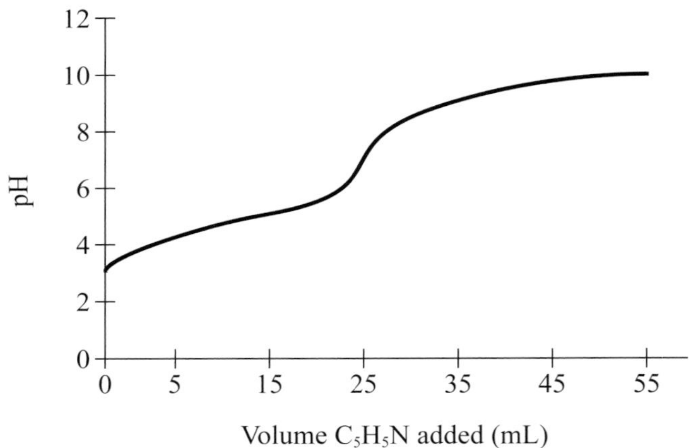

- A. shift the titration curve down.
- B. shift the titration curve up.
- C. shift the titration curve left.
- D. shift the titration curve right.

Question 59

Thymol blue is added to a reaction designed to determine the pK_a of acetylsalicylic acid. Which of the following statements best describes the purpose of thymol blue?

- A. Serve as a buffer for acetylsalicylic acid.
- B. Serve as a proton source for acetylsalicylic acid.
- C. Absorb a proton from acetylsalicylic acid.
- D. Donate a proton to solution upon reaching a certain pH.

TEST 7A

STOP. If you finish before time is called, check your work. You may go back to any question in this test.

ANSWERS & EXPLANATIONS for Test 7A can be found on p. 360.

Acids and Bases

MINI-TEST 7B

Time: 45 minutes
Questions 1–29

DIRECTIONS: Most of the questions in this test section are grouped with a passage. Read the passage, then select the best answer to each question. Some questions are independent of any passage and of one another. Select the best answer to each of these questions. If you are unsure of an answer, rule out incorrect choices and select from the remaining options. Indicate your selection beside the option you choose. A periodic table can be found on the last page of this book for you to use at any point during this test section.

Passage 1 (Questions 1-6)

It is estimated that norovirus gives rise to more than 267 million infections worldwide per year. The disease is usually contracted by ingestion of contaminated food, water, person-to-person contact, and touching contaminated surfaces. Norovirus typically causes self-limited gastroenteritis, but it is extremely infectious. It is responsible for many outbreaks in closed environments, such as cruise ships.

Cruise ships are particularly vulnerable because a large number of people are confined in a relatively small space. As a result, there is interest in improving the antiviral properties of materials which compose cruise kitchen equipment. Recently, a study used inoculative techniques to determine the virucidal properties of different copper alloys compared to stainless steel (SS). The use of antimicrobial alloys in high-risk closed environments may reduce the spread of disease. SS starts as iron ore mixed with coke in blast furnaces.

$$Fe_2O_3(s) + 3C(s) \rightarrow 2Fe(l) + 3CO(g)$$

The alloys investigated in this study were all homogenous solid state solutions of different metals. This data is shown in Figures 1 and 2.

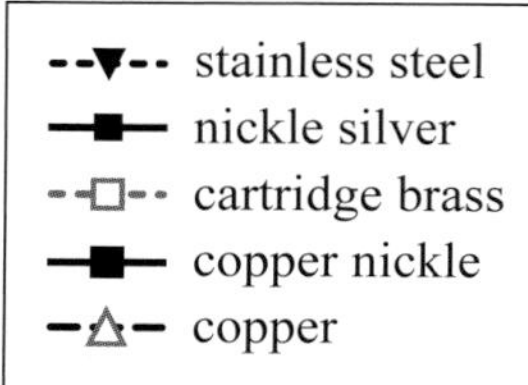

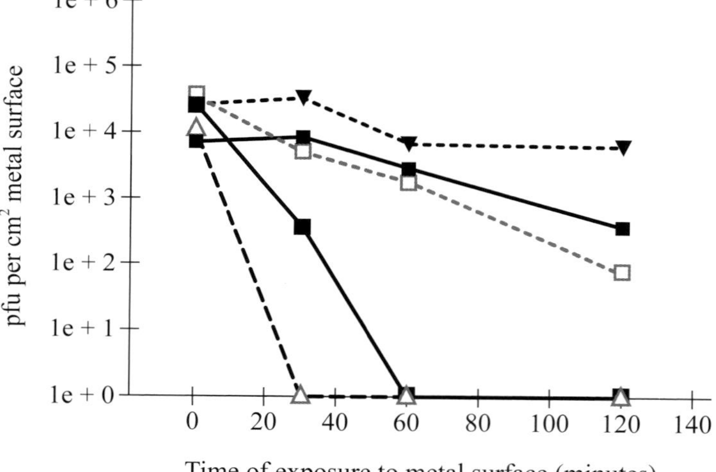

Figure 1 Virucidal properties of different alloys

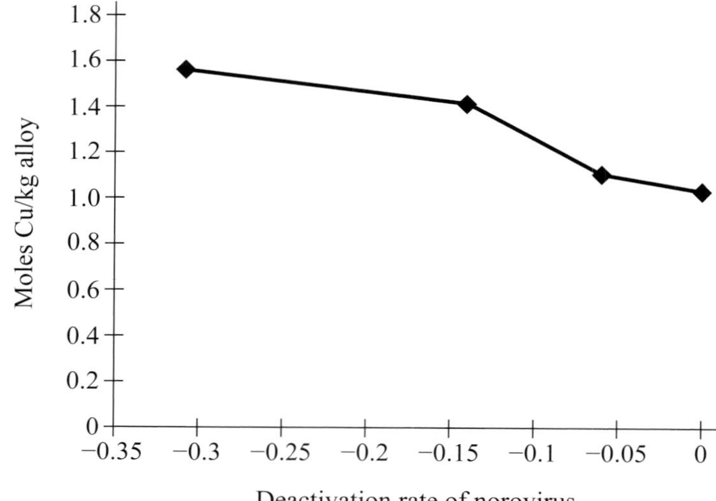

Figure 2 Dependence of inactivation rate on copper content

The inactivation rate, K, was calculated using equation 1, where N_o is the number of plaque forming units (PFUs) cultured from the alloy at the beginning of the study, N_f is the number of PFUs cultured from the alloy at the end of the study, and T is the time interval of the study.

$$K = \frac{\ln\left(\frac{N_f}{N_o}\right)}{T}$$

Additionally the mechanism of antiviral activity was investigated. Ethylenediaminetetraacetic acid (EDTA) and bathocuproinedisulfonic acid (BDS), both chelators that remove ionic copper species from solution, were added to the copper surface. EDTA removes ionic copper by forming octahedral complexes according to reaction 2.

EDTA + Cu^{2+} (Copper (II)) → Octahedral complex + $4H^+$

Reaction 2

It was observed that viruses could survive far longer in the presence of both EDTA and BDS.

This passage was adapted from "Inactivation of Norovirus on Dry Copper Alloy Surfaces." Warnes S, Keevil W. *PLoS ONE*. 2014. 9(5) doi: 10.1371/journal.pone.0098333 for use under the terms of the Creative Commons CC BY 3.0 Attribution license (http://creativecommons.org/licenses/by/3.0/legalcode).

Question 1

What is the correct Lewis structure of the gaseous product of Reaction 1?

- **A.** $C\equiv O:$
- **B.** $:C\equiv O:$
- **C.** $:C=\ddot{O}:$
- **D.** $\ddot{C}-\ddot{O}:$

Question 2

In reaction 2, copper(II) acts as a:

- **A.** Lewis acid.
- **B.** Lewis base.
- **C.** Brønsted-Lowry acid.
- **D.** Brønsted-Lowry base.

Question 3

Metal alloys were subjected to elemental analysis, shown below.

Alloy	Cu (g)	Zn (g)	Sn (g)	Ni (g)	Fe (g)	Cr (g)
X	89	—	—	10	1	—
Y	65	17	—	18	—	—
Z	—	—	—	8	74	18

Which, respectively, is expected to most and least rapidly inactivate norovirus?

- **A.** X, Z
- **B.** X, Y
- **C.** Y, X
- **D.** Z, X

Question 4

EDTA is a tetraprotic acid. Some tetraprotic acids have complex titration curves when neutralized with KOH. Where in this curve are the moles of KOH added equal to the moles of a tetraprotic acid in the solution?

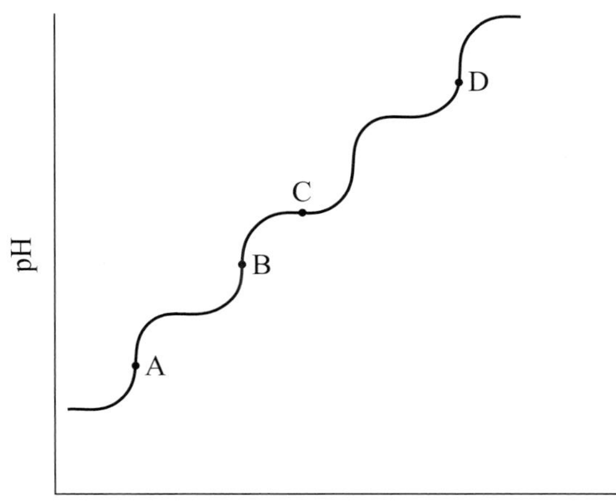

- **A.** A
- **B.** B
- **C.** C
- **D.** D

Question 5

EDTA has similar properties to other organic acids. What is the pH of a 1 M solution of butanoic acid? (pK_a butanoic acid $= 1.6 \times 10^{-5}$)

- **A.** 5.2
- **B.** 4.0
- **C.** 2.4
- **D.** 3.1

Question 6

Copper alloys are sensitive to corrosion in certain acidic solutions. If an acid indicator were added to a cleaning solution, and this indicator changes color when the protonated form is 1/10 of the initial concentration of the indicator, at what pH would it change color?

- **A.** $pH = pK_{a\ indicator} + 1$
- **B.** $pH = pK_{a\ indicator} - 1$
- **C.** $pH = pK_{b\ indicator} + 1$
- **D.** $pH = pK_{b\ indicator} - 1$

Passage 2 (Questions 7-11)

Glacial acetic acid (GAA) refers to solutions of pure anhydrous acetic acid. GAA cannot be effectively distilled from vinegar because the vapor phase of a vinegar solution does not significantly favor the exclusion of water.

In a domestic laboratory setting, GAA can be synthesized via the combination of an excess of sodium bisulfate and sodium acetate. Both of these chemicals exist as hydrates, and melt at relatively low temperatures. When the two are heated, GAA can be distilled.

$$NaHSO_4(l) + NaCH_3COO(l) \rightleftharpoons CH_3COOH(g) + Na_2SO_4(l)$$

Reaction 1

Reaction 1 is driven primarily through a disparity in the basicity of each anion. Excess sodium bisulfate is required, as it forms a liquid medium in which the reaction can proceed. Table 1 shows physical properties of these species.

Table 1 Physical Properties of Selected Chemicals in GAA synthesis

Chemical	pK_a of conjugate acid	Melting point (C°)	Boiling point of conjugate acid (C°)	MW (g/mol)
$NaHSO_4$	−3.0	58.30	337	138
$NaCH_3COO$	4.8	58.00	118	82
Na_2SO_4	2.0	32.38	Decomposes past 315	322

The purity of the GAA product can be assessed by observing its reaction with sodium bicarbonate.

Question 7

If the GAA were completely pure, it would:

- A. release bubbles upon exposure to sodium bicarbonate.
- B. not release bubbles upon exposure to sodium bicarbonate.
- C. release heat and bubbles upon exposure to sodium bicarbonate.
- D. not release heat and bubbles upon exposure to sodium bicarbonate.

Question 8

What is the K_a of $NaHSO_4$?

- A. 10^3
- B. 10^{-2}
- C. 10^{-3}
- D. 10^2

Question 9

100 mL of 1 M NaOH solution is mixed with 100 mL of 1 M acetic acid solution to form sodium acetate and water. What is the pH of the final solution?

- A. 13.5
- B. 7.0
- C. 9.4
- D. 6.1

Question 10

The contact of exposed skin to alkaline materials leads to a subjective "slippery" sensation. Which best explains this phenomenon?

- A. Epidermal surface lipids undergo aldol condensations via deprotonation of an α-hydrogen.
- B. Epidermal surface proteins lose their secondary structure via protonation of their basic groups.
- C. Epidermal surface proteins lose their primary structure via hydrolysis of the peptide bond.
- D. Epidermal surface lipids are converted to alkanoate salts.

Question 11

What mass of each reagent would allow Reaction 1 to proceed most effectively?

- A. 34.5 g of $NaHSO_4$ and 20.5 g $NaCH_3COO$
- B. 34.5 g of $NaHSO_4$ and 41 g of $NaCH_3COO$
- C. 34.5 g of $NaHSO_4$ and 10.3 g of $NaCH_3COO$
- D. 69 g of $NaHSO_4$ and 41 g of $NaCH_3COO$

Questions 12 - 15 do not refer to a passage and are independent of each other.

Question 12

Ibuprofen, shown below, has an approximate pK_a of 4.91. At a pH of 4.86, what fraction of ibuprofen molecules carries a negative charge?

- A. 0.05
- B. 0.48
- C. 0.73
- D. 1.0

Question 13

Which of the following amino acids is LEAST likely to participate in catalysis of an acid-base reaction?

- A. Histidine
- B. Arginine
- C. Lysine
- D. Isoleucine

Question 14

Given the table below, what is the charged state of the most basic amino acid at a pH of 14?

Amino acid	pK_a (COOH)	pK_a (NH^{3+})	pK_a (side chain)
Alanine	2.3	9.7	—
Arginine	1.8	9.0	12.5
Cysteine	1.7	10.8	8.3
Glutamic acid	2.2	9.7	4.3

- A. −2
- B. −1
- C. 0
- D. +1

Question 15

Which of the following best defines a Brønsted base?

- A. It accepts a proton.
- B. It accepts an electron.
- C. It donates a proton.
- D. It donates an electron.

Passage 3 (Questions 16-21)

Heat shock protein 90 (Hsp90) is a component of the cellular chaperone machinery, and is overexpressed in cancer cells. Recent evidence supports anticancer selectivity in Hsp90 inhibitors, and has inspired the development of small-molecule inhibitors as anticancer therapeutics.

Researchers evaluated the binding properties of an experimental agent, ICPD47, with isothermal calorimetric titration (ITC). The observed enthalpy of binding was highly dependent on the buffer used in the ITC experiment. For example, the observed enthalpy of binding $\Delta_b H_{obs}$ was approximately –28 kJ/mol in Tris buffer and –42 kJ/mol in phosphate buffer, at a pH of 7.5 and 37°C, as shown in Figure 1.

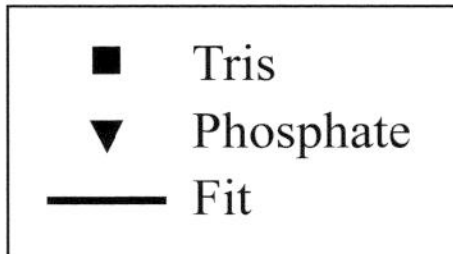

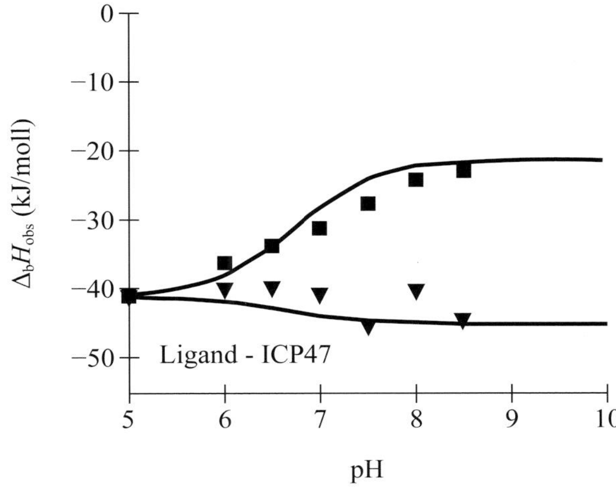

Figure 1 $\Delta_b H_{obs}$ in Tris and phosphate systems

These buffers have significantly different enthalpies of deprotonation, which affect the value of $\Delta_b H_{obs}$. Furthermore, analysis of observed enthalpies for ICDP47 binding as a function of pH shows a typical pH dependence indicating a single protonation event linked to inhibitor binding. The thermodynamic properties of various acid/base chemistry events between the buffer and ICPD47 are shown in Figure 2.

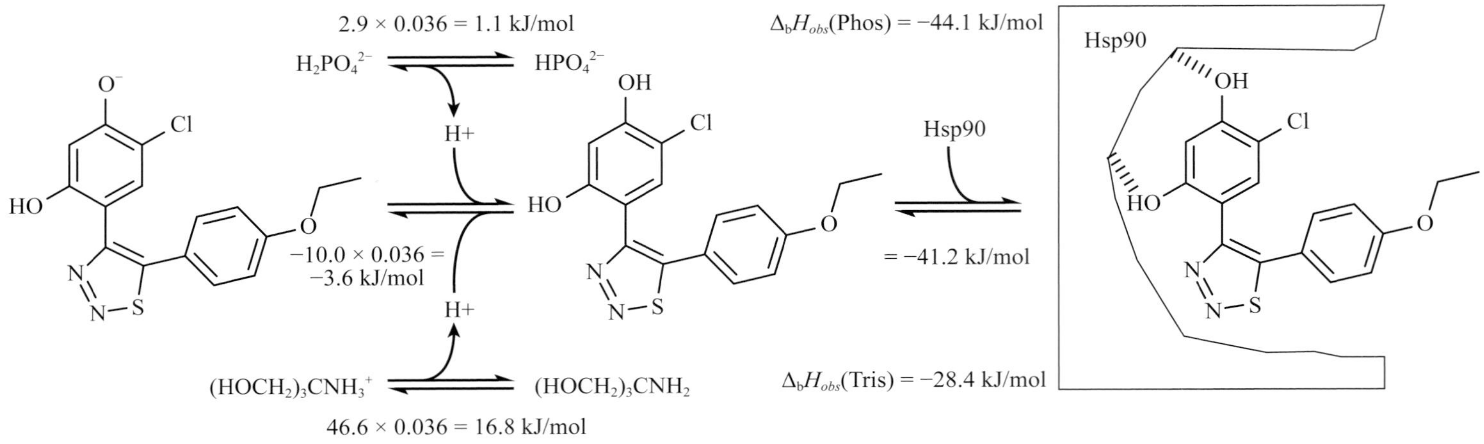

$2.9 \times 0.036 = 1.1$ kJ/mol

$H_2PO_4^{2-}$ ⇌ HPO_4^{2-}

H+

$-10.0 \times 0.036 =$
-3.6 kJ/mol

H+

$(HOCH_2)_3CNH_3^+$ ⇌ $(HOCH_2)_3CNH_2$

$46.6 \times 0.036 = 16.8$ kJ/mol

$\Delta_b H_{obs}$(Phos) = −44.1 kJ/mol

Hsp90

= −41.2 kJ/mol

$\Delta_b H_{obs}$(Tris) = −28.4 kJ/mol

Hsp90

Figure 2 Acid/base chemistry events that influence observed enthalpy of binding

This passage was adapted from "Thermodynamics of Aryl-Dihydroxyphenyl-Thiadiazole Binding to Human Hsp90." Kazlauskas E, et al. *PLoS ONE*. 2012. 7(5) doi:10.1371/journal.pone.0036899 for use under the terms of the Creative Commons CC BY 3.0 license (http://creativecommons.org/licenses/by/3.0/legalcode).

Question 16

The intrinsic binding enthalpy of ICDP47 with Hsp90 can be measured when a solution's pH is low enough that ICDP47 does not deprotonate the buffer when binding to Hsp90. What is the concentration of hydronium at this pH?

- **A.** 10^{-5} M
- **B.** $10^{-7.5}$ M
- **C.** $10^{-8.5}$ M
- **D.** 10^{-6} M

Question 17

The hydroxyl groups of ICDP47 are most likely to hydrogen bond with which residue in Hsp90?

- **A.** Isoleucine
- **B.** Aspartate
- **C.** Glycine
- **D.** Phenylalanine

Question 18

What ratio of monosodium phosphate to disodium phosphate should be mixed to create a buffer at a pH of 7.5? (Note: pK_a of $NaH_2PO_4 = 6.8$ and pK_a of $Na_2HPO_4 = 12.4$)

- **A.** $1:10^{0.7}$
- **B.** $10^{-4.9}:1$
- **C.** $10^{0.7}:1$
- **D.** $1:10^{-4.9}$

Question 19

Which of the following best explains how the K_w of pure water changes as the water's temperature increases?

- **A.** The ionization of water is an exothermic process, and increasing water's temperature favors its autoionization, increasing K_w.
- **B.** The ionization of water is an endothermic process, and increasing water's temperature favors its autoionization, increasing K_w.
- **C.** The ionization of water is an endothermic process, and increasing water's temperature favors its autoionization, decreasing K_w.
- **D.** The ionization of water is an exothermic process, and increasing water's temperature favors its autoionization, decreasing K_w.

Question 20

The pK_a of common buffer molecules are shown below. Which of the following molecules is best for a solution which is to be buffered at a pOH of 5.0?

Buffer	pK_a
Tris	8.06
HEPES	7.48
MES	6.15
PIPES	6.76

- **A.** PIPES
- **B.** HEPES
- **C.** MES
- **D.** Tris

Question 21

Which factor best explains the disparity between deprotonation enthalpies of the Tris and phosphate buffer conjugate acids?

- **A.** Phosphate buffer's conjugate acid requires less energy to undergo deprotonation because its O–H bond is less polarized than the N–H bond of Tris buffer's conjugate acid.
- **B.** Tris buffer's conjugate acid requires less energy to undergo deprotonation because the molecule gains a neutral charge following deprotonation, whereas phosphate buffer's conjugate acid gains a negative charge.
- **C.** Phosphate buffer's conjugate acid requires less energy to undergo deprotonation because the resulting negative charge is resonated between several oxygen atoms, but Tris buffer's conjugate base does not have any resonance structures.
- **D.** Tris buffer's conjugate acid requires less energy to undergo deprotonation because its N–H bond is more polarized than the O–H bond of phosphate buffer's conjugate acid.

Passage 4 (Questions 22-26)

Milk is an emulsion of proteins, carbohydrates, and dissolved minerals. It serves as a primary nutrition source for infant humans and other mammals. The chief class of proteins present in milk is caseins , which are insoluble phosphoproteins. Beyond their nutritional role in dairy products, caseins are also extracted and incorporated into a variety of semisynthetic materials, such as adhesives, plastics, and fabrics.

Casein based adhesives are first prepared by extracting casein from bovine milk. Bovine milk has a pH value of 6.6. Since casein has a pI of 4.6, casein exists as the caseinate anion in milk. During casein extraction processes, the pH of a milk sample is modified to generate the neutral and fully insoluble protein, which precipitates from the milk. After extraction, mixing dried casein powder with water and a strong base such as NaOH creates a solution that dries with powerful adhesive properties.

A study was conducted to calculate the adhesive strength of glue derived from various commercial sources of milk. The glue was generated from identical volumes of milk and used to glue two wooden boards together. Weights were added to the inferior board as shown in Figure 1 until board separation was achieved.

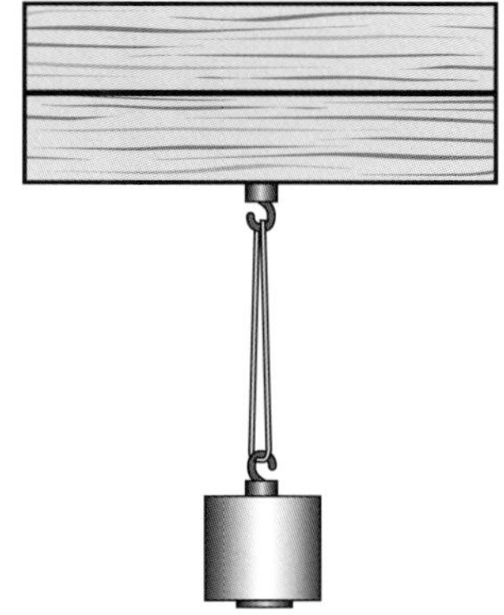

Figure 1 Adhesive strength experiment

Table 1 shows the relationship between the chemical properties of the milk and the adhesive strength of the glue derived from it.

Table 1 Adhesive Strength of Milk Glues

Milk	Percent butterfat (triglyceride) content	Glue strength (N)
Whole	3%	126.1
Skim	2%	127.4
Low fat	0%	130.0

TEST 7B

Question 22

Which of the following would best precipitate casein from milk?

○ **A.** N_2

○ **B.** HCl

○ **C.** NaOH

○ **D.** $NaCH_3CH_2OO$

Question 23

NaOH is not mixed with powdered casein in dry glue formulations because it prematurely activates the glue. Based on the solubility table below, which of the following dry formulations would release the most OH^- anion after mixing with water?

Chemical	K_{sp}
Calcium oxalate CaC_2O_4	2.7×10^{-9}
Calcium sulfite $CaSO_3$	6.8×10^{-8}
Calcium fluoride CaF_2	5.3×10^{-9}

○ **A.** Casein powder, sodium fluoride, and calcium hydroxide

○ **B.** Casein powder, sodium acetate, and calcium hydroxide

○ **C.** Casein powder, sodium oxalate, and calcium hydroxide

○ **D.** Casein powder, sodium sulfite, and calcium hydroxide

Question 24

The table below lists the hydroxide anion concentration of common beverages. Which of the following is true?

Beverage	$[OH^-]$
Lemon juice	10^{-12}
Orange juice	$10^{-9.8}$
Black tea	$10^{-6.8}$

○ **A.** Milk is less acidic than tea, orange juice, and lemon juice.

○ **B.** Milk is more acidic than orange juice but less acidic than tea.

○ **C.** Milk is less acidic than lemon juice, but more acidic than tea.

○ **D.** Milk is less acidic than lemon juice, but more acidic than orange juice.

Question 25

Which of the following hypotheses best explains the results in Table 1?

○ **A.** Milk with higher fat content better neutralizes the solution after addition of NaOH, allowing for the generation of a stronger glue.

○ **B.** Milk with lower fat content has a greater concentration of casein per unit volume, allowing for the generation of a stronger glue.

○ **C.** Milk with higher fat content has a lower concentration of casein per unit volume, allowing for the generation of a stronger glue.

○ **D.** Milk with lower fat content neutralizes less of the solution after addition of NaOH, allowing for the generation of a stronger glue.

Question 26

The conjugate acid of the imidazole side chain of a His residue in casein has a pK_a of 6.0. This residue is crucial for an enzyme catalyzed precipitation reaction used in the production of cheese. At a physiological pH of 7.4,

○ **A.** histidine's imidazole side chain is a zwitterion.

○ **B.** histidine's imidazole side chain is negatively charged.

○ **C.** histidine's imidazole side chain is about 25 times more likely to be neutral than protonated in solution.

○ **D.** histidine's imidazole side chain is about 25 times more likely to be protonated than neutral in solution.

TEST 7B

Questions 27 - 29 do not refer to a passage and are independent of each other.

Question 27

Theoretically, life could have evolved in an ethanol-only world, where water is replaced entirely by ethanol. Which of the following would describe the K_W of ethanol?

- O **A.** $[H^+][OH^-]$
- O **B.** $[H^+][OH^-]/[H_3C–CH_2OH]$
- O **C.** $[H^+][H_3C–CH_2O^-]$
- O **D.** $[H^+][H_3C–CH_2O^-]/[H_3C–CH_2OH]$

Question 28

A superacid is one which is more acidic than pure sulfuric acid. Which of the following would be the pK_a of a super acid?

- O **A.** 25
- O **B.** 2
- O **C.** –2
- O **D.** –25

Question 29

Which of the following is the most acidic hydrogen in the following structure?

$H_3C–CH_2–CH_2COOH$

A B C D

- O **A.** Atom A
- O **B.** Atom B
- O **C.** Atom C
- O **D.** Atom D

STOP. If you finish before time is called, check your work. You may go back to any question in this test.

ANSWERS & EXPLANATIONS for Test 7B can be found on p. 360.

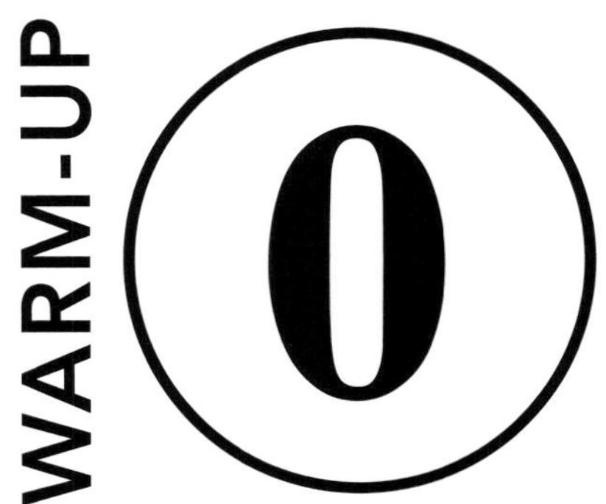

ANSWERS & EXPLANATIONS

Questions 1–5

ANSWER KEY
1. A
2. A
3. B
4. C
5. A

EXPLANATIONS FOR WARM-UP

Passage 1 (Questions 1-5)

1. **A is the best answer.** According to the passage, magnesium forms an ion with a cationic 2+ charge. In addition, magnesium is a transition metal. Magnesium would be likely to form two types of bonds—metallic and ionic. A metallic bond occurs when a metal becomes bonded to many other metals, allowing the sharing of electrons. An ionic bond forms between a metal and a non-metal, and is the other type of bond in which a metal is likely to participate. This makes choice A the most likely answer. Covalent bonds form between non-metals, eliminating choice B. Hydrogen bonds and Van der Waals bonds are intermolecular bonds that form between different molecules. Hydrogen bonds form between two compounds that possess a hydrogen atom that is bonded to a nitrogen, fluorine, or oxygen atom. Van der Waals bonds form between two separate molecules and is the result of transient interactions between the electron clouds of these molecules. This eliminates choices C and D.

2. **A is the best answer.** Notice that the answer choices use the condensed versions of the electronic configuration, meaning that the noble gas from the above row is used as a substitute for the full configuration. Manganese is in row four, meaning the condensed configuration would use Argon, [Ar], as the noble gas. This eliminates choices B and D. Manganese is the fifth element in the transition metal row, meaning that the d orbital has five electrons in it, as two electrons already filled the *s* orbital. This makes choice A a better answer than choice C.

3. **B is the best answer.** The first step in choosing the best answer is to decide whether the metal is diamagnetic or paramagnetic. A diamagnetic ion has an even number of electrons, where the spins of the electrons cancel out. A paramagnetic ion has an odd number of electrons, where the spins of the electrons do not cancel out. The 2+ charge on Mg means that it has lost two electrons. Since the normal electron configuration of Mg is $[Ne]3s^2$, the loss of two electrons would make the Mg^{2+} ion have a configuration of [Ne], which has a full octet. The magnesium ion thus has an even number of electrons, making it diamagnetic. Choices A and C can be eliminated. Figure 1 presents the relationship between the velocity of a reaction and the concentration of an enzyme at a fixed concentration of magnesium. Notice that the velocity of the reaction increases as more enzyme is added to the reaction mix. This means an excess of enzyme increases the overall velocity of the reaction, making choice B a better answer choice than choice D.

4. **C is the best answer.** Aspartate, Asp, is an amino acid, which is made of atoms that are non-metals. Some of the atoms in amino acids include carbon, oxygen, nitrogen, and hydrogen. A metallic bond is one between metals, where the electrons do not belong to any one atom, but are shared evenly between all atoms. Choice A can be eliminated. Ionic bonds form between metals and non-metals, but only when the metal atom has electrons to donate. Notice that Mg^{2+} has lost its two electrons in the *s* orbital, giving it a full octet. This likely means that it is unable to donate any additional electrons, making it less likely to form an ionic bond. Choice B is less likely to be the best answer for this reason. Electrostatic interactions occur between atoms of opposite charges that are spatially separated, as are the atoms of Asp and the magnesium ion. Associations of oppositely charged electron clouds describe this electrostatic interaction, likely making choice C the best answer. Choice D somewhat describes a metallic bond, but does not specify that the bond is between metals. Since Asp is not a metal, this type of bonding would not be expected. Choice D can be eliminated, as electrons are not completely shared in an ionic bond, but instead belong more to the non-metal atom.

5. **A is the best answer.** The oxygen atom of DNA likely has a negative charge, as it has given up the hydrogen on its hydroxyl group. Lysine and Arginine amino acids are positively charged at physiologic pH, meaning the positive charge of Lysine/Arginine would be attracted to the negative charge of the oxygen of DNA. This makes choice A most likely to be the best answer. All DNA bases are made up of non-metals, meaning that only ionic bonding could occur between the DNA bases and a metal. Choice B can be eliminated. Nitrogen is one of the three atoms that can undergo hydrogen bonding. N, F, and O can all help stabilize interactions with molecules that contain hydrogens, eliminating choice C. Nucleic acids usually associate via Van der Waals, non-covalent interactions, hydrogen bonds, or dipole-dipole bonds. No primary nucleic acid contains a sulfur atom, which is needed for a disulfide bond to form. Choice D can be eliminated.

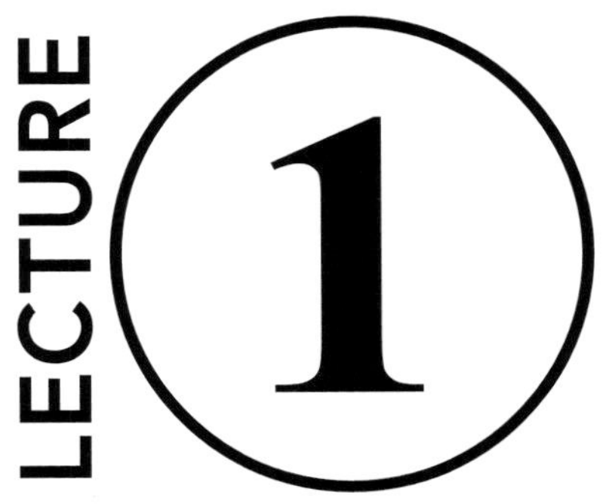

Introduction to General Chemistry

TEST 1A

ANSWERS & EXPLANATIONS

Questions 1–59

LECTURE 1 ANSWER KEY

TEST 1A		MINI-TEST 1B	
1. C	31. C	1. C	16. D
2. C	32. B	2. C	17. D
3. B	33. B	3. D	18. B
4. D	34. B	4. B	19. C
5. C	35. A	5. A	20. B
6. D	36. A	6. B	21. D
7. A	37. B	7. C	22. B
8. D	38. D	8. D	23. A
9. C	39. B	9. C	24. D
10. D	40. A	10. B	25. B
11. B	41. C	11. A	26. C
12. D	42. C	12. B	27. A
13. B	43. A	13. C	28. D
14. A	44. D	14. A	29. A
15. C	45. C	15. B	
16. C	46. B		
17. C	47. A		
18. A	48. C		
19. D	49. B		
20. B	50. B		
21. B	51. C		
22. D	52. A		
23. D	53. C		
24. C	54. C		
25. C	55. C		
26. D	56. D		
27. A	57. C		
28. C	58. C		
29. B	59. D		
30. B			

EXPLANATIONS FOR LECTURE 1

Passage 1 (Questions 1-4)

1. **C is the best answer.** The final paragraph of this passage explains that the Bohr model is only valid for systems with one point charge orbiting another. Such systems will have a nucleus which is a positive point charge and *only one* electron orbiting it. Atomic hydrogen satisfies these conditions and can be eliminated. Removal of three electrons from beryllium leaves it as the Be^{3+} cation. Shift backwards by one atomic number on the periodic table for each electron that is removed to find the resulting electron configuration after 3 electrons are removed. Be^{3+} has the electron configuration of H—i.e. it only has one electron—and can be eliminated. Li^+ fails this test as it has the electron configuration of He with two electrons. Since Li^+ has two point charges in orbit instead of just one, it does not satisfy the conditions necessary to be modelled by Bohr's model. Choice C is the best answer. He^+ has the same electron configuration as H and can be eliminated, as it will satisfy Bohr's model.

2. **C is the best answer.** Figure 1 describes the wavelengths associated with each region of the UVR spectrum. Remember that wavelength is inversely proportional to the energy of a photon, with the equation $E = hc/\lambda$. When the wavelength decreases, the energy increases and vice-versa. The smallest wavelengths will have the highest energy. UVC light has the highest energy and will be best for sterilizing water. Choice C is the best answer. Choices A and B are of lower energy and will be less effective. Infrared light has a far greater wavelength and lower energy than any form of ultraviolet light, also ruling out choice D.

3. **B is the best answer.** By thermodynamic convention, $\Delta E < 0$ kJ/mol when energy is being released by the system and such processes are called exothermic. When electrons relax to a lower orbital they *release* energy in the form of photons. Thus, photon emission is an exothermic process, ruling out choice A and making choice B a good answer. Since Equation 1 at least describes the relationship between the *reciprocal* of a photon's wavelength in terms of energy level transitions, it will be easiest to tackle the veracity of choice C before looking at choice D.

   In the first case, choice C, the electron moves from the third energy level to the second. Thus, $n_i = 3$ and $n_f = 2$. In the second case, choice D, the electron moves from the fourth energy level to the second: $n_i = 4$ and $n_f = 2$. The constant RZ^2 can be disregarded when comparing the resulting wavelengths using Equation 1. Plugging these values in to Equation 1 provides:

$$\frac{1}{\lambda_{3-2}} \propto \frac{1}{2^2} - \frac{1}{3^2}$$

$$\frac{1}{\lambda_{3-2}} \propto \frac{1}{4} - \frac{1}{9}$$

   Use the same approach for the second case:

$$\frac{1}{\lambda_{4-2}} \propto \frac{1}{2^2} - \frac{1}{4^2}$$

$$\frac{1}{\lambda_{4-2}} \propto \frac{1}{4} - \frac{1}{16}$$

   Thus: $\frac{1}{\lambda_{4-2}} > \frac{1}{\lambda_{3-2}}$ and $\lambda_{3-2} > \lambda_{4-2}$. The wavelength associated with a photon from an $n = 3$ to $n = 2$ electronic transition is greater than the wavelength associated with a photon from an $n = 4$ to $n = 2$ electronic transition. Choice C says the opposite and will not be part of the best answer. Choice C can be eliminated. By extension, since the wavelength is greater in the 3—2 transition than in the 4—2 transition, the 3—2 transition will release a photon with a lower energy than the 4—2 transition. Remember energy and wavelength are inversely proportional. For this reason, choice D can be eliminated, making choice B the best answer.

4. **D is the best answer.** The minimum wavelength is obtained when the other variables of Equation 1 provide the highest possible value for $\frac{1}{\lambda}$. Since Z and R are constants and the only variable left to change in this equation is n_i. In particular, increasing n_i in the $\frac{1}{n_i^2}$ term will cause the value of $\frac{1}{\lambda}$ to increase. Curiously, if n_i continuously increases the value of $\frac{1}{\lambda}$ does *not* continuously increase. It peaks around $\frac{RZ^2}{n_f^2}$ because once ni is great enough, $\frac{1}{n_i^2} \approx 0$. Thus the maximum value of $\frac{1}{\lambda}$ is equal to $\frac{RZ^2}{n_f^2}$. Conceptually, this result makes sense; the photon of maximum energy/minimum wavelength that can be emitted upon an electron relaxing to the third energy level results from a electron relaxing from a position infinitely high in energy to the third energy level. Using this simplified equation and plugging in the provided values provides:

$$\frac{1}{\lambda_{min}} = \frac{RZ^2}{n_f^2}$$

$\lambda_{min} = \frac{n_f^2}{RZ^2} = \frac{3^2}{(R \times 2^2)} = \frac{2.25}{R}$ Choice D is the best answer. Choice A is the reciprocal of the best answer. Choices B stems from failing to square both of the squared terms. Choice C stems from failure to square the Z term.

Passage 2 (Questions 5-9)

5. **C is the best answer.** In beta minus decay—which ^{188}Re experiences according to the passage—a neutron is converted into a proton, accompanied by the ejection of an electron. Since protons and neutrons have nearly identical masses, the molecular weight of the product is the same as the molecular weight of the reactant. Choice C is the best answer. Choice A comes from confusing beta minus decay with beta plus decay. During beta plus decay, a proton is converted to a neutron. If ^{188}Re underwent beta plus decay, its product would be ^{188}W, also sharing the same mass as ^{188}Re. Thus, choice A makes two mistakes. It uses the incorrect decay process to determine the product, and then uses a faulty method to determine the product's mass! Remember that periodic table masses for each element are the average mass of an element based on the natural abundance of all of their isotopes. The periodic table mass is not the proper mass of any particular isotope. Choice A would have resulted in using the periodic table to find the atomic mass of W. Since ^{188}Re does not experience beta plus decay, W is not a product. Choice A can be eliminated. Choice B reflects the same mistake of choosing the molecular mass from the periodic table instead of using the proper isotopic molecular mass of the decay product. Finally, choice D is a distractor.

6. **D is the best answer.** Z_{eff}, the effective nuclear charge, is NOT the same as formal charge. $Z_{eff} = Z - S$, where Z is the number of protons in the nucleus, and S is the number of non-valence electrons. Formal charge, in contrast, is dependent on the number of valence electrons. It is defined as FC = (# valence electrons in elemental atom) – (# bonds) – (# nonbonding electrons). Using the equation for Z_{eff} provides that the carbxoylate oxygen has a $Z_{eff} = 8 - 2 = 6$. Likewise, so does the ether oxygen. Choice D is the best answer. Choices A and B stem from using the equation for formal charge instead, by mistake. However, choice B takes resonance into account, whereas choice A does not. Choice C improperly adds the negative charge to the S term when calculating Z_{eff} of the carboxylate oxygen. Since this negative charge is from a valence electron, it does not need to be added. Choice C can be eliminated.

7. **A is the best answer.** The photoelectric effect describes one-to-one photon-to-electron collision and ejection, assuming that the incident photon has an energy greater than the work function, ϕ, of the material. Since the energy of the incident photon far exceeds the work function of lead, one electron will be ejected. Choices B and C can be eliminated on this basis. Lead shields may protect against other kinds of radiation, but gamma radiation can actually ionize the lead shield! This is why extremely thick lead or cement walls are required to absorb all of the energy of the ionizing radiation produced when gamma rays are released. In particular, the kinetic energy of the electron which is ejected is given by the equation:

   $KE = hf - \phi$, where hf is the energy associated with the photon based on the photon's frequency f and Planck's constant h.

   Plug and chug into this equation, but be careful with units as the energy of the γ-ray is expressed in keV, but the work function is expressed in eV.

$$KE = 50 \times 10^3 \text{ eV} - 4.1 \text{ eV} \approx 50 \times 10^3 \text{ eV}$$

   To convert this answer to J, remember the conversion factor of 1.6×10^{-19} J = 1 eV

   Thus, $(50 \times 10^3 \text{ eV})(1.6 \times 10^{-19} \text{ J/1 eV}) \approx 75 \times 10^{-16} \text{ eV} = 7.5 \times 10^{-15}$ eV. Choice A is the best answer. Choice D is a mistake that results from not converting the energy of the γ-ray from keV to eV, but instead treating it as if it were always in the units of eV. Choice D can be eliminated.

8. **D is the best answer.** The representative elements of the periodic table are the all of the groups which flank the transition metals on each side of the periodic table. Since Re is in the middle of the periodic table, it is a transition metal, and not a representative element. By not being a representative element, it cannot possibly be a chalcogen—which is a synonym for the oxygen group—or an alkaline earth metal, which is the group that starts with beryllium. Choice D is the best answer, and choices A, B, and C can be eliminated.

9. **C is the best answer.** Figure 2 shows the percent of cells which were fluorescently labeled, after exposing the cells to a solution of protease K. As its name suggest, protease K breaks down proteins. After exposure to protease K, the aptamers *all* demonstrated weaker binding behavior—evidenced by a smaller percentage of fluorescent cells. Since proteins were lost during the digestions process, it is reasonable to conclude that these aptamers were binding to proteins. Less proteins present would lead to less binding. If the aptamers were binding to genetic material, their binding properties should have been unaffected by digestion with protease K. Choices A and D can be eliminated on this basis. Finally, U8 always shows a greater percentage of fluorescently labeled cells. This means that U8 has a greater affinity for the proteins coded by EGFRvIII than does U2. Both transmembrane receptors and enzymes are different kinds of proteins so the answer choice that describes U8's superior performance will be the best answer choice. Choice C better answer than choice B, and is the best answer.

TEST 1A A&E

Passage 3 (Questions 10-13)

10. **D is the best answer.** Notice that Zn is a transition metal, while O is a nonpolar atom. This makes the bond between the two atoms an ionic bond. Even sharing of electrons between two atoms would be a nonpolar covalent bond, and will only occur between atoms of equivalent electronegativity, such as the diatomic molecule H_2. Choice A can be eliminated. In a polar covalent bond, the two atoms have differences in electronegativity, but both atoms are non-metals. As Zn is a metal, choices B and C can be eliminated. Oxygen is significantly more electronegative than zinc, meaning electrons are likely to transfer from zinc to oxygen, which is the defining characteristic of an ionic bond. Choice D is the best answer.

11. **B is the best answer.** The periodic table is divided up into multiple regions, corresponding to the physio-chemical properties of each element. Metalloids are found at the intersection of the transition metals and non-metals, and include elements such as B, Si, Ge, and As. Choice A can be eliminated. Transition metals are found in the middle of the periodic table and include metals like Cu, Zn, Mn, Ni, Co, and Fe. Transition metals have a unique ability to delocalize electrons across multiple atoms that are found in the same material through a bond called a metallic bond. It is the properties of transition metals and metallic bonds that allow electricity to flow through metal wires. Non-metals are hydrogen and those elements found to the right of the transition metals on the periodic table. Cu is a transition metal, not a non-metal, eliminating choice C. The lanthanides and actinides are often found in two rows below the periodic table, mainly to save space when displaying the table. The lanthanides and actinides are technically transition metals and are often radioactive. Copper is not a lanthanide or actinide, eliminating choice D and making choice B the best answer.

12. **D is the best answer.** A combination of the data contained in Figure 1 and a knowledge of atomic size trends on the periodic table will help answer this question. Notice that only the highest treatment dose of the metal oxide, 5000 mg/kg, is statistically significant in Figure 1. The control group and the two mouse groups treated at 50 mg/kg and 500 mg/kg all showed statistically similar body weights, meaning choices C and D are more likely to be the best answers than choices A and B. Even though most of the other answer choices are not metal oxides, they are combinations of metals and nonmetals. In order to distinguish between choices C and D, the atomic sizes of the metal oxides should be considered, as paragraph two suggests that some of the toxicity is due to the small size of the particles and their ability to transit into cells. Atomic size increases as one moves left and down the periodic table. Rb is further down the periodic table than Fe and B is further to the left on the periodic table compared to N. This suggests that RbB is a larger molecule than FeN and would have more difficulty transiting into cells. Choice D is more likely than choice C to be the best answer.

13. **B is the best answer.** Observing the additional figures presented in the question stem, it is apparent that increasing the dosing of nano-ZnO results in an increase in the relative mRNA expression of the MT1 and MT2 genes. The body operates to maintain homeostasis, meaning when the concentration of a certain molecule gets abnormally high, the body works to correct the imbalance. In this case, the increase in Zn likely means that the body would work to decrease the circulating levels of Zn. Zn is neither a metalloid nor a non-metal, making choices C and D less likely to be the best answer. A paramagnetic metal is one that includes unpaired in the outer valence shell, while a diamagnetic metal is one that has paired electrons in the outer valence shell. ZnO contains an ionic bond, meaning it would likely separate into Zn^{2+} and O^{2-} in solution. The condensed electron configuration of Zn is $[Ar]3d^{10}4s^2$. The Zn^{2+} ion would lose two electrons from the outer shell, meaning its configuration would be $[Ar]3d^{10}$. As the outer d shell contains an even number of electrons, the Zn ion is likely to be diamagnetic, not paramagnetic. This makes choice B a better answer choice than choice A.

TEST 1A A&E

Stand-alones (14-17)

14. **A is the best answer.** Choice A correctly defines the Pauli Exclusion Principle. There are only two spins possible for any electron, so many electrons share the same spin, and choice B can be eliminated. Every orbital has room for at least two electrons, so choice C can also be eliminated. It would be exceedingly unlikely for two electrons in the same atom to share the same ionization energy. Ionization energy typically increases with each electron removed. However, this is unrelated to the Pauli Exclusion Principle, so choice D can be ruled out leaving choice A as the best answer.

15. **C is the best answer.** The Heisenberg uncertainty principle states that the position and momentum of an electron can never be known at the same time. So choice C is the best answer. Since momentum is mass × velocity, by inference, the velocity of the particle also cannot be known. However, compared to choice C, choice A is not as accurate since the Heisenberg uncertainty principle refers most directly to momentum.

16. **C is the best answer.** The excited state describes a high energy state that is often associated with high temperatures and release of a photon upon relaxation to the ground state. The specific molecule mentioned in the question stem is irrelevant. Options I and III are true because they correctly define the excited state. Option II is confuses a proton for a photon and is inaccurate. So, choice C is the best answer.

17. **C is the best answer.** The effective nuclear charge describes the pull of the nucleus on orbiting electrons. Remember that electrons in higher energy orbitals experience a weaker "pull" because the electrons in lower energy orbitals "shield" them from the attractive forces of the nucleus. This effect is due to the repulsive force these intervening electrons exert on the electrons which are farther away from the nucleus. Thus, electrons which are closest to the nucleus will experience the least repulsive forces from intervening electrons between them and the nucleus; the closer to the nucleus an electron is, the greater its Z_{eff}. This question, then, is really asking, "Which of the following orbitals is closest to the nucleus?" As the principal quantum number increases so does its orbital's distance from the nucleus. Among the choices in this question, the 1*s* orbital will be closest to the nucleus because it has the smallest principal quantum number. Choice C is the best answer. Choices A, B, and D, can be eliminated as they describe orbitals further from the nucleus, subject to greater repulsive forces from intervening electrons and a weaker Z_{eff}.

Passage 4 (Questions 18-21)

18. **A is the best answer.** The passage states that the two possible atoms in the Ch position are sulfur and selenium. These atoms are in the same group. Electronegativity increases moving up a group, so choice A is the better answer between choices A and B. Choice C is the not the best answer because Pd is not in the Ch position. Choice D is not the best answer because although it is the most electronegative atom, fluorine is not found in the molecule in the passage.

19. **D is the best answer.** The monoatomic atom in Ta_2PdSe_5 is Pd. Uncharged, Pd has the electronic structure of the noble gas one period (row) above it. This means for formula should start with [Kr] and choices B and C can be ruled out. From Kr, Pd has 10 more electrons. Choice A only includes 9 electrons, so it is not the best answer and would possibly represent Pd^+. This leaves choice D as the best answer. Remember that transition metals do not always fill their *s* orbitals and instead preferentially fill their *d* orbitals first. Electron shells prefer to be empty, half filled or completely filled. So, if there are 10 electrons available, an atom would prefer to fully fill the *d* orbital and leave the *s* orbital empty. Use the image below for filling orbitals. All *s* orbitals have 2 electrons, *p* orbitals have 6 electrons, *d* orbitals have 10 electrons and *f* orbitals have 14 electrons. The preferential filling of d orbitals in the transition metals is an exception to the rule below.

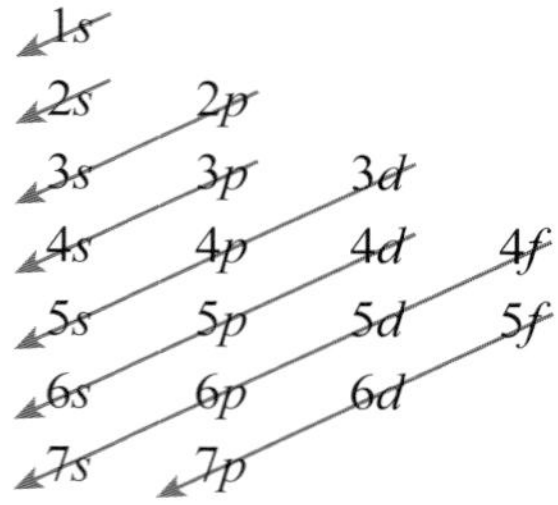

20. **B is the best answer.** In Ta_2PdSe_5, Ta and Pd are metals whereas Se is a nonmetal. So choice B is the best answer.

21. **B is the best answer.** The figure shows the electron density in the d orbitals of Ta and Pd relative to the energy of the system. At low energy ($E < 0$), electrons seem to prefer Pd, and at high energy, the electrons prefer Ta. At very low energy, the electrons appear to be absent from either d orbital. Choice A is the opposite of the findings in the figure, so it is not the best answer. Choice B is accurate and may be the best answer. Choice C is also the opposite of the findings in the figure, so choice C is not a strong answer. Choice D cannot be answered using the figure. The *s* orbitals may be full at low energy, but there is no way to be sure of that because the graph does not describe the *s*, *p* or *f* orbitals. So choice B is stronger than choice D.

Passage 5 (Questions 22-25)

22. **D is the best answer.** There are two separate processes which this question is asking about: emission and reflection. Emitted light is first absorbed as a photon by the molecule in question, causing an electron transition to a higher energy orbital. Eventually, the electron relaxes to its ground state, and releases the energy that it absorbed, reemitting the photon. Reflection occurs when some light strikes a material, and some or all of it bounces off of the material to the observer. The light which is bounced back to the observer is reflected light. If high energy light is absorbed and converted to heat, then low energy light can be reflected back to the observer. The appearance of any color can be a result of reflection, emission, or both. This question is asking about *what kinds* of emissions and reflections can explain the data in the table. Break this question into each point separately.

    Emission:

    Absorption of high energy visible light would result in the emission of high energy photons. Since high energy photons produce light of low wavelengths, the absorption and emission of high energy photons will be associated with a violet color. If the source of the color is emission, option IV is valid, but option I is not. Eliminate choices A and B.

    Reflection:

    Absorption of high energy visible light which is converted to heat means that the material which absorbs this high energy light will NOT have a color associated with high energy light; the high-energy light has been absorbed and cannot be "caught" by the eye. Instead, since the only light which reflects off the material is of low energy, the material will have a color that is associated with low energy light, such as red or yellow. If the source of the color is reflection, option II is valid, but option III is not. Eliminate choice C, and choose the best answer, choice D.

23. **D is the best answer.** Since halogens are diatomic materials comprised of the same atom, they are nonpolar. Each atom has the same negative charge density surrounding it, and the dipole vectors cancel each other out. Choice A can be eliminated. Although electronegativity dramatically decreases going down the halogen group, this is not expected to have a large effect on the phase of each element. The tendency of a material to have a high or low vapor pressure, or high or low melting point, is more related to the polarity of that material, and its size. Smaller molecules vaporize and melt at lower temperatures, and the opposite is observed for larger molecules. Although it appears that the more electronegative elements are more likely to be gases, the real trend going on here is that the halogens are capable of forming stable diatomic species, whereas the elements to the left of them form more massive extended metal networks or covalent rings, such as carbon or sulfur. Choice B can be eliminated. It is true that the quantity of valence electrons increases going down a group, but this does not seem to have any correlation with the phase of the element. Consider that sodium has more valence electrons than fluorine, and is a solid. Nonetheless, chlorine has even more valence electrons than sodium and is a gas! Increasing the number of valence electrons does not correlate very strongly with a reduction in the entropy of a material. Finally, as discussed above, there is direct correlation between increasing the mass of a material and decreasing its entropy. For a huge variety of molecular species, increasing the mass is related to the material having a greater tendency to exist as a solid, or to be a liquid with a lower vapor pressure. Choice D is the best answer.

24. **C is the best answer.** A single displacement reaction requires one component of a chemical to be lost and replaced with another. In Reaction 1, no components are lost, rather both compounds combine to form a single new compound. Choice A can be eliminated, and it looks like choice C may be the best answer. Lewis acid/Lewis base reaction requires one reactant to donate electrons to another reactant, which accepts them. This passage does not provide a lot of mechanistic or structural information about Reaction 1 or its product, so it is difficult to know about the fate of the electrons of each reactant. Choice C is a more certain and better answer than choice B, which can be eliminated. Finally, decomposition requires a reactant to be broken into smaller components. The opposite happened in Reaction 1, so choice D can be eliminated.

25. **C is the best answer.** Although it may be first instinct to start using division to determine how many moles there are of each reagent here, this approach is actually unnecessary. The passage describes the purple smoke reaction in the final paragraph, and it specifies that excess iodine sublimates from the heat of the reaction. This iodine gas has a rich violet color and is the source of the "purple smoke" this reaction produces. The more excess iodine there is, the more of it that can sublimate to create "purple smoke." Choose the protocol which has iodine in the greatest excess of aluminum, or choice C. Choice A does not have as much of an excess of iodine as does choice C, and can be eliminated. Choices B and D actually have iodine as a limiting reagent. These reactions will produce the least "purple smoke." They will quickly end since there is very little iodine to furnish the reaction, or sublime.

TEST 1A A&E

Stand-alones (26-29)

26. **D is the best answer.** The atomic and ionic radii increase with decreasing Z_{eff}. Essentially, in atoms with a smaller Z_{eff}, there is not as much of a positive charge pulling the orbiting electrons towards the nucleus. The hydrogenic species with the smallest Z_{eff} will have the greatest ionic/atomic radius. Remember that $Z_{eff} = Z - S$, where Z is the atomic number and S is the number on *non-valence* electrons. Since none of these atoms have any non-valence electrons, Z_{eff} will be their atomic number. H has the smallest atomic number and the smallest Z_{eff} here. It will have the weakest "pull" on its orbiting electron, causing its atomic radius to be larger than the other atoms who can "pull" their orbiting electron inwards more "tightly". Choice D will be the best answer. The other answer choices feature atoms with a greater Z_{eff} than H and can be eliminated.

27. **A is the best answer.** First, write the equation that describes this alpha decay to solve for the identity of the product:

$$^{187}_{75}\text{Re} \rightarrow {}^{4}_{2}\text{He} + {}^{M}_{Z}\text{X}$$

The sum of the mass numbers on each side of the equation must be equal to one another. Likewise, the sum of the atomic numbers on each side of the equation must also be equal to one another. Thus,

$$187 = 4 + \text{M}$$

$$\text{M} = 183$$

$$75 = 2 + \text{Z}$$

$$\text{Z} = 73$$

The decay product is $^{183}_{73}\text{X}$ or $^{183}_{73}\text{Ta}$. Compared to the reactant, $^{187}_{75}\text{Re}$, the decay product has both a smaller mass number and atomic number. Options III and IV will be part of the best answer. Choices C and D can be eliminated on this basis. Within the same row of the periodic table, atomic radius decreases moving left to right because of the stronger effective nuclear charge that comes from having more protons in the nucleus. Since Ta is to the left of Re, Ta has a smaller effective nuclear charge, and a larger radius. Option I will be part of the best answer, and option II will not be part of the best answer. Choice A is the best answer, and choice B can be eliminated.

28. **C is the best answer.** Tritium is an uncommon isotope of hydrogen. Uncommon isotopes of an element still share the same reactivity and bonding characteristics as the more abundant form of the element. They also occupy the same phase under given conditions. Since hydrogen is normally a diatomic gas under standard conditions, tritium is also a diatomic gas, making choice C the best answer. Hydrogen requires exceptionally low temperatures to solidify; this is true of tritium as well. Choice A can be eliminated. Although water is a liquid, elemental tritium is not, as discussed above, it is a gas. Choice B can be eliminated—be careful to properly read the question. Finally, plasmas occur when a gas is heated to very high temperatures, or subjected to strong electromagnetic fields. Since standard conditions are not this intense, there is no reason to expect tritium to exist as plasma. Choice D can be eliminated.

29. **B is the best answer.** Electron affinity is the willingness of an atom to accept an additional electron. More specifically, it is the energy released when an electron is added to an isolated atom. Elements that tend to have higher electronegativity also tend to have higher electron affinity. Electron affinity increases from left to right and from top to bottom across the periodic table. The best answer will be the element that is furthest to the right and near the top of the periodic table. Ca is found the furthest to the left on the periodic table of the elements listed, and choice A can most likely be eliminated. S is found furthest to the right and top of the table, likely making choice B the best answer. Se is found in the row below S, eliminating choice C. P is found to the left of S, eliminating choice D.

Passage 6 (Questions 30-33)

30. **B is the best answer.** Table 1 shows that every time the concentration of NO increases by a factor of 10, the time required to form NO_2 is reduced by a factor of 10. This is an inversely proportional relationship. It will be linear, so choices C and D can be eliminated. Choice A shows a directly proportional relationship with the parameters increasing together, and cannot be the best answer. Since one parameter increases while the other one decreases in choice B, it is the best answer.

31. **C is the best answer.** A net reaction is found by combining all the individual reactions that form a product. Chemicals which are on both the products and reactants side of the combined equation are eliminated because they have undergone no net reaction.

    The best way to solve this on test day is to mentally combine two reactions at a time that share reactants or products.

    Combining Reactions 1 and 2 provides:

$$^{\bullet}OH(g) + CO(g) + O2(g) \rightarrow HO_2{}^{\bullet}(g) + CO_2(g)$$

    Combining Reactions 3 and 4 provides:

$$HO_2{}^{\bullet}(g) + h\upsilon \rightarrow {}^{\bullet}OH(g) + O(g)$$

    Write Reaction 5 down separately:

$$O(g) + O_2(g) \rightarrow O_3(g)$$

    Combine any two of these three and then, add the third. The net reaction will be:

$$CO(g) + 2O_2(g) + h\upsilon \rightarrow CO_2(g) + O_3(g).$$

    Choose the best answer, choice C.

32. **B is the best answer.** When drawing Lewis structures, remember to provide each atom with a stable octet, unless it is an exception such as boron or aluminum. Next, minimize formal charges if possible, and if there are formal charges, distribute them in such a way the negative charges are near positive charges and vice-versa. Two of the oxygen atoms in choice A only have 7 electrons. This violates the octet rule, so choice A can be eliminated. All of the atoms have an octet and opposing charges are next to one another in choice B—it is the best answer, but look at the rest to be sure. The structure in choice C does not contain all 18 valence electrons that it requires, so choice C may be eliminated. The central oxygen atom in choice D violates the octet rule, and cannot be the best answer.

33. **B is the best answer.** Consider the easier part of this question, which deals with having unpaired electrons in the *p* orbital, first. The electron configuration of atomic oxygen is: $[He]2s^22p^4$. According to Hund's rule, subshells must be singly filled before they doubly filled. This means that of the three *p* subshells 2 of them will have unpaired electrons. Eliminate choices A and D. The dipoles created by the spin of the unpaired electrons will align the same way in an external magnetic field, giving the atom a net magnetic moment which will be attracted towards the field. Choice C should be eliminated—choose the best answer, choice B. This behavior of unpaired electrons causing an atom to be attracted to a magnetic field is called paramagnetism. Diamagnetism is the opposite. It occurs when an atom has completely paired electrons in all of its orbitals. The spins of each set of paired electrons oppose each other, so there is no net dipole caused by the spin of its paired electrons. As a result, diamagnetic materials are not attracted to a magnetic field.

Passage 7 (Questions 34-37)

34. **B is the best answer.** The passage specifies that sodium ferulate is a monoanionic sodium salt derived from FA. This means that there is only one negative charge on the molecule. It is formed from the reaction below:

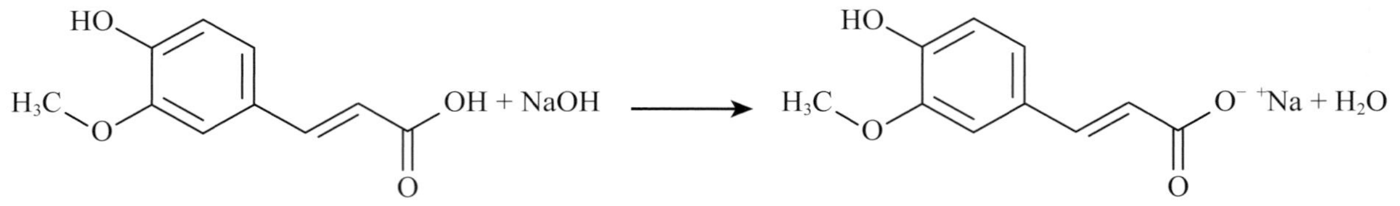

The carboxylic acid moiety ($pK_a \approx 5$) is far more acidic than the phenolic moiety ($pK_a \approx 10$). Exposure of FA to any of the alkaline solutions provided in the answer choices would result in deprotonation of the carboxylic acid first. However, if more than 1 equivalent of NaOH is used than the dianionic salt form may be accidentally synthesized via deprotonation of the phenolic group. Be careful to select the answer choice that furnishes the proper 1:1 ratio of moles of NaOH to moles of FA.

This amount can be solved using stoichiometry. First calculate how many moles of NaOH are required to form the desired salt.

(97.1 g FA)(1 mole FA/194.18 g) = **0.5 moles** of FA initially present. The solution which provides this many moles of NaOH will be the best answer.

Quickly use dimensional analysis to determine how many moles of NaOH are in each of the proposed solutions:

Choice A: (0.5 L)(0.1 mol/L) = 0.05 moles NaOH. Not enough.

Choice B: (0.5 L)(1 mol/L) = 0.5 moles NaOH. This is the best answer.

Choice C, like choice A, will produce a number of moles of NaOH in an order of magnitude that is too small to react with all of the FA. Finally, Choice D will provide 1 mole of NaOH. This is an excess of sodium hydroxide and will form the dianionic salt form of FA. Since this question requested the monoanionic salt, so choice D can be eliminated as well.

35. **A is the best answer.** According to the final paragraph of the passage, Figure 2 shows the survival probability of the rats for 30 days after exposure to the radiation, as a function of the daily dose of FA given before the exposure. A survival probability of 100% for 30 days means that the rat successfully survived the lethal effects of acute radiation sickness for thirty days. According to Figure 2, doses of 50 mg/kg, 75 mg/kg, and 100 mg/kg, all prevented the lethal effects of acute radiation sickness for 30 days. The lowest of these doses, 50 mg/kg, is the minimum dosage *per animal mass* per day required. Use dimensional analysis to determine what daily dose this would be for a 750 g rat.

$$(750 \text{ g rat})(10^{-3} \text{ kg rat/g rat})(50 \text{ mg FA/kg rat}) = 37.5 \text{ mg of FA.}$$

Choice A is the best answer. Choice B reflects the correct dose, but only if expressed in the units of mg/kg of rat. Since the units in the answer choices are mg, the dose must be scaled down for the specific rat in this question stem, and not pulled directly off of the graph. Choice C reflects the total mass of FA administered over the five day pre-exposure experimental period. Since the question only asked for the daily dose, choice C can be eliminated. Finally, choice D is a distractor and not the result of any specific computation error.

36. **A is the best answer.** In general, the ionization energies of an atom increase by roughly the same amount for each electron that is removed. The only substantial deviation from this trend is when an electron which is a member of an octet configuration is removed. Because of the greater stability of the octet configuration, removal of this electron requires far more energy. Thus, this question is really asking, "Which ionization of cobalt requires the greatest energy?" Remember, each ionization event leaves the element with the electron configuration of the element to its left. For example, the first ionization of cobalt leaves it with the electron configuration of iron, and its second ionization leaves it with the electron configuration of manganese. 10 ionizations will leave cobalt with the electron configuration of monoatomic chlorine—in other words, only seven valence electrons. The tenth ionization event breaks the octet configuration that cobalt had, forcing it have the same configuration as monoatomic chlorine. The chart which shows the dramatic increase in energy required for the tenth ionization will be the best answer. Choice A is the best answer as it shows this dramatic increase in energy. Choices B and C are distractors; they show the dramatic increase in ionization energy occurring at the improper ionization event. In particular, choice C is shows it one ionization too early. Finally, choice D shows *less* energy being required to ionize an atom multiple times. This strange result does not align with chemical principles; it should require more energy to cluster multiple negative charges on the same atom, not less. Choice D can be eliminated.

37. **B is the best answer.** According to the Henderson-Hasselbalch equation, pH = $pK_a + \log\left(\frac{[A^-]}{[HA]}\right)$, when a conjugate base's concentration $[A^-]$ is equal to the concentration of its acid form [HA] in solution, the pH = pK_a. pK_{a2} is the equilibrium constant that describes the second deprotonation of this molecule. Thus, for the pK_{a2}, the singly deprotonated form of FA can be considered the "acid form", and the doubly deprotonated form can be considered the conjugate base form. The point on the α plot where the singly deprotonated form and doubly deprotonated form have equal concentrations is where pH = pK_{a2}. This area occurs at a pH of around 10.2, making choice B the best answer. Choice A reflects the pH where the concentration of FA and its singly deprotonated form have the same concentration in solution. This value is pK_{a1} which the question did not ask for, so choice A can be eliminated. Choice C is a distractor, reflecting the pH at which the entire population of HA molecules exists in the doubly deprotonated form. Choice D is an analogous distractor, listing the pH at which the entire of population of HA exists in the singly deprotonated form.

TEST 1A A&E

Passage 8 (Questions 38-42)

38. **D is the best answer.** Calcium and strontium are both alkaline earth metals. It is important to know the properties of certain chemical groups for the MCAT®. Option I refers to the group's preference to lose two electrons to exist as the 2^+ cation when dissolved in solutions or making ionic bonds. This is because they have a full outer *s* orbital which can lose two electrons. So, options I is true and choices B and C can be ruled out. The alkaline earth metals are solid and silver in color at room temperature, so option III is true and choice A can be ruled out. This leaves choice D as the best answer. Interestingly, calcium and strontium are both red on the flame test so this can not be used to distinguish the metals. Notice this knowledge was not necessary to answering this question.

39. **B is the best answer.** A chalcogen is an element in the oxygen group. The oxygen group ionizes to the 2^- state, so the resulting ionic molecule would be SrCh where Ch is a chalcogen. This makes B the best answer. A monoatomic molecule is an oxymoron, a molecule implies more than one atom is present, so choice A is impossible and can be ruled out. A triatomic molecule would occur when Sr and a halide combine, resulting in the structure SrX_2 where X is a halide. Choice C is not the best answer. A molecule with four atoms may result when Sr combines with a transition metal and two halides, or a transition metal and two chalcogens. Numerous possibilities exist, and although this is a possible correct answer, it is not as precise as choice B so choice D can be eliminated.

40. **A is the best answer.** First decide if calcium or strontium has higher ionization energy. Ionization energy increases up a group and from left to right across a period. This means that calcium has the greater ionization energy, and choices B and C can be ruled out. Next, check Figure 1. The y-axis in Figure 1 is very unusual in that it has more counts at the bottom and less at the top. Sometimes on the MCAT®, data is presented in a strange way so always check the axes. According to Figure 1, calcium has more counts which would correspond to a greater concentration. So, choice A is the best answer.

41. **C is the best answer.** Electron affinity generally increases up a group and from left to right across a period. So, oxygen would be expected to have the greatest electron affinity, and choice C is the best answer.

42. **C is the best answer.** It is not completely clear what this question is asking, which is a common trick of the MCAT®. Since the passage uses Sr as a Ca substitute and both are alkaline earth metals, the best answer is likely an alkaline earth metal, so choice B can be eliminated. Next, consider why a certain mass of Sr was mentioned in the question. This mass corresponds to 2 moles of Sr because the atomic weight of Sr is about 87 g/mol. Choice A is 1 mole of Mg because the atomic weight of Mg is about 24 g/mol. Assume that the question mentioned a mass for a reason, and since choice A does not conform, it can be eliminated. Choices C and D are both 2 moles of alkaline earth metals. Radium is so named because it is highly radioactive. Radioactivity is associated with cancer development. For this reason, choice C is a better answer than choice D.

Stand-alones (43-46)

43. **A is the best answer.** Since concentration is usually expressed as moles of solute divided by the volume of solution, dimensional analysis needs to be performed in the numerator to solve this problem:

$$[(3.5 \text{ g Cl}^-) \times (1 \text{ mol}/35.45 \text{ g}) \times (10^3 \text{ mmol/mol})]/5.5 \text{ L} \approx 10^2/5.5 \approx 18$$

Choice B is a result of not using the mol to mmol conversion factor. Choice C is an error in using orders of ten. The molecular mass of chlorine gas is double that of the chloride ion. Nonetheless, there is not chlorine gas dissolved in human blood, and this question is only concerned about ionic chloride. If chloride's true molecular weight taken from the periodic table were improperly doubled, choice D would result.

44. **D is the best answer.** Elements that fall within the same column on a periodic table tend to exhibit similar chemistry. The best answer will be the compound that includes a metal in the same column as Zn. Cobalt is found in column 9, not column 12 of the periodic table, eliminating choice A. Similarly, Mn and Ca are found in columns 7 and 2, respectively, of the periodic table, not column 12. Choices B and C are less likely to be the best answer. Cd is also found in column 12, suggesting that it will exhibit similar chemistry to Zn. The likely reason behind similar chemistry between elements in the same column of the periodic table has to do with the number of valence electrons found in the outer shell of the element, which is common to elements of the same column.

45. **C is the best answer.** The amide bond occurs between two amino acids and involves the amine and carboxylic acid group. Electrons are often found closest to the atom with the greatest electron affinity and electronegativity. Oxygen is more electronegative than hydrogen, carbon and nitrogen, meaning the electron sharing between these atoms is likely to be polarized towards oxygen. Choice C is the better answer choice than choices A, B and D.

46. **B is the best answer.** The alkaline earth metals are the second group, moving towards the right, on the periodic table. They contain two valence electrons. Removal of both of these electrons is required to allow these metals to have a stable octet configuration. The alkali metals are the first group on the period table, starting on the far left side. They contain one valence electron. Removal of this electron allows alkali metals to have a stable octet configuration. Since only one electron needs to be removed from the alkali metals, but two need to be removed from the alkaline earth metals to reach an octet configuration, the first ionization of the alkali metals is expected to be more energetically favorable than the first ionization of an alkaline earth metal. Choice A can be eliminated. Noble gasses have extremely high first ionization energies, since their ionization requires destruction of the stable octet configuration. Eliminate choice C. The oxygen group is very electronegative—far more so than the alkali metals. Their great electronegativity makes it less energetically favorable to take one electron out of their outermost shell. Moreover, removal of one of their valence electrons does not result in a stable octet, as it does for the alkali metals. As a result of these two factors alkali metals are expected to have a more energetically favorable first ionization, as compared to the oxygen group. Choice D can be eliminated, and the best answer, choice B, can be chosen.

Passage 9 (Questions 47-51)

47. **A is the best answer.** Notice that the *p* orbital of N only contains three electrons, but each of these electrons is found in its own orientation. The three orientations of the *p* orbital are p_x, p_y, and p_z. Orienting the electrons in this manner would limit the repulsive forces between the electrons, lowering the overall energy of the atom. Choice A is most likely to be the best answer. Nitrogen does not contain any *d* orbitals, eliminating choice B. The valence shell of nitrogen is 2. Notice that nitrogen has two electrons in the 2*s* and three electrons in the 2*p*. This makes the number of valence electrons in nitrogen five, not three. Choice C can be eliminated. Oxygen has six electrons in its valence shell, and an additional electron to make O^- would give seven electrons in the valence shell. The electron configuration of N has five, not seven, electrons in the valence shell. Choice D can be eliminated.

48. **C is the best answer.** The answer choices provided show the condensed form of writing the electron configuration of an atom. The first part of correctly answering this question is to identify the most electronegative atom in the glutamine side chain. The Gln amino acid side chain is composed of N, C, H, and O. O is found near the top and right of the periodic table, making it the most electronegative. The best answer will be the electron configuration of O. The condensed form to write the electron configuration is the noble gas found on the previous row, which would be He in the case of O. The remainder of the electron configuration is the valence shell of the atom. Oxygen has six electrons in its valence shell, two in the 2*s* orbital and four in the 2*p* orbital. The electron structure of N is found in choice A, eliminating it as the best answer, as O is more electronegative than N. He, not Ne, is the noble gas found in the row above oxygen, eliminating choice B. Choice C correctly provides He as the noble gas reference, as well as shows six valence electrons in the outer orbital. Choice C is most likely to be the best answer. Similar to choice B, He, not Ne, is the noble gas reference. Choice D can be eliminated.

49. **B is the best answer.** The noble gases are found in the last column to the right on the periodic table. Their valence shells are filled with 8 electrons, making them highly resistant to reacting with other substrates. They are often used instead of atmospheric conditions to prevent oxidation and other unwanted reactions that would reduce reaction yield. Argon is a noble gas, meaning it would be highly unlikely to react with a substrate to protect it from further reactions, making choice A unlikely to be the best answer. Ne and other noble gases would take the place of atmospheric elements that can cause oxidation or other side reactions with the reactants of the Gabriel synthesis reactions. Choice B is most likely the best answer. Similar to choice A, Ar and Ne are unlikely to react with any substrates, eliminating choices C and D.

50. **B is the best answer.** This question is asking about the Heisenberg Uncertainty Principle, which states that the momentum and position of any particle cannot be known simultaneously. Notice how the question implies that the exact position of the electrons that would make up the electron density of the cation-π bond cannot be described. A hydrogen bond is between N, F, O and an H atom. There is no indication in the passage that a cation-π bond is similar to a hydrogen bond, making choice A unlikely to be the best answer. Choice B describes the Heisenberg Uncertainty Principle, likely making it the best answer. Paragraph one directly states that amino acids can form cation-π bonds, eliminating choice C. Amino acids such as tyrosine, tryptophan, and histidine all contain aromatic rings that can contribute π bonds, which are one of the two bonds found in a double bond. Choice D can be eliminated.

51. **C is the best answer.** According to Equation 1 and paragraph two, negative $\Delta E(\mathrm{a} - \mathrm{b})$ values represent attractive interactions. At the ion level, attractions occur between oppositely charged species. If the valence shell of one atom lacks electrons and the valence shell of another atom has too many electrons, the two atoms will be attracted in an attempt to lower their respective energies when isolated. The best answer will likely contain ions that are of opposite charges. The sodium and calcium ions are likely to repel each other, given that they are both positively charged. Choice A can be eliminated. H is uncharged in choice B, meaning it is not an ion and would be unlikely to be specifically attracted to the lithium ion. Choice B can be eliminated. The magnesium and oxygen ions are oppositely charged in choice C and would be likely to be attracted to each other. Choice C is most likely to be the best answer. Kr is a noble gas, meaning it has a full valence shell of electrons and is unlikely to interact with most other atoms. Choice D is unlikely to be the best answer.

Passage 10 (Questions 52-56)

52. **A is the best answer.** Equation 1 describes the remaining energy of the γ-ray following Compton scattering. Remember that as θ approaches zero, $\cos(\theta)$ approaches 1. This means that the smaller the scattering angle, the closer the denominator of Equation 1 will be to 1, leading to the maximum possible energy of the scattered gamma ray, which is its incident energy. Choice A is the best answer. Conversely, as θ increases in size, $\cos(\theta)$ decreases, approaching zero. This means that the larger the scattering angle the closer the denominator of Equation 1 will be to $(1 + E/m_0c^2)$. Any denominator greater than 1 will reduce the value of the energy of the scattered γ-ray relative to its initial energy. Choice B can be eliminated. Equation 1 demonstrates that the scattering angle has an effect on the energy of the scattered gamma ray, so choice C can be eliminated. Energy is not created or destroyed, so there is little reason to believe that a scattered ray could somehow gain more energy than it had before scattering. Choice D can be eliminated.

53. **C is the best answer.** First, write the balanced equation that describes this reaction:

$$2H_2(g) + O_2(g) \rightarrow 2H_2O(g)$$

Remember that according to the kinetic molecular theory, the volume a gas occupies at a given temperature and pressure is proportional to the number of molecules of gas particles. Thus, there are an equivalent amount of particles of hydrogen and oxygen gas. Nonetheless, the stoichiometry of the balanced equation indicates that during this reaction, twice as many moles of hydrogen are consumed for every mole of oxygen. Since the volumes of the gases are directly proportional to the number of moles consumed, twice the volume of hydrogen will be consumed for any given volume of oxygen. It is impossible to consume all of the oxygen because there is not enough hydrogen gas present. In order to consume all 20 L of oxygen gas 40 L of hydrogen gas would be required. This means that hydrogen is the *limiting reactant*, as the lack of it prevents this reaction from going to completion. Since oxygen is in excess of hydrogen, all of the hydrogen will be consumed. Use stoichiometry to determine what volume of steam will be produced: $(20\ \mathrm{L}\ H_2)(2\ \mathrm{L}\ H_2O/2\ \mathrm{L}\ H_2) = 20\ \mathrm{L}\ H_2O$ can be produced. Choice C is the best answer. Choice A stems from the assumption that the volumes of the reactant gases are additive, when they are not, even if every single particle in this reaction were consumed. The total volume of a gas is proportional to the number of its particles. During this reaction, the number of steam particles formed is less than the initial number of gas molecules. Choice A can be eliminated. Choice C represents the total volume of gas that was *consumed*, but not the volume of steam that was formed. Choice C can be eliminated. Choice D is a distractor.

54. **C is the best answer.** The passage specifies that the energy of a photoelectron is equal to the energy of gamma ray minus the electron binding energy E_B of the material. This equation is completely analogous to the equation which describes the energy of an electron ejected through the photoelectric effect. Use knowledge of the photoelectric effect to analyze this problem. The maximum velocity of an electron ejected from the surface of a metal during photoelectric effect experiments assumes that all of the energy of the ejected electron is in the form of kinetic energy. This approach also describes the maximum velocity of a photoelectron ejected from the active volume of the detector. The maximum velocity a photoelectron can reach is when all of its energy is in the form of kinetic energy. Put symbolically:

$$KE = E_\gamma - E_B$$

$$m_e v^2 = E_\gamma - E_B$$

$$v = \sqrt{\frac{E_\gamma - E_B}{m_e}}$$

"Plugging in" to this equation provides:

$$\sqrt{\frac{(661.66 - 360\ keV)\left(1000\frac{eV}{1keV}\right)\left(1.6 \times 10^{-19}\frac{J}{eV}\right)}{9.1 \times 10^{-31}\ \text{kg}}} \approx \sqrt{\frac{30 \times 1.5 \times 10^{-15} J}{9 \times 10^{-31}\text{kg}}} = \sqrt{5 \times 10^{16}} \approx 2 \times 10^{8}\ \text{m/sec}$$

Note the importance of converting eV into J.

Choice C is the best answer. Choices A and B are distractors with the improper order of magnitude. Choice D stems from omitting the final "taking the square root" step. It can be eliminated without a second thought since it is higher than c, the speed of light, the greatest possible speed in the universe.

55. **C is the best answer.** Consider what happens during Reaction 1. Two separate reactants combine to form two separate products. During a combination reaction, separate reactants combine to form *one* product. This reaction does not satisfy the conditions of a combination reaction, ruling out choice A. Decomposition reactions are the opposite process of combination reactions. In them, a single reactant is broken down into two or more products. Since this reaction started with two reactants and ended with two products, it does not satisfy the conditions of a decomposition reaction. Choice B can be eliminated. During oxidation-reduction reactions, electrons are transferred from one chemical species to another. A good method to determine whether or not an oxidation-reduction reaction has occurred is to pay attention to the oxidation number of the same atom in the reactant's and in the product's side of the balanced chemical equation. In this case, Zn starts with a oxidation number of 0 and ends with an oxidation number of +4. Hydrogen starts with an oxidation number of +1 and ends with an oxidation number of 0. Since there were four hydrogen atoms in this reaction, all four of zinc's electrons were transferred to them. This transfer of electrons is an oxidation-reduction reaction. Choice C may be the best answer, but rule out the last answer before choosing it. An Arrhenius acid/base reaction would require the loss/capture of a proton. Since the mechanism of this reaction is unclear, but does not seem to suggest loss/capture of a proton, choice D can be eliminated in favor of the best answer, choice C.

56. **D is the best answer.** Each half life that passes reduces the quantity and activity of ^{134}Cs by half. According to the passage, the half-life of ^{134}Cs is 2 years. Thus, 6.5 years represents a total of three and one-fourth half-lives. In other words, $(\frac{1}{2})^{3.25}$ multiplied by the original mass of the ^{134}Cs sample remains. This is slightly less than ⅛ of the initial quantity. Figure 1 indicates that the original activity of the higher energy 795.85 keV peak was about 10^3 counts/channel. After three and one-fourth half-lives, its new activity will be slightly less than $10^3/(\frac{1}{2})^3 = 10^3/8 = 125$ counts/channel. Choice D is the best answer. Choices A stems from assuming that one too many half-lives had passed. Choice B comes from scaling the activity by the number of half-lives which have passed, instead of properly multiplying the activity by ½ raised to the number of each half-life which have passed. Choice C is a distractor, too high in value, as it *exceeds* the activity remaining after three half-lives. Since more than three half-lives have passed, its activity should be even lower than this value. Choice C can be eliminated.

Stand-alones (57-59)

57. **C is the best answer.** The molecular weight provided for an element on the periodic table reflects the average of the molecular weights of all the naturally available isotopes of that element. This average will be closest in value to the molecular weight of the most common naturally available isotope. Since the periodic table says this average value is 238 g/mol, ^{238}U is probably the most common isotope, not ^{235}U. Option I will not be part of the best answer, and choice A can be eliminated. If a mole of UO_2 is reduced to metallic U, a mole of the pure metal will have a mass of 238.03 g as indicated by its mass number on periodic table. Option II will be part of the best answer. Since the average mass of uranium, given on the periodic table, is a little greater than 238, that means that there must exist naturally occurring isotopes which have a mass number greater than 238. Option III will be part of the best answer. The alpha emission product of ^{238}U is ^{234}Th. Option IV will not be part of the best answer. Choose choice C as it contains the best options, II and III.

58. **C is the best answer.** Alkali metals, found in the first column of the periodic table react explosively with water to form the metal hydroxide and hydrogen gas. Ni and Fe are transition metals are unlikely to produce hydrogen gas when exposed to water. Choices A and D can be eliminated. Calcium is also unlikely to be highly reactive with water, eliminating choice B. Lithium is an alkali metal which easily ionizes to Li^+ and can react with water to produce hydrogen gas and lithium hydroxide. Choice C is the best answer.

59. **D is the best answer.** Calcium does combine with the fluorine in HF to create an insoluble CaF_2 compound, preventing further damage. However, fluorine has seven, not six, electrons in its outer valence shell, eliminating choice A. Hydrogen would be unlikely to recombine with gluconate, as it is not a strong nucleophile on its own. Hydride, the H^- ion is a species that is highly nucleophilic. Choice B is unlikely to be the best answer. Calcium is not an unstable element, as its *s* orbital is complete with two electrons. Choice C can be eliminated. Calcium would react with the highly reactive F atom to form insoluble CaF_2, which would prevent additional damage. Choice D is the best answer. In general, the halides are highly reactive, as they contain seven electrons in their valence shells. They react to gain the additional electron to create a full octet.

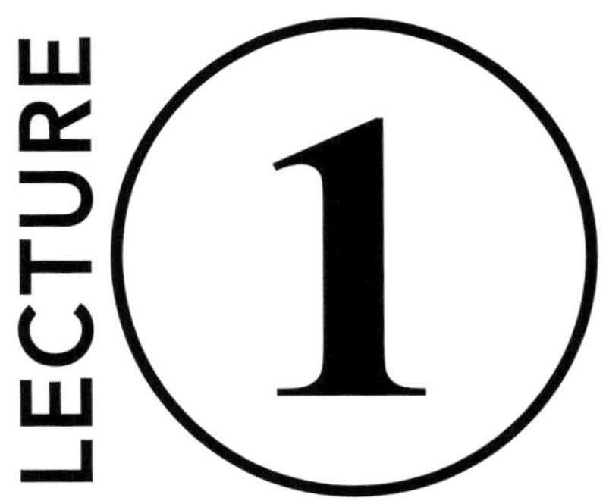

Introduction to General Chemistry

MINI-TEST 1B

ANSWERS & EXPLANATIONS

Questions 1–29

Passage 1 (Questions 1-6)

1. **C is the best answer.** Consider what is meant by the term LET. LET is the amount of energy released by a travelling particle for any given unit distance that it travels. In order to release energy over a distance, the particle must perform work—in other words, it is applying a force parallel to the distance that it is travelling. Whenever an energy unit is divided by a distance unit, much like the equation W/d = F, the result is a force unit. Consider this problem using dimensional analysis:

$$\text{keV}/\mu\text{m} = 10^{-16}\ \text{J}/10^{-6}\ \text{m} = 10^{-16}\ \text{N}\cdot\text{m}/10^{-6}\ \text{m} = 10^{-10}\ \text{N}.$$

Choice C is the best answer. Nowhere is any time unit mentioned. Without a time unit, coulomb and tesla are not viable answer choices as both of these derived units have a time term. In particular, they are $A \cdot s$ and $kg/Amp \cdot s^2$ respectively. Choices A and D can be eliminated on this basis. Joule is a unit of energy, and interconvertible with the electron volt. Nonetheless, dividing a work unit by a distance unit results in a force unit, as demonstrated above. Choice B can be eliminated as well, and choice C is the best answer.

2. **C is the best answer.** Remember the half-life decay equation: $A = A_o \times \frac{1}{2}^{t/h}$, where A is the final quantity, A_o is the initial quantity, t is the time of the decay process, and h is the half-life. Thus, each full half-life that passes reduces the count of the material by half. Any fraction of a half-life will reduce the count of the material by one-half raised to the power of that fraction of a half-life. Using this equation, but breaking the second term apart for each half-life and fraction of a half-life provides:

$$A = 10\ \text{cmp} \times \frac{1}{2}^{\frac{10}{10}} \times \frac{1}{2}^{\frac{5}{10}} = 5\left(\frac{1}{2}\right)^{\frac{1}{2}} = 5\sqrt{\frac{1}{2}} = 5 \times \left(\frac{1}{1.4}\right) \approx 5 \times \left(\frac{2}{3}\right) = 3.33$$

making choice C the best answer. Choice B is a distractor, and choice D comes misinterpreting $\left(\frac{1}{2}\right)^{\frac{1}{2}}$ as being ¼, when it is actually the $\sqrt{\frac{1}{2}}$ Choice D can be eliminated. This problem can also be solved using a little bit of intuition. The best answer should be between 5 and 2.5 because between 1 and 2 half-lives have passed. In particular, since this decay is halfway through the second half-life, choose the answer that is close to being half-way between 5 and 2.5, or a number close 3.75.

3. **D is the best answer.** Elemental actinium is used in Reaction 2. When determining its electron configuration, remember to start with *s* orbitals as they are highest in energy. For this reason when transition metals ionize, they tend to lose electrons from their *s* shells. Actinium is in the 7th row so its configuration will be $[Rn]7s^26d^1$. Choice D is the best answer. There is no stability benefit in having a partially filled *d* orbital, and a half-empty *s* orbital, when it is possible to completely fill the *s* orbital. Choices A can be eliminated. Choice B is even worse. At least a half-filled *s* orbital offers some stability. Choice B sacrifices a completely filled *s* orbital for a partially filled *d* orbital, and can be eliminated. In general, completely filled or half-filled orbitals are more stable than empty or partially filled orbitals. Although the actinium used in producing the radiolabeled monoclonal antibody has a mass number of 225 and "standard" actinium has a mass number of 227—as provided on the MCAT® periodic table—both of these atoms have the same number of protons. After all, they are the same atom! They will each attract the same number of electrons which will occupy the same orbitals. Choice C is a corruption that treats the *mass* number as the *atomic* number, dropping two electrons from the total electron count in order to balance the imagined lower proton count. Choice C can be eliminated.

4. **B is the best answer.** Normally, when an atom has a pi bond, it is sp^2 hybridized. The chelate is shown in Reaction 1. The sulfur atom here is bonded to a carbon atom which is bonded to a nitrogen atom, which has one bond to the rest of the molecule R. Without determining which atoms have multiple bonds, the set up looks like:

$$R-N-C-S$$

Since nitrogen has no formal charge, it must have 3 bonds and 1 lone pair. The additional bond to nitrogen must be between N and C because if it were between N and R, it would exceed R's valency of four bonds. A new structure is beginning to emerge:

$$R-\ddot{N}=C-S$$

To satisfy the central carbon atom's octet, it requires another bond to sulfur.

$$R-\ddot{N}=C=\ddot{S}\colon$$

Sulfur, in turn, requires two lone pairs, in addition to the double bond it shares with carbon, in order to have formal charge of zero. To determine the hybridization of the sulfur atom, count the number of sigma bonds and lone pairs of electrons on it. Match this number to the sum of the superscripts in a hybrid name. Remember, letters without superscripts are assumed to have the superscript 1. This sulfur atom has 2 LPs and 1 sigma bond, which results in 3, matching the sum of the superscripts of sp^2. Choice B is the best answer. The sum of the superscripts in choices A, C, and D do not equal three, and they can be eliminated.

5. **A is the best answer.** First, write the equation that describes this total decay scheme to solve the identity of the product. Remember, an α-particle is a helium nucleus, and a β-particle is an electron.

$$^{225}_{89}Ac \rightarrow {}^{4}_{2}He + {}^{4}_{2}He + {}^{4}_{2}He + {}^{4}_{2}He + {}^{0}_{-1}\beta^- + {}^{0}_{-1}\beta^- + {}^{4}_{2}He + {}^{M}_{Z}X$$

The sum of the mass numbers, M, on each side of the equation must be equal to one another. Likewise, the sum of the atomic numbers, Z, on each side of the equation must also be equal to one another. Thus,

$$225 = 4 + 4 + 4 + 4 + 0 + 0 + 4\ M$$

$$M = 205$$

$$89 = 2 + 2 + 2 + 2 - 1 - 1 + 2 + Z$$

$$Z = 81$$

Thus, the identity of the stable daughter product is $^{205}_{81}Tl$. Choice A is the best answer. Choice B reflects the most stable isotope of Ac, but compounds do not necessarily decay into *their* most stable isotope. After the decay process, the mass number and charge number on each side of the equation must be equal to one another since both mass and charged are conserved quantities. Choice B does not balance these terms, and is a weaker answer. Choice C is an error that could stem from not including one of the β-decay events in the overall equation. Choice D is an error that could stem from not including one of the α-decay events in the overall equation. Choices C and D can be eliminated.

6. **B is the best answer.** Based on the far right of Table 1, particles with energies near 0.2 keV/μm are β-particles. No matter what sort of β-emission occurred—whether β^+ or β^-—the mass number is conserved from parent to daughter. Either the number of protons will increase by one, in the case of β^- decay, or they will decrease by one, in the case of β^+ decay. Since Tl has an atomic number which is more than one proton away from Bi, choice A can be eliminated, as Tl cannot possibly undergo one β^- decay event to produce ^{209}Bi. Write a chemical equation to determine what sort of decay process could produce ^{209}Bi from ^{209}Pb or ^{209}Po.

$$^{209}_{82}Pb \rightarrow {}^{M}_{Z}X + {}^{209}_{83}Bi$$

The sum of the mass numbers on each side of the equation must be equal to one another. Likewise, the sum of the atomic numbers on each side of the equation must also be equal to one another. Thus,

$$209 = 209 + M$$

$$M = 0$$

$$82 = Z + 83$$

$$Z = -1$$

To decay from ^{209}Pb to ^{209}Bi the ejection of a massless negatively charged particle—a β^- particle—must occur. Applying the same approach to ^{209}Po reveals:

$$^{209}_{84}Po \rightarrow {}^{M}_{Z}X + {}^{209}_{83}Bi$$

From above, $M = 0$

$$84 = Z + 83$$

$$Z = 1$$

To decay from ^{209}Po to ^{209}Bi the ejection of a massless positively charged particle—a β^+ particle—must occur.

Use the right hand rule to determine that a positively charged particle will travel upwards in this magnetic field, and a negatively charged particle will travel downwards. Choice B is possible—if ^{209}Pb were the parent atom it would undergo β^- decay. The negatively charged β-particle would move downwards in the magnetic field. Evaluate the other answers before selecting choice B. In order for ^{209}Po to decay into ^{209}Bi, it must to release a β^+ particle. Such a particle would travel upwards in the magnetic field. Choice C is not a possible scenario and can be eliminated. As described, in order for ^{209}Pb to decay into ^{209}Bi, it must undergo β^- decay. The β^- it ejects will travel downwards, not upwards in the magnetic field, so choice D can be ruled out, making choice B the best answer.

TEST 1B A&E

Passage 2 (Questions 7-11)

7. **C is the best answer.** Use a periodic table and write the full nuclear equation that describes the transfer of mass and charge in this reaction. Since charge (Z) and mass (M) are conserved in nuclear reactions, two separate equations can solve for these variables.

$$^{141}_{56}\text{Ba} \rightarrow {}^{0}_{-1}\text{e} + {}^{M}_{Z}\text{X}$$

$$141 = 0 + \text{M}$$

$$\text{M} = 141$$

$$56 = \text{Z} - 1$$

$$\text{Z} = 57$$

The identity of X is $^{141}_{57}\text{La}$ choose the best answer, choice C. β^+ decay results in the release of a massless positive charge called a positron. If β^+ decay were mistakenly assumed, choice A would result. A beta particle has no mass. If β^- decay was confused for the emission of a negatively charged neutron, $_{-1}^{1}n$, which is not even a real decay particle, then choice B would result. If this equation were improperly written with a −1 in the mass number M instead of the charge number Z, choice D would result.

8. **D is the best answer.** The passage describes how the control rods undergo neutron capture, preventing neutrons released during the fission reaction from splitting more ^{235}U atoms. The control rods live up to their name, controlling the fission chain reaction, by slowing it down. A slower rate of reaction will be reflected by a reduced rate constant k. Decreasing the activation energy of this reaction, or increasing the pre-exponential factor A, will cause the value of k to increase so choices B and C can be eliminated. To distinguish between the remaining answer choices, consider the meaning of the pre-exponential factor, A. This number represents the fraction of atoms that will react when a reaction requires no activation energy, or if the average kinetic energy of the all of the atoms, RT, is infinitely greater than the activation energy. Since the control rods functionally remove a fraction of the ^{235}U from the reaction they reduce the value of A. Choice D is the best answer. The activation energy of this reaction has not changed. The atoms which remain accessible for fission still have the same chemical properties as they did before the control rods were lowered, so choice A can be eliminated.

9. **C is the best answer.** The easiest way to solve this problem is to pretend that there is a 1000 g of the material in question, and count how many half-lives it requires to drop to about 1/1000 of its original mass.

$$1000\text{ g} \rightarrow 500\text{ g} \rightarrow 225\text{ g} \rightarrow 112.5 \rightarrow 56.25 \rightarrow 28.125 \rightarrow \approx 14 \rightarrow \approx 7 \rightarrow \approx 3.5 \rightarrow \approx 1.75 \rightarrow \approx 0.85$$

$$\text{Hl}_1 \rightarrow \text{Hl}_2 \rightarrow \text{Hl}_3 \rightarrow \text{Hl}_4 \rightarrow \text{Hl}_5 \rightarrow \text{Hl}_6 \rightarrow \text{Hl}_7 \rightarrow \text{Hl}_8 \rightarrow \text{Hl}_9 \rightarrow \text{Hl}_{10}$$

Just a little under ten half-lives must pass to reduce the activity of ^{137}Cs by one-thousand fold. The best answer will be a little less than 30 years × 10 = 300 years so choose the best answer, choice C. If a little more than eight half-lives were used, instead of a little more than 9, choice A would result. Choices B and D are too large and can be eliminated.

10. **B is the best answer.** To solve this problem first use the equation given in the passage that relates how much energy can be converted into mass. $E = \Delta mc^2$. Since all of this energy is being converted into light, use the familiar equation that provides the energy of a photon in terms of its frequency, f, and Plank's constant, h. $E = hf$

Substitution provides that $hf/c^2 = \Delta m$

Use the other light equation $f = c/\lambda$ in place of f

This expression simplifies to $h/\lambda c = \Delta m$

Do not forget to make all of the units consistent when "plugging" into this equation:

$$\frac{6.6 \times 10^{-34}\text{ m}^2 \cdot \text{kg/sec}}{(4.9 \times 10^{-7}\text{ m})(3 \times 10^{8}\text{ m/sec})}$$

Choose the best answer, choice B.

Choices A describes the energy of a photon of the 490 nm wavelength light, using the equation $E = hc/\lambda$. Eliminate choice A. If wavelength was not properly converted into meters, choice C would result. If wavelength was not properly converted into meters, and the wrong equation, $E = hc/\lambda$, were used, choice D would result.

11. **A is the best answer.** Ionization energy is the energy needed to detach an electron from an atom. The first ionization energy is the energy necessary to remove an electron from neutral atom in its gaseous state to form a +1 cation. The energy required for the removal of a second electron from the same atom to form a +2 cation is called the second ionization energy. Third, fourth, fifth, and other ionization energies are named in the same manner. In general, as the positive charge of the cation increases, the ionization energy is expected to increase slightly as well, as a more positive and less stable cation is being formed. However, removing an electron that results in destruction of a stable octet has a far greater ionization energy than any ionization energy which comes from removing a non-octet electron. The correct graph will illustrate a nearly linear increase in ionization energy, and then a dramatic increase once the octet is destroyed. Removing three electrons from Ba, regardless of the isotope, will destroy its octet. Thus, the greatest increase of energy during ionization is expected during the third ionization, as this electron is completing an octet. Choice A is the best answer. If the number of electrons which must be removed to disrupt the octet were miscounted, choices B or C could result. Ionization energies do not show a directly linear relationship with the number of electrons that have been ionized. Choice D can be eliminated.

Stand-alones (12-15)

12. **B is the best answer.** Isotopes are elements that share the same number of protons and electrons, but not neutrons. As a result, they have the exact same reactivity, but they have different masses. Option II will be part of the best answer. If one of a pair of isotopes is stable and the other is not, the decay process of the unstable isotope can also be a means of distinguishing them. In the case presented in this question, one of the pair of isotopes is unstable and the other is stable. Thus, option IV will be part of the best answer. Choice A can be eliminated on this basis. The effective nuclear charge, Z_{eff}, on a valence electron is defined as $Z - S$, where Z is the atomic number of the element and S is the number of non-valence electrons. The effective nuclear charge does not change as a result of the number of neutrons in the nucleus of the atom. Option I will not be part of the best answer. Choices C and D can be eliminated, making choice B the best answer by the process of elimination. Remember, the atomic number is the number of protons in an atom. By definition, this number must be the same between two elements if they are to be isotopes; it is the mass number which distinguishes isotopes. Option III will not be part of the best answer because the atomic number does not change between isotopes.

13. **C is the best answer.** The question is asking which of the following agents is not an oxidizing or reducing agent. $LiAlH_4$ is a common reducing agent that donates hydride ions for reduction reactions, so choice A is not the best answer. CrO_3 is a common oxidizing agent, so choice B is not the best answer. Magnesium (Mg) is used in the Grignard reaction and is a reducing agent because it donates electrons in order to become Mg^{2+}. However, Mg^{2+} is already oxidized and cannot be used for redox reactions, so choice C is a strong answer. H_2O_2, hydrogen peroxide is a strong oxidizing agent but it can also act as a reducing agent in some reactions. This is a unique property of hydrogen peroxide and is worth memorizing.

14. **A is the best answer.** The first step in answering this question is to determine what the ionic state of Ca is in the ionic compound. Given that F usually has a formal charge of −1, the charge on Ca is most likely to be +2. The next step will be to determine the electron configuration of the normal Ca element, then subtract two electrons to get the electron configuration of the ion. Calcium is found in row four, column two, meaning that it likely has electrons in the $4s^2$ configuration normally. In the short form, the noble element in the preceding row is used to represent the configuration up to that point, which is Argon in this case. Losing two electrons would give the noble gas configuration of Ar, meaning choice A is likely to be the best answer. If Ca only lost one electron, choice B would be the best answer and can be eliminated. The electron configuration of the native element is $[Ar]4s^2$. However, the Ca^{2+} ion has lost two electrons, eliminating choice C. Addition of electrons to a *d* subshell would indicate that the element in question was a transition element, likely Ti in this case. Ca did not gain two electrons but instead lost two electrons. Choice D can be eliminated.

15. **B is the best answer.** The noble gases often show the lowest reactivity of any elements, predominantly due to their full octet in their outer valence shell. Bromine, which a diatomic element often found in a bond with a second bromine atom, is not a noble gas, but instead is missing one electron in its outer shell. Choice A can be eliminated. Argon is a noble gas that contains a full octet in its outer shell and highly unlikely to react with any other atoms. Choice B is likely to be the best answer. Fluorine, similar to Bromine, is a diatomic element, meaning that it is often found in a bond with a second fluorine atom. It is also missing an electron from its outer shell, making it more reactive than Argon. Choice C can be eliminated. Sulfur is missing two electrons from its outer shell, making it more reactive than Argon and the other noble elements found in column 18. Choice D can be eliminated, making choice B the best answer.

Passage 3 (Questions 16-21)

16. **D is the best answer.** Radium is in the same column as calcium in the periodic table. It has the same number of valence electrons, and very similar reactivity. In calcium chloride, calcium has a +2 charge. Radium-223-chloride behaves the same way. In both cases, donating two electrons from the metal to the halogen atoms allows every atom in the compound to reach an octet configuration. When dissolved, the calcium and radium ions maintain the +2 charge (choice D). Choice B comes from an easy mistake. It comes from assuming that the compound radium-223-chloride contains only one chlorine atom—it actually contains 2. Remember that the names of molecular compounds describe the number of atoms of each element, but the names of ionic compounds do not. Ionic compounds are named based on the most common ions produced by each element. Chloride ions have a −1 charge and radium, which is an alkaline earth metal, as a +2 charge. Choices C and A are incorrect. Since radium-223 is donating electrons, it will gain a positive charge.

17. **D is the best answer.** During decay processes, mass and charge are conserved. Since the vessel is sealed, the mass is unchanged. Choices B, C, and D assumed that the radium weighed 50 g and that there was no sealed container. This question is actually asking about the sealed container which houses radioactive material.

18. **B is the best answer.** Consider Equation 1. As the energy associated with the emitted particle increases, the ln(λ) becomes a smaller and smaller negative number. This means that the rate constant λ is actually increasing as the energy of the emitted particle increases. As the rate constant λ increases, the quantity of radioactive material at any time interval after T_0 decreases (see Equation 2). This will lead to a shorter half-life. This makes physical sense: material with shorter half-lives must be less stable than material with longer half-lives—they do not last as long! Because they are so much less stable, the particles they emit during decay have slightly higher energy.

19. **C is the best answer.** The energy level of electrons gets higher the further the electrons are from the nucleus. Electrons in higher shells are at a higher energy level and are further from the nucleus. Choices B, A, and D are all lower in energy because they are lower shells.

20. **B is the best answer.** Pay attention to the labels. Equation 2 allows the following expression to be derived:

$$\ln\frac{[^{223}\text{Ra}]_t}{[^{223}\text{Ra}]_o} = -kt$$

Since these expressions are equivalent, when one is plotted against the other, a straight line is the result.

21. **D is the best answer.** Look at Figure 1. All of the decay events that lead to the formation of ^{215}Po are alpha decay, and there are two decay events required. As explained in the passage, each alpha decay event releases a helium nucleus, $^4_2$He or . If two of these particles are released, than a total of 4 protons are lost from ^{223}Ra. Choice A is incorrect—it is the number of α-particles emitted. Choice B is a weaker answer—it is the total number of protons and neutrons lost. Choice C is can be eliminated as it is a counting error.

Passage 4 (Questions 22-26)

22. **B is the best answer.** The volume of the tantalum is 0.5 mm × 2.5 cm × 5.0 cm or 0.05 cm × 2.5 cm × 5.0 cm = 0.625 cm^3. To do mental math, move the decimals so the problem is more manageable.

0.05 cm × 2.5 cm × 5.0 cm = 0.5 cm × 0.25 cm × 5.0 cm = ½ cm × ¼ cm × 5 cm = 1/8 cm 2 × 5 cm = 5/8 cm^3 = 0.625 cm^3.

Now, multiply by the density to know the mass of the tantalum. 5/8 cm^3 × 16.99 g/cm^3 ≈ (5 × 16)/8 g = 5 × 2 g = 10 g. This is closest to choice B. Notice how MCAT® math can always be easily simplified. The other answer choices are calculation errors.

23. **A is the best answer.** Start with the number of grams calculated in question 1 then multiply by the atomic weight. The atomic weight of tantalum (Ta) is 180.95 g/mol. The simplified math is:

10 g/(200 g/mol) = 1/20 mol = 0.05 mol.

This is closest to choice A.

24. **D is the best answer.** The final product is Ta_2O_5. Assume the oxidation state of oxygen is −2 which would result in a −10 charge that must be balanced by the 2 tantalums. That makes each tantalum +5 and choice D is the best answer.

25. **B is the best answer.** The solvent in the passage contains phosphoric acid, H_3PO_4 which has one atom of phosphorus in every molecule. 1 L of a 1 M solution contains 1 mole of molecules. 1 mole contains 6.022×10^{23} molecules of H_3PO_4 and the same number of atoms of phosphorus. This makes choice B the best answer.

26. **C is the best answer.** As discussed previously, there were 0.06 moles of Ta used in the experiment. The final product is Ta_2O_5 which has a molecular weight of roughly 442 g/mol (181 + 181 + 16 + 16 + 16 + 16 + 16). 0.06 moles × 442 g/mol ≈ 0.05 × 500 = 25 g. That is the theoretical yield. The experimental yield will be 90% of 25 g which is 22.5 g. This is closest to choice C which is the best answer. Notice that the estimation used to simplify the math greatly reduced the time spent on this problem, and the correct answer was still obtained. Choice A is a miscalculation using the atomic weight for Ta rather than the molecular weight for Ta_2O_5. Choice B is the same miscalculation as choice A combined with forgetting to convert from theoretical to experimental yield. Choice D is a result of forgetting to convert from theoretical to experimental yield plus rounding up.

TEST 1B A&E

Stand-alones (27-29)

27. **A is the best answer.** The question stem suggests that the main difference between the two compounds that increases the half-life is the substitution of sulfur for the oxygen. Oxygen has a greater electronegativity than sulfur, meaning it is able to polarize the carbon-oxygen bond more than sulfur can polarize the carbon-sulfur bond. Remember that electronegativity increases as one moves up and right on the periodic table. The greater polarization makes the carbonyl subject to nucleophilic attack by water or other nucleophiles more so than the carbon-sulfur double bond. This would help prevent breakdown of the compound in solution. Remember that atoms in a column behave in a chemically similar manner, meaning the substitution of oxygen for sulfur would likely create an equally functional compound. Choice A is most likely to be the best answer. As sulfur has a decreased electronegativity compared to oxygen, it is less likely to encourage hydrolysis, eliminating choice B. The question stem does not provide enough information to ascertain whether a sulfur-substituted compound could be degraded more or less than the amide-containing compound. Choices C and D are weaker answer choices than choice A.

28. **D is the best answer.** Notice that the percent mass of potassium is provided in the question stem. The percent mass can be used to ascertain the molecule formula. Using the periodic table, K has an atomic weight of 39.1 g/mol, C has an atomic weight of 12 g/mol, and N has an atomic weight of 14 g/mol. As K is in the first column of the periodic table, it most likely adopts a +1 charge in an ionic compound, which is a compound that is composed of a metal and a non-metal. This most likely means that the CN complex has a −1 charge. Use the atomic weights to estimate the molecular formula. If the formula is most likely to be KCN, K at 39.1 g/mol is 60%, C at 12 g/mol is 18%, and N at 14 g/mol is 22% of the overall molecular weight of 65.1 g/mol. Oftentimes the charge that an atom would adopt in an ionic compound is beneficial in guiding the determination of the molecular weight.

29. **A is the best answer.** The question stem describes a disproportionate reaction, where there is an imbalance between the number of reactants and the number of products. The two reactants in the dissolution are water and KCl. Upon being dissolved in water, KCl, as an ionic compound, most likely dissociates into K^+ and Cl^-. Cl is one of the diatomic atoms, along with H, N, F, O, I, Cl, and Br, meaning that it prefers to exist as Cl_2 rather than Cl^-. This means that KCl breaks up disproportionately into more than two molecules, including K^+, Cl^-, and Cl_2. Choice A best describes a disproportionate reaction, making it the best answer.

Introduction to Organic Chemistry

TEST 2A

ANSWERS & EXPLANATIONS

Questions 1–59

LECTURE 2 ANSWER KEY

TEST 2A		MINI-TEST 2B	
1. B	31. D	1. D	16. A
2. A	32. A	2. C	17. D
3. A	33. C	3. B	18. A
4. A	34. B	4. B	19. B
5. C	35. B	5. C	20. A
6. D	36. D	6. A	21. B
7. C	37. A	7. D	22. D
8. C	38. C	8. C	23. C
9. A	39. B	9. A	24. C
10. B	40. C	10. B	25. D
11. D	41. A	11. D	26. D
12. C	42. C	12. C	27. C
13. D	43. C	13. B	28. C
14. C	44. A	14. B	29. D
15. B	45. B	15. B	
16. B	46. D		
17. D	47. C		
18. C	48. A		
19. C	49. C		
20. D	50. D		
21. A	51. D		
22. D	52. C		
23. C	53. A		
24. B	54. D		
25. A	55. D		
26. A	56. D		
27. B	57. A		
28. C	58. B		
29. A	59. B		
30. B			

EXPLANATIONS FOR LECTURE 2

Passage 1 (Questions 1-5)

1. **B is the best answer.** In order to successfully answer this question, the structure of butyric acid should be drawn. Paragraph one notes that butyric acid is a fatty acid, meaning it contains a carboxylic acid and a nonpolar hydrocarbon chain, as shown in the figure below. The but- prefix indicates that the molecule contains four carbons.

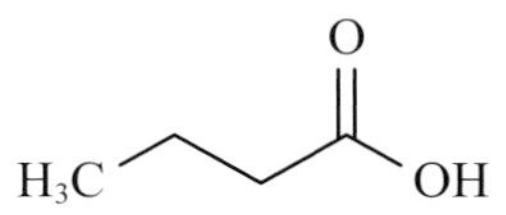

$$H_3C\text{–}CH_2\text{–}CH_2\text{–}C(=O)\text{–}OH$$

Carbon one is always the carbon with the highest priority, which means it is bonded to atoms with the highest molecular weights. The carboxylic acid carbon is bonded to two oxygens, meaning it is the highest priority, making it carbon one. The terminal methyl carbon is carbon four. An atom in *sp* hybridization is typically found in a triple bond and a single bond, which the carboxyl carbon is not, eliminating choice A. The carboxyl carbon is bound to three other groups, making it a sp^2 carbon, while the methyl carbon is bound to four different groups, making it an sp^3 carbon. Choice B is most likely to be the best answer. Carbon one would be a sp^3 carbon only if it was bonded to four different groups, not three, eliminating choice C as the best answer. Carbon cannot contain more than four bonds, meaning it could not exist in an sp^3d hybridization state. This eliminates choice D.

2. **A is the best answer.** A condensation reaction, also known as a dehydration reaction, creates a double bond from a single bond or a triple bond from a double bond, releasing water in the process. A hydrocarbon contains only hydrogens and carbons, so the maximum number of bonds to a carbon is four, resulting in sp^3 hybridization and tetrahedral geometry. After the reaction, one of the two of the single bonds would be replaced with a double bond, giving sp^2 geometry and a trigonal planar arrangement. The addition of the pi bond to the sigma bond to create a double bond shortens and strengthens the bond between the two carbons in the alkene, making choice A most likely to be the best answer. Double or triple bonds are not shorter, but rather longer, eliminating choices B and D. In addition, a shorter bond is stronger, not weaker, eliminating choice C and making choice A the best answer choice.

3. **A is the best answer.** A shortcut formula for the formal charge on an atom is: (# of valence electrons) – (# of nonbonded electrons + # of bonds). The number of valence electrons on carbon is four. Because the carboxyl carbon is in two single bonds and a double bond, it does not have any nonbonded, or free, electrons. The number of bonds is four, as a double bond counts as two bonds due to the presence of both a sigma and a pi bond. Using the shortcut formula above, the formal charge can be calculated as: $4 - (0 + 4) = 0$. This makes choice A the best answer choice, eliminating choices B-D.

4. **A is the best answer.** At first glance, this question seems complicated and particularly challenging, as it references specific bonds and groups in various enzymes. However, use principles of regulation and a knowledge of functional groups, in conjunction with Figure 1, to help solve this question. Knowledge of the steps of fatty acid synthesis, covered in Biology 1 Chapter 3, also helps confirm the best answer. An enoyl group involves the formation of a double bond from a single bond, with the release of water, which suggests that choice A is the best answer. However, knowledge of the enoyl functional group is not necessary to solve this question. Principles of regulation imply that a mutation in a protein causes the precursor molecules to increase in concentration and the products to decrease in concentration. If but-2-enoyl-ACP increased in concentration, it is likely that the enzyme that utilizes it as a substrate is mutated to be non-functional, suggesting FabR is at play by Figure 1. Choice A is likely to be the best answer. An enoyl group does not contain a triple bond and Fab A mutation would prevent but-2-enoyl-ACP formation, eliminating choice B. An enoyl group also does not contain a single bond and FabG mutation would likely lead to a decrease in but-2-enoyl-ACP, eliminating choice C. A bond must be formed between adjacent carbons, assuming the chain is linear, as it is likely to be in a four carbon molecule. Because a bond between carbons five and seven would be unlikely to form, choice D is less likely than choice A to be the best answer.

5. **C is the best answer.** Free fatty acids are able to help dissolve lipids, also known as fats, through a process called saponification. Fats are insoluble in solution and fatty acids are able to help create micelles. The absorption of fructose, a carbohydrate monomer, is unlikely to be impacted by the fatty acid butyric acid, eliminating choice A. Similarly, the absorption of glutamine, an amino acid, is unlikely to be impacted by a fatty acid, eliminating choice B. Vitamins A, D, E, and K are fat soluble vitamins, meaning they require fat in order to be absorbed. As butyric acid would likely create micelles of fatty acids that vitamin D is complexed with, it is possible that free butyric acid could help the molecular absorption of fat-soluble vitamins. Choice C is most likely to be the best answer. Cytosine is a nucleic acid, which does not depend on fatty acids for efficient absorption. Choice D can be eliminated.

Passage 2 (Questions 6-9)

6. **D is the best answer.** The most ionic bond will be one between atoms with greatly different electronegativities. The C=N bond, choice A, has a small difference in electronegativities with nitrogen being slightly more electronegative. The C–C bond, choice B, has no variation in electronegativity between the atoms, so choice B is not as strong as choice A. The C=O bond, choice C, has a greater difference in electronegativity than the C=N bond because O is more electronegative than N. Choice C is better than choice A. The O–H bond, choice D, has the greatest difference in electronegativity because H is less electronegative than C. This makes choice D the best answer.

7. **C is the best answer.** Think of the orbitals as synonymous with the types of bonds present. Single bonds are sp^3 hybridized. Double bonds are sp^2 hybridized. Triple bonds are *sp* hybridized. Methotrexate has single and double bonds so it must have sp^2 and sp^3 hybridized orbitals. There are no triple bonds so there are no *sp* hybridized orbitals. This makes options II and III true and option III false. Choice C the best answer.

8. **C is the best answer.** Deal with each answer individually. Increasing concentration of drug does not always result in more bacterial growth because, for the most part, increasing concentration results in more bacterial death, so choice A can be ruled out. Although more drug usually results in more death, for ampicillin from 4 to 8 μg/mL, there is actually less death so choice B can be ruled out. Ampicillin is the least effective drug because there is the most bacterial growth still occurring, so choice C is better than choice D.

9. **A is the best answer.** The electrons around methotrexate will be mostly distributed near the oxygens because oxygen is the most electronegative species. However, there will also be electrons near the aromatic rings because these have electrons in pi bonds. This makes choice A the best answer.

Stand-alones (10-13)

10. **B is the best answer.** Water is often able to serve as a nucleophile, especially when an electrophilic carbonyl is present in a molecule. Addition of water to the compound shown in the question stem would likely lead to water attacking one of the two carbonyl groups, forming a tetrahedral intermediate, and releasing a functional group. Notice that the carbonyl is also bound to a nitrogen atom. This highly resembles a peptide bond that forms between adjacent amino acids. The breakdown of glucose into pyruvate is through a series of enzymes and redox reactions. Water is involved in those reactions but there is no nitrogen in either glucose or pyruvate, making choice A a weak answer. Proteins are broken down in the proteasome via hydrolysis. Hydrolysis occurs when water attacks the carbonyl of a peptide bond, breaking the link between amino acids. Choice B is likely to be the best answer, as it shares similar chemistry to the reaction between water and the compound shown in the question stem. Emulsification occurs when fats are formed into micelles with the help of bile salts. This is not a reaction but instead a manifestation of hydrophobic interactions, eliminating choice C. Water is also not involved in forming the phosphodiester bond between nucleotides in a growing DNA strand, eliminating choice D.

11. **D is the best answer.** The length of a bond is inversely proportional to its strength. This means that shorter bonds are stronger, and longer bonds are weaker. Strong bonds occur when the electronegativities of the bonding atoms are similar, and double bonds are stronger than single bonds. With these facts in mind, recall the mnemonic for the electronegativity scale: FONCl BrISCH *(memorize this name, it will come in handy on test day).* Nitrogen is closer to carbon on the electronegativity scale; double bonds between nitrogen and carbon will be stronger than double bonds between carbon and oxygen—eliminate choice B. As mentioned above, double bonds are stronger (and shorter) than single bonds—eliminate choices A and B. Choice D is the best answer.

12. **C is the best answer.** Zwitterions occur when a molecule simultaneously contains both negative and positive charge(s). In biochemistry, zwitterions are typically found in structures that have carboxyl and amino groups—the acid-base properties of these functional groups lead to intramolecular proton exchange. In other words, the amino group acts as a base and deprotonates the carboxylic acid. When forming the positively charged part of the creatine zwitterion, there are three separate nitrogens to choose from. The best place to put the positive charge will be the location with the most resonance structures, so that the charge can be delocalized. Choice C can have the positive charge spread over three resonance structures, with the amino group of each side of the iminium contributing electrons. Choices A and B do not have any possible resonance structures so the there is no delocalization of the positive charge. Choice D should be eliminated—carbonyls are not basic. A protonated carbonyl is only seen in conditions of high acidity, and even then, it is only a transiently lived intermediate.

13. **D is the best answer.** The absorption of light by molecules occurs by conjugated double bond systems, in which a double bond, which is composed of a single sigma bond and one pi bond, is separated by a single bond, which is composed of a sigma bond. Seven sigma bonds would represent seven single bonds, which are unable to absorb light, eliminating choice A. Two pi bonds could either be one triple bond, composed of a sigma bond and two pi bonds, or two double bonds. Choice B is a possibility, as these two double bonds could be conjugated. One pi bond and seven sigma bonds would indicate only one double bond in the chain, and thus no conjugation. Choice C can be eliminated. Three pi bonds would indicate at least three triple bonds or one double bond and one triple bond. Given the increased number of pi bonds, it is most likely that the fatty acid described by choice D would have the highest probability of absorbing light, making it the best answer.

Passage 3 (Questions 14-17)

14. **C is the best answer.** The plot presented in the question shows the potential energy as a result of rotation around the $\sigma 2$ bond. The lower the potential energy, the less steric effects exist between the two aryl groups. At point A, the energy is at its lowest point, meaning the two aryl groups are most likely to be in their anti conformation, eliminating choice A. At point B, the energy is higher than at point A, meaning they are not at the anti position, but instead interacting to some extent. This is likely the gauche configuration, where the two aryl groups have some steric effects on one another. Choice B can be eliminated. Point C is at the highest potential energy point on the graph. This is likely to be the fully eclipsed position, where maximal steric effects occur between the two aryl groups, making choice C most likely to be the best answer. Point D represents another gauche interaction, similar to point B, and can be eliminated.

15. **B is the best answer.** A dipole moment is generated by the difference in electronegativity of two atoms in a bond. When the two atoms are the same, the generation of a dipole moment is unlikely, though differences in functional groups distant to the bond may also play some small role in creating a dipole moment, especially if strongly electronegative atoms are nearby. Each half of compounds 1, 3, 4, 5, and 6 is a mirror image of the other half, meaning the two atoms connecting the aryl functional groups are the same and the atoms distant to that bond are the same on each side. These compounds are unlikely to have a dipole moment. This also means that it is unlikely that one compound of compounds 1, 3, 4, 5, and 6 have more of a dipole moment than another, eliminating choices C and D. Compound 2 does not have the same atoms on either side of the bond linking the two aryl groups. It has a nitrogen on one side and a carbon on the other. Nitrogen is slightly more electronegative than carbon, so the bond will be polarized towards nitrogen, making compound 2 have a stronger dipole moment that all the remaining compounds. This eliminates choice A and makes choice B most likely to be the best answer.

16. **B is the best answer.** A Lewis dot structure and an understanding of formal charge help to figure out how many free electrons are on the nitrogen. Notice that the nitrogen does not have any formal charge, meaning it does not have a positive or negative charge depicted next to the atom in the structure. This means that the formal charge of the ion is 0. Using the periodic table, nitrogen should have 5 valence electrons. In the compound, the nitrogen is in a single bond with the carbon of the aryl ring and a double bond with the other nitrogen. There are a total of 6 electrons in these three bonds, 2 electrons per bond, but half of these electrons are assigned to each atom. This means the nitrogen has 3 electrons assigned to it from bonds that it is currently in. This leaves two electrons to account for the formal charge being zero. Choice B is most likely to be the best answer.

17. **D is the best answer.** The question asks for a comparison of the intermolecular interactions that could occur between the presented compounds and the allosteric regulatory site of the Pdcd4 protein. Van der Waals interactions occur between hydrophobic groups, including benzene rings, and would play a part in the compound's activity. However, all the other compounds also contain this group, eliminating choice A. An ionic bond is a type of intramolecular, not intermolecular bond, meaning it holds two atoms within a molecule together. Choice B can be eliminated. Electrostatic interactions are the intermolecular equivalent to an ionic bond. Notice that none of the compounds are charged, meaning they are not likely to participate in electrostatic interactions. Choice C can be eliminated. The substituents on the benzene ring in compound 6 are $-NO_2$ groups, which are also known as nitro groups. They contain oxygen with free electrons, which can participate in hydrogen bonding to amino acids inside proteins that contain hydrogens attached to N, F, or O, such as threonine and serine. As no other compound has nitro group or hydrogen bond donor groups on the aryl rings, choice D is most likely to be the best answer.

Passage 4 (Questions 18-21)

18. **C is the best answer.** Protoapigenone and apigenin are depicted in Figure 1. The key differences when comparing the two molecules will occur at the site that is different, carbon B. Carbon B has one more substituent and no double bond in protoapigenone. This means that compared to the carbon in apigenin, it has one more sigma bond. Choice A can be ruled out. Apigenin and protoapigenone have the same number of pi bonds, because they both have 8 double bonds, ruling out choice B. Carbon B in protoapigenone has sp^3 hybridization, making the molecule nonplanar. Meanwhile, all of the carbons in apigenin are sp^2 hybridized, and the entire molecule is in the same plane. Choice C is the best answer. Next, choice D is inaccurate because atom-wise, there is an extra oxygen and hydrogen in protoapigenone, making the opposite of choice D true.

19. **C is the best answer.** Looking at apigenin, every single carbon throughout the molecule has one double bond and 3 substituents, meaning they are all sp^2 hybridized. Based on this hybridization, every carbon is connected to other carbons that are in the same plane as it. Extending this relationship to the whole apigenin molecule means that all carbons are in the same plane. Options I and II are likely to be in the correct answer. The bond angle of 109.5° corresponds to sp^3, not sp^2, ruling out option III. Thus choice C is the best answer.

20. **D is the best answer.** London dispersion forces are the weakest intermolecular force and involve transient dipoles that can occur in any atom/molecule. Option I is likely to be in the correct answer, ruling out choices A and C. Hydrogen bonding can occur when a molecule has hydrogen atoms bonded to particularly electronegative atoms, such as N, O, or F. Since protoapigenone has hydroxyl groups, it can hydrogen bond. Dipole-dipole interactions can occur when dipoles are present in molecules. These occur when there are bonds between atoms of different electronegativities, like several of those in the protoapigenone molecule. Options II and III are also likely to be in the correct answer, so choice D is the best answer.

21. **A is the best answer.** Stereocenters are generally carbon atoms with four unique connected substituents. There is only one carbon bonded to four separate substituents, so choices C and D can be ruled out. Another rule that is important for this question is that the number of possible diastereomers is typically 2^n where n is the number of stereocenters, though this can be altered by the possibility of meso compounds. This 2^n rule is because a diastereomers are defined as any stereoisomers that have different configuration at least one stereocenter. Since there are generally 2 possibilities at any stereocenter, each new stereocenter doubles the number of possible diastereomers. Two of the potential stereocenter carbon's substituents are the two rings to the left and the –OH group. Next, there are two single bonds going along the rightmost ring in protoapigenone. Tracing along this ring through both of these bonds, it is important to recognize that these are actually identical. This means there are three unique substituents, not four, and this carbon is not a stereocenter. Choice A is the best answer, and choice B can be ruled out.

Passage 5 (Questions 22-25)

22. **D is the best answer.** This is a research based question disguised with chemistry jargon. To be correct, both parts of the answer choice must be correct. To know creatine's relationship with depression, its "psychological functionality," it is necessary to look at Figure 2. All the relevant chemistry can be learned from the structure of creatine provided in the passage. Although creatine is a zwitterion in the body, this passage never addressed the blood-brain barrier, so there is not enough information to know whether creatine can cross it. Polar molecules do not typically cross the blood brain barrier effectively, but there are special active transport mechanisms for certain molecules such as glucose. From the information provided, it is impossible to determine whether creatine may have such a transport mechanism or not. Choice A is not the best answer because of this doubt. When considering choice B, do not worry about whether or not creatine is a catecholamine. This is an intimidating detail to distract the test taker from the easier psychological part of the answer. When facing a two part answer, answer the easier part first; this is often enough to rule out an incorrect choice. Look at Figure 2. Creatine administration alone corresponds to slightly higher levels of depressive symptoms at the end of the study. Creatine is certainly not sufficient to reduce depression—eliminate choice B. Creatine is non-chiral so it cannot have a racemic mixture, as implied in choice C. Likewise, choice C also suggests that creatine must be administered to reduce depression. This claim is contradicted by the evidence provided in the placebo + exercise trial. A reduction in depression occurred in the total absence of creatine; creatine is not necessary to reduce depression—eliminate choice C. Based on Figure 2, creatine alone could not reduce depression, but exercise alone could! Creatine it is not sufficient to reduce depression, nor is it even necessary. Because of the amino groups and the stomach's low pH ≈ 1, creatine is expected to have a positive charge in the stomach. Choice D is the most correct of the choices.

TEST 2A A&E

23. **C is the best answer.** This question is testing interpretation of bond-line formulas. Remember to complete the valence of each carbon, by adding bonds to hydrogen until there are four bonds to the carbon. If the carbon already has four bonds, do not add any hydrogens. Also remember that empirical formulas represent the smallest whole number ratio of each element. The mistakes come from counting errors: Choice A ignores the carbon of the methyl group in the middle of the structure. Choice B ignores the hydrogens of the methyl group in the middle of the structure. Choice D forgets to add the hydrogen of the carboxylic acid.

24. **B is the best answer.** Single bonds are σ bonds. Adding one π bond to a single bond results in a double bond, and adding two π bonds to a single bond results in a triple bond. Since there are more than four σ bonds in the structure of creatine, choices A and C can't be right. For every double bond present in the structure, there will be a π bond in the structure. Since there are two double bonds, two π bonds are in this structure. π bonds have a lower bond energy than σ bonds—select choice B, and eliminate choice D.

25. **A is the best answer.** Compare these structures to the structure of creatine, and see that an amide/"peptide" bond has been formed and water has been lost. The MCAT® loves amide/"peptide" bonds. Anytime you see a carboxylic acid and an amine on a linear structure, be prepared for a cyclization reaction. The challenge of this question is to correctly make a five member ring and fuse it with a peptide bond. Since the imine is preserved in every structure, and the tertiary amine is too close to form a 5 member ring, know that the primary amine on the far left of the structure will be reacting with the carbonyl. Since the tertiary amine is too close to the carbonyl to form a 5 member ring, choice B can be eliminated. Number each atom, and form the ring. Two of these choices can be immediately eliminated—choices B and D are the same molecule. Whenever two answer choices are the exact same they both must be wrong. Choice C can be eliminated because there is no amide/"peptide" bond formed.

TEST 2A A&E

Stand-alones (26-29)

26. **A is the best answer.** After deprotonation, the resulting carbanion can be stabilized through resonance with oxygen. Although choice C can still resonate with the aromatic ring, any one of these resonance structures still places a negative charge on a carbon. It is more stable to put the formal negative charge on oxygen, as it is a more electronegative atom. Choices D and B are weaker answers for the same reason as choice C.

27. **B is the best answer.** Remember that the actual structure of a molecule is the average of its resonance structures. The carbon-nitrogen bond length in pyridine is an average between a double bond and single bond because of its two resonance forms. Take the average of the carbon-nitrogen double bond and the carbon-nitrogen single bond to approximate the answer.

$$(1.25\ \text{Å} + 1.47\ \text{Å})/2 = 1.36\ \text{Å}$$

The correct bond length must be closest to this number. The best answer is choice B. In fact, performing math was not even required to solve this problem. Choice B is the only choice which is between the single and double bond lengths of the average carbon-nitrogen bond. Choices A and D were too low. Choice C was too high. These choices could have been eliminated.

28. **C is the best answer.** The molecular formula is the true number of atoms present. The empiric formula is the simplest integer of atoms present. For example, the empiric formula for H_2O_2 is HO. And the empiric formula for C_6H_6 is CH. The molecular formula for levetiracetem is $C_8H_{14}N_2O_2$ which reduces to C_4H_7NO. This makes choice C the best answer.

29. **A is the best answer.** Recall that D- and L- amino acids refer to the stereochemistry for glyceraldehyde. D-glyceraldehyde is (*R*)-glyceraldehyde and L-glyceraldehyde is (*S*)-glyceraldehyde. However, for amino acids, D is not always *R,* and L is not always *S.* Nonetheless, the question is asking to convert from either *R* to *S* or *S* to *R*. This is a point worth memorizing- inversion of stereochemistry is best achieved with an S_N2 reaction. E2 reactions lose stereochemistry and create a double bond, so choice B is not the best answer. The Grignard reaction occurs at a carbonyl which lacks stereochemistry, so choice C is not the best answer. The Strecker reaction is used for amino acid synthesis. The question refers to amino acids but not to amino acid synthesis, just conversion from D- to L-. Choice A is more accurate than choice D, so choice A is the best answer.

Passage 6 (Questions 30-33)

30. **B is the best answer.** In reaction 1′, involving cisplatin and water as the two reactants, notice that the chlorine atom is replaced by a hydroxyl group. This means that the chlorine was replaced by water, and the second hydrogen of water was lost to the chlorine to form HCl. This makes the reaction a substitution reaction, not an elimination reaction. An elimination reaction forms a double bond or triple bond, with the loss of an atom bonded to the two atoms forming the ends of the double or triple bonds. Choices A and B can be eliminated, as E1 and E2 are elimination reactions. An S_N1 reaction has two steps and the rate of the reaction is dependent on the loss of an atom from one of the reactants. If reaction 1′ was an S_N1 reaction, cisplatin would first lose the Cl^- to form Pt^+ and then water would attack. Paragraph three states that Pt^+ is an unstable species, meaning it is unlikely to form this species on its own. An S_N1 reaction is probably not the most likely mechanism. An S_N2 reaction occurs in a single step and is dependent upon the nucleophile attacking the electrophile. In this case, because the Pt^+ would be an unstable species, the water is likely to attack the Pt of cisplatin and substitute for the Cl. Choice D is most likely to be the best answer.

31. **D is the best answer.** The change in molecular structure that occurs during reaction 3 involves the movement of a double bond from the carbonyl to between the carbon and nitrogen of the main ring. Notice that the hydrogen transfers from the nitrogen to the oxygen. This means the carbonyl turns into an enol, which is a hydroxyl group on an alkene. This keto to enol change is called tautomerism. Notice neither the oxygen nor the nitrogen move positions, meaning choices A and B are unlikely to be the best answer. Movement of a hydrogen and a proton are essentially equivalent here. The hydrogen, with its one electron, moves from the O to the N and a proton, a hydrogen without its electron, is the ion during the transfer itself. An enol is less stable than a ketone because a C=O is more stable than a C=C, as the electronegativity of the O is able to stabilize the electrons of the pi bond. In addition, the change in physical bonds between different atoms makes this a constitutional isoform. Choice D is more likely be the best answer compared to choice C.

32. **A is the best answer.** The diagrams shown in the answer choices are Lewis Dot Structure diagrams, which represent the number of electrons in the valence shells of atoms in the diagram. There are three main rules to drawing Lewis Dot structures: 1) Find the total number of valence electrons for all atoms in the molecule; 2) Use one pair of electrons to form a single bond between each pair of atoms; 3) Arrange the remaining electrons in lone pairs and double or triple bonds to satisfy the duet rule of hydrogen and the octet rule for all other atoms so that the total number of electrons matches the total found in step 1. After reaction 3′, the Pt has a double bond to O and two single bonds to N. This would be represented as four dots to oxygen and two dots to each nitrogen. No atoms have a formal charge, so the oxygen would get two more pairs of electrons to complete its octet and nitrogen would get one. This is found in choice A, likely making it the best answer. As there is no formal charge, the nitrogen atoms should have 5 electrons in its valence shell, meaning it would have one free electron. Choice B shows no electrons on nitrogen, eliminating it as a possible answer. Only one nitrogen has an electron in choice C, eliminating it as a possible answer. The bond to oxygen should be a single bond, but choice D shows only one bond between Pt and O, making choice D unlikely to be the best answer.

33. **C is the best answer.** The 1400–1600 cm^{-1} stretch usually corresponds to an alkene functional group, which is a C=C. The complexes also have C=N, which would appear at a similar frequency. The medium intensity peaks probably correspond to a mix of these two signals. Double bonds have one pi bond and one sigma bond, not two pi bonds. This eliminates choices A and B. The two carbons of a C=C would have equal electron affinities, as they are the same atom. A C=N would have unequal electron affinities, but this does not make choice C untrue, as some of the signal would come from the C=C. Three sigma bonds do not exist in any bond, which makes choice D an untrue statement. Choice D can be eliminated.

Passage 7 (Questions 34-37)

34. B is the best answer. The carbon that the iodine atom was lost on and replaced by a hydroxyl is a tertiary carbon. In substitution reactions, tertiary carbons undergo S_N1-mediated chemistry, where the leaving group first leaves and generates a carbocation that is subsequently attacked by a nucleophile, which is the hydroxide in this case. The extra charge density due to the increased substitution stabilizes the carbocation. This eliminates choices C and D. Because the carbocation intermediate is planar, the nucleophile can attack from above or below, which would result in a loss of stereochemistry. This makes choice B a better answer than choice A.

35. B is the best answer. Isomerization occurs around a double bond when the conformation changes. There are two ways to designate the stereochemistry of a double bond, namely *E* and *Z* or *cis* and *trans*. An *E* bond is the same as a *trans* bond, where the groups with the highest molecular weights on either side of the double bond are opposite one another in order to reduce steric interactions. *Z* and *cis* are the same, where the groups with the highest molecular weights on either side of the bond interact with greater steric interactions. Notice that the two rings are found on the same side of the double bond and would likely interact. This means the double bond is in the *cis* or *Z* conformation. Option I can be eliminated, and option II is a part of the best answer. There are no chiral carbons in CA-4, as no carbon is attached to four different groups. This means it cannot have an absolute stereochemical configuration of *R* or *S*, eliminating option III. Choice B is the best answer as it contains only option II.

TEST 2A A&E

36. D is the best answer. According to paragraph two, CA-4 and its analogues likely interact with β-tubulin via a hydrophobic pocket. Thus, the best substituent to be placed onto the CA-4 analogue would be able to interact via hydrophobic interactions. Substituent c contains a hydroxyl group on the benzene ring, which would make the ring polar. Choice A is unlikely to be the best answer. As with choice A, substituent e contains two hydroxyl groups, which make the ring structure polar. Choice B can be eliminated. The addition of the second aromatic ring would favor the formation of hydrophobic interactions, but the presence of the carbonyl and the oxygen create dipole moments that make the two-ringed structure polar overall. Choice C can be eliminated. Notice that substituent l has two aromatic rings and no electronegative atoms. The aromatic rings do not have an overall dipole moment, which makes them nonpolar. Substituent l would be able to participate in hydrophobic interactions, making choice D the best answer.

37. A is the best answer. Notice that the chlorine is substituted for the fluorine in the reaction shown in the question stem. Also notice that the carbon attached to the chloride leaving group is a primary carbon, as it is bound only to one other carbon in the aromatic ring. This likely means that the reaction occurs by S_N2 chemistry, which is a one-step reaction where the attacking nucleophile, fluoride in this reaction, attacks the carbon, kicking off the leaving group, which is chloride in this reaction. S_N2 chemistry occurs on primary carbons, as no stable carbocation could be generated due to the lack of substitution. Carbocation generation is a feature of the two-step S_N1 reaction. Choices C and D can be eliminated. Polar aprotic solvents have a dipole moment but no ability to hydrogen bond and help increase the rate of S_N2 reactions. This likely makes choice A a better answer than choice B. Ethanol is a polar protic solvent, which helps stabilize the carbocation in S_N1 reactions but inhibits S_N2 reactions as it would interact with reactants. Choice B can be eliminated.

Passage 8 (Questions 38-43)

38. C is the best answer. Remember that glycine is the simplest of the amino acids—it is achiral because its R-group is a bond to hydrogen. Like other amino acids, it has a carboxylic acid terminus, and an amino group terminus. Its structure is shown below:

$$H_2N - \underset{H}{\overset{H}{\overset{|}{C}}} - COOH$$

Glycine

A "cyano" group is any R–C triple bond, i.e. three parallel horizontal lines on top of each other N group. Since glycine lacks a triple bond to nitrogen, choice A can be eliminated. An imide is composed of two acyl groups bound to nitrogen. They are the nitrogen analogues of acid anhydrides. The structure of glycine lacks this functional group, and choice B can be eliminated. When amino acids combine together during the formation of proteins, the amino group of one attacks the carbonyl of another. A condensation reaction takes place, ejecting water, and forming a peptide bond. Peptide bonds refer to the connection between an amine and an acyl group. When these two groups are bonded together, the resulting functional group is also called an amide. Since this question is asking only about one amino acid, glycine, and not a full protein, there will be no peptide bonds and no amides in this structure. Eliminate choice D.

39. **B is the best answer.** With the exception of glycine, amino acids are chiral compounds and can rotate polarized light. Choice A can be eliminated. The imine intermediate in the Strecker synthesis undergoes nucleophilic attack by the CN^- anion, converting the intermediate from a planar molecule, into a new chiral species. Equal rates of attack on each face of the planar imine intermediate results in a racemic mixture which cannot rotate polarized light. Choice B may be the best answer, but eliminate the others before selecting it. It is difficult for amino acids to polymerize and form new amide bonds, especially without being exposed to an activating agent such as N,N′-dicyclohexylcarbodiimide, known as "DCC". Even if the alanine could somehow polymerize and remain soluble in solution, the polypeptide that it would form would still be chiral and would still be capable of rotating polarized light. For all of these reasons, choice C can be eliminated. If the pH of solution exceeded the isoelectronic point of alanine, then alanine would bear a negative charge as its carboxylic acid group would be deprotonated. Nonetheless, bearing a charge does not prevent a molecule from rotating polarized light. Choice D can be eliminated.

40. **C is the best answer.** Molecular geometry refers to the three-dimensional shape assumed only by the atoms of a molecule. This shape is influenced by the presence of lone pairs, as lone pairs increase the repulsive forces acting on the bonds. For example, water, or H–O–H is a non-linear structure. The two lone pairs on the middle oxygen atom compress the O–H bonds into a bent shape. Ammonia, or NH_3, has a lone pair on its central nitrogen. This lone pair pushes the three symmetrical N–H bonds away from it, creating a trigonal pyramidal shape. Choice C is the best answer. The electron domain geometry of ammonia is tetrahedral, as electron domain geometries describe the shape formed by atoms and lone pairs. Since this question did not ask for electron domain geometry, choice A can be eliminated. The lone pair on nitrogen pushes the three N–H bonds away from being in a plane. Choice B can be eliminated. On the MCAT®, square planar molecular geometries result from molecules with four separate bonds and two lone pairs such as XeF_4. Ammonia does not satisfy these structural conditions, and choice D can be eliminated.

41. **A is the best answer.** To be formed "as described in the passage" means to be formed via a Strecker synthesis, as this is what is described in the passage. Essentially, a classical Strecker synthesis combines an aldehyde, ammonia, and hydrogen cyanide to form a racemic mixture of an amino acid. During a Strecker synthesis, the R group of the nascent amino acid is derived from the non-hydrogen group bonded to the carbonyl of the aldehyde. The central carbon of this aldehyde will become the stereocenter of the new amino acid. Thus, the best answer will feature the R group of isoleucine bonded to the central carbon of the aldehyde. Choice A features this R group, and is the best answer. Choice B contains the R group of leucine, a molecule often confused for isoleucine because of its structural similarity. Choice C contains the R group of valine, which looks remarkably similar to the R group of leucine, commonly confused for isoleucine. Choice D contains the R group of another non-polar amino acid, alanine. If any of these other aldehydes were an electrochemically generated intermediate, they would undergo a Strecker synthesis. Ultimately, they would produce their corresponding amino acid, not the amino acid isoleucine. Choice B, C, and D can be eliminated.

42. **C is the best answer.** The retention factor, R_f, is a measure of how strongly attracted a substance is to the solvent in which it is dissolved. During thin layer chromatography, a solvent climbs up a thin plate covered in silica gel, carrying its solute with it. R_f is defined as the ratio of the height the solute reaches divided by the height the solvent reaches on the plate. The closer this ratio is to 1, the more attracted the solute is to the solvent, and the less it is attracted to the silica stationary phase. On this plate, the location of isoleucine can be determined by comparing the two standard samples on the left. Each of these standard samples contains Ala which will reach the same height in each trial. Thus, Ala reaches about 5 units, Gly reaches a little over 6 units, and Ile reaches about 3 units. $R_f = 3/10 = 0.3$. Choice C is the best answer. If the point which represents glycine were chosen by mistake, choice A would result. Choice B would result if the reciprocal of the R_f equation were used. Choice D follows the same error, except it uses the wrong point in addition to the reciprocal of the R_f equation.

43. **C is the best answer.** The first step to solving this problem is to draw a correct Lewis structure for carbon-monoxide. In general, try to provide each atom with an octet configuration, and then try to give the most electronegative atoms the negative charges if there are any. In this case, it is impossible to fulfill both of these considerations. The best Lewis structure, shown below, at least provides each atom with an octet configuration:

$$^{-}:C\equiv O:^{+}$$

Since triple bonds are stronger and shorter than double bonds, option I will not be part of the best answer. Choices A and D can be eliminated. Formal charge = (# valence electrons) – (# bonds) − (# nonbonding electrons). Using 6 as the number of valence electrons for oxygen and 4 for carbon, as well as this equation, demonstrates that options II and IV are true. Options II and IV will be part of the best answer. An octet refers to an atom being surrounded by 8 electrons. It does not matter whether these electrons are lone-pairs, or shared in a covalent bond—so long as there are 8. Carbon has 6 electrons shared via its bonds with oxygen, and 2 more in its lone pair. Thus, carbon has an octet configuration in this structure. Option III will not be part of the best answer, and choice B can be eliminated. Choice C is the best answer.

Stand-alones (44-47)

44. **A is the best answer.** A careful look at the anion pairs in this structure reveals that each anion is the exact same—one of the pair is just rotated 180° relative to the other. Since the solution is filled with the same chiral structure, it is expected to rotate polarized light, making choice A likely. Enantiomers are non-superimposable mirror images. The anions in calcium gluconate are not mirror images, and they are completely superimposable. Choice B should be eliminated. Meso compounds are compounds with stereocenters that also have an internal plane of symmetry, which causes each half of the compound to be its own mirror image. Meso compounds do not rotate polarized light because the optical effect of each half "cancels out" the other half. Since the anions in this structure do not have an internal plane of symmetry, they are not meso compounds. Choice C can be eliminated. Optical density refers to how quickly light can travel in a medium. In particular, it describes the ratio of the speed of light in a vacuum to the speed of light in a given medium. Being optically dense is not sufficient to rotate polarized light. Choice D can be eliminated.

45. **B is the best answer.** First determine the absolute configuration of this isomer of thalidomide. The nitrogen has highest priority, followed by the carbonyl carbon, then the saturated carbon. Conveniently, the lowest priority substituent, hydrogen, is in the back of this molecule. If needed, draw a circle from the highest priority substituent to the lowest priority substituent. The circle moves clockwise, so this molecule has an *R* configuration. According to the table, after digestion only 90% of the *R* enantiomer makes it to the blood. Once in the blood, 55% of it is bound to plasma proteins. This means that of the 90 mg from the 100 mg that actually enters circulation, only 45% will NOT be bound to plasma protein. To calculate what mass of the drug remains unbound in the blood, multiply the mass of the drug that entered the blood, 90 mg, by 0.45. The answer should be a little less than half of 90 mg, or a little less than 45 mg. Choice B is the best answer. Choice A is too high, it comes from multiplying 90 mg by 0.55—this is a trap—55% is the BOUND fraction of the drug, not the free fraction. Eliminate choice A. Choice C is weak for two reasons—it ignores the amount of drug lost during digestion, and confuses the percent of the drug which is bound to plasma proteins for the percent which is free. Choice D comes from performing the correct calculations for the *S* enantiomer. The thalidomide shown is the *R* enantiomer. Eliminate choice D.

46. **D is the best answer.** First determine the hybridization of this carbon radical. The sum of the number of lone pairs and sigma bonds of the intermediate must match the sum of the superscripts in the hybrid name of the correct hybridization. Remember that 1 is implied if no super script is written. This carbon radical has 2 bonds + 1 lone pair = 3. It is sp^2 (s^1p^2) hybridized. Choices A and C should be eliminated. To determine the formal charge, use the equation

$$\text{Formal charge} = (\#\text{ valence electrons}) - (\#\text{ bonds}) - (\#\text{ non-bonding electrons})$$

$$4 - 2 - 2 = 0$$

This radical carbon has formal charge of 0. Eliminate choice B, and select the best answer, choice D.

47. **C is the best answer.** Relative configuration is when two molecules differ by only one substituent and the other substituents are oriented identically about the chiral carbon. These structures satisfy those conditions, so they at least share the same relative configuration. Eliminate choice D. The absolute configurations of I and II are *R* and *S* respectively, so they do not share the same absolute configuration. Choices A and B cannot be the best answer. Since these structures share the same relative configuration, choice C is the best answer.

Passage 9 (Questions 48-51)

48. **A is the best answer.** A structural formula shows the arrangement of atoms in a molecule, with all of the bonds drawn out between atoms. Paragraph three describes that oxalylchloride is used to convert compound 2 to compound 3, so the molecular formula needed to draw the structural formula can be found in Figure 1. The molecular formula of oxalylchloride is $(ClCO)_2$, so the best answer will contain these atoms in an uncharged molecule. The valence shells of each atom are filled and the overall compound is uncharged in choice A, likely making it the best answer. Choice B shows a double bond between the carbon and chloride, which would give the chloride a net positive charge and the oxygen a net negative charge. This charge separation would be unlikely to give a stable molecule, making choice B less likely than choice A to be the best answer. Both oxygen atoms carry a negative charge in choice C, making the overall charge of the molecule −2. The molecular formula does not show a negative overall charge, eliminating choice C. The molecular formula also notes that there are two of each atom in the overall molecule. Choice D only shows one of each atom, eliminating it as a possible answer.

TEST 2A A&E

49. **C is the best answer.** Notice that the compound shown in the question stem resembles compound 1 at each position except the anomeric carbon. The anomeric carbon is the chiral carbon of an anomer, a cyclic diastereomers formed when a ring closes. A diastereomers is a chiral compound where at least one, but not all, chiral centers have the opposite configuration of a molecule with the same structural formula and bond connectivity. In compound 1, the functional group containing the nitrogen points up, which is the β configuration. The compound shown in the question stem has the nitrogen functional group pointing down, which is the α configuration. Meso compounds have a plane of symmetry through them. Neither compound 1 nor the compound shown in the question stem has a plane of symmetry, eliminating option I. Epimers have the same configuration at each position, except the anomeric carbon. The α and β forms of a sugar are epimers, making option II true. Epimers, by definition, are diastereomers that differ only at the anomeric carbon, meaning option III is also true. Choice C is the best answer, as it includes only options II and III.

50. **D is the best answer.** Valence electrons are electrons that are found in the outer shell of an atom. One straightforward way to find the number of valence electrons is to find the electron configuration of an atom. The electron configuration of carbon is $[\text{He}]2s^2 2p^2$, which means there are four valence electrons in carbon, two in the $2s$ orbital and two in the $2p$ orbital. Choice D is the best answer.

51. **D is the best answer.** While the MCAT® does not test the explicit knowledge of many sugars, the structure of glucose is one that is required. Fructose contains a furanose, which is a compound containing four carbons in the ring , instead of a pyranose, which contains five carbons in the ring, eliminating choice A as the best answer. Sucrose is a disaccharide combination of fructose and glucose. Compound 1 only contains one sugar derivative, eliminating choice B. Galactose is the carbon four epimer of glucose. Because glucose is shown in compound 1, choice C is less likely than choice D to be the best answer.

Passage 10 (Questions 52-56)

52. **C is the best answer.** Menthol has three stereocenters: the top methyl group, the lateral hydroxyl group, and the bottom isopropyl group. Each of these is a carbon atom bonded to four non-identical substituents. The number of possible stereoisomers for a molecule are 2^n, where n is the number of stereo-centers. $2^3 = 8$. Choice C is the best answer. Three is the number of *stereocenters* in this molecule, not the number of *stereoisomers* of this molecule. Choice A can be eliminated. A corruption of the correct equation, n^2, would result in choice B. Choice D could result if one of the stereocenters were not counted, and only two of the three were considered.

53. **A is the best answer.** Count the carbon atoms first. These are represented by line ends or vertices. There are 8 in the structure of methyl salicylate. Hydrogen atoms are not drawn explicitly, but rather are implied in the skeletal formula. They are added to each carbon atom until the carbon's valence is completed. In other words, every carbon atom has four bonds; bonds that are not drawn explicitly are assumed to be bonds to hydrogen. Thus, there are four hydrogen atoms attached to the ring, one on the hydroxyl group, and three bonded to the terminal methyl group at the top right of the structure. Finally, there are 3 oxygen atoms throughout this structure. The molecular formula of methyl salicylate is $C_8H_8O_3$. Since there are no common denominators between the subscripts of this formula, the molecular formula is also the empirical formula in this case. Remember the empirical formula is a description of the molecule using the smallest whole number ratio of atoms in the structure. In contrast, the molecular formula describes every atom present. If the carbon atom of the implied methyl group were accidently not counted, choice B would result. Since the aromatic ring has two substituents, it can only contain four hydrogen atoms. If a hydrogen atom were incorrectly assigned to ever carbon atom in the aromatic ring, choice C would result. Choice D looks like the most compelling empirical formula because it has smaller numbers. Nonetheless, it is not based on a correct census of each of the atoms present in this structure. $C_8H_8O_3$ represents the smallest whole number ratio of each atom to the next, and is the proper empirical formula. Choice D can be eliminated.

54. **D is the best answer.** Consider the "players" in option I: an alcohol, a carboxylic acid, and catalytic acid. These are the reactants in a Fischer esterification, where water is lost and an ester is formed from a carboxylic acid and an alcohol. Option I is a viable synthetic route, and will be part of the best answer. Both bases and acids are useful catalysts in *transesterification* reactions between and ester and an alcohol, but bases are not useful during *esterification* reactions between a carboxylic acid and an alcohol. If NaOH were mixed with salicylic acid, it would deprotonate the carboxylic acid moiety. Following deprotonation, the electrophilicity of the carbonyl carbon would plummet, as any subsequent addition reaction would form a dianion intermediate. No attack from methanol would take place, and the only product would be a sodium salicylate salt. Option II will not be part of the best answer. The alcoholic hydroxyl group is far more nucleophilic than the carboxylic hydroxyl group. Acetic anhydride or methanoic anhydride would react with this hydroxyl group, and not convert salicylic acid's carboxylic group into an ester. Options III and IV will not be part of the best answer. Choice D is the best answer as is contains the only true option, option I. Below are the results of each synthetic scheme. Where multiple, non-methyl salicylate products were possible, only one is shown:

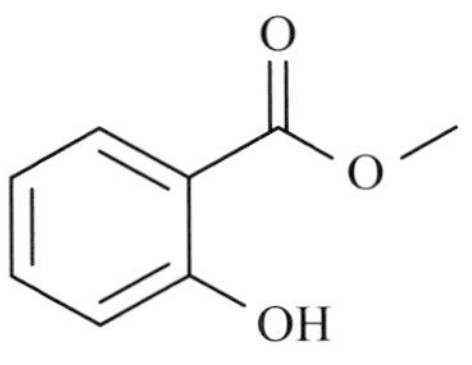

O O O O
O OH OH
OH OH O O O O
O⁻Na⁺
I 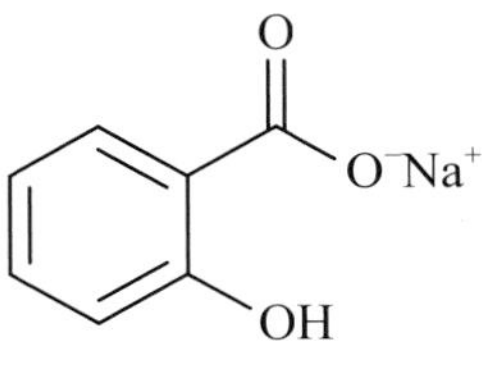 II 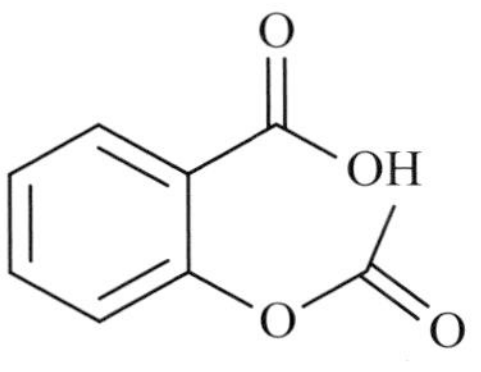 III 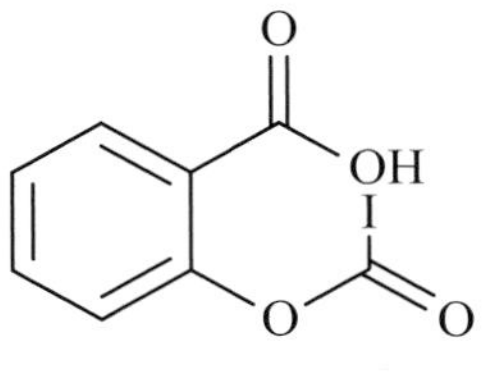 IV

55. **D is the best answer.** Whenever a strong acid is mixed with another chemical, the first thing to think is, "What will be protonated?" In menthol, the hydroxyl group is most basic, and will become protonated. Since the hydroxyl group is on a substituted 2° carbon, ejection of water and formation of a carbocation are possible. After the carbocation is formed, the reaction can proceed via an S_N1 or E1 mechanism. The answer choices here feature menthol rotated 180° horizontally relative to the way it is drawn in the passage. Do not be intimidated, these changes do not really affect the answer. Since the carbocation intermediate is planar, nucleophilic attack by the chloride anion on both sides is possible. Choices A and B can be eliminated as they are both direct products. Choice C has not experienced rearrangement—a hydrogen atom one bond length away from the carbocation has been lost in a traditional elimination reaction. Choice C can be eliminated. Choice D has experienced a hydride shift, moving the positive charge to a more stable 3° carbon, prior to the loss of a hydrogen atom from the central carbon of its isopropyl group. Hydride shifts are an example of rearrangement, so choice D is the best answer.

56. **D is the best answer.** Following deprotonation of methyl salicylate's hydroxyl group, the negative charge can be delocalized through resonance with the aromatic ring. This delocalization of negative charge means that the negative charge is less "available" to attack a proton and re-form the O–H bond. Choice D is the best answer. If a bond is weak, it is more likely to break. In acid/base chemistry if a bond to hydrogen is weak, the hydrogen atom is more likely to be lost as a proton, and vice-versa. Since menthol is *less* acidic than methyl salicylate, its O–H bond is expected to be *stronger*—i.e. it's more difficult to "pull" off the hydrogen atom. Choice A can be eliminated. Although hybridizations with greater *s* character are more acidic, this argument is generally applied to explain the higher acidity of alkynes vs. alkanes. The hybridization of C3 does not directly affect the oxygen atom of the hydroxyl group's bond with its hydrogen atom. Directly, it only causes the C–O bond to be shorter and stronger. The resonance of its π-system is what plays the larger role in contributing to the greater acidity. Choice B can be eliminated. Following deprotonation an excess *negative* charge is present, not a *positive* charge. Choice C can be eliminated.

Stand-alones (57-59)

57. **A is the best answer.** Specific rotation is an intrinsic property like density or molecular weight. By virtue of being defined by proportional extrinsic properties, specific rotation is constant. Choice A is not true, and is the best answer. Choice B is true—the observed rotation will need to double in order to keep $[\alpha]_{\lambda}^{T}$ constant. A racemic mixture consists of equal concentrations of each enantiomer from a pair of chiral molecules. Racemic mixtures do not observably rotate polarized light because the rotation caused by one enantiomer is canceled out by the opposite rotation caused by the other enantiomer. This effect will continue to occur even if the solution's concentration is doubled, and choice C is true as well. So long as a solution has an excess of one enantiomer, it will rotate polarized light. This is because there will be no other molecule to cancel out the rotation caused by the excess enantiomer—choice D is true.

58. **B is the best answer.** The number of stereoisomers for a molecule with n chiral centers is 2^n. There are no stereocenters in the planar aromatic ring system of this molecule, or on any atom one bond length away from the nitrogen—all of the atoms one bond length away from the nitrogen have two of the same substituent, namely, hydrogen. They cannot be chiral. The middle two carbon atoms, however, starting one bond length from the planar aromatic ring system are both chiral since they both have four separate substituents. $2^2 = 4$, so choose the best answer, choice B.

59. **B is the best answer.** Remember that anytime two atoms are covalently bonded to one another, there is at least one sigma bond. Every time an additional bond is created, they are formed by new pi bonds (double bonds have one sigma and one pi bond while triple bonds have one sigma and two pi bonds). Since the molecule has eleven single bonds, three double bonds, and one triple bond, it has a total of fifteen sigma bonds. If the N–H and O–H bonds were forgotten, then choice A might be chosen. Since every multiple bond has a sigma bond as well as the additional pi bonds, choice C is a weaker answer because it forgets to account for these sigma bonds. While triple bonds are formed by pi bonds, remember that a triple bond is composed of one sigma bond and two pi bonds. Choice D is a weaker answer that might be chosen if the triple bond was considered to have one pi bond.

Introduction to Organic Chemistry

MINI-TEST 2B

ANSWERS & EXPLANATIONS

Questions 1–29

TEST 2B A&E

Passage 1 (Questions 1-4)

1. **D is the best answer.** The structure of cadaverine indicates that it is a diamine. Remember that the amino nitrogen is somewhat basic—the lone pairs on it act as a Lewis base and can abstract protons from H^+ donors. Nonetheless, in weakly polar organic solutions, such as dicholormethane, its amino groups have a neutral charge. There are no free protons to abstract, and since cadaverine is a weakly-polar molecule, it dissolves. Thus, to extract cadaverine from dichloromethane, it is necessary to change its polarity relative to that of the solution, so that it will be preferentially dissolved in another solvent. Once cadaverine's polarity is changed relative to the solution, the two are *unalike*, and according to the adage, "like dissolves like," cadaverine will no longer be readily dissolved by the original solution. Toluene is another non-polar organic solvent. It will exert no effect on cadaverine's polarity. Choice A can be eliminated. Isopropyl alcohol is slightly-polar, and the O–H bond of an alcohol is more basic than the N–H bond of a protonated amine. Addition of isopropyl alcohol will not remarkably change the polarity of cadaverine because it will not donate any protons. Without more information, it is difficult to know what effects its addition will have on the solution. Perhaps it could form two phases and preferentially dissolve cadaverine in one of them? That might be helpful. Do not eliminate this answer choice right away, but look to see if there is something better. The 10% aqueous $NaHCO_3$ solution will form two layers, as it is way to polar to be miscible with dichloromethane. $NaHCO_3$ ionizes in solution to form Na^+ and the weak base HCO_3^-. This weak base will not have any effect on cadaverine, and will mostly be in the aqueous phase. Choice C can be eliminated. Addition of 10% aqueous HCl will protonate cadaverine. Although the protons are more soluble in the aqueous layer, at equilibrium a fraction of them will migrate to the organic layer, protonating cadaverine. Once protonated, cadaverine is no longer soluble in the organic layer, but is highly soluble in the aqueous layer. After enough shaking, most of the cadaverine is converted into a chloride salt and dissolved in the aqueous layer. Removal of the aqueous layer removes the bulk of the cadaverine from the solution, making it the ideal chemical for this extraction. Choice D is the best answer.

2. **C is the best answer.** The condensation reaction of a carboxylic acid and an amine form an amide. Choice C is the best answer. Although the dicarboxylic acids of Table 1, when reacted with putrescine, will form polymers linked with amide bonds, cinnamic and furoic acid are not dicarboxylic acids. They will not form a polymer with putrescine. Instead, they form a diamide with no further reactive sites on their sides. Since not *all* of the compounds in Table 1 can form a polymer, choice A can be eliminated. On the MCAT® nitriles are usually formed with the nucleophilic attack of the cyanide ion on an electrophile, such as in the Strecker amino acid synthesis. The reagents provided in this problem will not furnish a nitrile. Choice B can be eliminated. An imine is the nitrogen containing analog of a ketone or an aldehyde. They are formed from the condensation of primary amines with aldehydes, as well as ketones. Since there are no ketones or aldehydes in Table 1, no imines are expected to form. Choice D can be eliminated.

3. **B is the best answer.** The passage describes in the second-to-last paragraph that Compound A was neutral to litmus paper. This means that Compound A has neither basic nor acidic behavior. Since amines act as Lewis bases, choice A can be eliminated. Choice B contains an ester and an ether. Both of these classes of molecules are neutral, and choice B is the best answer. Although choice C contains an ether as its second option, it also contains a carboxylic acid as its first. Carboxylic acids react with litmus paper, causing it to turn red. Choice C can be eliminated. Choice D is weak for the same reason. Although it contains a neutral ether as the first option, it also contains a carboxylic acid as its second option. Choice D can be eliminated.

4. **B is the best answer.** The first step in solving IUPAC nomenclature problems is to rule out the improper names. Remember *E* and *Z* refer to the relative orientation of the two larger substituents coming off of the carbon-carbon double bond in the middle of the structure. *E* comes from the German word "*entgegen*" which means "opposed" and *Z* comes from the German word "*zusammen*" which means together. *Z* configurations about a carbon-carbon double bond denote cases where the two larger substituents are on the same side of the double bond. *E* configurations about a carbon-carbon double bond denote cases where the larger substituents are on opposite sides of the double bond. Cinnamic acid has its larger phenyl and carboxylic acid groups on opposite sides of the double bond. Thus, it has an *E* configuration. Choices A and C can be eliminated without further consideration. To distinguish between the remaining answer choices, remember that IUPAC nomenclature gives the most oxidized carbon atom the lowest number. C1 is the carbonyl carbon, C2 is the origin of the carbon-carbon double bond, and C3 is the phenyl carbon. Choice B is the best answer. Choice D reverses the correct numbering and can be eliminated.

Passage 2 (Questions 5-9)

5. **C is the best answer.** Notice that during reaction a, the bromine atom is substituted for a hydroxyl group that is subsequently lost in reaction b. Substitution reactions occur when one group leaves and is replaced by another, eliminating choices A and B, which are elimination reactions that would form a double bond. There are two types of substitution reactions of alkanes, S_N1 and S_N2. An S_N1 reaction has two steps, and the rate is dependent on only one of the reactants. The first step is carbocation formation and is the rate-determining step. The leaving group, in this case bromine, breaks away, and the nucleophile, the hydroxide in this case, attacks the carbocation. Both enantiomers are produced because the intermediate carbocation is planar, though only one of the two enantiomers is shown in Figure 1. An S_N1 reaction occurs on secondary and tertiary carbons, especially those that are substituted. This is because substitution around the carbon limits the spontaneous attack of a nucleophile. Only secondary and tertiary, but not primary, alkanes will undergo an S_N1 mechanism. Because the carbon is secondary and the groups around it likely would sterically hinder the attack of the nucleophile, choice C is probably the best answer. An S_N2 reaction occurs in one step when the nucleophile attacks a carbon, displacing the leaving group with inversion of stereochemistry. Typically only primary alkanes will undergo S_N2 reactions, as they are not sterically hindered. Additionally, if an S_N2 reaction occurred, the OH would be a wedge, not a dash. Choice D is not as good of an answer as choice C.

6. **A is the best answer.** Notice that the bromine atom is substituted for a hydroxyl group during reaction a, and that the carbon the bromine is attached to is a secondary carbon near groups that would provide a large degree of steric hindrance. This most likely makes the mechanism of action an S_N1 reaction, where the leaving group leaves, creating a planar carbocation, followed by the nucleophilic attack of the hydroxide. Because the intermediate is planar, there is no stereochemistry retained during the reaction, as it is equally likely that the nucleophile could attack from the top or the bottom. Only one of the enantiomers of compound 2 is shown in Figure 1, but the other enantiomer with the hydroxyl going into the page would be 50% of the product. Thus, the products of reaction a would be 50% *R* and 50% *S*, which is the definition of a racemic mixture. A racemic mixture does not rotate plane-polarized light, making choice A the best answer. Because a racemic mixture is produced, choices B-D can be eliminated.

7. **D is the best answer.** Both the amine and carboxylic acid contribute to the overall polar nature of all the starting compounds and intermediates of the reactions depicted in Figure 1. Both pentane and diethyl ether are non-polar solvents, meaning they would be unable to dissolve the various reactants and intermediates. Choices A and B can be eliminated. The last two solvents are both polar, but notice an important difference. Acetone is aprotic, meaning it does not contain an –OH or –NH bond that could contribute to hydrogen bonding, while *tert*-butanol is protic, due to the presence of the hydroxyl. In order to determine whether a polar protic or a polar aprotic solvent should be used, look at reaction a, which is a substitution reaction. The functional groups on either side of the bromine that is substituted for the hydroxyl group are bulky and would provide significant steric hindrance. In addition, the carbon attached to the bromine is a secondary carbon. This means reaction a likely occurs by an S_N1 mechanism, where the bromine would leave first, generating a carbocation that would later be attacked by the nucleophilic hydroxyl. Polar protic solvents increase the rate of S_N1 reactions by stabilizing the carbocation, while polar aprotic solvents decrease the rate of S_N1 reactions. Choice D is a better answer than choice C.

8. **C is the best answer.** According to paragraph two, a hydrophobic interaction between an inhibitor compound and Ile198 of CCR5 may be important in the overall mechanism of action. Ile is isoleucine, which is a nonpolar amino acid. Hydrophobic interactions occur between nonpolar groups, so the best answer will likely be nonpolar. A nitrile functional group is –CN, which is polar due to the electronegativity difference between the carbon and the nitrogen. This eliminates choice A. The carbonyl group is also polar, as there is an electronegativity difference between the carbon and the oxygen. A benzyl functional group is an aromatic ring that is nonpolar, which means it does not have an overall dipole moment. This would allow it to interact with the nonpolar isoleucine, likely making choice C the best answer. An amide functional group is a carbonyl bound directly to a nitrogen, which is polar due to the electronegativity differences between the carbon and both the oxygen and the nitrogen. Choice D can be eliminated.

9. **A is the best answer.** The first step to figuring out the hybridization and geometry of the carbon atom is to determine how many other atoms it is bonded to and how many free electrons it has. Notice the C of the nitrile group, which is –CN, is bound to a carbon in the aromatic ring and the nitrogen. This likely suggests that the geometry is *sp*, but double check to make sure the carbon does not have any free electron pairs, which also contribute to the geometry. Given that the carbon does not have a formal charge, it is likely sharing its electrons in other bonds, namely the triple bond that is present between the carbon and the nitrogen. Because the carbon is only attached to two other atoms and there are no free electron pairs, the *sp* hybridization and linear geometry of choice A is the best answer. If the carbon were attached to three other atoms, the hybridization would be sp^2 and the geometry trigonal planar. Choices B and C can be eliminated. If the carbon were attached to four other atoms, the hybridization would be sp^3 and the geometry tetrahedral. Choice D can be eliminated.

Passage 3 (Questions 10-13)

10. **B is the best answer.** While this question appears to ask about the stereochemistry at the specific stereocenters, notice that some answer choices have a unique number of stereocenters, meaning the most efficient way to determine the best answer is to determine the number of chiral carbons. The only two chiral carbons in the molecule are between the two five-membered rings, as each of these carbons connects to unique functional groups. Make sure to consider ringed structures carefully when determining whether the two functional groups that define the ring are unique, as they are in the case of both chiral carbons. Choices A and D can be eliminated, as (−)-phenserine has only two chiral carbons. The stereochemistry of carbon 3, which is the carbon found in both choices B and C, can be classified by the following priority order, ignoring the stereochemistry of the lowest priority group: (1) the bond to the bridging carbon, (2) the carbon connected to the aromatic ring, (3) the carbon connecting to the five-membered ring on the right, (4) the methyl carbon. This ordering appears to be the *R* configuration, but notice that the lowest priority group is coming out of the page, so reverse the configuration to *S*.

TEST 2B A&E

11. **D is the best answer.** A phenyl ring is a six-membered carbon-containing ring that is aromatic. A bond in an aromatic ring is intermediate between a single and a double bond, which makes it shorter and stronger than a single bond, but weaker and longer than a double bond. All of the bonds in the heterocyclic nitrogen-containing pyrrolidine ring are single bonds, which means that the bonds of the phenyl are stronger than the heterocyclic ring bonds. This eliminates choice A and B. Because the bonds of the aromatic ring have some double bond character, they are shorter than the single bond, making choice D a better answer choice than choice C.

12. **C is the best answer.** The carbon of the carbonyl in the amide functional group is predisposed to nucleophilic attack, as it has a partial positive charge on it due to the electronegativity of both nitrogen and oxygen. A pH of 12 indicates that the solution is basic and would have many OH^- molecules in solution. They hydroxide acts as an excellent nucleophile that would attack the carbonyl. A germinal diol contains two OH groups on the same carbon and could form if the tetrahedral intermediate created by the attacking hydroxide did not kick off a leaving group. However, the tetrahedral intermediate is likely to kick off either side of the (+)-phenserine, due to the leaving group's ability to stabilize the additional charge. Choice A is a possibility, but the other answer choices should be considered first. Methyl groups are unlikely to be substituted, as they are very poor leaving groups. Choice B can be eliminated. The tetrahedral intermediate created by the attack of the hydroxide would likely collapse to kick off one of the two original substituents of the amide, as these could stabilize the additional negative charge. Choice C is a better answer choice than choice A, likely making it the best answer. Remember that the majority of nucleophilic attacks will often result in no reaction, as the best leaving group is often the nucleophile that originally attacked the carbonyl. While the addition of an –OH to a molecule does result in oxidation, as an oxygen atom is added, the bond bridging the carbons between the two five-membered rings does not have functional groups that would be easily kicked off, making choice D less likely to be the best answer.

13. **B is the best answer.** Although the question references Figure 2, it is necessary to also use Figure 1 to answer this question. Notice that Figure 1 shows the derivatives of (+)-phenserine that are also tested for drug efficacy. According to paragraph two, (+)-phenserine is one of the most effective at preventing neuron death and may even increase the proliferation of neurons. As the methyl groups are substituted off (+)-phenserine and replaced with hydrogens, the drug derivatives begin to prevent less cell death, decreasing the efficiency of the drug at treating potential disease. By substituting hydrogen for the methyl group, the bond to nitrogen becomes slightly more polarized, as there is a greater difference in electronegativity between hydrogen and nitrogen, versus carbon and nitrogen. Remember that hydrogen has a slightly lower electronegativity than carbon. Choice A can be eliminated. The methyl group has tetrahedral geometry, with a hybridization of sp^3. As the number of methyl groups decreases, the drug becomes less effective, making choice B most likely to be the best answer. The number of single bonds between the main ring structure and the functional group does not change when the methyl group is substituted for the hydrogen, as both are single bonds. Choice C can be eliminated. sp^2 hybridized bonds are double bonds, which do not change as the methyl group is substituted, eliminating choice D.

Stand-alones (14-17)

14. **B is the best answer.** A structural isomer has the same molecular formula but different connectivity between bonds, which is unlikely to change as a solution cools, eliminating choice A. Conformational isomers have the same molecular formula and the same bond connectivity, but they have unique orientations in space. As the solution cools, functional groups that are bulky will tend to form an anti-staggered arrangement versus an eclipsed, fully eclipsed, or gauche conformation. This makes choice B most likely to be the best answer. Stereoisomers, including enantiomers, show unique configurations at chiral centers in terms of rotating plane-polarized light. The relative proportion of enantiomers should not change, as this would require a change in bond connectivity, eliminating choices C and D.

15. **B is the best answer.** An atom that is *sp* hybridized is found in a triple bond, while an atom with sp^2 hybridization is found in a double bond and two other single bonds, and an atom with sp^3 hybridization is found in four single bonds. There are no triple bonds in the ring, eliminating choices A and C. Four of the atoms, including the two carbonyl carbons and the carbons in the alkene, are sp^2 hybridized, as they are in a double bond and are also single bonded to two other atoms. This makes choice B most likely to be the best answer, and eliminates choice D.

16. **A is the best answer.** Functional groups that contain conjugated double bonds, such as benzene, and long chain alkenes with double bonds separated by single bonds are able to absorb light. Remember that double bonds are composed of one sigma bond and one pi bond. Notice that aspirin contains a benzene right that has an aromatic arrangement of double bonds, likely making choice A the best answer. The carboxyl group does contain one double bond, but it cannot absorb light on its own, eliminating choice B. A methyl group, composed of CH_3 is also unable to absorb light, eliminating choice C. As with a carboxyl group, an ester group contains a carbonyl carbon that is not conjugated, preventing it from absorbing visible light. Choice D can be eliminated.

17. **D is the best answer.** Electron density around an atom is determined by the functional groups and atoms near it. Oxygen is an electronegative atom, meaning it concentrates electrons from other atoms that it shares bonds with. In terms of priority and naming, carbon one is bound to the atom with the greatest atomic weight, which is oxygen in this case. Carbon four is in a double bond and a single bond. Double bonds have increased electron density, meaning carbons four and three are likely to have more electrons than carbons such as carbon five. This makes choices A and B less likely to be the best answer. Carbon two is in a double bond, meaning is it has some increased electron density, making choice C less likely to be the best answer. Carbon one has some increased electron density due to the double bond, but it is also bound to an electronegative oxygen, which withdraws electrons. As the other answer choices are also contained in double bonds, the addition of the oxygen atom will likely create decreased electron density for carbon one compared to the other answer choices. Choice D is the best answer.

TEST 2B A&E

Passage 4 (Questions 18-21)

18. **A is the best answer.** In all of these molecules, sulfur has a neutral charge. In order to have a neutral charge, each sulfur atom in this group of molecules must have two lone pairs of electrons. These lone pairs provide a great negative charge density that is not evenly distributed about the molecule. In molecules where sulfur is in the center, these lone pairs comprise two vertices of the tetrahedral structure, but not all four, as shown:

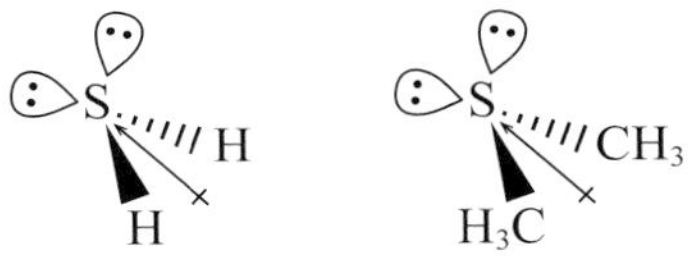

Thus, both hydrogen sulfide and dimethyl sulfide have a net dipole moment—their lone pairs have a greater negative charge density than do their other substituents, and the distribution of negative charge on these molecules is asymmetric. Similarly, the sulfur atom in methanethiol is far more electronegative than the C–H bonds in the methyl group. There is a greater charge density on this atom, which leads to methanethiol also having a net dipole moment. All options will be part of the best answer, choice A. Choices B, C, and D can be eliminated.

19. **B is the best answer.** Remember that double bonds cannot rotate about their axes because π-bonds are both on top and beneath of the atoms they bond together. A food analogy is a nice to way imagine this: it is impossible to vertically rotate the cheese (atoms) in a cheese sandwich because the bread (π-bond) keeps it in place along both its top and bottom aspects. Bonds, which through resonance adopt a π-bond system, also do not rotate for the same reason. Consider this resonance form of the dipeptide:

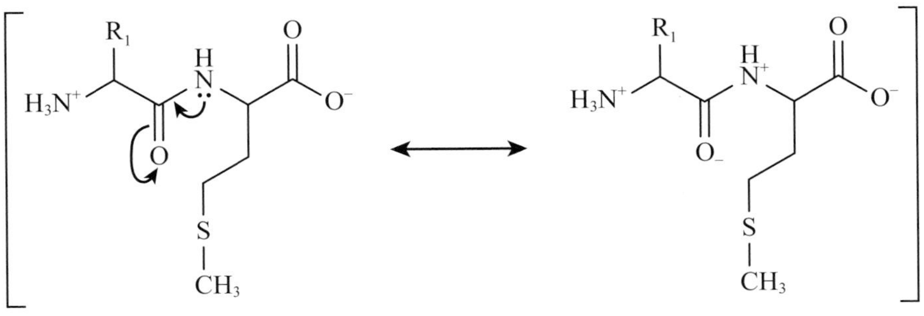

Thus, both option II and III *cannot* rotate and will be part of the best answer. Choices C and D can be eliminated on this basis. Option I and IV are both sigma bonds which can rotate freely. Options I and IV will not be part of the best answer, and choice A can be eliminated, leaving the best answer, choice B.

20. **A is the best answer.** Remember that the COOH group is called a "carboxylic acid" for a reason. This functional group is among the most acidic of the organic functional groups. Carboxylic acids are much more acidic than thiols and alcohols, making option II the first of the compounds in these lists. Choices B and D can be eliminated on this basis. Because compound I has a ketone group on the alpha position, it can better stabilize the resulting negative charge from deprotonation of its carboxylic acid moiety. Its alpha carbon has a δ^+, and exerts a slight inductive effect, increasing the acidity of compound I relative to compound IIII, making choice A the best answer. Choice C can be eliminated.

21. **B is the best answer.** There are two kinds of stereoisomers: enantiomers and diastereomers. This molecule is chiral, having four separate substituents which means it has an enantiomer. Choice A can be eliminated on this basis. However, besides its enantiomer, it does not have any other stereoisomer. Remember, in order for it to have a diastereomer which is a non-cis/trans diastereomer, it would require at least another stereocenter, which it does not have. Thus, there are only two stereoisomers of this molecule. Choice B is the best answer. Although this molecule has four substituents, each substituent is does *not* lead to another stereoisomer. The substituents can freely rotate resulting in infinitely many *conformational* isomers but all of these conformational isomers are in fact the same structure. Choices C and D can be eliminated.

TEST 2B A&E

Passage 5 (Questions 22-26)

22. **D is the best answer.** Immediately after receiving the second dose of STI-571, the patient will have the full dose of the second day of treatment in his body (600 mg) in addition to what remains of his first dose, taking its half-lives into account. The drug's half-life of 18 hours is hinted at in the last sentence of the passage, where it describes how long it takes for 50% of the drug to be excreted.

    To determine how much STI-571 remains from the first dose, calculate how many half-lives have passed using dimensional analysis:

    $$(24 \text{ hours})(1 \text{ half life}/18 \text{ hrs}) = 1.33 \text{ half lives}$$

    This means that (600 mg)($0.5^{1.33}$) remains of the first day's dose. Because of the exponential term, less than ½ of the original quantity of the first day's dose is in the patient's body. In other words, a little less than 300 mg of this dose remains in the body. Therefore, the correct answer must be less than 900 mg, but greater than 750 mg, because two half-lives have not yet passed. Choices A and C should be eliminated because they are greater than 900 mg. Choice D should be eliminated since it is too low—this actually comes from calculating the half-life as if 48 hours have passed since taking the first dose. Be careful, the question implies that the patient takes the second dose only 24 hours after the first dose. By the process of elimination, choice B is the best answer.

23. **C is the best answer.** Bimolecular nucleophilic substitution is jargon for an S_N2 reaction. S_N2 reactions change the absolute configuration of chiral centers because the nucleophile attacks the electrophile from the back, effectively causing the substituents on it to be brought from "behind the page" to "coming out of the page." Since amines have a nucleophilic lone pair they can participate in S_N2 reactions. Eliminate choice A. As discussed above, S_N2 reactions can cause a molecule's absolute configuration to change—eliminate choice B. 1° alkyl halides are not necessarily chiral centers, especially if the central carbon is bonded to two hydrogens as well as a halogen atom, just like the top of the larger reactant in Reaction 2. Since this alkyl halide is not a chiral center, it does not matter if its substituents are brought from "behind the page" to "coming out of the page." Since it is achiral, its absolute configuration does not change. Choice C may be the best answer. Although steric interactions can prevent the polyalkylation of a 2° amine with a haloalkane, nonetheless, monoalkylation is not prevented. If the monoalkylation proceeds via an S_N2 mechanism, than an inversion of absolute configuration is expected. In other words, the prevention of polyalkylation will not prevent the inversion of configuration, which happens after the first alkylation event. Choice D is not as good as choice C for this reason.

24. **C is the best answer.** Protons and halide ions are released during amide formation via the combination of an amine and an acyl halide. These side-products are expected to form pyridinium chloride salts when they combine with pyridine, in an acid-base reaction. Since answer choice A is discussing how the protocol of the reaction makes a side-product, there may be a better answer choice that addresses the necessity of this protocol to make the *target* product. Keep on looking at the answers. Amide cleavage is possible in very acidic environments. Nonetheless, it is unlikely that the amount of acid released as a side product could lower the pH of the solution meaningfully enough to catalyze amide hydrolysis, especially if the solution is very dilute. Moreover, because STI-571 has so many basic amino functional groups in it, its structure acts like a "proton sponge" protecting its amide functionality from acid catalyzed hydrolysis. Keep going down and looking at the choices, there may be something better. Protonation of the attacking amine would greatly harm its nucleophilicity—it would actually prevent the reaction from occurring. Choice C is stronger than choice A and B and may be the best answer. Compound 1 is soluble in THF without pyridine. It is a fairly non-polar molecule and would quickly dissolve in an ether solvent. Arguably, pyridine may even hurt the solubility by saturating the solvent. Eliminate choice D. Choice C is the best answer because it directly answers the question. Remember the question wants to know why pyridine needs to added to the solvent for Reaction 2 to proceed. Choice C correctly explains how the reaction will not occur in pyridine's absence. All of the other answer choices are either irrelevant to the goals of the reaction, such as choice A, less likely to affect the reaction, such as choice B, or not scientifically true, such as choice D.

TEST 2B A&E

25. **D is the best answer.** If structures I and II were enantiomers they would need to be non-superimposable mirror images of each other. Look closely at structures I and II and realize that they are shown as if there is a mirror in between them. The problem is, they are not mirror images. If they were mirror images, drawn as if there is a mirror between them, then their dashes and wedges would be going the same direction. Since they are not mirror images of each other, they are not enantiomers. Eliminate choice A. Diastereomers are isomers which are non-superimposable, non-mirror images of each other that share the same bond-to-bond connectivity. Structures I and II are completely super-imposable after rotating one of them 180°. They are not diastereomers for this reason. In fact, they are the same structure! Eliminate choice B. "Stereoisomer" is an umbrella term for molecules that share many features besides their three dimensional structure. Since structures I and II are the same molecule, they share a three dimensional structure. They are not stereoisomers—eliminate choice C. Choice D is the best answer because they are the same structure—by definition they must be non-isomeric.

26. **D is the best answer.** Aromaticity describes an increased stability experienced by cyclic planar molecules that have $4n + 2\pi$-electrons, and contiguous *p*-orbitals. Aromatic molecules have a lower heat of combustion than expected because of their enhanced stability. The key to solving this question is to determine which molecule is non-aromatic. Instead of going through cumbersome calculations to determine which structure fails Hűckel's rule, consider the structures. 2H-thiopyran does not have contiguous *p*-orbitals. It is not aromatic, and is expected to release the most heat during combustion. Choice D is the best answer. The other structures are aromatic and will not release as much heat. Remember that the lone pairs on pyrimidine and pyridine are not π–electrons since they do no occupy *p*-orbitals—for this reason they do not affect the π–electron count ($n = 1$) of these molecules. Eliminate choices A, B, and C.

Stand-alones (27-29)

27. **C is the best answer.** The chemotherapeutic helps to increase the activity of a tumor suppressor gene by binding to a site other than its active site to stabilize the protein. This suggests that the chemotherapeutic helps make the protein structure more rigid and stable. Additionally, the question stem notes that the activity is known to increase in an additive manner, meaning the more of the compound that is added, the stronger the increase in activity. Choice A shows a relatively modest increase before a large jump, which is not additive in nature. Choice A can be eliminated. Choice B shows no change, even though the concentration is changing, eliminating it as the best answer. The plot in choice C shows increasing activity with increasing drug dose, which is described in the question stem, likely making choice C the best answer. Similar to choice A, choice D shows a drastic increase in activity at a high concentration, but little to no effect at lower concentrations. This does not suggest an additive benefit, eliminating choice D as the best answer.

28. **C is the best answer.** The proteasome is an organelle in the cell that is responsible for breaking down proteins into individual amino acids. In order to break the proteins down, the peptide bonds between individual amino acids need to be hydrolyzed. The serine serves as the attacking nucleophile at the carbonyl carbon of the peptide bond, which creates a tetrahedral intermediate that collapses to release the nitrogen and its associated chain. The peptide bond is found between the carbonyl and the nitrogen, marked C on the diagram above. This makes choice C the best answer.

29. **D is the best answer.** Notice that the platinum atom has four other groups bonded to it. However, it is also a transition metal, meaning it has *d* orbitals that need to be filled. Pt has two lone pairs of electrons, ones that will sit oriented along the y-axis. One set will be in the positive y direction and the other in the negative y direction (see the image below). This makes the hybridization of cisplatin sp^3d^2. A linear molecule only has two bonds, with one being a triple bond and the other being a single bond. It would have *sp* hybridization, eliminating choice A. Trigonal planar geometries are bonded to three groups, typically with bond being a double bond and the other two being single bonds. Choice B can be eliminated. Tetrahedral arrangement is bonded to four groups, but all the orbitals are *s* and *p* orbitals. As Pt is a transition metal, it also has *d* orbitals, which need to be filled. It is due to these *d* orbitals that Pt takes a square planar geometry and has sp^3d^2 hybridization.

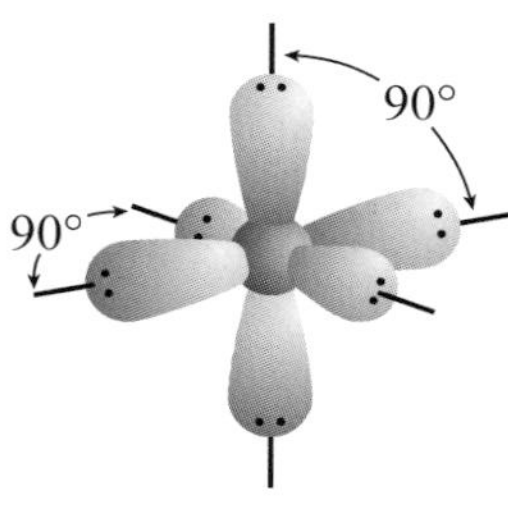

TEST 2B A&E

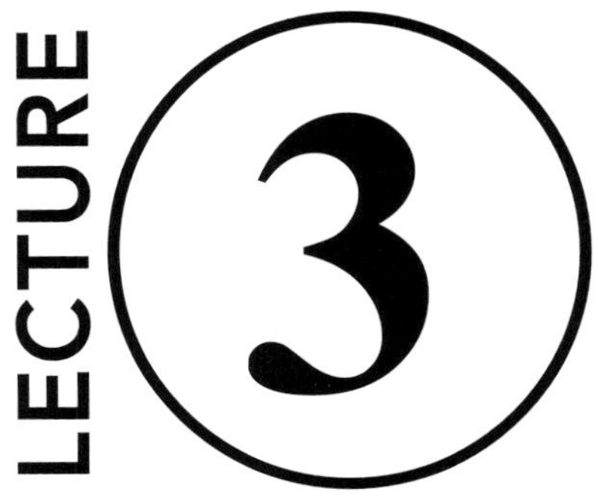

Oxygen Containing Reactions

TEST 3A

ANSWERS & EXPLANATIONS

Questions 1–59

LECTURE 3 ANSWER KEY

TEST 3A		MINI-TEST 3B	
1. B	31. A	1. A	16. C
2. D	32. A	2. B	17. B
3. B	33. B	3. D	18. D
4. D	34. C	4. A	19. A
5. C	35. D	5. C	20. D
6. D	36. D	6. C	21. D
7. B	37. A	7. D	22. D
8. C	38. B	8. C	23. A
9. A	39. C	9. C	24. C
10. B	40. D	10. A	25. D
11. B	41. A	11. D	26. C
12. B	42. B	12. C	27. D
13. A	43. D	13. B	28. D
14. D	44. D	14. D	29. A
15. A	45. A	15. B	
16. B	46. B		
17. C	47. B		
18. B	48. B		
19. B	49. D		
20. D	50. A		
21. A	51. D		
22. A	52. B		
23. B	53. B		
24. D	54. B		
25. B	55. C		
26. C	56. D		
27. B	57. B		
28. A	58. D		
29. A	59. B		
30. B			

EXPLANATIONS FOR LECTURE 3

Passage 1 (Questions 1-5)

1. **B is the best answer.** Ether cleavage can be accomplished by strongly acidic solutions. The first step of the reaction is protonation of the target ether oxygen atom in order to convert it into a better leaving group. After protonation, a nucleophile, the Cl^- anion in this particular reaction, attacks the methyl carbon via an S_N2 mechanism, ejecting a substituted phenol, and forming methyl chloride. Choice B provides both the acidic protons and the chloride anions, and is a strong answer. Ethers are impervious to bases. Although some radical addition reactions are possible with Cl_2, these reactions will not necessarily cleave the ether bond. Choice B is stronger than choice A for this reason. The ether bond is not electrophillic and is highly inert, even to alkyl halides such as methyl chloride which can generally perform substitution/addition reactions. Choice C can be eliminated. For the same reasons, the Cl^- anion is unexpected to perform any reactions with the ether bond of Compound 1 without the presence of an acidic environment. Choice D can be eliminated.

2. **D is the best answer.** Consider what has changed between reactant and product. An aldehyde group has been exchanged for a primary alcohol. No new carbon atoms have been added, ruling out the alkylating organometallic agent methylmagnesium iodide. Choice A can be eliminated. Methyl bromide will probably undergo no reaction if mixed with Compound 1. It will not exhibit any reactivity with the aldehyde group, and the chlorine atoms will not react with it. Methylbromide is a reactant that would be particularly susceptible to S_N2 reactions, but Compound 1 is not a good nucleophile, so no reaction would be expected. Choice B can be eliminated. Choice C provides reagents that can be used in an transesterification reaction, but transesterification is not pertinent to aldehydes; aldehydes lack the C–O bond which must be broken to allow the transesterification reaction to move from an unstable tetrahedral intermediate to a stable product. Moreover, an alcohol is the final product, not an ester. Choice C can be eliminated. Finally, sodium borohydride ($NaBH_4$) is a weak reducing agent, which is able to convert aldehydes/ketones into alcohols; their carbonyl carbon has a strong $\delta+$. $NaBH_4$ generally cannot reduce esters, carboxylic acids, or amides, as their carbonyl has a weaker $\delta+$. The more aggressive metal hydride reagent, lithium aluminum hydride, can reduce these less reactive molecules. To remember this difference in reactivity, use the mnemonic, "*weak* people **SOB**": **SO**dium **B**orohydride.

3. **B is the best answer.** "Aryl substitution" is organic chemistry jargon for an aromatic ring bonded to the carbon of interest. In Compound 1, the aromatic ring is bonded to the carbonyl carbon of an aldehyde. Remember in carbonyl chemistry, C1 is the carbonyl carbon. Since there are no other carbons bonded to this aldehyde, the name of this molecule will be a derivative of methanal. Choice A can be eliminated because it uses the suffix for ketones, not aldehydes. The phenyl group is bound to C1, the only carbon possible, making choice B a better answer than choice C. Choice D makes the error of counting one of the phenyl carbons as part of the aldehyde chain, when those carbons are in fact part of the aryl substituent. Choice D can be eliminated as well. Choice B is the best answer.

4. **D is the best answer.** Consider the structure of the product and of the proposed reactants. A lactol or cyclic hemiacetal has been formed from a ketone. The reaction conditions, namely, an acidic solvent and a dehydrating agent fit the profile for hemiacetal/acetal formation. Remember, this reaction releases water as a product. Removal of water shifts the equilibrium to favor the lactol. To determine which open chain form will give rise to the cyclic form, count the number of ring members, including heteroatoms. The hydroxyl group of the lactol used to be the oxygen of the carbonyl of the original ketone form. The oxygen within the ring used to be the hydroxyl group at the end of the chain. Using these as landmarks, number the ring as shown, and find the answer choice that contains the same number of future ring members.

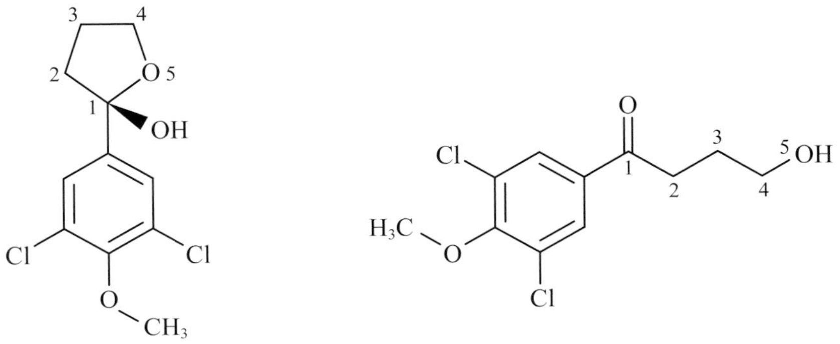

Choice D is the best answer. The other answer choices have either too many or too few atoms in their chain to form a ring of the appropriate size. Counting atoms is often a quick and easy way to eliminate weaker answer choices. Choices A, B, and C can be eliminated.

5. **C is the best answer.** Sodium borohydride is a relatively weak reducing agent. It can reduce aldehydes and ketones since their carbonyl carbon has a strong δ+, but it generally cannot reduce esters, carboxylic acids, or amides, as their carbonyl has a weaker δ+. Choice A can be eliminated as both Compound 1 and Compound 3 are capable of being reduced with sodium borohydride. Metalorganic reagents are great for performing nucleophilic addition reactions at carbonyl carbons. However, this reactivity is not shared with alcohols. Instead, the highly basic alkyl part of the metalorganic reagent deprotonates the alcohol, forming an alkoxide metal salt. Choice B can be eliminated. Alcohols are far more polar than their analogous aldehydes. As a result they have a higher boiling point. Moreover, the alcohol shown here has a greater molecular weight than does Compound 1. These two factors together are likely to increase Compound 2's boiling point relative to Compound 1's. Choice C may be the best answer, but, rule out choice D before choosing it. Compound 1 and Compound 3 have an electrophilic carbonyl which can transiently form bonds to alcohols with the loss of water. The acid catalyst is necessary to initiate the hemiacetalization reaction for both of these compounds and the desiccating agent shifts the equilibrium to favor the hemiacetal. Choice D is a weaker answer and can be eliminated, making choice C the best answer.

Passage 2 (Questions 6-10)

6. **D is the best answer.** $LiAlH_4$ (LAH) is a strong reducing agent capable of reducing aldehydes, ketones, and carboxylic acid derivatives. There are two carbonyl groups on oseltamivir: the ester and the amide. With two molecules of LAH for every one molecule of oseltamivir, two reductions may occur. Both carbonyls would be expected to be reduced by LAH. In the reaction, LAH generates a hydrogen anion, known as a hydride, which attacks the carbonyl carbon to form a new carbon-hydrogen bond and breaks the pi-bond of the double-bonded oxygen. If there are any leaving groups attached to the carbonyl carbon, the carbon-oxygen pi-bond will re-form as the bond between the carbonyl and the leaving group breaks. This will result in an aldehyde. If there is no leaving group, the oxygen is protonated and an alcohol is formed.

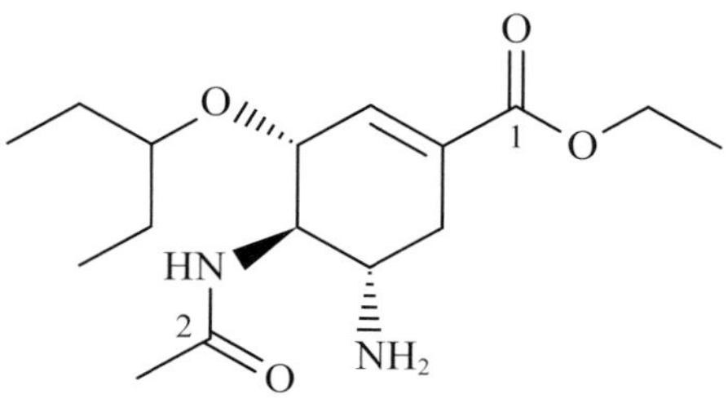

Carbon 1 in the ester has an ethoxyl bonded to it. When attacked by the hydride, this group leaves as ethanol, creating an aldehyde. When carbon 2 in the amide group is attacked, the nitrogen of the amide is protonated to form an amino group and is capable of acting as a leaving group. Carbon 2 will become a separate aldehyde that is now separate from the main molecule. This creates the structure seen in choice D. Because choice A does not include the reduction of the amide group, it is not a strong answer. Choice B shows an unchanged structure, so it can be eliminated. This would be correct if the student used $NaBH_4$, which is a weaker reducing agent that is incapable of reducing carboxylic acid derivatives. Choice C shows two hydroxyl groups where the ester group was. If the LAH were to work twice on the ester, it would convert it to a primary alcohol, not a geminal diol, so it is a weaker answer.

7. **B is the best answer.** The passage states that oseltamivir is activated in the liver after it undergoes ester hydrolysis. In this process, water attacks the carbonyl carbon of the ester and the alkoxide group that is bound to the carbonyl carbon acts as a leaving group and is eventually protonated to become an alcohol. This group is replaced by the water, which is deprotonated to become a hydroxyl group. A hydroxyl group bound to a carbonyl group forms a carboxylic acid. An amide group has a nitrogen atom bound to a carbonyl group. A new nitrogen atom would not be attached during ester hydrolysis, so choice A is a weak answer. Hydrolysis is a general term for a reaction that uses water to break a bond between two molecules. Ester hydrolysis adds a hydroxyl group to a carbonyl group, forming a carboxylic acid. This makes choice B a strong answer. An amine group consists of a nitrogen atom bound to at least one carbon atom that is not a carbonyl. As in choice A, ester hydrolysis would not add a new nitrogen to oseltamivir, so choice C can be eliminated. An ester group would also not be formed in ester hydrolysis, which uses water to remove ester groups. A transesterification reaction where a different alcohol was used as a nucleophile could result in the formation of a new ester. Since water is the nucleophile in this reaction, choice D is a weak answer.

8. **C is the best answer.** The best way to approach this question is by considering which of the atoms attached to the hydrogen can best handle a negative charge after the hydrogen leaves. This reasoning is similar to the reasoning behind deciding which group is the least nucleophilic because groups that are weak nucleophiles are very stable with a negative charge. Factors that stabilize negative charges include having a large electron shell, high electronegativity, and the ability to spread out the negative charge through resonance. Hydrogen 1 is a tempting choice because the negative charge can be stabilized by resonance, but carbanions are not very stable because carbon is not very electronegative. This eliminates choice A. While hydrogen 2 may seem like a possibly correct choice because the nitrogen it is bound to is electronegative, this nitrogen is unable to form resonance structures to stabilize the negative charge. This makes choice B a weaker answer. Hydrogen 3, the hydrogen bound to the nitrogen in the amide group, is most acidic. Nitrogen is very electronegative and it can also form resonance structures to spread the negative charge to the oxygen in the carbonyl group. Oxygen is also very electronegative, making this a stable resonance structure. As a result, choice C is a strong answer. For hydrogen 4, while the carbon can form resonance structures with the oxygen of the carbonyl group to form an enolate, carbon is not as electronegative as nitrogen, so choice D can be eliminated, which leaves choice C as the best answer.

9. **A is the best answer.** The carboxylic acid group of shikimic acid is the only functional group that can undergo esterification. Esterification occurs when alcohols or alkoxides attack a carboxylic acid derivative. Esters have about the same amount of reactivity as carboxylic acids, which would make esterification of shikimic acid a process with a low yield that would require a very large excess of alcohol to push the reaction to completion. $SOCl_2$, the reagent in choice A, can react with the carboxylic acid to form an acyl chloride, which is the most reactive carboxylic acid derivative. This will quickly react with an alcohol to form an ester. This makes choice A a strong answer. $NaBH_4$ is a reducing agent, which is useful for the reduction of aldehydes and ketones. Because this reagent would not aid in the esterification of shikimic acid, choice B can be eliminated. $KMnO_4$ is an oxidizing agent, which would react with shikimic acid's hydroxyl groups to form ketones. This would not aid in the esterification reaction, so choice C is a weak answer. Ethanol is the specific alcohol that would be used in this esterification, but high amounts of ethanol would be required to push the esterification reaction to completion. Because of this, choice D can be eliminated.

10. **B is the best answer.** Monosaccharides can be classified by their number of carbons and by whether they have an aldehyde (aldose) or ketone (ketose) functional group in their straight chain form. To classify a monosaccharide in its cyclic form as an aldose or ketose, it is necessary to look at the anomeric carbon, which is found next to the oxygen that is participating in the ring. The anomeric carbon is usually depicted in diagrams to the right of the oxygen in the ring, but this is not always the case, and may sometimes be found to the left of the oxygen. The anomeric carbon will always be the carbon next to the oxygen in the ring that has a hydroxyl group bound to it. An easy way to remember carbon which is the anomeric carbon, look for the carbon that is bonded to two oxygen molecules as this will be the anomeric carbon. Aldoses will have hydrogen and a hydroxyl group bound to the anomeric carbon while ketoses will have a hydroxyl group and an alkyl or acyl group bound to the anomeric carbon. For neuraminic acid, the anomeric carbon is the carbon to the left of the oxygen because the carbon to the right of the oxygen is not bound to a hydroxyl group. The anomeric carbon is bound to both a hydroxyl group and an acyl group, so it must be a ketone when in its straight chain form. This means neuraminic acid is a ketose. Also, there are nine carbons in total in the molecule, so neuraminic acid is a ketononose. Because choice A describes neuraminic acid as having six carbons and an aldose, it can be eliminated. Choice B correctly describes neuraminic acid as a ketononose and is the best answer. Choice C correctly describes neuraminic acid as a nonose, but it mistakenly characterizes it as a aldose, so it is a weaker answer. Because choice D mislabels neuraminic acid as having six carbons and as being an aldose, so it can be eliminated.

Passage 3 (Questions 11-14)

11. **B is the best answer.** Consider the effects of adding dilute acid to a mixture of Compound 1 dissolved in Compound 2. The protons introduced to the solution will immediately protonate the amino groups on both Compound 1 and Compound 2. This will cause each to gain a positive charge and be paired with an anion from the acid. Such a dramatic change in polarity of each compound is expected to reduce their solubility in the solvent, which is most likely also Compound 2. This would remove them from the reaction and hurt the overall yield. Choice B best states this idea and is the best answer. The addition of acid only increases the electrophilicity of a carbonyl carbon when it can protonate the carbonyl oxygen. As discussed, the carbonyl oxygen in Compound 1 will not be protonated, and no increases in the electrophilicity of Compound 1 are expected. Choice A can be eliminated. Nucleophilicity refers to the tendency of positively charged molecules to be attracted to the reactant. Following protonation, the last thing Compounds 1 and 2 will try to gain is another positive charge. Choice C can be eliminated. During this transesterification reaction, water is not a leaving group: methanol is. Choice D can be eliminated.

TEST 3A A&E

12. **B is the best answer.** Pyridnium chlorochromate, or "PPC" as it is fondly known in organic chemistry classrooms, is a fairly gentle oxidizing agent. It can oxidize primary alcohols to aldehydes and secondary alcohols to ketones. It is not strong enough to oxidize a material all the way to a carboxylic acid, and will not be the best answer. Eliminate choice A. Sodium dichromate, water, and sulfuric acid is a very strong oxidizing mixture. Sodium dichromate is more powerful, and can oxidize benzylic, or methyl groups directly bonded to benzene, C–H bonds to carbonyl compounds. It will also oxidize alcohols all the way to carboxylic acids. It has the strength to perform Reaction 2 and will be the best answer. Lithium aluminum hydride is a powerful reducing agent. It adds hydrogen to molecules, and will not be the best answer. Ozone is an oxidizing agent used during the cleavage of alkenes into carbonyl compounds. P-nitrotoluene has three double bonds, and they react with ozone analogously to alkenes. The primary difference is that complete cleavage and the resulting carbonyl products are not obtained until the unstable triozonide product is mixed with water. Nonetheless, ozone will not react with the methyl group of toluene, so this oxidation will not provide the target product. Choice D can be eliminated.

13. **A is the best answer.** NaOEt is added to this reaction to deprotonate Compound 2 so that Compound 2 can add to the carbonyl carbon in Compound 1. After the attack, Compound 1 and Compound 2 form a tetrahedral intermediate. This tetrahedral intermediate either collapses back to the starting materials, or ejects an ethoxide ion, ultimately forming the transesterified product. Since the ethoxide anion is regenerated during this reaction, it does not undergo a net reaction, but rather only facilitates the combination of Compound 1 and Compound 2. In other words, NaOEt is a catalyst. It allows the reaction to be performed with a reduction in activation energy, shown as X on the graph. Eliminate choice D. The only net reaction that occurs is the esterification of Compound 1 with Compound 2. There is a fixed energy change associated with this reaction. Adding a catalyst will not affect this fixed energy change, represented by Y on the graph. Eliminate choices B and C. Since Y remains the same and X is reduced, choice A is the best answer.

14. **D is the best answer.** Acyl halides are extremely reactive to electrophiles. In a basic solution of sodium ethoxide, the sodium ethoxide will rapidly consume the acyl halide, and prevent it from ever reacting with the alcohol. Whatever remains of the acyl halide will be able to form tetracaine with the alcohol, but this reaction scheme is very inefficient and will lead to wasted precursors. Choice A can be eliminated. The carboxylic acid shown in choice B will also be consumed by the sodium ethoxide solution, resulting in a very non-reactive carboxylate ion. Choice B can be eliminated. If the reagents in choice C undergo a transesterification, the carbonyl will be too far from the aromatic group—the resulting structure is not tetracaine. Finally, choice D will undergo a transesterification and form tetracaine properly. Choice D is the best answer.

Stand-alones (Questions 15-18)

15. **A is the best answer.** This substitution reaction relies on the ability for X to act as a leaving group when the hydroxyl group attacks. Since fluorine, by virtue of its more strongly basic behavior, is a poorer leaving group than the other halogens, tosyl fluoride will least readily undergo this reaction, and choice A is the best answer. When thinking about the trends in halogen leaving group ability, remember the more basic, i.e poorer, leaving groups will have weaker conjugate acids. In order of acidity, HF < HCl < HBr < HI.

16. **B is the best answer.** In this reaction scheme, the chloride ion of step 2 acts as the nucleophile. While step 1 is capable of producing chloride ions, these are not better nucleophiles than chloride ions that would normally be found in a solution, which makes choice A a weaker option. In step 1, the alcohol is converted into a tosylate, which has the capacity to resonate. This resonance makes the tosylate a better leaving group since it can better stabilize the negative charge that is formed, making choice B a strong answer. As mentioned above, resonance is achieved by converting the alcohol to a tosylate, but remember that S_N2 reactions occur via a single step and do not form a carbocation intermediate like S_N1 reactions, making choice C a weaker option. The tosylate formed is larger and more sterically hindered than the primary alcohol, making choice D a weaker choice than choice B.

17. **C is the best answer.** An alkyl alcohol is any alkyl group attached to an alcohol, and can be approximated as R–OH. Since there is an OH group, hydrogen bonding is possible, and choice A can be eliminated. The hydrogen attached to the oxygen is weakly acidic, making choice B a weaker answer. The oxygen–carbon bond has a large electronegativity difference, which gives the bond polarity. Since an alkyl alcohol does not have any double bonds or atoms with lone pairs near it, it will not be able to participate in resonance. Choice C is the best answer.

18. **B is the best answer.** Propanoic acid and butanol have a similar molecular weight of about 74 g/mol. Propanoic acid is a 3-carbon carboxylic acid while butanol is a 4-carbon alcohol. A carboxylic acid is capable of forming two hydrogen bonds with another carboxylic acid, essentially forming a dimer and effectively doubling the molecular weight of the molecule. This increase in effective molecular weight as well as the ability to form two hydrogen bonds while alcohols can only form one hydrogen bond, will result in propanoic acid having a higher boiling point, so choice A can be eliminated. The dimerization of carboxylic acids allows them to be soluble in nonpolar solvents. Carboxylic acids with less than 5 carbons are usually soluble in water as well. In contrast, butanol would not be expected to be very soluble in hexane which is a nonpolar solvent but slightly soluble in water, so choice B is a strong answer. The carbonyl carbon of carboxylic acids is very reactive and readily undergoes nucleophilic attack. While butanol is capable of participating in S_N2 reactions, OH is not the best leaving group and would require the assistance of an acidic environment to facilitate a nucleophilic attack. Choice C is a weaker answer for this reason and can be eliminated. As mentioned earlier, propanoic acid is actually capable of forming two hydrogen bonds due to the presence of a partial negative charge on the carbonyl oxygen and the polarity of the O–H bond of the hydroxyl group. Choice D can be eliminated, so choice B is the best answer.

Passage 4 (Questions 19-23)

19. **B is the best answer.** Phenyllithium is an organometallic reagent. These reagents often act as nucleophillic reducing agents because the organic-metal bond is weak, with a tremendous $\delta-$ on the organic group. To predict the reactivity of these molecules, pretend they are a carbanion-metal salt. As such, any protic solvent is at risk for rapid deprotonation, consuming the organometallic reagent, and preventing the reduction of the ketone group of Compound 1. Likewise, any electrophillic solvent may become reduced by phenyllithium. Benzene is inert, and will not interfere with the alkylation of Compound 1. Choice A can be eliminated. Ethyl acetate has an electrophillic carbonyl group which can be alkylated by phenyllithium. The resulting ketone product is *even more* electrophilic and will again undergo alkylation by another molecule of phenyllithium, resulting in a tertiary alcohol upon dilute acid work-up. Thus, every mole of ethyl acetate consumes two moles of phenyllithium. This side reaction prevents the alkylation of the original target, Compound 1. Choice B is an unsuitable solvent for this reaction, but the other answer choices should be ruled out before choosing it. Both hexane and diethyl ether are inert, and will not interfere with the alkylation of Compound 1. Choices C and D can be eliminated. Choice B is the best answer.

20. **D is the best answer.** Disregard the first part of this IUPAC name, and instead focus on the end, as this is the only difference in three of the answer choices. The names of esters are derived from their parent carboxylic acids, except the ending, "-oic acid", is replaced with "-oate". When naming a parent carboxylic acid chain, the carbonyl carbon counts in the chain length. Thus, MPPP has a three carbon or "propanoate" chain. Choices A and C stem from not counting the carbonyl carbon when calculating the parent chain length, which would result in a parent chain that is one short of the correct length. Choices A and C can be eliminated. Choice B improperly counts the ether oxygen which should not be included in the parent carbon chain length. Choice D is the best answer because it correctly identifies the parent chain as having a three-carbon chain.

21. **A is the best answer.** Consider the reaction:

Propionic acid + Propionic acid ⇌ (?) Propionic anhydride + H_2O

Carboxylic acids are more stable than anhydrides. This is evident in the greater reactivity that anhydrides possess. In general, to bring a stable molecule to a higher energy state, energy must be added. Since temperature is a proxy measurement of energy, increasing the temperature results in increasing the energy of the system. Most likely, higher temperatures are required, making choice C a weaker answer. Adding a catalytic base to this reaction would hinder this reaction by deprotonating the propionic acid. Deprotonation of propionic acid would form the propionate anion which has a weaker $\delta+$ on its carbonyl carbon, which would inhibit the addition of the hydroxyl group of one propionic acid molecule to the carbonyl of another. Choices B and D can be eliminated on this basis. Acids are effective catalysts in this reaction as they protonate the carbonyl oxygen resulting in a greater $\delta+$ on the carbonyl carbon. This change converts propionic acid into a better electrophile, and makes the carbonyl carbon more susceptible to nucleophillic attack. Since anhydride formation is an equilibrium reaction that forms water as a product, water removal with a desiccating agent shifts the reaction to the right, further favoring anhydride formation. Choice A is the best answer.

22. **A is the best answer.** The first step in solving this problem is to draw the structure of 4-methyl-pentanoic anhydride. Remember, the name of symmetric anhydrides is derived from the name of the parent carboxylic acid, but the word "acid" is replaced with the word anhydride. The numbering scheme of carboxylic acids is based on the most oxidized carbon, which is the carbonyl carbon, being C1. Draw 4-methyl-pentanoic acid and combine it with itself, as shown:

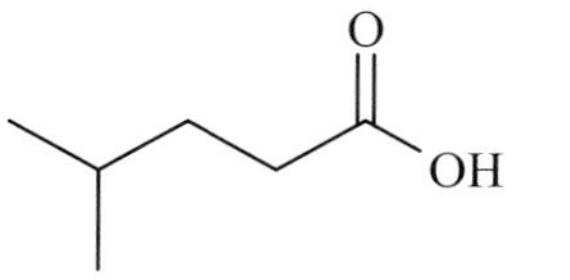

4-methyl-pentanoic acid

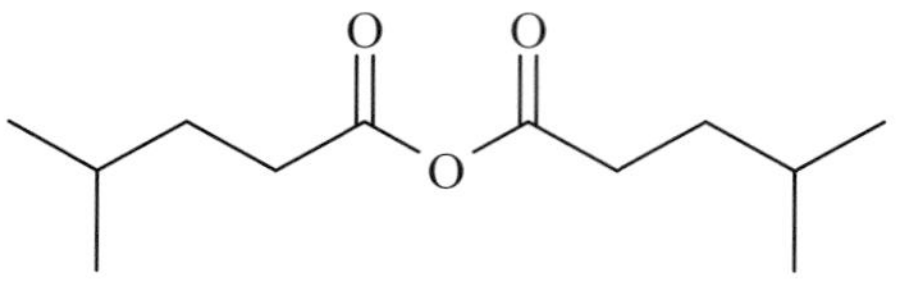

4-methyl-pentanoic anhydride

Choice B would be chosen if the parent chain was numbered with C1 being at the end of the parent chain furthest from the carbonyl carbon. Choice B can be eliminated. Remember that the carbonyl carbon "counts" as one of the carbons in the chain of a carboxylic acid. In other words, pentanoic acid has a chain of five carbons, not six. Choices C and D make the mistake of not counting the carbonyl carbon as a member of the parent chain and can be eliminated as well. Choice A is the best answer.

23. **B is the best answer.** Reaction 3 only competes with Reaction 2 when the temperature of the solution rises above 30°C. Remember that temperature is a proxy measurement of the average kinetic energy of a system. In other words, until the energy of Reaction 3 is increased, it does not compete with Reaction 2. This means that the activation energy barrier of Reaction 3 is greater than that of Reactions 2. Reaction 3 will have a greater peak than will Reaction 2, so choices C and D can be eliminated. Choice A implies that Reaction 2 has a lower activation energy barrier and a more thermodynamically stable product. According to choice A, Reaction 3 is both kinetically and thermodynamically unfavorable. Systems tend to progress towards stability, and if choice A accurately describes these reactions, then Reaction 3 would occur negligibly; there is neither a kinetic or thermodynamic reason for it to outcompete Reaction 2. Choice B on the other hand shows that Reaction 3 is kinetically unfavorable, but thermodynamically more stable. Under higher temperature conditions, where the activation energy barrier can be overcome, the greater stability of the product of Reaction 3 drives the reaction forward. Choice B is better than choice A because it describes why a kinetically unfavorable reaction would occur. Choice B is the best answer.

Passage 5 (Questions 24-27)

24. **D is the best answer.** Benzyl chloroformate is an acyl halide. It is extremely reactive to nucleophilic substitution reactions and is used to produce carboxylic acid derivatives. In particular, reaction of an acyl halide with a carboxylic acid produces an anhydride, and the reaction of an acyl halide with an amine produces an amide. If Compound 1 were first exposed to benzyl chloroformate, the benzyl chloroformate would react with both hydroxyl groups and the amine of Compound 1. It would form two anhydride groups on each side, as well as an amide in the middle of the structure. In fact, the amino group is expected to undergo acylation first, before the hydroxyl groups, because amines are stronger nucleophiles. Choice A can be eliminated. Next, exposure of this dianhydride/amide containing molecule to benzyl alcohol and catalytic acid would result in the formation of Compound 3. Since compound 3 is regenerated and demonstrates the capacity to undergo selective hydrolysis, choices B and C can be eliminated. The amide functionality would not be hurt since amides are more stable than esters. In general, it is possible, with harsh conditions, to convert an ester into an amide, but not the reverse. Compound 3 can undergo selective hydrolysis. Thus, reversing the order of these steps does not hurt the synthesis. Choice D is the best answer.

25. **B is the best answer.** A dipeptide contains two amino acids and a single peptide bond. A tripeptide contains three amino acids and two peptide bonds. This molecule only contains a single peptide bond and is only linking two amino acids together. For it to be a tripeptide, there would need to be at least three nitrogen atoms present in the molecule. Choices A and D can be eliminated. To distinguish between choices B and C, the name of the residue to the left of phenylalanine needs to be determined. If the stereocenter of each amino acid is a point of origin, then glutamic acid has its carboxylic acid in the γ-position and aspartic acid has its carboxylic acid in the β-position. See their structures below:

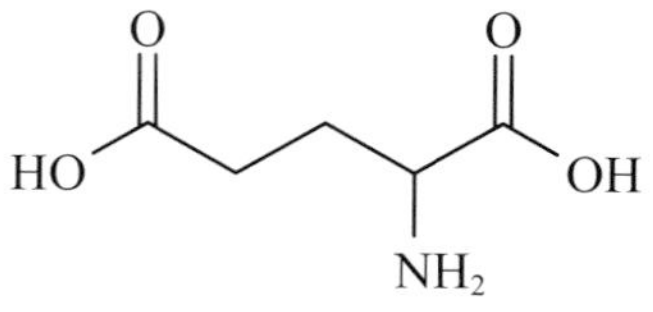

Glutamic acid

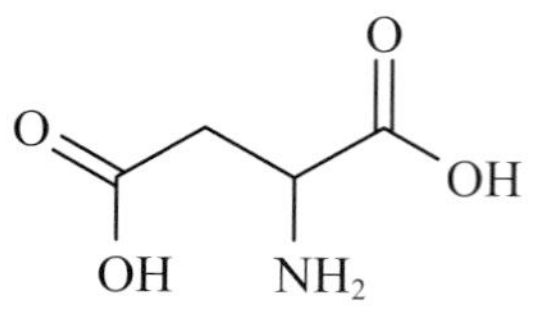

Aspartic acid

A useful mnemonic is that aspartic acid is smaller, and that is why it is alphabetically first—this is not actually the reason these amino acids were named, but it's a good way to remember the difference between them. Since aspartame also has its carboxylic acid in the β-position, choice B is the best answer, and choice C can be eliminated.

26. **C is the best answer.** Reaction 3 introduces a protecting group onto the amine, transiently turning it into an amide. Without this protecting group, heating Compound 2 could result in a variety of undesirable side products. For instance, two molecules of Compound 2 could dimerize via an amide bond, an intramolecular amidification reaction may occur resulting in a β-lactam, or three molecules of Compound 2 could trimerize via amide bonds. Using benzyl chloroformate to convert the amine of Compound 2 into an amide prevents these undesirable side reactions from occurring. This is especially important because the presence of catalytic base encourages ester aminolysis—the formation of an amide through cleaving an ester with an amine. Although Reaction 3 has more than a catalytic quantity of base, and base mediated ester hydrolysis is more likely to occur, the competing amidification reaction could still decrease the yield of the desired product. For this reason, it is necessary to first protect the amine in Compound 2. The best answer to this question will demonstrate a product that arises from failure to protect the amine functionality. Choices A and B are both undesirable side products, but they come as a consequence of the base mediated hydrolysis. Protecting the amine by performing Reaction 2 will have a minimal effect on preventing these side reactions, so its purpose cannot be to prevent these side products. Choices A and B can be eliminated. Since no inversion of absolute configuration is expected, choice D can be eliminated, which leaves Choice C as the best answer.

27. **B is the best answer.** This question is really asking, "What functional groups in aspartame are prone to destruction by acidic conditions? What products come as a result?" Looking at the structure, the methyl ester on the far right can b hydrolyzed into a carboxylic acid and methanol by the strongly acidic conditions. This reaction is the reverse of a traditional Fischer esterification. Option I will be part of the best answer. Eliminate choice A. The next functional group to be hydrolyzed by the acid is the amide bond in the middle of the molecule. Hydrolysis of this bond results in the release of two amino acids, aspartic acid and phenylalanine. Remember that the carboxyl terminus of phenylalanine has already been formed by releasing its methyl group. Option II will be part of the best answer. No other parts of this molecule are subject to alteration under these conditions, and no other products are expected. The R group in glutamic acid is one methyl group longer than the R group in aspartic acid—the structures of the amino acids I a commonly tested subject on the MCAT®. Option III can be eliminated, removing choices C and D. Choose the best answer, choice B.

TEST 3A A&E

Stand-alones (Questions 28-31)

28. **A is the best answer.** The reaction described in the question is between 4-toluenesulfonyl chloride (TosCl) and an alcohol. This is a classic way of making an alcohol group into a better leaving group, so it can participate in a substitution reaction. In this reaction, after the formation of the tosyl group, a Cl ion acts as a nucleophile in an S_N2 fashion. In an S_N2 reaction, a nucleophile attacks a carbon with a strong leaving group attached. Once this nucleophilic attack occurs, the leaving group is kicked off. S_N2 reactions result in inversion of the stereochemistry of the molecule being attacked and are more likely to occur when both the nucleophile and electrophile are not hindered by sterics, or bulky substituents. Since it is a substitution reaction, the reactant can be drawn as the structure provided, but with an OH group replacing the Cl atom, as seen below.

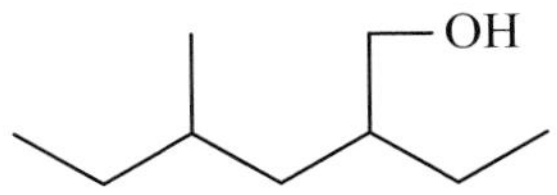

OH

All of the answer choices are alcohols, so this question requires knowledge of the nomenclature rules. The first step is identifying the largest, continuous carbon chain that contains the highest priority group, which is the OH molecule. For this molecule, the parent chain is a six-carbon chain, so the molecule is a substituted hexanol. Choices B and C can be eliminated. Choices A and D correctly identify the parent chain but start numbering the carbons at opposite ends. Numbering should always result in the highest priority group having its lowest possible number. Since choice D has the OH group on carbon 6 and choice A has it on carbon 1, choice D can be eliminated. Choice A is the best answer.

29. **A is the best answer.** The strain of the small four atom amide ring makes it easily broken when exposed to heat. Choice B can be eliminated because cyclic esters are called lactones, not lactams. Choice C is a weaker answer because lactams are not aromatic compounds. Choice D can be eliminated because lowering the temperature would make something like a strained ring *more* stable, instead of less stable.

30. B is the best answer. All four of the compounds listed in the answer choices are either a carboxylic acid derivatives or a carboxylic acid (choice A). The two major factors to consider for boiling point estimation are the size of the molecule and the strength of the intermolecular forces. Larger the molecule have higher boiling points. Molecules with stronger intermolecular forces will also have a higher boiling point. The molecular weight of choices A and B are roughly the same at about 60 g/mol. Ethanoyl chloride and methyl acetate are both larger molecules, but are not significantly larger, with both molecules having a molecular mass between 75 and 80 g/mol. When comparing boiling points of different molecules, assessing the strength of the intermolecular forces is critical. Since choices C and D are unable to form hydrogen bonds, these molecules are expected to have a much lower boiling point than a molecule of similar mass that is capable of forming a strong hydrogen bond. Both acetic acid and ethanamide are capable of participating in hydrogen bonding, so choices C and D can be eliminated. Both carboxylic acids and amides have unusually high boiling points for molecules of their size due to the hydrogen bonds they can form. Ethanamide is capable of forming up to three hydrogen bonds since it has two N–H bonds and one polar carbonyl bond that is also capable of hydrogen bonding. Since acetic acid is only capable of forming two hydrogen bonds, it is expected to have a lower boiling point than ethanamide, so choice A can be eliminated. Choice B is the best answer.

31. A is the best answer. Since this esterification reaction requires a nucleophilic attack of an alkoxide ion or alcohol molecule on a carbonyl, there are a couple of potential problems that can arise. If the α-carbon (neighboring carbon) of the carbonyl group has large groups bonded to it, then those groups can sterically hinder a nucleophilic attack on that carbonyl. In the case of this reaction, the 2 methyl groups will provide enough steric hindrance that the only way to overcome this is to make the carbonyl extremely electrophilic or to make the nucleophile very strong and small. Changing the carboxylic acid so the methyl groups are further away from the carbonyl will decrease the steric hindrance and increase the likelihood of the esterification occurring, so choice A is a strong answer. The adjustment in choice B will increase the size and bulkiness of the nucleophile, which would further impede the reaction from occurring, so it can be eliminated. Amide groups are more stable than carboxylic acids. Another way to state this property is that the amide moiety is a poor leaving group. This explains why hydrolysis of amides only occurs under extreme conditions. The reaction is much more likely to result in the formation of an ester if a carboxylic acid is used, so choice C can be eliminated. A catalytic amount of acid would be expected to increase the likelihood of this reaction by increasing the electrophilicity of the carbonyl by increasing the polarity of the bond after the oxygen is protonated. A base, on the other hand, is not expected to increase the polarity of this bond and would not improve the likelihood of this reaction occurring. Choice D can be eliminated.

TEST 3A A&E

Passage 6 (Questions 32-35)

32. A is the best answer. Compound 1 is an enol. Enols exist in equilibrium with ketones, and this equilibrium favors the ketone. This explains the need to add acid to the solution to facilitate enol formation. During the tautomerization reaction, which interconverts the two structures, the hydroxyl group of the enol is deprotonated, forming a carbonyl, and the unsaturated bond attacks the proton. Choice A is a strong answer because it is the product of this reaction. In particular, it has the correct R group bonded to the carbonyl. Choice B reverses the positions of the R groups. Choice C shows a structure in which two hydrogen atoms have been removed from the original structure rather than the one that is moved during tautomerization. Since tautomers are constitutional isomers, a structure which has lost atoms cannot be a valid tautomer. Choice D is not a ketone, which would be the tautomer of an enol. Choice A is the best answer.

33. B is the best answer. The mechanism which describes iminium formation is included below:

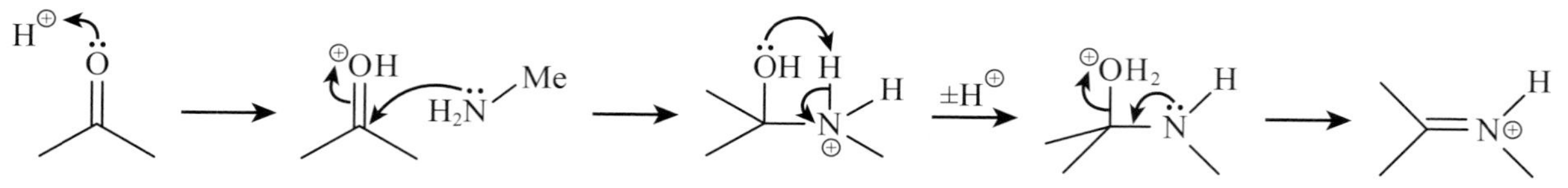

In the second line of the mechanism it is apparent that water is a leaving group. Eliminate choice A. After nitrogen acts as a nucleophile and attacks, the resulting hemiaminal is tetrahedral, not planar. Choice B may be the best answer. Choice C describes the first step of this mechanism and should be eliminated. Choice D is also part of the mechanism and should be eliminated. Since choice B is the only mechanistic step that does not occur, it is the best answer.

34. C is the best answer. Choice A is a weaker answer because all kinds of carboxylic acids take advantage of this resonance stabilization after protonation. The question stem is concerned with what is unique about Compound 2 that gives it this reactivity. Greek letters are often used to describe the locations of carbons on carboxylic acids. The α carbon is the carbon adjacent to the carbonyl carbon, and the next atom away from the carbonyl carbon is the β carbon, and so one. This notation scheme is most often seen with carboxylic acids, but other molecules can use it too. Just remember that the α carbon is the one that is bonded to the functional group of interest. Compound 2 is a β-keto acid because it has a ketone in the position of the β-carbon. Some β-keto acids actually form a 6 member intermediate during decarboxylation, but not a five member intermediate, so choice B is a weaker answer. β-keto acids use resonance to stabilize the anionic intermediate, so choice C is probably the best answer, if it is better than choice D. Choice D is weaker than choice C because Compound 2 is not a γ-keto acid, the ketone on it is in the β-position. Choice C is the best answer.

35. D is the best answer. Consider the functional groups that are in this reaction. A 3° amine, an alcohol, a carboxylic acid, and catalytic acid. The 3° amine cannot act as a nucleophile because after attacking the carbonyl carbon, it cannot undergo deprotonation to lose the resulting unstable +1 charge. Since the amine will not attack, the only remaining viable reaction pathways is esterification. In this esterification, the alcohol on tropine will attack the carbonyl carbon of tropic acid. The formal term for an acid catalyzed esterification between an alcohol and a carboxylic acid is a "Fischer-Speier esterification." Since the alcohol of one species will only attack the carbonyl carbon of another, choice A is a weaker answer. It features an ether formation between two alcohol groups on each of the molecules. Choice B can be eliminated for the same reason. These reaction conditions will result in the formation of an ester at the carbonyl carbon, not an ether at the hydroxyl group. Choice C is unlikely because the 3° amine cannot act as an effective nucleophile. Choice D is the best answer because it represents the product of a proper esterification reaction between the alcohol of tropine and the carbonyl carbon of tropic acid.

Passage 7 (Questions 36-39)

36. D is the best answer. Although an aqueous solution with an acid may be helpful for deprotection via hydrolysis of the acetate esters, the acidic conditions will lead to an undesired side reaction: the hydrolysis of the acetal linkage between each of the sugar subunits in sucralose. For this reason, basic deprotection should be employed to obtain the product, as acetals are impervious to bases. Choices A and B can be eliminated. Since choices C and D both use bases to accomplish deprotection, consider which choice will better perform the halogenation reaction. Sodium chloride is unable to convert an alcohol into a haloalkane. Eliminate choice C. The process of elimination makes choice D the best answer. Sulfuryl chloride, SO_2Cl_2, much like thionyl chloride, converts alcohols into haloalkanes. Choice D is the best answer.

37. A is the best answer. Remember that a reducing sugar is a sugar that has a free aldehyde or free ketone group in its open chain form. This group acts as an electron donor in certain diagnostic reactions such as Tollen's test. For a sugar to be able to isomerize into its open chain form, its anomeric carbon must contain a hemiacetal or hemiketal. In the case of a polysaccharide, at least one of the sugar residues must have a hemiacetal or hemiketal functionality. Sucrose has both anomeric carbons bound together via an acetal linkage. As a result, sucrose does not contain a hemiacetal or hemiketal, and there is no possibility of either sugar residue isomerizing into an open chain form. Sucrose is a nonreducing sugar, so choices C and D can be eliminated on this basis. The simple nomenclature rule of α = hydroxyl group pointing down and β = hydroxyl group pointing up for describing an anomeric carbon cannot be applied to the fructose residue of sucrose, as this rule only applies when a sugar is drawn in its conventional form, with C6 pointing up. This fructose residue is drawn "upside down" relative to its conventional structure. Imagine rotating the entire sucrose molecule such that C6 of the fructose residue points up, to determine the configuration of the anomeric carbon of the fructose residue. After mentally rotating the structure, realize that the anomeric carbon has a hydroxyl group pointing up and thus has the β configuration. Choice A is the best answer, and choice B can be eliminated.

38. B is the best answer. After deprotonation of the hydroxyl group of C6 of the glucose residue, an alkoxide is in close proximity to an ester. These reagents are present during base catalyzed transesterification reactions between an alcohol and an ester. Conversely, basic ester hydrolysis occurs between a metal hydroxide and an ester, with no alkoxide. Since the reagents here do not result in ester hydrolysis, choices C and D can be eliminated. To distinguish between choices A and B, consider the reactivity of the alkoxide: it will donate its negative charge to the nearest electrophile, which in this case is the carbonyl of the acetate ester on C4 of the glucose residue. After donating its electrons, a tetrahedral intermediate will be formed, and one of the bonding pair electrons from the carbonyl double bond rests entirely on the oxygen atom. The ring formed between all of these structures has 6 members, consisting of four carbon atoms and two oxygen atoms, making choice B better than choice A. Choice B is the best answer.

39. **C is the best answer.** Look at Reaction 1. The first step involves adding triphenylmethyl chloride in a pyridine solvent. Draw the structure of triphenylmethyl chloride as shown:

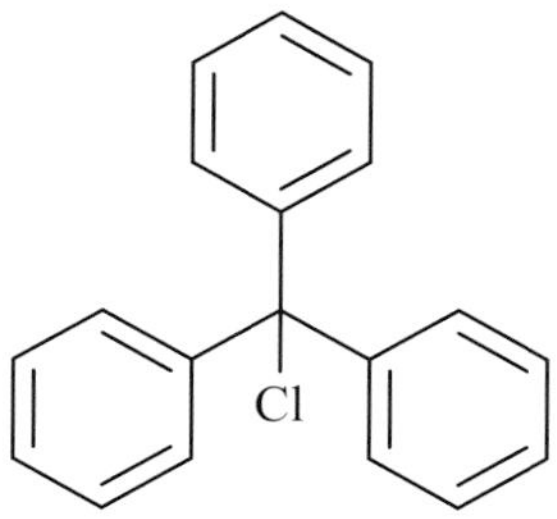

Triphenyl methyl chloride

The center of this highly conjugated structure is a 3° carbon. If "normal" 3° carbons can undergo S_N1 reactions, then a system where the positive charge can be delocalized over three benzene rings is especially capable of participating in S_N1 reactions. Based on the reaction shown in the passage, it seems that this reagent only leads to the etherification of 1° alcohols. Otherwise, every hydroxyl group on the sucrose molecule would be converted into a triphenyl ether. If this occurred, after initial conversion to triphenyl ethers, subsequent esterification with acetic anhydride would be impossible. Since esterification with acetic anhydride *did* occur on every hydroxyl group except the 1° alcohols, it can be concluded that this reagent is selective for 1° alcohols. The selectivity for 1° alcohols probably stems from steric effects due to the three phenyl groups. However, in the case of this problem, acetic anhydride is used first. This reagent will make acetate esters out of every hydroxyl group, ruling out choices A and D. To distinguish between choices C and B, determine whether or not this reaction can result in the cleavage of the glycosidic bond. The glycosidic bond is an acetal linkage, and it can be broken in acidic conditions. The by-product of esterification with acetic anhydride is acetic acid, which will lower the pH of the solution, and could, in theory, break the glycosidic bond, permitting the esterification of the anomeric carbon. To combat this scenario, pyridine is used as a solvent. Pyridine is a nitrogen containing heterocycle that can act as a weak base by abstracting protons released during the esterification reaction. This basic behavior "traps" the free protons and keeps the solution slightly basic, protecting the glycosidic bond from acid catalyzed hydrolysis. Choice C is the best answer because it shows the preserved glycosidic bond. Choice B can be eliminated.

Passage 8 (Questions 40-43)

40. **D is the best answer.** Although organometallic reagents are typically used in addition reactions, by virtue of their extremely basic carbon, they may also be used as strong bases. The strength of the base used in Reaction 2, CH_3MgBr, can be understood by the weakness of its conjugate acid, methane, with a pka $\approx$ 48. Such a powerful base is capable of deprotonating the alkyne group of the reactant species of Reaction 2 into a carbanion. The carbanion which results from this reaction is less basic than the organometallic reagent because it is sp hybridized. The 50% S character of this bond allows for greater electrostatic stabilization of the lone pair electrons because they are held closer to the nucleus. After turning this alkyne into a carbanion, it becomes an extremely powerful nucleophile in its own right, and can attack $CO_2(g)$, adding a carboxylate group to itself. Unless a dilute acid work-up is performed on this newly formed carboxylate group, it will exist as a magnesium bromide salt.

The extreme basicity of the organometallic reagent used in Reaction 2 renders it useless in any protic solvent because it would simply deprotonate the solvent, and never attack the target reagent. As a result, this reaction should be performed in an ethereal or otherwise aprotic solvent, such as THF or diethyl ether. Since Reaction 2 requires both I) an aprotic solvent and II) a dilute acid work up, choice D is the best answer.

41. **A is the best answer.** Look at the difference between the products and the reactants of Reaction 4. A cycle ester, also known as a lactone, has been formed. This ring has come from an intramolecular esterification reaction. Remember that acids are used to catalyze an esterification reaction between an alcohol and a carboxylic acid. Choice C, the weak base, sodium acetate, can be eliminated on this basis. To determine which acid is best, realize that the other carboxylic acids may form their own non-intramolecular esters with the hydroxyl groups of the alcohols of the reactant. They are also far weaker acids than toluene sulfonic acid. Since toluene sulfonic acid is stronger, it will act as a better catalyst and it does not run the risk of generating undesired side products. For this reason, choice A is the best answer.

42. **B is the best answer.** Consider this reaction. An aldehyde, a ketone, and NaOH are the players. NaOH can form an enolate by deprotonating the alpha carbon of the ketone. This enolate will attack the other carbonyl carbon and add to it, forming an aldol. Ultimately, an aldol condensation will occur. A nice way to choose between the answer choices without rewriting the entire mechanism is to remember that aldol condensations always produce an enone, or alkene conjugated to a ketone. This will look like a carbonyl that has a carbon-carbon double bond one bond length away from it. Of these choices, only choice B has the necessary enone in the product. Choice A lacks the enone, choice C is missing a carbon atom in the linkage altogether, and choice D has a hydroxyl group instead of a carbonyl carbon on the five member ring. Choice B is the best answer.

43. **D is the best answer.** Look at the structure of spironolactone. Esters are sensitive to cleavage in the presence of base—they revert into alcohols and carboxylic acids. Since sulfur is in the oxygen column of the periodic table, thioesters share a lot of the same reactivity patterns as conventional esters. They are more sensitive to attack, because $R–S^-$ is a better leaving group than $R–O^-$ since it is less basic. Choice D shows both ester and thioester functionalities following basic cleavage. Glycerol is simply used here as a solvent. Because of its many hydroxyl groups, it is capable of dissolving the polar NaOH. It does not act in this reaction, so choice A should be eliminated. Choice B fails to include the thioester cleavage and should be eliminated. Choice C actually created a new hydrogen atom and "magically" cleaved an inert ketone. This reaction is not possible, so eliminate choice C.

Stand-alones (Questions 44-47)

44. **D is the best answer.** $KMnO_4$ is an oxidizing agent, which will react with pentanal, an aldehyde, to form a pentanoic acid, which is a carboxylic acid. $NaBH_4$ is a reducing agent, but it is too weak to reduce a carboxylic acid to an aldehyde. It can only reduce aldehydes and ketones to alcohols. The net reaction will yield a carboxylic acid with five carbons, so choice D is the best answer.

45. **A is the best answer.** Propanone is a 3-carbon ketone, propanol is a 3-carbon alcohol and butanol is a 4-carbon alcohol. Boiling points are determined by intermolecular bond strengths and molecular weight. Propanone is incapable of hydrogen bonding with itself, while both propanol and butanol can form hydrogen bonds with themselves using their hydroxyl groups. This means propanone must have the lowest boiling point. Proponol must then have a lower boiling point than butanol because butanol has a higher molecular weight. This makes choice A the best answer.

46. **B is the best answer.** Carboxylic acids, like ketones and aldehydes, are capable of reacting via multiple mechanisms depending on the other reactant. If there is a strong nucleophile present, it will attack the carbonyl carbon and either displace a good leaving group when the carbonyl reforms, or form a tetrahedral carbon if there is no good leaving group. Cl_2 is not a strong nucleophile, and is more likely to undergo nucleophilic attack given that Cl^- is a good leaving group since it is a weak base. Substitution reactions at the α-position are possible through a mechanism that utilizes an enolate intermediate. In this situation, a hydrogen on the α-carbon is removed via a base which initiates the formation of the enol. The double bond is capable of acting as a nucleophile and will attack the Cl_2 molecule. This will result in the addition of a chloride at the α-position, which in this case is carbon number 2. Choices A and D can be eliminated. Choice A would be the result of the nucleophilic substitution reaction at the carbonyl carbon, which is less likely to occur given the fact that an attacking Cl^- would be a better leaving group than the OH. This would result in no net product being formed. In a situation where the OH^- acted as the leaving group to form an acyl halide, the presence of OH^- in the solution would readily attack the newly formed acyl halide and regenerate the carboxylic acid. Remember that acyl halides are the most reactive carboxylic acid derivative and will readily hydrolyze to the carboxylic acid if water is present. Choice D would be the result if CH_3Cl was used instead of Cl_2. Choice C indicates that the methyl group at carbon 2 was replaced by the Cl^- atom. While this is a substitution reaction, it is a hydrogen atom on carbon 2 that is replaced. Choice B accurately reflects this and is the best answer.

47. **B is the best answer.** The question stems says that the reaction proceeds through an enolate intermediate. Basic conditions form an enolate through the direct deprotonation of an α-hydrogen. This question is really testing the acidity of α-hydrogens. Since the product of this reaction has an electron withdrawing halogen on the α-carbon, the remaining α-hydrogen is more acidic because the electron withdrawing group stabilizes the α-carbon by allowing it to partially delocalize the resulting negative charge that follows deprotonation. This will favor subsequent base catalyzed enolate formation—in other words, the product of this reaction is more enolizable. Choices A and C can be eliminated. The mechanism of the halogen addition makes the most sense if the enolate's unsaturated bond acts as a nucleophile, and attacks the diatomic halogen atom. Since the enolate is far more basic than the halide leaving group, a successful substitution reaction is expected, without the reverse reaction occurring. The ability to readily form another enolate is expected to result in further halogenation. Choice D can be eliminated, making choice B the best answer.

Passage 9 (Questions 48-51)

48. **B is the best answer.** Remember that the Greek letter is used to describe the anomeric carbon. If the bond is pointing upwards relative to the anomeric carbon, then the bond is **b**eta. Think **b**irds fly up. If the bond is pointing downwards relative to the anomeric carbon then the bond is **a**lpha. Think **a**nts crawl down. The anomeric carbon is the most oxidized carbon in the molecule, having two bonds to oxygen. In the case of digoxin, the anomeric carbon is in the β-configuration. This anomeric carbon shares a glycosidic bond with C4 in the sugar molecule. The best answer is choice B. Choices A assign the wrong configuration to the anomeric carbon. To know in which direction the carbons are counted, remember to imagine the molecule as an aldehyde. In a sugar molecule, the carbon of the aldehyde represents C1. Do this by pretending that the bonds of the anomeric carbon to each oxygen atom are broken. Treat the front-most C–O bond as the aldehyde's carbonyl. The carbon that remains bonded to C1, is C2 and the other numbers follow that order. Choices C and D use a counting scheme that goes in the opposite direction, increasing in number value in the direction that the carbon number should decrease.

49. **D is the best answer.** $H_2SO_4(aq)$ is a strong acid and can catalyze both acetal hydrolysis and ester hydrolysis. During acetal hydrolysis, two molecules of alcohol leave the parent acetal carbon, and the acetal carbon is converted to a ketone. Since the answer choices do not feature the parent acetal carbon, but rather a moiety which was bound to this acetal carbon via ether linkage, a hydroxyl group is expected at the old position of the ether linkage. Eliminate choices B and C. Since the lactone in the upper right of the structure of digoxin is just a cyclic ester, it will share the reactivity that esters have in acidic solutions, and undergo hydrolysis, liberating an alcohol and forming a carboxylic acid. Choice A shows an unreacted lactone, but choice D shows the lactone after acid catalyzed hydrolysis. Choice D is better than choice A and is the best answer.

50. **A is the best answer.** During the acid catalyzed hydrolysis of an acetal, water attacks the acetal carbon after one of the alkoxy groups is protonated and leaves. To shift the equilibrium towards the hydrolyzed product, it is important to keep the concentration of water high, as it is continually consumed during the reaction. Removal of water has the opposite effect, favoring acetal formation with the sugar or the ethanol solvent. Choice A is a strong answer, and since choice B is the opposite of choice A, it can be eliminated. Adding methanol to the reaction vessel will allow the formation of a methoxy-acetal in addition to the ethoxy-acetal, but it will not help form any hemiacetal products, so choice C is not as good as choice A. Reducing the temperature will slow the rate of this reaction, but not favor the formation of hemiacetals, so choice D can be eliminated.

51. **D is the best answer.** A lactone is an ester which is in a closed ring. This can be seen in the ring attached to C17 in the general steroidal motif of CGs in Figure 1. Choice A can be eliminated. A polysaccharide is a chain of sugar molecules. There is a chain of three sugar molecules that eventually attach to the steroidal motif of CGs at C3 in Figure 1, so choice B can be eliminated. Alcohols are R–OH groups. There are six of them in this structure, so choice C can be eliminated. Lactams are amides which are in a closed ring. There are no lactams in this structure, which makes choice D the best answer.

Passage 10 (Questions 52-56)

52. **B is the best answer.** Count the number of equivalents of HCl released during each step of this synthesis. During the formation of an acyl halide from a carboxylic acid with the use of $SOCl_2$, SO_2 gas and HCl are released. The first step of this synthesis releases 1 equivalent of HCl. Next, the amidation of the acyl chloride also releases another equivalent of HCl. In total, there are 2 equivalents of HCl produced during DEET synthesis. Choice B is the best answer.

53. **B is the best answer.** $SOCl_2$ is a halogenating agent typically used to convert alcohols into alkyl halides, and carboxylic acids into acyl halides. Choice A is a tempting distractor. While the structure provided is an accurate depiction of the theoretical polymerization of *m*-toluic acid, this structure is highly unlikely to form because methyl groups are too inert to react with most chemicals, including carboxylic acids. The only moieties $SOCl_2$ can halogenate are carboxylic acids or alcohols. Halogenation of carboxylic acids, as shown in the first step of the synthesis of DEET, creates acyl halides. Acyl halides are extremely reactive, and can react with carboxylic acids, forming acid anhydrides. Choice B is an example of this likely outcome and is a strong answer. Choice C features halogenation on a benzene ring, and while benzene rings can be halogenated, $SOCl_2$ is not capable of participating in this reaction. Choice C can be eliminated. While choice D is tempting given the present of sulfur in $SOCl_2$, it is the chlorine atoms, rather than the sulfur atom, that are reactive enough to participate in these reactions. Since choice D shows the sulfur reacting with *m*-toluic acid atom, it can be eliminated.

54. **B is the best answer.** When heated with HCl and water, DEET will be subject to undergoing hydrolysis just as other carboxylic acid derivatives. The amide group, although more stable than other acid derivatives, is capable of being hydrolyzed under these harsher conditions. Any carboxylic acid derivative will produce the parent carboxylic acid after hydrolysis. Choice A is a possible product. After undergoing nucleophilic attack by a water molecule, the carbonyl will attempt to reform and kick off the best leaving group. R-groups, even those with aromatic stability, are not as strong of leaving groups as amines, so a benzyl alcohol would not be expected to be liberated from this hydrolysis. Choice B is a strong answer. After protonation of the nitrogen of the amide group, it becomes a much better leaving group and is capable of being displaced as the amine shown in choice C. This allows choice C to be eliminated. Since amides are the most stable of the carboxylic acid derivatives, it is possible that some of molecules of DEET will not undergo hydrolysis. Choice D can be eliminated in this case, leaving choice B as the best answer.

55. **C is the best answer.** If a molecule with a complex name is given, and a structure is provided, do not be intimidated by the name. Look at the structure and simplify the problem. The molecule provided in this question is a ketone. Ketones are more reactive than carboxylic acids and undergo nucleophilic addition in the presence of an amine with catalytic acid. In particular, if the attacking amine is a 2° amine, an enamine is formed. An enamine is analogous to an enol product, but rather than a hydroxyl group, there is an amine group bonded to a carbon that also has a double bond to a neighboring carbon atom. If a 1° amine is used in the reaction, than an imine is formed. Since $(C_2H_5)_2NH$ is a 2° amine, it will form an enamine product. The best answer is choice C.

56. **D is the best answer.** If the final step of the reaction was contaminated by ethanol, an additional reactant would be available to participate in the nucleophilic substation reaction. Ethanol would attack the acyl halide, which would be kicked off since it is a good leaving group. As long as the amine is present in solution, it will be capable of attacking the carbonyl carbon of any acyl halide in solution as well as the newly formed ester groups. Amines are stronger nucleophiles, and will outcompete ethanol for the nucleophilic substitution reaction. Addition of an amine to an ester will most likely result in the formation of an amide with the ethanol group acting as a leaving group. To understand this, remember that amines are not as good of leaving groups as alcohols, which explains the relative reactivity of amides being less reactive than that of esters. While choice A accurately states this, remember that this reactivity has to do with the ability of the carboxylic acid derivative to react with a nucleophile and undergo substitution. Since esters are more reactive than amides, it is more likely that any ester that forms will be attacked by an amine group to form DEET, so choice A can be eliminated. DEET is still expected to be the major product, but since choice B states that amides are more reactive than esters, it can be eliminated. For the final product to contain both an ester and amide group, the benzyl group would have to act as a leaving group. A general rule is that R-groups, even those that are capable of stabilizing a negative charge through resonance, are not going to be the best leaving groups. Choice C can be eliminated. Choice D is the best answer.

TEST 3A A&E

Stand-alones (Questions 57-59)

57. **B is the best answer.** Oxidizing agents remove electrons from the molecules with which they are interacting. Atoms with high affinity for electrons can usually act as oxidants. This explains why molecules that contain multiple oxygen atoms are often oxidants. $KMnO_4$ is an example of such a molecule and readily accepts electron density from a compound, making choice A a weaker answer. Na metal has a very low electron affinity and acts as a reducing agent by donating its electrons to the other compound with which it is reacting, making choice B a strong answer. H_2O_2 is similar to $KMnO_4$ in that it has multiple oxygen atoms with high electron affinity that are capable of accepting electron density. Choice C is a weak answer. Since fluorine has the highest electron affinity, it would be expected to accept electron density when reacted with a molecule. This would make it an oxidizing agent, eliminating choice D and making choice B the best answer.

58. **D is the best answer.** This is a classic two by two question. To answer it, first determine the effect that protonation of the oxygen has on the reactivity of the carbonyl. By being protonated, the oxygen gains a positive charge, increasing the polarity of the C–O bond and creating a larger partial positive charge on the carbonyl carbon. This increases the ability of the molecule to undergo a nucleophilic attack by CN and would increase the rate of the reaction. Since choice A is deprotonated, it would be expected to react slower than choice C. The same can be said of choice B as it relates to choice D, making choices A and B weaker answers. To differentiate between choices C and D, the sterics of the molecule have to be considered. While choice D has a bulkier group towards one end of the molecule, note that this is not as close to the carbonyl as the bulkier portion of choice C. Since the carbonyl is the portion of the molecule that is going to undergo the nucleophilic addition of CN, decreasing the availability of this portion of the molecule by having large groups near it would slow down the reaction, making choice C a weaker answer than choice D.

59. **B is the best answer.** There are two ways to approach this problem. Either you can recognize PCC as a soft oxidizer, which is unable to oxidize the newly formed aldehyde into a carboxylic acid, or you can use process of elimination. Both choices I and III are strong oxidizers and will bring a primary alcohol all the way to the carboxylic acid without stopping at the aldehyde. Options I and III can be eliminated since they will be unable to generate an aldehyde without further oxidizing it to the carboxylic acid. Option II will be in the best answer choice, which is choice B.

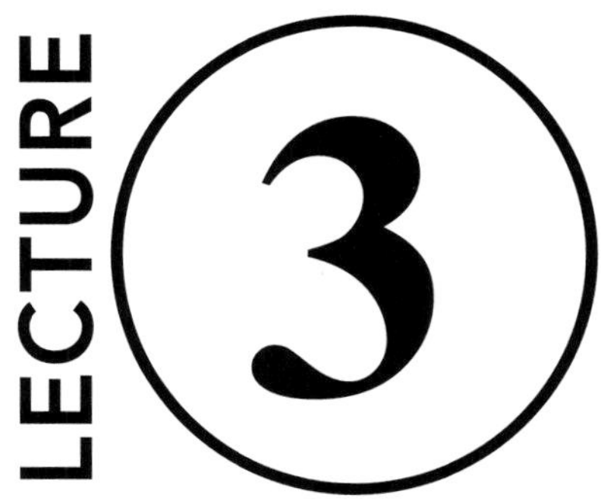

Oxygen Containing Reactions

MINI-TEST 3B

ANSWERS & EXPLANATIONS

Questions 1–29

Passage 1 (Questions 1-6)

1. **A is the best answer.** Look at Reaction 1. It provides a "formula" for solving this problem. However, unlike other science formulas, instead of plugging and chugging with numbers, plug and chug with functional groups. This is how generic reactions are designed to be used. It may be helpful to redraw the reactants and label them as shown:

   Determine the product of this Ugi reaction by attaching the R groups of each reactant to the "frame" provided in Reaction 1. This process reveals that choice A is the best answer. The other answer choices stem from failure to substitute the frame accurately. Choice B can be eliminated because the carbonyl group in each of the amides does not follow the pattern shown on the "frame" given in Reaction 1. In Reaction 1, moving from left to right on the product, the pattern is shown to be carbonyl, nitrogen, carbonyl, nitrogen. In choice B, this pattern is not followed, instead it is arranged as carbonyl, nitrogen, nitrogen, carbonyl. Choice B can be eliminated. Choice C places the amino group near R_5 as a tertiary amine, when the formula stipulates that it should be a secondary amine. Choice D features a ring formation reaction that is impossible, as a new carbon atom has been added to the ring from out of nowhere. Choice D can be eliminated.

2. **B is the best answer.** Reduction is gaining electrons and oxidation is losing electrons. In organic chemistry, oxidation can usually be simplified as resulting in an increase in bonds to oxygen or halogen atoms, or loss of C–H bonds. Likewise, reduction is often an increase in bonds to hydrogen or R groups or the loss of bonds to oxygen or a halogen. During Reactions *A* and *B* the double bond from carbon to oxygen is converted into a single bond. Since this is a loss in bonds to oxygen, reduction has occurred, eliminating choices A and C. To reach artesunate from either dihydroartemisinin or artemether, nucleophilic attack by the bottom-most oxygen atom on a carbonyl containing species probably occurred. Whether that added carbonyl containing species was an anhydride, acid chloride, or carboxylic acid is not fully clear, but the identity of the carbonyl containing species does not matter for this question. Esters cannot add to carbonyl carbons because the resulting oxonium cation cannot regain a neutral charge; regaining a neutral charge would require cleavage of a C–O bond. Choice D can be eliminated on this basis. Conversely, the oxonium cation that results from addition of the lactol (cyclic hemiacetal) to a carbonyl carbon can regain a neutral charge via deprotonation. Thus, Reaction *A* should occur first to transform artemisinin into a proper nucleophile, prior to the esterification in Reaction *C*. Choice B is the best answer.

3. **D is the best answer.** Consider what will change during this reaction: a cyclic hemiacetal, or $R_1R_2C(OH)OR_3$ group, will be converted into a cyclic acetal, or $R_1R_2C(OR_3)OR_4$ group. Acetals are formed from the condensation of a ketone or aldehyde with an alcohol, and proceed via a hemiacetal intermediate. Once the acetal is formed, very little of it reverts back to the hemiacetal. Acetals are more stable molecules. Catalytic acid is required to activate the carbonyl group in order to make it more nucleophilic during this reaction. In addition, since this conversion is an equilibrium reaction, a desiccating agent is required to remove water from the solution to shift the equilibrium to favor condensation and acetal formation. Choice D has all of the proper "ingredients": an alcohol, acid, and dehydrating agent. Choice d is most likely the best answer, but eliminate the other choices before selecting it. Acetic anhydride is an acylating reagent that forms carbonyls, not ether linkages. Choice A can be eliminated. NaOH is a strong base that would deprotonate the hydroxyl group of the hemiacetal, leading to a reopening of the hemiacetal ring and formation of an aldehyde. Choice B can be eliminated. Methylmagnesium bromide is strong base and powerful nucleophile. It would participate in a similar reaction as NaOH. Choice C can be eliminated as well.

4. **A is the best answer.** Substituents on the α-carbon of a carbonyl group can alter the rate of nucleophilic substitution via two mechanisms—electronic or steric effects. If there is a large, bulky group on the α-carbon, then the ability of a nucleophile to gain access to the carbonyl carbon and react with it decreases. Since the rate determining step is the nucleophilic attack, this will result in a decreased rate. The α-carbon for choice A has a single methyl group and two hydrogen atoms, so it is a relatively small substituent. Comparatively, choice B consists of a carbon bonded to three additional methyl groups, which is considered a bulky group and would have a decreased rate of nucleophilic substitution. Choice B can be eliminated. Choice C only has two methyl groups bonded to it, but this would still be a bulkier group than that of choice A and would increase the steric hindrance of the reaction. Choice C can be eliminated. Choice D is similar to choice B, except that it is bonded to three ethyl groups rather than three methyl groups. Since this would still be a bulkier R group that that of choice A, it can be eliminated.

5. **C is the best answer.** In the last paragraph of this passage, the unique stability of the endoperoxide bridge of the trioxane ring is mentioned. In other words, the peroxide group is most likely inert to the proper derivitization reagents. Nonetheless, even without knowing about the stability of this peroxide group, it is a better strategy to select the best answer based on what *is* known: a carbonyl has become a hydroxyl. Consider what reagents will perform this reduction. Hydrochloric acid and water would lead to hydrolysis of the lactone, opening the ring, and forming an alcohol and carboxylic acid. Choice A can be eliminated. Hydrochloric acid and methanol would lead to an acid catalyzed transesterification, also opening the ring, but instead forming an ester and an alcohol. Choice B can be eliminated. Sodium borohydride is a gentle reducing agent, perfect for adding hydrogen to ketones and aldehydes. Under short enough reaction times, it is gentle enough not to react with non-acidic alcoholic solvents. The hydrogen addition to the carbonyl group forms a negatively charged tetrahedral intermediate which can be converted into an alcohol, with acidic work-up. Choice C may be the best answer, but eliminate choice D before selecting it. Sodium hydroxide is a powerful base, it will attack the lactone, hydrolyzing it, and turning it into a carboxylic acid and an alcohol. Just like the acid and water example, this reaction will result in opening the ring as well. Choice D can be eliminated, and choice C is the best answer.

6. **C is the best answer.** Imines are the nitrogen analog of ketones, and enamines are the nitrogen analog of enols. Imines are formed when primary amines attack an aldehyde or ketone, and enamines are formed when secondary amines attack aldehydes or ketones. Amines are the simple nitrogen atoms bonded to R groups, and amides are the nitrogen analog of esters. Since this product has a nitrogen with a double bond, and was formed from a primary amine attacking a ketone/aldehyde, it is an imine. Choice C is the best answer. The reagents used do not support any other product being formed, and the product that is formed does not match the other categories. Choices A, B, and D can be eliminated.

Passage 2 (Questions 7-11)

7. **D is the best answer.** A hydride is an H^- ion. Hydride transfer refers to a hydrogen atom acting as nucleophile and adding to a molecule, as shown in Reaction 1. This occurs during the reduction of the aldehyde to an alcohol in the Cannizarro reaction. If the alcohol product is formed via a hydride transfer from the aldehyde reactant, then the alcohol will not have a deuterated α-carbon because the hydrogen that adds at the α-carbon is from the original aldehyde which does not have the deuterium isotope to donate. If, however, the hydrogen atom is taken from the solution, a source of deuterium, and not added via hydride reduction, then the product alcohol will have a deuterated α-carbon. To support the hypothesis that reduction occurs via a hydride transfer from the reactant, the final product cannot have a deuterated α-carbon. Choice D is the best answer because it restates this idea. Choice A can be eliminated because it states the opposite of Choice D. Choice B is a weaker answer because the hydroxyl group of the alcohol can be deuterated regardless of the original mechanism by which the intermediate alkoxide is formed. Since observing the presence of a deuterated hydroxyl group will not provide evidence for or against the mechanism of reduction, choice B can be eliminated. Choice C is weaker than choice D. For the results of choice C to occur, only half, but not all, of the alcohol product would be formed via hydride transfer from the reactant.

8. **C is the best answer.** Although it may be tempting to select choice B, as this best resembles the reaction given in the passage, there is a major difference between cyclohexanecarboxaldehyde and benzaldehyde. Cyclohexanecarboxaldehyde contains bonds to hydrogen in the α-position. This means that it cannot behave as a substrate in a Cannizarro reaction, but rather will undergo an aldol addition. Eliminate choices A and B. The reaction stops once the molecule becomes a β-hydroxy-carbonyl, and will not proceed to the condensation step, because cyclohexanecarboxaldehyde only has 1 α-hydrogen, not two. Choice C is the β-hydroxy-carbonyl, and a strong answer. Choice D is a perversion of a typical aldol condensation product—note that it lacks the conjugated unsaturated bond at the coupling site. Choice D is a weaker answer for two reasons. No condensation will occur in this reaction since cyclohexanecarboxaldehyde doesn't have a second α-hydrogen that is required for the condensation reaction to occur. If this reaction did occur, the condensation product would not look like choice D, as the double bond that would be formed from the reaction is not present in choice D. Choice C is the best answer.

9. **C is the best answer.** Remember in the first paragraph of the passage what one of the key requirements of the Cannizarro reaction was no bond to hydrogen in the α-position. Choices A and B both have a bond to hydrogen in the α-position and should be eliminated—in fact, choice A is not even an aldehyde, it is a ketone. Choices C and D both lack a bond to hydrogen in the α-position. To distinguish between these two choices, remember the mechanism of the nucleophilic attack on the acyl chloride. This is something that is familiar and may help eliminate choice D. Essentially, OH^- will attack the carbonyl, forming a negatively charged tetrahedral intermediate shown here:

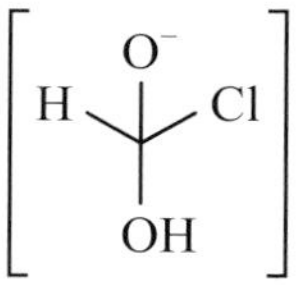

[H–C(O⁻)(Cl)–OH]

Cl^- is a much better leaving group than H^- because H^- is a very strong base, and Cl^- is a weak base. Cl^- is expected to leave this molecule, converting the intermediate into a carboxylic acid. Once a carboxylic acid, this molecule will no longer be able to participate in the Cannizarro reaction. Conversely, choice C has no "easy" leaving groups. After it is attacked by OH^-, it will most likely reform the original reactant via the reverse reaction as the OH^- would be the best leaving group. Choice C is the best answer.

10. **A is the best answer.** Remember that the oxidizing agent is oxidizing the other molecule. In order to do this, it must remove electrons from that molecule, thus becoming reduced itself. Whenever the word "oxidizing agent" is used, remember that it means the same thing as "molecule that gets reduced." This question simplifies to "Which of the two molecules provided will be reduced to an alcohol?"

Looking at the mechanism in Reaction 1 provides the first hint. The first step of this reaction is a nucleophilic attack on the carbonyl. In this reaction, that means OH^- adding to the carbonyl carbon. Next, the species which is attacked will ultimately transfer a hydride ion to the other species, reducing it to an alcohol. Since methanal is a smaller aldehyde than benzaldehyde and does not have the advantage of resonance, it has a greater δ+ on its carbonyl carbon. This renders it more nucleophilic, and means it will get preferentially attacked by OH^-. As discussed, this means that methanal will ultimately reduce benzaldehyde. Benzaldehyde is the oxidizing agent, so eliminate choices B and D. Since it has the weaker δ+, choice A is the better than choice C.

11. **D is the best answer.** Carboxylic acids engage in more hydrogen bonding than alcohols because of the carbonyl group. This increased hydrogen bonding gives them considerably higher boiling points than their corresponding alcohols. For example, ethanol boils at 78°C and formic acid boils at 101°C, despite both molecules having nearly identical molecular weights. Option I is true. Resonance does not prevent hydrogen bonding. All that is required for hydrogen bonding is for hydrogen to be bound to either F, N, or O. Option II is false. Finally, consider what happens during the second step of this reaction. The alkoxy grouped formed during the hydride shift would deprotonate the newly formed carboxylic acid, yielding an alcohol and metal carboxylate salt. Dilute acid work-up is required to protonate the carboxylate. Upon protonation, the carboxylate is no longer negatively charged. Since it is less polar, it is expected to be less soluble in water. Option III is true. Select the answer choice with the options I and III. Choice D is the best answer.

Stand-alones (Questions 12-15)

12. **C is the best answer.** Enolates are formed under basic conditions when the molecule is deprotonated at the α-carbon, which is the carbon directly neighboring the carbonyl. The hydrogens bound to the α-carbon are acidic due to the electron-withdrawing effects of the neighboring carbonyl carbon. The carbonyl carbon withdraws electron density from the C–H bonds in order to stabilize its partial positive charge. Choice A is not the best answer since the α-carbon will be negatively charged and highly nucleophilic after being deprotonated by potassium tert-butoxide. Electron-withdrawing groups remove electron density from the C–H bonds at the α-position, increasing the acidity. Electron-donating groups increase the electron density of the C–H bonds, decreasing the acidity. Choice B can be eliminated since the nitro group is a strong electron-withdrawing group. The nitrogen atom in the nitro group has a full positive charge, which it will stabilize by removing negative electron density from the nearby C–H bonds, making these bonds more acidic and increasing the rate of the reaction with base. Answer choice C is the best answer since the addition of an electron-donating methyl group to the α-carbon of acetyl acetone would decrease the acidity of the molecule and the rate of reaction with potassium tert-butoxide. Acetyl acetone contains two electron-withdrawing carbonyl groups. Removing one of the carbonyl groups would decrease the acidity of the alpha hydrogens since there would be fewer electron-withdrawing groups near the α-carbon. Choice D can be eliminated since an increase in pK_a corresponds to a decrease in acidity.

13. **B is the best answer.** A cyanohydrin is a compound that has a carbon atom bonded to both an alcohol group and a cyano (CN) group. Since the question stem states that the unknown compound will react with an aldehyde or ketone, an easy way to solve this question is to work backwards by assessing what reaction will occur between an aldehyde and each of the answer choices. Water with catalytic H_2SO_4 will not react with an aldehyde to create a new product. Since there is not a good leaving group, after water attacks the carbonyl, the carbonyl will most likely reform, and the originally attacking water molecule will leave. There is a possibility of a diol forming under the right conditions, but since this is not a cyanohydrin, choice A can be eliminated. Since KCN is a salt, it will dissociate into K^+ and CN^- once in solution. CN^- is a very strong nucleophile and poor leaving group, so once it attacks the carbonyl, the new negative charge on the oxygen molecule will be stabilized by deprotonating an acidic hydrogen from the solvent. This will result in a cyanohydrin, so choice B is a strong answer. Similar to KCN, $NaNH_2$ will produce a strong NH^{2-} nucleophile in solution, but after nucleophilic attack, the final product will have an NH_2, rather than a carbon triple bonded to a nitrogen, so choice C can be eliminated. HNO_3 is a strong acid that will completely dissociate in solution. Since it is a strong acid, its conjugate base, NO^{3-} is a weak base and will not attack the carbonyl, so choice D can be eliminated.

14. **D is the best answer.** Although the question stem does not provide the structures of the compounds in the reaction, they can be drawn using their chemical name. Iodomethane is a methane molecule with one iodine atom substituted for a hydrogen atom, (CH_3I). 2-pentanone is a 5-carbon chain with a carbonyl at the second carbon. Since CH_3I is not a strong nucleophile, but rather an electrophile, it will not attack the carbonyl carbon to form a new carbon-carbon bond. For carbonyl chemistry, it is important to remember the possibility of a second type of reaction involving the α-carbon, which is the more likely reaction in this case. The rate determining step for enolate chemistry is usually the deprotonation of the α-carbon, so any change in the reaction conditions that increases the acidity of these hydrogen atoms will increase the rate. While pentanal would be expected to have slightly more acidic hydrogens on the α-carbon, this increase is largely outweighed by the decrease in the number of hydrogens on α-carbons. Since 2-pentanone has 2 α-carbons and a total of 5 hydrogens on these carbons, while pentanal only has one α-carbon and its associated 2 hydrogen atoms, there is a smaller probability of deprotonation occurring. This will likely lower the expected rate of the reaction and is probably a weaker answer. Adding catalytic H_2SO_4 would increase the rate of the reaction, but it accomplishes this by protonating the carbonyl oxygen, not the α-carbon. Remember that the formation of the enol requires deprotonation of the α-carbon. Choice B can be eliminated. Using a better nucleophile, such as the alkoxide, would increase the rate if the reaction was proceeding through a nucleophilic attack of the carbonyl. Since that is not the main reaction in this case, choice C can be eliminated. Halogenation of the 4-position of 2-pentanone will place an additional electron-withdrawing group next to the α-carbon. This will increase the acidity of those hydrogens and the rate will likely increase, making choice D the best answer.

15. **B is the best answer.** Ketones are capable of reacting via a nucleophilic addition reaction at the carbonyl carbon or through the formation of an enolate following deprotonation of the α-carbon, which is the carbon that neighbors the carbonyl. Since the question stem is asking for the reactant that will favor the product that results from substitution at the α–carbon, reactants that are more likely to attack the carbonyl, i.e. strong nucleophiles, are less likely to react at the α-carbon. The α-position of a ketone can participate in electrophilic addition reaction via a mechanism that involves an enolate ion. The enolate ion is generated when a proton on the α-carbon is removed, forming a double bond between the α-carbon and carbonyl carbon. This double bond participates in an electrophilic addition reaction just like other alkenes. Since this mechanism does not involve the nucleophilic attack on the α-carbon, choice A can be eliminated. A bulky nucleophile that is a strong base would increase the likelihood of a reaction occurring at α-carbon, but this would be the result of the base preferentially deprotonating the α-carbon rather than attacking the carbonyl. This is similar to the situation described in choice B, so it is a strong answer. A strong nucleophile with less steric hindrance will be more likely to attack the carbonyl of the ketone rather than act as a base and deprotonate the α-carbon. Choice C can be eliminated. If a nucleophile is stabilized by resonance, then it is less likely to be a strong nucleophile or strong base. This would result in a decreased likelihood of either reaction occurring, so choice D can be eliminated.

Passage 3 (Questions 16-21)

16. **C is the best answer.** Aldoses are carbohydrates that contain an aldehyde, and ketoses are carbohydrates that contain a ketone. Glucose contains an aldehyde, and fructose contains a ketone, so glucose is an aldose and fructose is a ketose. Choice C is the best answer.

17. **B is the best answer.** This question is asking about two kinds of stereoisomers, anomers and epimers. An epimer describes a member in a pair of molecules that shares the same absolute configuration at all stereocenters except one. An anomer is a specific kind of epimer. In particular, it is the epimer that comes from changing the absolute configuration of a single stereocenter, the anomeric carbon. In other words, *all anomers are epimers, but not all epimers are anomers*. The anomeric carbon is the hemiacetal carbon of these structures. Since the sugar given in the question has an α configuration, its anomer must have a beta configuration. α configurations have the anomeric carbon's hydroxyl group pointing down, and β configurations have the anomeric carbon's hydroxyl group pointing up. A good mnemonic to remember this is that **α**nts crawl and **β**irds fly. Eliminate choice A, since it is an α configuration. To distinguish between the other β structures it would be easiest to draw α-D-glucose from memory, and choose the structure that perfectly matches it, except for the anomeric carbon. This structure is choice B, which is the best answer.

TEST 3B A&E

18. **D is the best answer.** This question looks like an intimidating question on IUPAC number conventions, but it is simpler than it appears. It is actually just an α vs. β configuration question in disguise. Look at the structure and realize that the anomeric carbon in glucose is in the α configuration, and the anomeric carbon in fructose is also α. α configurations have the anomeric carbon's hydroxyl group pointing down, and β configurations have the anomeric carbon's hydroxyl group pointing up. A good mnemonic to remember this is that **α**nts crawl and **β**irds fly Since the correct answer must have each anomeric carbon in the α configuration, choice D is the best answer.

19. **A is the best answer.** Xylose is the sugar form of xylitol, which as shown in Figure 1 has 5 carbon atoms, making it a pentose. Since the question does not specify whether the D or L form is desired, the stereochemistry is not as important as identifying the carbon that will be oxidized or reduced and the reaction it will undergo. Xylitol lacks a carbonyl group, so one of the alcohol substituents will need to be converted to a carbonyl in order to achieve the sugar xylose. This will result in an increase in the number of bonds to an oxygen atom, so the reaction can be defined as an oxidation. Remember that this is not the precise definition of an oxidation reaction, but is an easy shortcut that will work most of the time for organic chemistry questions. The conversion of an alcohol to an aldehyde is the result of an oxidation reaction. If a strong enough oxidizing agent is present, the aldehyde can be further oxidized to form a carboxylic acid. The reverse reaction for each of these steps can be characterized as reduction reactions. Choices B and D can be eliminated. The question stem states that xylose is an aldose. Since aldoses have an aldehyde group, the oxidation reaction must take place at either carbon 1 or 5. Oxidation of carbon 2 will result in a ketose, so choice C can be eliminated. Choice A is the best answer.

20. **D is the best answer.** Do not be intimidated by these large structures. The reaction can be simplified as substituting acetic esters for the alcohols of the sugar. Considering the reactivity of each reagent in order is the best way to solve this problem. Acetone is a fairly inert ketone. It is not very reactive to nucleophillic attack at the carbonyl unless there is a very strong nucleophile such as a hydride anion. Under the conditions of this problem, acetone is not expected to react, so choice A can be eliminated. Acetic acid is a tempting answer, but like other acids, it is capable of hydrolyzing the glycosidic bond between the two sugars. In addition, due to the negative formal charge, the acetate anion is unlikely to be attacked by the alcohols of the sugar. Acetic acid will not provide the target product of this problem, so choice B can be eliminated. Sodium acetate is a weak base. Although it is unable to hydrolyze the glycosidic bond, like acetic acid, the resulting acetate anion which forms through its ionization is unlikely to be attacked by the alcohols of the sugar. No reaction is expected to occur with sodium acetate, so choice D can be eliminated. Acetic anhydride is readily attacked by alcohols, converting the alcohols into acetic esters, like the product of this problem. This makes choice D the best answer.

21. **D is the best answer.** D-glucose is an aldohexose that can be converted to D-fructose, which is a ketohexose, via tautomerization. Tautomerization is the process of switching between a keto and enol form. The keto form, which is a traditional ketone or aldehyde, and the enol form, which consists of a C–C double bond ("en") and an alcohol group ("ol"), exist in equilibrium. These tautomers do not represent different resonance structures of the same molecules, as bonds must be broken and reformed between different atoms to create the different molecules. Once the enol is formed, it can either revert back to the original keto and regenerate glucose, or form a new carbonyl at carbon 2 and create fructose. The mechanism of this transformation is shown below.

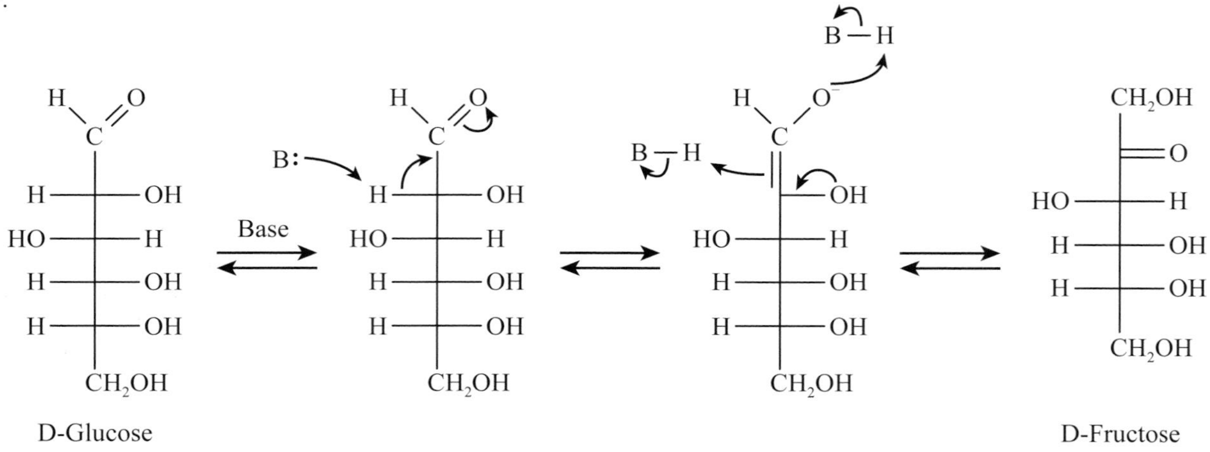

D-Glucose

D-Fructose

Choice A is a trap answer that tries to take advantage of the common misconception that tautomers are resonance structures of one another. Choice A can be eliminated. As mentioned before, the transformation of a keto to an enol occurs in an equilibrium and is a reversible process. Choice B can be eliminated. The process of tautomerizing from a keto to an enol starts by the deprotonation of the α-carbon, not the alcohol group. Choice C can be eliminated. The deprotonation of the α-carbon results in the formation of the double bond between the α-carbon and the carbonyl. This increase in electron density on the carbonyl carbon is relieved by the electronegative oxygen, which eventually becomes protonated to form the alcohol portion of the enol. The use of a bulky base lowers the chance of the base attacking the carbonyl carbon in a nucleophilic manner. Since the first step of this transformation requires the deprotonation of carbon 2, using a base that is less likely to attack the carbonyl, improves the likelihood of the conversion of glucose to fructose, so choice D is the best answer.

Passage 4 (Questions 22-26)

22. **D is the best answer.** The passage describes in the third paragraph that phospholipids are composed of a DAG and a phosphoric acid ester. Serine will be everything beyond the phosphoric acid ester. Remember that during an esterification reaction, often times, the H of a hydroxyl group is lost so that the esterified molecule's oxygen atom may be able to form the ester bond. Break phosphatidylserine in the middle of its right side P–O bond, and re-form the hydroxyl group to produce the structure of serine. Choice D is the best answer. Choice A improperly keeps the phosphate group as part of the structure of serine. If this moiety were part of the structure of serine, there would be no reason to call it "phosophatidyl". The phosphate group is an additional motif. Choice C can be eliminated for the same reason, as it includes atoms further away than the phosphate group, all the way to the glycerol core. Finally, choice B improperly reconstructs serine, using a carboxylate group, instead of a hydroxyl, as its new head. Carboxylate groups cannot easily undergo esterification—even if they could, the result would be an anhydride like species, not the ester bond shown in this structure. Choice B can be eliminated.

23. **A is the best answer.** The melting point of fatty acids increases as their number of double bonds decreases. This is because double bonds put kinks in the structure which make forming a neatly packed solid more difficult. A nice way of conceptualizing this idea is to imagine putting scotch tape into a small box. If the pieces are cut into neat strips, they stack on top of each other very easily. If the pieces are rolled into sticky, double sided rings, they will not pack nearly as well. The neat strips are fully saturated fatty acids, and the rings are the unsaturated fatty acids. Since erucic acid's only double bond is lost during this process, the melting point of the product will increase relative to erucic acid. Choice A is probably the best answer, and choice B can be eliminated. Based on the passage, TAGs require three FAs in their structure. The process in this question starts with one FA and ends with one FA. Esterification of Compound 1 does not occur during this process. In other words, Compound 1 does not start as a TAG nor does it end as a TAG. Choices C and D can be eliminated. Choice A is the best answer.

24. **C is the best answer.** This problem can be challenging because, at first glance, both types of products may seem possible. The enamine can behave as either an alkylating agent or may react directly with (*S*)-1-deutero-1-bromoethane via the lone pairs on its nitrogen atom.

The alkylating activity of this enamine stems from the resonance form shown below:

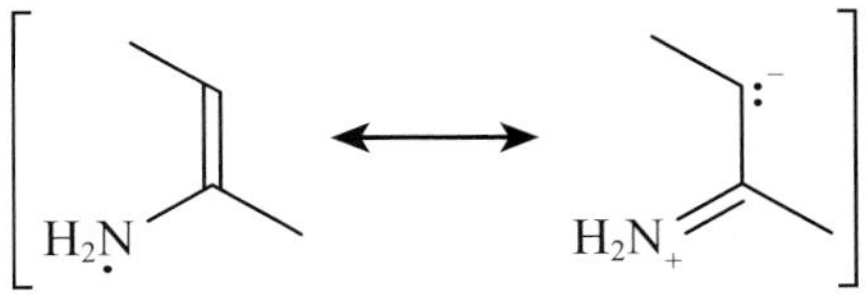

H_2N ⟷ H_2N^+

Despite whether the carbon or nitrogen act as the nucleophile, this reaction will proceed via an S_N2 mechanism. Thus, the best way to answer this question is to rule out the impossible choices first. One of the criteria for an S_N2 mechanism is an inversion of stereochemistry. Draw (*S*)-1-deutero-1-bromo-propane in the same way that choices A and B are drawn.

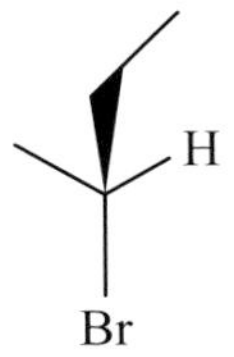

H

Br

Conveniently, replicating the style of choices A and B forms the (*S*)-enantiomer. With this reactant in mind, look at the proposed substitution products, choices A and B. The nitrogen atom is in the same position as the bromine atom in the reactant. If an S_N2 reaction with the nitrogen atom acting as nucleophile occurred, the nitrogen atom would be above the plane of deuteron, hydrogen, and ethyl groups. In other words, choices A and B do not show an inversion in stereochemistry. Choices A and B can be eliminated on this basis. Choice B is a tempting distractor as it shows the possibility of polyalkyation, one of the synthetic risks of using primary amines in these sorts of reactions. Choice C shows the proper inversion of stereochemistry after being attacked by the nucleophilic carbon of the enamine, but choice D lacks this inversion. Choice C is the best answer.

25. **D is the best answer.** Saponification is the alkaline hydrolysis of TAGs. The OH^- anion attacks the carbonyl of each of the stearic acid esters, and the glyceroxide acts as a leaving group resulting in the formation of a free fatty acid out of each of the stearic acid esters. After forming each new carboxylic acid, they are rapidly deprotonated by the newly released glyceroxide anion. The resulting negative charge on the fatty acid is stabilized by combining with ionic sodium, from the NaOH that was used. Thus, the product of this reaction will be a carboxylate sodium salt, ruling out choices B and C. Since choice A is not a carboxylate anion, but rather an alkoxide, choice A is a weaker answer. Choice D is a carboxylate anion, so it is the best answer, and choice A can be eliminated.

26. **C is the best answer.** No alkylation occurs during this reaction. Stearic acid, as both its name and the provided structure suggest, is an acid. Organometallic reagents such as phenyl lithium are powerful bases and nucleophiles. Instead of attacking the carbonyl carbon of stearic acid and forming an unstable tetrahedral intermediate, it is far easier for phenyllithium to deprotonate the carboxylic acid moiety at the end of the molecule. This reaction leads to the formation of a lithium carboxylate salt. Since choice C is the only lithium carboxylate salt, it is probably the best answer, but eliminate the other choices before choosing it. Phenyl octadecanoate is the hypothetical product if alkylation via addition at the carbonyl carbon occurred. Since this reaction is less likely than the acid-base reaction described above, choice A can be eliminated. Choice B contains a similar error by assuming the alkylation reaction will occur, but it confuses the nomenclature rules for the theoretical product. Whenever an ester is named, "—oate" gets attached to the name of the chain that contains the carbonyl carbon and "—yl" gets attached to the name of the moiety connected via ester linkage. Choice B can be eliminated. With the given reagents, the formation of an ether would not occur, as even the alkylation reaction would preserve the carbonyl functionality. Choice D can be eliminated.

Stand-alones (Questions 27-29)

27. **D is the best answer.** Assuming the fever does not reach an extreme temperature, it is likely that the increase in body temperature will result in an increase in rate of the reaction catalyzed by the enzyme. Choice A is less likely to be the best answer. Breaking a glycosidic bond occurs via hydrolysis. This is the opposite of a dehydration reaction, which is also called a condensation reaction. A dehydration reaction is capable of forming a glycosidic bond, so choice B can be eliminated. It is important to remember that dehydration reactions describe what is happening to the reactant. The reactant is being dehydrated and losing a molecule of water, but the environment is gaining a water molecule, or becoming hydrated. An ester is a carboxylic acid derivative with an OR group, with R being any alkyl chain, rather than an OH. While this compound consists of an oxygen atom bonded to an R group that is also bound to a second oxygen atom, in the cyclic form as that of disaccharides, there is not a carbonyl present at this position, so the glycosidic bond is not characterized as an ester bond. Choice C can be eliminated. As mentioned earlier, a disaccharide can be broken into two monosaccharides via a hydrolysis reaction. This reaction utilized water to break apart the glycosidic bond. Choice D is the best answer.

28. **D is the best answer.** The Strecker amino acid synthesis results in the production of racemic amino acids. In the first step of the mechanism, the cyanide anion acts as a nucleophile toward the carbonyl of each aldehyde substrate, by attacking each side of the carbonyl. Since this molecule has a planar structure, each side of the molecule has the same probability of being attacked. During the work up step of each molecule, both members of the nascent amino acid chiral pair are dissolved in the aqueous solution in equal concentration, so it is optically inactive, and will not rotate polarized light. Choice D is the best answer.

29. **A is the best answer.** When an acetal is exposed to acidic solutions, it undergoes hydrolysis, regenerating the hydroxyl groups which originally formed the acetal bonds. One useful strategy for answering this question is to look at the answer choices first and evaluate which of the structures would form the products mentioned in the question stem after acetal hydrolysis via reflux with sulfuric acid. After acetal hydrolysis, a cyanohydrin and glucose is released from choice A. This cyanohydrin is transiently lived, as it is not stable. During the neutralization step, it decomposes into HCN and benzaldehyde. Choice A looks like the best answer, but rule out the others before selecting it. Ethers will not break in acidic conditions. Since choice B has the benzaldehyde group attached to the glucose molecule via an ether bond, this bond will not be broken under the reaction conditions proposed and a free benzaldehyde group would not be formed. Choice B is not likely to be the best answer. Following cyanohydrin decomposition, choice C does not release benzaldehyde. In fact, since the carbonyl is bonded to a methyl group rather than a hydrogen atom, it releases acetophenone, which is a ketone. As a result, choice C is unlikely to be the best answer. After acetal hydrolysis, choice D releases benzoic acid, not benzaldehyde—it is also unlikely to be the best answer.

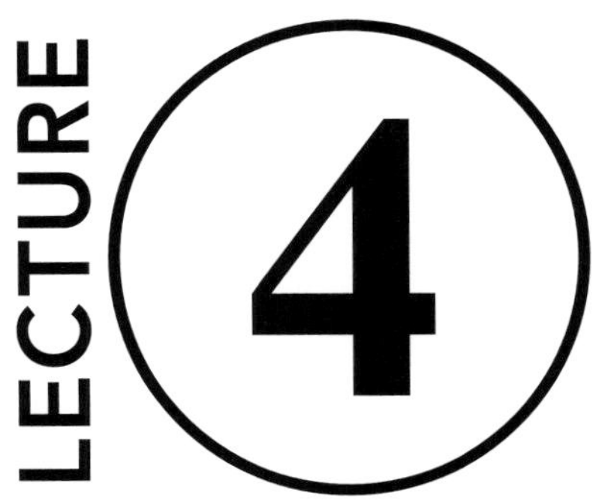

Thermodynamics and Kinetics

TEST 4A

ANSWERS & EXPLANATIONS

Questions 1–59

LECTURE 4 ANSWER KEY

TEST 4A		MINI-TEST 4B	
1. D	31. A	1. D	16. B
2. B	32. D	2. C	17. B
3. C	33. A	3. B	18. B
4. D	34. B	4. C	19. D
5. C	35. C	5. D	20. D
6. B	36. C	6. C	21. A
7. B	37. A	7. D	22. B
8. C	38. D	8. A	23. C
9. D	39. B	9. C	24. D
10. B	40. B	10. B	25. A
11. C	41. D	11. D	26. A
12. A	42. C	12. D	27. A
13. C	43. B	13. D	28. D
14. D	44. B	14. D	29. B
15. A	45. B	15. B	
16. B	46. A		
17. C	47. C		
18. B	48. D		
19. A	49. B		
20. C	50. D		
21. A	51. B		
22. C	52. B		
23. A	53. C		
24. C	54. B		
25. C	55. C		
26. D	56. D		
27. D	57. C		
28. D	58. B		
29. B	59. C		
30. C			

EXPLANATIONS FOR LECTURE 4

Passage 1 (Questions 1-5)

1. **D is the best answer.** The average rate of a reaction is the change in the concentration of a species divided by the change in time. Of these figures, only Figure 1 provides all of the information required to perform this calculation. The other figures show information regarding the rate constant's behavior in different systems. This question stem indicates which of the four lines to choose from in Figure 1. Since $pH = -\log[H^+]$, an H^+ concentration of 10^{-3} M refers to a pH of 3. The results of the experiment at a pH of 3 are represented by the bottom curve on the graph in Figure 1. The label on Figure 1 indicates that this experiment was performed with 50 μM of ODNs. To calculate the change in concentration over the change in time, select two Y values, and two corresponding x-values, and plug these values into the equation $R = \frac{y_2 - y_1}{x_2 - x_1}$.

   For convenience let $y_1 = 0\%$, $y_2 = 60\%$, $x_1 = 0$ hours, and $x_2 = 70$ hours.

   These numbers must be manipulated slightly before plugging directly into the equation. Since this reaction started with a concentration of 50 μM of ODN, and at y_2, 60% has been depurinated, the concentration of depurinated ODNs at y_2 is 50 μM × 0.6 = 30 μM. The time units in the denominator must also be converted to seconds using dimensional analysis:

   $$(70\text{ hr})(60\text{ min/hr})(60\text{ sec/min}) = 252 \times 10^3\text{ sec}.$$

   Thus, the rate $R = (30\ \mu\text{M} - 0\ \mu\text{M})/(252 \times 10^3\text{ sec} - 0\text{ sec}) \approx -10^{-4}\ \mu\text{M/sec}$. Choose the best answer, choice D. The other answer choices fail to perform all of the manipulations before plugging into the equation for R. If the hours were converted to seconds, but the percent depurination was not converted to a concentration, choice A would result. If both values were directly pulled from the graph with no manipulation whatsoever, choice B would result. Choice C makes the same mistake as choice B, except uses 40% instead of 60%.

2. **B is the best answer.** Figure 3 describes the effect of NaCl concentration on the depurination rate constant. Under strongly acidic conditions, a 0.5 M solution of NaCl is required before an appreciable effect on the rate constant is observed. Conversely, in the less acidic, i.e. more basic, solution, even a small addition of salt has a profound effect on the rate constant. For lack of further information, the more acidic a solution is, the less sensitive the depurination reaction is to the concentration of NaCl. In order for these other researchers to not observe any effect of NaCl concentration on the depurination rate constant, they likely performed their experiments under highly acidic conditions. Choice B is the best answer. If they used an alkaline solution, they would have observed an effect similar to that in graph B of Figure 3. Choice A can be eliminated. This passage does not provide adequate information as to the effects of dissolved ions from other salts. Choices C and D can be eliminated.

3. **C is the best answer.** Use algebra to manipulate the Arrhenius equation into slope intercept form in order to solve this problem:

   $$k = Ae^{-\frac{E_a}{RT}}$$
   $$\ln(k) = \ln(A) + \ln(e^{-\frac{E_a}{RT}})$$
   $$\ln(k) = \left(\frac{-E_a}{R}\right)\left(\frac{1}{T}\right) + \ln(A)$$

   The y-intercept occurs when the x-axis has a value of 0. If $1/T = 0$, then $\ln(k) = \ln(A)$. Choice C is the best answer. The slope of this graph is $-E_a/R$. This question did not ask for the slope, and choice A can be eliminated. Choices C and D are distractors which could be chosen if the equation was not simplified to slope-intercept form.

4. **D is the best answer.** The rate of any reaction is dependent on its rate limiting step. Figure 2 indicates that increasing the pH of the reaction causes the value of $\lg(k)$ to become more negative. This means that k is becoming a smaller number and the reaction is proceeding more slowly. Eliminate choice A. According to the Arrhenius equation, decreasing the temperature of a reaction causes k to be a smaller number, and for the reaction to proceed more slowly. Eliminate choice B. The rate determining step is the one which is expected to proceed most slowly, often as a result of its energetic non-favorability. In this reaction, formation of an oxocarbenium ion is far more difficult than protonating two nitrogen atoms. Nitrogen is more basic than oxygen and will be protonated to some extent even in neutral solutions. Oxygen is a strongly electronegative atom—it is not expected to be stable with a positive formal charge. The facility with which nitrogen is protonated is evidence that double protonation of a nucleotide is not the rate determining step. Doubly protonating a molecule "costs" less energy than forming the oxocarbenium ion. Choice C can be eliminated. Addition of an enzyme that reduces the activation energy required to form the rate determining oxocarbenium intermediate will increase the rate of the overall reaction. Choice D is the best answer.

5. **C is the best answer.** The rate of a first order reaction is proportional to the concentration of one reagent: Rate = $k[A]^1$. Alternatively, especially in cases where an enzyme E is saturated with substrate S, the rate law can also be first order with two reagents if it satisfies the condition Rate = $k[S]^0[E]^1$ because this rate law simplifies to Rate = $k[E]^1$. The decomposition of $H_2O_2(l)$ into $O_2(g)$ and $H_2(g)$ is only dependent on the concentration of $H_2O_2(l)$ and is probably not the best answer. Choice A can be eliminated. The solvolysis of triphenyl methyl bromide in methanol proceeds via an S_N1 mechanism because it features a weak nucleophile, a good leaving group, and a highly substituted bulky tertiary haloalkane. The rate of S_N1 mechanisms are dependent only on the concentration of the carbocation forming species, and are thus first order reactions. Choice B can be eliminated. The bromination of iodomethane with NaBr(*aq*) in $H_2O(l)$ proceeds via an S_N2 mechanism because it features an unhindered primary haloalkane with a good leaving group and relatively good nucleophile. S_N2 reactions are dependent on the concentration of both the electrophile and the nucleophile and are second order reactions. Choice C is a strong answer. Radioactive decay is only dependent on the concentration of the decaying isotope. Choice D can be eliminated. Choice C is the best answer.

Passage 2 (Questions 6-9)

6. **B is the best answer.** In the cleavage of ozone, rather than radical chlorine being consumed by the reaction, it is regenerated at the end of a cycle and proceeds to cleave more ozone. This behavior of being an unconsumed reagent is a hallmark of catalytic behavior. Moreover, in the absence of radical chlorine, the net reaction does not occur so rapidly, otherwise ozone depletion would be more common throughout the world. This passage only discusses ozone depletion in the context of it being caused by CFC decomposition products. All of these points suggest that chlorine is acting as a catalyst. Catalysts act by reducing the activation energy of a reaction. Choice B is probably the best answer, but the others should be ruled out before choosing it. Enthalpy and entropy are both state functions. This means that changes in these quantities are the same, regardless of the path taken to affect the change because these quantities only describe the equilibrium state of the system. Likewise, in this problem, the change in entropy and enthalpy only describe the equilibrium state of the reactants and the equilibrium state of the products of the net reaction. Relying on a chlorine-containing intermediate species during the cleavage of ozone does not change the equilibrium state of the reactants or the products of the net reaction. In other words, whatever happens between the beginning and end of a reaction coordinate diagram has no effect on the first or final point of the diagram. Chorine has no effect on the change in entropy or enthalpy in this reaction, so choices A, C and D can be eliminated, and choice B is the best answer.

7. **B is the best answer.** Remember that $W = P\Delta V$, in conditions of constant pressure. Since the pressure of the tube is provided, solve this problem by converting kPa to Pa and multiplying by the change in volume expressed in m^3.

$$\Delta V = 5000 \text{ cm}^3 - 1000 \text{ cm}^3 = 4000 \text{ cm}^3 \text{ which in cubic meters is:}$$

$$(4000 \text{ cm}^3)\left(\frac{1 \text{ m}}{100 \text{ cm}}\right)\left(\frac{1 \text{ m}}{100 \text{ cm}}\right)\left(\frac{1 \text{ m}}{100 \text{ cm}}\right) = \mathbf{4 \times 10^{-3} \text{ m}^3}$$

$$P = \mathbf{68 \times 10^3 \text{ Pa}}$$

$$(68 \times 10^3 \text{ Pa})(4 \times 10^{-3} \text{ m}^3) = 272 \text{ J}$$

The best answer is choice B. Choice A comes from improperly converting cm^3 to m^3, and treating 1000 cm^3 as equal to 1 m^3. Remember to continue canceling units until the correct exponent is on the target unit. Choice C only uses the final volume of the gas, and does not consider the *change* in volume. Choice D does not consider the change in volume and does not properly convert to m^3.

8. **C is the best answer.** As the refrigerant expands, the gas will occupy a greater volume and can be arranged in more configurations—the entropy has increased in the gas/pipe system, and option I will be part of the best answer. Choice A can be eliminated. ΔG is only equal to 0 at equilibrium, and a condition of being at equilibrium is that no net reaction is occurring in the system. Since expansion is occurring, this system is NOT at equilibrium, and option II will not be in the best answer. Choices B and D can be eliminated. Expansion is an endothermic process, and the enthalpy of the system must increase in order to permit gas expansion to occur. Option III will be in the best answer. Choice C has the correct options, I and III, and is the best answer.

9. **D is the best answer.** Remember in a PV diagram that the area under the curve represents the work performed on or by the gas. The work is performed on the gas when its volume is reduced, but performed by the gas, when it expands. To determine the upper and lower boundaries of work, pretend that the pressure remained constant throughout this process. If the pressure remained constant at 50 kPa, the lower pressure of the process, then the work performed would be the area under that curve, 50 kPa × 2 L = 100 J. Since the pressure actually started at a greater value during this process, the area must be greater than 100 J, and more than 100 J of work was actually performed on the gas. Choice A is true. Next, test choice B using the same method. Pretend the pressure remained constant throughout the process at its starting pressure. This would result in a total work of 100 kPa × 2 L = 200 J performed on the gas. Since the pressure did not remain as high as 100 kPa throughout this process, the area under the curve must be less than 200 J. Choice B is true as well. Consider choice C in light of the ideal gas law, $PV = nRT$. Remember that isothermal processes are processes in which temperature (T) remains constant. The process which occurs to this gas must result in the parameters, P, V, n, R, and T capable of satisfying the ideal gas law.

Let the initial case be $PV = nRT$. For simpler algebra, let PV = A and nRT = B. This means that A = B.

At the end of the process, and with the conditions described in choice C, a new description of this system would be: $\frac{1}{2}P\frac{1}{2}V = \frac{1}{4}nRT$, which, expressed in terms of A and B is $\frac{1}{4}\text{A} = \frac{1}{4}\text{B}$. Which means that A = B and that PV remains equal to nRT, so the process described in C is a valid process.

Test choice D the same way:

Let PV = A and nRT = B. As before, this means that A = B. At the end of the process, and with the conditions described in choice D, a new description of this system would be:

$\frac{1}{2}P\frac{1}{2}V$ for the left side of the equation, and $\frac{1}{2}nRT$ for the right side. This does not work mathematically because $\frac{1}{4}\text{A} \neq \frac{1}{2}\text{B}$. The process cannot be achieved by performing choice D since it does not agree with the ideal gas law. Choice D is the best answer.

Stand-alones (Questions 10-13)

TEST 4A A&E

10. **B is the best answer.** Remember the generic equation for a rate law: $R = k[A]^{\alpha}[B]^{\beta}$. A third order reaction means that $\alpha + \beta = 3$. Since the units of A and B are both mol/L and R has the units mol/L · s, k must have units such that:

$$\text{Mol/L} \cdot \text{s} = \text{Mol}^3/\text{L}^3 \times k$$

If k has the units $\text{mol}^{-2} \cdot \text{L}^2 \cdot \text{s}^{-1}$, then the equation works. Choice B is the best answer. Remember that $\text{mol}^{-2} \cdot \text{L}^2 = \text{M}^{-2}$.

11. **C is the best answer.** The question stem describes an S_N2 reaction, which always proceeds with inversion of stereochemistry. S_N2 reactions are so named because the kinetics are second order since the rate depends on the concentration of both reactants. S_N1 reactions are first order because the rate depends on the reaction of the electrophile only. The addition of the nucleophile occurs immediately and is not relevant to the rate law. The answer choices depict a zero-order reaction (choice A), a first order reaction (choice B), a second order reaction (choice C), and a third order reaction (choice D). The y-axis is derived through calculus and may not be completely intuitive. Of note, the y-axes used in the answer choices apply to rate laws that depend on the concentration of one molecule (A). For second and third order kinetics, the y-axes may include two or three molecules, respectively. It is important to commit these figures to memory. Since choice C shows a second order reaction, it is the best answer. Theoretically, an S_N2 reaction could display third order kinetics if the reaction was $AC + 2B \rightarrow AB_2 + C$. This would make the rate law rate = $k[AC][B]^2$. Since rate laws describe the actual reaction, this would be very unlikely because it would require two molecules of B to simultaneously attack AC. Choice D is not impossible, but it is not the best answer.

12. **A is the best answer.** The contaminant in the final product is less thermodynamically favored than the major product that the research group is trying to isolate. This product is most likely forming because it is the kinetically favored product despite its decreased stability. To drive the reaction to the more thermodynamically favored product, the researchers can increase the temperature of the reaction, making choice A a strong answer. Decreasing the temperature would increased the amount of the kinetic product formed and would result in a larger amount of the contaminant. Increasing the rate of the reaction would not increase the purity of the final product since this would not increase the likelihood of forming the thermodynamic product. Choices C and D both would have this effect and are weaker options than choice A.

13. **C is the best answer.** When the starting concentration of citrate is quadrupled, as seen by comparing trials 1 and 2, the rate also quadruples. This means that the reaction is first order with respect to the concentration of citrate. When comparing the rates of trial 2 and 3, it can be seen that the rate doubles when the concentration of Ca^{2+} is doubled, but it must be noted that the concentration of citrate in this trial has also doubled. Since both of the reactant concentrations are doubled and the rate is only doubled, one of the reactants is not contributing to the rate law (or is zero order). Choices A and B state that the reaction is first order with respect to Ca^{2+}, but as shown in trial 3, changing the concentration of Ca^{2+} does not affect the reaction making the exponent in the rate law equal to zero. Choices A and B can be eliminated. The exponent on y is determined via the changes made between trials 1 and 2. Since the concentration is quadrupled and the rate law is also quadrupled, the reaction is first order with respect to citrate, making choice C a better answer than choice D.

Passage 3 (Questions 14-17)

14. **D is the best answer.** A transition state is a temporary molecule that is at a higher energy level than either the reactants or products. The rate of a reaction can be increased if the energy in the system is increased so more molecules are capable of reaching this unstable state. Increasing the energy of the transition state would make it more difficult for reactants to achieve a sufficient energy level and would make the reaction slower, weakening choice A. Lowering the activation energy of the reaction would increase the rate, but increasing the temperature just provides more energy for the system so that more reactants can overcome the activation energy. Since the activation energy is unchanged, choice B is a weaker answer. Decreasing the energy level of the product would make the reaction more thermodynamically favorable, but would not be expected to affect the rate of the reaction, making choice C a weaker option. For a reaction to occur, molecules must collide with enough energy and at the right orientation to form an unstable intermediate compound. By increasing the temperature, the molecules have a larger amount of kinetic energy on average, which increases the likelihood of a successful reaction, making choice D the best answer.

15. **A is the best answer.** Before AA is solvated in the ionic liquid, the ionic liquid is a pure solution and has an ordered arrangement of molecules. Addition of AA would disrupt this ordered arrangement, which is also called a lattice, as noted in the last paragraph. Entropy is a measure of disorder, so the more disordered the solution becomes due to breaking the ordered lattice structure of the ionic liquid, the greater the entropy. This means choice A is most likely to be the best answer. As the solution is getting more disordered, the entropy is unlikely to decrease, eliminating choice B. The entropy increases due to increasing disorder, eliminating choice C. The entropy increases initially when the AA is added, eliminating choice D.

16. **B is the best answer.** AA is being dissolved in an ionic liquid. Heat transfer can occur in three ways: 1) conduction, 2) convection, and 3) radiation. Transfer of heat by conduction occurs when two objects physically touch, such as a pot to a hot stove. Option I is unlikely to be part of the best answer, eliminating choices A and C. Convection is the transfer of heat by a circulating fluid, such as circulating air in an oven or the warmed fluid in the experiment described in the passage. Option II is likely part of the best answer. Transfer of heat by radiation does not involve a circulating fluid but rather the transfer of heat via electromagnetic waves, eliminating option III from the best answer. Choice B is a better answer than choice D.

17. **C is the best answer.** The two expansion coefficients can be used to estimate the attractive forces between AA and [DEEA][Pro], according to the last paragraph of the passage. Notice that as the temperature increases, the value decreases, suggesting the molecules are less attracted to each other. This makes sense because as temperature increases, the molecules gain more kinetic energy and are less likely to maintain close proximity with one other to participate in intermolecular interactions like hydrogen bonding and electrostatic interactions. The formula $KE = \frac{3}{2}kT$ shows that the kinetic energy increases with increasing temperature. The increase in kinetic energy would also further disrupt the ordered arrangement of [DEEA][Pro], which would occur by intermolecular interactions. This raises the entropy of the reaction. Choices A and B can be eliminated. Decreasing temperature would have the opposite effect and increase attractive forces, eliminating choice D and making choice C the best answer.

TEST 4A A&E

Passage 4 (Questions 18-21)

18. B is the best answer. The first paragraph of the passage notes that PA is highly volatile and easily evaporates at room temperature. Molecules evaporate when they gain enough kinetic energy to overcome to attractive forces in the liquid solution, allowing the compound to escape into the vapor phase. Kinetic energy is directly proportional to temperature by the following equation: $KE = \frac{3}{2}kT$. Decreasing the temperature would decrease kinetic energy, which would decrease the number of molecules of PA that are capable of evaporating. Option I is a component of the best answer. Vaporization occurs when the vapor pressure above the liquid and the atmospheric pressure are equal. A higher atmospheric pressure would likely prevent as much vaporization, as the vapor pressure would need to increase by that much as well. Option II is likely a component of the best answer. A large surface area would allow the PA compounds to space out even further, minimizing the attractive forces between compounds. This would likely increase vaporization, eliminating option III. Choice B is the best answer, as it contains a combination of options I and II.

19. A is the best answer. The passage provides the equation that should be used to solve this question: $\Delta G_b° = E_{complex} - E_{\beta-CD} - E_{PA}$. Plugging in the numbers provided in the table gives $\Delta G_b° = -781$ kcal/mol – (–744 kcal/mol) – (–27 kcal/mol) = –10 kcal/mol. Choices C and D can be eliminated, which would result from –781 kcal/mol – 744 kcal/mol – 27 kcal/mol. Next choose whether the reaction is spontaneous. Since the ΔG value is negative, the reaction is exergonic or spontaneous. If the ΔG value was positive, then the reaction would be endergonic or non-spontaneous. This eliminates choice B and makes choice A the best answer.

20. C is the best answer. Both the passage and the provided reaction show that the reaction is stoichiometric, meaning one PA combines with one β-CD. Because the reaction is described as elementary, the coefficient of the compounds in the chemical reaction can be used to predict the overall order of the reaction. Remember that the reaction order can only be predicted from the chemical equation if it is described as elementary. Otherwise, the reaction order needs to be experimentally determined. The coefficient in front of β-CD is one, meaning the order with respect to β-CD is also one. Choice A can be eliminated. To get the overall order of the reaction, combine the coefficients in front of the two reactants. 1 + 1 = 2, so the overall order with respect to the reactants is the overall order of the reaction. Choice B can be eliminated, and choice C is most likely to be the best answer. Only when the reaction is described as elementary can the coefficient be used to predict the overall order. Choice D can be eliminated, as the question stem notes that the reaction is elementary.

21. A is the best answer. This question is asking about the change in free energy, ΔG, the change in the activation energy, E_a, and $\Delta G^‡$, of the solubility reaction. Notice that the acidic condition has greater solubility in a shorter amount of time, while the basic condition has lower solubility and a longer solubility time. If the acid acted as a catalyst to lower the activation energy, the reaction would proceed more quickly, making choice A a possible answer. This can be confirmed with the equation, $k = Ae^{-Ea/RT}$, where A is the Arrhenius constant, R is the gas constant, and T is the temperature. By this formula, if E_a decreases, the rate of the reaction, k, increases. The addition of a catalyst can only change the activation energy of a reaction, not the thermodynamic properties of the reactants or products, meaning the ΔG cannot be changed by a catalyst. Choices B and D can be eliminated. The reaction with the longest amount of time would likely have the greatest activation energy, meaning the basic pH likely raises the $\Delta G^‡$ the most. Choice C is less likely than choice A to be the best answer. Notice that the solubility values provided in the table are more of a distractor and are not important in choosing the best answer.

Passage 5 (Questions 22-25)

22. C is the best answer. Use the equation:

$$\Delta H°_{reaction} = \Delta H°_{f\ products} - \Delta H°_{f\ reactants}$$

Remember that elements in the native form, such as the carbon liberated at the end of Reaction 2, have a heat of formation of 0 kJ/mol.

$$[6\Delta H_f°(C(s)) + 6\Delta H_f°(H_2O(l))] - [1\Delta H_f°(C_6H_{12}O_6(s))]$$

$$[(6 \text{ mol of C} \times 0 \text{ kJ/mol}) + (6 \text{ mol of } H_2O \times -285.8 \text{ kJ/mol})] - [-1271 \text{ kJ/mol}] \approx -1800 + 1271 = -529 \text{ kJ/mol.}$$

Choice C is the closest answer to this calculated value and is the best answer.

Remember to multiply the heat of formation by the number of moles in the reaction according to Hess's Law of Summation. Also, do not forget that the order of this equation is the heat of products minus the heat of reactants, not the reverse. In thermochemistry, negative energy values mean that energy leaves the system. Positive energy values mean that energy is being put into the system. The negative answer here means that this decomposition reaction is exothermic, releasing energy from the system into the surroundings.

23. **A is the best answer.** According to Le Châtelier's principle, equilibrium reactions respond to perturbations by readjusting to counteract the change. If more products are added, the reaction will seek to remove products by forming the original reactants, and vice-versa. Adding $CO_2(g)$ and $H_2O(g)$ will drive the reaction to the left to try to remove these species by re-forming $NaHCO_3(s)$. Options I and II should be part of the best answer.

Since this reaction is performed in a sealed vessel, and some of the products are gaseous, pressure is also a product of the reaction. Although adding helium gas will increase the pressure in the vessel, don't be misled. The addition of an inert gas to an equilibrium mixture is an important exception to Le Châtelier's principle. This change does not affect the equilibrium, and no change in the concentration of any chemical is expected. A way to understand this exception is to remember that the equilibrium constant, K_{eq}, is based on the concentration of products and reactants. Addition of an inert gas to a sealed container does not change these concentrations. Option III is not part of the best answer. Choice A is the best answer.

24. **C is the best answer.** Temperature is a measure of the average kinetic energy of a system, and reactions depend on collisions between particles. At a higher temperature, more and higher energy collisions are able to occur, and it is easier for the particles to react. If the temperature requirements to start a reaction are high, that means that the activation energy of that reaction is high as well. The expansion reaction with the highest activation energy will be the material that begins to expand at the highest temperature and vice versa. LLC should be first because it requires the least energy to begin expanding. Eliminate choices B and D. Next, should be KKC, with SSC at the very end of the list. Select the best answer, which is choice C. Choice A is tempting, but it has the order of the last two items reversed.

25. **C is the best answer.** Remember that if $E_{a\ forwards}$ increases or decreases, so will $E_{a\ backwards}$. Also, remember that catalysts only reduce the activation energy of the reaction but have no effect on the equilibrium. In the presence of a catalyst, the reaction requires less energy to proceed, which generally increases the speed of the reaction. K_{eq} remains the same in the presence of a catalyst, because even though it is easier for the reaction to produce more products, it is also easier to produce more reactants! The activation energy is reduced in both directions. Choice C is the best answer, and the second part of this answer choice is really just a distractor. Changing E_a in one direction means that it will change by that same magnitude in the other direction. So this answer choice could really be read, "does not have an effect on K_{eq} because $E_{a\ reaction}$ has decreased. Since addition of a catalyst has no effect on the value of K_{eq}, choices A, B, and D, can be eliminated.

Stand-alones (Questions 26-29)

26. **D is the best answer.** It is true that a catalyst would increase the rate of the reaction, but it would do so by stabilizing the transition state, which lowers the activation energy, rather than stabilizing the final products, which would make the reaction more thermodynamically favorable, so choice A is a weaker answer. The rate is under more influence by the concentration of B, but the concentration of A has an effect on the rate law since it was determined to be first order experimentally. Changing the concentration of A will change the rate of the reaction, making choice B a weaker answer. The order of the overall reaction is calculated by adding the order of each reactant together. In the case of this reaction, the overall order would be three, eliminating choice C. Since the reaction is zero order with respect to C, the rate is not affected by changes to the concentration of C. The rate is determined by the slowest step of the reaction, which means molecule C is not participating in this step, making choice D the best answer.

27. **D is the best answer.** While a transition state is a high energy intermediate, under normal reaction conditions, it is too unstable to be isolated, making choice A a weaker choice. If the transition state is stabilized, less energy is required for it to be created, which makes the reaction go quicker. This is the mechanism for most catalysts including enzymes. Increasing the temperature provides more molecules with a sufficient amount of energy to reach the transition state rather than stabilizing the intermediate, making choice B a weaker option. While the second half of choice C is accurate, the transition state is a high-energy complex, eliminating choice C. The transition state is capable of proceeding to the products of the reaction or breaking apart into the original reactants, making choice D the best answer.

28. **D is the best answer.** The thermodynamics of the reaction cannot be used to determine the kinetics, or speed, of the reaction. A classic example of this is the thermodynamic stabilities of diamond and graphite. Under STP, graphite is lower in energy and the reaction of diamond being converted to graphite is spontaneous. The reaction however, moves incredibly slow. Choices A, B and C can be eliminated, which leaves choice D as the best answer.

29. **B is the best answer.** Raney Ni is a catalyst. Catalysts make reactions proceed faster by reducing the activation energy of a reaction. Remember that even though catalysts can change the activation energy of a reaction, catalysts have no effect on the net change in free energy of a reaction. Choices A and D can be eliminated because they are true. Catalysts like Raney nickel are, by definition, not consumed during a reaction. Eliminate choice C since it is true of Raney nickel.

Finally, increasing the concentration of a catalyst in a reaction will cause the reaction to go faster...up to a point. This point in the above reaction is when all of the substrate molecules, H_2, are saturated with the catalyst, Raney Ni. Adding excess Raney Ni at this point will have no further effect on rate. In other words, increasing the concentration of Raney Ni does not always increase the rate of this reaction. Choice B is the best answer because it is not always true of this reaction. When the MCAT® provides answers that all seem true, one of them is likely to not always be true. Watch out for this trap.

Passage 6 (Questions 30-35)

30. **C is the best answer.** The passage states that the folding of protein Y has a standard enthalpy of −20 kJ/mol. Negative change in enthalpy means that heat is released, and it is an exothermic reaction. As a result, option I is a component of the best answer, and choice B can be eliminated. It is also stated in the passage that the folding of protein Y has a standard Gibbs free energy change of −14 kJ/mol. When the Gibbs free energy change is negative, the process is exergonic, so option II is also a component of the best answer, eliminating choice A. A process is second order if the reaction is bimolecular. Without kinetics experiments, it is impossible to conclude that a reaction is second order. In addition, the passage states that protein X is a monomer, so its folding is more likely to be unimolecular. As a result, option III is not a strong answer, so choice D can be eliminated. After these eliminations, choice C is the best answer.

31. **A is the best answer.** Le Châtelier's principle states that when a system at equilibrium is stressed, the system will shift in a direction that reduces that stress. In this reaction, gaseous carbon dioxide is formed. The carbon dioxide escapes into the atmosphere because the reaction is being performed in an open vessel. The escape of carbon dioxide removes product, causing the reaction to run to completion because no equilibrium can be established. As a result, choice A is not likely to be a true statement. Urea is the limiting reagent because it is dissolved in water, so there will be more molecules of water than urea. As a result, choice B can be eliminated. As ammonia is produced, the molecules can deprotonate water using its electron pair. This process will generate hydroxide ions, which will make the solution basic, so choice C is a weak answer. Nucleophiles are bases, and since ammonia is a base, it is a nucleophile. It is also a nucleophile because of its electron pairs, which can attack electrophiles. As a result, choice D can be eliminated. Choice A, which is most likely to not be a true statement, is the best answer.

32. **D is the best answer.** First, it is important to remember the difference between positive and negative Gibbs free energy values. A negative Gibbs free energy change means that a reaction will occur spontaneously, while a positive Gibbs free energy change means that the reaction will not occur spontaneously. Next, it is important to note that the question is asking for the free energy change of folding for protein Y in pure water. In pure water, the concentration of urea is 0 M. Figure 2 shows the Gibbs free energy change of unfolding at different concentrations of urea. Using linear regression, the data can be extrapolated to determine the Gibbs free energy change of unfolding at 0 M urea. As stated in the passage, it is important to remember that Figure 2 is depicting the Gibbs free energy change of protein unfolding, which is the reverse reaction of protein folding, so any value obtained from the figure needs to be negated if solving for Gibbs free energy change of protein folding. Choice A is the value of ΔG at the highest urea concentration. This data point would provide the Gibbs free energy of unfolding at that urea concentration, not at 0 M urea, eliminating choice A. Choice B uses the y-intercept, where there is no urea present in the solution. The y-intercept would be the best answer, except that this number is not negated, so it depicts the free energy change of unfolding. As a result, choice B is a weak answer. Choice C is a weak answer for the same reason as choice A. Choice D uses the value given by the y-intercept, and negates the value to give the free energy change of folding. As a result, choice D is the best answer.

33. **A is the best answer.** A negative control in an experiment is often used to ensure the experimental procedure is working correctly. A negative control uses a very similar setup to the experimental group, except its omits results are not expected to fluctuate with changes in the independent variable. This set-up allows the experimenter to establish what effect the remaining reagents will have on the experimental measurements. Ideally, in this situation, chancing the independent variable, which is the concentration of urea, should be not change in the dependent variable, which is the measured fluorescence that serves as an indirect way of measuring protein folding in this experiment. Choice A leaves urea and removes protein, which enables researchers to assess if the urea is contributing to any of the measured fluorescence. The researcher does not expect any fluorescence when no protein is present, making choice A a good negative control. Choice B is not a strong answer because it uses the same conditions as the experimental group. The fluorescence is caused by tryptophan in the protein under investigation, so it makes the most sense to remove the protein in the control group. The presence of protein and absence of urea is one of the experimental conditions tested. While this would establish a baseline fluorescence, it would not allow the researcher to determine if the concentration of urea was influencing the fluorescence independent of the effect it has on protein folding. This reasoning makes choice C a weaker answer than choice A. Because the reaction is in equilibrium does not mean that a negative control is not required. It is still necessary to validate the experimental procedure Choice D can be eliminated. As a result, choice A is the best answer.

34. **B is the best answer.** The relationship between Gibbs free energy, enthalpy, and entropy, is given by the following equation: $\Delta G° = \Delta H° - T\Delta S°$, where $\Delta G°$ is standard Gibbs free energy change, $\Delta H°$ is standard enthalpy change, T is absolute temperature in Kelvin, and $\Delta S°$ is standard entropy change. All of these calculations use Kelvin for temperature because it always has a positive value, so it is important to convert temperature from Celsius to Kelvin using the equation K = °C + 273. The temperature in Kelvin is K = 25°C + 273 = 298 K. The first equation can be rearranged to find that $\Delta S° = \frac{\Delta H° - \Delta G°}{T}$. Now the values from the passage are plugged in: $\Delta S° = \frac{\left(-20\frac{\text{kJ}}{\text{mol}}\right)-\left(-14\frac{\text{kJ}}{\text{mol}}\right)}{298\ K} = 0.0201\frac{\text{kJ}\cdot\text{mol}}{K} = -20.1\frac{\text{kJ}\cdot\text{mol}}{K}$. Choice A does not convert the temperature from Celsius to Kelvin. Choice B does convert temperature from Celsius to Kelvin and has the correct sign. Choice C is a good answer, except it has the entropy as positive, as opposed to negative. Choice D can be eliminated because it both has positive entropy and also fails to convert the temperature from Celsius to Kelvin. As a result, choice B is the best answer.

35. **C is the best answer.** The incorrect calibration of the fluorometer will result in all data points being shifted upwards by the same amount. Bias occurs when all data points are shifted by the same degree and in the same direction away from the true value. The incorrect calibration of the fluorometer introduces bias. Bias does not have to result from an intentional manipulation of the data. As a result, option I is a component of the best answer, and choice B can be eliminated. Accuracy refers to how close measurements are to the true value. Because the incorrect calibration resulted in all data being shifted away from the true value, accuracy was affected, so option II is likely a component of the best answer. As a result, choice A can be eliminated. The experimental method calculates Gibbs free energy from the equilibrium constant. The equation relating the two is $\Delta G° = -RT\ln K_{eq}$. It is important to remember that the temperature in the equation needs to be in Kelvin, not centigrade. The thermometer recorded a temperature of 50°C, which is twice the actual value of 25°C. Once the conversion is made from centigrade to Kelvin, the relative difference between actual and measured temperature is much smaller because K = °C + 273.So while the error in temperature measurement would increase the Gibbs free energy change, the value would not double. This reasoning eliminates option III and choice D. As a result, choice C is the best answer.

Passage 7 (Questions 36-39)

TEST 4A A&E

36. **C is the best answer.** Equation 1 solves for the energy released during the combustion of the analyte. This quantity can be determined without knowing the mass of the analyte. Option I is false. It is tricky because heat capacity, another common thermochemical value, relies on knowing the mass of the analyte.

If the saturation vapor pressure of water is reached inside the calorimeter, then no water can vaporize. This is important because, if this is not the case, some of the heat released during the reaction will vaporize the water, which is a product of the combustion reaction. If this heat vaporizes water, it will not heat the water bath, and the measurement of energy released during combustion will be artificially low. The assumption of maintaining a saturated water vapor pressure inside the bomb calorimeter is necessary for Equation 1 to be valid. Option II is true. Although the vapor may become unsaturated as the temperature inside the calorimeter increases during the reaction, it is assumed that the heat inside the calorimeter is dissipated too rapidly into the water bath for it to rise significantly enough to change the saturation vapor pressure.

If the iron fuse is not completely consumed during the reaction, then performing the calculation as written in Equation 1 will lead to an artificially low measurement of energy released. The experimenter would be subtracting energy from the total energy released during the reaction that was never released by the reaction to heat the water. Option III is true. It is necessary for the entire mass of iron to be consumed for this equation to remain valid. The best answer will contain options II and III. Choice C is the best answer.

37. **A is the best answer.** ΔT is defined as $\text{Temperature}_{\text{final}} - \text{Temperature}_{\text{initial}}$. The final temperature will be the maximum temperature the bomb calorimeter reaches, and, by proxy, the water bath, before they start losing energy to the surroundings. This temperature is the best measurement of the total energy that the water absorbed. According to Figure 1, this final temperature is about 36°C. The initial temperature, an average of the first few points on the graph before combustion began, is 25°C. ΔT = 36°C – 25°C = 11°C. Choice A is the best answer. Choice B has the wrong sign. Remember in thermodynamics that when the temperature of a system increases, its temperature change is positive. Choices C and D were calculated using the final point on the graph for $\text{temperature}_{\text{final}}$. The final temperature, as explained above, is the highest measured temperature during the experiment, not the last point on the graph. Eliminate choices C and D.

38. **D is the best answer.** Figure 1 indicates that the water temperature was initially well above room temperature. Energy flows from regions of higher temperature to lower temperature, never the reverse. In other words, energy was not gained from the surroundings in this experiment because the surroundings were "colder" than the system. Eliminate choice A. Since the water bath eventually cooled down, it had to release its energy into the surroundings. Since the second part of choice B states the opposite, choice B can be eliminated. Remember the first law of thermodynamics, $\Delta E = q + w$, says that the change in internal energy of a system is equal to the sum of the heat gained or lost by the system and the work done on/by the system. The system of this experiment is the bomb calorimeter and its water bath. The surrounding system is everything else in the universe. As described above, in order to return to room temperature from a state of higher energy, the water must release energy into the surroundings. Remember that when energy is released, $q < 0$. Since no PV work was performed, $w = 0$. This means that $\Delta E < 0$ as well. Choice D is better than choice C because choice C states that $\Delta E = 0$. Choice D is the best answer.

39. **B is the best answer.** Consider the process by which oxidation occurs inside the calorimeter. First, a current, consisting of electrical energy, travels through an iron fuse in a highly pressurized oxygen atmosphere. Next, the iron fuse becomes hot because of the current travelling through it, which manifests as thermal energy. The hot iron achieves the activation energy necessary to react with the oxygen in the bomb calorimeter, initiating the primary oxidation reaction and liberating more energy because it is forming a more stable iron oxide. This is an example of a change to chemical energy. Finally, heat from this oxidation reaction is dissipated into the water, in the form of thermal energy, which surrounds the bomb calorimeter. Since this reaction begins with a current travelling through the fuse, electrical energy must be the first part of the answer. Choices A and D should be eliminated. In order, energy is converted from electrical, to thermal, to chemical, and back to thermal energy. Choice B restates this, and is the best answer. The heat caused by the current is what initiates the chemical combustion of the fuse, not the electrical energy. For this reason, choice B is stronger than choice C and is the better answer.

Stand-alones (Questions 40-43)

40. **B is the best answer.** The reaction order can be cited with respect to a particular reactant or with respect to the overall reactants. When the reaction is an elementary reaction, the coefficients in front of the molecule can be used to determine the overall order of the reaction. When a number does not explicitly appear in front of a molecule, the understood coefficient is one. As the question stem asks for the order of the reaction with respect to only oxygen, the best answer is most likely one. The overall order of the reaction is three, with a value of two coming from the SO_2 compound and a value of one coming from the O_2. Choice B is the best answer.

41. **D is the best answer.** The dependence of reaction rate upon temperature is described by the Arrhenius Equation, $k = Ae^{-E_a/RT}$, where A is the Arrhenius constant, E_a is the activation energy, R is the gas constant, and T is temperature. A decrease in temperature would result in a lower rate of reaction, causing more pyruvate to remain and less to be converted to lactic acid. This makes choices A and B both true, eliminating them as best answers because the question is asking for the LEAST likely result. The reaction rate is likely to decrease, eliminating choice C, and making choice D the best answer.

42. **C is the best answer.** Enzymes are biological catalysts that reduce the activation energy of the reactions in which they are participating. According to the Arrhenius equation, $k = Ae^{-E_a/RT}$, decreasing the value of the activation energy, E_a, increases the value of the rate constant k, increasing the rate of the reaction. Option I will be part of the best answer, and choice B can be eliminated. After the addition of catalase, less activation energy is required to initiate the reaction. In other words, the particles do not require the same amount of kinetic energy to initiate the reaction. Since temperature is a measure of the average kinetic energy of a system, if a reaction will proceed with less kinetic energy, at the macroscopic level, the reaction will proceed at a lower temperature. Option II will be part of the best answer as well. Choice A can be eliminated. Finally, catalysts do *not* change the equilibrium constant of a reaction. After addition of a catalyst, the reverse reaction and forward reaction are both made equally "easier" by virtue of having a smaller activation energy "hill" to overcome. The reaction reaches the same equilibrium, just at a quicker rate. Option III will not be part of the best answer, and choice D can be eliminated. Choice C is the best answer.

43. **B is the best answer.** The larger number of bonds that are broken, the greater the enthalpic change. Denaturation of DNA is a process that separates 2 DNA strands, and the major change in terms of bonding is the breaking of hydrogen bonds. Thus, the DNA with higher C/G content, and more hydrogen bonds to break, would have a greater magnitude of enthalpic change. This eliminates choices C and D. Entropy is a measure of disorder in a system. In the denaturation of both strands, the primary change in entropy is due to the conversion of a single paired strand into two unpaired strands. This is fairly constant in both reactions, so choice B is the best answer. The entropic change will be comparable.

Passage 8 (Questions 44-48)

44. **B is the best answer.** The x-axis of Figure 1 shows increasing pH, while the y-axis shows the change in enthalpy, or ΔH, of the binding reaction. Entropy is a measure of disorder and is represented by ΔS, which is not plotted in Figure 1. Choice A is less likely to be the best answer, as the entropy of the reaction is not determined. Notice that as the pH decreases, the ΔH of the reaction becomes more negative. This indicates that the reaction is becoming more exothermic, likely making choice B the best answer. Notice that all the values for the enthalpy are negative, meaning that the reaction is exothermic. As the pH increases, the reaction becomes less exothermic but the ΔH never becomes positive, meaning the reaction does not become endothermic. Choice C can be eliminated. Because entropy is not considered in Figure 1, choice D is less likely than choice B to be the best answer.

45. **B is the best answer.** The binding of the inhibitor can be described by the following chemical reaction, where the interaction of the inhibitor and the protein form one complex.

$$\text{Geldanamycin} + \text{Hsp90} \leftrightarrow \text{Geldanamycin-Hsp90}.$$

Notice that there are two reactants and one product, meaning the entropy of the reaction decreases, not increases, as there is less disorder. This eliminates choices A and C. For any chemical reaction to occur, the entropy change of the universe must either be zero or positive, as the Second Law of Thermodynamics states that the entropy of an isolated system will never decrease. The fact that the entropy of the universe cannot decrease makes choice B more likely to be the best answer than choice D.

46. **A is the best answer.** Figure 2 provides the best information to help answer this question. The ΔG of a reaction predicts whether the reaction will be spontaneous or not. Notice that the binding of all inhibitors produces a negative ΔG, ΔH, and $T\Delta S$. The ΔG can be calculated by $\Delta G = \Delta H - T\Delta S$, meaning that both enthalpy and entropy contribute to the spontaneity of the reaction. The bar corresponding to enthalpy, ΔH, is significantly more negative than the $T\Delta S$ bar corresponding to entropy. This suggests that the enthalpy contributes more to the spontaneity of the reaction than the entropy, likely making choice A the best answer. The contribution of the entropy to the reaction is much less than the enthalpy, eliminating choice B. The bars do not contribute equally to the free energy change of the reaction, eliminating choice C. As both entropy and enthalpy contribute to the spontaneity of a reaction, choice D can be eliminated.

47. **C is the best answer.** Radicicol binding to Hsp90 decreases the entropy of the reaction, as the enzyme and inhibitor form a complex. Thus, the reaction goes from two compounds to one compound, decreasing entropy and eliminating choice A. Both Figures 1 and 2 show that the enthalpy of the reactions between the inhibitor and Hsp90 is negative. It is reasonable to assume that the binding of a similar compound radicicol would also give a negative enthalpy, meaning that no heat would be needed. Choice B can be eliminated. Epoxide rings are highly sterically strained, and a reaction with a strong nucleophile would be likely to break the epoxide ring in an energetically favorable reaction, which would also be exothermic. The reaction is highly exothermic due to the relief of the high energy ring strain. Breaking bonds actually requires an input of energy, but the energy released due to relieving the ring strain makes the overall reaction exothermic. Choice C is most likely to be the best answer. The Gibbs Free Energy values for all the ICPD compounds binding to Hsp90 are negative, meaning the reaction is spontaneous. Choice D can be eliminated.

48. **D is the best answer.** The movement of the piston represents changes to the volume of air that is present in box. The scientist uses the position of the piston to estimate changes in heat, as the volume of the air is proportional to the temperature of the air by $PV = nRT$. A reaction that is exothermic releases heat into the environment, which would increase the volume of the air inside the box, pushing the piston up. This expansion of the volume generates the work necessary to move the piston, as the movement of the piston increases the volume to allow for the pressure to remain constant. Under constant pressure, the volume change is proportional to the change in temperature. If no change in heat were expected, the piston would remain stationary, eliminating choice A. The piston would be expected to rise over the course of the experiment as more heat was released due to the binding of the inhibitor to Hsp90. It would not be expected to fall, as the reaction is not endothermic. Choices B and C can be eliminated. The piston would most likely rise until the end of the reaction, when no additional heat was being generated, making choice D the best answer.

Passage 9 (Questions 49-52)

49. B is the best answer. The fourth paragraph of the passage describes that ΔH can be found in the first enthalpic measurements taken during the experiment. Since Compound 1 was added to a solution containing HS fragments, the first addition of Compound 1 will be the source of the first enthalpic measurement. This first addition is represented by the smallest concentration of Compound 1 to the concentration of HS fragments in the x-axis, and is the first point on Figure 2 moving left to right. The value of this measurement is about −32 kJ/mol. However, before plugging this value into the right side of Equation 1, convert the units of this measurement into cal/mol because the answer choices and ΔS are in this unit. Table 1 provides that the ΔS for Trial 1 is 4.46 cal/mol. Do not forget that this equation needs the temperature to be expressed in Kelvin.

$$37°\text{C} + 273.15 = 310.15\text{ K}$$

Now, plug into Equation 1:

$$\Delta G = \Delta H - T\Delta S$$

$$\Delta G = (-32\text{ kJ/mol})(1000\text{ J/kJ})(1\text{ cal}/4.2\text{ J}) - [(310.15\text{ K} \times 4.46\text{ cal/mol} \cdot \text{K})]$$

$$\approx (-32 \times 10^3\text{ J})(1\text{ cal}/4\text{ J}) - (300\text{ K} \times 4.5\text{ cal/mol} \cdot \text{K}) = 9350\text{ cal/mol.}$$ Choice B is the best answer.

If the final enthalpic measurements instead of the initial enthalpic measurements been used, choice A would result. If the enthalpy provided in Figure 2 were not converted to cal/mol, choice C would have been calculated. Had the temperature in Celsius not been converted to absolute temperature, choice D would result.

50. D is the best answer. Figure 2 shows that the reaction between Compound 1 and HS-fragments is an exothermic reaction. If the solution containing Compound 1 has a lower temperature than the experimental cell, then some of the heat liberated during Reaction 1 will be used to heat the solution that contained Compound 1, and less will be available to heat the combined solutions in the experimental cell. Thus, the power applied to the experimental cell to keep it at thermal equilibrium with the reference cell will be greater than it was in the original experiment because energy is lost through warming the colder solution. Choice A can be eliminated. The passage explains that less power is applied during exothermic processes, and more power is applied during endothermic passages. This relationship indicates that more power is needed to be applied to the experimental cell during a weakly exothermic reaction, compared to a strongly exothermic reaction. Essentially, the reaction occurring in the experimental cell does a poor job "heating itself up," and "keeping up" with the reference cell, which receives a steady amount of power. In other words, greater energy input will be associated with a lower ΔH. Choice D is the best answer. Choices B and C can be eliminated.

51. B is the best answer. This is an algebra substitution problem involving logarithms. Remember a property of logarithms: If log(x) = y, then $\log(x^{-1}) = -y$. This property is true of logarithms to any base, including *e*. In the second to last paragraph of the passage, the relationship between K_a and K_D is provided: $K_a = K_D^{-1}$

Suppose $RT\ln(K_D) = x$.

According to the property above, $RT\ln(K_D^{-1}) = -x$.

Thus, $-[RT\ln(K_D^{-1})] = x = -[RT\ln(K_a)] = RT\ln(K_D) = \Delta G$.

Choice B is the best answer. Choice C can be eliminated because substituting one non-equivalent variable into an expression changes the value of the expression. The other answer choices look like sophisticated algebra is needed to be performed to reach them, but they are distractors and not the result of any specific error.

52. B is the best answer. All of the cells contain the same mass of fluid, and mercury has a far lower specific heat capacity than benzene. For any given input of power, the mercury containing experimental cell's temperature (cell X) will increase more substantially than the benzene containing experimental cell (cell Y). Eliminate choice A. This question is really testing the zeroth law of thermodynamics, namely, that temperature exists, and represents the average kinetic energy of the particles whose temperature is being measured. To state this law more precisely: If systems A and B are in thermal equilibrium with one another, and systems B and C are in thermal equilibrium with one another, then systems A, B, and C are all in thermal equilibrium with one another. This means they all share the same temperature. Since temperature is just a measurement of the average kinetic energy of a group of particles, systems A, B, and C also all share the same average kinetic energy. Apply this rule to the case described in this problem. The experimental cells X and Y and the reference cell are all in thermal equilibrium with one another. This means that all three cells share the same temperature, and that the particles in them share the same average kinetic energy. Choice B is the best answer, and choices C and D can be eliminated.

Passage 10 (Questions 53-56)

53. **C is the best answer.** The first step to answer this question is to rewrite the given reactions by reversing and/or multiplying them as needed, so when they are added together, they result in Reaction 2. Remember that anytime a reaction is reversed, its change in enthalpy must have its sign reversed as well.

$2 \times (2Fe(s) + 6H_2O(l) \rightarrow 2Fe(OH)_3(s) + 3H_2(g))$	2×321.0 kJ/mol
$3 \times (2H_2(g) + O_2(g) \rightarrow 2H_2O\,(l))$	-3×571.7 kJ/mol
$+\,2 \times (2\,Fe(OH)_3(s) \rightarrow 3H_2O\,(l) + Fe_2O_3(s))$	-2×288.6 kJ/mol
$4Fe(s) + 3O_2(g) \rightarrow 2Fe_2O_3(s)$	$\Delta H° \approx 642 - 1713 - 576 = -1650$ kJ/mol

Choice A is an error that comes from multiplying each thermochemical equation by the appropriate coefficient but not changing the sign for each time a thermochemical equation is rotated about its reaction arrow. Choice B uses a positive sign for the second reaction, and choice D uses a positive sign for the bottom reaction—after multiplying to correct for the stoichiometry. Choices B and D can be eliminated, which makes choice C the best answer.

54. **B is the best answer.** According to Hess's law, the total enthalpy change for a given reaction is the sum of the enthalpy changes of all the steps that lead to that given reaction. Hess's law makes it possible to add reactions and their enthalpies together to determine the enthalpy of the net reaction. Molecules or elements found on both sides of the reaction arrows in different equations can be crossed out as shown below. Since the goal is to calculate the enthalpy of the net reaction, and there is no net gain or loss of these species, they do not contribute to the change in enthalpy. Adding Reaction 1, after flipping the equation and multiplying it by 2, to the reaction provided in the question stem provides the final net thermochemical equation, as shown:

$-2[\cancel{NaCl(s)} + \frac{3}{2}O_2(g) \rightarrow NaClO_3(s)$	$\Delta H° = -45.76$ kJ/mol)]
$+\,2Na(s) + Cl_2(g) \rightarrow \cancel{2NaCl(s)}$	$\Delta H° = -411$ kJ/mol
$2Na(s) + Cl_2(g) + 3O_2(g) \rightarrow 2NaClO_3(s)$	$\Delta H° = -319.5$ kJ/mol

Although choice A correctly changes the sign of $\Delta H°$ after rotating the equation, it fails to use the appropriate coefficient of 2 to multiply the molecules so they "cancel" one another out to provide the target equation. Choice A can be eliminated. Choice C reflects the simple addition of all of the $\Delta H°$ values. This approach does not result in the final net equation as the stoichiometry has not been appropriately scaled to provide the target net equation. Finally, choice D, although successfully scaling the equations to cancel out terms that are not in the net equation, fails to change the sign of $\Delta H°$ of the first equation, after rotating it. Remember if an equation is rotated, then its $\Delta H°$ must be multiplied by -1. Choice D can be eliminated.

55. **C is the best answer.** The first law of thermodynamics describes how the internal energy of a closed and isolated system is conserved, being equal to the heat put into the system minus the work performed by the system. The second law of thermodynamics describes how the entropy, or disorder, of the universe is always increasing. Among these answer choices, the constancy of the energy in the closed candle-mine system, despite energy loss from the candle (gained by the air), is an example of the first law. The ever increasing dispersal of energy throughout this same system is an example of the second law. Choice A can be eliminated, as it attaches the first law of thermodynamics with an example of the second law. Remember the third law of thermodynamics describes the existence of an absolute zero, where a system exists with the minimum possible energy. Choice B attaches an example of the first law of thermodynamics to the third law and can be eliminated. Choice C describes energy becoming more spread out throughout the universe, and properly connects it with the second law. Choice C is probably the best answer, but eliminate choice D to be sure. The zeroth law of thermodynamics describes the existence of temperature, and that thermal energy does not pass between two items that have the same temperature. An example of the zeroth law would be putting two cups of warm water, at the same temperature, into thermal contact with each other, and noting that one cup does not become cooler as the other one becomes hotter. Since choice D does not discuss temperature at all, it can be eliminated. Choice C is the best answer.

56. **D is the best answer.** The terms spontaneity, entropy and enthalpy are all contained in the equation for the change in Gibb's free energy: $\Delta G = \Delta H - T\Delta S$. A reaction is spontaneous if $\Delta G < 0$ kJ/mol, and a reaction is non-spontaneous if $\Delta G > 0$ kJ/mol. Since Reaction 1 has a negative change in enthalpy as evidenced by its negative ΔH value, and choice A claims it experiences a positive change in enthalpy, it can be eliminated. Reaction 1 is spontaneous at all temperatures because $\Delta H < 0$ kJ/mol and $\Delta S > 0$ kJ/mol—for every 2 moles of solid reactants consumed, 2 moles of solid product and 3 moles of gaseous products are produced. ΔG will be a negative number regardless of the temperature. Choices B and C can be eliminated on this basis. Finally, choice D is the best answer because it explains why ΔG is less than zero at any temperature for this reaction. Knowing how to interpret this equation is a high yield concept tested on the MCAT®.

TEST 4A A&E

Stand-alones (Questions 57-59)

57. C is the best answer. The units here can be tricky! Remember that a Pascal is just 1 N/m^2. The volume needs to be converted to cm^3 in order to properly use this equation. Dimensional analysis is a great tool for solving difficult conversions. Use the equation $W = P\Delta V$ to solve this problem, where ΔV is equal to 2.3 L.

$$\left(10^5 \frac{N}{m^2}\right)(2.3\ L)(1000\ cm^3/L)\left(\frac{1\ m}{100\ cm}\right)\left(\frac{1\ m}{100\ cm}\right)\left(\frac{1\ m}{100\ cm}\right) = (1 \times 10^5\ N/m^2) \times (2.3 \times 10^{-3}\ m^3) = 230\ J$$

Choice C is the best answer. If the volume was not converted to m^3, then choice A would be selected. If the pressure and volume were both not converted, then choices B or D would be chosen.

58. B is the best answer. The change in enthalpy is the bottom half of a reaction coordinate energy diagram. This would be the value of Y. X is the activation energy. Z is the sum of the activation energy and the change in enthalpy for this reaction. In other words, $X + Y = Z$. Since Y is not listed as a choice alone, it can be re-expressed algebraically as $Y = Z - X$, and choice B is the best answer. If the activation energy were confused for the change in enthalpy, choice A would result. The sum of the change in enthalpy and the activation energy is choice C. This is not what the question is asking, so eliminate choice C. Adding any value to Y will generate a value which exceeds the change in enthalpy. Choice D can be eliminated.

59. C is the best answer. The second law of thermodynamics describes that the entropy of the universe is always increasing. The best answer will describe a step during the formation of a macromolecule-ligand complex that increases the entropy of the universe. Two molecules coming together to form a single larger complex decreases the entropy in the universe. Choice A can be eliminated. The aqueous solvation layer is the highly ordered water layer that surrounds a non-polar material in solution. The formation of this layer requires a decrease in entropy, as the water molecules which participate in it are less free to move elsewhere in solution. If this layer decreases in size, then the entropy of the universe increases, as the water molecules which were in the layer are now free to move elsewhere in the solution. Choice B can be eliminated, and choice C is a strong answer. Although choice D represents a process with a positive change in entropy, this step does not occur during the *formation* of macromolecule-ligand complexes. Choice D can be eliminated, and choice C is the best answer.

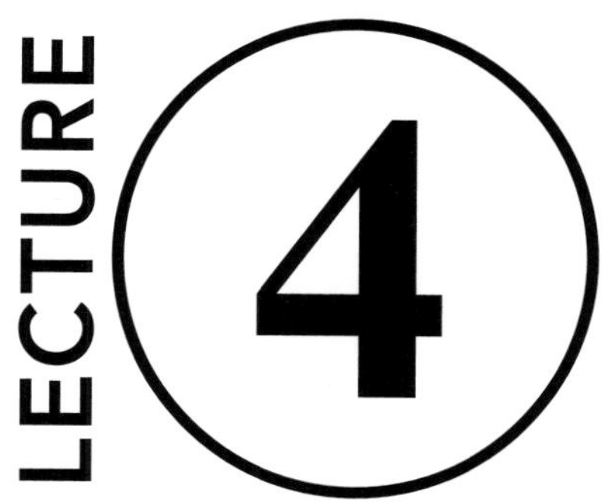

Thermodynamics and Kinetics

MINI-TEST 4B

ANSWERS & EXPLANATIONS

Questions 1–29

Passage 1 (Questions 1-4)

1. **D is the best answer.** The enthalpy of a reaction can be determined by comparing the bond energies of the broken bonds that were initially present with those newly formed. To answer this question, carefully confirm that the changes described in each choice are in fact occurring and also accurate in terms of energy release or absorption. Bonds stabilize compounds and bring them to a lower energy level, releasing energy. Meanwhile, breaking bonds requires increasing the energy of the participants in a bond to a higher energy level. All four choices correctly pair energy absorption with bond breaking and energy release with bond formation. Next, there is a C–N bond present that is broken after step 1. There is also a new C–O and a new N–H bond. Though there is a new hydroxyl functional group after step 1, the O–H bond did not form as a result of step 1, so choice D is the best answer.

2. **C is the best answer.** Enzymes are biological catalysts, and this category of molecules do not impact the equilibrium of a reaction. This fact rules out choices A and B. Enzymes reduce the energy required to reach the transition state of a reaction, speeding it up. Compare the ΔG of the transition state for the catalyzed steps 1 and 2 to the ΔG of the transition state for the uncatalyzed steps. The reduction in this value is greater according to the statement at the end of paragraph 1, so choice C is the best answer. The greater effect on step 1 suggests that speed of step 1 is increased by HOGG1 more than step 2, ruling out choice D.

3. **B is the best answer.** Use the equation $\Delta G = \Delta H - T\Delta S$ and the data in Table 1 to solve this problem. Numbers from the table can be directly plugged into this equation. There is only one unknown, temperature. –6.4 kcal/mol = −2.8 kcal/mol − $T \times$ 11.2 cal/(K × mol)). The key mistake to avoid is with the conversion of units for entropy since the unit scale is generally different. Solving for T provides a value of 321.4 K, closest to choice C.

4. **C is the best answer.** This question can be answered using the equation $\Delta G = \Delta H - T\Delta S$ and the data provided in Table 1. Step 1 should always be spontaneous because a reaction is spontaneous when ΔG is negative. Since the ΔH of step 1 is negative and ΔS is positive, ΔG will always be negative. This makes choices A and B unlikely. Step 2 has a positive ΔH and a positive ΔS. Thus, the entropy term is what could make this reaction spontaneous. It can be spontaneous at some temperatures, so choice D is unlikely. Choice C is the best answer because a high temperature amplifies the effect of ΔS on spontaneity, and this condition is needed for ΔS to outweigh ΔH.

TEST 4B A&E

Passage 2 (Questions 5-9)

5. **D is the best answer.** Since each answer is comparing the amount of heat per unit time, the question is essentially asking for the comparison of power output by the two stars. The heat the sun radiates is proportional to $r^2 \times T^4$. Calculating the ratio of this value in the distant star and comparing it to that of the sun helps to solve by what factor the radiation power has changed.

$$\frac{\left(\frac{1}{2}r\right)^2(2T)^4}{r^2T^4} = \frac{\frac{1}{4}r^2 16T^4}{r^2T^4} = 4$$

   The distant star radiates 4 times as much heat as the sun. The other answer choices come from carefully laid traps. As shown by the calculation above, the two stars differ in their power output, so choice A can be eliminated. Choice B results from using 4^2 instead of $(\frac{1}{4})^2$ as the factor by which the radii differ. Choice C results from not accounting for the different radius of the distant star.

6. **C is the best answer.** Conduction is thermal energy transfer via molecular collisions. It is typically associated with hotter solid objects touching colder solid objects. Convection is thermal energy transfer via the movement of a fluid between two objects. Since the R-value is a measure of heat transfer from one side of a solid object to the other side, it is a measure of the conduction ability of a material. A large R-value implies that despite a large temperature difference at each side of a material, very little heat is transferred. In other words, a large R-value shows that the material is a poor conductor of heat. Wood has a large R-value and brick has a low R-value. This means that wood is a poor conductor of heat relative to brick, which eliminates choice A and makes choice C a strong answer. Since the R-value measures the ability to transfer heat via conduction, not convection, there is not any evidence to support choices B and D.

7. **D is the best answer.** Remember that solids are not included when writing an equilibrium constant expression, and that the concentration of the products is divided by the concentration of the reactants. Since solids are not included in the equilibrium expression, choices A and B can be eliminated. Choice C is the reciprocal of the equilibrium constant expression—watch out for this trap, and eliminate choice C. Choice D has the expression correctly written and is the best answer.

8. **A is the best answer.** The reaction quotient, Q, is an indicator of which direction a reaction will proceed. If the reaction quotient is less than K_{eq}, the reaction will proceed towards the product side. If the reaction quotient is greater than K_{eq}, the reaction will proceed towards the reactant side. Since the reaction in this question is proceeding towards the product side, $K_{eq} > Q$. Choice A is a strong answer, and choice C can be eliminated.

   When a reaction is at equilibrium, the concentration of products and reactants is not observably changing. The reaction in this problem is not at equilibrium since hydrogen gas is being produced and released. Since this reaction is not at equilibrium $K_{eq} \neq Q$ and choice B can be eliminated. A K_{eq} with a value of 1 is possible for unique chemical systems, but does not need to be true for a reaction to proceed forward. It is a weaker answer than choice A, so choice D can be eliminated.

9. **C is the best answer.** The energy difference between the reactants and the products is the change in enthalpy. Since the arrow does not go between reactant and product energy levels it is not describing enthalpy—eliminate choices A and D. The energy difference between the reactants and the transition state is $E_{a\,forwards}$ Since this is not represented by the arrow, choice B can be eliminated. and the energy difference between the products and the transition state is $E_{a\,reverse}$. This arrow indicates the $E_{a\,reverse}$, so choice C is the best answer.

Passage 3 (Questions 10-13)

10. **B is the best answer.** Remember that when the exponent of a number is a fraction, the denominator of the fraction represents a root function to apply to the number, and the top of the fraction represents an exponential function to apply to that given root function. In other words, $X^{3/2} = \sqrt{X}^3 = X\sqrt{X}$. If the concentration is doubled, the same logic applies. $2^{3/2} = \sqrt{2}^3 = 2\sqrt{2}$. Choice B is the best answer. The other errors come from not calculating the exponent properly.

11. **D is the best answer.** K_{eq} is sensitive to changes in temperature. Nonetheless, it is not sensitive to isothermal changes in volume. Since K_{eq} is defined as $\frac{[\text{products}]}{[\text{reactants}]}$, quadrupling the volume of the reaction vessel is the same thing as saying that the new $K_{eq} = \frac{\frac{1}{4}[\text{products}]}{\frac{1}{4}[\text{reactants}]} = \frac{[\text{products}]}{[\text{reactants}]}$. K_{eq} does not change with isothermal volume expansion. Choose the best answer, choice D.

12. **D is the best answer.** A catalyst will reduce the activation energy of this reaction, depicted as the highest point on the coordinate energy diagram, but it will not affect the change in energy of the reaction, depicted as the difference in height between the beginning of the graph and the end of the graph. Although choice A correctly shows a greater activation energy than the catalyzed reaction diagram, it shows a change in the energy of this reaction, which is not expected to occur with removal of the catalyst. Choice A can be eliminated. Choice B shows the same activation energy as the catalyzed reaction and also shows a change in the energy of this reaction, so it can be eliminated. Choice C displays a lower activation energy for the uncatalyzed reaction compared to the catalyzed reaction, and it also alters the energy difference that occurs during this reaction. Choice C can be eliminated. Choice D accurately displays an increase in the activation energy while maintaining the overall change in energy between the reactants and products, so it is the best answer.

13. **D is the best answer.** The equilibrium constant will only change if the temperature of the reaction is changed. According to Le Châtelier's principle, the reaction will shift in such a way to reestablish the equilibrium. Reaction 1 is exothermic with a negative reaction enthalpy. This means it releases heat as a "product" and the reverse reaction is endothermic. To partially undo the increase in temperature, the reaction will run in reverse to consume the "excess" heat. Increasing the propensity to run in the reverse direction to relieve the increase in temperature favors the formation of reactants and will increase their concentration. Since $K_{eq} = \frac{[\text{products}]}{[\text{reactants}]}$, the value of K_{eq} will decrease as a result. Choice A would be the expected effect of increasing the temperature of a endothermic reaction (($\Delta H_{reaction} < 0$), but since this is an exothermic reaction, it can be eliminated. By definition, whenever the concentration of products at equilibrium increases, K_{eq} must also increase, so choice B can be eliminated. The same logic applies to choice C. Since an increase in the K_{eq} is expected to result in an increase in the products at equilibrium, choice C can be eliminated. Choice D best predicts the outcome of increasing this particular reaction and is the best answer.

TEST 4B A&E

Stand-alones (Questions 14-17)

14. **D is the best answer.** The entropy of a system as it is heated from a solid to liquid to gas increases because the molecules become less organized. For this reason, choices A and C can be eliminated. The entropy for a system is relatively linear until a state change when there is an abrupt change in the entropy of the system. This is especially pronounced in the liquid to gas transition. The curve most closely resembles choice D.

15. **B is the best answer.** Use the equation $\Delta G = \Delta H - T\Delta S$. In order for a reaction to proceed, ΔG must be less than zero. The question stems provides ΔH. Since the question is asking for the minimum value of entropy that will result in a spontaneous reaction, set up the equation as an inequality.

$$0 \text{ kJ/mol} > 26.4 \text{ kJ/mol} - (298.15 \text{ K} \times \Delta S)$$

Do not forget the units of ΔS are kJ/K · mol, so convert the temperature to Kelvin.

$$\Delta S > (26.4 \text{ kJ/mol})/298.15 \text{ K}$$

$$\Delta S > 0.1 \text{ kJ/K} \cdot \text{mol}$$

Choose the best answer, choice B, as it is closest to the estimated answer. Choice A uses the wrong sign. Choices C and D would result from not converting the temperature units into K, and calculating with temperature in Celsius.

16. **B is the best answer.** Use Hess's law to solve this problem. Multiply Reaction 1 by two, and change the direction of the reaction arrow. Remember to double the change in enthalpy and reverse its sign as well.

$$C_6H_{12}O_6(s) + 6O_2(g) \rightarrow 6CO_2(g) + 6H_2O(l) \quad \Delta H = -2808 \text{ kJ}$$
$$+\ 6CO_2(g) + 6H_2O(l) \rightarrow 2C_3H_6O_3(s) + 6O_2(g) \quad \Delta H = 2688 \text{ kJ}$$
$$C_6H_{12}O_6(s) \rightarrow 2C_3H_6O_3(s) \qquad \Delta H = -120 \text{ kJ}$$

If the enthalpy of Reaction 1 were not doubled, choice A would result. If the sign of the enthalpy of Reaction 1 was not reversed during the addition step, choice C would result. If the two enthalpies were added together, and none of the required manipulations were performed, choice D would result.

17. **B is the best answer.** The first step for solving this reaction is establishing a balance equation. Since the question states this is a hydrolysis reaction, H_2O must be included in the reactants along with urease. The two products formed are carbon dioxide, CO_2, and ammonia, NH_3. The final balanced equation is as follows:

$$(NH_2)_2CO + H_2O \rightarrow CO_2 + 2NH_3$$

Since the ΔH values for these molecules are not provided, an additional way to solve for the ΔH of the reaction is to calculate the total bond dissociation energy in the reactants and subtract it from the total bond dissociation energy of the products. These bond dissociation energies (BDE) can be calculated as follows:

$$\text{BDE of } CO_2 = (\text{moles of } CO_2)(\text{\# of C=O bonds/mol of } CO_2)(\text{BDE of C=O bond}) = (1 \text{ mol})(2 \text{ bonds})(799 \text{ kJ/mol})$$

$$\text{BDE of } CO_2 = 1598 \text{ kJ}$$

$$\text{BDE of } NH_3 = (\text{moles of } NH_3)(\text{\# of N—H bonds/mol of } NH_3)(\text{BDE of N—H bond}) = (2 \text{ mol})(3 \text{ bonds})(391 \text{ kJ/mol})$$

$$\text{BDE of } NH_3 = 2346 \text{ kJ}$$

$$\text{BDE of } H_2O = (\text{moles of } H_2O)(\text{\# of O—H bonds/mol of } H_2O)(\text{BDE of O—H bond}) = (1 \text{ mol})(2 \text{ bonds})(463 \text{ kJ/mol})$$

$$\text{BDE of } H_2O = 926 \text{ kJ}$$

$$\text{BDE of } (NH_2)_2CO = (\text{moles of } (NH_2)_2CO)[(\text{\# of N—H bonds/mol of } (NH_2)_2CO)(\text{BDE of N—H bond}) + (\text{\# of N—C bonds/mol of } (NH_2)_2CO)(\text{BDE of N—C bond}) + (\text{\# of C=O bonds/mol of } (NH_2)_2CO)(\text{BDE of C=O bond})]$$

$$\text{BDE of } (NH_2)_2CO = (1 \text{ mol } (NH_2)_2CO)[(4 \text{ N—H bonds})(391 \text{ kJ}) + (2 \text{ N—C bonds})(305 \text{ kJ}) + (1 \text{ C=O bond})(799 \text{ kJ})$$

$$\text{BDE of } (NH_2)_2CO = 1564 \text{ kJ} + 610 \text{ kJ} + 799 \text{ kJ} = 2973 \text{ kJ}$$

$$\Delta H = \text{BDE}_{\text{products}} - \text{BDE}_{\text{reactants}}$$

$$\Delta H = (1598 \text{ kJ} + 2346 \text{ kJ}) - (926 \text{ kJ} + 2973 \text{ kJ})$$

$$\Delta H = 45 \text{ kJ}$$

If the total bond dissociation energy for the products was subtracted from the reactants, –45 kJ would have been calculated. Choice A can be eliminated. Choices C and D stem from not balancing the equation properly and thus forgetting that there are 2 moles of NH_3 produced, so the BDE for NH_3 has to be multiplied by 2 when calculating the ΔH. Choice B is the best answer.

Passage 4 (Questions 18-21)

18. **B is the best answer.** Use Equation 2 to help answer this question. Notice that the question stem asks for the experimental results at two temperatures, suggesting that this variable should be the first examined. The question stem does not indicate that the concentration of the initial reactant, glucose, differs in the two experiments, eliminating choice A. Equation 2 allows for the concentration of an enzyme to be determined at a particular ratio between reactants and products, w^+, a net reaction rate, v, and a given thermodynamic driving force, $\Delta G'$. During exercise, the temperature of the body is higher, which would decrease the magnitude of the denominator, increasing the concentration of the enzyme that is needed to achieve a given reaction rate and thermodynamic driving force. Choice B is most likely to be the best answer. Additionally, hexokinase is the first enzyme in glycolysis, which converts glucose into glucose-6-phosphate. During exercise, the cell is most likely to break down glycogen into glucose for additional use in glycolysis, eliminating choice C. As the concentration of enzymes required to process glycolytic intermediates increases, due to the increase in temperature according to Equation 2, choice D can be eliminated.

19. **D is the best answer.** The key to answering this question is knowing how to interpret the change in free energy, or ΔG of a reaction. Notice that the ΔG is +22.8 kJ/mol in this reaction. A positive change in free energy is considered non-spontaneous, eliminating choices A and B. A non-spontaneous reaction is thermodynamically unfavorable, making choice D a better answer than choice C.

20. **D is the best answer.** The reaction quotient is used when the reaction is not at equilibrium, as is the case when a reaction just begins. Q represents the reaction quotient, while K represents the equilibrium constant. This immediately allows for choices B and C to be eliminated, as K represents the equilibrium constant, not the reaction quotient. The reaction quotient can be computed by placing the concentrations of the products in the numerator and the concentrations of the reactants in the denominator. This makes choice D a better answer than choice A.

21. **A is the best answer.** In order for any reaction to occur, the entropy of the universe must increase, meaning the universe must get more disordered. Option I is most likely true and should be included in the best answer. The entropy of the overall reaction increases, as one glucose molecule is converted into two pyruvate molecules. Since one molecule is converted into two, the entropy increases, eliminating option II from the best answer. Enzyme catalysis does not impact the thermodynamic properties of a reaction, only the kinetic properties. In other words, enzymes speed up reactions, but do not change the energy levels of the reactants or products. Option III is unlikely to be part of the best answer. Since only option I has evidence that suggests that it should be part of the best answer, choice A is the best answer.

TEST 4B A&E

Passage 5 (Questions 22-26)

22. **B is the best answer.** A few options can be eliminated because they wrongly compare information given in the question stem. The body is kept at a higher temperature than room temperature. Since the experiment was performed at room temperature, any answer that justifies an observed difference as being the result of the *in vivo* experiment being performed at a lower temperature, such as choices C and D, can be eliminated. To decide between choices A and B, consider the equation used to calculate binding affinity, or ΔG: $\Delta G = \Delta H - T\Delta S$. At a higher temperature, entropy is multiplied by a larger number, so entropy plays a larger role than enthalpy when compared to the same reaction at a lower temperature. Thus, choice A is unlikely, and choice B is the best answer.

23. **C is the best answer.** The equation for the calculation of ΔG is $\Delta G = \Delta H - T\Delta S$. All of the information required to perform this calculation is given in Table 1. $\Delta H = -18.1$ kcal/mol while $T\Delta S = 17.7$ kcal/mol. The best answer is −18.1 kcal/mol − 17.7 kcal/mol = −35.8 kcal/mol. Choice C is the best answer. Choice A is the result of multiplication of these two terms, so it is unlikely. Choice B is unlikely because it is the result of addition of the two values. Choice D is unlikely as it is the result of subtracting the enthalpy term from the entropy term, reversing the equation to calculate binding affinity.

24. **D is the best answer.** The effect of pH is not explored by the experiments in this passage, but it is stated that only the deprotonated sulfonamides can bind to carbonic anhydrases. Thus, it is likely that high pH, where a greater fraction of any given compound would be deprotonated, would improve binding of sulfonamides to CA active sites. Choices A and B are unlikely. Temperature impacts the $T\Delta S$ term by increasing its magnitude. A more negative value would be favorable in terms of impact of ΔG, so high temperature would be best for 1b binding. Choice D is the best answer, and choice C can be ruled out.

25. **A is the best answer.** Option I discusses enthalpy, which is the difference between bonds broken and bonds formed for a given interaction or reaction. The enthalpy (ΔH) is larger in magnitude for 2b than 1b, as the value for 2b is −31.7 while the value for 1b is −16.6. Thus, choice A is a likely answer. Choice A is essentially saying that the enthalpy value for 1b binding is smaller than the enthalpy value for 2b, meaning that more energy is released based on bond breaking and forming with 2b. The negative sign indicates that the products are lower energy, and a bond was likely formed. Choice B is hard to determine because the data provided in Table 1 only gives information about equilibrium, not kinetics. Thus, it is unlikely to be the correct answer. Choice C is unlikely because temperature impacts the entropy term when determining binding affinity only in magnitude. Since the entropy of 1b binding is positive, and enthalpy is negative, the binding is always spontaneous. Similarly, 2b is spontaneous at all temperatures. Choice D is unlikely because the kinetics cannot be predicted based on the given data. Determination of kinetics would require the energy change to reach the transition state of the reaction, which is the key determinant of reaction speed. Choice A is the best answer.

26. **A is the best answer.** The answer to this question is within the data shown in Table 1. All of the answers are based on 2a and/or 1a. 1a and 2a both have large, negative enthalpies. Meanwhile, 1a has a larger, positive $T\Delta S$ term while 2a has a smaller positive $T\Delta S$ term. Considering A and B, fever affects temperature primarily, which would increase the magnitude of the $T\Delta S$ term. A larger magnitude to begin with indicates a larger change that would occur with fever, so choice A is likely to be the best answer. 2a has a smaller entropic contribution to binding affinity, indicating it is likely to be more stable during a fever. Choice B can be eliminated. Choice C is unlikely because 2a has a positive $T\Delta S$ term, so binding affinity would be reduced at lower temperature. Choice D is unlikely because 1a actually binds better at higher temperature given the positive $T\Delta S$ term. As a further note, temperature can impact many characteristics of pharmacologic behavior, including how quickly drugs are metabolized and cleared from the system, as well as how effectively they bind to and exert their effects.

Stand-alones (Questions 27-29)

27. **A is the best answer.** First, balance the reaction. The problem does not give the formula for glucose. Recall that all sugars are carbo*hydrates* meaning they have the formula $[C(H_2O)]_n$. Glucose is a hexose, so the formula has n = 6 or $C_6H_{12}O_6$. This makes the balanced equation:

$$C_6H_{12}O_6 + 6O_2 \rightarrow 6CO_2 + 6H_2O$$

Next, use the following formula:

$$\Delta H^\circ_{rxn} = \Sigma\, \Delta H^\circ_{f,\,products} - \Delta H^\circ_{f,\,reactants}$$

or

$$\Delta H^\circ_{rxn} = 6[\Delta H^\circ_f(CO_2)] + 6[\Delta H^\circ_f(H_2O)] - \Delta H^\circ_f(C_6H_{12}O_6) - 6[\Delta H^\circ_f(O_2)]$$

Now plug and chug

$$\Delta H^\circ_{rxn} = 6(-393.5\text{ kJ/mol}) + 6(-285.8\text{ kJ/mol}) - (-1275\text{ kJ/mol}) - 6(0\text{ kJ/mol})$$

$$\Delta H^\circ_{rxn} = -2361\text{ kJ} - 1714.8\text{ kJ} + 1275\text{ kJ}$$

Do the following MCAT® math

$$\Delta H^\circ_{rxn} = 6(-393.5\text{ kJ}) + 6(-285.8\text{ kJ}) - (-1275\text{ kJ}) - 6(0) \approx 6(-400\text{ kJ}) + 6(-275\text{ kJ}) - (-1275\text{ kJ}) - 6(0)$$

$$\approx -2400\text{ kJ} - 1650\text{ kJ} + 1275\text{ kJ} = -2775\text{ kJ/mol}$$

This is closest to choice A, so choice A is the best answer.

Choice B results from not balancing the equation. Choice C results from not correctly subtracting H°_f reactants from products. Choice D repeats the error in choice B and incorrectly identifies a reaction with a positive ΔH° as exothermic.

28. **D is the best answer.** This is a basic definition. Enzymes lower activation energy, often referred to as E_a (energy of activation) or $\Delta G^\ddagger$. Choice D correctly defines an enzyme. It is a common misconception that enzymes make a reaction "more spontaneous" or lower ΔG°_{rxn}. This is not true. They only change the activation energy, which is completely independent of the overall ΔG°_{rxn}.

29. **B is the best answer.** This question asks about the equilibrium constant versus the reaction quotient. The reaction quotient has the same structure as the equilibrium constant, but is used when a reaction is not at equilibrium. A reaction at its start is not at equilibrium, making an expression involving the reaction quotient more appropriate than an expression involving the equilibrium constant. Choices A and C can be eliminated. The reaction quotient is the concentration of the products divided by the concentration of the reactants, making choice B a better answer than choice D. Notice that the concentration of carbon dioxide is not included in the equilibrium expression. This is because it is a gas and is not truly in solution. Gasses and solids are not included in equilibrium expressions.

Phases

TEST 5A

ANSWERS & EXPLANATIONS

Questions 1–59

LECTURE 5 ANSWER KEY

TEST 5A		MINI-TEST 5B	
1. D	31. C	1. A	16. C
2. B	32. C	2. C	17. C
3. B	33. A	3. A	18. D
4. C	34. A	4. C	19. A
5. C	35. C	5. C	20. B
6. A	36. D	6. B	21. C
7. B	37. D	7. B	22. B
8. B	38. C	8. C	23. C
9. B	39. A	9. A	24. B
10. C	40. B	10. B	25. D
11. D	41. C	11. A	26. A
12. A	42. C	12. C	27. D
13. A	43. B	13. B	28. A
14. A	44. B	14. A	29. C
15. C	45. B	15. B	
16. C	46. A		
17. D	47. D		
18. B	48. C		
19. A	49. D		
20. C	50. B		
21. C	51. D		
22. D	52. A		
23. A	53. A		
24. A	54. D		
25. C	55. A		
26. A	56. B		
27. C	57. A		
28. B	58. A		
29. B	59. C		
30. B			

EXPLANATIONS FOR LECTURE 5

Passage 1 (Questions 1-5)

1. **D is the best answer.** The passage states that the concentration of CO_2 in the atmosphere (0.04%) remains constant despite the elevation change. This means that with each breath, the alveoli are flushed with fresh air that contains essentially no CO_2. A difference in partial pressure across the alveoli is the driving force for CO_2 diffusion out of the capillaries. Since this driving force is relatively conserved, CO_2 exchange is not largely affected, weakening choice A. If the partial pressure of O_2 in the blood decreases significantly more than the partial pressure of O_2 in the atmosphere, then the pressure difference and rate of diffusion of oxygen into the capillaries would increase. As shown by Figure 1, the partial pressure of O_2 in the venous blood has a much smaller decrease with increasing elevation when compared to the atmospheric partial pressure. This lowers the pressure difference which would decrease the rate of diffusion. Since the sharp decline in atmospheric partial pressure, not venous partial pressure, is the direct cause of the lower diffusion rate, choice B is a weaker answer. As mentioned in the passage, the percentage of oxygen, which can be represented as the mole fraction, remains constant. This means that a change in the amount of oxygen in the lungs is due to a decrease in the total atmospheric pressure. If the answer stated that the partial pressure of O_2 is too low, then this would be a strong answer , but because it states that the mole fraction changes, choice C is a weaker option. By looking at Equation 1, it can be seen that a major factor in the rate of diffusion is the pressure gradient across the membrane. As the climbers ascend, eventually they reach an altitude where the partial pressure of oxygen in the air is similar to the partial pressure of oxygen in the venous blood. As a result, the rate of diffusion is insufficient to provide enough oxygen for the climber's metabolic needs, and other methods of compensation are required, making choice D the best answer.

2. **B is the best answer.** Altering the temperature of the system will change the rate of diffusion, but as long as the temperature is constant between every trial, then the results and the conclusions drawn from them should not be altered, weakening choice A. By looking at Equation 1, it can be seen that the rate of diffusion is affected by the difference in pressure of the two chambers. As a result, trials that have the same ratio of partial pressures are not expected to have a similar rate of diffusion. If trial 1 has a pressure of 50 mmHg in container A and 100 mmHg in container B, then it has a difference in pressure of 50 mmHg and a ratio of 1:2. If the pressure in each container is doubled, the ratio is still 1:2, but the difference is now 100 mmHg (200 mmHg in container B minus 100 mmHg in container A). This will result in a faster rate of diffusion for the second trial. If the researchers assume the two trials are replicates of each other, the reliability of the experiment will be largely affected, making choice B a strong option. Since the completion of a trial occurs when equilibrium between the two containers is reached, it is expected that the volume of gas in each container is equal. Because both containers still have the same initial conditions, there will not be as large of an effect on the results as that caused by choice B, which eliminates choice C. The choice of gas should not cause significant error as long as the gas used behaves in an ideal manner. The diffusion constant in Equation 1 would be different depending on the gas chosen since it accounts for the density of the gas used, but as long as the experimenter is aware of which gas is being used, there should not be a major effect on the results, making choice D a weaker answer than choice B.

3. **B is the best answer.** The volume of individual gas particles is considered to be negligible due to the small volume each one occupies when compared to the volume of the container. This assumption is made due to the relative volume of the molecules, not their energy level, making choice A a weaker answer. The kinetic molecular energy theory states that an increase in temperature results in an increase in the average kinetic energy of the system. Since an increase in kinetic energy corresponds to an increase in velocity ($KE = \frac{1}{2}mv^2$), choice B is a strong answer. The ideal gas law can be simplified to show that temperature and pressure are directly proportional. As the temperature of the system increases, the pressure would be expected to increase as well, making choice C a weaker option. Liquids have stronger intermolecular forces than gasses, so conditions that would cause a gas to condense (higher pressure, lower temperature) increase the intermolecular forces. Since an increase in temperature would not have this effect, choice D is a weaker answer.

4. **C is the best answer.** This question can be answered in multiple ways. One option is to use the equation $P_A = X_A P_{total}$ where X_a is the mole fraction of gas A, P_{total} is the total pressure of the gas mixture, and P_A is the partial pressure of gas A. Since the question states that the atmosphere is composed of 80% nitrogen and the graph in Figure 1 shows that there is a total pressure of about 750 mmHg at sea level, multiplying these two values yields a partial pressure of 600 mmHg. If the partial pressure of oxygen at sea level was used in this equation instead of the total atmospheric pressure, a value of approximately 120 mmHg would be calculated, eliminating choice A. By using Figure 1 to estimate the total pressure at 8000 m, which is roughly 80% of the maximum altitude displayed on the graph, a value close to 270 mmHg would be obtained, so choice B can be eliminated. A second way of answering this question is by realizing that nitrogen and oxygen are by far the biggest contributors to the atmosphere (78% and 21% respectively). This means that the contribution of trace gasses to the partial pressure can be cautiously ignored when answering this question. By utilizing Dalton's law and the estimates obtained from Figure 1, the partial pressure of oxygen can be subtracted from the total atmospheric pressure, which would yield a value around 600 mmHg, making choice C a strong answer. Dividing the total pressure at sea level by 0.80 would yield an answer close to choice D, which can be eliminated and makes choice B the best answer.

5. **C is the best answer.** When comparing two containers of gas molecules, if the volume, temperature, and pressure of the two gasses are the same, then the number of molecules in the container is also the same. Since the volume of gas in Chamber B is four times larger than Chamber A, a ratio of 1:1 would not be expected, eliminating choice A. Regardless of the mass of the gas molecules, under standard temperature and pressure, 1 mole of gas will occupy a volume of 22.4 L. Despite the fact that water vapor has half the molar mass of fluorine, it still occupies four times as much volume meaning there are four times as many gas molecules. Choice B is not the best answer because it factors in the molar mass of the molecules when calculating the ratio. A ratio of 1:8 can be calculated if the assumption is made that having half the molar mass means that twice as many molecules can occupy the same relative volume, making choice D a weaker answer. As mentioned previously, since the containers are at standard temperature and pressure, the volume of gas is directly proportional the number of molecules of gas. Because the volume of gas in Chamber B is four times greater than Chamber A, Chamber B also has four times as many molecules, making choice C the best answer.

Passage 2 (Questions 6-9)

6. **A is the best answer.** Let the equation as described in the passage represent the initial conditions. Doubling the larger radius results in a new volume $V_l = \pi\frac{h}{3}(4R^2 + 2Rr + r^2)$. Conversely, doubling the smaller radius results in another new volume $V_s = \pi\frac{h}{3}(R^2 + 2Rr + 4r^2)$. If $V_l > V_s$ then $V_l - V_s > 0$.

   Perform this subtraction to determine if V_l, the volume generated by doubling the larger radius, is indeed greater than V_s, the volume generated by doubling the smaller radius:

$$\begin{array}{r} \pi\frac{h}{3}(4R^2 + 2Rr + r^2) \\ -\pi\frac{h}{3}(R^2 + 2Rr + 4r^2) \\ \pi\frac{h}{3}3R^2 - \pi\frac{h}{3}3r^2 \end{array}$$

   Remember that R > r. Thus, $\pi\frac{h}{3}3R^2 - \pi\frac{h}{3}3r^2 > 0$. The volume generated by doubling the larger radius is greater than the volume generated by doubling the smaller radius. At a given pressure and temperature, the number of particles of gas that can occupy a space is proportional to the volume of the container. The change which most increases the volume of the ear canal—increasing the larger radius—most increases the number of gas particles it can contain. Choice A is consistent with this reasoning and is probably the best answer. Choice B describes doubling the smaller radius as most effectively increasing the volume of the ear canal. This is false, as increasing the larger radius most effectively increases the volume of the ear canal. Choice B can be eliminated. For the same reason, choice C can be eliminated; the effects of doubling each volume are not identical to each other. Finally, choice D implies that the number of molecules of gas which can occupy the ear canal are unrelated to the ear canal's volume. This statement contradicts the ideal gas law, $PV = nRT$. Remember that when temperature and pressure are constant, reasonable assumptions for this problem, that $\frac{P}{RT}$ can be described as a constant K. The ideal gas law simplifies to $KV = n$. The number of particles of a gas is proportional to the volume the gas occupies, ruling out choice D.

7. **B is the best answer.** Figure 2 shows the relationship between overpressure, blast exposure duration, and survival probability. The "50% survival" curve shows the values of overpressure and blast exposure that are lethal to half of the victim population. According to the first paragraph, overpressure is the pressure generated that is greater than atmospheric pressure. In other words, the absolute pressure that results in casualties is the OP + atmospheric pressure. This value is 482 kPa + 100 kPa = 582 kPa. Since temperature (T) is provided as a constant, and the number of particles (n) is also a constant in this problem, the ideal gas law simplifies to $PV = K$, where K is a constant equal to nRT.

Let the subscripted 1 represent normal non-blast conditions and the subscripted 2 represent blast conditions.

$$P_1V_1 = K = P_2V_2$$

$$P_1V_1/P_2 = V_2$$

Under standard conditions, i.e., 0°C and 1 atm, one mole of any gas has a volume of 22.4 L. Use the absolute pressure that results in a 50% survival for 1 second as P_2 and 22.4 L as V_1.

$(10^2 \text{ kPa})(22.4 \text{ L})/(582 \text{ kPa})$ = a little less than 4 L, so choice B is the best answer.

Choice A stems from misreading the units on the X-axis. The units are milliseconds. Because 1000 msec = 1 sec, the intersecting points at the end of the graph should be used to determine the OP that is lethal to half of blast victims for 1 second of exposure. Choice A stems from using the points that define the intersection at 1 *msec*, not 1 *sec*, so it can be eliminated. Choice C stems from "plugging in" only the OP instead of the absolute pressure into the equation above. Remember that the OP is a derived measurement and does not reflect the actual pressure of the air. Choice C can be eliminated. Pressure and volume are inversely proportional. Since the air from the blast is at a higher pressure, it should have a lower molar volume than "normal" air. In other words, it should have a smaller molar volume than 22.4 L/mol. Choice D can be eliminated on this basis. It stems from an error in "plugging in" atmospheric pressure in Pa instead of kPa.

8. **B is the best answer.** This problem specifies that the reaction goes to completion and excess heat is dissipated. This means that before the reaction and after the reaction, the temperature of the gasses within the container remain at the same starting point, matching the surroundings. Since the vessel was sealed, all of the particles which were formed could not escape. The volume the gasses occupy before and after the reaction also remains the same—that of the container. With these assumptions, namely, a constant T and V, the ideal gas law can be simplified as follows:

$$PV = nRT$$

$$P = nR\frac{T}{V}$$

$$P = nK, \text{ where } K \text{ is a constant equal to } \frac{TR}{V}.$$

Let the subscripted 1 represent pre-reaction conditions and the subscripted 2 represent post-reaction conditions.

$$\frac{P_1}{n_1} = K = \frac{P_2}{n_2}$$

$$\frac{P_2}{P_1} = \frac{n_2}{n_1}$$

In other words, the ratio between the number of particles after the reaction to the number of particles before the reaction is equivalent to the factor by which the pressure has changed. The number of particles before and after the reaction can be estimated by counting the number of moles of reactant and products in the gaseous state in the balanced equation:

22 moles of products/7 moles of reactants $\approx$ 3.

Choice B is the best answer. Choice A represents the factor by which it would increase if the number of moles of TNT were factored in to the calculation. Since solid particles do not contribute significantly to the pressure of a system, they are not included when using the ideal gas law. Choice A can be eliminated. Choice C subtracts the relative number of gaseous reactants from the sum of the relative number of gaseous products. Since this question is asking about a factor by which the pressure has increased, a ratio is required, so calculating the net gain or loss of gaseous particles will not suffice. Choice C can be eliminated. Choice D stems from adding all of the "equivalents" of gas of the reactants, but not factoring in the original pressure created by the moles of gas on the reactants side of the reaction. Addition will not directly answer this question, as the ratio between the initial and final conditions is required. Choice D can be eliminated.

9. **B is the best answer.** The image of a pneumothorax indicates that trapped air is compressing the lung. Boyle's law states that volume and pressure are inversely proportional. As the lung expands during inhalation, the trapped air has less space to occupy and will exert an ever increasing pressure on the lung, making inhaling additional air more difficult. Choice A states the opposite of this and can be eliminated. Choice B seems to summarize these expectations and may be the best answer, but eliminate the other choices before selecting it. The pressure exerted against the lungs by the trapped air makes inhalation very difficult, and can even result in death—this is a dramatic contrast to the relatively effortless breathing mechanics of a healthy lung. Choice C can be eliminated on this basis. Finally, exhalation is actually expected to be easier in a lung that has a pneumothorax. Consider the forces acting on the lung to push the inhaled air out: the lung's elastic recoil and the force derived from the pressure exerted by the trapped air acting on the surface of the lung. There are more forces acting on the lungs to push the air out with a pneumothorax than there are in a healthy lung that only has the recoil force. Exhalation is easier, not more difficult in patients that have a pneumothorax, so choice D can be eliminated.

Stand-alones (Questions 10-13)

10. **C is the best answer.** A mixture of gases will be homogenous regardless of polarity differences, which is unlike liquids. This occurs because gas molecules are often so far apart that they exert negligible attractive or repulsive forces on one another. This is one of the tenants of the kinetic molecular theory of gases. However, gases do separate according to density at low temperatures, due to the force of gravity that acts upon them. The densest gas will settle at the bottom and the least dense will rise to the top. This eliminates choice A. Initial mixing will likely evenly distribute the gas molecules, but they will begin to settle when the container is moved to a low temperature. Halothane, not sevoflurane is the densest gas, meaning it will be at the bottom. Choice B can be eliminated. Nitrogen is the least dense gas, while halothane is the densest. Choice C is most likely the best answer. Initially, the gases are likely to be evenly dispersed, especially at room temperature. Moving the container to a colder temperature would allow the gases to settle. Choice D can be eliminated.

11. **D is the best answer.** In order for hydrogen bonding to occur, the hydrogen must be bound to a highly electronegative atom and interact with an N, F, or O atom in a separate molecule. While isoflurane contains F and O, it does not have a hydrogen atom that is bound to a highly electronegative atom, as its only two hydrogens are bound to carbon. Option I is likely to be part of the best answer. Ionic bonding occurs between a metal and a non-metal within the same uncharged molecule, not between molecules. Notice how the molecule is also not charged, giving additional evidence that it is unlikely to contribute to ionic bonding. Option II is likely to be part of the best answer. Electrostatic interactions occur when part of the molecule has a partial positive charge and a part of a separate molecule has a partial negative charge. Given the opportunity for significantly polarity in isoflurane, due to the electronegative F, Cl, and O atoms, electrostatic interactions could occur in a non ideal, or real world situation. Since the question is asking for the interactions that would occur if the gas acted as an ideal gas, electrostatic interactions would not be expected to occur. This is because one of the assumptions of ideal gasses is that they do not experience intermolecular interactions. For this reason, all three interactions presented in the question would not be expected to occur, so choice D is the best answer.

12. **A is the best answer.** The question stem alludes to the idea gas equation, $PV = nRT$. The constant volumetric flow rate suggests that the volume per minute being administered is relatively consistent, allows for the comparison of pressure at various temperatures. P and T are directly proportional, so increasing the temperature will increase the pressure of the gas in the airways. Choice A is most likely to be the best answer, and choice B can be eliminated. Unless the volumetric flow rate is adjusted, the increase in pressure would be unlikely to drop, eliminating choice C. The pressure would be expected to increase due to the increased pressure, eliminating choice D.

13. **A is the best answer.** At a constant temperature, the pressure and volume of a gas are inversely related. The first step in answering this question is to determine whether the lungs expand or deflate as the patient inhales. Inhaling causes air to enter and expand the lungs, eliminating choices C and D. At a constant temperature, the expansion of the lungs would result in the inverse effect on pressure, decreasing the pressure in the lungs, and allowing air to flow from the higher pressure outside into the lower pressure inside. This is due to the relationship established by the ideal gas law, which states that pressure and volume are inversely related. Choice A is a better answer than choice B.

Passage 3 (Questions 14-17)

14. **A is the best answer.** According to Boyle's law, provided in Equation 1, the pressure P and volume V of an enclosed gas must multiply together to provide the same constant. In other words, by whatever factor V increases, P must decrease and vice-versa; V and P have an inversely proportional relationship. The height of the plunger above the syringe tip, h, is a proxy measurement of the volume *within the syringe*. This volume is formally given by πr^2h, where πr^2 is the cross sectional area of the syringe barrel. Because h is proportional to $V_{syringe}$ reducing h by any factor reduces $V_{syringe}$ by some factor and increases the pressure *within* the syringe by that same factor. Thus, decreasing h will increase the pressure *within* the syringe. This pressure acts to compress the balloon, increasing the pressure within the balloon, and decreasing the balloon's volume. Thus, h $\propto V_{balloon}$. Choice A is the best answer. Since V_b and h are directly proportional, choices B and C can be eliminated because they show a square root and inversely proportional relationship respectively. Choice D relates an exponential increase in volume when pressure is increased, which is not expected based on Boyle's law. Choice D can be eliminated.

15. **C is the best answer.** All gas particles are equivalent according to the ideal gas law. In other words, helium does not exert any more pressure than does any other gas under identical conditions. For an identical depression of the syringe, the same pressure increase inside the syringe will lead to the same reduction in volume of the balloon. Likewise, for an identical retraction of the syringe, the same pressure decrease inside the syringe will lead to the same increase in volume of the balloon. Choice C best summarizes the expected identical behavior and is the best answer. Choices A, B, and D suggest that helium particles exert more or less pressure within the balloon than do air particles. Based on the ideal gas law, which describes gas behavior in terms of the *number* of particles, not the *identity* of particles, this makes choice A, B, and D weaker answers. Remember, according to the kinetic molecular theory of gasses, gas particles do not occupy volume.

16. **C is the best answer.** Dalton's law of partial pressures says that the mole fraction of a gas in a mixture of gases is equal to its fraction of the total pressure in a system. In symbols, $\frac{\text{moles } O_2}{\text{moles of gas}} = \frac{P_{O_2}}{P_{gas}}$

Use stoichiometry to determine what the mole fraction of oxygen is in the balloon, based on its mass fraction. It is easiest to do this is to pretend that there are 100 g of gas in the balloon.

$$(100 \text{ g gas})(25 \text{ g } O_2/100 \text{ g gas})(1 \text{ mole } O_2/32 \text{ g } O_2) \approx 0.80 \text{ moles } O_2$$

$$(100 \text{ g gas})(75 \text{ g } N_2/100 \text{ g gas})(1 \text{ mole } N_2/28 \text{ g } N_2) \approx 3 \text{ moles } N_2$$

Calculate the partial pressure of O_2 by using the equation $\left(\frac{\text{moles } O_2}{\text{moles of gas}}\right)(P_{gas}) \approx (0.80/3.8)(1 \text{ atm}) < 0.25$, but it is greater than 0.12 atm. Choice C is the best answer. Choice A stems from confusing mass percent with mole percent. Only the *mole* fraction of a component gas can be used as a scaling factor with the total pressure of a gas to determine the partial pressure of that particular component gas. The mass percent, or the mass fraction, cannot be used for this purpose. Choice A stems from using the mass fraction as a scaling factor instead of the mole fraction. Choice B is a distractor based on dividing choice A by two, possibly based on the premise that oxygen is a diatomic gas. Choice D is the mass fraction of nitrogen. This is a distractor that can be eliminated.

17. **D is the best answer.** Pressure is force per area. The force applied to the syringe plunger is the mass of the weight multiplied by the acceleration due to gravity. This force is acting on the surface area of the plunger. Symbolically, this can be shown as: P = F/A = mg/A.

Substitute this term for pressure into Equation 1.

$PV/2$ = K Remember in the final state—the state at which the pressure, mg/A, caused by the weight's presence, is acting—the volume has been reduced by a factor of 2 since the height has been halved and h $\propto V$.

Substitution provides:

$$\text{mg}V/2\text{A} = \text{K}.$$

Algebraically solving for m provides: 2KA/Vg = m. Choice D is the best answer. Choice A is an algebra error that stems from accidently dividing by A, rather than multiplying by it. Choice B does not reduce the volume by a factor of 2. Choice C is an error that results from not including gravitational acceleration in the force term, while developing the other pressure expression to substitute into Equation 1. It also does not reduce the volume by a factor of 2. Choices A, B, and C can be eliminated.

Passage 4 (Questions 18-21)

18. **B is the best answer.** Use the ideal gas law to predict the effect of temperature on the volume of a gas at constant pressure. $PV = nRT$ since P, n, and R are all constants, this equation can be simplified to $V = KT$. Volume is directly proportional to temperature. By whatever factor the temperature decreases, the volume will also decrease. Since the ideal gas uses absolute temperature, it is necessary to convert the temperatures used in the two experiments to the Kelvin scale.

$$25°C + 273°C = 298\ K$$

$$-78°C + 273°C = 195\ K$$

The ratio of these temperatures is 195/293 ≈ 2/3 Thus, the volume of the gas, now at −78°C and 1 atm of pressure, is expected to be 2/3 of its original volume at 25°C and 1 atm. Based on Table 1, this man most likely has a VC of around 4.4 L at room temperature and pressure—the 3.2 L measurement can be disregarded because it deviates from the other values. (2/3)(4.4) = a number greater than 2. Choice B is the best answer. Choice A is a distracting answer that is too low and can be eliminated. The volume of air shrinks with colder temperatures, and does not remain the same. Choice C can be eliminated. If 3/2, the reciprocal of the absolute temperature ratio, is used by mistake, choice D would result.

19. **A is the best answer.** Until the hole is opened at the base of the inverted volumetric cylinder, the pressure of the fluid and air in the cylinder is atmospheric pressure. Since the top is sealed, this pressure acts on the cross-sectional area at the bottom of the fluid column, generating an upwards force. Once a hole is opened, atmospheric pressure generates a downwards force. This force acts on the upper exposed area of the fluid column beneath the air which has bubbled into the cylinder. With the upwards force from the pressure and the downwards force from the pressure balanced, gravity is the only net force, and the fluid in the volumetric cylinder will fall until it is the same height as the rest of the fluid in the trough. Choice A is the best answer. Gravity will pull the water down until it is at its lowest potential energy possible. This occurs when its level is equal to that of the rest of the water in the trough. Eliminate choice B. Since a net force is now acting on the water, it cannot remain stationary. Eliminate choice C. The water will not exit the hose. While a participant is measuring their VC, the hose is filled with air, whose pressure exceeds that of the water in the inverted cylinder. When the participant stops breathing and removes his mouth from the hose, water will rush into it. This is because there is only atmospheric pressure pushing the water out of the hose, but there is hydrostatic pressure and atmospheric pressure pushing water into the hose. Despite the fact that water will rush into the hose, there is a limit to how high it will rise. It will rise only to the height that the hose is submerged in the trough. At this height, the hydrostatic pressure in the portion of the hose which is beneath the cylinder and the portion of the hose which is submerged, but not beneath the cylinder, is the same. Both have a pressure of $\rho_{H_2O}gh$ where h is the height of the water in the trough. Choice D can be eliminated.

20. **C is the best answer.** Nitrogen gas is a diatomic molecule, and at 0°C and 1 atm, an ideal gas has a volume of 22.4 L. Use dimensional analysis to solve this problem.

$$(0.8\ L)(1\ mol/22.4\ L)(6.022 \times 10^{23}\ molecules/mol)(2\ atoms\ of\ N/1\ molecules\ of\ N_2) = \frac{(0.8 \times 6.022 \times 10^{23} \times 2)}{22.4\ atoms\ of\ nitrogen}$$

Choice C is the best answer. Since nitrogen gas is a diatomic molecule, every molecule of nitrogen gas actually contains 2 atoms. Choice A fails to multiply the number of particles by 2, and can be eliminated. Choices B and D multiply by 22.4 L instead of dividing by it. They can both be eliminated.

21. **C is the best answer.** Manipulate the equation that relates changes in energy with specific heat capacities and temperature changes: $q = mc\Delta T$ or, re-expressed for this problem , $q/mc = \Delta T$. Since this question provides every term of this equation except ΔT, isolating this variable allows for it to be calculated. Be careful to keep all units consistent when putting numerical values into the equation.

$$6270\ J/(3000\ g \times 4.18\ J/g \cdot C°) = 0.5°C$$

Choose the best answer, choice C. If an algebra error of multiplying by 4.18 J/g · C°, instead of dividing, were made, choice A would result. Choice B is simply a distractor somewhat close in value to the best answer. If the energy added to the water were not converted to J, choice D would result.

TEST 5A A&E

Passage 5 (Questions 22-25)

22. **D is the best answer.** At the end of exhalation, the concentration of CO_2 will be at a maximum in the FFR. Thus, CO_2 has an exhalation concentration of 5% without the AVS, or 2% with the AVS. Dalton's law states that the partial pressure of a gas is proportional to its mole fraction in a mixture of gases. At constant temperature and pressure—reasonable assumptions for the interior of an FFR—Avogadro's law states that the volume a gas occupies is proportional to the number of particles of that gas. Since the volume fraction of CO_2 has been reduced from 5% to 2%, that means that only $\frac{2}{5}$ of the original number of particles of CO_2, which were in the FFR, remain in the FFR. This loss of CO_2 particles results in a proportional reduction in the partial pressure of CO_2. As a percentage, the drop in partial pressure can be calculated as the change in CO_2 fraction divided by the initial fraction of CO_2 particles. $\frac{5-2}{5} \times 100\% = 60\%$. Choice D is the best answer. Choice A represents the *absolute* fraction of CO_2 exhaled with an AVS. This number is not helpful for answering this question as it is asking about the *relative* reduction in P_{CO_2}. Choice B represents the *difference* between the volume fractions of CO_2 with and without the AVS. In order to be meaningful with respect to a *percent* pressure reduction, this value would need used in a ratio. Choice B can be eliminated. If the percentage of P_{CO_2} which remains were accidentally calculated, choice C would result , so it can be eliminated. Choice D is the best answer.

23. **A is the best answer.** Boltzmann's constant, *k*, is analogous to the gas constant *R*, but rather than being pertinent to an entire mole of particles, it is pertinent to one or several particles. It is defined as R/N_A where N_A is Avogadro's number, or 6.022×10^{23}. As a result, it can be used in place of *R* when the ideal gas law is being applied to individual particles. This variation of the Ideal Gas Law is: $PV = nkT$ where *n* is the number of particles, *k* is Boltzmann's constant, *T* is the absolute temperature of the sample, and *P* and *V* are the pressure and volume of the sample, respectively. Since N_A is a constant, the only parameters necessary to calculated *R* are pressure, volume, temperature, and mass. From mass, it is possible to determine how many moles of the sample are present. The best answer will include options I, II, III, and IV. Choice A is the best answer. Even though mass is not explicitly mentioned in the ideal gas law, "n" can be directly calculated from it. Choice A makes the error of not including this term because it is not explicitly mentioned in the ideal gas law. Choices C and D lack options that are necessary to solve for R, and ultimately *k*.

24. **A is the best answer.** The volume and temperature do not change in the flask, and the flask is isobaric to the mercury column. Thus, the pressure acting on the mercury column is the same pressure within the flask. With tedious calculations, it is possible to calculate the initial and final pressures using $P = \rho_{Hg}gh$ and then substitute P_{ini} and P_{final} into the Ideal Gas Law to solve for n_{ini} and n_{final}. However, remember that atmospheric pressure is, by definition, 760 mmHg. It is easier to recognize that the drop in pressure is 76 mmHg or 10% of the total pressure of 1 atm. In other words, the new pressure inside the flask is 0.9 atm.

Rearrange the Ideal Gas law to solve for *n*: $PV/RT = n$

Since *V*, *R*, and *T* are constant in this situation, the equation can also be expressed as $PC = n$, where $C = V/RT$. Thus, since *P* has dropped by 10%, so has *n*. Choice A is the best answer. Choice B does not stem from a particular error in the calculation, but is just a distractor. Although the height of the mercury column is proportional to the number of particles in the flask, these parameters do not share a one to one correspondence. In other words, each mm that the height of the column rises or falls does not represent an increase or decrease in the number of particles in the flask by 1%. Choice C stems from this assumption and can be eliminated. If the number of particles which remain in the flask were calculated by mistake, choice D would result.

25. **C is the best answer.** Remember that a temperature on the Kelvin scale is always 273 units higher than it is on the Celsius scale. Thus, this temperature is the same as 0°C. The volume a gas occupies at 0°C and 1 atm is always 22.4 L/mol. This value should be memorized before test day. 5 L of CO_2 can react with $Ca(OH)_2$ in a 1 mol of CO_2 to 1 mol of $Ca(OH)_2$ ratio as shown in the balanced equation provided by the question stem. The mass of $Ca(OH)_2$ required to trap 5 L CO_2 can be calculated using dimensional analysis:

$$(5\text{ L }CO_2)(1\text{ mol }CO_2/22.4\text{ L})(1\text{ mol }Ca(OH)_2/1\text{ mol }CO_2)(74\text{ g/mol }Ca(OH)_2) \approx (1/4)(74) = 18.5\text{ g}$$

Since the rounding that was used to solve this calculated a value which was artificially high, it is important to keep this in mind when evaluating the answer choices. Choice A is a distractor, not due to any specific calculation error. If the molecular mass of only one OH group were added to the molecular mass of Ca, instead of the mass of 2 OH groups, choice B would result. Choice C is similar to the estimated value calculated, but on the lower end. Choice D matches the artificially high rounded answer, and should be considered as a possible answer but compared with choice C, it is a weaker answer. Choice C is the best answer.

Stand-alones (Questions 26-29)

26. **A is the best answer.** First look at the labels on each graph. PV is on the Y-axis, and nT is on the X-axis. A nice way to solve these problems is to rearrange the equation that relates the graphed variables to each other, until it is in a form easily interpreted for graphing purposes. The ideal gas law states that $PV = nRT$. Thus, PV and nT are directly proportional. Graphically, this relationship appears as a line which increases or decreases by the same factor in each axis. Choice A is the best answer. When PV/nRT is plotted against P for a non-ideal gas, the graph of choice B results. This question does not ask about a non-ideal gas. Choice B can be eliminated. Life experiences can serve as a good reminder that the pressure and volume of a gas do not remain constant with a change in temperature. This is the reason why whipped cream containers all have strong warnings not to expose them to heat. Such exposure can result in dangerous explosions, as the internal pressure will increase due to the increased temperature, possibly bursting the container. Choice C describes a scenario of pressure and volume not responding to a change in temperature, which would not occur, so choice C can be eliminated. Choice D represents an inversely proportional relationship between the variables and can be eliminated.

27. **C is the best answer.** The ideal gas law states that $PV = nRT$. The volume of the lungs and the moles of air in the lungs are constant in the situation proposed by the question. R is also a constant, so P is proportional to T. Since pressure is directly proportional to temperature, the higher the temperature is, the higher the corresponding pressure will be. Therefore, choice C is the best answer because it has the highest temperature.

28. **B is the best answer.** Remember that the definition of molecular weight is the ratio of the mass of a chemical to the quantity of moles present in that mass. The ideal gas law can be used to provide n, the moles of the gas in question. Dividing the mass m of the gas by n provides the gas's molar mass. The derivation is below:

$$PV = nRT$$

$$PV/RT = n$$

$$\frac{\mathrm{m} \times RT}{PV} = \frac{\mathrm{m}}{n} = \text{molecular weight}$$

Plug and chug to solve this problem:

$$(0.026\ \text{g})(0.82\ \text{L} \cdot \text{atm/mol} \cdot \text{K})(423.15\ \text{K})/(0.5\ \text{atm})(0.2\ \text{L}) \approx (0.02 \times 423)/0.1 = 84.6\ \text{g/mol}$$

Choose the closest answer, choice B. Using the temperature in Celsius, not Kelvin, would result in choice A. Choices C and D are distractors that do not stem from a specific error in performing these calculations.

29. **B is the best answer.** The above statements are the four requirements for an ideal gas except for one small difference. Molecules must exert zero force on each other, not very little force. Recall that the ideal gas equation assumes that there are no intramolecular interactions. If molecules exert force on each other, then there are intermolecular interactions. This is a small nuance, but it makes choice B the best answer.

Passage 6 (Questions 30-34)

30. **B is the best answer.** There are only two constants in the van der Waals equation. The best answer will be the algebraic solution for one of them. This question really is asking which one of the constants, "a" or "b," corrects for the deviations of a non-ideal gas caused by intermolecular forces? Consider the effects that intermolecular forces could have on the behavior of a gas. Attractive intermolecular forces can decrease the pressure a gas can exert on the walls of its container. Instead of directly colliding against the walls of the vessel, since there is an attraction between gas particles, they tend to pull each other *away* from the walls of the vessel. This results in less forceful collisions, and a lower pressure. Thus a real gas's pressure will be too low to maintain the relationship of the ideal gas law $PV = nRT$. The "a" constant allows for a number to be added to P, correcting for the lower pressure that a true gas has. The "b" constant actually corrects for molar volume. For real gases, the space in which gas molecules are free to move is not simply the volume of the container. This is because the actual volume of each gas particle is large enough that it significantly lowers how much volume the gases can actually occupy. Gas molecules cannot occupy spaces already occupied by other gas molecules! The volume of all of these particles has to be subtracted from the total volume of the container to calculate the true volume in which the gas can travel. Since "a" corrects for intermolecular attractions, the best answer will be an algebraic solution for "a", or choice B. If "b" was mistakenly isolated instead of "a", choice A would result. If T were solved for instead of "a," choice C would result. Finally, an algebra error from not using the reciprocal of n^2/V^2 would result in choice D.

31. **C is the best answer.** The goal of this experiment was to calculate the van der Waals constant "*a*." To do so, physical properties such as the temperature, pressure, and the mass of the gas used were recorded. If water remained in the flask during the course of the experiment, the mass of the gas would be artificially high during the final weighing step. This would increase the value of n, and lead to an artificially low "*a*" constant. Choice A represents a failure in maintaining the purity of the flask. It is not a necessary assumption for the results of this experiment to be valid. In fact, if choice A were assumed, the results of this experiment would be invalid, as the mass obtained after weighing the flask would be artificially high due to the water's presence. Since this experiment relies on the van der Waals equation to solve for "*a*," and the constant "*b*" represents the molar volume of each gas particle, the volume that each gas particle occupies is not negligible. Eliminate choice B. If air enters the flask at a negligible rate after the flask is removed from the hot water bath, this means that the only material in the flask is the gas. Whatever air was present in the flask before the vaporization step should have already been chased out when most of the sample entered the gas phase and escaped the flask. When only gas remains in the flask, measurements of mass can be converted to n without n being artificially high or low. As a result, "*a*" can be calculated accurately. Choice C is the best answer. If air did not escape the flask during the vaporization of the volatile liquid, then during the weighing step, the mass of the re-condensed gas would be made artificially high by the presence of air. Once again, this would lead to an artificially low number for the value of "*a*." Choice D can be eliminated.

32. **C is the best answer.** There are many examples of other media that are better for thermal energy transfer than water, such as a hot metal or a direct flame. The boiling water's chief goal was not to act as a thermal energy transfer agent, but rather to keep the flask at constant temperature. Choice A can be eliminated. Once water reaches its boiling point, it will remain at that temperature until every last drop of water evaporates, regardless of how much energy is added. Choice B can be eliminated as it contradicts this observation. In the third paragraph, the passage describes that the van der Waals constant can be found from a gas at a given temperature and pressure. In other words, the van der Waals equation only predicts the behavior of a gas at a given temperature. If the temperature of the gas does not stay constant during the vaporization part of the experiment, it is impossible to use Equation 1 to solve for "*a*". Choice C is a strong answer because it describes the constant temperature of a boiling water bath, which is the main purpose of the water bath in this apparatus. Atmospheric pressure can be considered approximately constant for experiments such as this one. In other words, this system is isobaric. Nonetheless, maintaining a constant pressure was not the purpose of the boiling water. Eliminate choice D.

33. **A is the best answer.** The only way variables in an equation can be meaningfully added or subtracted from one another is if they utilize the same unit. Thus, in the quantity $(V - nb)$ both V and nb must be in the same units. V is in liters, so nb must also be equal to liters. An algebraic approach can solve the problem:

$$[\mathrm{L}] = [\mathrm{mol}][b]$$

$$[\mathrm{L}]/[\mathrm{mol}] = [b]$$

The units of b are L/mol—this allows for both terms in the quantity $(V - nb)$ to have liters as their unit. Choose the best answer, choice A. The other answer choices would not result in nb having the unit of liters. Choice B results in $\mathrm{mol}^2/\mathrm{L}$, choice C results in mol^2, and choice D is actually the units of the "*a*" constant, not the b constant. Eliminate choice D.

TEST 5A A&E

34. **A is the best answer.** This is not an equation you need to memorize for the MCAT®. This problem can be solved with the "limiting cases" approach and dimensional analysis. In the limiting cases approach, pretend that a certain variable is very small and see if the equation still predicts what should be expected in the real world. If the density of the mercury were very small, a lot of mercury would have to rise up the tube before enough weight was generated to counteract the force of atmospheric pressure acting on the entrance of the evacuated tube. In other words, the lower the density of the fluid, the greater the height to which it can rise. This implies an indirectly proportional relationship between density and height. Choice C can be eliminated since it displays a direct relationship. Next, use dimensional analysis to rule out the other answer choices. The target unit of the height of the column is meters. Rewrite each expression with the units that each variable represents. The expression that results in the correct units will be the best answer.

Choice A is shown as an example below:

$$\left(\frac{\mathrm{N}}{\mathrm{m}^2}\right)\left(\frac{\mathrm{kg}}{\mathrm{m}^3} \times \frac{\mathrm{m}}{\mathrm{sec}^2}\right)^{-1} = \left(\frac{\mathrm{N}}{\mathrm{m}^2}\right)\left(\frac{\mathrm{kg}}{\mathrm{m}^2 \times \mathrm{sec}^2}\right)^{-1} = \mathbf{N} \times \frac{\mathbf{sec^2}}{\mathbf{kg}}$$

Since $\mathrm{N} = \mathrm{kg} \times \mathrm{m/sec}^2$, this can substituted into the numerator of the bolded term. $\frac{\mathrm{kg} \times \mathrm{m}}{\mathrm{sec}^2} \times \frac{(\mathrm{sec}^2)}{\mathrm{kg}} = \mathrm{m}$. Choice A has the right units, and will be the best answer. Repeating this process with the other answer choices will not provide the proper units. Using dimensional analysis or the limiting cases approach can be very helpful if the MCAT® uses a question with an obscure equation like this one.

Passage 7 (Questions 35-38)

35. C is the best answer. Evaporation requires heat input; it occurs when a liquid gains enough kinetic energy that its particles can break free of their intermolecular bonds and enter the gas phase. Condensation is the reverse process. Particles leaves the gas phase and enter the liquid state; the particles have less kinetic energy and are no longer moving with a large enough velocity to escape each other's intermolecular attractions. This energy must go somewhere since energy is neither created nor destroyed. Typically, it is released into the surroundings, or in this case, the CPAP pipe. Since condensation releases heat, it is an exothermic process—choices A and B can be eliminated because they describe condensation as an endothermic process. Because the energy is released into the pipe, the temperature of the pipe is expected to increase somewhat. Select choice C and eliminate choice D.

36. D is the best answer. Remember the equation $P = \rho gh$. The lower the height of a column of fluid, the lower the pressure is at the bottom of the fluid. The atmosphere acting on a person follows the same rules. If someone is further from the top of the atmosphere, they experience a greater pressure because the column of fluid acting on them is larger. If they are closer to the top of the atmosphere, they experience a smaller pressure because the column of fluid acting on them is smaller. In other words, without pressurizing devices, the higher in altitude someone stands, the lower the partial pressure of oxygen is around them. At a high enough altitude, physiological compensatory mechanisms of respiration will not be able to deliver enough oxygen to the body and anoxia will occur. The passage states, "..the cornea can swell under conditions of inadequate oxygen perfusion." The highest elevation without pressurized devices will lead to the poorest oxygen delivery and the most swollen cornea. Of these choices, the climber 5500 m above sea level will experience the lowest partial pressure of oxygen—this will be the first part of the best answer. The second part of the best answer will be the person who is breathing air with the most oxygen. The submarine operator 300 m below sea level must be surrounded by air that is equal in pressure to the deep sea water surrounding the submarine, otherwise the submarine would implode. This high pressure air has a higher partial pressure of oxygen than atmospheric air. The submarine operator is expected to have the most oxygenated and least swollen cornea; the submarine operator is the second part of the best answer, so select choice D. The pressurized plane and the car are at roughly similar pressures. The operators of these vehicles won't experience the significant changes in pressure and oxygen partial pressure that the climber and submariner will experience. Choices A and C can be eliminated.

37. D is the best answer. 1 atm of pressure and 0°C is considered STP, or standard temperature and pressure. At these parameters, a mole of gas occupies 22.4 L. This conversion is used often by the MCAT® and would be helpful to know on test day. Since the ideal gas law is assumed to be in effect for this situation, the fact that a mole of gas occupies a volume of 22.4 L is true regardless of the identity of the gas—select choice D. Choices A, B, and C are all the result of attempting to account for the partial pressure of oxygen when calculating the volume.

38. C is the best answer. The passage states that, "This kind of corneal swelling is well-known, especially in relation to contact lens wear when the contacts have a low oxygen diffusion flux, J…" In other words, if the contacts have a low J, then less oxygen will reach the cornea, and it will swell. Since J is inversely proportional to the thickness of the lens, a thicker lens will lead to a lower J and will result in swollen corneas. Match the more swollen cornea to the thicker lens, and the less swollen cornea to the thinner lens. Patient Y wore contact 1, and patient X wore contact 2. Select choice C. Choice A is unlikely; if both patients wore the same lens, they would be expected to experience similar swelling, which they did not. Eliminate choice A. Choice B is the opposite of the best answer and can be eliminated. There is enough information to answer the question, so choice D may be eliminated as well.

Passage 8 (Questions 39-42)

39. **A is the best answer.** Don't be intimidated by this question. There is ALWAYS enough information to solve the problem on the MCAT®. First, it's necessary to figure out how many protons were consumed in this reaction. The initial concentration of the protons was 10^{-6} M. The new neutralized concentration will be 10^{-7} M because a neutral solution has a pH of 7. Since the solution is 1 L in size, these molarities are also the number of moles of protons in solution.

    The subtraction can be simplified using scientific notation.

    First, express the quantity of moles to the same power of ten. Then, subtract the final number of moles of protons from the initial number to determine how many moles or protons were consumed.

    10^{-6} moles $H^+ = 10 \times 10^{-7}$ moles H^+ initial. This step makes both quantities of moles the same power of ten.

    $10 \times 10^{-7} - 10^{-7} = 9 \times 10^{-7}$ moles H^+ lost. This step shows how many moles were consumed in the reaction.

    Next, write the balanced formula for this neutralization reaction to solve for the quantity of gas liberated.

    $$CaCO_3(s) + 2HCl(aq) \rightarrow CaCl_2(aq) + H_2O(l) + CO_2(g)$$

    For every 2 moles of protons consumed, 1 mole of CO_2 is produced. Remember that the volume a gas occupies at STP is 22.4 L/mol—this value is important to know for test day.

    $(9 \times 10^{-7}$ moles of protons lost$)\left(\frac{1 \text{ mol } CO_2}{2 \text{ mol } H^+}\right)\left(\frac{22.4 \text{ L}}{\text{mol } CO_2}\right) \approx 4.5 \times 10^{-7} \times 20 = 9 \times 10^{-6}$ L of gas produced. This is closest to choice A—select the best answer, choice A.

40. **B is the best answer.** Remember that the contact angle is determined while the material is in the liquid phase. Each of the options indicates a different phase of matter. The best answer will include only the liquid phase. Use extremes to rule out the non-liquid regions of the diagram. At a minimum of pressure and a maximum of temperature the material will be in the gas phase—this region is the bottom right of the diagram. Option IV represents the gaseous phase, so choice D can be eliminated. At a maximum of pressure and minimum of temperature the material will be in the solid phase—this region is the upper left of the diagram. Option I represents the solid phase, so choice A can be eliminated. The middle of the diagram where all of the lines intersect is the proverbial triple point. At this temperature and pressure, all three phases of the material coexist in equilibrium. Although liquid is present, the sample is not fully liquid. This answer is weaker than option II, in which most of the sample is in the liquid phase. Eliminate choice C, and select the best answer, choice B.

41. **C is the best answer.** Materials that have lower boiling points tend have greater vapor pressures than materials with greater boiling points. A lower boiling point due to the molecules of a certain substance requiring less kinetic energy for their atoms to escape the liquid phase and become a gas. Since their atoms require less kinetic energy to escape, at any given temperature there will be more particles in the gas phase; this leads to a greater vapor pressure. In other words, materials with low boiling points have high vapor pressures. If choice A is true, then choice B must be true as well, and vice-versa. Both choices cannot be the best answer, so they both can be eliminated. Since neither trimethylsilanol nor *t*-Butyl alcohol have any chiral centers, choice D is also false.

    A lower vapor pressure is expected in tremethylsilanol because of the greater polarity of the Si–O bond. Silicon is less electronegative than carbon. The greater polarity of this bond increases the strength of the intermolecular attractions. This leads to a greater boiling point and lower vapor pressure than its carbon analog, *t*-Butyl alcohol. Select the best answer, choice C.

42. **C is the best answer.** Dalton's law is $P_{total} = P_n + P_{n+1} + P_{n+2}\ldots$ This law means that the total pressure in a container is equal to the partial pressures of all the gases in the container. The lid must be able to support the total pressure in the container in order for the container to remain sealed. Use Dalton's law to calculate the total pressure of the container.

    $$P_{total} = P_n + P_{n+1}$$

    $$P_{total} = P_{H_2O} + P_{CO_2}$$

    $$P_{total} = 1875 \text{ mmHg} + 289.1 \text{ mmHg} = 2164.1 \text{ mmHg}$$

    Select the best answer, choice C.

TEST 5A A&E

Stand-alones (Questions 43-46)

43. **B is the best answer.** According to the ideal gas law ($PV = nRT$), temperature and moles of gas are inversely related. That would make choice A a tempting option, except for the fact that the number of moles of gas is held constant in this situation. The amount of gas particles can only be changed by adding or removing gas from the tank, weakening choice A. As the temperature of a gas decreases, the gas molecules slow down. This, in conjunction with the fact that the gas molecules are under a high amount of pressure due to the way in which the tank was filled, increases the likelihood of individual gas molecules interacting with one another. As a result, the molecules will behave in a less ideal way, and an increase in intermolecular forces is possible, making choice B a likely answer. Since the question stem states that the tanks are rigid, the volume of the tank and the gas contained within it would not be expected to change, making choice C a weaker answer. According to the kinetic molecular theory, as a volume of gas is heated, the gas molecules increase in velocity. Since choice D reverses this relationship, it is a weaker answer, making choice B the best answer.

44. **B is the best answer.** First, determine the molecular weight of phosgene.

2 Cl	71 g/mol
1 C	12 g/mol
+1 O	16 g/mol
$COCl_2$	99 g/mol

Next, use dimensional analysis to calculate the total number of moles of air in the room. Since a lethal dose is 3 ppm, or 3 parts per million, a lethal dose would result if a room contained a concentration of phosgene at 3 mol of phosgene for every one million moles of total air. This can be represented as 3 mol of phosgene/3×10^6 mol of air or as 3×10^{-6} moles of phosgene/mol of air in the room. Next, calculate how many grams of phosgene will produce that number of moles. Remember that at STP, 1 mole of gas occupies a volume of 22.4 L.

$$(22 \times 10^3 \text{ L})(22.4 \text{ mol of gas/L})(3 \times 10^{-6} \text{ mol phosgene/mol of gas})(99 \text{ g/mol phosgene})$$

Choice B is the best answer because it matches this dimensional analysis. Choice A seems like a strong answer, except it is missing the conversion unit, 22.4 L/mol, and so is unlikely to be the best answer. The power of ten in choice C results in several thousand kilograms of phosgene being calculated. This is much larger than the mass required to create a toxic dose in this situation, so choice C can be eliminated. Choice D also looks good, except it uses the reciprocal of the molecule weight instead of the molecular weight.

45. **B is the best answer.** The non-volatile solutes in the saliva will decrease the vapor pressure of the saliva. As water evaporates from the pure water beaker, it will then condense into the beaker containing the solutes. This will continue until all of the pure water has vaporized. As the concentration of non-volatile solutes in the saliva decreases due to increasing water, its vapor pressure will increase, but it will never match the vapor pressure of pure water. Therefore the process continues until all the water is in the saliva beaker, and choice B is the best answer. Choice A is the opposite of the expected observation and can be eliminated. Because the vapor pressure between the two liquids is different, a net change in the amount of water in each beaker is expected, so choice C can be eliminated. Because the vapor pressure of the solutions in each beaker will always differ, the beakers would not be expected to have the same amount of water at equilibrium, so choice D can be eliminated.

46. **A is the best answer.** Since the packaging is flexible, an increase in temperature would be expected to change the volume rather than the pressure, making this question an application of Charles's Law. As the temperature increases, the volume of the gas also increases, making choice A a strong answer. Using the ideal gas law ($PV = nRT$) it can be seen that if everything except for volume and temperature are held constant, then there is a direct relationship between V and T, making choice B a weaker answer. Since the question states that the container is compliant, it does not require much force to increase its volume. This means that a change in pressure as a result of increase temperature would result in an expansion of volume that returns the pressure to the original level, making choice C a weaker answer than choice A. Pressure and temperature are directly related, and choice D would result from an inverse relationship making it a weaker choice.

Passage 9 (Questions 47-52)

47. **D is the best answer.** The key change that occurs in the desorption process is that the VOCs go from liquid to gas phase. Liquids are denser and more compact, so the same number of molecules generally takes up more space in the gas phase than in the liquid phase. Choice A is unlikely. Choice B is unlikely as gases often have a higher heat capacity compared to the liquid phase. Choice C can be ruled out because the strength of intermolecular forces usually follows this trend: solid > liquid > gas. Choice D is the best answer because deposition is the process by which a gas undergoes a phase change to form a solid. This can only occur following desorption because the VOCs are not gases before the desorption step.

48. **C is the best answer.** Desorbing the VOCs from the fibers involves first extracting VOCs in the sample using fibers and then successfully desorbing the VOCs by converting them from the liquid to gas phase. Consider what conditions favor liquid to gas exchange. These conditions are low pressure and high temperature. Option I is likely to be in the best answer since it will increase the likelihood of the VOCs remaining in the liquid phase. Option II is unlikely to be included in the best answer as it would increase the ability of the experiment to desorb the VOCs. Based on Table 1, increasing fiber number increases the percentage of VOCs successfully isolated. Since option III is the opposite of this, it is likely to be in the best answer. Choice C is the best answer.

49. **D is the best answer.** Heat capacity of the VOCs is unlikely to be significantly impacted by pressure, and this would not necessarily impact the experiment. Choice A is unlikely. The VOCs are in the liquid phase during the extraction step according to the passage. Sublimation is the phase change going from solid to gas, so choice B is unlikely. It is true that solids exist at high pressures, but the solid fibers used for extraction would only convert to liquid or gaseous phase under extreme conditions that are unlikely in this experiment. It is unlikely that the designers of this experiment would choose a fiber that is unstable in the solid phase as this could cause contamination of the sample during desorbing process if the fibers also entered the gaseous phase. Choice C is unlikely. Evaporation of VOCs is a concern. They are defined as volatile, meaning they readily evaporate. If they evaporate, they would not adhere to the solid extraction fibers and would be lost. High pressure can increase the temperature required for high rates of evaporation, so choice D is the best answer.

50. **B is the best answer.** The best answer to any question will generally be true and accurate, as well as relevant to the question. In this case, all of these options are factually correct. Consider which one has the most relevance to the experiment. The small molecular weight is unlikely to affect the experiment, ruling out choice A. Being nonreactive, on the other hand, provides a large benefit. If helium was readily reactive, it could alter the VOC metabolites isolated in the gaseous phase. This would confound the experimental results, which makes choice B a strong answer. Choice C is true but would not provide a benefit to this experiment, so it can be eliminated. The same is true of choice D. Choice B is the best answer.

51. **D is the best answer.** Real gases have several key differences. Their behavior is defined by the Van der Waals' equation: $[P + n^2a/V^2](V - nb) = nRT$. In this equation, b accounts for volume of actual gas molecules and a reflects the strength of intermolecular attractions. The P and V terms in the ideal gas equation, $PV = nRT$, have been adjusted based on real behavior. Since the term including b is subtracted from volume, the actual volume of a real gas is larger. Real gases have higher volume because the molecules actually take up volume. This eliminates choices A and B. To distinguish between choices C and D, consider the impact of intermolecular forces on pressure. Because the term including a is actually added to pressure, this implies that the real pressure is lower. Pressure is related to the force of collisions between gas molecules and the container walls. The intermolecular forces acting between real gas molecules are primarily attractive, and this reduces the number of collisions on the container wall. This results in a decrease in pressure relative to pressure in ideal behavior. Choice C can be ruled out, and choice D is the best answer.

52. **A is the best answer.** Density of gases is directly proportional to molecular weight. This is because regardless of the size or mass of each molecule of gas, each molecule takes up the same amount of volume. The determinant of density in this case is molecular weight.

    Compound A has a molecular weight of:

    $$(12 \text{ mol of C} \times 12 \text{ g/mol}) + (10 \text{ mol of H} \times 1 \text{ g/mol}) + (1 \text{ mol of O} \times 16 \text{ g/mol}) = 170 \text{ g/mol}$$

    Compound B has a molecular weight of:

    $$(10 \text{ mol of C} \times 12 \text{ g/mol}) + (7 \text{ mol of H} \times 1 \text{ g/mol}) + (1 \text{ mol of O} \times 16 \text{ g/mol}) + (1 \text{ mol of H} \times 1 \text{ g/mol}) = 144 \text{ g/mol}$$

    Compound C has a molecular weight of:

    $$(3 \text{ mol of C} \times 12 \text{ g/mol}) + (5 \text{ mol of H} \times 1 \text{ g/mol}) + (1 \text{ mol N} \times 14 \text{ g/mol}) + (1 \text{ mol of O} \times 16 \text{ g/mol}) = 71 \text{ g/mol}$$

    Compound A has the highest molecular weight, so choice A is the best answer. Choices B, C, and D can be eliminated.

Passage 10 (Questions 53-56)

53. A is the best answer. Increasing the weight of the mass is expected to decrease the height of the piston. Choice B should be eliminated as it shows a direct relationship between the weight on the piston and the height of the piston. To distinguish between the remaining choices, it is best to consider the ideal gas law.

$$PV = nRT$$

To solve this problem it will be easiest to consider the simple case of only having one weight on the massless piston. Remember, the pressure of the gas is also equal to the force applied to the stationary piston by the weight, divided by its area, or $\frac{mg}{\pi r^2}$. The volume is equal to the volume of the piston chamber, $\pi r^2 h$. After substitution, the following equation describes this system.

$$\left(\frac{mg}{\pi r^2}\right)(\pi r^2 h) = nRT$$

After simplifying, this reduces to:

$$m = \frac{nRT}{gh}$$

Since $\frac{nRT}{g}$ is a constant, rewrite it as "K".

$$m = \frac{K}{h}$$

For this equation to remain balanced, the mass of the weight depressing the piston will be inversely proportional to the height of the piston. Choice A best demonstrates this inverse relationship and should be selected. Although choices C and D show the added masses decreasing the height of the piston, they do not show a linear relationship as evidenced by the curve line in both graphs. These answers are not as good as choice A, which shows the inverse, linear relationship.

54. D is the best answer. Consider the phase diagram provided in Figure 1 and use extremes to determine what phase each region of the diagram represents. At a minimum of pressure and a maximum of temperature the material will be in the gas phase. This region is located on the bottom right of the diagram. At a maximum of pressure and minimum of temperature the material will be in the solid phase. This region is located on the upper left of the diagram. The region whose boundaries are the solid and gas phases is the liquid phase. The point where all three lines intersect is the proverbial "triple point." The triple point is where all three phases exist in equilibrium. Since the triple point occurs at −57°C and 5.1 atm, choice A does describe carbon dioxide's phase behavior and should be eliminated.

The area on the phase diagram which is no longer above or below the liquid-gas boundary is the supercritical fluid phase. Here, CO_2 exists as neither gas nor liquid. This area on the phase diagram occurs at 31°C and 72.8 atm, so choice B does describe carbon dioxide's phase behavior and should be eliminated.

Connect −60.5°C and 10 atm in the graph to determine what phase CO_2 will exist as in these conditions. CO_2 is well within the solid phase with these conditions, so choice C properly describes carbon dioxide's phase behavior. Eliminate choice C.

The line that separates the liquid and solid phases provides the freezing point at different pressures. Since choice D is a point along this line, it means these conditions will allow CO_2 to freeze. Choice D does not describe the phase behavior of CO_2 and is the best answer.

55. **A is the best answer.** First consider the ideal gas law.

$$PV = nRT$$

In the case of this problem, the pressure is also equal to the force applied to the stationary piston by the weight divided by the area of the top of the piston, or $\frac{\text{mg}}{\pi r^2}$. The volume is equal to the volume of the piston, $\pi r^2 h$. After substitution the following equation describes this system.

$$\left(\frac{\text{mg}}{\pi r^2}\right)(\pi r^2 h) = nRT$$

Since the goal is to determine the mass of CO_2,and the question states that the entire mass of dry ice enters the gaseous phase, or sublimates, the next step is to solve for n.

$$n = \left(\frac{\text{mg}h}{RT}\right)$$

Since n refers to the number of moles of gas, multiplying this number by the molecular mass will provide the mass of dry ice added to the piston.

$$n \times \text{MW}_{CO_2} = \text{mass of } CO_2 \text{ added} = \left(\frac{\text{mg}h}{RT}\right) \times \text{MW}_{CO_2}$$

The best answer is choice A, which restates this expression. Choices B is an algebraic error that stems from multiplying instead of dividing by RT. Choice C arises from a mistake with units. Since MW_{CO_2} is in g/mol, and n is in mol, to solve for grams, multiplication of n by MW_{CO_2} is required. Choice D can be eliminated by using the equation to assess the effects of a hypothetical situation. The height of the piston should increase when a greater mass of dry ice is added, not decrease. This expression shows the height of the piston decreasing with a greater mass of dry ice. Without using algebra, choice D can be eliminated.

56. **B is the best answer.** When a substance goes from liquid to gas, the particles have more freedom, and their energy is more distributed in the universe. The entropy of the system has increased, and $\Delta S > 0$. Choices A and C can be eliminated. When a substance enters the gas phase, the process is endothermic and energy must be absorbed, so $\Delta H > 0$. Eliminate choice D, which makes choice B the best answer.

Stand-alones (Questions 57-59)

57. **A is the best answer.** If 5% of air on a humid day is composed of water, 5% of the original air sample must have been displaced to provide the necessary volume for the water vapor. Since ideal gasses are equally mixed, 5% of each separate gas had to leave the original air mixture.

Nitrogen: 80% × 0.05 = 4%

Four percent of the total loss of the air particles is from nitrogen. Nitrogen's new mole percent in air would be 76%

Oxygen: 20% × 0.05 = 1%

One percent of the loss of the air particles is from oxygen. Oxygen's new mole percent in air would 19%.

The ratio of new percent of oxygen particles to the old percent is 19%/20% = 0.95. Since the partial pressure is directly proportional to the number of particles, this ratio also reflects the ratio of the new partial pressure of oxygen to its initial partial pressure. Thus, the new partial pressure of oxygen is 95% of its initial partial pressure. Choose the best answer, choice A. If the 5% of air, which had to leave, was assumed to be comprised of equal numbers of particles of each gas (i.e. modeled as an absolute loss of 2.5% from each gas) choice B would result. This weakens choice B, as 5% of *all* of the *mixed* gasses left. This does not result in a subtraction of 2.5% from each separate gas's mole percentage. To better understand this point, pretend there were 100 particles comprising a sample of air. 5% of the 80 particles of nitrogen are removed along with 5% of the 20 particles of oxygen. Although the fraction that leaves from each population of particles is the same, the actual number of particles that leave from each gas is different. Eliminate choice B. If all 5% of the displaced air consisted of from oxygen molecules, choice C would result. Choice D contradicts Dalton's law. The partial pressure of a gas is directly proportional to its mole fraction in a mixture of gases. Since the mole fraction of oxygen changed, its partial pressure also had to change. Choice D can be eliminated.

58. A is the best answer. The universal gas constant, R, relates all of the terms in the ideal gas law, $PV = nRT$. To determine R's units, first isolate it algebraically:

$$\frac{PV}{nT} = R$$

Re-express each of the variables with examples of the units by which they are described:

$$\frac{\text{Pressure} \times \text{volume}}{\text{particle number} \times \text{temperature}}$$

These units can be (atm × L)/mol × K. Since unit multiplication also obeys the commutative property, atm × L = L × atm, making choice A the best answer. The other answer choices stem from algebraic errors. In particular, choice B improperly divides by the volumetric term and choice C is the reciprocal of the best answer. Choice D lacks a unit for temperature. Choices B, C, and D can be eliminated.

59. C is the best answer. STP is standard temperature and pressure. The standard temperature is 273 K and the standard pressure is 1 atm. For this reason it is easiest to use the 0.08206 L atm K^{-1} mol^{-1}. Solve $PV = nRT$ for volume to have $V = nRT/P$ = 4 mol × 0.08206 L atm K^{-1} mol^{-1} × 273 K / 1 atm = 4 mol × 22.4 L mol^{-1} = 89.6 L. It is worthwhile to memorize 22.4 L mol^{-1} as the value of 0.08206 L atm K^{-1} mol^{-1} × 273 K. Choice A occurs from an error in decimal placement. Choice B occurs by forgetting that the problem mentions 4 moles. Choice D occurs by using 298 K instead of 273. Many experiments are run at 298 K—conveniently this is room temperature—but the problem specifically mentioned STP, so choice C is the best answer.

Phases

MINI-TEST 5B

ANSWERS & EXPLANATIONS

Questions 1–29

Passage 1 (Questions 1-5)

1. **A is the best answer.** Reorder the evaporative heat loss equation to solve for the unknown variable, which in this case is *E*.

$$E = h_e A \Delta P$$

Pretend that the equation as written is the initial case with the shirt on. With the shirt off, since the effective radiating surface area, A, has increased by half, the shirtless case can be described as follows:

$$E = h_e(1.5)A\Delta P$$

The shirtless case has increased evaporative heat loss by 50% of its original value. Select the best answer, choice A.

Choice B is a mistake that could be made if an assumption was made that this problem was asking about the change in h_e if everything else but A remained constant. Since h_e is a constant, it does not make sense for it to change by 66%. Eliminate choice B. Choice C is an error in numerical reasoning. Increasing a value by half of its original value is a 50% increase. In order to be a 150% increase, it would involve increasing a number by a factor of 2.5. Eliminate choice C. Choice D would be a possible answer if the equation was not rearranged properly, or if h_e was solved for rather than E.

2. **C is the best answer.** Paragraph 2 of the passage provides the crucial hint to solving this problem by stating that when humidity is equal to the saturation vapor pressure of the sweat on the surface of the skin, sweat will no longer evaporate. When sweat no longer evaporates, evaporative heat loss is prevented. Since Figure 1 shows saturation vapor pressures at different temperatures, find the saturation vapor pressure that is relevant to sweat at thermal equilibrium with skin at 40°C. At this vapor pressure, no more sweat can evaporate, and evaporative heat loss is prevented. Since the temperatures in the graph are expressed in Kelvin, remember to add 273.15 to 40°C to convert it to Kelvins. The best answer will be the vapor pressure that is found on the curve at 313.15 K or 55 torr.

The other weaker answer choices do not correspond with the vapor pressure at 313.15 K. They come from not carefully reading the question. Choice A is the saturation vapor pressure at room temperature. Since the problem specified that the skin is not at room temperature, choice A can be eliminated. Choice B is the saturation vapor pressure at body temperature. Since the problem specified that the skin is actually at a higher temperature than body temperature, choice B should also be eliminated. Do not assume that all body measurements occur at 310.15 K. Choice D is the end of the graph. The end of this graph is not the point where sweat can no longer evaporate but is simply the last value that scientists recorded. Choice D should be eliminated.

3. **A is the best answer.** To compare these quantities, do some quick stoichiometric calculations to convert them into the same units. The values of the heat capacity and heat of vaporization of water are provided in the passage.

Vaporizing 1 g of boiling water

$$\left(\frac{40.7\text{ kJ}}{\text{mol}}\right)\left(\frac{1\text{ mol}}{18\text{ g}}\right)\left(\frac{1000\text{ J}}{1\text{ kJ}}\right) \approx 2000\text{ J}$$

Bringing 1 g of water from 0°C to 100 °C

$$\left(\frac{4.18\text{ J}}{\text{g} \times {}^\circ\text{C}}\right)(100^\circ\text{C})(1\text{ g}) = 418\text{ J}$$

$$2000\text{ J}/418\text{ J} \approx 5$$

Vaporizing the boiling water requires a little over 5 times as much energy, and choice A is the closest and best answer.

Choice B is an error that comes from not converting the units. $\left(\dfrac{40.7\text{ kJ/mol}}{4.128\dfrac{\text{J}}{\text{g} \times {}^\circ\text{C}}}\right)$ These units do not cancel each other out to result in a final unit of Joules. Remember that units must be the same when comparing values of the same physical property. Choice C is an error that comes from failing to convert the enthalpy of vaporization into kJ/g. Choice D is simply a tempting distractor. It is tempting because it is the only answer choice that implies that vaporization here takes less energy, not more.

4. **C is the best answer.** This is a trick question. Equilibrium does not mean that the system stops changing. It means that there is no net change in the system. In other words, water continuously evaporates from the skin while also condensing onto it, but there is no net change in the amount of water on the skin, or in the atmosphere. Choices A, B, and D imply that the system can no longer change, when, in fact, it can. Eliminate these choices. Choice C is the best answer because it is true, even though it may feel "wrong" compared to the other choices.

5. **C is the best answer.** If a fabric is permeable to gases, that means that sweat can vaporize off the skin and diffuse trough the fabric to the air in the room. Not a lot of sweat is expected to be found when the fabric is removed from the skin if the fabric is permeable to gases. Conversely, if the fabric is impermeable to gases, then sweat vapor will not be able to escape from between the skin and fabric. Eventually the saturation vapor pressure will be reached under the fabric, and the body will continue to produce sweat, which cannot evaporate. A lot of sweat is expected in the trial with impermeable fabric. Fabric Y is the most permeable to gases and fabric Z is the least permeable to gases—some form of this hypothesis will be expressed in the best answer. Since choice A has fabric W as the least permeable fabric, it should be eliminated. Choice B states the opposite of the logical hypothesis, and should be eliminated. Choice C looks like a strong answer because it restates the logical hypothesis. Choice D is not the best answer because fabric Y is more permeable than fabric X. Choice C is the best answer.

Passage 2 (Questions 6-11)

6. **B is the best answer.** As explained in the passage, Equation 1 describes the approximate relationship between M and c. The two variables are inversely proportional, meaning that as c increases, M must increase by the same magnitude. Choice B depicts this behavior accurately and is the best answer. Choice A shows an opposite relationship where an increase in M leads to a proportional increase in c, and can be eliminated. Equation 1 predicts a continuous relationship, with variety of values for c depending on M. Since choice C is a discrete graph with a limited number of values of c, it can be eliminated. Choice D shows a changing relationship between c and M. Based on Equation 1, a linear graph would be expected, so choice D is unlikely to be the best answer and can be eliminated.

7. **B is the best answer.** The major goal of this experiment is described in the first sentence of the first paragraph. Reading through the jargon , this first sentence describes calculating how well certain elements absorb heat, i.e. determining their specific heat capacity. The procedure described here is analogous to the coffee-cup calorimetry performed in freshman chemistry labs. Since all of the elements in Table 1 are metals, and conservation of energy is a necessary assumption when using a calorimeter to calculate specific heat, choice B is the best answer.

   Although water's capacity to resist a change in temperature is a useful property that lends it great utility in thermochemical analyses, water was not being directly evaluated in this study. Instead, it was used as a heat-absorbing medium to calculate the specific heat of the metals in Table 1, so choice A can be eliminated. Equation 1 describes a constant that relates specific heat capacity to molecular weight, but the first paragraph of this passage provides no reason to believe that this was the goal of the experiment. Moreover, introducing this equation with the expression, "In pre-modern times…" makes it seem much more likely to be background information rather than meaningful content relevant to the goal of this study. Choice C does not answer the question as well as choice B, which directly addresses the goal of the study as stated in the first sentence of the passage. Choice C can be eliminated. Finally, the relationship between density and specific heat capacity is never mentioned in this passage. It is unlikely to be the best answer, and choice D can be eliminated.

8. **C is the best answer.** Remember that the metal will always end in thermal equilibrium with the solution, and that energy is transferred from the metal into the solution until the two are in thermal equilibrium with one another. If the new solution has a lower specific heat than the original solution, as ethanol does relative to water, then the temperature of the solution will change with a smaller input of energy. This is implied by the units of specific heat: J/g · K. Specific heat describes how many Joules it takes to raise 1 gram of a substance by 1 Kelvin. If the specific heat is smaller, then less Joules, i.e. energy, are required to change the substance's temperature. The energy that is transferred from the metal to the solution, until the two materials reach thermal equilibrium, will lead to a greater increase in ethanol's temperature with less energy being lost by the metal. In other words, for a smaller amount of energy donated by the metal, the ethanol solution experiences a far greater increase in temperature than the water solution experienced. The net result is that the metal will cool of slightly compared to its initial temperature, and the ethanol's temperature will rise dramatically. Since the ethanol solution will rise to a higher temperature, and the metal loses less energy to achieve this change, the equilibrium temperature of the metal will also be higher than what it was in the water solution. As a result, the magnitude of ΔT_e will decrease, and choice A can be eliminated. The magnitude of ΔT_s will also increase, so choices B and D can be eliminated. Choice C is the best answer.

TEST 5B A&E

9. **A is the best answer.** Remember that the specific heat capacity of a material is equal to how many Joules must be added or removed to raise or lower the temperature of 1 gram of the material by 1 Kelvin. The units of specific heat capacity are J/g • K. A quick way to potentially eliminate weaker answer choices is to investigate what the final unit would be for each expression. For this question, ensure that energy units are in the numerator, and mass and temperature units are in the denominator. Choices B and D can be eliminated because they do not have mass or temperature units in the denominator. Since each sample was 0.1 moles of material, and M represents the molecular weight (g/mol) the mass of each sample will be equal to 0.1 M. Since 0.1 M can be rewritten as $\frac{1}{10}$ M, this is mathematically equivalent to having 10 in the numerator and M in the denominator of each expression. Remember that in specific heat measurements, energy units must be in the numerator, and the energy absorbed/released by a system is given by the equation $q = mc\Delta T$. When using this equation, the change in temperature, ΔT, is for the material with mass, m, and specific heat capacity, c, that are also being multiplied together. Otherwise, the equation does not make sense. Choice A properly represents the energy released by the metal/gained by the water, divided by the mass of the metal sample times its change in temperature, and is the best answer. Choice C does not use properties of the same material in its numerator, and can be eliminated.

10. **B is the best answer.** By definition boiling occurs when a solution's vapor pressure is equal to atmospheric pressure, so choice A can be eliminated. To evaluate choice B, calculate how much energy is required to change the water's temperature from 25°C to 100°C:

$$q = mc\Delta T$$

$$q = (100\text{ g})(4.2\text{ J/g}\cdot{}^\circ\text{C})(100^\circ\text{C} - 25^\circ\text{C}) = (420\text{ J/}^\circ\text{C}) \times 75^\circ\text{C} = 31500\text{ J} = 31.5\text{ kJ}$$

31.5 J is the energy required to raise the water to 100°C, but this is NOT the energy required to boil it. Once at 100°C, the water must receive additional energy to overcome the enthalpy of vaporization and actually boil. During this process of overcoming the enthalpy of vaporization, the extra energy that is added does not change the water's temperature, but acts instead to break intermolecular bonds in the liquid state. Since *more* than 31.5 kJ are required for the water to boil, choice B is a strong answer. Liquid water will reach a maximum of 100°C under atmospheric conditions—any more energy it receives goes into forming more vapor and will no longer raise the temperature of the water solution. Choice C can be eliminated. Two objects in thermal equilibrium have the same temperature. Since temperature is directly correlated with the average kinetic energy, and thus average velocity, of a solution or mass, choice D is true. Choice D can be eliminated.

11. **A is the best answer.** Table 1 shows the specific heat capacities of the different metals that were tested during this experiment. Aluminum has a specific heat capacity that is double that of nickel. This means to reach a given temperature, a mass of aluminum must receive twice as much energy as an identical mass of nickel. By extension, when placed in the water solution, the aluminum will have twice as much energy to donate to the solution before reaching thermal equilibrium with the solution, and the temperature change of the solution will be double that of the solution that received the Ni. This makes choice A the best answer. Choice B would be the best answer if the question was asking for the temperature of the solution that received the nickel sample with respect to the solution that received the aluminum sample. Choice C is tricky because it seems logical that two metals with the same initial temperature would bring the water solution to the same final temperature at equilibrium. The trick to answering this question is understanding that the amount of energy stored in the aluminum sample is twice as large as that of the nickel sample due to the difference in specific heat capacity. This means that the aluminum sample will contribute more energy to the solution and the final equilibrium temperature will be higher.

Stand-alones (Questions 12-15)

12. **C is the best answer.** Both choice A and B are true statements. The MCAT® would never require memorization of melting or boiling points, so that is the first warning sign that these may not be the best answers. Additionally, they do not clearly relate to the question. Boyle's law states that PV is constant assuming constant T. Charles' law is that V/T is constant assuming constant P. Since Boyle's law includes P, it best relates to the barometer, which measures pressure. Another way of thinking about it is that Boyle's law assumes constant T, so it could not be measuring different temperatures as a thermometer does. Since Charles' law includes T, it relates to the thermometer, which measures temperature. Neither Boyle's nor Charles' law fully explain a barometer or thermometer because these laws are only applicable to ideal gases, and liquid mercury does not behave like an ideal gas, but choice C is the best answer.

13. **B is the best answer.** The van der Waal's equation is $(P + n^2a/V^2)(V - nb) = nRT$. The larger the value of a and b, the greater deviation from ideal behavior. The table indicates that bromine has the largest a and b so choice B is the best answer. Through process of elimination, choice D and choice A should have been ruled out since they had intermediate values. Deciding between choice B and C could then be reasoned by remembering that the molecules of an ideal gas are assumed to not have volume. Bromine is a massive atom, so it is most likely to deviate from ideal behavior, and choice B is the best answer.

14. **A is the best answer.** This question is addressing the two different heat capacities a substance can have: constant volume heat capacity, C_v, and constant pressure heat capacity, C_P. The answer to this problem can be predicted by remembering the First Law of Thermodynamics, $\Delta U = q + w$. In the case where the volume stays constant, the system cannot perform PV work. With the inability to perform this work, most of the energy which is added must contribute to a temperature change. On the other hand, when pressure is held constant and the substance is allowed to expand, some of the energy can leave the system as PV work is done on the surroundings as the volume changes. This means that at constant pressure, a substance can absorb energy with less change in temperature, by expelling some of the energy to the surroundings as work. A general conclusion that can be drawn is that C_P is greater than C_v. Choice A is the best answer, and choice B can be eliminated. Since one of these paths prevents the performance of work, and the other path allows some of the energy, which the system acquires, to perform work, the energy which remains available to change each system's temperature will be unequal. In other words, for a given input of energy, the temperature change will be different for each system. Choice C can be eliminated. The ideal gas law $PV = nRT$ prohibits a change in temperature that is not accompanied by at least a change in either volume or pressure if the number of molecules in the sample remains unchanged. When n is constant, if T changes without P or V, or P and V changing, the equation is not be balanced on each side. Contradictions of this sort are not possible on the MCAT®. Choice D can be eliminated.

15. **B is the best answer.** The formula $C_v = q/\Delta T$ can be used to calculate the required heat, q.

$$q = C\Delta T = (3600 \text{ J/kg/°C})(0.5 \text{ kg})(25°\text{C}) = 45 \text{ kJ}$$

Forgetting to multiply by the 3600 J/kg/°C would lead to choice A, eliminating it as the best answer. Choice B best matches the calculated answer, so it is most likely to be the best choice. Forgetting to multiply by 0.5 kg would lead to choice C, eliminating it as the best answer. Forgetting to multiply by 25°C would lead to choice D, so it as the best answer.

Passage 3 (Questions 16-20)

16. **C is the best answer.** Use the equation $q = mc\Delta T$. This equation provides the energy required to change the temperature of an object of a given a mass. It will help solve how much energy must be added to the water to raise the temperature to its the boiling point. Don't forget to also add the heat of vaporization as just getting to the boiling point is not enough.

$$(60 \text{ g})\left(\frac{4.1 \text{ J}}{\text{g} \cdot °\text{C}}\right)(100°\text{C} - 25°\text{C}) \approx (240 \text{ J/°C})(75°\text{C}) = 18{,}000 \text{ J} = 18 \text{ kJ}.$$ **This is the energy required to reach 100°C.**

$$(60 \text{ g})\left(\frac{1 \text{ mole}}{18 \text{ g}}\right)\left(\frac{40 \text{ kJ}}{\text{mole}}\right) = 133.2 \text{ kJ}.$$ **This is the energy required to vaporize the water after it reaches 100°C.**

The sum of these energies is the total energy required to create steam.

$$18 \text{ kJ} + 133.2 \text{ kJ} = 151.2 \text{ kJ}$$

Choice A results from only solving the first part of this problem and not adding the heat of vaporization. Choice B results from solving both parts of the problem, but failing to convert to kJ after calculating the energy required to raise the temperature—**it is helpful to write out units to avoid these kinds of mistakes.** Choice D arises from only solving for the heat of vaporization and not adding the energy required to reach 100°C. Eliminate choice D.

17. **C is the best answer.** This question is really asking for the options that will increase the boiling point of the water in the bag. If the boiling point is increased, then the liquid water will be able to achieve a higher temperature before boiling. Remember that a liquid cannot exceed its boiling point, as additional energy put into a liquid at this point will be used to change phase from a liquid to a gas. Dissolving ions in a solvent increases its boiling point. This effect is proportional to the amount of ions dissolved and is maximized in a saturated solution. If the solution is saturated with sodium chloride, the water will reach a higher temperature before boiling. Option I will be part of the best answer. Expanding the surface area of the bag may allow water to boil more rapidly, but it does not change its boiling point. The water in the bag will not achieve a higher temperature before boiling. Option II can be eliminated. Sealing the exhaust would cause the steam to accumulate in the bag, and its vapor pressure would rapidly exceed atmospheric pressure. For additional water to boil, more thermal energy would be required to overcome this greater pressure barrier. This results in a greater boiling point, and the liquid water in the bag can acquire a higher temperature before boiling. Option III will also be part of the best answer. Choice C has the best options included, so it is the best answer.

18. **D is the best answer.** Look at the table in the passage. In the experiment, the researchers paired three different FFRs with two different MSBs to find out which combination was most sterile after being heated. The mechanism of heat transfer was convection, since steam, a heated gas, performed the bulk of the heating—select choice D. Although it is arguable that radiation from the microwaves themselves played a role, this is not an answer choice. Conduction was not the primary mechanism of heat transfer because the inner pleat in the MSB prevented the FFR from directly touching the hot water—eliminate choice C. The passage never discusses calculating vaporization energy or heat capacity and does not have any data to suggest that these fields were explored—choices A and B can be eliminated as well.

19. **A is the best answer.** Specific heat capacity is the quantity of energy required to change the temperature of 1 gram of material by 1°C. It can be solved using an algebraic variation of the $q = mc\Delta T$ equation, namely, $C = \frac{q}{m\Delta T}$

    In this problem the temperature change is the same and the energy applied is the same. The only difference is that the Moldex FFR is twice the mass of the KC FFR. $C_{moldex} = \frac{q}{2m\Delta T}$. This is ½ of the original specific heat capacity, or 1 J g^{-1} K^{-1}. Select choice C. Choices C and D are traps that arise from incorrectly assuming that specific heat has a directly proportional relationship with mass. Choice B can be eliminated—the heat capacity will not be the same as the KC FFR because, per unit mass, this material requires less energy to change temperature.

20. **B is the best answer.** A greater specific heat means that a material can absorb more energy before its temperature increases. A material with a greater heat capacity will require a longer period of time on the heater to reach 70°C. Arrange these in order from lowest to highest specific heat—Benzene, Olive Oil, Ethanol, Water—and select choice B. Choice A can be eliminated as it is the opposite of the best answer. It has the substances listed in order from highest specific heat to lowest specific heat. Choice C can be eliminated—it has the middle substances out of order. Choice D can be eliminated because it starts with a substance with the highest specific heat, not the lowest specific heat.

Passage 4 (Questions 21-26)

21. **C is the best answer.** The third paragraph and Figure 1 both describe that DSC measurements rely on the energy difference required to bring the reference and sample cells to the same temperature. Since both cells are brought to the same temperature and contain the same solvent, any disparity in energy that is added comes from overcoming phase changes of the solutes in the sample solution. Choices A and D can be eliminated because they would require using solvents which do not match the sample solution's solvent. Energy differences between these systems are not due solely to the presence of solute molecules. If the reference medium contained the same solutes in the same concentration as in the sample solution, the two solutions would be identical! There would be no disparities between either systems' thermal behavior. As a result, it would be impossible to measure the energy difference caused by phase transitions of the solute. There would be no reference control, without solute, with which to compare it. Choice B can be eliminated. The same mass of solvent receiving the same quantity of energy is expected to experience the same change in temperature unless its solute experiences a phase transition. A system where both the reference and sample cell have the same mass of solvent will be perfect for elucidating the thermochemical differences that occur during the solute's phase transitions. Choice C is the best answer.

22. **B is the best answer.** There are numerous equivalent expressions for power, such as $P = iV$ or $P = V^2/R$. When approaching this problem, if the latter of these equations was not remembered, Ohm's law can be used to substitute the desired variables into a different power equation. Even with the second expression, the power of this heater is not provided explicitly in the passage. It must instead be calculated, using the definition of power, which is energy, or work, expended over time. Thus, $P = W/t = V^2/R$. The energy this resistor releases into the sample solution will heat the sample solution and can be solved from the thermochemical equation, $w = q = mc\Delta T$. After dividing by time, power is derived: $\frac{w}{t} = \frac{q}{t} = \frac{mc\Delta T}{t} = \frac{V^2}{R}$.

23. **C is the best answer.** Look at the thermogram provided in Figure 2. At least while being heated, there is no real change in heat capacity between 50°C and 55°C. This means that between these two temperatures, no phase change is experienced by the solute particles. Cooling the solution through this temperature change will not result in any phase transition. Since a phase transition is the only process that requires a change in the heat necessary to maintain the same temperature in both the sample and the reference solutions, in the absence of a phase transition, there will be no difference in the heat required to maintain the same temperature in the sample and reference solutions. In other words, the cooling rate of the sample cell will not need to increase/decrease relative to the reference cell. Choice C shows a uniform cooling rate and is the best answer. Choice A is what would be expected if the solute solidified in this temperature range. More energy would need to be removed to overcome the negative enthalpy of fusion, in order to keep the sample cell at the same temperature as the reference cell. Choice A can be eliminated. Choice B looks like the opposite of the thermogram and is a tempting distractor. Choice D shows a linearly decreasing rate of cooling—since the two solutions will exhibit the same thermochemical behavior in this temperature range, a flat line is expected. Choice D can be eliminated.

24. B is the best answer. When a nonvolatile solute, i.e. a solute with no vapor pressure, is added to a liquid, some solute molecules reach the surface of the solution and reduce the surface area available for the liquid molecules. Since solute molecules do not break free from the solution but do take up surface area, the number of molecules breaking free from the liquid decreases while the surface area of the solution and the volume of open space above the solution remain the same. Thus, the vapor pressure of a solution is lower than the vapor pressure of the pure solvent. Choice B is the best answer. Choice A says the opposite and can be eliminated. Choice C may have been true if the reference medium had a very small concentration of solute, as there would not be enough solute to exert any effect. Nonetheless, the reference medium is actually quite concentrated with a non-volatile solute—as stated in the question stem—in contrast with the pure solvent, which contains no solutes. As described above, these solutes reduce the reference medium's vapor pressure, making choice C less likely than choice B. There is no reason to expect that the solution will have a larger vapor pressure since adding a solute decreases the vapor pressure if compared to the pure solvent. Choice D can be eliminated.

25. D is the best answer. For all sera, during this temperature interval, $C_p^{ex} = 0$. Remember that C_p^{ex} is a measure of excess heat capacity, or essentially, how much *more* energy was required to raise the sample solution's temperature by a given amount more than the reference solution. $C_p^{ex} = 0$ means that the same energy is required to raise both the reference and sample solutions to the same temperature. Otherwise, there would be a non-zero value for the excess specific heat capacity, C_p^{ex}. Thus, $q_s = q_r$ and $\Delta q = 0$. Choice D is most likely the best answer, but check the other choices before choosing it. If the thermochemical equation $q = mc\Delta T$ were used, the magnitude of the q solved from this equation is equal to q_r and q_s. However, since the question asked for Δq and not these other values, choices A and B can be eliminated. Choice C would result had the numerical values plugged into that equation been rounded, and not compensated for when choosing an answer. Choice D is the best answer.

26. A is the best answer. Sublimation describes the process whereby a solid becomes a gas, and never transitions through the liquid phase. It is commonly observed with solidified CO_2, known as dry ice. Water can also sublimate, assuming the pressure is low enough. To determine where this spot is on the phase diagram, first figure out what phases are within each boundary. The top left of the graph represents the solid phase because this area has the greatest pressure and lowest temperatures. The water particles are packed tightly together and do not have a lot of energy to move around. The bottom right of the graph represents the gas phase. These water particles are packed very loosely together because there is the least pressure acting on them. They also have the greatest kinetic energy. The middle bounded region is the liquid phase. Every point on the line, starting in the lower left, which separates the solid phase from the gas phase, is an area where solid water will be in equilibrium with gaseous water. Choice A is the best answer. The middle point of the graph, II, is known as the triple point. It is the temperature and pressure at which all three phases of water coexist in equilibrium. When water goes from a pure solid to the triple point, it will also melt, so this point does not *only* represent sublimation, and choice B can be eliminated. Point III is a melting point—here ice becomes water. Point IV is a boiling point—here, water becomes steam. Choices C and D can be eliminated. Remember any point on a line which separates phase boundaries is a phase transition point.

Stand-alones (Questions 27-29)

27. D is the best answer. The work done in expanding a gas under constant pressure can be calculated using $W = P\Delta V$. Since the change in volume is not provided in the question stem, it must be calculated using the equation that is provided.

$$\Delta V = \frac{4}{3}\pi(r_f^3 - r_o^3)$$

Since $r_o = 5$ cm, it is possible to substitute integers into this equation and "plug and chug."

$$W = P\frac{4}{3}\pi(r_f^3 - r_i^3)$$

$$W = [(1.022\text{ atm})(10^5\text{ Pa/atm})]\left(\frac{4}{3}\pi\right)(20^3 - 25^3\text{ cm}^3)\left(\frac{1\text{ m}}{100\text{ cm}}\right)\left(\frac{1\text{ m}}{100\text{ cm}}\right)\left(\frac{1\text{ m}}{100\text{ cm}}\right)$$

$$= 1.022 \times \left(\frac{4}{3}\pi\right)(20^3 - 25^3\text{ cm}^3)(10^{-1})\text{ or }\frac{1.022 \times 4\,(20^3 - 25^3) \times \pi}{30}\text{ J}$$

Choice D is the best answer. Choice A does not convert the radius from cm^3 to m^3 and does not provide the answer in joules. Choice B lacks the conversion of the pressure units into Pa, and also lacks the conversion of cm^3 to m^3, and can be eliminated. Finally, choice C does not properly convert cm^3 to m^3. To convert square units, repeated division, as shown above, is required. Remember $Pa \times m^3 = J$ but $atm \times m^3 \neq J$. Likewise, $Pa \times cm^3 \neq J$, This is why it is so important to be careful with units when applying equations, otherwise the answer may not be in the appropriate units.

28. A is the best answer. Sublimation is the transition from a solid to a gas, so choice A is inaccurate and likely the best answer. Vaporization is the transition from a liquid to a gas, so choice B is true and can be eliminated. Condensation is the transition from a gas to a liquid, so choice C can be eliminated. Deposition is the transition from a gas to a solid, allowing choice D to be eliminated.

29. C is the best answer. Remember that when the refrigerant evaporates, it is absorbing heat from its surroundings, breaking the intermolecular bonds which hold it in the liquid phase, and entering the gas phase—this process is what allows it to cool other parts of the system. This increase of heat that the refrigerant experiences is expressed with an increasing ΔH. Choices B and D are oriented in the opposite direction and can be eliminated. According to the second paragraph, gas expansion occurs in a low pressure pipe within the system. Since the transition observed between points 4 and 1 occurs at a lower pressure than the transition seen between 3 and 2, choice C is better than choice A and is the best answer.

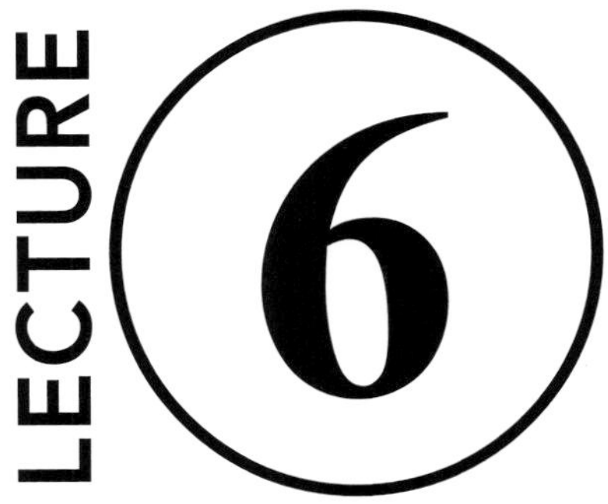

Solutions and Electrochemistry

TEST 6A

ANSWERS & EXPLANATIONS

Questions 1–59

LECTURE 6 ANSWER KEY

TEST 6A		MINI-TEST 6B	
1. B	**31. B**	**1. B**	**16. B**
2. A	**32. D**	**2. C**	**17. C**
3. D	**33. A**	**3. C**	**18. A**
4. B	**34. A**	**4. A**	**19. C**
5. A	**35. B**	**5. C**	**20. C**
6. D	**36. C**	**6. C**	**21. C**
7. B	**37. A**	**7. C**	**22. D**
8. D	**38. C**	**8. A**	**23. D**
9. C	**39. D**	**9. D**	**24. B**
10. D	**40. C**	**10. D**	**25. C**
11. D	**41. D**	**11. C**	**26. C**
12. B	**42. D**	**12. D**	**27. A**
13. A	**43. A**	**13. A**	**28. D**
14. B	**44. D**	**14. B**	**29. A**
15. C	**45. D**	**15. D**	
16. B	**46. D**		
17. D	**47. B**		
18. B	**48. D**		
19. B	**49. D**		
20. C	**50. A**		
21. D	**51. B**		
22. D	**52. B**		
23. C	**53. C**		
24. A	**54. C**		
25. D	**55. B**		
26. B	**56. D**		
27. C	**57. C**		
28. A	**58. A**		
29. A	**59. C**		
30. C			

EXPLANATIONS FOR LECTURE 6

Passage 1 (Questions 1-5)

1. **B is the best answer.** Since calcium ions have a +2 charge, they are expected to form an ionic bond with ions carrying a negative charge, but hydronium ions, also known as H_3O^+ are positively charged and would not be expected to associate with calcium, weakening choice A. Phosphate ions have a −3 charge and are capable of forming an ionic bond with calcium in a two to three ratio, so choice B is a strong option. Ammonium, like hydronium, has a +1 charge, making choice C a weaker option. Chloride has a −1 charge and would be able to form an ionic bond with calcium to form $CaCl_2$. In water, which is the main solvent of urine, compounds containing halogens are soluble (except when those compounds contain mercury, lead, or silver). Since $CaCl_2$ is soluble, it would not be expected to form kidney stones, making choice B a stronger answer than choice D.

2. **A is the best answer.** When in solution, calcium ions are completely surrounded by water molecules which can interact with the positive ions due to the polar nature of water. To form a new ionic bond with oxalate ions, some of those intermolecular bonds between water and calcium ions must be broken, making choice A a strong answer. Since oxalate can be considered a non-metal and calcium is a metal, an ionic bond rather than a covalent bond would form between them, which makes choice B a weaker option. K_{sp} is an equilibrium constant , which is a value that describes the relative amount of reactants and products for a given reaction at equilibrium. A larger equilibrium constant indicates that the more products than reactant will be present once equilibrium is achieved. Equilibrium constants are calculated at specific temperatures and will change if the temperature of the reaction is altered. Since K_{sp} is an equilibrium constant, it is not expected to change unless the temperature of the solution changes, making choice C a weaker answer. As calcium oxalate dissolves in water, intermolecular bonds between water molecules are broken and replaced by intermolecular bonds between water and oxalate. Since the question is asking about a precipitation reaction, the opposite would be expected, making choice D a weaker answer.

3. **D is the best answer.** Lowering the concentration of the hydrogen ions in the urine would result in an increase in the pH. This is an important distinction to make since the x-axis of Figure 1 is representing pH and not hydrogen ion concentration. As the pH increases, the solubility of magnesium ammonium phosphate decreases. As a result, the concentration of ions that make up this stone would be expected to decrease as they crash out of solution as a precipitate. Because choice A claims the opposite would occur, it is probably not the best answer. Since calcium oxalate solubility is not significantly affected by a change in the pH, the amount of calcium oxalate stones should not change with an increase in pH, making choice B a weaker answer. From Figure 1, it can be determined that the solubility of uric acid actually increases as urine pH increases, eliminating choice C. Figure 1 shows that the solubility of magnesium ammonium phosphate decreases as the pH increases, which would result in an increased amount of precipitate, making choice D the best answer.

4. **B is the best answer.** Since the temperature of the urine remains the same, an increase in the risk of kidney stone formation will be largely increased if there is a significant increase in the concentration of certain ions needed for precipitation. This can be achieved through the common-ion effect. Since Na^+ and Cl^- are very soluble and are not found in kidney stones, increasing their concentration is not expected to increase the risk of kidney stones, weakening choice A. A sports drink that contains $CaCl_2$ could potentially increase the concentration of Ca^{2+} in the urine, which could increase the risk for kidney stones, making choice B a strong option. Since $CaCO_3$ is relatively insoluble, it would not be expected to increase the concentration of Ca^{2+} in the urine, making choice C a weaker choice than choice B. As shown in Figure 1, black tea should probably be avoided because it would increase oxalate ions in the urine, but since green tea with milk has very few oxalate ions, choice D is a weaker answer than choice B.

5. **A is the best answer.** When water solvates a polar molecule, the water molecules becomes oriented so the oxygen atoms face the positively charged compound and the hydrogen atoms face the negatively charged compounds. Since calcium ions has a +2 charge, oxygen would be expected to be oriented towards these ions, making choice A a strong option. The oxalate ions would interact with the partially positively charged hydrogen ions, allowing choice B to be eliminated. Given that calcium oxalate is insoluble, interaction between it and the water molecules would be very minimal. In this insoluble form, the charge of neighboring calcium oxalate molecules stable each other leading to the formation of a crystal structure. Since water is not significantly interacting with calcium oxalate, choice C is a weaker answer. Water molecules that are not solvating other polar molecules will align so that the oxygen atoms are interacting with the hydrogen atoms of neighboring water molecules due to them having an opposite charge, making choice D a weaker answer.

Passage 2 (Questions 6-9)

6. **D is the best answer.** It is worthwhile to memorize the molecular formulas for common ions. Phosphate is PO_4^{3-}. PO_3^{2-} is not an ion that is commonly seen in solution. In fact, it does not even have a name, so choice A is not the best answer. Phosphite is PO_3^{3-}, so choice B is not the best answer. PO_4^{2-} is not an ion commonly seen in solution and is also not a named ion, so choice C is not the best answer. PO_3^{2-} and PO_4^{2-} are possible polyatomic anions and would be composed of phosphorus (IV) and phosphorus (VI), respectively. However, phosphorus (V) and (III) are much more common and result in PO_4^{3-} and PO_3^{3-} respectively. The MCAT® does not require memorization of the oxidation states of atoms, but it does benefit to know the names of common polyatomic anions.

7. **B is the best answer.** Dipole interactions occur when a bond is very polarized due to a large difference in electronegativities of two species. Alanine (Ala) and phenylalanine (Phe) are nonpolar amino acids, so their side chains have no noticeable dipoles. Tyrosine (Tyr) and glutamine (Gln) both have oxygen atoms, which would create a dipole. Glutamine also includes a nitrogen atom, which would have a slight dipole moment. Between Gln and Tyr, choice B is the best answer. Notice that both molecules can participate in hydrogen bonding, which is common in molecule with strong dipoles. Molecules capable of hydrogen bonding always have strong dipoles, but the reverse is not always true.

8. **D is the best answer.** A steroid is a hydrophobic molecule with a multi-ringed structure. Like all steroids, methylprednisolone is relatively insoluble in the blood and other aqueous fluids and must be transported on a carrier protein. The forces that allow a steroid to interact with the hydrophobic interior of carrier protein are Van der Waal's forces because these are the only forces that do not require a charged molecule or dipole. Ionic bonds occur between charges molecules. The question states that methylprednisolone is hydrophobic so it cannot be charged, and choice A is not the best answer. Hydrogen bonds occur when a hydrogen atom that is covalently bound to a polar atom experiences a strong partial positive charge that interacts with another polar atom nearby that has a strong partial negative charge. The question stem states methylprednisolone is hydrophobic so it should not have many polar atoms, and choice B is not the best answer. Dipole interactions occur when nearby dipoles interact. Again, dipoles are a result of bond polarization, which only occurs where there is a large difference in the electronegativities of atoms. Methylprednisolone is not polar, so choice C is not the best answer.

9. **C is the best answer.** This question requires knowledge of neuronal physiology. The resting membrane potential of a neuron is −70 mV. This potential is the same concept as an electromotive force that is created in an electrochemical cell in the lab. A neuron depolarizes to 40 mV when an action potential fires. The signal is propagated down the cell by insulating fat, also known as myelin. Without myelin, the signal will dissipate and the cell will be unable to depolarize. This is most consistent with choice C, where initially the axon depolarizes, but the signal fails to propagate down the axon. Choice A depicts a failure of action potential firing, which is not the best answer. Choice B shows the axon potential firing and propagating down the axon to the dendrites. This would be a normal axon, and choice B is not the best answer. Choice D shows a sustained depolarization of the axon. A voltage gated potassium channel is used to repolarize the cell. A mutation in that channel or an absence of potassium may cause choice D, but it is not the best answer.

Stand-alones (Questions 10-13)

10. **D is the best answer.** Any molecule that produces hydrogen ions would increase pH so choice A is not accurate. The mechanism by which citrate achieves this result is by forming a complex ion with calcium. A complex ion forms when a metal ion becomes covalently bound to multiple molecules that are acting as Lewis bases, and the metal ion is prevented from interacting with other molecules. Choice B describes this process correctly, but states that citrate binds to oxalate, which is not a metal, to form the complex ion making it a weaker choice. Choice C is a distractor that is impossible. The presence of a new molecule in solution is not able to decrease the mass of an atom. The only way to decrease the mass of an atom would be through nuclear decay. So, choice C is not the best answer. The formation of the complex ion occurs as described in choice D. A small number of citrate complexes are able to remain dissolved in solution. This is one of the reasons citrate is added to beverages.

11. **D is the best answer.** First consider the disassociation equilibrium of $ZnCl_2$:

$$ZnCl_2(s) \rightleftharpoons Zn^{+}(aq) + 2Cl^{-}(aq)$$

Raise the concentration of the products, to their coefficient in the disassociation equilibrium.

$$K_{sp} = [Zn^{+}][Cl^{-}]^2$$

Select the correct answer, choice D. The incorrect answer choices are all perversions of the correct equilibrium expression meant to intimidate students. Be confident and select the correct answer.

TEST 6A A&E

12. B is the best answer. The common ion effect takes advantage of disturbing the solubility equilibrium with another chemical, in order to enhance the solubility of the compound in question. To explain this, let's consider the dissociation of $CaSO_4(s)$ in water:

$$CaSO_4(s) \rightleftharpoons Ca^{2+}(aq) + SO_4^{2-}(aq)$$

$$K_{sp} = [Ca^{2+}][SO_4^{2-}]$$

Once the ions of Ca^{2+} and SO_4^{2-} have concentrations such that they can satisfy the K_{sp} expression, no more solid can dissolve. Reducing the concentration of Ca^{2+} or SO_4^{2-} in solution would increase the solubility of $CaSO_4(s)$ because more of it would need to dissolve in order to satisfy the solubility product constant. Adding a chemical that precipitates either Ca^{2+} or SO_4^{2-} out of solution would accomplish this. Option I will be part of the best answer because of the remarkably lower K_{sp} that barium sulfate has compared to calcium sulfate. Addition of barium nitrate will lead to the formation of barium sulfate, removing sulfate ions from solution, and forcing more calcium sulfate to dissolve. Conversely, adding a chemical that increases the concentration of either of these ions in solution would decrease the solubility of $CaSO_4$; the concentration of one of the ions would be greater and prevent more new ions from dissolving. Option II will not be part of the best answer. Choices A and C can be eliminated. The solubility of a solid increases as the temperature of its solution increases, as the solute particles have greater kinetic energy to overcome the solute-solute interactions which keep them held together as a solid. Option III will be part of the best answer. Finally, adding more water will decrease the concentration of each ion in solution. More of the solid will need to ionize in order to satisfy the K_{sp}. Option IV will also be part of the best answer. Choice D can be eliminated, and choice B is the best answer.

13. A is the best answer. The first step in solving this problem is to start with the solubility equation, $S = [H_2U] + [UH^-]$. Recall the formulas for K_D and K_{sp} as well:

$$K_{sp} = [H^+][UH^-]$$

$$K_D = \frac{[H^+][UH^-]}{[H_2U]}$$

Now solve for $[H_2U]$ and $[UH^-]$.

$$H_2U = \left(\frac{1}{K_D}\right)(K_{sp}) = \frac{K_{sp}}{K_D} \text{ and } [UH^-] = \frac{K_{sp}}{[H^+]}$$

Remember, according to the definition of pH, $pH = -\log[H^+]$, that $[H^+] = 10^{-pH}$. Substitute this term into the UH^- expression for $[H^+]$.

$$[UH^-] = \frac{K_{sp}}{[10^{-pH}]}$$

Substitute these bolded expression into the solubility equation:

$$S = \frac{K_{sp}}{[K_D]} + \frac{K_{sp}}{[10^{-pH}]}$$

Simplify this expression by multiplying the numerator and denominator of each fraction by the denominator of its neighbor to provide the new expression:

$$\frac{[(10^{-pH})(K_{sp})] + K_{sp}K_D}{10^{-pH}K_D}$$

Further simplification reveals that this expression is equivalent to:

$$\left(\frac{K_{sp}}{K_D}\right)\frac{(10^{-pH} + K_D)}{10^{-pH}}$$

Stop here. The left-hand term is enough to rule out choices B and D, and the right-hand term can rule out choice C, as addition, not subtraction, is occurring. Often times on the MCAT®, fully simplifying the algebra can be wasteful if a partial solution suffices to choose the best answer. Choice A is the fully simplified best answer.

Passage 3 (Questions 14-17)

14. **B is the best answer.** Unless otherwise specified, assumed room temperature. At room temperature, $K_w = 10^{-14}$. Since $K_w = [H^+][OH^-]$ then $-\log(K_w) = -\log([H^+]) + -\log([OH^-])$

In other words, **14 = pH + pOH**. This is a very useful relationship, and is worth memorizing. It makes solving this problem a lot easier than relying on equilibrium equations.

$$14 = pH + pOH$$

$$14 - pH = pOH$$

$$14 - 4 = pOH$$

$$10 = pOH$$

$$10^{-10} = [OH^-]$$

Select the correct answer, choice B.

15. **C is the best answer.** The only reactions occurring at the anode are oxidation reactions. Oxidation reactions are reactions in which the reactant loses electrons. Eliminate choice D, as H^+ does not lose electrons. The next hint in solving this problem comes from the passage itself in the final paragraph. The passage says that there is a pH gradient in the electrolyte, with a low pH being near the anode. A low pH means that the solution surrounding the anode is acidic, having a greater local concentration of $H^+(aq)$. The only way for the anode to have this greater local concentration of $H^+(aq)$ is for it to be continuously producing it, otherwise the protons would rapidly diffuse away. The correct side reaction will be producing protons. Select the best answer, choice C. Choices B and A are poor choices because they are not decreasing the local pH of the anode.

16. **B is the best answer.** The passage provides a pretty strong hint in the last sentence where it describes how membrane lipids will change their orientation in response to the electric field generated by the cell. The positively charged protonated amino group of the molecule will orient itself towards the negative pole of the battery, and vice-versa for the negatively charged phosphate group. The negative pole of the battery will be the cathode, where reduction is occurring, because it is coated in electrons. The positive pole of the battery will be the anode, were oxidation is occurring, because it has a local lack of electrons. The passage hints in the last paragraph that LMO is the cathode and zinc metal is the anode. The amino group will be oriented towards the LMO, and the phosphate group will be oriented towards to zinc metal. Eliminate choice A and select the best answer, choice B. Choice C is scientifically wrong, as having a net charge of zero will not prevent the molecule from responding to an electric field. Moreover, the passage explains in the last sentence that membrane lipids change their orientation in response to electrical fields. Eliminate choice C. Choice D would be true if the field changed directions. In the case of this battery, the field's location is constant because the poles of the battery are not moving. Eliminate choice D.

17. **D is the best answer.** All of these answer choices are partially true. Be sure to select the best answer choice, which will be fully true. Choice A is not the best answer choice. At an electrolyte concentration of 0.2 M, *B. subtilis* survived better than *E. coli*. Eliminate choice A. Choice B is also weak, as *E. coli* far better survived the intense 0.3 M electrolyte solution than did *B. subtilis*. Although choice C is factual, this experiment never established that there was a concentration threshold. At all concentrations, the bacteria in this experiment survive and are viable for a few days. Choice C is NOT supported by the experiment, and should be eliminated. Choice D is the best, and is supported by the experiment. Look at the 0.3 M part of the graph, and see that acclimated *E. coli* are better capable of surviving this most lethal concentration of electrolyte. Choose the best answer, choice D.

Passage 4 (Questions 18-21)

18. B is the best answer. When comparing the solubility of materials using K_{sp}, remember that K_{sp}, the solubility product constant, is a proxy measurement of solubility. It is derived by raising the equilibrium molar solubility of each chemical to the power of its coefficient in its dissociation equation, and then multiplying these terms together. For example, let AB_2 represent a molecule that dissociates sparingly in water:

$$AB_2(s) \leftrightarrow A^+(aq) + 2B^-(aq)$$

$$\text{Thus, } K_{sp} = [A^+]1[B^-]^2$$

All of the chemicals in this table dissociate into two ions. The real molar solubility *could* be found by taking the square root of each K_{sp}, but this is unnecessary. Since all of the K_{sp} values in this table reflect the square of each molar solubility they can be directly compared to each other! The compound with the smallest K_{sp} value is the least soluble, and the compound with the greatest K_{sp} value is the most soluble. Choice B is the best answer, as it is the most soluble. The other answer choices have smaller K_{sp} values and are less soluble. Choice A, C, and D can be eliminated. Choice A stems from an error in interpreting scientific notation. Remember, the lower an exponent is on the number-line, the *smaller* the number, not the reverse.

19. B is the best answer. When comparing the solubility of materials using K_{sp}, remember that K_{sp}, the solubility product constant, is only a *proxy measurement* of solubility. It is derived by raising the molar solubility of each chemical to the power of its coefficient in its dissociation equation, and then multiplying these terms together. For example, let AB_2 represent a molecule that dissociates sparingly in water:

$$AB_2(s) \leftrightarrow A^+(aq) + 2B^-(aq)$$

$$\text{Thus, } K_{sp} = [A^+]^1[B^-]^2$$

Apply the same equation to calculate the molar solubility of each of these compounds before comparing them to each other. The waters of hydration can be disregarded in writing the dissociation expression for calcium sulfate dehydrate because the concentration of water is assumed to be constant.

$$CaSO_4(s) \leftrightarrow Ca^{2+}(aq) + SO_4^{2-}(aq)$$

$$K_{sp} = [Ca^{2+}][SO_4^{2-}]$$

The solubility of any one of these ions represents the molar solubility of the compound, because for every mole of one ionic species in solution, a mole of the parent compound had to dissolve. Thus, the solubility of $CaSO_4 = \sqrt{K_{sp\,CaSO_4}} = \sqrt{13.1 \times 10^{-5}}$.

By the same approach, the solubility of $BaSO_4 = \sqrt{K_{sp\,BaSO_4}} = \sqrt{1.1 \times 10^{-10}}$

The relationship between the solubility of these compounds can be found by taking the ratio between them:

$$\frac{\sqrt{K_{sp\,CaSO_4}}}{\sqrt{K_{sp\,BaSO_4}}} = \frac{\sqrt{13.1 \times 10^{-5}}}{\sqrt{1.1 \times 10^{-10}}} = \frac{\sqrt{3.1} \times 10^{-2.5}}{\sqrt{1.1} \times 10^{-5}} \approx \frac{1.7 \times 10^{-2.5}}{1 \times 10^{-5}} = 1.7 \times 10^{5/2}$$

Choice B is closest to this rounded answer. Choices A and D are algebra errors that stem from not taking the square root of everything under the square root symbol. Choice C is an error that comes from directly comparing the K_{sp} values to each other. Remember K_{sp} value are only a *proxy measurement* of solubility—it is necessary to convert them into molar solubility to solve solubility comparison problems.

20. C is the best answer. First determine the balanced chemical equation that describes this reaction:

$$CaCH_3COO(aq) + NH_4CO_3(aq) \rightarrow CaCO_3(s) + NH_4CH_3COO(aq)$$

Since the K_{sp} of calcium carbonate is very small, the amount of calcium carbonate which remains dissolved in solution can be disregarded for this calculation. In other words, assume that every particle of calcium carbonate will precipitate during this reaction.

Use stoichiometry to calculate what volume of the 3 M ammonium carbonate solution must be added to consume all of the calcium acetate solution. This volume added to the initial volume is the final volume of the solution, once a precipitate will no longer form.

$$(50 \times 10^{-3}\ \text{L})(1\ \text{mol}\ CaCH_3COO/\text{L})(1\ \text{mol}\ NH_4CO_3/1\ \text{mol}\ CaCH_3COO)(1\ \text{L}/3\ \text{mols}\ NH_4CO_3) = 16.6 \times 10^{-3}\ \text{L}$$

$$V_f = V_i + V_{added}$$

V_f = 50 mL + 16.6 mL = 66.6 mL. Choice C is the best answer. Choice A is the amount of ammonium carbonate solution which must be *added*, but it is not the final volume of the solution. Choice A can be eliminated. Choice B is a distractor with the same order of magnitude as the best answer, and choice D stems from an error in stoichiometry. The carbonate anion has a −2 charge. As a result, there is a 1:1 ratio between this anion and ionic calcium when they form a compound. Choice D stems from ascribing a −1 charge on the carbonate anion, doubling the ratio of this anion to calcium, and artificially doubling the amount of solution which must be added. Choice D can be eliminated.

21. D is the best answer. This reaction occurs in two steps: 1) Nitric acid decarboxylates silver carbonate, forming water, carbon dioxide, and silver nitrate. 2) the ionic silver in silver nitrate is reduced by the copper in the wire, forming solid silver and releasing ionic copper into the solution.

1. $2HNO_3(aq) + Ag_2CO_3(s) \rightarrow H_2O(l) + 2AgNO_3(aq) + CO_2(g)$

In general, a carbonate salt mixed with an acid typically forms water and carbon dioxide. This is a useful rule to keep in mind when approaching these sorts of problems.

2. $2AgNO_3(aq) + Cu(s) \rightarrow Cu(NO_3)_2(aq) + 2Ag(s)$

In terms of charge transfer, this second reaction can be understood as:

$$2Ag^+(aq) + Cu^\circ(s) \rightarrow Cu^{2+}(aq) + 2Ag^\circ(s)$$

Nitric acid is consumed during his reaction. Since catalysts are not consumed, choice A can be eliminated. Electrons left copper and reduced silver. This means that silver has a greater reduction potential than does copper. It is far more energetically favorable to reduce silver with copper than to reduce copper with silver—this first reaction *releases* energy, the second requires energy *to be added.* There is no reason to expect the reduction of copper via the oxidation of silver, regardless of the presence of nitric acid. Choices B and C can be eliminated. Carbon dioxide is released from silver carbonate, after nitric acid has been added. This carbon dioxide gas will originate from the solid silver carbonate, appearing as bubbles in solution. Choice D is the best answer.

Passage 5 (Questions 22-25)

22. **D is the best answer.** The first step to solving this problem is to balance these two redox equations by multiplying them by coefficients which leave each reaction producing or consuming the same amount of electrons:

Multiply Reaction 2 by three, and Reaction 3 by two and add them together as shown:

$$2 \times [\text{Al}(s) \rightarrow \text{Al}^{3+}(aq) + 3\text{ e}^-]$$
$$+\,3 \times [\text{Ag}_2\text{O}(s) + 2\text{ e}^- \rightarrow 2\text{ Ag}(s) + \text{O}^{2-}]$$
$$2\text{ Al}(s) + 3\text{ Ag}_2\text{O}(s) \rightarrow 2\text{ Al}^{3+}(aq) + 6\text{ Ag}(s) + 3\text{O}^{2-}$$

After balancing these redox equations, the ratio of moles of elemental silver which are formed to moles of aluminum which are oxidized can be determined as a 3:1 ratio.

Use dimensional analysis to determine how many nanograms of silver are formed for every nanogram of aluminum which is oxidized.

$$(1\text{ ng Al})(1\text{ mol Al}/27 \times 10^9\text{ ng Al})(3\text{ mol Ag}/1\text{ mol Al})(108 \times 10^9\text{ ng Ag/mol Ag}) = 4 \times 3 = 12\text{ ng.}$$

Choice D is the best answer. Choice A stems from reading directly from Equations 1 and 2 without balancing them. In particular, it uses the native coefficients in front of each compound to determine an improper 2:1 ratio of moles of silver formed to moles aluminum oxidized. Choice A can be eliminated. Choice B stems from properly balancing the equation, but accidentally using the reciprocal of the appropriate mole ratio between moles of silver formed to moles of aluminum oxidized. Choice B can be eliminated. Choice C is a distractor based on the false assumption that the mass of one lost reactant must equal the mass of one newly formed product. This is a misstatement of the conservation of mass which actually states that the *sum* of the masses of the reactants is equal to the *sum* of the masses of the products.

23. **C is the best answer.** Remember that K_{sp}, the solubility product constant, is a proxy measurement of solubility. It is derived by raising the equilibrium molar solubility of each chemical to the power of its coefficient in its dissociation equation, and then multiplying these terms together. For example, let AB_2 represent a molecule that dissociates sparingly in water:

$$\text{AB}_2(s) \leftrightarrow \text{A}^+(aq) + 2\text{B}^-(aq)$$
$$\text{Thus, } K_{sp} = [\text{A}^+]^1[\text{B}^-]^2$$

Applying the same technique to hydroxyapatite provides that $K_{sp} = [\text{Ca}^{2+}]^{10}[\text{PO}_4^{3-}]6[\text{OH}^-]^2$. The next step is to pick the concentration of an ion and determine its relationship to the amount of hydroxyapatite which must dissolve to form it. For this answer explanation, $[\text{OH}^-]$ will be used , as it has the simple ratio of 2:1 with respect to the concentration of dissolved hydroxyapatite. However, note that any other ion could be used during this step of solving the problem. Let the $[\text{OH}^-] = \text{X}$. Substituting this term in, the K_{sp} expression changes to $K_{sp} = [5\text{X}]^{10}[3\text{X}]^6[\text{X}]^2$

$$K_{sp} = 5^{10} \times 3^6 \times \text{X}^{18}$$
$$\sqrt[18]{\frac{K_{sp}}{5^{10} \times 3^6}} = [\text{X}]$$

Remember that the ratio of $[\text{OH}^-]$ to $[\text{Ca}_{10}(\text{PO}_4)_6(\text{OH})_2]$ which dissolves is 2:1. Thus, $2\text{X} = [\text{Ca}_{10}(\text{PO}_4)_6(\text{OH})_2]$ which dissolves.

The best answer will have the form of $2 \times \sqrt[18]{\frac{K_{sp}}{5^{10} \times 3^6}} = [\text{Ca}_{10}(\text{PO}_4)_6(\text{OH})_2]$

Choice C is the best answer. Choice A stems from not properly writing the K_{sp} expression. In particular, it improperly puts the coefficient from the dissociation expression "in the box" as well as using the coefficient as the exponential term. In other words, it substituted $[10]^{10}$ for $[\text{Ca}^{2+}]$. The coefficient does not go "in the box," instead it is only used as the exponential term. However, a scaling factor from the balanced equation is often required to go "in the box." Choice A can be eliminated. Choice B properly solves the problem, but does not include the very last step where the concentration of dissolved OH^- is appropriately scaled to become the solubility of hydroxyapatite. Choice B can be eliminated. Choice D is a distractor based on making the errors which would have resulted in Choice A, except that is also contains an extraneous coefficient as well.

24. **A is the best answer.** In the "standard" galvanic cell, electrons travel from the anode to the cathode through the wire and counter ions are provided by the salt bridge to prevent each half cell from over-polarizing during the reaction. The mouth is not truly an electrochemical cell, rather it is the site where an electrochemical reaction is occurring. Saliva is an electrolytic solution that allows the transfer of electrons from the aluminum metal to the amalgam filling. In this sense, it is most akin to a wire, which also allows the transport of electrons from one material to another. Choice A is probably the best answer, but consider the other ones before choosing it. During these reactions, saliva is neither reduced nor oxidized. Thus, it is not the cathode or anode, respectively. Choices B and D can be eliminated. Finally, the saliva does not need to provide counter ions during this reaction because no positive or negative charges are lost from the solution, i.e. the saliva, as they would be lost from each half cell in a galvanic cell. Choice C is not as strong as the best answer, choice A.

25. **D is the best answer.** Remember the definition of pH: pH = $-\log[H^+]$. Every decrease in a pH unit reflects a 10 fold increase in the concentration of H^+. Likewise, every decrease in a pH unit also leads to a 10 fold increase in the solubility of hydroxyapatite. If the solubility of hydroxyapatite were expressed as a base ten logarithm, every decrease in a pH unit would result in an identical increase in the log base ten of the solubility of hydroxyapatite. Thus, $\log[Ca_{10}(PO_4)_6(OH)_2]$ should *increase* linearly as the pH decreases. Choice D best shows this behavior and is the best answer. Choices A and B show exponential behavior instead of linear behavior and can be eliminated. Choice C stems from accidently illustrating the relationship between $-\log[Ca_{10}(PO_4)_6(OH)_2]$ and pH. Choice C can be eliminated.

Stand-alones (Questions 26-29)

26. **B is the best answer.** The principle behind solvents is that "like dissolves like." The MCAT® requires memorization of the structures of the DNA bases and amino acids. For this question, it is only necessary to know that guanine is an organic polar molecule with numerous hydrogens available to hydrogen bond. Water is a polar protic solvent, meaning that it has polarized bonds and can give away its hydrogen to become a strong base. A protic solvent is often one that has an –OH group that is able to donate a hydrogen as a Bronsted acid and can often hydrogen bond to help solvate compounds. This makes choice A a candidate for the best answer, but the other choices should be considered. Ethanol also can hydrogen bond, and contains two carbons, which may be able to interact with the carbon-containing rings of G. Its polar protic nature, like water, helps solvate polar compounds like G, and the addition of the extra carbon helps further solvate organic molecules. Choice B is likely a better answer choice than choice A. Methane and nonane are both nonpolar molecules that are unlikely to solvate a polar molecule, eliminating choices C and D.

27. **C is the best answer.** Remember that K_{sp} is derived from the dissociation equilibrium of iron(III) hydroxide:

$$Fe(OH)_3 \rightleftharpoons Fe^{3+} + 3OH^-$$

Raise the concentration of each ion to its coefficient in the balanced dissociation equilibrium to create the K_{sp} expression:

$$K_{sp} = [Fe^{3+}][OH^-]^3.$$

Division provides the solubility of $[Fe^{3+}]$:

$$K_{sp}/[OH^-]^3 = [Fe^{3+}]$$

Remember that pOH = 14 – pH and that $10^{-pOH} = [OH^-]$

In neutral water: pOH = 14 – 7 = 7 and $10^{-7} = [OH^-]_{neutral}$

In water with a pH of 8: pOH = 14 – 8 = 6 and $10^{-6} = [OH^-]_{basic}$

$$\frac{[Fe^{3+}]_{basic}}{[Fe^{3+}]_{neutral}} = \frac{K_{sp}/[OH^-]^3_{basic}}{K_{sp}/[OH^-]^3_{neutral}} = \frac{[OH^-]^3_{neutral}}{[OH^-]^3_{basic}} = \frac{[10^{-7}]^3}{[10^{-6}]^3} = \frac{10^{-21}}{10^{-18}} = 10^{-3}.$$

Choice C is the best answer. Choice A is an algebra error from adding the cubed terms to the exponent, instead of multiplying. Choices B and D are distractors, each an order of ten away from the best answer.

28. **A is the best answer.** First, determine how many moles of sulfuric acid are in this solution:

$$(1\text{ L})\left(\frac{1000\text{ mL solution}}{\text{L solution}}\right)\left(\frac{1\text{ g solution}}{\text{mL solution}}\right)\left(\frac{0.30\text{ g }H_2SO_4}{\text{g solution}}\right)\left(\frac{1\text{ mole }H_2SO_4}{\approx 100\text{ g }H_2SO_4}\right) = 3\text{ moles of }H_2SO_4$$

Molarity is given by moles of solute/liters of solution:

$$3\text{ mol }H_2SO_4/1\text{ L} = 3\text{ M}$$

Select the best answer, choice A.

29. **A is the best answer.** The solubility product is the equilibrium of a solvation reaction. The first step in solving these problems is to write out the reaction that is occurring as the sodium bicarbonate dissolves:

$$NaHCO_3(s) \leftrightarrow Na^+(aq) + HCO_3^-(aq)$$

Pure solids and pure liquids are not included in a solubility product expression, likely making choice A the best answer. Choice B can be eliminated, as only one sodium molecule is dissolved per sodium bicarbonate molecule. Pure solids are not included in the solubility product expression, eliminating choice C. Water is also not included in the equilibrium expression, eliminating choice D.

Passage 6 (Questions 30-33)

30. **C is the best answer.** Consider Reaction 2. In order to produce a current for the detector, the electrode must be *reduced* by the ferrocyanide complex. In other words, ferrocyanide should have a more positive oxidation potential than the electrode which is to be reduced. This means that ferrocyanide is more "eager" to give its electron to the electrode than the electrode is to give it to ferrocyanide. Ferrocyanide has a more positive oxidation potential than electrode Y, making choice C the best answer. Choices B and D can be eliminated, as these electrodes have a greater value for the standard oxidation than ferrocyanide. They are more likely to be oxidized by ferrocyanide than ferrocyanide is to be oxidized by them. Remember if the standard reduction potential between two materials is the same, no reaction will occur. There is no energy difference to promote the reaction. For this reason, choice A can be eliminated as one of the electrodes in this choice will not establish a potential difference when electrically connected with ferrocyanide.

31. **B is the best answer.** Remember, the molecular *shape* is the shape whose vertices come from the positions of the atoms in the molecule, while ignoring the positions of the lone pair electrons. For example, even though ammonia has one lone pair, its shape is trigonal pyramidal—the lone pair of electrons is treated as if it were invisible and only the atoms are used. Since there are no lone pairs in the ferricyanide complex, the effects of bond angle compression due to the presence of lone pairs can be disregarded, and only the locations of the bonding domains need to be considered. Each of these bonding domains is the vertex of whatever shape this molecule will form. Since this molecule has six total bonding domains, it will form an octahedron. Choice B is the best answer. The other shapes can only be formed when lone pairs are present in the molecule and/or if the molecule has fewer than 6 bonding domains. Choice A, trigonal bipyramidal, occurs in a molecule with 5 bonding domains and no lone pairs. Choice A can be eliminated. Choice C, square planar occurs in molecules with 4 bonding domains and two lone pairs. Finally, choice D, T-shaped, requires 4 bonding domains, and one lone pair. Choices C and D can be eliminated.

32. **D is the best answer.** There are numerous ways to solve this, but the best way will require the least amount of steps. Do not convert to moles, as that step is not necessary to solve this problem. First use dimensional analysis to calculate how much sugar the hypoglycemic patient has in their blood before treatment:

(50 mg/dL)(10 dL/1 L)(5 L) = 2500 mg of glucose in the entire patient's body.

Next, calculate how much glucose the patient needs in their blood:

(100 mg/dL)(10 dL/1 L)(5 L) = 5000 mg of glucose in the patient's body post-treatment.

The difference between these values is how much glucose the patient must ingest: 5000 mg – 2500 mg = 2500 mg of glucose or 2.5 g of glucose. Choice D is the best answer. Choices A and B are distractors, and choice C is the total glucose the patient will have dissolved in their blood after treatment, but not the amount which they must ingest to treat their hypoglycemia. Choices A, B, and C can be eliminated.

33. **A is the best answer.** Remember that reduction occurs at the cathode and that oxidation occurs at the anode. A useful mnemonic for this rule is "**An Ox** and **Red Cat** = **an**ode **ox**idizes, and **cat**hode **red**uces. According to Reaction 2, which occurs on the solid state catalyst, ferricyanide *gains electrons* to become ferrocyanide. This is evinced by it gaining a negative charge. This *reduction* reaction occurs at the cathodic terminal of the solid state catalyst, ruling out choices B and D. During Reaction 3, the cyanide containing complex loses the negative charge it gained during Reaction 2 and reverts to being ferricyanide again. This *loss of electrons* is oxidation and occurs at the anodic terminal of the electrode, ruling out choice C, and making choice A the best answer.

Passage 7 (Questions 34-37)

34. **A is the best answer.** The solubility product constant for calcium hypochlorite is given by: $K_{sp} = [Ca^{2+}][ClO^-]^2$. The solubility of calcium hypochlorite that is provided in the passage can be used for the concentrations in the equation, but it must first be converted to molar concentration. Using a periodic table, calcium hypochlorite has a molar mass of 142.98 g/mol. The molar solubility of calcium hypochlorite is: s = 0.21 g/mL × 1000 mL/L × 1 mol/142.98 g = 1.47 mol/L. It is important to remember that when calcium hypochlorite dissolves, one calcium ion is produced for every two hypochlorite ions. As a result, $K_{sp} = (s) \times (2s)^2 = 4s^3$. After plugging in 1.47 mol/L for s, it is found that $K_{sp} = 12.67$. This reasoning makes choice A a strong answer. Choice B ignores the fact that two hypochlorite ions are produced for every one calcium ion, and can be eliminated. Because choice C does not convert the solubility to molar solubility and does not double the number of hypochlorite ions, it can be eliminated. Choice D is a weak answer because it both does not convert solubility to molar solubility. As a result, choice A is the best answer.

35. **B is the best answer.** In this situation, copper ions are being formed while hydrogen gas is being produced. The hydrogen ions are being reduced, and the half-reaction is given a reduction potential of zero because it is the standard hydrogen electrode. As a result, the net voltage produced by the reaction is the negated reduction potential of copper. The net reaction for the production of either Cu^{2+} or Cu^+ creates a negative reduction potential, so an outside voltage source is required to force the reaction to occur. 0.5 V are being applied to the copper rod, so only Cu^{2+} ions may form, since they have a reduction potential below 0.5 V ($E = -0.337$ V). First, the number of electrons required to reduce 500 g of copper needs to be determined. Copper has a molar mass of 63.5 g/mol, and two moles of electrons are required to oxidize one mole of copper. As a result, 500 g × 1 mol Cu/63.5 g · 2 mol e^-/1 mol Cu = 15.75 moles of electrons are needed. 1 ampere of current provides 1 C/s of electrons, and there are 96,485 coulombs per mole of electrons. The number of seconds to provide 15.75 moles of electrons is 15.75 mol e^- × 96485 C/mol e^- × 1 s/1 C = 3.0×10^6 seconds. This reasoning makes choice B the best answer.

36. **C is the best answer.** In a galvanic cell, the reactions must be spontaneous because there is no outside source to power them. The reductions of Cu^+ and Cu^{2+} have a reduction potential of 0.521 V and 0.337 V, respectively. The oxidation of chlorine gas has an oxidation potential of −1.62 V. The overall potential of a reaction is given by the reduction potential plus the oxidation potential. For either copper ion reduction, a net negative potential exists. While the reaction is nonspontaneous, the reverse reaction will spontaneously occur. As a result, option I is a weak answer, and choice A can be eliminated. Because the reverse reaction will form, hypochlorous acid will actually be reduced to form chlorine gas, while copper will be oxidized to release copper cations. This reasoning makes choice II a weak answer, and choices B and D can be eliminated. Because copper is being oxidized, copper must be the anode, making option III a strong option and choice C the best answer.

37. **A is the best answer.** Calcium hypochlorite will dissociate in solution to form Ca^{2+} and ClO^- ions. Because hypochlorous acid is weakly acidic, its conjugate base, hypochlorite, must be strongly basic. As a result, the following reversible reaction will occur: $ClO^- + H_2O \leftrightarrow HClO + OH^-$. This reaction will favor the formation of products because hypochlorous acid is a weak acid, and is therefore more stable than its strong conjugate base. By Châtelier's principle, the removal of hypochlorite will result in more calcium hypochlorite to dissolve. The reaction of hypochlorite with water is most favored when there is a low concentration of hydroxide ions in the solution. This situation occurs at low pH, so choice A is a strong answer. Choice B can be eliminated because pH 7.5 has a higher concentration of hydroxide ions than choice A. Choice B uses a pH number in the pH range for chlorine-based pools mentioned in the passage, but it is important not to pick a number simply because it looks familiar from the passage. The pH of the water used in pools is not necessarily chosen for solubility purposes. Choice C also has a higher concentration of hydroxide ions than choice A, so it can be eliminated. The reaction between hypochlorite and water to produce hypochlorous acid and hydroxide ions result in an increased solubility for calcium hypochlorite. The concentration of hydroxide ions determines the extent of this reaction, with a decreased concentration meaning that the reaction is pushed more towards the products. As a result, pH does have an effect on solubility. This reasoning makes choice D a weak answer. Choice A is the best answer.

Stand-alones (Questions 38-41)

38. **C is the best answer.** Dipole-dipole interactions occur between different molecules (intermolecular) not between atoms of the same molecule (intramolecular). Mixing up these two terms is a common trap answer of the MCAT®, and is the reason Choice A is not the best answer. These forces occur when two molecules that have some polarity, or charge separation, experience a force due to the opposite charges attracting one another. While dipole-dipole forces are often present between polar molecules, choice B states that they occur between atoms of the same molecule. This is alluding to a polar bond which often results in the formation of a dipole (positive on one side and negative on the other). Remember that dipole-dipole interactions occur between two different molecules that have a separation of charge, which makes choice B a weaker answer. Hydrogen bonds occur when molecules that have a hydrogen atom bonded to an extremely electronegative molecule (O, N, or F) experience a strong force with neighboring molecules. This intermolecular force results from the extreme dipole that is created by the polar bond between the hydrogen and electronegative atom, making choice C a strong answer. While dipole-dipole interactions allow the participating molecules to achieve a lower energy state, this occurs by separating similar charges from one another and allowing opposite charges to be oriented next to each other, making choice D a weaker option and choice C the best answer.

39. **D is the best answer.** Addition of SrCl would have the net effect of increasing the concentration of Sr^{2+} which would decrease the amount of $Sr(OH)_2$ dissolved in solution via the common ion effect, weakening choice A. Pressure only has a measurable effect on the solubility of gasses and since $Sr(OH)_2$ is not a gas, choice B is a weaker answer. Stirring a solution affects the rate at which a compound dissolves by increasing the surface area that is exposed to the solvent, but it does not have an effect on the final amount dissolved. Since this is a saturated solution, the amount dissolved will not be increased by stirring, which makes choice C a weaker option. By decreasing the pH, there will be an increase in the amount of H^+ ions available in solution. This will cause more OH^- ions to undergo a condensation reaction with the hydrogen ions to produce water molecules. The net result will be a decrease in the concentration of OH^- ions, which will increase the solubility of $Sr(OH)_2$.

40. **C is the best answer.** The mole fraction of a solute in solution is equal to the moles of the solute divided by the total moles of all solutes and solvent in solution. In order to determine the mole fraction, the moles of solute and solvent need to be determined first. Sodium chloride has a molar mass of 58.44 g/mol, and water has a molar mass of 18 g/mol. The number of moles of sodium chloride in solution is found by dividing the grams of sodium chloride by its molar mass: 150 g · 1 mol/ 58.44 g = 2.57 moles. The number of moles of water is found by first converting 750 milliliters to 750 grams, and then dividing the mass of water by water's molar mass: 750 g · 1 mol/18 g = 41.67 moles. The mole fraction of sodium chloride is then found by dividing the moles of sodium chloride by the moles of sodium chloride and water: 2.57 mol/(2.57 mol + 41.67 mol) = 0.058. It is important to remember that the number of moles of sodium chloride is NOT doubled even though sodium chloride dissociates to form two ions in solution. Solution concentrations are always based on the solute before concentration. In this case, this is the compound sodium chloride. This makes choice C the best answer.

41. **D is the best answer.** In a standard reduction potential table, the strongest reducing agents are the ones with the most negative reduction potential, meaning they are more easily oxidized. The zinc ion has the most negative reduction potential, meaning it is most likely the strongest reducing agent compared to the other biologically important metals found in the table. Choice D is the best answer.

Passage 8 (Questions 42-47)

42. **D is the best answer.** Remember "**LEO** the lion says **GER.**" **L**ose **e**lectrons **o**xidation and **g**ain **e**lectrons **r**eduction. Since Reaction 1 causes water to lose 4 electrons, it is oxidation. Eliminate choices B and C, as they claim that Reaction 1 is reduction. Reaction 2 is reduction because it adds 4 electrons to water. Reaction 3 is oxidation because PEDOT° loses 1 electron. The correct answer must be oxidation, reduction, oxidation—this is choice D. Choice A is a weaker answer because the last reaction is listed as reduction instead of oxidation.

43. **A is the best answer.** PEDOT:PSS is a "shield" for the water. It undergoes oxidation and reduction in order to prevent the water from undergoing these reactions. This is hinted in the passage where it says, "To protect water from electrolysis, and still maintain a potential difference across the terminals of the gel, it is possible to oxidize and reduce material that remains attached to or within the electrodes."

Reaction 2 leads to oxidized $PEDOT^+$. If $PEDOT^+$ comprised the cathode material, it will be able to absorb more electrons than PEDOT°. Reaction 2 should be performed on the cathode material because this will increase the life of the cell before it starts attacking water. Choose choice A. If the anode material were pre-oxidized there would be very few electrons to donate before the material over-oxidized, and the reaction started attacking water. In fact, pre-oxidizing the anode material would shorten the life of the cell. This is the opposite of the goal of the instrument. Choice B is a weaker answer. Performing this reaction on both materials is less advantageous than performing it on just the cathode material because the anode material would still become over-oxidized. Choice D is a weaker answer because oxidizing the cathode material is useful to increase the life of the cell.

44. **D is the best answer.** Remember that one ampere is equal to a Coulomb of charge passing a point in a circuit every second. It will be necessary to use Faraday's constant to convert from μA to moles.

$$\left(\frac{30 \cdot 10^{-3}\text{ Coulombs}}{\text{sec}}\right)\left(\frac{60\text{ sec}}{1\text{ minute}}\right)(2\text{ min})\left(\frac{\text{moles e}^-}{9.6 \cdot 10^4\text{ Coulombs}}\right)\left(\frac{1\text{ mole PEDOT}^+}{1\text{ mole e}^-}\right) = \frac{3 \cdot 6 \cdot 2 \cdot 10^{-1}}{9.6 \cdot 10^4}\text{moles PEDOT}^+$$

$$\approx 4 \times 10^{-5}\text{ moles PEDOT}$$

The correct answer should be a little bit less than 4×10^{-5} mole because the value in the denominator is somewhat greater than 9; choice D is the closest number and should be chosen. Choice C is a mistake that comes from forgetting that two minutes passed. Choice B is a mistake that comes from forgetting to convert to seconds. Choice A is a mistake that comes from improper scientific notation.

45. **D is the best answer.** Concentration is defined as moles of solute per liter of solvent. Whenever a question is asking for the concentration of a chemical, convert the mass of the chemical into moles, and divide this quantity by the volume of solvent that is used to dissolve it.

$$\frac{3\text{g}}{121.14\text{ g}} \cdot \text{mol}^{-1} \approx \frac{1}{40}\text{ mol}$$

Don't forget to divide the quantity of moles by the volume of the solvent:

$$\frac{\frac{1}{40}\text{ mol}}{0.5\text{ L}} = 0.05\text{ M}$$

The incorrect answer choices stem from math errors, or are there to serve as tempting distractors. In particular, choice C comes from dividing by 2 instead of multiplying by the reciprocal of ½.

46. **D is the best answer.** SDS denatures proteins because its hydrophobic end strongly associates with the portion of the protein that is hydrophobic, and gives the protein negative charges which are roughly evenly distributed over the structure of the protein. The even distribution of negative charges cause the protein structure to become rod-like in solution, effectively destroying the 2°, 3°, and 4° structures of the protein. Since the proteins all have negative charges, they will migrate to the positively charged side, or the anode. Select choice D. They will be repelled by the cathode, so choice C is wrong. Since all the proteins carry a net charge regardless of pH, they will not stop moving at the pI—eliminate choice B. Choice A is wrong because even without SDS, if the pH were lower than the pI, the proteins would continue to move in the gel matrix because they would still bare a net charge.

47. **B is the best answer.** Use the equation $\Delta G = \Delta H - T\Delta S$. In case it's difficult to remember this equation, use the mnemonic **G**et **H**igh **T**est **S**cores to remember the arrangement of the variables. During dissolution, the entropy will increase, so $\Delta S > 0$, and the best answer will contain option I. In order for a reaction to occur ΔG must be less than 0, so the best answer will also contain option III. With this in mind, it is possible to eliminate other answer choices. Choice A must be incorrect because it does not include a negative ΔG.

ΔH is not necessarily greater or less than 0; it depends on how large the value of ΔS is, and whether or not ΔG can remain negative. A positive ΔH can be present with a very large ΔS or high temperatures, and the reaction will still be spontaneous. Consider that dissolving NaOH has $\Delta H < 0$, but dissolving $NH_4(NO_3)$ has a $\Delta H > 0$. Choices C and D can be eliminated.

Passage 9 (Questions 48-51)

48. **D is the best answer.** Remember that oxidation occurs at the anode, and reduction occurs at the cathode. Choices B and C both feature electron loss—these reactions are oxidation, not reduction. The reactions of choices B and C cannot occur at the cathode; eliminate these choices. To distinguish between the reduction choices, A and D, remember the hint the passage gives in the last paragraph. It says that the SM undergoes oxidation. Choice A shows the SM being reduced; this choice can't possibly be describing this cell—eliminate choice A. Finally, choice D features a reduction reaction which is true of the cell in the passage. It is reduction because the reactant is gaining electrons, and it's true of the cell in this passage because an oxidized metal is being made pure again by having its rust removed. Select choice D.

49. **D is the best answer.** The final paragraph explains that electrolysis drives the rust removal. Electrolysis requires a current to be passed between the terminals of the cell. To quickly pass a current in solution, there must be dissolved ions to acts as charge carriers. Without an ionic charge carrier, current cannot effectively pass through the solution, and the electrolysis will slow down dramatically. Of the choices, only glucose will not form ions in solution. If it is used instead of NaCl, then the current will slow down dramatically, and rust will not be effectively removed via electrolysis. Select choice D. The other choices are incorrect; they all form ions in aqueous solution.

50. **A is the best answer.** Do not be intimidated by this question! All the reactions in this passage that lead to the formation of rust are dependent on the reactions that precede them. If Reaction 2 does not occur, then Reaction 3 will not occur, and there will be no iron(II) formed to react with the hydroxide anion in solution. Reaction 2 requires the presence of dissolved oxygen gas. If there is no dissolved oxygen gas, then Reaction 2 will not occur, and rust will never have the opportunity to form.

Reducing the partial pressure of a gas above a solution decreases the concentration of that gas that can remain dissolved in the solution. At higher elevations, oxygen has a far lower partial pressure. A container at this higher elevation cannot contain as much dissolved oxygen as a container at a lower elevation. This means that Reaction 2 will not occur to the same extent at the higher elevation. The rate of rust formation is expected to decrease in the container at the higher elevation—select the best answer, choice A.

Choice B is the opposite of the correct answer—eliminate it. With less oxygen available, rust formation will slow down—choice C cannot be true—there will be a detectable change in the rate of rust formation. There is enough information to solve this problem, so eliminate choice D as well.

51. **B is the best answer.** Use the periodic table to calculate the MW of $Fe(OH)_2$

Fe	55.8
2O	32
+ 2H	2
	89.8 ≈ 90 g/mol

Next, use stoichiometry to find out how many Coulombs must have passed through the cell:

$$\frac{(5\text{ g Fe(OH)}_{2\text{ removed}})\left(\frac{1\text{ mol Fe(OH)}_2}{90\text{ g}}\right)\left(\frac{2\text{ mol e}^-}{1\text{ mol Fe(OH)}_{2\text{ removed}}}\right)\left(\frac{9.5\times10^4\text{ C}}{1\text{ mol e}^-}\right)}{(8\text{ hours})(60\text{ min/hour})(60\text{ sec/min})}$$

The incorrect choices come from missing steps in this problem. Choice A forgets that two moles of electrons are passed into the material for every mole of reduced iron that is produced—eliminate choice A. Choice C does not properly convert the time to seconds in the denominator—remember that an amp is 1 C/sec, not per hour. Eliminate choice C. Choice D does not use the MW of $Fe(OH)_2$ properly—eliminate choice D.

Passage 10 (Questions 52-56)

52. **B is the best answer.** The passage explains in the third paragraph that the phosphoric acid is added to make the solution clear after it turns yellow. Table 1 shows that $Fe(OH)_3$ is both insoluble and yellow. It must be that the Fe^{3+} produced during Reactions 1 and 2 hydrolyzes the water it's in to form $Fe(OH)_3$. For lack of further information, this hypothesis explains the yellow color the solution adopts. The iron in $Fe(OH)_3$ is not Fe^{2+}, as this compound has three hydroxide groups in it. Each hydroxide group has a −1 charge, and for this compound to be neutral, Fe must be in the +3 state. By forming a soluble complex with Fe^{3+}, phosphoric acid prevents Fe^{3+} from hydrolyzing water, and prevents the formation of the yellow precipitate—choice B is the best answer. Since phosphoric acid is reacting with Fe^{3+}, choice A, which states that it is reacting with Fe^{2+}, can be eliminated. If phosphoric acid formed insoluble complexes with Fe^{3+}, then putting it into solution would cause the solution to become cloudy, not clear as described in the passage, so choices C and D can be eliminated.

53. **C is the best answer.** The net ionic equation which describes this reaction will be the balanced sum of the two half-reactions. The first half reaction is:

$$8H^+(aq) + MnO_4^-(aq) + 5e^- \rightarrow Mn^{2+}(aq) + 4H_2O(l)$$

The second half reaction is:

$$Fe^{2+}(aq) \rightarrow Fe^{3+}(aq) + e^-$$

This problem does a lot of the work already by providing the protons and water which were needed to balance each half reaction. Since the number of electrons on each side of the reaction arrow must be equal, multiply Reaction 2 by five. After doing this, adding the two reactions together cancels out the electrons and provides the balanced net ionic equation.

$$\begin{array}{l} 8H^+(aq) + MnO_4^-(aq) + \cancel{5e^-} \rightarrow Mn^{2+}(aq) + 4H_2O(l) \\ +\ 5Fe^{2+}(aq) \rightarrow 5Fe^{3+}(aq) + \cancel{5e^-} \\ \hline 8H^+(aq) + MnO_4^-(aq) + 5Fe^{2+}(aq) \rightarrow Mn^{2+}(aq) + 4H_2O(l) + 5Fe^{3+}(aq) \end{array}$$

This is the best answer, choice C. FeO is not a product of either half reaction. It cannot possibly be a product of the net reaction, so eliminate choice A. Five ferrous and five ferric iron ions are required to balance the number of electrons in the net reaction. Since choice C does not have the correct amount of iron ions it can be eliminated. The formation of Fe^{3+} from Fe^{2+} is only one half reaction, and is not the net ionic equation. Choice D can be eliminated.

TEST 6A A&E

54. **C is the best answer.** Use dimensional analysis to determine how many moles of $KMnO_4$ 50 mL of solution contains:

$$(0.1 \text{ mol/L})(50 \times 10^{-3} \text{ L}) = 50 \times 10^{-4} \text{ moles of } KMnO_4$$

According to Reaction 1, one molecule of $KMnO_4$ requires 5 electrons for reduction to Mn^{2+}. Since each iron atom only releases 1 electron during oxidation, five moles of iron(II) were consumed every time one mole of $KMnO_4$ was consumed.

$(50 \times 10^{-4} \text{ mol } KMnO_4)(5 \text{ mol } Fe^{2+}/1 \text{ mol } KMnO_4)(56 \text{ g/mol } Fe^{2+}) \approx 5 \times 10^{-3} \times 5 \times 5.5 \times 10 = (125 + 12.5) \times 10^{-2} = 1.375$ g of iron were in the tablet.

Divide the mass of iron in the table by the total tablet's mass to find its mass percent of iron:

$100\% \times (1.37 \text{ g}/2.8 \text{ g}) \approx 50\%$ so choose the best answer, choice C.

Choice A incorrectly assumes a 1:1 mole ratio of $KMnO_4$ to Fe^{2+}. Choice B uses a 1:4 mole of $KMnO_4$ to Fe^{2+}. Choice D uses a 1:3 mole ratio of $KMnO_4$ to Fe^{2+}.

55. **B is the best answer.** In the absence of phosphoric acid, the solution turned yellow. Table 1 provides the hint that this yellow compound is $Fe(OH)_3$. The iron in $Fe(OH)_3$ is not Fe^{2+}, as this compound has three hydroxide groups in it. Each hydroxide group has a −1 charge, and for this compound to be neutral, Fe must be in the +3 state, i.e. ferric iron. Since the solution the ferric iron is in is acidic, there is no reason to expect that the ferric iron reacted with OH^- in solution. It more likely hydrolyzed water according to the reaction below:

$$Fe^{3+}(aq) + 3H_2O(l) \rightarrow Fe(OH)_3(s) + 3H^+(aq)$$

In this case, Fe^{3+} is acting as an electron acceptor. This behavior makes it a Lewis acid. Choice A says the opposite, so it can be eliminated. Brønsted-Lowry acids are proton donors. Fe^{3+} does not donate a proton during this reaction, and cannot be a Brønsted-Lowry acid. Choice C can be eliminated. Brønsted-Lowry bases are H^+ acceptors. Since Fe^{3+} does not accept H^+ during this reaction, it is not a Brønsted-Lowry base, and choice D can be eliminated.

56. **D is the best answer.** Reaction 1 and 2 from the passage describe the reactivity of the permanganate ion and the ferrous iron ion. When the two are combined in acidic media, permanganate is reduced and iron(II) is oxidized. This reactivity will occur if the two materials are together in solution, or even if they are separated by a wire, like the cell in this question. Since iron is getting further oxidized, it will not form on the platinum wire, and choice A can be eliminated. Reaction 1 explains that acid is consumed during the reduction of the permanganate ion. The consumption of acid will increase the pH of $KMnO_4$'s half-cell, not reduce it, so choice B can be eliminated, and the best answer, choice D can be chosen. The passage explains that the permanganate anion is colored violet, and that its reduction product, Mn^{2+}, is colorless. Since the permanganate anion is being reduced to Mn^{2+} while this cell runs, its half-cell will gradually lose its color and become clear. Choice C can be eliminated.

Stand-alones (Questions 57-59)

57. **C is the best answer.** In order to find the reduction potential of the four DNA bases, the sign of the voltage for the oxidation potential needs to be reversed, making the four values negative, as shown below.

DNA base	Oxidation potential (V)
G	−1.29
A	−1.42
C	−1.60
T	−1.70

The base with the least negative reduction potential is LEAST likely to be reduced. Another way of phrasing least likely to be reduced is most likely to be oxidized. The least negative reduction potential belongs to *G*, making choice C the best answer. Remember that the free energy of a reaction can be calculated if the potential of the cell is known, by the equation $\Delta G = -nFE_{cell}$, where n is the number of moles of electrons that are transferred in the balanced reaction, *F* is the charge on one mole of electrons (96,486 C/mol^{-1}), and *E* is the potential of the chemical cell.

TEST 6A A&E

58. A is the best answer. Reduction always occurs at the cathode, regardless of the type of electrochemical cell. Because this is true for both galvanic and electrolytic cells, option I is a weak answer and choices C and D can be eliminated. In a galvanic cell, the cathode is given a positive charge, while in an electrolytic cell the cathode is given a negative charge. One way to remember this in a galvanic cell is that electrons are attracted to the positive charge of the cathode. Option II is correct, and eliminates choice B. An outside voltage source is only required for an electrolytic cell, in which a nonspontaneous reaction occurs. Galvanic cells do not require an outside voltage source because the reactions are already spontaneous. As a result, option III is incorrect. This makes choice A the best answer.

59. C is the best answer. This question is concerned with the distinction of conventional current vs. electron flow, and interpreting circuit diagrams. Remember that conventional current describes the flow of positive charges. In a circuit diagram, conventional current flows from the higher of the vertical lines representing the battery, to the lower of the vertical lines representing the battery. In this case, conventional current flows from electrode Y to electrode X. Option II is false, and choices A and B can be eliminated. Electrons move the opposite direction of conventional current. The electrons will leave electrode X and enter electrode Y. Option III is false, and choice D can be eliminated. No more work is required at this point to select the correct answer, choice C, but it is worthwhile to explain why option IV is true. Option IV is true because, as mentioned earlier, electrons leave it and enter electrode Y. This means electrode X is experiencing a loss of electrons, or oxidation. The anode always describes the terminal where oxidation takes place.

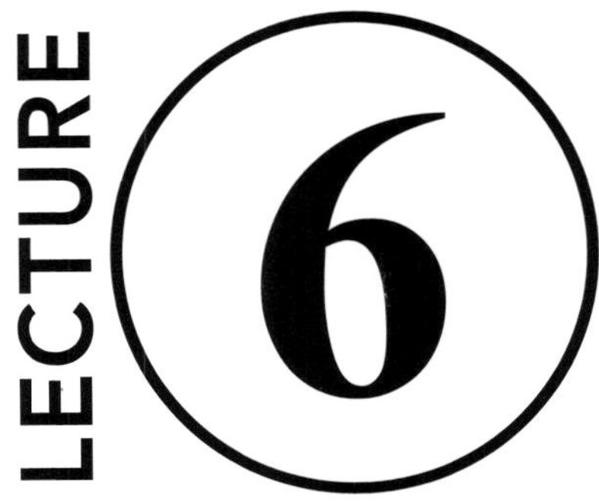

Solutions and Electrochemistry

MINI-TEST 6B

ANSWERS & EXPLANATIONS

Questions 1–29

Passage 1 (Questions 1-4)

1. **B is the best answer.** The molality of a solution is determined by the moles of solute, in this case oxidized G, divided by the kilograms of solvent. Water has a mass of 1 kg/L, meaning the mass of the solvent is 2 kg. Dividing 2.5 moles by 2 kg gives 1.25 mol/kg, or 1.25 molal. Choice B is most likely to be the best answer, as the other answer choices do not equal the calculated molality.

2. **C is the best answer.** Notice that the reaction of guanine with the chromium species results in the loss of an electron from guanine to form the two free-radical products. This means that guanine was oxidized and chromium reduced to Cr(III). A Brønsted acid or base donates or accepts a hydrogen, respectively. As hydrogen transfer does not occur in this reaction, but rather movement of an electron, choices A and B are unlikely to be the best answer. Because Cr(IV) results in the oxidation of guanine, it serves as an oxidizing reagent, not a reducing reagent, making choice C a better answer choice than choice D.

3. **C is the best answer.** Both Pathway 1 and Pathway 2 are oxidation reactions, which are generally highly exothermic reactions. The question stem describes that the reaction occurs in a vessel surrounded by water, which would be able to increase or decrease in temperature if the reaction was exothermic or endothermic, respectively. Choice A shows an exothermic reaction, as the water temperature increases over time, making it a possible answer choice. Choice B shows no temperature change, which is unlikely to occur when a reaction is exothermic. Choice B can be eliminated. Similar to choice A, choice C shows an exothermic reaction, as the temperature increases over time. However, towards the end of the reaction, the temperature change becomes less, as would be the case when the reactants begin to run out and the reaction comes to completion. Choice C is likely a better answer choice than choice A for this reason. Choice D shows an endothermic reaction, not an exothermic reaction, as the temperature decreases over time. Choice D can be eliminated.

4. **A is the best answer.** The question stem asks for the equilibrium constant of the reaction, which can be found by placing the concentrations of the reactants over the concentrations of the products. Remember that H_3O^+ is often represented by H^+ on the MCAT®, so choice A is most likely to be the best answer. Choice B can be eliminated, as the reactant is not the radical G but instead guanine itself. The equilibrium constant always has the concentrations of the products over the concentrations of the reactants. Choice C can be eliminated, as the arrangement of the guanine derivatives is not correct. At first glance, the products and reactants seem in the appropriate positions in choice D. However, remember that pure liquids, like water, are not included in equilibria expressions, making choice A a better answer choice than choice D.

Passage 2 (Questions 5-9)

5. **C is the best answer.** First determine the molar mass of lead nitrate, $Pb(NO_3)_2$

Pb	207.2
N(2)	28
+ O(6)	96
	331.2 g/mol

Long division and tedious conversions are not necessary. Just keep in mind that molarity is a measure of a ratio. 5 M means that there is 5 moles of $Pb(NO_3)_2$ per every 1 liter of water. So long as this ratio of 5:1 is maintained, the solution will be 5 M.

Since 100 g is only 0.1 L of water, 0.5 moles of $Pb(NO_3)_2$ must be added. Likewise, since 200 g is 0.2 L of water, 1.0 moles of $Pb(NO_3)_2$ must be added. 1.0 moles of $Pb(NO_3)_2$ is just the molecular weight calculated above. Select choice C as it has the correct ratio. The incorrect answer choices have the incorrect ratio. Choice D is a tempting distractor, but just consider the following to eliminate it:

$\frac{152.6 \text{ g}}{331.2 \text{ g/mol}} < 0.5$ moles. Choice D cannot be correct as it is less than 0.5 moles of solute and the ratio is not 1:5.

6. **C is the best answer.** Write out the full definition of K_{sp} and the Nernst equation:

$$K_{sp} = [Pb^{2+}][I^-]^2$$

If the [Pb] = x, then $K_{sp} = [x][2x]^2 = 4x^3$

The full Nernst equation is:

$$E_{cell} = E^\circ_{cell} - \left(\frac{RT}{nF}\right)\ln\left(\frac{[Pb^{2+}_{anode}]}{[Pb^{2+}_{cathode}]}\right)$$

Since $[Pb^{2+}_{anode}]$ is equal to the concentration of lead dissolved in the PbI_2 solution, it can be substituted for X in the K_{sp} equation above.

$$K_{sp} = 4[Pb^{2+}_{anode}]$$

Use algebra to solve for $[Pb^{2+}_{anode}]$ and substitute it into the bold equation above.

$$e^{\left(\frac{(E^\circ cell - Ecell)nF}{RT}\right)}[Pb^{2+}_{cathode}] = [Pb^{2+}_{anode}]$$

$$K_{sp} = 4\left(e^{\left(\frac{(E^\circ cell - Ecell)nF}{RT}\right)}[Pb^{2+}_{cathode}]\right)^2$$

Select the correct answer, choice C.

7. **C is the best answer.** Evaluate whether or not each option is true. If an answer choice contains a true option, eliminate it. Remember that electrons will flow so as to make each half-cell have the same concentration of dissolved Pb^{2+}. This means the lead nitrate cell will receive electrons, and undergo reduction—lowering its concentration of Pb^{2+} ions. The lead iodide cell needs a lot more Pb^{2+} ions in solution to match the higher concentration of the lead nitrate cell. It will give up electrons from its lead electrode and undergo oxidation—increasing its concentration of Pb^{2+} ions. Electrons will flow from the lead iodide half-cell to the lead nitrate half-cell. Option I is true, and option II is false. Eliminate choice D, as it contains option I. Option II will be in the correct answer choice.

Look at the Nernst equation. Realize that the cell voltage becomes zero when $\frac{[Pb^{2+}_{anode}]}{[Pb^{2+}_{cathode}]} = 1$. Since every second that the cell runs brings this ratio closer to 1, that means that its voltage is gradually dropping throughout its entire discharge. Option III is false, and will be part of the correct answer choice. Since choices A and B do not include option III, they should be eliminated. It is not necessary to consider the last option, option IV, because the only answer which includes the required false options is choice C.

As it turns out, option IV is true. Mass and charge are conserved in chemical reactions. In other words, however many electrons are lost from the anodic electrode, will be gained by the cathodic electrode. According to Faraday's law, this number of electrons is directly proportional to the mass of lead which will be lost on one side and deposited on the other. Option IV is true and not part of the correct answer choice.

8. **A is the best answer.** The first hint this question gives is when it describes the crystals as "new." That means the crystals were not in the half-cell to begin with. Since PbI_2 is highly insoluble, there were already crystals of it in the cell to begin with. Choice C can be eliminated. This question is really asking about the role of the salt bridge. Remember that as lead is being oxidized in the lead iodide half-cell, more Pb^{2+} is being generated in solution. The cell would stop because of the repulsive effect of an over-accumulation of positive charges, unless they were counter balanced with negative charges—which they are. The salt bridge gradually leaks nitrate anions into the lead iodide half-cell in order to maintain electrical neutrality. Likewise, as Pb^{2+} is reduced in the lead nitrate half-cell, Pb^{2+} disappears and leaves a surplus of NO_3^{1-} anions. Once again, the salt bridge gradually leaks potassium cations to prevent an over accumulation of negative charges in the lead nitrate half-cell. This process continues throughout the total run-time of the cell. As a result, when the experiment is over, there will be $Pb(NO_3)_2$ dissolved in the lead iodide half-cell, and KNO_3 dissolved in the lead nitrate half-cell. When the cells evaporate, these compounds will crystalize. The "dried out" lead iodide half-cell will contain crystals of $Pb(NO_3)_2$. Select the correct answer choice A. Choice B, KNO_3 will be present as a crystal, but only in the lead nitrate half-cell. Eliminate choice B. Choice D is a distractor. Since there was no chloride ions present at any point in this experiment, it is impossible to have this compound. Eliminate choice D.

9. **D is the best answer.** The salt bridge functions to deliver ions to each half-cell solution, in order to help the solutions maintain electrical neutrality against their changing ion concentrations. If the salt bridge suddenly crystallized, it couldn't deliver ions very well. Look at all of these choices and realize that they are soluble in the presence of $Pb^{2+}(aq)$ except for choice D, sodium chloride. If the cotton of the salt bridge were impregnated with sodium chloride, upon immersion in the half-cells, it would crystalize, and be unable to effectively deliver ions—this would cause the cell to quickly stop running. Choice D is least appropriate for the cell. Choice D should be chosen. All of the other answer choices are fully soluble in the presence of $Pb^{2+}(aq)$, and equally appropriate for the cell described in the passage. Choices A, B, and C should be eliminated.

Stand-alones (Questions 10-13)

10. **D is the best answer.** The salt bridge allows the ions dissolved in it to travel to the cathode and anode, to "compensate" for the growing number of negative and positive charges the terminals generate. If there were no salt bridge, the reaction would quickly stop. The accumulation of negative charges at the cathode and positive charges at the anode would generate a very high electrostatic potential. Remember the equation for electrostatic potential energy $U = \frac{kQq}{r}$. As the magnitude of Q increases (through an accumulation of charges), it will require more and more energy to transport electrons to/from the electrodes. Eventually, the energy required to transport electrons will exceed the voltage of the cell, and they will no longer be any net movement. In other words, an increasing electrostatic potential difference will prevent further movement of electrons. Select the best answer, choice D. Since the salt bridge is not part of the circuit, and does not have electrons flowing in it, resistance is not relevant to it. Eliminate choice A. Copper wire could not be used as a substitute for the salt bridge, as it would not be able to deliver ions to counteract the accumulation of charges. Eliminate choice B. Despite the fact that no current would travel without a salt bridge, there would still exist a potential difference, or voltage, across the electrodes. The EMF would not be equal to zero. Eliminate choice C.

11. **C is the best answer.** Loss of an electron is oxidation, which is the opposite of reduction. The species that has the most positive reduction potential is more likely to undergo oxidation. As guanine has the most positive reduction potential, choice C is the best answer.

12. **D is the best answer.** Electrolytes are ions in solution, and the more electrolytes in solution, the better the solution becomes at conducting electricity. The solution that has the most ions in solution will likely be the best conductor of electricity. To determine which solution has the most electrolytes in it, first check the number of ions that the compound will dissociate into, and then multiply that by the molarity of the solution. Choice A has 3 moles of electrolytes per liter, choice B has 4 moles of electrolytes per liter, choice C has 5 moles of electrolytes per liter, and choice D has 8 moles of electrolytes per liter. As a result, choice D is the best answer because it has the highest concentration of electrolytes.

13. **A is the best answer.** Notice that the sign only changes one unit to go from 1+ to 2+ during the electron transfer reaction. Loss of an electron would generate an additional positive charge, resulting in oxidation. Choice A is most likely to be the best answer. As the sign only changes from 1+ to 2+, only one electron is involved, eliminating choice C. Cu^+ loses an electron to become Cu^{2+}, meaning it is oxidized, not reduced. Choices C and D can be eliminated.

Passage 3 (Questions 14-17)

14. **B is the best answer.** During Reaction 3, iron donates two electrons to ionic copper. This process is spontaneous because copper has a greater reduction potential than iron. Standard reduction potentials can be considered a quantification of how much an atom "wants" electrons. The more positive the number, the more the atom wants the electrons. To determine which way the electrons will flow in these choices, consider how much each pre-reduced species "wants" electrons and what can happen in the reaction. If $Cu^{2+}(aq)$ is mixed with $Sn^{2+}(aq)$ either there will be no reaction, or $Sn^{2+}(aq)$ will be oxidized and $Cu^{2+}(aq)$ will be reduced. According to Table 1, the reduction of $Cu^{2+}(aq)$ has a greater potential than that of $Sn^{4+}(aq)$. This means $Cu^{2+}(aq)$ is a stronger oxidizing agent than $Sn^{4+}(aq)$. When $Cu^{2+}(aq)$ takes electrons from $Sn^{2+}(aq)$, the resulting Sn^{4+} is too weak as an oxidant to take them back. Choice B is probably the best answer, but go through the rest to be sure. A fun way to remember this principle is to imagine each pre-reduced species in a redox pair, in this case $Cu^{2+}(aq)$ and $Sn^{4+}(aq)$ as being in a battle for electrons. The stronger, i.e. having a greater reduction potential, of the pre-reduced species will always win, either undergoing the reduction reaction, or, if it started in the reduced state, keeping its electrons and not reacting. Choices A and D have reduction potentials which are greater than that of $Cu^{2+}(aq)$. These materials are stronger oxidants than Cu^{2+} and will not donate their electrons to $Cu^{2+}(aq)$. Choices A and D can be eliminated. Finally, oxidation of $Cu(s)$ with $Cu^{2+}(aq)$ results in no net reaction: $Cu(s) + Cu^{2+}(aq) \rightleftharpoons Cu(s) + Cu^{2+}(aq)$ Nothing would occur, and choice C can be eliminated.

TEST 6B A&E

15. **D is the best answer.** This electrolytic cell described in Figure 1 and in the second-to-last paragraph purifies copper by oxidizing it into solution and then re-reducing it onto the pure electrode. Since the impure copper electrode is oxidized from elemental to ionic copper, the impure electrode is the anode. The pure copper electrode performs the reduction; it is the cathode. For every mole of Cu^{2+} ions which are produced at the anode, two moles of electrons will move to the cathode and reduce a mole of Cu^{2+} ions. Thus, there is no *net* change in the concentration of Cu^{2+} ions in this cell. Choice D is the best answer, and choices A and B can be eliminated. $CuSO_4$ is used as an electrolyte because once in solution, all copper ions are equivalent. It does not matter whether the copper ion which is reduced onto the cathode comes from the anode or from the solution. The concentration of the $CuSO_4$ solution will remain the same, the anode will still shrink, and pure copper will plate out onto the cathode. However, by the end of the process, the majority of the reduced copper ions will have come from the anode because the anode has far more copper ions to donate than what is present in solution. Using a different electrolyte may result in the undesired deposition of a non-copper metal onto the cathode. Electrodes do have local effects. In this case, since oxidation is rapidly occurring at the anode, a slightly higher concentration of copper ion is expected to form there, before they can all diffuse away. Likewise, since reduction is rapidly occurring at the cathode, a slightly lower concentration of copper ions is expected to form there because new ions have not yet diffused to replace the ones which were reduced. Choice C states the opposite of what would occur and can be eliminated.

16. **B is the best answer.** The resistivity ρ of materials is constant at a given temperature. Resistivity is useful for comparing the resistance to passing an electric current that different materials have. It is defined as $\rho = R\left(\frac{A}{l}\right)$ for a wire, where A is the cross-sectional area of the wire, l is the length of the wire and R is the resistance in the wire. Since ρ cannot change, decreasing the radius of the wire will decrease its cross sectional area, ultimately increasing its resistance. With a greater resistance, less current will be passed through it, and less copper will be purified. Choice A can be eliminated. Conversely, increasing the radius of the wire by 50% increases the area of the wire by a factor of 2.25. Remember $A_{initial} = \pi r^2$ With this change, $A_{final} = \pi(1.5r)^2 = 2.25\pi r^2$. According to the resistivity equation, the resistance R must decrease by the same factor that the area increased to keep ρ constant. Choice B may be the best answer, but consider the other choices before choosing it. In the question stem, it is revealed that platinum has a higher resistivity than does copper. For a wire of identical dimensions, a platinum wire will have a greater resistance. Choice C can be eliminated. Using two wires to connect the electrodes instead of one wire essentially creates a circuit with double the initial cross sectional area. This will reduce the resistance by a factor of 2. Since choice B led to a greater reduction in resistance, it is the best answer. Choice D can be eliminated.

17. **C is the best answer.** Remember a positive standard reduction voltage means that the reaction is spontaneous. A negative standard reduction voltage means that energy must be supplied to run the electrochemical reaction—such a reaction is non-spontaneous. To calculate the standard reduction voltage of the cell, E°_{cell} use the equation $E^\circ_{cell} = E^\circ_{red} + E^\circ_{ox}$. The standard oxidation voltage E°_{ox} has the same magnitude, but opposite sign of the standard reduction voltage. Thus, $E^\circ_{ox} = -E^\circ_{red}$ of the species that will be oxidized. The species which is oxidized is the species with the smaller standard reduction potential. In this case, zinc will be oxidized, and copper will be reduced.

$$E^\circ_{cell} = E^\circ_{red} + E^\circ_{ox} = E^\circ_{red\ of\ Cu} + -E^\circ_{red\ of\ Zn}$$

$$E^\circ_{cell} = 0.337\text{ V} + -(-0.763\text{ V}) = +1.1\text{ V}$$

Choice C is the best answer. Since the answer is positive, this reaction will spontaneously occur, and choices A and B can be eliminated. Had the negative sign in front of zinc's standard reduction potential been omitted, −0.43 V would have been obtained, resulting in the numerical value shown in choices B and D. Choice D can be eliminated because it improperly combines a negative standard reduction voltage with a spontaneous reaction.

Passage 4 (Questions 18-22)

18. **A is the best answer.** According to the final paragraph of the passage, "z" must be substituted with the number of moles of electrons transferred during each half-reaction. The best way to determine this number is to look at how many electrons were removed from glucose during its oxidation, by comparing its structure to that of gluconolactone. Two hydrogen atoms have been removed, as well as two electrons. Choice A is the best answer. Although *this* is not what actually happened, it may be convenient, for the sake of "electron bookkeeping," to imagine the removal of a hydride ion, $H:^-$, and a proton. In order to form the new double bond to oxygen, an H–C bond must be removed. Otherwise, carbon's valence of four bonds will be exceeded. Removal of the hydride ion allows carbon to accept the new lone pair on oxygen, following oxygen's deprotonation, forming a double bond, resulting in a stable molecule. Choice B would be the result if the stoichiometry of the reaction were doubled for the sake of the *net* reaction. However, this question in only concerned with using the Nernst equation for the glucose containing cell's half-reaction. Choices C and D would come from not properly counting the electrons which were transferred.

TEST 6B A&E

19. **C is the best answer.** Use the Nernst equation provided in Equation 2 of this passage because a *full*-cell reaction is provided in the question stem.

$$E_{red} = E^{\circ}_{red} - \left(\frac{RT}{ZF}\right)\ln(Q_r)$$

When $[Zn^{2+}] = [Cu^{2+}]$, $\ln(Q_r) = 0$. Under these conditions, $E_{red} = E^{\circ}_{red}$. Thus, the voltage measured when $[Zn^{2+}] = [Cu^{2+}]$ is the same as the standard reduction potential of this cell. This voltage occurs when $[Cu^{2+}] = 0.01$ M because the concentration of zinc ion is fixed at this same value. The reduction potential of the half-cell is 1.10 volts. Choice C is the best answer. The other choices stem from choosing "tempting" points on the graph. Choice A is a maximum voltage from the study, choice B is an "in between" value, and choice D is the minimum voltage from the study. Tempting as they may be, they do not represent the standard reduction voltage and can be eliminated.

20. **C is the best answer.** Remember E° is a standard value of the potential difference between the cells when they are configured under specific settings. It describes the energy that *can* be liberated when electrons move from the oxidant to the reductant. Even though no reaction may be occurring, a cell still has a voltage. An easy way to remember this is that batteries still have voltages even if they are just sitting on store shelves. Thus, the standard reduction potential remains the same, even if the activation energy of this electrochemical reaction is no longer achievable without the catalyst. Choice C is the best answer. Choices A, B, and D, do not recognize that the standard reduction potential of an electrochemical reaction is a constant value. They can be eliminated.

21. **C is the best answer.** M, or molarity, refers to moles of solute divided by the liters of solvent, in this case water. The molecular formula of glucose, $C_6H_{12}O_6$, is discernible from the structure provided in the passage, but it is better to have this molecular formula and structure memorized before Test Day. Glucose will show up in a variety of contexts across multiple subject areas in the MCAT®.

Calculate its molecular weight:

C: 12 g C/mol C × 6 mol C/mol of glucose= 72 g C/mol of glucose

H: 1 g H/mol H × 12 mol H/mol of glucose = 12 g H/mol of glucose

O: 16 g O/mol O × 6 mol O/mol of glucose = 96 g O/mol of glucose

96 g O/mol of glucose + 12 g H/mol of glucose + 72 g C/mol of glucose = 180 total g/mol of glucose

Next, set up an algebraic expression for molarity:

$$\frac{\left(\frac{\text{X g}}{\text{180 g/mol}}\right)}{\text{0.05 L}} = 1\text{M}$$

X = 9 g. Choice C is the best answer. Remember that the molecular mass of oxygen, as given on the periodic table, refers to 1 mole of *mono*atomic oxygen. If this convention was forgotten and the molecular mass of oxygen was incorrectly divided by two "so it wouldn't be too large," and then multiplied by six, as above, choice A would result. Choice B stems from an order of magnitude error. Choice D is a distractor that does not stem from a computational error.

22. **D is the best answer.** The power output of an electrical appliance is given by the equation $P = iV$ where i is the current in amperes and V is the voltage. Since the voltage of this cell is provided in the question stem, the current i must be determined in order to calculate the power output of this cell. Remember that an ampere, the SI unit for current, is one coulomb of charge passing a point per second. It has the units C/sec. The number of moles of gluconolactone formed in a given time has a proportional relationship to the number of electrons passing through the current within the same span of time. Dimensional analysis can be used to solve this exact relationship. Reaction 1 shows the gluconolactone has a molecular mass which is only two hydrogen atoms—2 amu—less than that of glucose, $C_6H_{12}O_6$. Gluconolactone has a molecular mass of 178 g/mol.

$$(\text{1.78 g gluconolactone})\left(\frac{\text{1 mole gluconolactone}}{\text{178 g gluconolactone}}\right)\left(\frac{\text{2 moles of } e^-}{\text{1 mole gluconolactone}}\right)\left(\frac{96.5 \times 10^3}{\text{mol } e^-}\right) \approx 1.9 \times 10^3 \text{ C}$$

All of this charge was passed in 10 hours. To obtain the final answer, this time must be converted to seconds.

$$(\text{10 hours})(\text{60 min/hour})(\text{60 sec/min}) = 36 \times 10^3 \text{ sec}$$

The current i can be calculated from the ratio of the charge which was passed to the time in which it was passed.

$$1.9 \times 10^3 \text{ C}/36 \times 10^3 \text{ sec} \approx 0.05 \text{ amps}$$

Substitute this current into the equation for electrical power, $P = iV$. $P = (0.05\text{ A})(0.5\text{ V}) = 25 \times 10^{-3}$ W, or 25 mW. Choice A is the closest and best answer. If the reciprocal of moles of electrons transferred per moles of gluconolactone produced, i.e. 0.5 as opposed to 2 were used, choice B would result. If the time were not properly converted to seconds, but instead directly used with the units of hours, choice C would result. The current, *i,* is not a measure of power until it is multiplied by the voltage. If the current were calculated but not multiplied by voltage to calculate power, choice D would result.

Passage 5 (Questions 23-26)

23. **D is the best answer.** Look at the Reactions 1 and 2. At both terminals, lead sulfate will be the product, so options I and II are both correct. Eliminate choice A. When the battery is fully discharged, there is no more chemical potential energy. The reaction is complete, and is in a condition of equilibrium, so $\Delta G_{\text{reaction}} = 0$ kJ/mol. Option III is correct. Only choice D has all three correct options together. By the process of elimination, it must be the correct answer. Although it is not necessary to know why option IV is incorrect to solve this problem, it is worth knowing how to eliminate option IV.

    The net reaction of this cell is:

    $$Pb°(s) + PbO_2(s) + 2HSO_4^-(aq) + 2H^+(aq) \rightarrow 2PbSO_4(s) + 2H_2O(l)$$

    When the battery is fully discharged, the concentration of water has increased, and the concentration of H^+ has decreased. This means the solution is more basic, and its pH has increased. Option IV can be eliminated.

24. **B is the best answer.** Eliminate the answer choices which correctly describe the electrolysis of water in this cell. Looking at the equations, it seems that the protons liberated in the first reaction become the reactants in the second reaction. At the end of both of these reactions, there is 1 mole of O_2 gas produced for every 2 moles of H_2 gas. Since the MCAT® assumes ideal behavior, remember that the volume a gas occupies is proportional to the number of molecules of that gas, and is not influenced by the gas's composition. Since there are twice as many moles of H_2 than there are of O_2, H_2 will occupy twice the volume of O_2. Eliminate choice A.

    During this water splitting, protons are reduced to form hydrogen gas. In other words, H_2 gas will form at the cathode. To determine which terminal is the cathode, see which one undergoes reduction, or gains electrons during the cell's operation. Lead dioxide gains electrons. Lead dioxide is the cathode, and H_2 gas will form on it. Select choice B as it is does not occur in this cell.

    Oxygen gas forms through the oxidation of water. Since oxidation occurs at the anode, choice C is true and should be eliminated. When this reaction is complete, 2 moles of liquid water have become three moles of gas. The entropy of the system has dramatically increased because there are more separate molecules generated, and the gas phase leads to a greater distribution of energy than does the liquid phase. Choice D occurs and should be eliminated.

25. **C is the best answer.** First write the equilibrium expression for the disassociation reaction of $PbSO_4$:

    $$PbSO_4(s) \leftrightarrow Pb^{2+}(aq) + SO_4^{2-}(aq)$$

    Next, use the products of this reaction to write the equilibrium equation. In this case, since there are no coefficients in the disassociation reaction, there will not be any exponential terms in the equilibrium equation.

    $$K_{sp} = [Pb^{2+}][SO_4^{2-}]$$

    Use algebra to solve for the desired term:

    $$[Pb^{2+}] = \frac{K_{sp}}{[SO_4^{2-}]}$$

    $$[Pb^{2+}] = \frac{2.13 \times 10^{-8}}{0.5\text{ M}} = 4.26 \times 10^{-8}\text{ M}$$

    This is closest to the best answer, choice C. Choice D does not use the correct power of 10, and choices A and B are simply distractors not based on any computation error.

26. **C is the best answer.** Don't be intimidated by the cell notation. The key to solving this problem is to have a qualitative understanding of the Nernst equation, shown below:

    $$E = E° - \left(\frac{0.06}{n}\right)\log(Q)$$

    $$\text{Q in this case is defined as } \frac{[Pb^{2+}_{\text{anode}}]}{[Pb^{2+}_{\text{cathode}}]}$$

    So long as the ratio of the concentration of lead ions in each half of the cell remains the same, the emf will also remain the same. The ratio of lead ions in the cell of the problem is $1_{\text{anode}}:6_{\text{cathode}}$. The correct answer choice will also have a $1_{\text{anode}}:6_{\text{cathode}}$ ratio of lead ions. Choice C has this ratio, and should be selected. The incorrect choices do not have the appropriate ratio. It is worth noting that choice D can be eliminated on the basis that it has the same concentration of lead ions in each side. It will have an emf = 0. Since the cell of the problem has different concentrations in each half cell, it will produce a non-zero emf.

Stand-alones (Questions 27-29)

27. **A is the best answer.** The battery in a cardiac pacemaker is most likely to be a galvanic cell, where the electrons flow spontaneously between the two termini due to a difference in reduction potentials of the metals. In galvanic cells, oxidation always takes place at the anode, eliminating choices C and D. This means that the opposite reaction, reduction would take place at the cathode, making choice A a better answer choice than choice B.

28. **D is the best answer.** The MCAT® requires specific knowledge about nickel-cadmium batteries. Nickel-cadmium batteries are a type of rechargeable battery, so choice A is not the best answer. Like all batteries, nickel-cadmium batteries function by undergoing a redox reaction to produce energy. Redox reactions are caustic meaning they cause chemical irritation and burns, so choices B and C are not the best answer. Although being rechargeable makes nickel-cadmium batteries superior to alkaline batteries, they have a "memory effect" that makes them inferior to lithium batteries. The memory effect results in the battery holding less charge if recharged before completely emptying. So, choice D is the best answer.

29. **A is the best answer.** Recall the convention for naming polyatomic anions. In order of increasing oxidation state, the nomenclature is hypo-X-ite, X-ite, X-ate, per-X-ate; where X is the prefix associated with the non-oxygen ion. So, hypochlorite must be the lowest oxidation state of chlorine which occurs in choice A. Choice B is chlorite. Choice C is chlorate. Choice D is perchlorate.

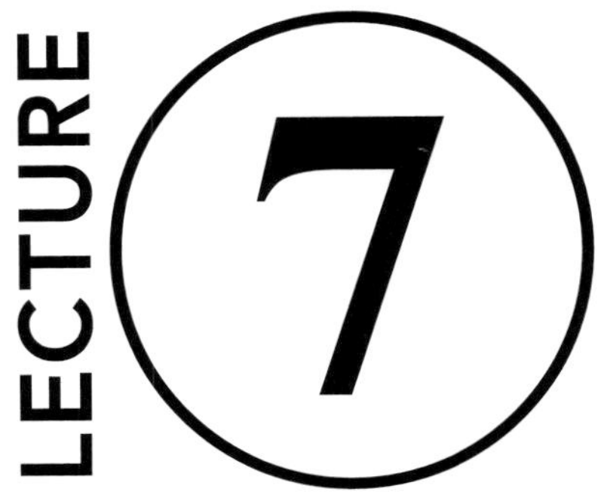

Acids and Bases

TEST 7A

ANSWERS & EXPLANATIONS

Questions 1–59

LECTURE 7 ANSWER KEY

TEST 7A		MINI-TEST 7B	
1. A	31. B	1. B	16. A
2. C	32. B	2. A	17. B
3. A	33. A	3. A	18. A
4. D	34. D	4. A	19. B
5. D	35. C	5. C	20. D
6. C	36. A	6. A	21. C
7. C	37. B	7. D	22. B
8. C	38. B	8. B	23. C
9. A	39. C	9. C	24. C
10. C	40. B	10. D	25. B
11. D	41. D	11. C	26. C
12. A	42. B	12. B	27. C
13. C	43. C	13. D	28. D
14. D	44. A	14. B	29. D
15. A	45. A	15. A	
16. D	46. B		
17. C	47. B		
18. D	48. D		
19. D	49. A		
20. A	50. A		
21. D	51. A		
22. D	52. B		
23. D	53. B		
24. C	54. C		
25. B	55. D		
26. D	56. B		
27. C	57. D		
28. C	58. A		
29. A	59. D		
30. A			

EXPLANATIONS FOR LECTURE 7

Passage 1 (Questions 1-5)

1. **A is the best answer.** The indicator's purpose in an acid/base titration is to establish the end point of the experiment, or when the experiment has reached the desired pH. Oftentimes, the end-point is chosen to be the equivalence point, as the volume of titrant required to reach the equivalence point can be used to calculate the concentration of the analyte. This experiment is no exception to the general goal of using an indicator to establish when the equivalence point is reached. This question is really asking what will be the pH of the end point, which is also the equivalence point of this titration. Since free fatty acids are weak acids—they are essentially carboxylic acids with long alkane "tails"—the conjugate base has some "strength" in solution, and can raise the pH somewhat. At the equivalence point of this titration, the pH will be greater than 7 because of the basic activity of the conjugate bases from the free fatty acids. In order for the indicator to indicate a basic equivalence point, it will need to become colored in an alkaline, or basic, solution. Choice A is the only answer that describes the indicator becoming colored in a basic solution and is the best answer. Choice B states the opposite and can be eliminated. Choices C and D assume that the equivalence point of this titration has a neutral pH, when, in fact, it does not. Choices C and D can be eliminated as well.

2. **C is the best answer.** Whenever conjugate bases, conjugate acids, and pH are mentioned in a question, think about the Henderson-Hasselbalch equation which describes the relationship between these values.

$$\text{pH} = \text{p}K_\text{a} + \log\left(\frac{[\text{A}^-]}{[\text{HA}]}\right)$$

The question stem indicates that the color change is only visible when the conjugate base form, A^-, comprises 10% of the concentration of its acid form, HA. In other words the ratio $\frac{[\text{A}^-]}{[\text{HA}]} = 0.1$. Nonetheless, it is still not possible to "plug and chug" until the $\text{p}K_\text{b}$ given in the question stem is converted into a $\text{p}K_\text{a}$. Use the formula $\text{p}K_\text{a} + \text{p}K_\text{b} = 14$.

$$14 - \text{p}K_\text{b} = \text{p}K_\text{a}$$

$$14 - 4.39 = \text{p}K_\text{a} = 9.61$$

Plug this $\text{p}K_\text{a}$ value and the numerical value of the ratio of $\frac{[\text{A}^-]}{[\text{HA}]}$ into the Henderson-Hasselbalch equation to solve this problem:

$$\text{pH} = 9.61 + \log(0.1)$$

$\text{pH} = 8.61$. C is the best answer. Choice A stems from plugging in the $\text{p}K_\text{b}$ instead of the $\text{p}K_\text{a}$ into the Henderson-Hasselbalch equation and can be eliminated. Choice B stems from putting a minus sign in front of the logarithmic term in the Henderson-Hasselbalch equation by mistake. Choice B can be eliminated. Choice D is combination of both of these approaches, namely, using the $\text{p}K_\text{b}$ instead of the $\text{p}K_\text{a}$ and also improperly putting a minus sign in front of the logarithmic term in the Henderson-Hasselbalch equation. Choice D can be eliminated.

3. **A is the best answer.** The titration which is proposed here will result in the re-formation of fatty acid molecules from the soap molecules. Their carboxylate terminus will be converted into a carboxylic acid, dramatically reducing their polarity. Since "like dissolves like," reducing the polarity of these molecules will reduce their aqueous solubility and cause them to precipitate out of solution. By the equivalence point, every single soap molecule should be protonated. They are expected to form a larger greasy insoluble precipitate in the solution because now fewer molecules can be dissolved. Choice A best summarizes this expectation and is most likely the best answer. With a reduced solubility of the soap molecules, the precipitate will grow in size, not shrink, or remain the same size. Choices B and C can be eliminated. As discussed, adding acid *reduces* the solubility of the soap molecules. Even at the half-equivalence point, sufficient acid has been added to promote the growth of a precipitate. Choice D is weaker than choice A and can be eliminated.

4. **D is the best answer.** Remember the definition of K_b. Consider the reaction of a base, A^- with water to from the conjugate acid, HA:

$$A^-(aq) + H_2O(l) \rightleftharpoons OH^-(aq) + HA(aq)$$

For these reactions, pK_b is defined as $-\log\left(\frac{[OH^-][HA]}{[A^-]}\right)$

Or using stearic acid instead, $pK_b = -\log\left(\frac{[CH_3(CH_2)_{16}COOH][OH^-]}{[CH_3(CH_2)_{16}COO^-]}\right)$

The problem is that [OH] is not provided as a variable in any of these expressions. However, this is no cause for alarm. Remember that $10^{-pOH} = [OH^-]$ and that $14 - pH = pOH$. Thus, $10^{-(14-pH)} = [OH^-] = 10^{pH-14}$. Since this question defined x as the pH, the best answer, will be: $-\log\left(\frac{[CH_3(CH_2)_{16}COOH][10^{x-14}]}{[CH_3(CH_2)_{16}COO^-]}\right)$, or choice D. Choice A is the reciprocal of the expression for pK_a; this is not the definition of pK_b, and choice A can be eliminated. Instead of including an $[OH^-]$ in the numerator, choice B includes a term which is equivalent to $[H^+]$. Choice B can be eliminated. Choice C is an error that stems from improperly distributing the negative sign into the exponential figure when calculating $[OH^-]$ from the pH. Choice C can be eliminated.

5. **D is the best answer.** At the equivalence point, there are no carboxylate anions left to abstract the protons which are added to the solution from the strong acid titrant. As a result, the pH rapidly plummets, appearing as a vertical asymptote on the titration curve. Thus, at 100 mL enough HCl has been added to protonate all of the carboxylate anions. The caption beneath Figure 2 indicates that the HCl solution had a concentration of 0.1 M. Use dimensional analysis to determine how many moles of acid were added to neutralize all of the carboxylate anions. Remember, for every 3 moles of carboxylate anion, or saponified products, 1 mole of triglyceride was originally in the solution. This is because each mole of triglyceride is hydrolyzed into three moles of fatty acid salts during saponification.

(100 mL)(10^{-3} L/mL)(0.01 mols HCl/L)(1 mol fatty acid/1 mol HCl)(1 mol triglyceride/3 mols fatty acids) = 0.33×10^{-3} mols of triglycerides = 3.3×10^{-4} mols of triglycerides.

To find the concentration of the triglycerides, divide the number of moles of triglycerides by the total volume of the blood extract, 100 cm^3 = 100 mL = 0.1 L

3.3×10^{-4} moles triglycerides/0.1 L = 3.3×10^{-3} M choice D is the best answer. Choice A reflects the error of not using the conversion factor to convert from moles of fatty acids to moles of triglycerides initially in the blood. Choice A can be eliminated. Choice B makes that same error, but also never divides the moles of fatty acids by the volume of the blood extract. Choice B can be eliminated. Choice C makes an analogous mistake. Although it properly identifies the number of moles of triglycerides in the blood extract, it never divides this number by the volume of the blood extract in order to express it as a concentration. Choice C can be eliminated.

Passage 2 (Questions 6-10)

6. **C is the best answer.** Look at Figure 1. It shows that phenolphthalein solutions just turn fuchsia at a pH of 8.2. Since pH + pOH = 14, the pOH = 5.8.

Use the definition of pOH to solve this problem.

$$[OH^-] = 10^{-pOH}$$

$$[OH^-] = 10^{-5.8}$$

C is the best answer. Choices A and B both fail to include the negative sign which should be in front of the exponent when converting from pH or pOH to concentration. Eliminate these choices. Choice D is the concentration of H^+ when the solution turns fuchsia. This value is 10^{-pH} and should be eliminated.

TEST 7A A&E

7. **C is the best answer.** The molecular mass of a substance is defined as the number of grams that provides one mole of that substance. To solve for the molecular mass of a substance, divide the mass of the substance by how many moles of the substance the mass in question provides. Since the mass of the unknown acid is provided in Table 1, put this value, 2.3 g, in the numerator.

For a diprotic acid, the number of moles of NaOH required to neutralize the solution is twice the number of moles of acid that was initially dissolved in the solution.

The following neutralization reaction of a generic diprotic acid, H_2A, with NaOH should help illustrate the point:

$$H_2A(aq) + 2NaOH(aq) \rightarrow Na_2A(s) + 2H_2O(aq)$$

Dimensional analysis is a powerful way to solve this part of the problem:

$$(0.140 \text{ L NaOH})\left(\frac{0.08 \text{ moles NaOH}}{1 \text{ L NaOH}}\right)\left(\frac{1 \text{ moles unknown acid}}{2 \text{ moles NaOH}}\right).$$

This term will go in the denominator.

$$(14 \times 10^{-2} \times 8 \times 10^{-2})/2 = 56 \times 10^{-4} \text{ moles of unknown acid in denominator.}$$

$$2.3 \text{ g}/56 \times 10^{-4} \text{ mol} \approx 400 \text{ g/mol}$$

Select the closest answer, choice C. The incorrect answer choices come from errors in stoichiometry regarding the ratio of NaOH needed to neutralize a diprotic acid.

8. **C is the best answer.** The evidence which will most contradict this hypothesis must feature phenolphthalein existing as a planar structure and not reflecting colored light. At a pH < 0, phenolphthalein does not exist as a planar structure. The central carbon only has single bonds around it, and can rotate. In fact, it will rotate in order to reduce unfavorable steric interactions. Choice A can be eliminated because the behavior of non-planar phenolphthalein is not relevant to this question. Choice B features a planar phenolphthalein that is reflecting colored light. The molecule is planar because it consists entirely of alternating single and double bonds. Any single bond which is between two double bonds cannot rotate because the double bonds lock it in place. This behavior strongly supports the hypothesis of the question and should be eliminated. At a pH > 13 phenolphthalein is still planar, but cannot reflect colored light. If it could, then a viewer would be able to see a color. Since the solution is clear, this means that all of the light is passing right through it. This behavior strongly contradicts the hypothesis of the question, and makes choice C the best answer. Choice D does not feature a planar phenolphthalein. Much like the overly acidic case, choice A, it should be eliminated, as it is not relevant to this question.

9. **A is the best answer.** This question is asking about the ratio between a weak acid and its conjugate base, and it provides the pK_a of the acid in question. These terms hint to use the Henderson-Hasselbalch equation, which includes all of them. The weak acid is the lactone form of phenolphthalein, and the conjugate base is the fuchsia form.

$$pH = pK_a + \log\left(\frac{[A^-]}{[HA]}\right)$$

When the solution just turns fuchsia with the addition of base, according to Figure 1, the pH is 8.2. "Plug and chug" from here to find the ratio of the colored form to the lactone form.

$$8.2 = 9.3 + \log\left(\frac{[A^-]}{[HA]}\right)$$

$\frac{[A^-]}{[HA]} = 10^{-1.1} < \frac{1}{10}$ which means it must be a little less than 1:10. Choice B can be eliminated. Choice C is too great a value and should be eliminated. Choice D would mean that $\frac{[A^-]}{[HA]} = 10^{-2}$. This is way too small and should also be eliminated. Choice A is a little less than $\frac{1}{10}$ and is the best answer. Select choice A.

TEST 7A A&E

10. **C is the best answer.** According to the Henderson-Hasselbalch equation, pH = pK_a + $\log\left(\frac{[A^-]}{[HA]}\right)$, when the amount of strong base added is equal to half the concentration of the acid in solution, $\frac{[A^-]}{[HA]} = 1$ and pH = pK_a. In other words, each half equivalence point indicates the pK_a of the acidic species which is currently undergoing neutralization at that area in the acid titration curve. Since this question asks about pK_{a3}, look at Figure 1, and find the third half-equivalence point. The first half-equivalence point will be right between the start of the experiment and the first vertical rise in the graph. The second and third half-equivalence points will be midway between the vertical rises of the graph, moving left to right past the first vertical rise. The numerical value of the third half-equivalence point will be equal to pK_{a3}. Select choice C, 7.1, because it looks closest to the third half-equivalence point. Choice A is the third equivalence point as it is vertical rise. In a monoprotic titration, the equivalence point is reached when an equal number of moles of acid have been mixed with moles of base. In a polyprotic titration, each equivalence point describes when the molar quantity of added base matches the molar quantity of a specific acidic group which is undergoing neutralization on the molecule. The pH rises sharply at the equivalence points because once an acidic group is consumed by base, it can no longer buffer the solution against changes in alkalinity. The third equivalence point should be eliminated because it is not what the question wanted. Choices B and D are the second and first equivalence points respectively. They should be eliminated because they are not what the question wanted either.

Passage 3 (Questions 11-14)

11. **D is the best answer.** Look at (R)-(+)-omeprazole to answer this question. The sulfur atom has a lone pair of electrons. This lone pair would pick up an H^+ which makes the sulfur basic, more specifically a Brønsted base. Note that on the MCAT®, the terms "acid" and "base" usually refer to the Brønsted definition which defines acidity based on movement of protons. The sulfur does not have a spare H^+ so it is not acidic and choice A can be ruled out. An acidic carbon would be one that release H^+ to become a carbanoin. This is very uncommon and no carbon in (R)-(+)-omeprazole would release a proton so choice B can be ruled out. An acidic oxygen would be one in a carboxylic acid. Two oxygens in (R)-(+)-omeprazole are in the form of ethers which are not acidic so choice C can be ruled out. There is also a S=O oxygen that would behave like a carbonyl and could become protonated to make S–O–H. This is oxygen acting as a Brønsted base, so choice D is the best answer.

12. **A is the best answer.** The principle acid in the stomach is HCl, which is a strong acid that behaves by donating H^+. Acids that donate H^+ are Brønsted acids, so choice A is the best answer.

13. **C is the best answer.** The passage states the pancreas releases K^+ and HCO_3^-. Although not explicitly stated, it can be assumed that these ions associate together as a solvated salt. HCO_3^- is a weak base because it can pick up H^+ to become H_2CO_3, so choice C is the best answer.

14. **D is the best answer.** It is difficult to know what this question is asking so the easiest way to tackle it is to deal with the answers systematically. There is a problem with both choice A and choice C in that HCl is not made in the nephron, unlike NH_4^+ which is a principle nitrogenous waste product. So, choices B and D are better than choices A and C. Between choice B and choice D, it is necessary to find the vessel that would affect the nephron. The afferent arteriole is the one going to the nephron so this one could directly affect the nephron. The efferent arteriole occurs following the glomerulus but is capable of modulating renal function as well. However, since the afferent arteriole is upstream of the glomerulus, choice D is the best answer.

Stand-alones (Questions 15-18)

15. **A is the best answer.** Lewis acids are electron acceptors. Arrhenius acids and Brønstead-Lowry acids are both proton donors. In other words, Arrhenius acids and Brønstead-Lowry acids release the H^+ cation into solution. Since protons react with other species by gaining electrons, Arrhenius acids and Brønstead-Lowry acids are also Lewis acids, but Lewis acids are not necessarily Arrhenius acids or Brønstead-Lowry acids. A good analogy to understand this idea is that all squares are rectangles, but not all rectangles are squares. In this analogy, Lewis acids are rectangles, and Arrhenius acids and Brønstead-Lowry acids are squares.

    Choice A seems safe, as the Fe^{3+} ion accepts electrons from oxygen, and behaves as a Lewis acid. Choices B and C are poor, since iron(III) chloride never donates a proton in this reaction. Lewis bases are electron donors, and since Iron(III) chloride is accepting electrons, not donating them, choice D is wrong. Choose the best answer, choice A.

TEST 7A A&E

16. **D is the best answer.** The only way K_{sp} can be directly compared between compounds is if the compounds form the same number of ions when they dissociate. Among these, both $CaCO_3$ and $MgCO_3$ form two ions. Since $MgCO_3$ has a greater K_{sp}, it is more soluble, and choice C should be eliminated.

Determine the solubility of the remaining salts in the table by disregarding the significance of their K_{sp} value. The base 10 and its exponent in the K_{sp} value, and the number of ions that will form when each salt dissociates is all the information needed to solve this problem. The number of ions the salt forms in solution will determine the root function used to calculate the solubility of the salt in question, as shown below:

$$[Mg(OH)_2] \approx \sqrt[3]{10^{-11}} = 10^{-3.66}$$
$$[CaCO_3] \approx \sqrt{10^{-9}} = 10^{-4.5}$$
$$[Al(OH)_3] \approx \sqrt[4]{10^{-34}} = 10^{-8.5}$$

$Al(OH)_3$ is dramatically less soluble than the other salts, and choice D is the best answer.

17. **C is the best answer.** Since pH is defined as $-\log[H^+]$ the lower the value of pH, the greater the acidity. As acidity increases, pH decreases, and vice-versa. Choices A and B should be eliminated since they confuse the effects of acid concentration on the value of a pH unit.

Think about the effects of hyperventilating. This means that the person is rapidly inhaling and exhaling. With each inhalation, he brings oxygen into his blood stream, and with each exhalation he removes carbon dioxide from his blood stream. According to Le Châtelier's principle, the removal of carbon dioxide should shift this equilibrium to the right, consuming H^+ ions from the blood to generate more carbon dioxide. As the concentration of H^+ ions in the blood falls, the acidity will decrease and the pH will increase. Choice D states the opposite and should be eliminated. Choice C best describes this process, and is the best answer.

18. **D is the best answer.** The ideal buffer consists of a weak acid and a conjugate salt, with the pK_a of the weak acid close to the pH of the desired solution. Blood is buffered at 7.4 so the ideal acid will have a pK_a closest to this. Going from K_a to pK_a involves taking the negative log, so by pure estimation, the pK_a's of hydrocyanic acid and carbonic acid are not close to 7.4, making choice A and B incorrect. The pK_a's of hypochlorous and dihydrogen phosphate acids are both within 7 to 8. The negative log of 6.2×10^{-8} is closer to 7.4 however, because 6.2×10^{-8} is closer to 10^{-7} than 10^{-8}. On the other hand, 3.5×10^{-8} is closer to 10^{-8} than 10^{-7}, meaning the pH is around 7.7. This makes choice D the better answer over choice C.

Passage 4 (Questions 19-22)

19. **D is the best answer.** When water is at temperatures higher than 25°C, its autoionizes to a greater degree. This is because the autoionization of water is an endothermic process. After all, a neutral molecule is being broken into two charged ions.

$$H_2O + \text{heat} \rightleftharpoons H^+ + OH^-$$

When heat is added, the equilibrium will shift to the products according to Le Chatlier's principle. If the water started at 25°C, then at the new temperature $[H^+][OH^-] > 10^{-14}$. Since $[H^+] = [OH^-]$ in pure water, that means the concentration of each must be slightly greater than 10^{-7}. This forces the solution to actually have a pH lower than 7—select choice C. At this higher temperature, that lower pH means that the water is neutral! A pH of 7 indicates a neutral solution ONLY at 25°C and 1 atm of pressure.

Choices B, and D are false for the same reason. Since $[H^+][OH^-] > 10^{-14}$ and $[H^+] = [OH^-]$ The concentration of each must be greater than $\sqrt{10^{-14}}$ or 10^{-7}. This leads to a pH which is necessarily lower than 14 and 7. A is incorrect because this pH is too low, and cannot be obtained via autoionization processes at 55°C. Remember that 55°C is roughly the temperature of a bath tub. Life experience teaches us that bath tubs are not as acidic as battery acid!

20. **A is the best answer.** By convention conjugate acids and conjugate bases are shown on the product side of the chemical equation. Since water is on the reactant side, it cannot be a conjugate acid or a conjugate base. Eliminate choices B and D. Water acts as a proton acceptor and an electron donor. This makes it a base by the Brønsted-Lowry and Lewis definitions of acids and bases so choice A is the best answer. Since water is accepting a proton, not donating one, it is not an acid—choice C can be eliminated.

21. **D is the best answer.** The 1% weak acid discussed in the question stem refers to 1% vinegar; bleach is a base, and dish soap could only behave as a very weak base. Consider Figure 1. Pfu (plaque forming units) are on the Y axis—this value represents the number of active virions. Since short applications of 1% vinegar still leave some active flu viruses, it CANNOT be relied on to fully inactive flu viruses on contaminated surfaces. Choice A is incorrect. However, the 1% vinegar does have some virucidal properties, as there are less active virions present after the vinegar application than there are after the control trial and the water trial; to a limited degree, the 1% vinegar can be relied upon to inactivate flu viruses on contaminated surfaces. Choice B is false. Choice C is false—there are NO active virions present after hot water treatment for an hour, but there were active virions present after the short 1% vinegar treatment.

22. **D is the best answer.** This question is really two questions in disguise. 1) What is the effect of acidity on flu viruses? 2) Is trifluoroacetic acid stronger or weaker than vinegar and why?

The passage answers the first part, when it explains that vinegar's antiviral properties stem from the low pH-dependent denaturation of certain flu-virus proteins. In other words, vinegar inactivates flu-viruses by lowering the pH of the solution. The more acidic the media is, the more viruses will be inactivated. To answer the second part of the question, remember some acid-base trends. Electron withdrawing groups increase acidity, and so do weak O–H bonds. A molecule with weaker O–H bonds and more electron withdrawing groups than vinegar will be able to deactivate more viruses. Trifluoroacetic acid is one such molecule.

Trifluoroacetic acid is more acidic than vinegar because of fluorine's electronegativity. The fluorine atoms pull electron density from the O–H bond, thereby weakening it. In addition, once deprotonated, the trifluoroacetate anion can delocalize the negative charge by spreading it over the electronegative fluorine atoms. This causes trifluoroacetate to be a weaker base than acetate. Trifluoroacetate will be more acidic than vinegar, and will inactivate more viruses. Select choice D.

To eliminate the wrong answers, remember that conditions which favor a stable conjugate base or a weak O–H bond will increase the acidity of a molecule, and allow it to inactivate more viruses. Choice B can be eliminated—this produces a weaker acid. Choices A and C can be eliminated—the stronger acids produced these ways are expected to deactivate more viruses, not less.

Passage 5 (Questions 23-27)

23. **D is the best answer.** The passage provides a hint that primary burns are related to the acidity of the acid. In particular, it describes the hydrolysis of amide bonds and acid induced conformational changes of proteins as causes of primary burns. Both of these effects will intensify and lead to a more severe burn, with a more acidic solution. The question really becomes, "Which of these solutions is most acidic?"

The ionic radius of each halide increases going down their period in the periodic table. A larger ionic radius means that the negative charge which follows deprotonation will be more diffuse and spread out. As a result, the larger anions will be weaker bases/stronger acids, and less capable of attracting and "holding on" to their proton. In addition, the longer X–H bonds which the larger halogens form, are weaker than the shorter X–H bonds that the smaller halogens form. This makes the larger halogens more capable of giving up their protons and more acidic, and the smaller halogens less acidic. In other words, acidity increases in the following order F < Cl < Br < I. HI will be the most acidic, and is the best answer. Select choice D.

24. **C is the best answer.** The definition of K_{sp} can be used to solve this problem. Remember that the solubility product constant of $CaF_2 = [Ca^{2+}][F^-]^2$

If x is used to represent the concentration of calcium, this equation simplifies to:

$$[x][2x]^2 = 4x^3 = K_{sp}$$

From here, use algebra to solve for x:

$$4x^3 = 3.9 \times 10^{-11}$$

$$x \approx \sqrt[3]{10^{-11}} = 10^{-3.66}$$

Select the closest answer, choice C, $0.991 \times 10^{-3.66}$ or as written there, $9.91 \times 10^{-4.66}$.

25. **B is the best answer.** Start by considering the chemical equation which describes the precipitation of fluoride:

$$2HF(aq) + CaGlu_2 \rightarrow CaF_2(s) + 2HGlu(aq)$$

Since CaF_2 is so highly insoluble, for the sake of this problem, it is easiest to imagine that every mole of CaGlu which is added will precipitate two moles of F^-. This leads to a mole ratio of CaGlu to HF of 1:2. Option III is correct and option II should be eliminated. Next, look at the structure of gluconate. It is the conjugate base of a carboxylic acid, and is expected to have weakly basic behavior. Since it will be a weak base, even though the mole ratio of gluconate to protons is 1:1, not every proton will be captured by gluconate. Since there will be an excess of protons in solution, the pH will be less than 7. Option I is correct, and option IV should be eliminated. Select the answer choice that has the correct options, choice B. The incorrect answers have only half of the correct options, or are fully incorrect.

TEST 7A A&E

26. D is the best answer. Write the pK_a expression for that describes this dissociation.

$$pK_a = -\log\left(\frac{[0.008\ H^+][0.008\ F^-]}{[0.1 - 0.008\ HF]}\right)$$

This equilibrium equation is labeled to indicate what happens when 8% of the 0.1 M solution disassociates. Use scientific notation and don't forget to round to make working with these numbers easier.

$$pK_a = -\log\left(\frac{64 \times 10^{-6}}{\sim 0.1}\right) = -\log(6.4 \times 10^{-4}) = 4 - \log(6.4)$$

The answer will be less than 4, but greater than 3. Select choice D, as it is closest to the answer.

27. C is the best answer. In this question, once the solution is neutral, adding a few mL of NaOH will dramatically raise the pH of the solution. Look for an area on the graph where the addition of a few mL of NaOH causes the pH to rapidly increase. Option III best satisfies these conditions, so choice C is most likely the best answer. Choice A is the beginning of the titration. Here the pH < 7 and the solution is acidic. Eliminate choice A. Choice B is part way through the titration. Again, the pH < 7 here, so choice B can be eliminated. Choice D is the end of the titration. It is when the experimenter has decided to stop adding more NaOH. At this point enough base has been added that the solution has a pH > 7. Eliminate choice D.

Stand-alones (Questions 28-31)

28. C is the best answer. The method outlined in 7.3 can be used to solve this problem :

1. Write down the reaction:

$$CH_3COOH(aq) + H_2O(l) \rightleftharpoons H_3O^+(aq) + CH_3COO^-(aq)$$

Set up the equilibrium equation and solve for K_a using pK_a:

$$10^{-pK_a} = K_a = \frac{[H_3O^+][CH_3COO^-]}{[CH_3COOH]}$$

2. Since it is a 10% solution of acetic acid, $[CH_3COOH] = 0.1$ M let $x = [H_3O^+] = [CH_3COO^-]$

$$10^{-4.7} = K_a = \frac{[x][x]}{[0.1 - x]} \approx \frac{[x]^2}{0.1}$$

x is small enough that it can be disregarded.

3. Solve for x.

$$10^{-3.7} = x^2$$

$$\sqrt{10^{-3.7}} = x = 10^{-1.85}$$

$$-\log[10^{-1.85}] = 1.85$$

1.85 is the pH.

29. A is the best answer. A strong acid by definition dissociates 100% in solution whereas a weak acid does not. The acid dissociation constant measures this and a higher constant measures greater dissociation in solution. Therefore, a strong acid has a higher K_a than a weak acid, making choices B and D incorrect. Converting K_a to pK_a requires taking the negative log, which means a larger K_a value produces a smaller pK_a. Strong acids have lower pK_a values, typically negative, compared to weak acids. Choice C is a weaker answer, and choice A is the best answer.

30. A is the best answer. $LiCO_3$ will dissociate into Li^+ + and CO_3^- ions. Li^+ does not exert any appreciable acid base properties, but CO_3^- is a weak base. It can from the bicarbonate ion. As a result, the pH is expected to be slightly basic, and choice A is the best answer.

31. **B is the best answer.** A buffer solution is a solution of a weak acid and its conjugate base. During the addition of acid or base to buffer solutions, buffers prevent the pH of the solution from changing dramatically because they act as "proton sponges" and "proton reservoirs". When a base is added to solution, they donate protons. When an acid is added to solution, they accept protons. Since they are weak acids, after they accept a proton, they are not likely to lose it back to the solution. Likewise, if a base is added, they are weaker than the strong base, and donate their protons without deprotonating water afterwards. In this way, they keep the pH of the solution from changing dramatically, within their effective pH range. Ammonia and ammonium sulfate is a combination of a weak acid and its conjugate base, and will make an effective buffer. Eliminate choice A. Hydrochloric acid is a strong acid and cannot be a member of a weak acid and conjugate base buffer pair, so choice B is the best answer. Sodium acetate and acetic acid is a combination of a weak acid and its conjugate base, and will make an effective buffer. Eliminate choice C. Finally, nitrous acid, HNO_2, is a weak acid, unlike the similar HNO_3 which is a strong acid. Since this weak acid is paired with its conjugate base, choice D will also make an effective buffer and can be eliminated.

Passage 6 (Questions 32-35)

32. **B is the best answer.** Intensive properties are properties which do not depend on the size of the sample being tested. Density is an intensive property because no matter how large the mass of the object, its volume is proportionate. Consequently, the ratio between mass and volume, i.e. density, is constant. Mass, on the other hand, is an extensive property. It is dependent on the size of the sample. The larger the sample, the greater the mass. Choices C and D are both extensive properties. The more antacid added to the burette, the more CO_2 gas will be released. The moles of CO_2 gas released are dependent on the size of the antacid tablet. Likewise, in choice D, the more antacid that is added to the burette, the greater will be the change in pH.

Choices A and B are both intensive properties. Every tablet contains a certain number of moles of $CaCO_3$ per mass of tablet which will neutralize two moles of HCl, releasing a proportional quantity of CO_2 gas. In other words, the mass of the tablet is proportional the moles of $CaCO_3$ within the tablet, which is proportional the volume of CO_2 gas released. Since all of these parameters are proportionally related, a ratio between two of them will be constant, and is an intensive property. To choose between choices A and B, remember the other condition of the question, that the value of the unit must increase with increasing ability of the antacid to neutralize acid. The stronger the antacid is, the greater the amount of CO_2 gas it can release for a given mass. The ratio, L of CO_2 gas released/mass of antacid tablet, will increase with increasing antacid strength. Conversely, the ratio, mass of antacid tablet/L of CO_2 released, will decrease with a stronger antacid. Eliminate choice A, and choose the best answer, choice B.

33. **A is the best answer.** Remember that the pH of the acidified solution must be 1. This is equal to a $[H^+] = 10^{-1}$ M. Do not forget to consider that adding the acid actually further dilutes the solution! This is an easily avoided mistake

$$\text{Mathematically, } \frac{\text{concentration of HCl} \times \text{volume of HCl solution dispensed}}{\text{amount of HCl solution dispensed} + \text{ initial solution volume}} \text{ must equal } 10^{-1} \text{ M.}$$

$$(12\text{M})(\text{X L})/(\text{X L} + 0.3 \text{ L}) = 10^{-1} \text{ M}$$

$$12\text{X} = 0.1\text{X} + 0.03$$

$$12.1\text{X} = 0.03$$

$$\text{X} = 0.03/12.1 = 3 \times 10^{-2}/12.1 \approx 0.25 \times 10^{-2} \text{ L} = 2.5 \text{ mL}$$

The real answer will be a little less than 2.5 mL because the denominator was rounded down. Select the best answer, choice A. Choice B comes from failing to consider the dilution caused by adding the acid. Choices C and D are too small to be the best answer.

34. **D is the best answer.** When in doubt, write the balanced chemical equation for the reaction described in the question stem:

$$2HCl(aq) + Mg(OH)_2(s) \rightarrow MgCl_2(aq) + 2H_2O(l)$$

No CO_2 will be produced whatsoever in this reaction! It is a standard neutralization reaction, where an acid and a base form water and a salt. Eliminate choices A and C because they suggest that $Mg(OH)_2(s)$ will produce more carbon dioxide gas than $CaCO_3(s)$, when, in fact, it will not produce any at all. Since the OH^- anion is a far stronger base than the CO_3^{2-} anion, choice B is not as strong of an answer as choice D. Choice D is the best answer because it indirectly addresses why $Mg(OH)_2(s)$ does not produce carbon dioxide gas.

35. **C is the best answer.** According to Reaction 1, there are 2 moles of acid consumed for every 1 mole of $CO_2(g)$ that is produced. According to the ideal gas law, $PV = nRT$ as applied to the $CO_2(g)$ of this experiment , $2(PV/RT) = 2n$, and this is equal to the number of moles of hydronium, H^+, that were consumed. The number of moles of hydronium that were initially present is equal to the volume of the solution multiplied by 10^{-pH}. Algebraically, the new pH will be:

$$-\log\left[\frac{\left((V_{\text{of solution}} \times 10^{-\text{pH}}) - \left(\frac{2PV_{\text{H}_2\text{O displaced}}}{RT}\right)\right)}{V_{\text{of solution}}}\right]$$

Do not forget that when using the ideal gas law, the other units must match the gas constant R. R is usually provided as 8.31 L · atm/mol · K. Be sure to convert from Celsius to K, and from mL to L.

Using actual numbers, this expression becomes.

$$-\log\left[\frac{\left((0.300 \times 10^{-1}) - \left(\frac{2 \times 0.75}{8.31 \times 298}\right)\right)}{0.300}\right]$$

Select choice B, as it restates this.

Choice A can be eliminated without much thought because pH is the negative $\log_{10}$ of the concentration of hydronium, not just the $\log_{10}$. Choice C fails to convert the temperature and volume units into units which would match the gas constant. Choice D is correct except it forgets to consider the mole ratio of $CO_2(g)$ to HCl. The coefficient, 2, is required to determine the moles of hydronium from the ideal gas law using moles of $CO_2(g)$.

Passage 7 (Questions 36-39)

36. **A is the best answer.** The water dissociation constant is equal to the product of the hydrogen ion and hydroxide ion concentrations, totaling 7.4×10^{-7} at pH 7.4. When a large influx of chloride occurs, the SID predicts a decrease, which is correlated with acidosis. The best answer should reflect an increase in $[H^+]$ for this reason, making choice B incorrect. The water dissociation constant also implies a balance between the two species, so if the hydrogen concentration increases, the hydroxide concentration should follow suit, making choice D incorrect. The overall constant should be increased, due to larger $[H^+]$ and $[OH^-]$, making choice A better than choice C.

37. **B is the best answer.** According to Table 1, the mean increase in blood pH after 24 hour NIV treatment is 0.09 (from 7.26 to 7.35). It can be rounded to 0.1 for simplicity in calculations. When pH increases by 0.1 in this exact interval, blood is becoming more basic, meaning hydrogen ion concentration decreases, eliminating choice A and C. Specifically, the hydrogen ion concentration decreases from something between 10^{-7} and 10^{-8}. Any change greater or less would produce dramatic changes to pH more than 0.1. Choice D is incorrect because 5×10^{-7} is between the range 10^{-6} and 10^{-7}. Choice B is the best answer.

38. **B is the best answer.** Identifying the acidity or basicity of a salt depends on its anion and cation. To restore acidotic blood to normal pH equilibrium, a basic salt is needed and acidic salts will further exacerbate the problem. The answer to this question is identifying the acidic salt. Sodium bicarbonate is a basic salt, because the sodium will form sodium hydroxide in aqueous solution while the bicarbonate will form carbonic acid in solution. The sodium hydroxide is a stronger base than the carbonic acid is an acid, hence the salt is basic, and choice A can be eliminated. Ammonium chloride is an acidic salt because the ammonium forms ammonia in solution while chloride forms hydrochloric acid, a strong acid. Because ammonia is a weak base, ammonium chloride is an acidic salt. Sodium acetate is a basic salt because the sodium forms sodium hydroxide, a strong base, while the acetate forms acetic acid, a weak acid. Similarly, potassium cyanide is a basic salt because potassium forms potassium hydroxide, a strong base, while cyanide forms hydrocyanic acid, which is weak. Choices C and D are basic, which are incorrect, while choice B is acidic and the best answer.

39. C is the best answer. In Table 1, the blood pH fluctuates throughout the 24 hours, while the other parameters show one-way change. This question is best assessed by POE. Choice A is incorrect because pH is a function of hydrogen ion concentration, not CO_2 levels, and "strictly" is a strong word. Nothing in the passage suggests that blood pH is determined strictly by $PaCO_2$. Choice B is also incorrect because as lactate concentration decreases, blood pH both increases and decreases, violating proportionality. The best answer is choice C, which implies that different factors modulate pH during NIV to varying degrees depending on how long the ventilation has been applied. It could be that respiratory factors such as respiratory rate and heart beat have stronger influence in the short term while metabolic factors such as oxygen, carbon dioxide, and lactate concentrations have more weight in the long term, or vice versa. This moderate statement is the best approach to answering this question which doesn't have a "clear" solution presented in the passage.

Choice D is poor because factors such as oxygen, carbon dioxide, lactate content, and respiratory rate certainly play a part in modulating blood pH on a physiological basis. Blood pH cannot be independent of these, which is far too strong of a statement.

Passage 8 (Questions 40-43)

40. B is the best answer. "Salification" means "salt forming". This question is really asking which atom on doxycycline is the most basic. HCl has been added, and answer choices A–C are the same except they feature protonation at a different site. The choices indicate that this is a "who is the most basic" type of question. Since sodium was a never a reactant here, choice D can be eliminated. It is a distractor, and is actually the basic salt which follows the reaction of doxycycline and NaOH. To solve what the salification product will look like, remember that the most basic atom will be the one which is protonated after the reaction. Choice A is an enol that tautomerizes with its ketone form. In the ketone form, the nitrogen's lone pair can be delocalized through resonance. This will reduce the basicity of choice A in comparison to choice B. Choice B's nitrogen does not have any resonance to delocalize its lone pair. It is more basic than choices A and C, and is the best answer. A protonated carbonyl oxygen is extremely acidic, and only a transiently lived intermediate in many reactions. Choice C is not stable enough to persist as an ionic solid, and can be eliminated.

41. D is the best answer. After completely dissolving, the drug will exist as $DoxH^+$ and Cl^-. This question is asking about the equilibrium that occurs when $DoxH^+$ behaves as an acid:

$DoxH^+ \rightleftharpoons Dox + H^+$. The free base refers to the deprotonated drug.

Remember, $pH = pK_a + \log \frac{[A^-]}{[HA]}$. This is the Henderson-Hasselbalch equation, which describes the relationship between pH, pK_a, and the dissociation of a weak acid. The percent of the drug which is a free base relative to the protonated form is simply the ratio $\frac{[A^-]}{[HA]}$. The passage also explains that the stomach is 0.1 M HCl.

Use the equation $pH = -\log[H^+]$ to determine the pH of the stomach

$-\log(0.1) = 1$. The stomach has a pH of 1.

Use algebra to isolate the ratio before using actual numbers to solve the problem.

$$10^{(pH - pK_a)} = \frac{[A^-]}{[HA]}$$

Now substitute the numbers given in the passage.

$$10^{(1-3.1)} = \frac{[A^-]}{[HA]}$$

$\frac{[A^-]}{[HA]} = 10^{-2.1}$ This is slightly less than 1%, so choice D is the best answer.

42. B is the best answer. Think about Equation 1, $R = \frac{DA(C_s - C_b)}{h}$, and consider the effects of each of the proposed changes. If h is reduced by a factor of 2 then R will double. Cutting the sphere in half will increase its effective surface area by $2 \times \pi r^2$. Its new surface area will be $6\pi r^2$. The factor by which its surface area has increased will be $\frac{6\pi r^2}{4\pi r^2} = 1.5$ If choice B is chosen, then R will only increase by 50% of its initial value. Choice A increases R by 100% of its original value, and choice B should be eliminated.

Choice C will lower C_s. Since the drug has just been added to the solution C_b is still very low, but since C_s has decreased, the difference between them is also lower, and R will also decrease. Eliminate choice C. Pouring out half of the solution will increase C_b because the surrounding solvent will become more concentrated. Since C_s starts as greater than C_b, narrowing the difference between them once again decreases R. Eliminate choice D.

TEST 7A A&E

43. **C is the best answer.** Neutral water has a pH of 7. In the second paragraph of the passage it explains that stomach acid has a $[H^+] = 0.1$. This corresponds to a pH of 1. Each pH unit is 10× greater in concentration of H^+ ion than the one above it because they are on a logarithmic scale.

pH	7 → 6 → 5 → 4 → 3 → 2 → 1
Factor of increasing $[H^+]$	Initial → × 10 → × 10 → × 10 → × 10 → × 10 → × 10

Between 7 and 1 on the pH scale there is difference in 10^6 in concentration of H^+. 10^6 is a million, so select the best answer, choice C.

Stand-alones (Questions 44-47)

44. **A is the best answer.** The pH that allows an amino acid to be neutrally charged, i.e. the pI, is the average of the pK_as of its carboxy-terminus and of its amino-terminus. Symbolically, this relationship is: pI = (pK_{a1} + pK_{a2})/2. First, remember that the dissociation of the carboxy terminus will be described with pK_{a1} since it is more acidic and will be deprotonated first. The dissociation of the amino-terminus will be described with pK_{a2} since it is more basic and will be deprotonated second. pK_{a2} > pK_{a1}, so choice C can be eliminated. Since choice A satisfies the relationship of the pI equation, it is the best answer. The sum of the two pK_a values ≠ pI, so choice B can be eliminated. The difference of the two pK_a values ≠ pI so choice D can be eliminated.

45. **A is the best answer.** Lactic acid is a weak acid, while ammonia is a weak base. In addition, lactic acid has a hydrogen on the carboxyl group, as well as on the hydroxyl group, meaning it is a diprotic acid. A diprotic acid has two equivalence points, accounting for the shape of the titration curve above. Bicarbonate is a base, so adding bicarbonate to the titration mixture will mean that less ammonia needs to be added in order to reach the equivalence point. This would result in shifting the curve to the left, making choice A most likely to be the best answer. If acid was added to the titration, then the curve would be shifted to the right, as more base would have to be added to reach the equivalence point. This is because some of the added base would react with the acid that was added to the titration mix. Only a change in the identity of the weak acid or weak base would shift the curve up or down, which is not true in this case. Choices C and D are less likely than choice A to be the best answer.

46. **B is the best answer.** This is a point worth memorizing but also can be reasoned from the question. Neutralization reactions are often exothermic meaning they release heat. This is true on the lab bench where fires may spontaneously ignite and is also true in the human body where the release of heat can cause burns. Based on the formula $\Delta G = \Delta H - T\Delta S$, neutralization reactions are often exergonic as well but this is not directly related to what makes them lethal. The release of heat is what is harmful and exergonic reactions are not always exothermic, so choice B is the best answer.

47. **B is the best answer.** Buffers have the effect of flattening a titration curve over a specific pH range, known as the buffer zone. Without a buffer, the pH of a titration curve is nearly vertical since pH is measured on a logarithmic scale. The buffer zone is the area where additions of acid (or base) result in only small changes in pH and is the horizontal region of the curve. This makes choice B the best answer. Point A is at region of very low pH where the amount of acid is rapidly exceeding the amount of base causing a change in pH. The pH is relatively constant in the buffer zone, so choice A is not the best answer. Points C and D are both at areas of very high pH where the amount of base is exceeding the amount of acid and causing a change in pH. For the same reason as choice A, choices C and D are not the best answer.

Passage 9 (Questions 48-51)

48. **D is the best answer.** A normal pH, according to information contained in the passage, is 7.4. Using Figure 1 as a guide, when DIDS is added, the pH value decreases by 0.2. This means the pH goes from 7.4 to 7.2. This means the change in pH can be found by:

$$pH = -\log[H^+]$$

pH 7.4	pH 7.2
$7.4 = -\log[H^+]$	$7.2 = -\log[H^+]$
$[H^+] = 10^{-7.4}$	$[H^+] = 10^{-7.2}$

$$\Delta[H^+] = 10^{-7.2} - 10^{-7.4} \approx 2 \times 10^{-8}\,M$$

While these pH values are not whole numbers, notice that the difference in pH between the two conditions is less than 1×10^{-7}, meaning the difference is likely to be an order of magnitude smaller, or some value on the order of 1×10^{-8}. The difference is less than 1×10^{-7} because both exponents contain a −7 and the difference between the two numbers is 0.2. A difference of 1 or more between the numbers would increase the magnitude of the difference, which would give an exponent less than 7. Choices A and B represent a change in four orders of magnitude, which would yield a final pH around 3.4. Choice C is close to 10^{-6}, which would correspond to a pH of 6, not 7.2, making choice C less likely to be the best answer. Choice D describes a concentration difference that is less than an order of magnitude, which would be nearly the difference between the two pH values. Notice that it is not necessary to do a full calculation, as the best answer, choice D, can be approximated from the order of magnitude.

49. **A is the best answer.** Notice that the addition of DIDS to the medium, as shown in Figure 1, inhibits the transport of bicarbonate. This question can best be thought of as an application of Le Chatlier's principle. Bicarbonate serves to carry carbon dioxide in a solvated form from tissues to the lungs for excretion. It also serves as the main buffer of blood pH. The chemical equation for bicarbonate production in blood and body tissues is:

$$H_2O + CO_2 \rightleftharpoons H_2CO_3 \rightleftharpoons H^+ + HCO_3^-.$$

By blocking the transport of bicarbonate into the cytosol with the use of DIDS, as is shown in Figure 1, there would now be more bicarbonate in the medium of the dish than normal, shifting the equation to the right. This would result in more protons combining with bicarbonate, decreasing the concentration of protons in solution and increasing the pH in the cell culture dish, likely making choice A the best answer. Because bicarbonate is a base and it is no longer being imported into the cytosol of the cell, the pH should decrease, as shown in Figure 1. This eliminates choice B. As the chemical equation would shift to the left, the proton concentration would decrease in the cell culture dish, eliminating choice C. As shown in Figure 1, the cytosol of the cancer cell acidifies after being treated with DIDS, meaning there is an increase in the concentration of protons in the cytosol, not a decrease, eliminating choice D.

50. **A is the best answer.** According to Figure 2, as the pH decreases, the levels of phosphorylated MKK3 (pMKK3) rise. This could mean increased activity of a kinase or decreased activity of a phosphatase, according to the passage. The pH and the proton concentration have an inverse relationship, meaning that as the pH decreases, the proton concentration increases. If protons serve as an allosteric activator of a kinase, then a decreased pH would lead to an increase in pMKK3, which is shown in Figure 2. Choice A is most likely to be the best answer. Decreased activation of a kinase would result in less pMKK3 with decreasing pH, eliminating choice B. If decreasing the proton concentration resulted in decreased allosteric activation of a phosphatase, the levels of pMKK3 would be expected to be high at high pH, which is not shown in Figure 2, eliminating choice C as the best answer. A phosphorylase, similar to a kinase, adds a phosphate onto an organic molecule. A phosphorylase is unique from a kinase, however, in that it breaks apart a molecule when it phosphorylates it, while a kinase just adds a phosphate group, without breaking apart the molecule. Allosteric activation of a phosphorylase would increase the levels of pMKK3, which occurs with a decrease in pH, or an increase in proton concentration. This is the opposite of the relationship suggested in choice D, eliminating it as the best answer.

51. **A is the best answer.** When an acid dissociates into a proton and its conjugate base in an aqueous solution, the proton really exists as the hydronium ion, H_3O^+. Lactate is the conjugate base of lactic acid, which has free electrons on the carboxyl oxygen, which can serve as a nucleophile to remove a hydrogen from the hydronium ion to generate lactic acid and water. Choice A is most likely to be the best answer. Lactate has an excess of electrons, making it more likely to be a nucleophile, not an electrophile. Choices B and D can be eliminated. While it is theoretically possible that lactate could remove a hydrogen from bicarbonate, it is highly unlikely, as the p*K*a of the hydrogen on bicarbonate would be very high, and bicarbonate would be resistant to becoming doubly negatively charged. Choice C is less likely than choice A to be the best answer.

Passage 10 (Questions 52-56)

52. B is the best answer. Use the definition of pK_a to solve this problem: $pK_a = -\log\left(\frac{[H^+][A^-]}{[HA]}\right)$. When the 1.5 M solution ionizes, some of the acetic acid, HA, will be lost. For every mole of HA which is lost, a new mole of H^+ and A^- will form. This means that $[H^+] = [A^-]$. If $x = [H^+]$ then $pK_a = -\log\left(\frac{[x^2]}{[HA-x]}\right)$

Solve for x to determine $[H^+]$.

$10^{-pK_a} = \left(\frac{[x^2]}{[HA-x]}\right)$ because x is so small in comparison to HA, it can be ignored in the denominator. Thus,

$$\sqrt{[HA]\times 10^{-pK_a}} = x$$

$$x = \sqrt{4\times 10^{-4.75}} = 2 \times 10^{-2.375}$$

$$-\log(x) = pH = -\log(2 \times 10^{-2.375}) = 2.375 - \text{"something less than 1"} \approx 2$$

Choice A represents a pH value that is too high and choice C represents a pH value that is too low, based on the partially estimated approach above. Choice D can be eliminated without even performing any work, as it is a pH well above 7. This is not possible in an *acidic* water solution at room temperature. By definition acids are solution have a pH < 7.

53. B is the best answer. Figure 1 shows the concentration of AA and its effect on biofilm inhibition. The figure's title stipulates that the percent AA is given as volume AA per volume of solution. Curiously, it seems that PS_1586 thrives in slightly more acidic environments, reaching it peak growth with a 16% AA concentration by volume. A solution with this concentration of AA will be the most conducive for the growth of PS_1586, and will be the best answer. Since the concentration is given in volume per volume in Figure 1, convert the mass of AA to volume in order to determine if the ratios given in each answer choice are proper. Choice A: (16.8 g)(1 mL/1.05 g) = 16 mL of AA. If it is mixed with 100 mL of broth, the solution will be too dilute, being less than 16% by volume, so choice A can be eliminated. Choice B: (16.8 g)(1 mL/1.05 g) = 16 mL of AA. It if is mixed with 84 mL of broth, the solution will be 16% AA by volume, and will be most conducive for growing PS_1586. Choice B is the best answer. Because AA has a density > 1, the solutions proposed in choices C and D will be too dilute. They will be less than 16% AA by volume. Choices C and D can be eliminated.

54. C is the best answer. A conjugate base, non-dissociated acid, and solution pH are all terms in the Henderson-Hasselbalch equation. Since the question is providing these terms, it is a strong hint to use the Henderson-Hasselbalch equation. The amount of acetic acid which ionizes prior to adding calcium acetate is negligible in comparison to the amount of conjugate base which has been added. Remember that calcium is a divalent cation, requiring two equivalents of acetate to form a salt. For every 1 mole of calcium acetate introduced into the solution, 2 moles of acetate will be released. In addition, 2000 mL is the same thing as 2 L because 1000 mL = 1 L. With these ideas in mind, "plug and chug" using the Henderson-Hasselbalch equation:

$$pH = pK_a + \log\left(\frac{[A^-]}{[HA]}\right)$$

$$pH = 4.75 + \log\left(\frac{2 \text{ moles}/2 \text{ L of } A^-}{1 \text{ M of HA}}\right)$$

$$pH = 4.75 + \log(1) = 4.75$$

B is the best answer. If only one mole of acetate were plugged into this equation instead of 2, choice C would result. Choices A and D are just distractors.

55. D is the best answer. A negative control and a positive control were performed in addition to the experimental trials shown in Figure 1. Compared to the positive control, there was almost no biofilm formed in the negative control. In general, negative implies "lack of something." With this in mind, it is reasonable to conclude that the negative control did not have any added bacteria in it, but the positive control did have bacteria added to it. The negative control was performed to determine if there were any endogenous bacteria already living in the broth solution that could skew the results. The positive control was to determine how the added bacteria would fare in the absence of added AA. The positive control provided a baseline so that the experimental results could be conclusive, and the negative control established that there were no endogenous bacteria present in the broth to skew results. Finally, because of the way pH is defined, $pH = -\log[H^+]$, increasing the concentration of an acid *lowers* the pH of a solution. Choice D is the best answer because it identifies the role of the negative control trial and correctly describes the pH as decreasing throughout the experiment, as described in the passage. Although choice A identifies the role of the negative control trial, it makes the mistake of describing the pH of the solution as increasing throughout the experiment. Choice A can be eliminated. Choices B and C describe the role of the positive control instead of the negative control and can be eliminated. Choice B is particularly weak as it also incorrectly describes the pH of the broth as increasing during the experiment, when, in fact, it decreased.

56. B is the best answer. There are a lot of problems with choice A. Since AA is a weak acid, it does not completely ionize. In order for a solution of AA to have the same pH as a solution of HCl, which completely ionizes, far more AA must be added to the solution. This means that a solution of AA with an equivalent pH to a solution of HCl has far more solutes dissolved in it. Such a solution will have a *greater* osmolarity as well. A solution with a high osmolarity would most likely cause a cell to shrivel, not fill with water and burst—the definition of cytolysis. Furthermore, bacterial cells have cell-walls which protect them against shriveling or bursting due to changes in their environments tonicity. Choice A can be eliminated. The acid form of acetic acid is far less polar than its deprotonated form, and can probably cross the bacterial cell membrane. This may be a good answer, so do not eliminate it yet. HCl is a stronger acid than AA. This means that Cl^- is a weaker base and has less "control' of its protons than does AA. The opposite of choice C is true, and choice C can be eliminated. Finally, the deprotonated version of AA is very polar, having a −1 charge. It is probably unable to cross the hydrophobic cell membrane. Choice D is not as strong as choice B. Choice B is the best answer.

Stand-alones (Questions 57-59)

57. D is the best answer. Carbonic acid, H_2CO_3, and bicarbonate, HCO_3^-, are two of the main compounds responsible for buffering blood pH. Bicarbonate contains one less hydrogen than carbonic acid, meaning carbonic acid gave up a hydrogen to generate bicarbonate. This makes bicarbonate the conjugate base of carbonic acid. Choices A and B show bicarbonate, not carbonic acid, eliminating them as possible answers. Carbonic acid donated a hydrogen to water in solution to become bicarbonate, eliminating choice C and making choice D the best answer.

58. A is the best answer. The question stem implies that a weak acid is being substituted for a strong acid. This means the starting pH of the titration would be that of a strong acid, which is around a pH of 1. This would shift the whole titration curve down, making choice A most likely to be the best answer. Substitution of acetic acid with a weaker acid would shift the titration curve up, as the initial starting pH would be higher. Choice B can be eliminated. Addition of a base to the titration reaction would require more acid to reach the equivalence point, shifting the reaction to the left. This eliminates choice C. A shift to the right would mean acid was added to the titration mix, eliminating choice D.

59. D is the best answer. Thymol blue is an example of an indicator that functions in an acidic range. An indicator undergoes a color change upon reaching a certain pH, typically by donating or accepting a proton. When a compound is added to a titration reaction, which is usually used to determine the pK_a of an acid, it is usually an indicator for the pH of the solution. It does not necessarily serve as a buffer, eliminating choice A. It would also not necessarily serve as a proton donor or acceptor specifically for the acetylsalicylic acid compound, but rather for many molecules in solution, eliminating choices B and C. As an indicator, it could donate a proton or accept a proton from solution to undergo a color change, making choice D more likely to be the best answer.

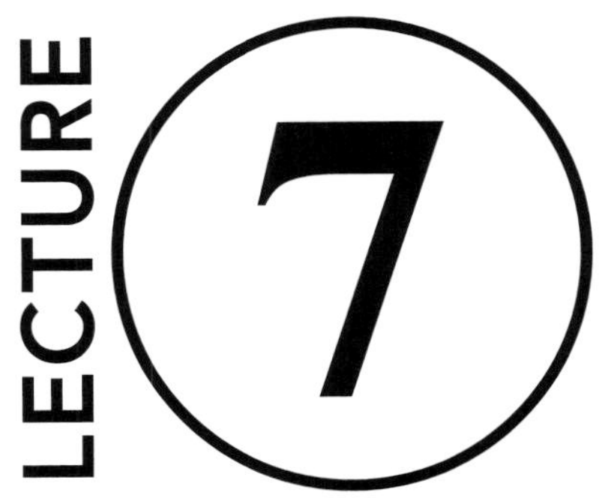

Acids and Bases

MINI-TEST 7B

ANSWERS & EXPLANATIONS

Questions 1–29

Passage 1 (Questions 1-6)

1. **B is the best answer.** CO has a total of ten valence electrons. Since all of the structures provided have 10 electrons, it will be impossible to eliminate wrong answer choices this way. The next thing to consider is that the atoms in the structures should satisfy the octet rule—this is generally true except for a few exceptions such as B, Al, and Be. Carbon does not have an octet in choices C and D. Oxygen does not have an octet in choice A. Choices A, C, and D, are less likely structures than choice B because in choice B, both atoms have a complete octet. Select choice B.

2. **A is the best answer.** Both the Brønsted-Lowry and Lewis acid/base definitions will be tested on the MCAT®. According to the Brønsted-Lowry definition, a base is a proton acceptor, and an acid is a proton donor. The Lewis definition is just a generalization of this definition. According to the Lewis definition, an acid is an electron acceptor, and a base is an electron donor. The Lewis definition is important because it allows non-protic systems to also be described in terms of acid-base chemistry.

   No proton is being exchanged with copper(II) in this reaction, the Brønsted-Lowry definition has no relevance here—eliminate choices C and D. Since the copper(II) accepts electrons from EDTA during the formation of the octahedral complex, it is a Lewis acid. Select the correct answer, choice A, and eliminate choice B.

3. **A is the best answer.** Do not be intimidated. This is a challenging research based question, but the passage provides a lot of hints to answer it. First, use numeric intuition on Equation 1. When a virus is very rapidly deactivated, the ratio of N_f/N_o will be a very small number. This will translate to a large negative value once the natural log of this ratio is taken. In other words, the more negative the deactivation rate, the more rapidly the alloy deactivates the virus.

   Figure 2 shows that as the copper content of the alloy increases, the deactivation rate becomes more rapid. The alloy with the greatest copper content will most rapidly inactivate norovirus, and the alloy with the least copper content will least rapidly inactivate norovirus.

   The chart in this question gives the masses of different alloy components. Conveniently, in all the alloys, their masses add up to 100 g. This means that the mass percent of each element will be proportional to the mole fraction of each element; by looking at the masses, it is possible to know which material has the greatest concentration of copper. Alloy X has the most copper and alloy Z has the least copper. Alloy X will most rapidly inactivate the virus, and alloy Z will least rapidly inactivate the virus—select the correct answer, choice A. Although other elements are provided, since the passage only describes the effect of copper, this is the only element that allows conclusions to be drawn. The other elements are only provided to distract and intimidate. Some of the incorrect answer choices, such as choice D, are a perversion of the correct answer—after all the hard work of solving this problem, don't make a careless error here! In this problem, the other incorrect choices are simply distractors.

4. **A is the best answer.** A tetraprotic acid can lose 4 protons. Some, like the one in this problem have four distinct equivalence points. Each equivalence point indicates the pH at which a specific acidic moiety is fully deprotonated. There is only 1 mole of acid present for every 4 protons in solution. When the first acidic moiety is fully deprotonated, the number of moles of KOH required to accomplish this is equal to the number of moles of acid in solution. This stage in the titration occurs at the first equivalence point—select the correct answer choice A. Choice B is the second equivalence point; at this stage the moles of KOH added is double the moles of acid present in solution—eliminate choice B. Choice C is a tempting distractor. It is in the middle of the graph and looks symmetrical. Choice C is actually useless for this problem because it does not represent a quantity of KOH which is even a whole number multiple of the moles of acid in solution. **The MCAT® loves to make distracting options look symmetrical and "clean." Be suspicious.** Eliminate choice C. Choice D is the fourth equivalence point; at this stage the moles of KOH added is quadruple the moles of acid present in solution—eliminate choice D.

5. **C is the best answer.** First , write the disassociation reaction and set up the equilibrium expression:

$$CH_3CH_2CH_2COOH + H_2O \rightleftharpoons CH_3CH_2CH_2COO^- + H_3O^+$$

$$K = \frac{[CH_3CH_2CH_2COO^-][H_3O^+]}{[CH_3CH_2CH_2COOH]} = 1.6 \times 10^{-5}$$

If 1 M of is $CH_3CH_2CH_2COOH$ is added, then "X" amount of that will disassociate. There will be "X" mol/L of $CH_3CH_2CH_2COO^-$ and "X" mol/L of H_3O^+.

$$K = 1.6 \times 10^{-5} = \frac{[x][x]}{[1-x]} \approx \frac{x^2}{1}$$

$$X = \sqrt{16 \times 10^{-6}} = 4 \times 10^{-3}$$

$-\log(4 \times 10^{-3})$ will be less than three and greater than 2—select choice C.

This is because of a property of logs, included here:

$-\log(4 \times 10^{-3}) = -\log(4) + -\log(10^{-3}) = 3$ – a small number between one and zero

6. **A is the best answer.** Recognize that the answer choices are all variations of the Hendersohn-Hasselbalch equation. Use this equation and the values given in the question stem to find the answer.

$$pH = pK_{a\ indicator} + \log\left(\frac{[A^-]}{[HA]}\right)$$

Since the protonated form is 1/10 the initial concentration, this equation can be rewritten:

$$pH = pK_{a\ indicator} + \log\left(\frac{[10]}{[1]}\right) = pH = pK_{a\ indicator} + 1$$

Choices C and D are incorrect variations of the Hendersohn-Hasselbalch equation; pK_b is not a term in the equation. Typically, pK_b is seen in the context of pOH. These choices can be eliminated. Choice A comes from incorrectly substituting the concentrations of the different forms of the indicator into the Hendersohn-Hasselbalch equation—it should also be eliminated.

Passage 2 (Questions 7-11)

7. **D is the best answer.** If the GAA were completely pure, it would be totally anhydrous. Without water present, the acid will not dissociate because there is no medium in which to dissociate. All of the H^+ would be covalently bound to the acetate group. Since no protons would be free in the solution, the classic gas releasing reaction of an acid and sodium bicarbonate would not occur. Mixing these chemicals together would result in no reaction. Choose the best answer, choice D.

8. **B is the best answer.** Careful here. Table 1 provides the pK_a of the **conjugate acid** of each chemical listed. That means each pK_a is provided for the protonated version of the listed chemical. The conjugate acid of Na_2SO_4 is $NaHSO_4$, so use the pK_a provided to the right of Na_2SO_4. Since $pK_a = -\log(K_a)$ then $10^{-pKa} = K_a$.

   $10^{-2} = K_a$ of $NaHSO_4$. Choose the best answer, choice B. 10^3 is the K_a of sulfuric acid. This not what question wanted, so choice A can be eliminated. Choice C is the K_a of sulfuric acid, but calculated without the appropriate sign. Choice D is the K_a of $NaHSO_4$, but calculated without the appropriate sign. Both of these choices can be eliminated as well.

9. **C is the best answer.** Although this problem can be solved by deriving the pK_b of acetic acid from the pK_a provided in Table 1, and doing some extensive calculations, it really is not necessary to do all that work. Sodium acetate is a weak base. A solution of sodium acetate will have a pH somewhat higher than 7.0, but nowhere near 14. This logic alone allows the best answer, choice C, to be chosen. The more complicated derived approach is shown below:

pK_a of acetic acid is provided in Table 1 and is 4.8.

Use the relationship pK_a + pK_b = pK_w = 14.

$$\text{p}K_b = 10.2 \text{ and } K_b = 10^{-10.2}$$
$$K_b = \left(\frac{[\text{HA}^+][\text{OH}^-]}{[\text{A}^-]}\right)$$
$$\sqrt{K_b[\text{A}^-]} = [\text{OH}^-]$$
$$-\log(\sqrt{\text{p}K_b[\text{A}^-]}) = \text{pOH}$$

Remember that pH + pOH = 14.

$$14 - \text{pOH} = \text{pH}$$

The final pH is:

$$14 - (-)\log(\sqrt{\text{p}K_b[\text{A}^-]})$$

[A$^-$] is a little bit less than 1 M, but use 1 M so simplify the calculation.

$$\approx 14 + \log(10^{-5.1})$$
$$14 - 5.1 = 9.8$$

Choose the best answer, choice C.

10. **D is the best answer.** Lipids are just carboxylic acids with long aliphatic tails. "Alkaline" is chemistry jargon for basic. Exposure of a lipid to alkaline materials results in deprotonation of the carboxylic acid terminus, and the formation of an ionic bond between the newly formed carboxylate group and a cation. Such metal alkanoate salts are called soaps. They can form micelles, and are used to dissolve fat and oil, in solutions which are otherwise too polar to dissolve those materials. Soaps feel slippery. It is soap formation at the surface of the skin which results in the slippery feeling people experience when exposed skin contacts an alkali material.

Lipids will undergo deprotonation at the carboxylic acid group with far greater ease than they will undergo deprotonation at an α-hydrogen. Following deprotonation at the carboxylic acid group, the negative charge can be delocalized over two oxygen atoms. Deprotonation at the α-hydrogen only allows the negative charge to be delocalized over one oxygen atom. This is why the carboxylic acid hydrogen is more acidic than the α-hydrogen. Choice A is weaker than choice D. Since a base is being used in this question, no protonation is expected. Eliminate choice B. Choice C is possible, but base mediated amide hydrolysis requires a very high concentration of base. Moreover, destruction of tissue proteins would not feel slippery—it would ultimately result in blisters and chemical burns. Since the reaction conditions for choice C are difficult to achieve and are not expected to feel slippery, choice D is the best answer.

11. **C is the best answer.** The passage explains in the third paragraph that an excess of $NaHSO_4$ is required for this reaction because it melts and forms a liquid medium in which the reaction can occur. Of these choices, choose the choice with the mole ratio with the least moles of $NaCH_3COO$ and the most moles of $NaHSO_4$. No math is required. Choose the ratio with greatest mass of $NaHSO_4$ to the lowest mass of $NaCH_3COO$. Choice C is better than choices A and B. To distinguish between choices C and D consider the division below.

Choice C: $4 > 34.5/10.3 > 3$

Choice D: $2 > 69/41 > 1.5$

Choice C has a greater mass ratio of $NaHSO_4$ to $NaCH_3COO$. By extension, it has a greater mole ratio of $NaHSO_4$ to $NaCH_3COO$ and is the best answer.

TEST 7B A&E

Stand-alones (Questions 12-15)

12. **B is the best answer.** The Henderson-Hasselbalch equation, $pH = pK_a(-)\log\left[\frac{H^-}{HA}\right]$, helps to answer this question. When the concentration of the conjugate base, H^-, is equal to the concentration of the acid, HA, the pH is equal to the pK_a. The conjugate base of ibuprofen loses the hydrogen from the carboxylic acid to become negatively charged. As the pK_a is very close to the pH of the solution, the mixture is nearly 50% H^- and 50% HA. Choice B is most likely to be the best answer. If a very low fraction of the molecules carries a negative charge, this means most of the molecules are protonated, which would be found at a very low pH. Choice A is less likely than choice B to be the best answer. If the pH is greater than the pH, nearly all of the acid will be deprotonated. As the pH is less than the pK_a, choices C and D can be eliminated.

13. **D is the best answer.** Acid base reactions involve the donation or acceptance of a proton, so the best answer will be an amino acid that is unlikely to donate or receive a proton on its amino acid side chain. Histidine, arginine, and lysine all contain nitrogen atoms on their side chains that can donate or accept protons, depending on the pH of the solution. Isoleucine is a non-polar amino acid that is unable to donate or accept a proton, making choice D the best answer.

14. **B is the best answer.** The first important step is to identify the most basic amino acid, which can be done by looking at the pK_a of the side chains. The higher the pK_a, the weaker the acid, or stronger the base. Arginine, with a side chain of 12.5, is the most basic (alanine, without a side chain pK_a, is neutral). The pH mentioned in the question stem is very basic meaning all available protons will be stripped from the amino acid. Arginine has a carboxyl group an amino group, and a guanidinium group. At very high pH, the carboxyl group will be deprotonated to carry a −1 charge. The amino group and guanidinium groups will both be deprotonated to carry a neutral charge. So −1, choice B is the best answer.

15. **A is the best answer.** A Brønsted base accepts a proton and choice A is the best answer. The Brønsted definition of acids and bases is proton-centric whereas the Lewis definition is electron-centric. Choice B describes a Lewis acid. Choice C describes a Brønsted acid. Choice D describes a Lewis base.

Passage 3 (Questions 16-21)

16. **A is the best answer.** The difference in the binding enthalpies in the two buffer systems is a result of the energy costs that come from the associated acid/base reactions while binding. Figure 2 shows the enthalpic cost of deprotonating the buffer molecules. In particular, since deprotonating Tris—H^+ while binding "costs" +16.8 kJ/mol and deprotonating sodium phosphate while binding only "costs" +1.1 kJ/mol, the observed enthalpy of binding, which takes into account the concurrent protonation of ICDP47, will be more negative in the sodium phosphate buffer. At a low enough pH, ICDP47 is already protonated and will not need to deprotonate one of these buffer molecules while binding with Hsp90. Thus, if the pH is low enough, regardless of the buffer system, there will only be one value for the binding enthalpy. Only the binding reaction occurs, without the associated acid/base reactions. The correct pH will be the pH that shows an equivalent $\Delta_b H_{obs}$ for both buffer systems. Graphically, these will be overlapping points on Figure 1. This points occur at a pH of 5. $[H^+] = 10^{-pH}$. $[H^+] = 10^{-5}$. Choice A is the best answer. At an $[H^+] = 10^{-6}$ two separate points are first observed for each buffer system. This means that acid/base reactions are occurring as well as the binding reaction. Although this is the first pH at which these side reactions are observed to occur, since the question did not ask about when these acid/base reactions first occur, choice B does not answer the question. A pH of 7.5 is mentioned in the passage, but this value also has two separate enthalpies for each buffer system. Choice C cannot be the best answer. Choice D features the $[H^+]$ associated with the greatest disparity in binding enthalpies—this is the opposite of the best answer, as side acid/base reactions play a significant role in producing a final enthalpy value. The MCAT® likes to offer answer choices that are extreme in order to distract students. Be careful of this trap.

17. **B is the best answer.** Technically, carbonyls can act as hydrogen bond acceptors. Since all amino acids contain carbonyl groups, this question must be looking for a stronger hydrogen bond. A stronger hydrogen bond would be found between the hydroxyl groups of ICDP47 and the more electronegative member of any sort of N–H, O–H, or F–H bond. Of the amino acids listed in the answer choices, aspartate is the only one which contains an O–H bond in its R-group. It will be able to provide the strongest hydrogen-bonding with ICDP47. Choice B is the best answer. Choices A, C, and D lack the capacity to hydrogen bond within their R-groups.

18. **A is the best answer.** The Henderson-Hasselbalch equation relates pK_a and the concentration of an acid to its conjugate base, to the pH of a solution. It can be used to solve buffer formulation problems, and is written: $pH = pK_a + \log\left(\frac{[A^-]}{[HA]}\right)$ HA refers to the acid, and A^- refers to the conjugate base. This problem adds one thinking step, and that is selecting the correct pK_a to plug into this equation. The correct pK_a will be the pK_a which describes the behavior of the acid, not the conjugate base. In this case HA is NaH_2PO_4 and A^- is Na_2HPO_4. Use the pK_a of NaH_2PO_4 to solve this problem.

$$7.5 = 6.8 + \log([Na_2HPO_4]/[NaH_2PO_4])$$

$10^{0.7} = [Na_2HPO_4]/[NaH_2PO_4]$ Choice A is the best answer. Two errors would result in choice B: using of the wrong pK_a, and then using the opposite of the ratio that the wrong pK_a provided, when "plugged" into the Henderson-Hasselbalch equation. The ratio of disodium phosphate to monosodium phosphate is $10^{0.7}$:1, but this is not what question asked for, so eliminate choice C. Choice D makes the first of the two mistakes of choice B, namely "plugging in" the incorrect pK_a value.

19. **B is the best answer.** Consider the violent exothermicity of a neutralization reaction. Forming water from H^+ and OH^- is clearly an exothermic reaction. By extension, performing the reverse reaction $H_2O \rightarrow H^+ + OH^-$ must be very endothermic. In general, it often requires energy to break bonds, energy is usually released when new bonds are formed. Eliminate choices A and D. According to Le Châtelier's principle, after heating water, which is an equilibrium mixture of H_2O, H^+, and OH^-, the system will try to remove the heat that was added. It can do this by endothermically forming more ions. Thus, K_w will increase because the concentration of H^+ and OH^- has increased. Choice B is the best answer, and choice C can be eliminated.

20. **D is the best answer.** The best buffer will have a pK_a closest to the target pH. Since pOH + pH = 14, the target pH is 9. Thus, Tris has the closest pK_a and will make the best buffer. Choice D is the best answer. If pOH were mistakenly treated as pH, choice C would result. Choices A and B are not as close as the best answer, choice D, and can be eliminated.

21. **C is the best answer.** Use the acronym FONCl BrISCH (pronounced "Fon-kel-brish") to remember the relative electronegativities of common atoms. O is more electronegative than N. Thus, an O–H bond will be more polarized than an N–H bond. Eliminate choices A and D. In addition, more polarized bonds increase acidity, not the reverse. Look at the top and bottom of the left side of Figure 2. Phosphate buffer's conjugate acid requires +1.1 kJ/mol to undergo deprotonation, but Tris buffer's conjugate acid requires 16.8 kJ/mol. Deprotonating Tris buffer's conjugate acid requires more energy, so choice B can be eliminated. The conjugate acid of the phosphate buffer is an oxyacid. The oxygen atoms in the conjugate base of an oxyacid can share the negative charge, spreading it over a larger area and thus stabilizing the ion, and increasing acidity, or the ease with which the molecule is deprotonated. Choice C is consistent with Figure 2 and chemical science. It is the best answer.

Passage 4 (Questions 22-26)

22. **B is the best answer.** The passage provides a great hint for solving this problem. It explains that changing the pH of a milk sample can precipitate casein. Remember that the pI is the pH of a solution that will cause casein to have a net neutral charge. If the pH of the solution surrounding the casein is greater than casein's pI, the casein will have a net negative charge. Conversely, if the pH < pI, the casein will have a net positive charge. According to the passage, neutrally charged casein will precipitate from milk. Thus, if the pH of milk is dropped to casein's pI, casein will precipitate. Of the choices, the only acid which can lower the pH of milk is HCl. Choice B is the best answer. N_2 is a fairly inert gas. Besides causing the solution to bubble up, it will not do very much else. Choice A can be eliminated. NaOH and $NaCH_3CH_2COO$ are both bases, and will raise the pH of the solution, increasing the concentration of caseinate. Since caseinate is charged, it is more soluble in the polar, primarily aqueous, milk than is casein. Converting casein to caseinate will increase the solubility of this protein in milk, and choices C and D can be eliminated.

TEST 7B A&E

23. **C is the best answer.** The passage states that the mixture of casein powder, sodium hydroxide, and water makes glue. The best dry formulation will form these chemicals when mixed with water. Calcium hydroxide is one of the dry chemicals, and it is the only possible source for the hydroxide ion. Unfortunately, it is only scantly soluble in water. Its dissociation equilibrium strongly favors the left side.

$$Ca(OH)_2(s) \rightleftharpoons Ca^{2+}(aq) + 2OH^-(aq)$$

However, if ionic calcium could be precipitated, according to Le Châtelier's principle, the equilibrium would shift to the right. More OH^- would be released into solution.

The sodium salt which will most effectively precipitate ionic calcium, shifting the equilibrium to the right, will be the salt whose anion forms the least soluble calcium salt. This sodium salt will allow the most ionic calcium to be precipitated. It will also cause the most OH^- to be released. Remember that the root function which provides the molar solubility of salt from its K_{sp} is always based on the number of ions the salt forms when it dissociates.

Thus, the molar solubility of Ca^{2+} in a CaF_2 solution which dissociates into three ions is:

$$\sqrt[3]{5.3 \times 10 - 9} \approx 10^{-3}$$

Since the $CaSO_3$ and CaC_2O_4 both only dissociate into two ions, their molar solubilities are $\sqrt{6.8 \times 10^{-8}} \approx 10^{-4}$ and $\sqrt{2.7 \times 10^{-9}} \approx 10^{-4.5}$ respectively. Sodium oxalate is expected to precipitate the most ionic calcium and will release the most OH^- into solution. Choice C is the best answer. Sodium acetate will not precipitate any calcium at all, as calcium acetate is very soluble in water. Choice B can be eliminated. Calcium fluoride and calcium sulfite both have greater molar solubilities of ionic calcium than does calcium oxalate. They will allow more calcium ion to remain in solution, and less OH^- will be able to dissociate from $Ca(OH)_2$ and enter solution. Eliminate choices A and D.

24. **C is the best answer.** pH is defined as $-\log[H^+]$. pOH is defined as $-\log[OH^-]$. A lower pH value means a substance is more acidic, and a higher pH value means that it is more basic. Conversely, a lower pOH value means a substance is more basic, and a higher pOH value means that it is more acidic. For room temperature solutions, the relationship between pH and pOH is: pH + pOH = 14.

The items in the table have the following pOH values:

Lemon juice: 12

Orange juice: 9.8

Black tea: 6.8

The passage says that milk's pH is 6.6. Thus, the pOH value of milk is 14 – 6.6 = 7.4. Milk is more acidic than black tea, but less acidic than orange and lemon juice. Choice C is the best answer.

25. **B is the best answer.** Remember that a triglyceride is three fatty acid connected via ester linkage to glycerol. A generic triglyceride is shown below :

$$\begin{array}{l} H_2C-O-\overset{O}{\overset{\|}{C}}-R' \\ \;| \\ HC-O-\overset{O}{\overset{\|}{C}}-R'' \\ \;| \\ H_2C-O-\overset{O}{\overset{\|}{C}}-R''' \end{array}$$

A triglyceride will undergo hydrolysis in the presence of a strong base, releasing an alkoxide anion. Since the alkoxide ion is a strong base, it is still expected to react with casein to produce glue. Three equivalents of NaOH producing three equivalents of alkoxide anions does not really neutralize the amount of base present in the nascent glue solution. Choices A and D can be eliminated. Moreover, choice A suggests that the fattier milks produce a stronger glue. This is contradicted by the results of the experiment, which suggest that less fatty milks produce stronger glues. Choice C can be eliminated as well. Choice B is the best answer because it supports the results of the experiment, having a less fatty milk produce a stronger glue, and uses a scientifically valid explanation to explain why.

26. C is the best answer. First, remember the structure of histidine, shown below. Its imidazole side chain is made bold:

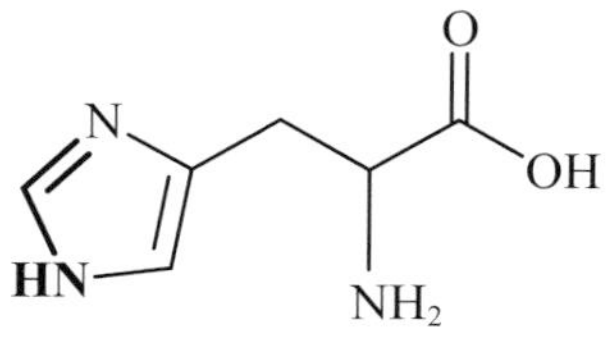

Zwitterions occur when an equal number of both negative and positive charges are present on a molecule, leaving it with a net charge of zero. With a slightly alkaline solution pH, and no reason to acquire a positive charge, the imidazole side chain is not expected to exhibit zwitterionic behavior. Choice A can be eliminated. Careful here. The tricky part of choice A is that the amino acid histidine, as a whole, may exist as a zwitterion, since the nitrogen of its amino terminus may deprotonate the acidic carboxyl terminus. Nonetheless, since the question only asked about the imidazole side chain, or R group, there is no concern of zwitterion formation. In general, creating a negatively charged amino group via deprotonation requires a solution far more basic than 7.4. Choice B is unlikely. To distinguish between choice C and D, use the Henderson-Hasselbalch equation.

$$\mathrm{pH} = \mathrm{p}K_a + \log\left(\frac{[\mathrm{A}^-]}{[\mathrm{HA}]}\right)$$

$$7.4 = 6.0 + \log\left(\frac{[\mathrm{A}^-]}{[\mathrm{HA}]}\right)$$

$$101.4 = \left(\frac{[\mathrm{A}^-]}{[\mathrm{HA}]}\right)$$

This means that in solution, the concentration of A^-, or the neutrally charged imidazole side-chain, is $10^{1.4}$ times greater than the concentration of its conjugate acid, HA. $10^{1.4}$ is about 25, so choice C is the best answer. If the conjugate acid were confused for the neutral imidazole side chain, choice D would result.

Stand-alones (Questions 27-29)

27. C is the best answer. The question is not completely clear but it is asking to define K_w for ethanol. Keep in mind, K_w is simply K_a for water. $K_a = \frac{[\mathrm{H}^+][\mathrm{A}^-]}{[\mathrm{HA}]}$ where HA is an acid and A^- is the acids conjugate base. For ethanol, $K_a = [\mathrm{H}^+][\mathrm{H_3C{-}CH_2O^-}]/[\mathrm{H_3C{-}CH_2OH}]$. For K_w the $[H_2O]$ in the denominator is removed because it is impossible to define the concentration of a molecule in a pure solution of that molecule. So, K_w for water is $[\mathrm{H}^+][\mathrm{OH}^-]$. This means K_w for ethanol will be $[\mathrm{H}^+][\mathrm{H_3C{-}CH_2O^-}]$. Choice C is the best answer. Choice A does not include the correct conjugate base. Choice B combines errors in choice A and choice D. Choice D includes the concentration of ethanol in the denominator which is not the best answer because the concentration of the liquid is not included in the K_w equation. Choice D would be the best answer for describing an ethanol solution dissolved in water. However, the question assumes the predominant liquid in the world is ethanol which would make the concentration of ethanol irrelevant to the K_w equation.

28. D is the best answer. The strongest known superacid is fluoroantimonic acid which has a pK_a of −25. Other strong acids include sulfuric acid which has a pK_a of −3 and hydrochloric acid which has a pK_a of -6. This is not something that should be memorized for the MCAT®. pK_a is the $-\log(K_a)$ where K_a is the $\frac{[\mathrm{A}^-][\mathrm{H}^+]}{[\mathrm{HA}]}$. So, a very large K_a would favor acid production and be associated with a very large, negative pK_a. The largest negative pK_a is −25, choice D.

29. D is the best answer. Atom A is a methyl hydrogen. The pK_a of methyl is about 50 meaning it is a very weak acid. Likewise, the hydrogens in an alkane chain are very weakly acidic. These are slightly more acidic than the methyl hydrogen but still very weak. COOH describes a carboxylic acid which is a weak organic acid. The pK_a of a carboxylic acid is about 4. To put it in perspective, the pK_a of HCl is about −6. So a carboxylic acid is still a weak acid but it is the strongest acid in the above molecule. Choice D is the best answer.

PHYSICAL SCIENCES

DIRECTIONS. Most questions in the Physical Sciences test are organized into groups, each preceded by a descriptive passage. After studying the passage, select the one best answer to each question in the group. Some questions are not based on a descriptive passage and are also independent of each other. You must also select the one best answer to these questions. If you are not certain of an answer, eliminate the alternatives that you know to be incorrect and then select an answer from the remaining alternatives. A periodic table is provided for your use. You may consult it whenever you wish.

PERIODIC TABLE OF THE ELEMENTS

1 **H** 1.0																	2 **He** 4.0
3 **Li** 6.9	4 **Be** 9.0											5 **B** 10.8	6 **C** 12.0	7 **N** 14.0	8 **O** 16.0	9 **F** 19.0	10 **Ne** 20.2
11 **Na** 23.0	12 **Mg** 24.3											13 **Al** 27.0	14 **Si** 28.1	15 **P** 31.0	16 **S** 32.1	17 **Cl** 35.5	18 **Ar** 39.9
19 **K** 39.1	20 **Ca** 40.1	21 **Sc** 45.0	22 **Ti** 47.9	23 **V** 50.9	24 **Cr** 52.0	25 **Mn** 54.9	26 **Fe** 55.8	27 **Co** 58.9	28 **Ni** 58.7	29 **Cu** 63.5	30 **Zn** 65.4	31 **Ga** 69.7	32 **Ge** 72.6	33 **As** 74.9	34 **Se** 79.0	35 **Br** 79.9	36 **Kr** 83.8
37 **Rb** 85.5	38 **Sr** 87.6	39 **Y** 88.9	40 **Zr** 91.2	41 **Nb** 92.9	42 **Mo** 95.9	43 **Tc** (98)	44 **Ru** 101.1	45 **Rh** 102.9	46 **Pd** 106.4	47 **Ag** 107.9	48 **Cd** 112.4	49 **In** 114.8	50 **Sn** 118.7	51 **Sb** 121.8	52 **Te** 127.6	53 **I** 126.9	54 **Xe** 131.3
55 **Cs** 132.9	56 **Ba** 137.3	57 **La*** 138.9	72 **Hf** 178.5	73 **Ta** 180.9	74 **W** 183.9	75 **Re** 186.2	76 **Os** 190.2	77 **Ir** 192.2	78 **Pt** 195.1	79 **Au** 197.0	80 **Hg** 200.6	81 **Tl** 204.4	82 **Pb** 207.2	83 **Bi** 209.0	84 **Po** (209)	85 **At** (210)	86 **Rn** (222)
87 **Fr** (223)	88 **Ra** 226.0	89 **Ac**= 227.0	104 **Unq** (261)	105 **Unp** (262)	106 **Unh** (263)	107 **Uns** (262)	108 **Uno** (265)	109 **Une** (267)									

*	58 **Ce** 140.1	59 **Pr** 140.9	60 **Nd** 144.2	61 **Pm** (145)	62 **Sm** 150.4	63 **Eu** 152.0	64 **Gd** 157.3	65 **Tb** 158.9	66 **Dy** 162.5	67 **Ho** 164.9	68 **Er** 167.3	69 **Tm** 168.9	70 **Yb** 173.0	71 **Lu** 175.0
=	90 **Th** 232.0	91 **Pa** (231)	92 **U** 238.0	93 **Np** (237)	94 **Pu** (244)	95 **Am** (243)	96 **Cm** (247)	97 **Bk** (247)	98 **Cf** (251)	99 **Es** (252)	100 **Fm** (257)	101 **Md** (258)	102 **No** (259)	103 **Lr** (260)